Riding Lawn Mower (1992 and Later)

SERVICE MANUAL ▪ 1ST EDITION

PRIMEDIA Business Directories & Books
P.O. Box 12901 ▪ Overland Park, KS 66282-2901
Phone: 800-262-1954 Fax: 800-633-6219
www.primediabooks.com

Cover photo courtesy of:
John Deere

Riding
Lawn
Mower *(1992 and Later)*

SERVICE MANUAL ■ *1ST EDITION*

Riding Lawn Mower Manufacturers:

- AGCO-ALLIS
- Ariens
- Cub Cadet
- John Deere

- Honda
- Massey-Ferguson

- MTD
- Simplicity

- Snapper
- Wheel Horse (Toro)
- White

CONTENTS

CONTENTS (Cont.)

FUNDAMENTALS

INTRODUCTION

Correct-fast-easy service may not be possible if the servicing mechanic does not have an understanding of how the machine is supposed to operate. Understanding these fundamentals will not, however, repair worn or damaged equipment. Knowledge of the machine design fundamentals, familiarity with standard accepted service procedures, specific repair information, proper tools and necessary new parts can be combined by service personnel to repair damaged equipment. The mechanic should also be aware that his safety and the safety of others is most important. **Do not take chances** (Fig 1). Be prepared to handle crises (such as spills, fires or run-away equipment) quickly and safely, even before an emergency occurs.

SAFETY INTERLOCK SYSTEMS

Riding lawn mowers may be equipped with two or more interlock safety switches which prevent the engine from starting if blade clutch or drive clutch is engaged or if transmission is in gear. Various types of interlock safety starting systems are used and safety switches may be lo-

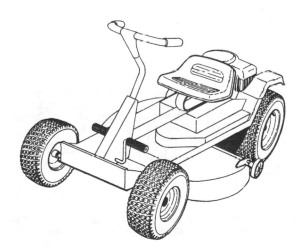

Fig. 1–Operate and service all power equipment carefully and safely.

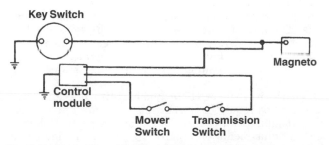

Fig. 2–Typical wiring diagram of interlock safety starting system used on some models equipped with recoil starter. Refer to text.

cated on blade clutch, main drive clutch, transmission, under mower seat or on recoil starter rope handle lock.

Always inspect the interlock safety starting system and make sure it is in good operating condition before checking the basic ignition system.

NOTE: Never return a mower to service with any safety interlock system switches bypassed. The switches are installed to encourage safe operation. Defeating any of the system will permit unsafe operation, which may result in injury.

The interlock safety starting system show in Fig. 2 is equipped with an electronic control module. Before engine can be started, mower switch and transmission switch must be closed (mower blade clutch disengaged and transmission in neutral). When engine is operating, current feedback from engine magneto switches the control module, isolating the safety switch circuit. At this time, mower blade clutch can be engaged and transmission shifted from neutral without affecting engine operation. If engine will not start with blade clutch disengaged and transmission in neutral or if engine will start with blade clutch engaged or transmission in gear, check and repair safety starting system.

CAUTION: Use extreme care when checking the system as the interlock switches may be bypassed at times during tests.

If engine will not start with blade clutch disengaged and transmission in NEUTRAL, disconnect wires to safety switches at the control module. Install a bypass wire on the control module where switch wires were removed. If engine will start now, use a continuity light or ohmmeter and test for faulty safety switches or switch circuit wires. If engine will not start disconnect control module wire from engine magneto terminal. If engine will still not start, check basic ignition system as trouble is not in safety starting system.

If engine will start with blade clutch engaged or transmission in gear, disconnect wires to safety switches at control module. If engine will not start, inspect safety switches and switch circuit wiring and replace as necessary. If engine will start with safety switch wires disconnected, but will not start with the magneto terminal grounded to the frame, control module is faulty and must be replaced.

NOTE: Always make certain that interlock safety starting system is in good condition and that all safety switches are connected before returning mower to service.

Another type of safety starting system is shown in Fig. 3. Safety switches (5 and 6) must be open (drive clutch locked in fully disengaged position and mower lift and blade disengagement lever in fully disengaged position) before engine can be started. When recoil starter handle (3) is unlocked, spring leaf type safety switch (4) moves to ground against the frame. After the engine is started, the recoil starter handle must be locked in position in frame pushing safety switch (4) open, before the blade or drive clutch is engaged. If the engine will not start with drive clutch and blade fully disengaged, check for faulty switches (5 and 6) and wiring using a continuity light or ohmmeter. Replace faulty components as required.

NOTE: Always make certain the interlock safety system is in good condition and that all safety switches are connected before returning mower to service.

On models equipped with safety starting system shown in Fig. 4, the safety switch (5) is located under the lawn mower seat. When the operator is off the seat, the switch (5) is closed. Before the engine can be started, the safety switches (3 and 4) must be open (mower blade clutch disengaged and drive clutch pedal locked in fully depressed position). After the engine is started and operator is seated on the riding mower, the weight of operator on the seat (normally 100 pounds is required) pushes switch (5) to open position. At this time, blade clutch and drive clutch can be engaged without affecting engine operation. However, if operator raises off the seat while blade clutch or drive clutch is engaged, engine will stop. If engine will not start when blade clutch and drive clutch are in disengaged position, use a continuity light or an ohmmeter and check for faulty safety switches (3 and 4) or grounded switch wires. Replace faulty switches as required.

NOTE: Always make certain that interlock safety system is in good condition and that all safety starting switches are connected before returning mower to service.

Many electric start models are equipped with the safety starting system shown in Fig. 5. On this system, safety switches are in the electric starter solenoid switch circuit instead of the magneto ignition circuit as on recoil start models. Transmission must be in neutral and mower blade clutch in disengaged position (both switches closed) before the key switch will operate the electric starter solenoid (magnetic) switch.

If electric starter will not operate when transmission is in neutral and blade clutch is disengaged or if starter will operate when transmission in gear or blade is engaged, use a continuity light or an ohmmeter and check for faulty safety switches. Replace faulty switches when necessary.

NOTE: Always make certain the safety starting system is in good condition and all safety starting switches are connected before returning mower to service.

MAINTENANCE

Normal maintenance should include a complete check of the equipment, making sure that equipment is adequately lubricated and adjusting components/controls as required. These normal maintenance procedures can effectively reduce the amount of damage that will require repair.

Encourage operators to check all systems as described in the operating instructions, each time the equipment is to

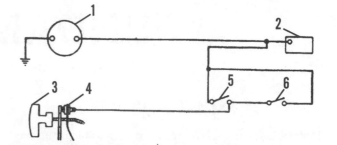

Fig. 3–Typical wiring diagram of interlock safety starting system used on some recoil starter models. Refer to text.
1. Key switch
2. Engine magneto
3. Recoil starter handle
4. Safety Switch
5. Drive clutch pedal safety switch
6. Blade disengagement safety switch

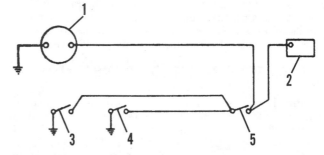

Fig. 4–Typical wiring diagram of interlock safety starting system used on some recoil starter models. Refer to text.
1. Key switch
2. Engine magneto
3. Drive clutch safety switch
4. Blade clutch safety switch
5. Seat safety switch

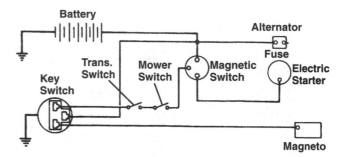
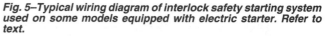

Fig. 5–Typical wiring diagram of interlock safety starting system used on some models equipped with electric starter. Refer to text.

be used. Additional regular inspections by service personnel should be encouraged, usually at the beginning and end of normal operating seasons.

Follow the manufacturer's lubrication recommendations. The manufacturer recommends the type of lubricant and frequency of lubrication service to reduce damage to the equipment. Altering recommended lubrication intervals or changing lubricant may result in extensive damage.

Adjust drive belt or chain tension, tire pressure, controls, ect., as required. Checks may indicate the need for adjustments, repair or installation of new parts. Delaying needed adjustments or repairs may result in increased wear rate and/or extensive damage to otherwise usable parts.

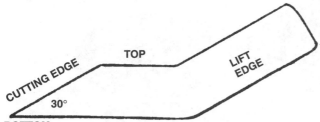

Fig. 6–Drawing of typical blade cross-section identifying parts of blade. The cutting edge should form approximately 30° angle with bottom.

Fig. 8–View of a commonly used cone type balancer. Alignment of the two parts of the cone indicate balanced blade.

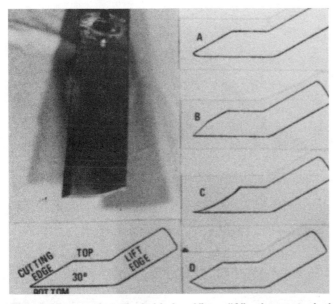

Fig. 7–Views of typical blade. View "A" shows typical cross-section of dull blade. View "B" is incorrect because of sharpening at too much angle. View "C" is sharpened at less than 30° angle. View "D" shows incorrect method of sharpening caused by grinding lower edge of blade.

CUTTING BLADES

INSPECTION

Mower blades should be inspected frequently for sharpness, balance and straightness. Dull blades will cause ragged grass cutting and can cause excessive load on engine. Bent or out-of-balance blades cause excessive vibration.

CAUTION: Always remove wire from engine spark plug before performing any inspection or service of blades.

Dull blades can normally be sharpened, but bent or cracked blades must be replaced. Refer to the following paragraphs for blade servicing.

SHARPENING

Slightly dulled blades can normally be restored with a few strokes of a file. Badly dulled or nicked blades should be removed and sharpened on a grinder. Ideal cutting edge is sharpened at a 30° angle as shown in Fig. 6. Blades wear

on the underside as shown at A–Fig. 7. If blade is not worn excessively, the 30° angle cutting edge and flat underside can be obtained without excessive grinding. Do not sharpen bottom edge as shown at (D). Sharpen both ends of blade evenly so that blade remains balanced. Always check blade for balance after sharpening.

BALANCING

An unbalanced blade can cause severe vibration resulting in damaged blade spindle bearings and cracked mower housing. Various types of blade balancers are available. A popular blade balancer is the cone type shown in Fig. 8. Before balancing blade, make sure blade is clean and properly sharpened. Place the blade center mounting hole over the cone balancer and check balance. Mark heavy end of blade. Resharpen blade to remove metal from heavy end. DO NOT grind away the lift edge to balance blade.

BLADE TRACKING

Mower blades should cut on a plane parallel to the level mower housing. With the riding mower on a smooth floor, measure the distance from the end of the blade to the floor. Rotate blade 180° and measure the distance from the opposite end of the blade to the floor. Measurements should be the same with $\frac{1}{16}$ inch (1.6 mm). If not, blade or blade spindle (sometimes crankshaft) is bent and should be replaced.

DRIVE BELTS, BELT GUIDES AND PULLEYS

Drive belts should be checked periodically and adjusted if necessary to prevent slippage under normal operating conditions. Belts should be kept clean and dry. Wipe belts with a clean rag to remove any oil or dirt and carefully check condition of belts. Install new belt of correct size if old belt is stretched or damaged. Refer to Fig. 9. A damaged belt may be normal after much use, but premature damage may be caused by other failure.

Pulleys should be aligned. The straight edge (C–Fig. 10) should indicate that all are in line. If the side of the pulley (A) is thicker than the side of the pulley (B), clearance (E & F) should be the same as the difference in thickness of the sides when the straight edge is touching at the points (D). If the side of pulleys are the same, clearance at (E & F) indicates that pulley (B) is lower than pulley (A). Method indicated in text for moving pulley should be employed to align pulleys. If the clearance (E & F) is different, the pulley may be bent or one of the shafts is not in line with the other shaft. Correct alignment to improve belt operation and increase operating life. Check pulleys and install new pulley and belt if nicked (N–Fig. 11), worn (W) or bent (B). Condition and alignment of pulleys is critical to life of belt.

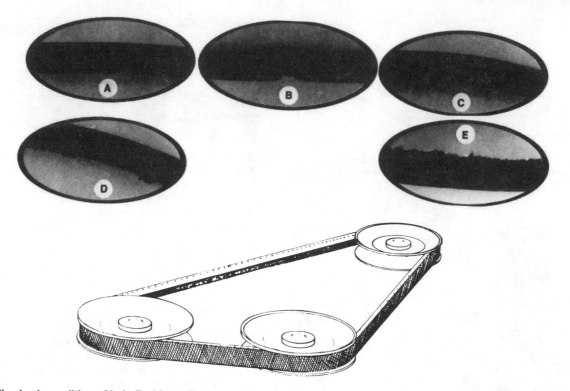

Fig. 9–Visually check condition of belt. Problems illustrated in the insets should be corrected and new belt installed. Inset "A" shows cracks or cuts in belt. Inset "B" shows localized burned section of belt caused by drive pulley turning with belt not moving. Inset "C" shows frayed and worn friction sides. Inset "D" shows notched belt with sections broken loose or out. Inset "E" shows frayed and worn backside of belt which is usually caused by incorrectly adjusted belt guard.

Belt guides and belt stops must be positioned so they will be free of the belt when the clutch is engaged but will hold belt free of drive pulley when the clutch is disengaged. If the belt guide specified clearance is not available, position belt guides for ⅛ inch (3mm) clearance with the clutch engaged and check operation. Be sure to reinstall all guards to prevent injury or belt damage.

DRIVE CHAIN

On models equipped with a drive chain, make certain the chain sprockets are aligned to prevent excessive wear on chain and sprockets. Drive chain should be adjusted so the chain has about ¼ inch (6.4 mm) slack. If chain is too tight, excessive wear and stretch will result. If chain is too loose, it may jump off the sprocket or ride into the sprocket teeth resulting in excessive wear on the sprockets and chain. Under normal operating conditions, open drive chain should be lubricated with engine oil each 10 hours of operation.

Sprocket tooth profile (B–Fig. 12) is precisely ground to fit the roller diameter and chain pitch (A). When chain and sprocket are new, the chain moves around the sprocket smoothly with a minimum of friction, and the load is evenly distributed over several sprockets teeth. Wear on pins and bushings of a roller chain results in a lengthening or "stretch" of each individual chain pitch as well as lengthening of the complete chain. The worn chain, therefore, no longer perfectly fits the sprocket. Each roller contracts the sprocket tooth higher up on the bearing area (C) and that tooth bears the total load until the next tooth and roller make contact. Chain wear will therefore quickly result in increased sprocket wear.

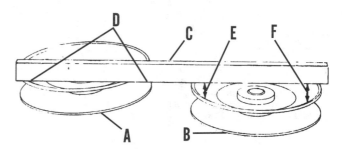

Fig. 10–Be sure that pulleys are correctly aligned so that belt will move smoothly from one pulley to the other. Sometimes belt is used to drive pulleys that are not aligned, but special guides are employed to change direction of belt. Refer to text.

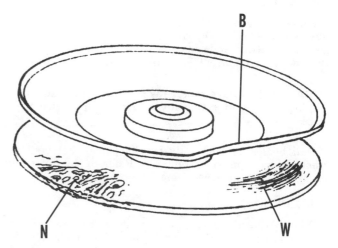

Fig. 11–Damage to pulley such as rough surface (N), cupped surface (W) or bent sides (B) will quickly wear belt out.

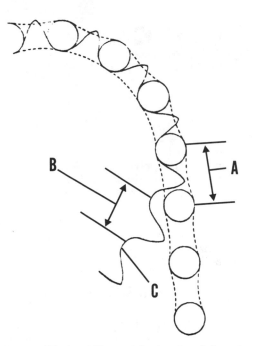

Fig. 12–Chain pitch (A) should be matched to the pitch and contour of sprocket tooth (B).

As a rule of thumb, a new chain should be installed whenever chain stretch exceeds 2%, or ¼ inch (6.4 mm) for 1 foot (304.8 mm) of length. Replace #40 chain when a 24 pitch length of chain measures 12¼ inches (311.2 mm). Check sprockets carefully for wear if chain wear is substantially greater than 2%, and replace sprockets when in doubt. Sprocket wear usually shows up as a hooked tooth profile. A good test is to fit the sprocket to a new chain. Wear on sides of sprocket indicates misalignment. If sprockets must be replaced because of wear, always replace the chain. Early failure can be expected if a new chain is mated with worn sprockets or new sprockets with a worn chain.

REPAIR

Adjustment and repair information for the individual mower units is included within the MOWER SERVICE section. Engine application is listed in the MOWER SERVICE section; however, specific engine repair information is described in ENGINE REPAIR section. Transmission, transaxle and differential application is listed in the MOWER SERVICE section, but procedure for servicing the more common units is described in the TRANSMISSION REPAIR or DIFFERENTIAL REPAIR sections of this manual.

BELT SERVICE

V-BELTS

V-belts may be the item most overlooked during equipment maintenance, but proper care and maintenance of V-belts and their pulleys can yield great rewards. The nature of V-belts makes preventive maintenance relatively easy. Unlike fatigue or flaws in direct drives that are very often invisible until an abrupt failure stops the equipment, V-belts and pulleys wear gradually and usually give advance warning of failure. Nonetheless, it is important to recognize the warnings.

Before attempting any maintenance, disconnect the battery negative terminal wire and be sure the ignition switch is in the OFF position. Other safety procedures—such as blocking—may be required to assure safety.

All belts and pulleys will wear as part of their life's cycle. As wear occurs, the belts will ride lower in the grooves. Because the pulley center distance must be increased to compensate for wear and stretching, a used belt is, in effect, longer than a new one.

V-belts grip by wedging in the pulley grooves. Belts that are too loose cause slippage, loss of power, loss of speed and rapid wear to both the belt and the pulley. A howl or squeal indicates that the belt is too loose or the load is too heavy.

ALIGNMENT AND TENSION

Check to be sure pulleys are properly aligned because misalignment can cause excessive wear to the belt sidewall. Unusual wear of the belt outer cover is an indication of more serious mechanical trouble. Belts engineered to operate without an outer cover, such as cut or raw-edge belts, will become narrow as they wear. This wear decreases belt tension and may cause the belt to slip.

Belts that are too tight will wear rapidly and the excessive side loads may damage the drive shafts, bushings and bearings.

Inspect the drive elements when removing belts. Relieve belt tension by loosening the drive take-up adjustment. Remove belt guards as necessary, then remove the old belts. Remove any rust and dirt from the take-up rails and lubricate the rails if necessary so tensioning the new belt will be easier. Inspect and repair damaged machine elements such as worn bearings and bent shafts to reduce the likelihood of future mechanical trouble and to ensure maximum service from new belts.

V-belts are designed to operate by making clean, dry-surface contact with the sidewall of the pulleys. Inspect the belts periodically to assure that they are not contaminated with grease or oil. Don't allow mud, rust or any other foreign matter to build up in the pulley grooves. Clean pulleys carefully with a wire brush.

SIGNS OF TROUBLE

Never install new V-belts without carefully inspecting the pulleys. Focus special attention on these conditions:

- Worn groove sidewalls.
- A shiny pulley groove bottom.
- Wobbling pulleys.
- Damaged pulleys.

Pulley sidewalls must be perfectly straight because the wedging action of the V-belt is impaired and its gripping power is reduced when the walls are worn or dished out.

A shiny pulley groove bottom is an indication that the belt, pulley or both are badly worn and the belt is bottoming in the groove. This condition may first be evident on the smaller pulley.

INSTALLING NEW BELTS

Where multiple V-belt drives are used, install all matching belts at the same time. After prolonged operation, V-belts will stretch and if only one belt (of a multiple drive) is new, the belt will have to carry most of the load. It Is more economical to install matched sets of all-new belts from the same manufacturer.

Store new belts in a cool, dry place to assure maximum V-belt performance when they are installed. Deterioration is likely to occur if belts are stored near heat sources or piled on damp floors.

If pulleys are not properly aligned, check to be sure the drive and driven shafts are parallel both horizontally and vertically. The center of the drive and driven pulleys should be a straight line.

Set the belt take-up adjustment at its minimum position and place the new belt in the correct position by hand. Never pry belts over the pulley with a screwdriver or other hard object.

Tighten the drive until slack in the belt is removed. All V-belt drives must operate with the correct belt tension to provide the optimum wedging action of the belt against the groove sidewalls. Refer to the equipment operator's book for the tension adjustment procedure.

Allow a reasonable break-in period of a few hours, and then check again for proper belt tension. New belts tend to elongate slightly until they are seated in the pulley groove and initial stretch is removed from the belt.

Be sure to reinstall all belt guides, guards and shields.

BELT REPLACEMENT

Always replace a used belt with a new belt that is an exact replacement. Belts are designed for specific applications. Installing an incorrect belt may cause excessive slippage, premature wear to pulleys and short belt life.

Belts are available from the equipment manufacturer or from aftermarket belt manufacturers. The equipment model number, model year and unit serial number are usually necessary to obtain the correct belt.

AGCO Allis

Model	Make	Engine Model	Horsepower
1692175	B&S	*	12
1692176	B&S	*	12
1692394	B&S	*	8.5
1692399	B&S	*	13
1692819	B&S	*	11
1692821	B&S	*	12
1693042	B&S	*	11
1693044	B&S	*	12
1693046	Kohler	*	14

*Note the engine model number and refer to the engine service section in this manual for engine specifications.

FRONT WHEELS

LUBRICATION

Each front wheel hub is equipped with a grease fitting. Front wheels should be injected with lithium-base grease after every 25 hours of operation. Lubricate the front wheels more frequently when ambient temperature exceeds 85° F (39° C) or when operating in dusty conditions.

REMOVAL AND INSTALLATION

The front wheels are equipped with replaceable bushings. To remove the wheel and bushings, proceed as follows:
1. Remove the wheel cover (8–Fig. AG1-1).
2. Remove the retaining ring (7).
3. Remove the wheel with the bushings.
4. Separate the bushings from the wheel.

5. Inspect the spindle and bushings for wear and damage.
6. Inspect the wheel for rim and hub damage.
7. Reverse the removal steps to reassemble and install the wheel and bushings. Lubricate the bushings after assembly

FRONT SPINDLE

LUBRICATION

Lubricate the front wheel spindles after every 25 hours of operation. Inject lithium-base grease into the front axle main member through the grease fitting (A–Fig. AG1-2) at each end.

OVERHAUL

1. Raise and support the side to be serviced.
2. Remove the wheel and tire.
3. Disconnect the tie rod end and drag link end, if necessary, from the spindle.
4. Detach the snap ring (B–Fig. AG1-2) securing the top of the spindle, then withdraw the spindle from the axle.
5. Reverse the removal steps to install the front spindle. Lubricate the spindle after assembly.

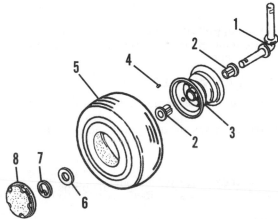

Fig. AG1-1—Exploded view of wheel assembly.

1. Spindle	5. Tire
2. Bushing	6. Washer
3. Wheel	7. Snap ring
4. Grease fitting	8. Wheel cover

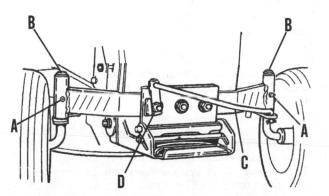

Fig. AG1-2—Inject grease into front axle member through grease fittings (A). The spindles are retained by snap rings (B).

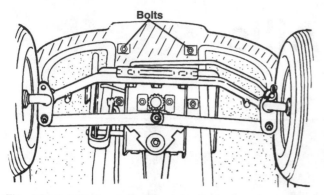

Fig. AG1-3–Adjust gear backlash by loosening the bolts and moving the steering shaft. Refer to text.

FRONT AXLE MAIN MEMBER REMOVAL AND INSTALLATION

1. Remove the mower deck, then raise and support the front of the machine.
2. Remove the steering link (C–Fig. AG1-2).
3. Remove the spindles.
4. While noting the parts arrangement for the steering pivot (D), remove the three bolts securing the axle main member.
5. Remove the axle main member.
6. Install the axle main member by reversing the removal procedure.

STEERING SECTOR AND SHAFT

LUBRICATION

Lubricate the steering gears with lithium-base grease after 25 hours of operation, or more frequently when operated in a dusty environment.

ADJUSTMENT

Adjust steering gear backlash by loosening bolts (Fig. AG1-3) and moving the steering shaft. Be sure the steering gears move smoothly without binding after adjustment.

OVERHAUL

1. Remove the mower deck as described in this section.
2. Remove the steering wheel cap (1–Fig. AG1-4).
3. Drive out the roll pin (3).
4. Remove the steering wheel.
5. Remove the shaft cover (4).
6. Remove the shaft retaining pin (5).
7. Remove the washers (6).
8. Raise and support the front of the machine.
9. Remove the steering shaft from the bottom of the machine.
10. Detach the tie rods from the sector gear.
11. Remove the sector gear pivot bolt (28) and remove the sector gear (25).
12. Inspect components and replace if damaged.
13. Reassemble the steering components by reversing the disassembly procedure. Check steering gear backlash after installation and, if necessary, adjust as previously described.

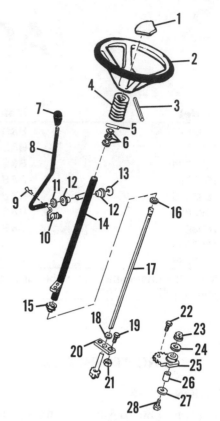

Fig. AG1-4–Exploded view of steering shaft assembly

1. Cap	15. Bushing
2. Steering wheel	16. Washer
3. Pin	17. Steering shaft
4. Cover	18. Washer
5. Pin	19. Bolt
6. Washers	20. Plate
7. Knob	21. Nut
8. Shift lever	22. Bolt
9. Pin	23. Nut
10. Spring	24. Washer
11. Washer	25. Sector gear
12. Bushings	26. Spacer
13. Washer	27. Washer
14. Shift tube	28. Bolt

ENGINE

Refer to the appropriate engine section in this manual for tune-up specifications, engine overhaul procedures and engine maintenance.

REMOVAL AND INSTALLATION

1. Remove the engine cover and disconnect the spark plug wire.
2. On electric start models, disconnect and remove the battery.
3. Disconnect any interfering electrical wires from the engine.
4. Disconnect the throttle cable from the engine.
5. Remove the mower as outlined in the MOWER DECK section.
6. Remove the traction drive belt from the engine pulley.
7. Detach the pulley from the engine crankshaft.
8. Remove the engine mounting fasteners.
9. Remove the engine.
10. Install the engine by reversing the removal procedure.

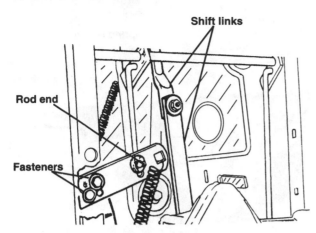

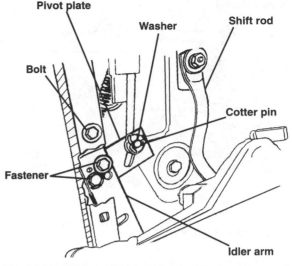

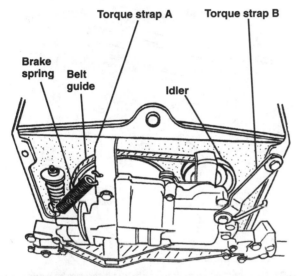

Fig. AG1-5–Refer to text for clutch adjustment procedure on models equipped with a gear transaxle.

Fig AG1-7–Refer to text for clutch adjustment procedure on models equipped with a hydrostatic transaxle.

1. Remove the mower deck as described in this section.
2. Raise and support the rear of the machine.
3. Detach the brake spring.
4. Remove the torque strap (A).
5. Remove the belt guide.
6. Remove the torque strap (B).
7. Loosen the transaxle mounting bolts.
8. Loosen the idler axle sufficiently so the belt can pass between the idler and belt guide.
9. Disconnect the shift links (Fig. AG1-5).
10. Disconnect the PTO clutch electrical wire.
11. Remove the drive belt.
12. Reverse the removal procedure to install the drive belt. Position the idler belt guide so it is ⅛ inch (3.2 mm) from the idler. Perform the transaxle neutral adjustment procedure described in this section.

Fig. AG1-6–Refer to text for drive belt removal procedure on models equipped with a gear transaxle.

TRACTION DRIVE CLUTCH AND DRIVE BELT (MODELS WITH HYDROSTATIC TRANSAXLE)

ADJUSTMENT

If the rear wheels continue to drive the machine when the clutch/brake pedal is depressed, adjust the clutch idler position as follows:
1. Disconnect the spark plug wire.
2. Loosen the fasteners on the pivot plate (Fig. AG1-7).
3. Move the pivot plate so the forward edge of the washer on the control rod aligns with the end of the slot in the plate.
4. Tighten the fasteners.
5. Check operation. The drive belt should not rotate when the parking brake is engaged and the engine is running.

REMOVAL AND INSTALLATION

Refer to Fig. AG1-8 when performing the following procedure.
1. Remove the mower deck as described in this section.
2. Raise and support the rear of the machine.
3. Loosen the fasteners retaining the belt guides.
4. Loosen the fasteners retaining torque strap (A).
5. Loosen the fasteners retaining torque strap (B).

TRACTION DRIVE CLUTCH AND DRIVE BELT (MODELS WITH GEAR TRANSAXLE)

ADJUSTMENT

If the rear wheels continue to drive the machine when the clutch/brake pedal is depressed, adjust the clutch idler position as follows.
1. Disconnect the spark plug wire.
2. Loosen the fasteners on the idler arm (Fig. AG1-5).
3. Engage the parking brake.
4. Move the idler arm against spring tension and retighten the fasteners.
5. Check operation. If the clutch rod end is against the slot end in the idler arm and belt slippage occurs, replace the belt. Also inspect components for wear that may allow belt slippage.

REMOVAL AND INSTALLATION

Refer to Fig. AG1-6 when performing the following procedure.

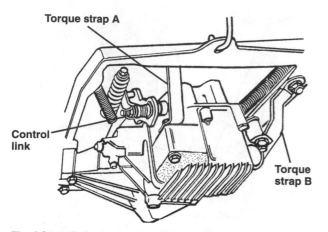

Fig AG1-8–Refer to text for drive belt removal procedure on models equipped with a hytorstatic transaxle.

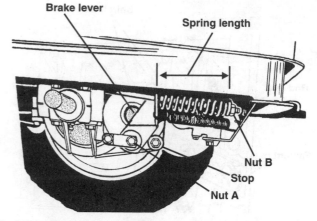

Fig.AG1-9–Rotate nut A to adjust brake on models equipped with a gear transaxle. Refer to text.

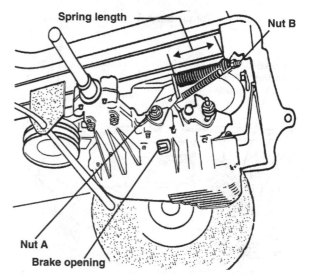

Fig. AG1-10–Insert a feeler gauge through the brake opening in the transaxle housing to measure brake disc clearance. Refer to the text.

6. Loosen the transaxle mounting bolts.

7. Detach the idler spring from the frame.

8. Refer to Fig. AG1-7. Remove the cotter pin and washer from the control rod end, then separate the rod from the pivot plate.

9. Remove the idler arm attaching bolt (Fig. AG1-8) and spacer. The idler may now rest against the belt.

10. Note the position of the belt guide on the idler.

11. Disconnect the upper and lower shift rods.

12. Loosen the transaxle control link.

13. Disconnect the PTO clutch electrical wire.

14. Remove the drive belt.

15. Reverse the removal procedure to install the drive belt. Perform the transaxle neutral adjustment and the return-to-neutral adjustment procedures described in this section.

GROUND DRIVE BRAKE ADJUSTMENT

MODELS WITH GEAR TRANSAXLE

Refer to Fig. AG1-9 when performing the following procedure.

1. Remove the left rear wheel.

2. Push the brake lever forward and measure the gap between the lever and stop. The gap should be $\frac{1}{8}$ inch (3.2 mm).

3. Rotate nut (A) to obtain the specified gap.

4. Engage the parking brake. Measure the spring length. Specified spring length is $2\frac{9}{16}$ to $2\frac{5}{8}$ inches (65-66.6 mm).

5. Rotate nut (B) to obtain specified spring length.

MODELS WITH HYDROSTATIC TRANSAXLE

These models are equipped with a Hydro-Gear hydrostatic transaxle equipped with brake discs inside the transaxle housing. Check for correct brake adjustment using the following procedure.

1. Insert a feeler gauge between two brake discs through the opening on the housing's underside (Fig. AG1-10).

2. Measure the gap between the brake discs. The gap should be 0.025-0.030 inch (0.64-0.76 mm).

3. Rotate the brake lever retaining nut (A) to obtain the specified gap.

4. Engage the parking brake. Measure the spring length. Specified spring length is $2\frac{11}{16}$ to $2\frac{23}{32}$ inches (68.3-69.1 mm).

5. Rotate nut (B) to obtain the specified spring length.

TRANSAXLE (MODELS WITH GEAR TRANSAXLE)

LUBRICATION

The outer ends of the transaxle are equipped with grease fittings (Fig. AG1-11). Inject lithium-base grease into the grease fittings after every 25 hours of operation. One or two shots from a hand-held grease gun should be sufficient. Refer to the repair section for internal lubrication information.

NEUTRAL ADJUSTMENT

Adjust the shift linkage so the transaxle neutral position and the shift lever are synchronized. Refer to Fig. AG1-12 when performing the following procedure.

1. Raise and support the rear of the machine.

2. Move the shift lever so the transaxle is in NEUTRAL.

3. Loosen the nut securing the shift links.

4. Move the shift control lever to the neutral position indicated on the control panel.

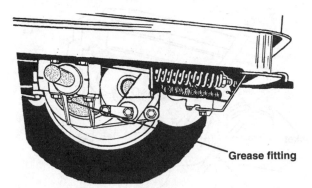

Fig. AG1-11—On gear transaxle, inject grease into fittings on each end of axle housings.

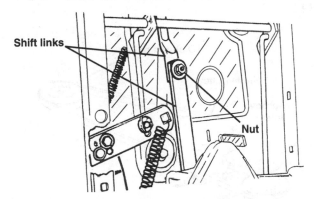

Fig. AG1-12—Loosen nut and reposition shift links as described in text for neutral adjustment.

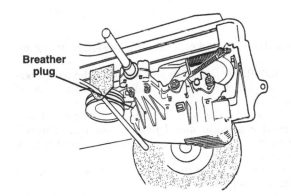

Fig AG1-13—Drawing showing location of breather plug on hydrostatic transaxle.

5. Retighten the nut to 17 ft.-lb. (23 N•m) and check adjustment.

REMOVAL AND INSTALLATION

To remove the transaxle, proceed as follows.
1. Remove the mower deck.
2. Raise and support the rear of the machine.
3. Remove the rear wheels.
4. Remove the drive belt.
5. Disconnect the shift linkage.
6. Disconnect the brake link.
7. Disconnect neutral switch wire from the switch on the transaxle.
8. Detach the torque straps (Fig. AG1-6).

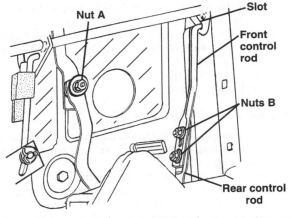

Fig. AG1-14—Refer to text for neutral adjustment procedure on models equipped with a hydrostatic transaxle.

9. Support the transaxle.
10. Remove the transaxle mounting bolts.
11. Remove the transaxle.
12. Install the transaxle by reversing the removal procedure.

OVERHAUL

Models equipped with a gear transaxle use a Peerless 915 transaxle. Refer to the repair section in this manual for overhaul information.

TRANSAXLE (MODELS WITH HYDROSTATIC TRANSAXLE)

LUBRICATION

Recommended oil is SAE 20W50 with an API rating of SG. To check or fill the transaxle, clean the area around the breather plug (Fig. AG1-13), then unscrew the breather plug. To check the oil level, measure from the boss surface to the oil. The oil level should be 1.75-2.00 inches (44-51 mm).

NEUTRAL ADJUSTMENT

Adjust the shift linkage so the transaxle's neutral positions and the shift lever are synchronized. Refer to Fig. AG1-14 when performing the following procedure.

NOTE: Operate the machine in Step 1 to verify the transaxle is in NEUTRAL.

1. Move the shift lever so the transaxle is in NEUTRAL.
2. Raise and support the rear of the machine.
3. Loosen the nut (A) securing the shift rods together so the rods can move independently.
4. Move the shift control lever to the neutral position indicated on the control panel.
5. Retighten the nut to 17 ft.-lb. (23 N•m) and check adjustment.

NOTE: Be sure the forward control rod is not binding in the frame slot before proceeding. If needed, lubricate the rod.

6. Loosen the nuts (B) securing the front and rear control rods so the rods can move independently.
7. Move the speed control lever to the full forward position.
8. Push the forward control rod back fully until it contacts the rear of the slot.
9. Tighten the nuts (B).
10. Check operation.

PURGE AIR IN TRANSAXLE

Air trapped inside the transaxle during overhaul or service must be purged for proper operation and to prevent internal damage.
1. Position the machine on a level surface.
2. Pull the pressure release lever located under the right, rear frame corner back to the PUSH position.
3. Run the engine at slow idle speed.
4. Move the speed control lever alternately to the full FORWARD and full REVERSE positions three times. Keep the lever in the FORWARD or REVERSE position for five seconds each time.
5. Move the speed control lever to NEUTRAL.
6. Push the pressure release lever forward to the DRIVE position.
7. Run the engine at full speed and operate the speed control lever so the machine moves forward and reverse alternately at least five feet in each direction. The speed control lever must be at the maximum speed position. Operate the machine three times in each direction.
8. Repeat the purging procedure as needed until the machine operates smoothly.

REMOVAL AND INSTALLATION

To remove the transaxle, proceed as follows.
1. Remove the mower deck.
2. Raise and support the rear of the machine.
3. Remove the rear wheels.
4. Remove the drive belt.
5. Disconnect the brake link and detach the brake return spring.
6. Disconnect the shift linkage.
7. Detach the torque straps (Fig. AG1-8).
8. Support the transaxle.
9. Remove the transaxle mounting bolts.
10. Remove the transaxle.
11. Install the transaxle by reversing the removal procedure.

OVERHAUL

Models equipped with a hydrostatic transaxle use a Hydro-Gear 310-0500 transaxle. Refer to the repair section in this manual for overhaul information.

ELECTRIC PTO CLUTCH

TESTING

Use the following procedure to locate the cause if the PTO clutch malfunctions.
1. Turn the ignition switch ON.
2. Actuate the PTO switch.
3. If the clutch does not engage, disconnect the wiring connector at the clutch.
4. Use a 12-volt test lamp to check continuity of the wire coming from the PTO switch.
5. If the lamp lights, the PTO is either defective or the wiring connector at the clutch field coil is faulty.

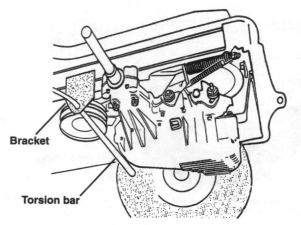

Fig. AG1-15—Drawing showing location of the torsion bar and brackets.

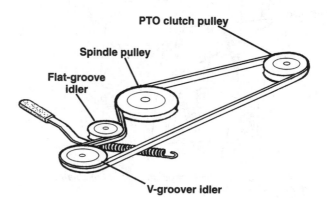

Fig. AG1-16—Mower belt routing diagram for 30-inch mower deck.

6. To check the PTO field coil, perform the following procedures:
a. Clutch installed—connect an ohmmeter to the clutch terminals. The ohmmeter should indicate a resistance of 6.59-7.29 ohms.
b. Clutch removed—apply a 12-volt source to the clutch terminals. Hold a piece of metal next to the coil. The coil should attract the metal. There should be an audible click when the clutch engages.
7. If the PTO clutch fails the preceding tests, replace the coil or entire clutch assembly.

REMOVAL AND INSTALLATION

1. Remove the mower deck as described in this section.
2. Raise and support the rear of the machine.
3. Remove the torsion bar bracket and torsion bar (Fig. AG1-15).
4. Disconnect the PTO clutch electrical wire.
5. Hold the spacer below the clutch by placing a wrench on the two flats on the spacer.
6. Remove the clutch retaining bolts.
7. Remove the clutch assembly from the crankshaft.
8. Reverse the removal procedure to install the PTO clutch. Apply antiseize compound to the engine crankshaft. Tighten the clutch retaining bolts to 45-50 ft.-lb. (63-68 N•m).
9. If installing a new clutch or components, run the engine at full speed and engage the clutch several times after the mower is installed to burnish the clutch surfaces.

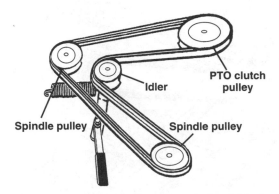

Fig. AG1-17–Mower belt routing diagram for 34-inch mower deck.

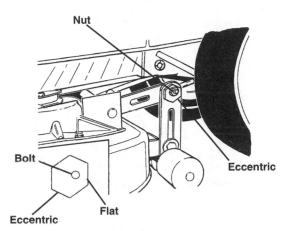

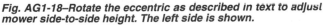

Fig. AG1-18–Rotate the eccentric as described in text to adjust mower side-to-side height. The left side is shown.

MOWER DRIVE BELT REMOVAL AND INSTALLATION

30-INCH MOWER DECK

Refer to Fig. AG1-16 when performing the following procedure.

1. Place the mower height control lever in the lowest position.
2. Move the moveable idler away from the belt and remove the belt from the PTO pulley and mower spindle pulley.
3. Remove the mower drive belt.
4. Reverse the removal procedure to install the belt.

34-INCH MOWER DECK

Refer to Fig. AG1-17 when performing the following procedure.

1. Place the mower height control lever in the lowest position.
2. Move the moveable idler away from the belt and remove the belt from the PTO pulley and idler.
3. Remove the cover over the left mower spindle pulley.
4. Remove the mower drive belt.
5. Reverse the removal procedure to install the belt. The flat side of the belt must contact the idler.

MOWER DECK

LUBRICATION

Lubricate the spindles and idler arm after every 25 hours of operation. Inject multipurpose grease through the grease fittings. One or two shots from a hand-held grease gun should be sufficient. Apply clean engine oil to the contact surface of all moving parts.

Lubricate more frequently when ambient temperature exceeds 85° F (39° C) or when operating in dusty conditions.

ADJUSTMENT

Before attempting any adjustment, the machine must be on level ground and the tires must be properly inflated. Disconnect the spark plug wire and tie it out of the way.

SIDE-TO-SIDE HEIGHT

1. Position the mower deck in the DOWN position at mid-height.
2. Loosen the rear mower deck hanger links so the deck rests on the rear rollers.

> NOTE: The deck must rest on the rollers. If not, adjust the roller position, then readjust the roller position after performing the leveling adjustment.

3. Measure the height of the blade tip above the ground. Measurement should be within $\frac{1}{8}$ inch (3.2 mm) of blade tip on opposite side.
4. Note the position of the eccentric (Fig. AG1-18) on the deck's left side. The flat on the eccentric near the bolt must be toward the rear of the deck. If not, reposition the eccentric and tighten the nut to 30 ft.-lb. (41 N•m).
5. Adjust the blade side-to-side height by rotating the eccentric on the deck's right side.
6. Recheck the blade height.
7. Tighten the rear hanger link fasteners and reposition the rear rollers, if moved.

FRONT-TO-REAR HEIGHT

1. Measure the distance from the ground to the blade from front to rear.
2A. 30-inch Mower Deck– The front of the blade should be level with the rear of the blade or up to $\frac{1}{8}$ inch (3.2 mm) higher.
2B. 34-inch Mower Deck– The front of the blade should be level with the rear of the blade or up to $\frac{1}{4}$ inch (6.4 mm) higher.
3. To adjust the front-to-rear dimension, adjust the position of the nuts (Fig. AG1-19) on the height adjustment rod.

Transport Height Adjustment

When the mower lift lever is in the transport position, the rollers on the rear of the mower deck should be $\frac{1}{8}$-$\frac{1}{4}$ inch (3.2-6.4 mm) above the ground. Refer to Fig. AG1-20 and use the following procedure to adjust the transport height.

1. Adjust the mower height to 3 inches (76 mm) on 30-inch mower deck or $2\frac{3}{4}$ inches (70 mm) on 34-inch mower deck.
2. Loosen the nut and move the spacer against the trailing arm. Retighten the nut. Perform on both sides of the mower deck.

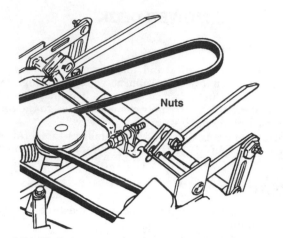

Fig. AG1-19—Rotate nuts to adjust mower height. Refer to text.

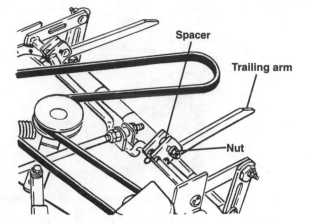

Fig. AG1-20—Refer to the text for the roller height adjustment procedure.

3. Check the roller height. If incorrect, repeat the procedure.

REMOVAL AND INSTALLATION

1. Turn the front wheels fully to the left.
2. Move the mower deck to the lowest position.
3. Push the idler arm and remove the mower belt from the mower pulleys.
4. Support the front of the mower deck with a block of wood.
5. Detach the lift cable hook from the mower deck eye.
6. Pull out the hitch lever (Fig. AG1-21), disengage the hitch and place it out of the way.
7. Remove the mower deck by moving it out from the right side of the machine.
8. Reverse the removal procedure to install the mower deck. Be sure the open portion of the hook on the lift cable is toward the rear of the machine. The trailing arms (Fig. AG1-20) must be above the torsion bar.

MOWER DECK SPINDLE

Two spindle configurations have been used. Early spindles are identified by the use of a bolt to secure the pulley. Later spindles are equipped with a nut to hold the pulley on the spindle.

OVERHAUL

Early Models (Fig. AG1-22)

1. Remove the mower deck as previously described.
2. Remove the blade.
3. Note the position of the belt guides attached to the spindle housing, then unscrew the spindle housing mounting screws and remove the spindle assembly.
4. Secure the blade adapter (15) in a vise.
5. Remove the bolt (1), lockwasher (2), washer (3), pulley (4) and shield (5).
6. Free the unit from the vise, then remove the collar (16) from the blade adapter.
7. Remove the blade adapter (15), shield (14) and shim (13).
8. Separate the spindle housings by prying apart.
9. Press the bearings off the spindle.
10. Assemble the spindle by reversing the disassembly procedure. Note the following:

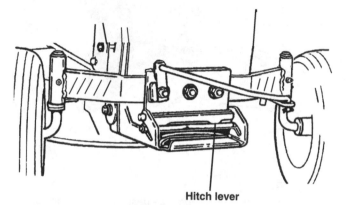

Fig. AG1-21—Pull the hitch lever to detach the hitch.

a. If a foam gasket is not available, apply RTV sealant to the upper and lower spindle housing mating surfaces.
b. Fill the lower spindle housing with lithium-based grease.
c. Install the pulley so the long end of the hub is toward the housing.
d. Tighten the pulley retaining screw to 50-70 ft.-lb. (68-95 N•m).
e. Maximum spindle end play is ⅛ inch (3.2 mm).
f. Install the long spindle housing screws at the belt guide location.

Later Models (Fig. AG1-23)

1. Remove the mower deck as previously described.
2. Remove the blade.
3. Unscrew the spindle housing mounting screws and remove the spindle assembly.
4. Secure the spindle in a vise.
5. Remove the nut (1), Belleville washers (2), pulley (3) and spacer (4).
6. Pry apart the spindle housings.
7. Disassemble the remainder of the spindle housing components.
8. Inspect the components for damage.
9. Install the washer (11) onto the shaft with the concave side toward the flange on the spindle.
10. Install the bearings and spacer (7) into the lower spindle housing.

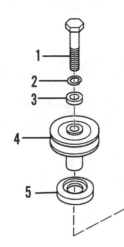

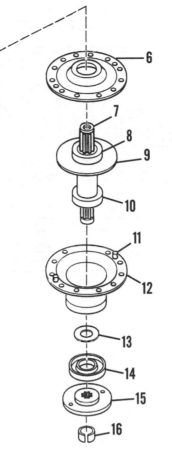

Fig. AG1-22–Exploded view of a mower spindle used on a 30-inch mower deck.

1. Bolt
2. Lockwasher
3. Washer
4. Pulley
5. Shield
6. Upper spindle housing
7. Spindle
8. Bearing
9. Foam gasket
10. Bearing
11. Pin
12. Lower spindle housing
13. Shim
14. Shield
15. Adapter
16. Collar

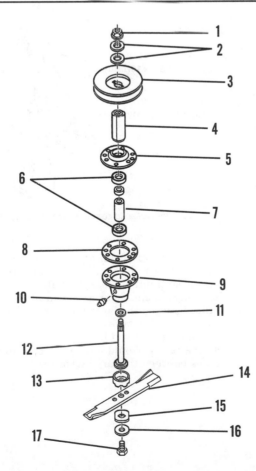

Fig. AG1-23–Exploded view of a mower spindle used on a 34-inch mower deck.

1. Nut
2. Belleville washer
3. Pulley
4. Spacer
5. Upper spindle housing
6. Bearing
7. Spacer
8. Foam gasket
9. Lower spindle housing
10. Grease fitting
11. Bearing
12. Spindle
13. Collar
14. Blade
15. Washer
16. Lockwasher
17. Bolt

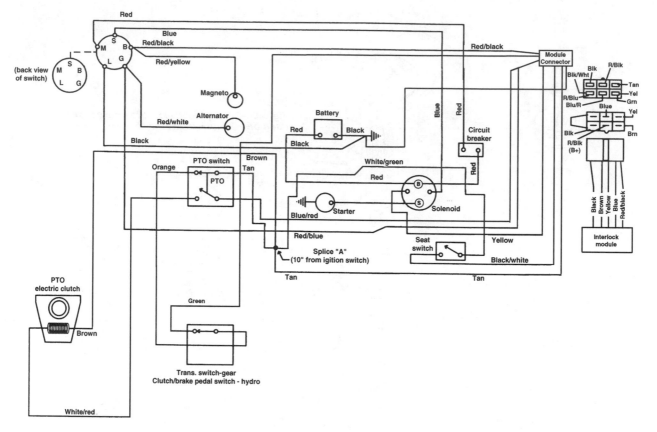

Fig AG1-24–Typical wiring schematic.

11. Install the spindle into the lower spindle housing and bearings.

12. Install the foam gasket. If a foam gasket is not available, apply RTV sealant to the upper and lower spindle housing mating surfaces.

13. Fill lower spindle housing with lithium based grease.

14. Install the remainder of the components while noting the following:

   a. Tighten pulley retaining nut to 50-70 ft.-lb. (68-95 N•m).

   b. Maximum spindle end play is ⅛ inch (3.2 mm).

ELECTRICAL

Refer to Fig. AG1-24 for a wiring schematic. Note the following points:

1. The transaxle must be in NEUTRAL, the mower must be disengaged and the operator must be in the seat for the engine to start.

2. The engine should stop if the transaxle is in gear or the mower is engaged and the operator leaves the seat.

STARTER RELAY TESTING

Note the location of the small and large terminals on the relay (Fig. AG1-25) when performing the following test.

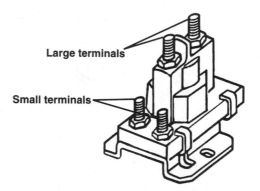

Fig. AG1-25–Refer to text for starter relay testing procedure.

1. Using an ohmmeter or continuity tester, check for continuity between the small terminals. The tester should indicate a continuity of less than 10 ohms.

2. Using an ohmmeter or continuity tester, check for continuity between the large terminals. The tester should indicate no continuity.

3. Connect a 12-volt battery to the small terminals.

4. The tester should indicate a continuity of less than 10 ohms between the large terminals.

AGCO-ALLIS
ZT SERIES

Model	Make	Engine Model	Horsepower
1692907	Kohler	CV14S	14
1692908	Kohler	CV16S	16
1693232	B&S	*	18
1693296	Kohler	CV14S	14
1693298	Kohler	CV16S	16
1693469	Kohler	CV14S	14
1693475	B&S	*	16

*Note the engine model number and refer to the engine service section in this manual for engine specifications.

FRONT WHEELS

LUBRICATION

Each front wheel hub is equipped with a grease fitting. Front wheels should be injected with a lithium-base grease after every 25 hours of operation. Lubricate the front wheels more frequently when ambient temperature exceeds 85° F (30° C) or when operating in dusty conditions.

REMOVAL AND INSTALLATION

The front wheels are equipped with replaceable bushings. To remove the wheel and bushings, proceed as follows:
1. Remove the hub cap (8–Fig. AG2-1).
2. Remove the retaining ring (7).
3. Remove the wheel with the bushings.
4. Separate the bushings from the wheel.
5. Inspect the spindle and bushings for damage.

6. Inspect the wheel for rim and hub damage.
7. Reverse the removal steps to reassemble and install the wheel and bushings. Lubricate the bushings after assembly

FRONT SPINDLES

MAINTENANCE

Lubricate the front wheel spindles after every 25 hours of operation. Inject lithium-base grease into the grease fitting on the spindle housing. Lubricate the spindles more frequently when ambient temperature exceeds 85° F. (30° C.) or when operating in dusty conditions.

OVERHAUL

Refer to Fig. AG2-2 for an exploded view of the spindle assembly. To remove a front spindle, proceed as follows.
1. Raise and support the side to be serviced.
2. Remove the wheel and tire as previously described.
3. Remove the E-ring (1–Fig. AG2-2) from the top of the spindle.

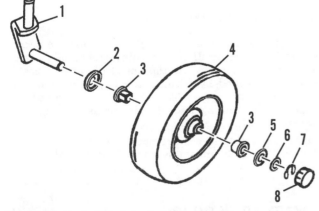

Fig. AG2-1–Exploded view of wheel assembly.

1. Spindle
2. Cup washer
3. Bushing
4. Wheel
5. Larger washer
6. Small washer
7. E-ring
8. Hub cap

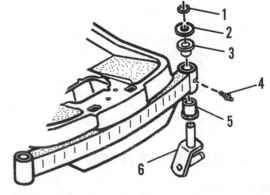

Fig. AG2-2–Exploded view of spindle assembly

1. E-ring
2. Washer
3. Bushing
4. Grease fitting
5. Bushing
6. Spindle

4. Remove the spindle (6).
5. Inspect the components for damage.
6. Install the spindle by reversing the removal procedure. Lubricate the spindle after assembly.

ENGINE

Refer to the appropriate engine section in this manual for tune-up specifications, engine overhaul procedures and engine maintenance.

REMOVAL AND INSTALLATION

1. Remove the engine cover and disconnect the spark plug wire.
2. Electric start models–Disconnect and remove the battery.
3. Disconnect any interfering electrical wires from the engine.
4. Disconnect the throttle cable from the engine.
5. Remove the mower as outlined in MOWER DECK.
6. Remove the traction drive belt from the engine pulley.
7. Detach the pulley from the engine crankshaft.
8. Remove the engine mounting fasteners.
9. Remove the engine.
10. Install the engine by reversing the removal procedure.

TRANSAXLE DRIVE BELT

Early models use five wire-type belt guides (A-Fig. AG2-3A) to hold the belt in place. Later models use three wire-type belt guides (A and D–Fig. AG2-3B).

REMOVAL AND INSTALLATION
Early Models

1. Remove the engine cover and disconnect the spark plug wire.
2. Remove the mower deck.
3. Remove the PTO clutch (P-Fig. AG3-3A) as described in this section.
4. Push down the clutch pedal.
5. Remove the drive belt (B-Fig. AG2-3A) by sliding the belt between the pulleys and the belt guides.
6. Install the belt by reversing the removal procedure. Adjust the belt as needed so there is ⅛ inch (3.2 mm) clearance between the belt and the guides.

Later Models

1. Remove the engine cover and disconnect the spark plug wire.
2. Remove the mower deck.
3. Remove the PTO clutch as described in this section.
4. Remove the carrier assembly as described in this section.
5. Remove the wire belt guide (D–Fig. AG2-3B) from the transmission pulleys.
6. Remove the drive belt (B–Fig. AG2-3B) by sliding the belt between the pulleys and the belt guides.
7. Install the drive belt by reversing the removal procedure. Adjust the belt guides as needed so there is ⅛ inch (3.2 mm) clearance between the belt and the guides.

STEERING CONTROL LINKAGE

LUBRICATION

Periodically lubricate all rubbing contact surfaces with engine oil. Apply oil more frequently when the machine is operated in dusty conditions.

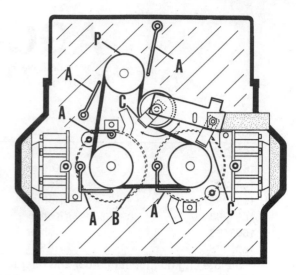

Fig. AG2-3A–Drawing of tractor drive belt components on early models. Five belt guides (A) are used on early models.

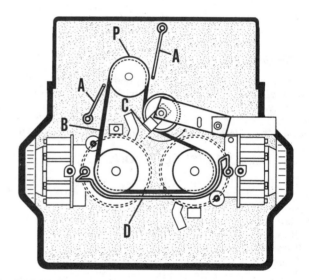

Fig. AG2-3B–Drawing of traction drive belt components on later models. Three belt guids (A and D) are used on later models.

RUNNING ADJUSTMENT

Each transaxle is independently controlled to permit zero-radius turning. If the machine tracks slightly off course while running, the top speed of each transaxle may be controlled by turning the appropriate adjustment knob (Fig. AG2-4). Minor adjustment may be necessary while running because the transaxles may not operate equally.

If the operating levers are not parallel within ⅜ inch (3.2 mm) when the machine is traveling straight ahead, perform the linkage adjustment as described in this section.

LINKAGE ADJUSTMENT

Before performing the following adjustment, be sure the machine is situated on level ground and the tires are properly inflated.

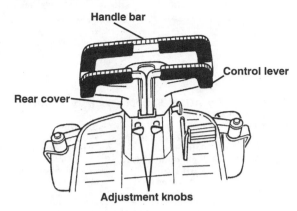

Fig. AG2-4–*Refer to text for steering linkage adjustment procedure.*

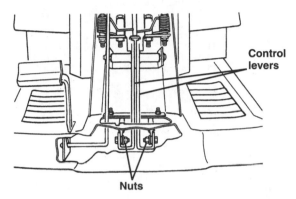

Fig AG2-5A–*Refer to text for steering linkage adjustment procedure.*

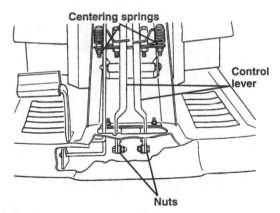

Fig. AG2-5B–*Refer to text for steering linkage adjustment procedure.*

1. Rotate the adjustment knobs (Fig. AG2-4) fully counter-clockwise.

NOTE: The front shroud is shown removed in the following drawings for clarity. Front shroud removal is not necessary to perform the adjustment.

2. Loosen the adjustment nuts shown in Figs. AG2-5A or AG2-5B.
3. Move the bolts to the bottom of the slots in the control levers.

4. Tighten the nuts and check operation. If the machine does not track properly, proceed to Step 5.
5. Loosen the adjusment nut in one of the control levers and move the bolt in the control lever slot. Retighten the nut and check machine operation.

NOTE: Perfectly straight tracking is not necessary when performing Step 6. See Step 7.

6. After noting the directional change caused by Step 5, relocate the bolts in the control lever slots to obtain tracking as straight as possible.
7. Turn the adjustment knobs shown in Fig. AG2-4 as needed to obtain straight tracking.

CONTROL LEVER POSITION ADJUSTMENT

When the machine is in neutral, the distance from each control lever (Fig. AG2-4) to the handlebar should be $2\frac{1}{4}$ to $2\frac{3}{8}$ inches (57-60 mm). If incorrect, perform the following adjustment procedure.
1. Remove the mower deck as described in this section.
2. Remove the rear handlebar cover (Fig. AG2-4).
3. If so equipped, disconnect the wires from the headlight switch.
4. Remove the front handlebar cover (4–Fig. AG2-6).
5. If so equipped, remove the headlight.
6. Remove the covers from the top of the front control tower cover (39–Fig. AG2-6) and the screws underneath the frame. Remove the front control tower cover.
7. Loosen the fastener (A–Fig. AG2-7) on each transaxle control rod.

NOTE: To assist in obtaining an equidistant space, attach a suitably sized board to the control levers.

8. Loosen the bolt in each centering spring (Fig. AG2-5B). Move the bolt in the slot to obtain the desired distance from each control lever to the handlebar, then retighten the bolt.
9. Reassemble the covers.
10. Perform the neutral adjustment as described in this section.

REAR CARRIER

The transaxles and transaxle drive belt idler are mounted on a carrier at the rear of the machine. The carrier permits the rear of the machine to pivot independently during operation. Use the following procedure to remove the carrier for service to the carrier or if removing both transaxles.

REMOVAL AND INSTALLATION

1. Disconnect the engine spark plug lead.
2. Remove any weights attached to the carrier.
3. Remove the mower deck.
4. Raise and support the rear of the machine.
5. Remove the rear wheels.
6. Remove the PTO clutch as described in this section.
7. Disconnect the electrical lead from the clutch/brake switch on the clutch rod.
8. Disconnect the transaxle control rods (B–Fig. AG2-7).
9. Disconnect the brake rod (C) from the linkage inside the carrier.
10. Detach the oil reservoirs (Fig. AG2-8) from the main-frame.

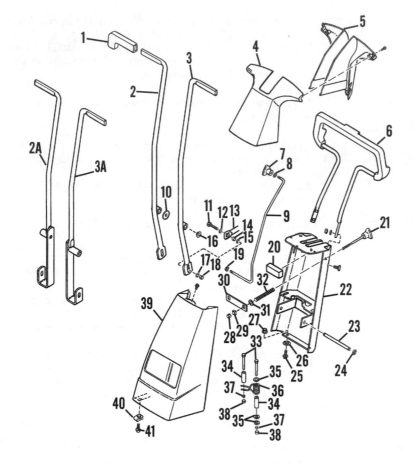

Fig AG2-6–Exploded view of control tower assembly

1. Grip	19. Nut
2. Right control lever (later models)	20. Pad
2A. Right control lever (early models)	21. Speed adjustment knob
3. Left control lever (later models)	22. Control tower
3A. Left control lever (early models)	23. Shaft
4. Front cover	24. E-ring
5. Rear cover	25. Screw
6. Handlebar	26. Washer
7. Parking brake knob	27. Nut
8. Washer	28. Locknut
9. Parking brake rod	29. Nut
10. Washer	30. Stop bar
11. Bolt	31. Washer
12. Washer	32. Spring
13. Transaxle control knob	33. Bolt
14. Spacer	34. Spacer
15. Washer	35. Washer
16. Washer	36. Spring
17. Washer	37. Lockwasher
18. Nut	38. Nut
	39. Front shroud
	40. Nut plate
	41. Screw

11. Support the carrier assembly with a jack.

12. Remove the carrier retaining bolts, then lower the carrier assembly out of the mainframe.

13. Refer to Fig. AG2-9 if disassembling carrier components.

14. Reverse the removal procedure to install the carrier assembly. Tighten the carrier retaining bolts to 75 ft.-lb. (102 N•m).

HYDROSTATIC TRANSAXLE

The machine is equipped with two hydrostatic transaxles. Each transaxle drives a rear wheel, which allows zero-turn-steering through independent operation of the transaxles.

LUBRICATION

Normal Operation

The oil level should be at maintained at the FULL mark on the oil reservoirs (Fig. AG2-8). If necessary, add oil to the tanks. Recommended oil is Simplicity Multipurpose Hydro Oil, Mobil DTE-26.

Refill and Bleed Transaxle

To refill the hydrostatic transaxle with oil and bleed air from the system after the transaxle has been serviced, proceed as follows.

CAUTION: Be sure the machine is adequately supported and cannot move when performing the following procedure.

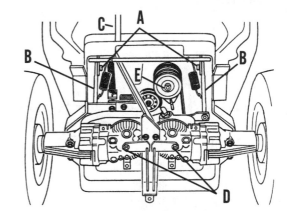

Fig. AG2-7–Drawing of transaxle carrier underside.

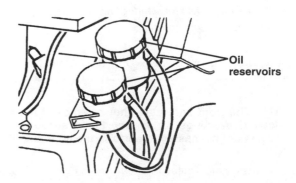

Fig. AG2-8–Drawing showing transaxle oil reservoir used on later models. On early models, only a single hose connects the oil reservoir to the transaxle.

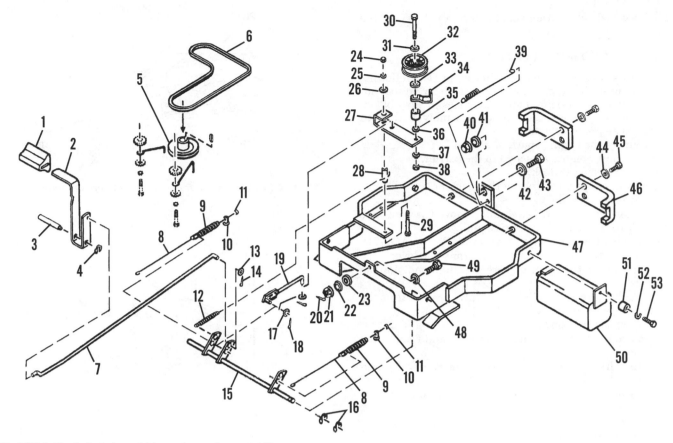

Fig AG2-9–Exploded view of transaxle carrier assembly.

1. Pedal pad
2. Clutch/brake pedal
3. Shaft
4. Clip
5. Engine pulley
6. Drive belt
7. Clutch/brake rod
8. Brake rod
9. Spring
10. Trunnion pin
11. Lock nut
12. Spring
13. Washer
14. Cotter pin
15. Pivot shaft
16. Clips
17. Washer
18. Cotter pin
19. Clutch rod
20. Cotter pin
21. Locknut
22. Belleville washer
23. Bushing
24. Nut
25. Lockwasher
26. Washer
27. Idler arm
28. Pivot spacer
29. Bolt
30. Bolt
31. Washer
32. Pulley
33. Washer
34. Belt guide (18 hp models)
35. Spacer
36. Spacer
37. Lockwasher
38. Nut
39. Spring
40. Locknut
41. Bushing
42. Washer
43. Bolt
44. Washer
45. Bolt
46. Weight (18 hp models)
47. Carrier
48. Washer
49. Bolt
50. Weight
51. Spacer
52. Lockwasher
53. Bolt

1. Fill the oil reservoirs to the full line.

2. Raise and support the rear of the machine so the rear wheels are off the ground.

3. Start the engine and run at idle speed for about three minutes.

4. Move the steering control levers from full forward to full reverse in 15-second intervals for three minutes.

5. Return the levers to NEUTRAL for five seconds.

6. Add oil to the oil reservoirs as needed.

7. Repeat the procedure until the oil level stabilizes.

8. Check operation. Repeat the procedure if the machine does not function normally.

NEUTRAL ADJUSTMENT

When released the control levers should return to the neutral position. Check, and if necessary, adjust the control lever positions as described in this section.

CAUTION: Be sure the unit is adequately supported and cannot move when performing the following procedure.

1. Position the machine on level ground with the parking brake disengaged.

2. Raise and support the rear of the machine.

3. Loosen the fastener (A–Fig. AG2-7) on each transaxle control rod so the rods can move freely.

4. Move each transaxle control rod (B) until it engages the positive neutral detent in the transaxle.

5. Without moving the rods, tighten the fastener (A) on each rod.

NOTE: Place a weight in the operator's seat to activate the seat switch so the engine will run.

6. Start the engine, then run it at half-throttle.

7. Operate each control lever and check the operation of the respective rear wheel. When the control lever is re-

leased, rear wheel rotation should stop. If not, repeat the neutral adjustment procedure.

REMOVAL AND INSTALLATION

The transaxles are mounted in a carrier. The following procedure describes the removal procedure for an individual transaxle. If servicing both transaxles, it may be advantageous to remove the carrier assembly with both transaxles as previously described.
1. Disconnect the engine spark plug lead.
2. Remove any weights attached to the carrier.
3. Remove the mower deck.
4. Raise and support the rear of the machine.
5. Remove the rear wheel.
6. Push down the clutch pedal and remove the transaxle drive belt from the transaxle drive pulley.
7. Disconnect the transaxle control rod (B–Fig. AG2-7).
8. Disconnect the brake rod from the transaxle lever.
9. Disconnect the transaxle oil reservoir hose and plug the openings.
10. Detach the pressure relief dump valve arm (D) from the transaxle.
11. Support the transaxle.
12. Remove the transaxle mounting bolts and remove the transaxle.
13. Install the transaxle by reversing the removal procedure. Note the following:
   a. Perform the neutral adjustment procedure as described in this section.
   b. Perform the brake adjustment procedure as described in this section.

OVERHAUL

All models are equipped with two Eaton Model 778 hydrostatic transaxles. Refer to the HYDROSTATIC TRANSAXLE REPAIR section for service information.

BRAKE ADJUSTMENT

Refer to Fig. AG2-10 when performing the following procedure.
1. Raise the seat.
2. Push the brake lever on the transaxle forward as far as possible.
3. Pull the brake rod to the rear.
4. Measure the gap between the nut on the brake rod and the pivot.
5. Rotate the nut so the gap is $\frac{1}{8}$ inch (3.2 mm).
6. Repeat the procedure on the opposite transaxle.

ELECTRIC PTO CLUTCH

Early and late models have been equipped with different PTO clutch units. The clutch unit may be identified by the color of the electrical wires. The electrical wires connected to early units are colored brown and white/red. Late model clutches are connected to wires colored orange and black/white.

TESTING

Use the following procedure to locate the cause if the PTO clutch malfunctions.
1. Turn the ignition switch ON.
2. Actuate the PTO switch.

Fig AG2-10–Refer to text for brake adjustment procedure.

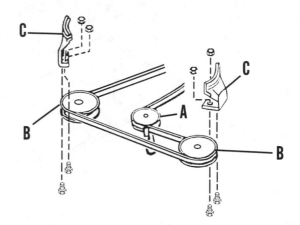

Fig. AG2-11–Drawing showing mower drive belt on 38-inch mower deck

A. Idler pulley
B. Mower spindle pulley
C. Belt guide

3. If the clutch does not engage, disconnect the wiring connector at the clutch.
4. Use a 12-volt test lamp to check continuity of the wire coming from the PTO switch.
5. If the lamp lights, the PTO is either defective or the wiring connector at the clutch field coil is faulty.
6. To check the PTO field coil, perform the following procedures:
   a. Clutch installed–Connect an ohmmeter to the clutch terminals. The ohmmeter should indicate a resistance of 6.59-7.29 ohms on early units or 2.74-3.02 ohms on late units.
   b. Clutch removed–Apply a 12-volt source to the clutch terminals. Hold a piece of metal next to the coil. The coil should attract the metal. There should be an audible click when the clutch engages.
7. If the PTO clutch fails the preceding tests, replace the coil or entire clutch assembly.

REMOVAL AND INSTALLATION

1. Remove the mower deck as described in this section.
2. Raise and support the rear of the machine.
3. Disconnect the PTO clutch electrical wire.
4. Remove the clutch retaining bolt (E–Fig. AG2-7).
5. Remove the clutch assembly from the crankshaft.
6. Reverse the removal procedure to install the PTO clutch. Apply antiseize compound to the engine crankshaft. Tighten the clutch retaining bolt to 35 ft.-lb. (47.6 N•m).

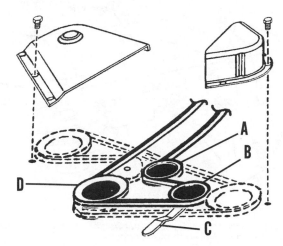

Fig. AG2-12–Drawing showing mower drive belt on 44-inch and 50-inch mower decks.

A. Idler pulley
B. Idler pulley
C. Lever
D. Center mower spindle pulley

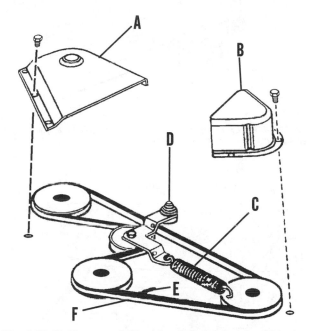

Fig. AG2-13–Mower spindle drive belt routing for 44-inch and 50-inch mower decks.

7. If installing a new clutch or components, run the engine at full speed and engage the clutch several times after the mower is installed to burnish the clutch surfaces.

MOWER DECK DRIVE BELT

REMOVAL AND INSTALLATION

38-inch Mower Deck

Refer to Fig. AG2-11 when performing the following procedure.
1. Remove the mower deck as described in this section
2. Loosen the idler (A) bolt and relocate the belt guide.
3. Loosen and move the belt guides (C) adjacent to the mower spindle pulleys (B).
4. Remove the belt.

5. Install the belt, then move the belt guides into proper position.
6. Install the mower deck.

44-inch and 50-inch Mower Deck

Refer to Fig. AG2-12 when performing the following procedure.
1. Place the mower height control lever in the lowest position.
2. Move the moveable idler (B) away from the belt using the lever (C) attached to the idler.
3. Remove the belt from the PTO pulley, then remove the mower drive belt.
4. Reverse the removal procedure to install the belt.

MOWER SPINDLE DRIVE BELT REPLACEMENT (44-INCH AND 50-INCH MOWER DECK)

Refer to Fig.AG2-13 when performing the following procedure.
1. Remove the mower deck as described in this section.
2. Remove the mower deck drive belt as described in this section.
3. Remove the belt covers (A and B).
4. Detach the spring (C) from the idler arm.
5. Loosen the idler arm bolt (D).
6. Remove the spring (E).
7. Remove the spindle drive belt (F) from the deck pulleys.
8. Reverse the removal procedure to install the belt.

MOWER DECK

LUBRICATION

Lubricate the spindles and idler arm after every 25 hours of operation. Inject grease through the grease fittings. One or two shots from a hand-held grease gun should be sufficient. Use a lithium-base grease. Apply clean engine oil to the contact surface of all moving parts.

Lubricate more frequently when ambient temperature exceeds 85° F (39° C) or if operating when dusty conditions.

ADJUSTMENT

Before attempting any adjustment, the machine must be on level ground and the tires must be properly inflated. Disconnect the spark plug wire and tie it out of the way.

SIDE-TO-SIDE HEIGHT

1. Position the mower deck in the highest cutting position.
2. Position the blades so they are perpendicular to the machine centerline.
3. Measure the height of the blade tips above the ground. Measurement should be within $\frac{1}{8}$ inch (3.2 mm) from side-to-side. If the dimension is incorrect, proceed to Step 4.
4. Loosen the nut (Fig. AG2-14) adjacent to the eccentric.
5. Loosen the screw (Fig. AG2-14).
6. Adjust the blade side-to-side height by rotating the eccentric.
7. Retighten the nut and screw.
8. Recheck the blade height.

FRONT-TO-REAR HEIGHT

38-inch and 44-inch Mower Deck

1. Measure the distance from the ground to the blade from front to rear.

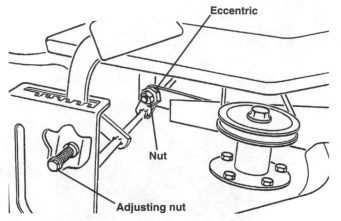

Fig AG2-14–Side-to-side adjustment for all models.

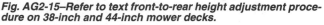

Fig. AG2-15–Refer to text front-to-rear height adjustment procedure on 38-inch and 44-inch mower decks.

2A. 38-inch Mower Deck–The front of the blade should be level with the rear of the blade or up to $\frac{1}{8}$ inch (3.2 mm) higher.

2B. 44-inch Mower Deck–The front of the blade should be $\frac{1}{8}$-$\frac{1}{4}$ inch (3.2-6.4 mm) higher then the rear.

3. To adjust front-to-rear dimension, loosen the nut on the eccentric (Fig. AG2-15) and rotate the eccentric.

4. Tighten the nut and recheck the blade heights.

5. If the mower height control lever drops out of the quadrant, rotate the spring adjusting nut (Fig. AG2-15) clockwise to increase spring tension. Do not totally compress the spring.

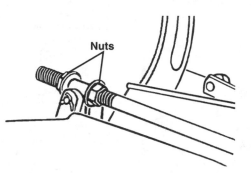

50-inch Mower Deck

1. Measure the distance from the ground to the blade from front to rear.

2. The front of the blade should be $\frac{1}{8}$-$\frac{1}{4}$ inch (3.2-6.4 mm) higher then the rear.

3. To adjust front-to-rear dimension, rotate the nuts on the height control rod (Fig. AG2-16).

4. Tighten the nuts against the bracket and recheck blade height.

Fig. AG2-16–Refer to text for front-to-rear height adjustment procedure on 50-inch mower deck.

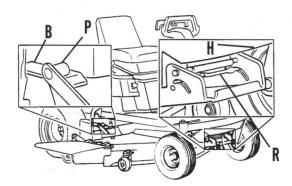

Fig. AG2-17–Mower hitch components

REMOVAL AND INSTALLATION

38-inch and 44-inch Mower Deck

1. Turn the front wheels fully sideways.

2. Move the mower deck to the lowest position.

3. Push the idler arm lever and remove the mower belt from the PTO clutch pulley.

4. Pull out the hitch release rod (R–Fig, AG2-17) and disengage the front mower deck hitch (H).

5. Slide the mower deck forward so the support pins (P) on each side disengage from the support brackets (B).

6. Remove the mower deck by moving it out from the right side of the machine.

7. Reverse the removal procedure to install the mower deck.

50-inch Mower Deck

1. Turn the front wheels fully sideways.

2. Set the mower height control to the middle height position.

3. Push the idler arm lever and remove the mower belt from the PTO clutch pulley.

4. Pull out the hitch release rod (R–Fig. AG2-17) and disengage the front mower deck hitch (H).

5. Remove the hitch rod pin (Fig. AG2-18), then remove the hitch rod and disengage the hitch from the mower deck.

6. Slide the mower deck forward so the support pins (P–Fig. 2-17) on each side disengage from the support brackets (B).

7. Remove the mower deck by moving it out from the right side of the machine.

8. Reverse the removal procedure to install the mower deck.

MOWER DECK SPINDLE

OVERHAUL

Refer to Fig. AG2-19 for 38-inch mower deck or Fig. AG2-20 for 44-inch and 50-inch mower decks when performing the following procedure.

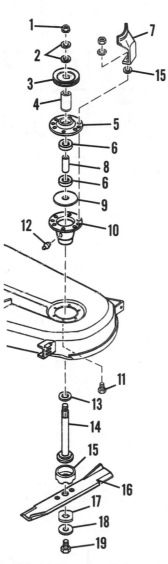

Fig. AG2-18–Remove the pin and rad to detach the hitch from the 50-inch mower deck.

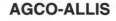

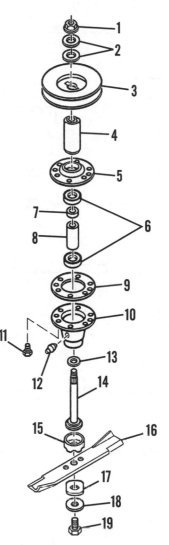

Fig. AG2-19–Exploded view of spindle assembly used on 38-inch mower decks.

1. Nut	11. Screw
2. Belleville washers	12. Grease fitting
3. Pulley	13. Washer
4. Spacer	14. Spindle
5. Spindle upper housing	15. Grass shield
6. Bearings	16. Mower blade
7. Belt stop	17. Washer
8. Spacer	18. Spring washer
9. Foam gasket	19. Screw
10. Spindle lower housing	

Fig. AG2-20–Exploded view of mower spindle asssembly used on 44- and 55-inch mower decks.

1. Nut	10. Lower spindle housing
2. Belleville washer	11. Bolt
3. Pulley	12. Grease fitting
4. Spacer	13. Washer
5. Upper spindle housing	14. Spindle
6. Bearing	15. Collar
7. Spacer (44-&	16. Blade
55-inch decks)	17. Washer
8. Spacer	18. Spring washer
9. Foam gasket	19. Bolt

1. Remove the mower deck as previously described.

2. Remove the blade.

3. Unscrew the spindle housing mounting screws and remove the spindle assembly.

4. Secure the spindle in a vise.

5. Remove the nut (1), Belleville washers (2), pulley (3) and spacer (4).

6. Pry apart the spindle housings.

7. Disassemble the remainder of the spindle housing components.

8. Inspect the components for damage.

9. Install the washer (13) onto the shaft with the concave side toward the flange on the spindle.

10. Install the bearings and spacer (8) into the lower spindle housing.

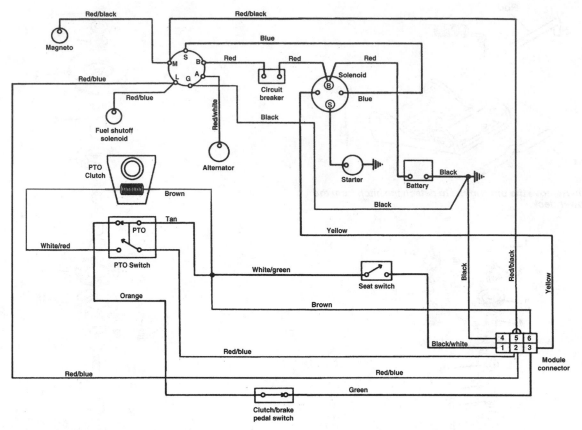

Fig. AG2-21–Wiring diagram for early models. Early models are equipped with an interlock module.

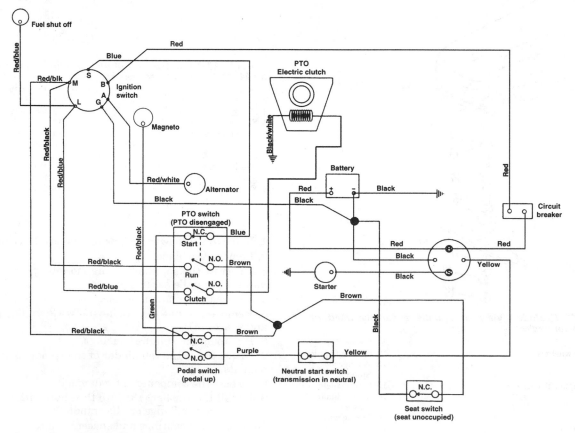

Fig. AG2-22–Wiring diagram for later models.

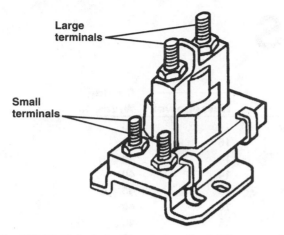

Large terminals

Small terminals

Fig. AG2-23–Refer to text for starter relay testing procedure.

11. Install the spindle into the lower spindle housing and bearings.

12. Install the foam gasket. If a foam gasket is not available, apply RTV sealant to the upper and lower spindle housing mating surfaces.

13. Fill the lower spindle housing with lithium-base grease.

14. Install the remainder of the components while noting the following:

    a. Tighten the pulley retaining screw to 55-75 ft.-lb. (75-100 N•m).

    b. Maximum spindle end play is ⅛ inch (3.2 mm).

    c. Tighten the blade retaining screw to 45-55 ft.-lb. (61-74 N•m).

ELECTRICAL

Refer to Fig. AG2-21 or AG2-22 for a wiring schematic. Early models are equipped with a safety interlock module. The module grounds the engine ignition if the PTO is operated when the operator is out of the seat, or if the brake pedal is up when the operator is out of the seat.

Note the following points:

1. The transaxle must be in NEUTRAL, the mower must be disengaged and the operator must be in the seat for the engine to start.

2. The engine should stop if the transaxle is in gear or the mower is engaged and the operator leaves the seat.

STARTER RELAY TESTING

Note the location of the small and large terminals on the relay (Fig. AG2-23) when performing the following test.

1. Using an ohmmeter or continuity tester, check for continuity between the small terminals. The tester should a indicate continuity of less than 10 ohms.

2. Using an ohmmeter or continuity tester, check for continuity between the large terminals. The tester should indicate no continuity.

3. Connect a 12-volt battery to the small terminals.

4. The tester should indicate a continuity of less than 10 ohms between the large terminals.

INTERLOCK MODULE TESTING (EARLY MODELS)

The interlock module should be considered faulty only after all other wiring and devices have been tested or checked. An accurate testing procedure is not available. Replace the unit with a new or good unit and recheck operation.

ARIENS

Model	Make	Engine Model	Horsepower	Cutting Width, In.
915001 (EZR1440)	*	*	14	40
915002 (EZR1648)	*	*	16	48
915003 (EZR1540)	*	*	15	40
915004 (EZR1440)	B&S	28P777	14	40
915005 (EZR1540)	Kohler	PS	15	40
915006 (EZR1640)	Tec.	OHV16	16	40
915007 (EZR1648)	B&S	303777	16	48
915301 (EZR1440)	B&S	*	14	40
915302 (EZR1648)	B&S	*	16	48
915303 (EZR1440)	B&S	*	14	40

*Note the engine model number and refer to the engine service section in this manual for engine specifications.

FRONT WHEELS

LUBRICATION

Each front wheel hub is equipped with a sealed bearing. Periodic lubrication is not required.

REMOVAL AND INSTALLATION

Each front wheel is equipped with a replaceable bearing. To remove the wheel and bearing, refer to Fig. AR1-1 and proceed as follows:
1. Support the front of the mower.
2. Remove the nut (19–Fig. AR1-1) and withdraw the axle bolt (23).
3. Remove the wheel with bearing.
4. Separate the bearing from the wheel.
5. Inspect the bearing for damage.
6. Inspect the wheel for rim and hub damage.
7. Reverse the removal steps to reassemble.

FRONT SPINDLES

MAINTENANCE

Lubricate the front wheel spindles after every 50 hours of operation. Inject grease to the spindles through the grease fitting (7–Fig. AR1-1) at each end of the axle. One or two shots from a hand-held grease gun should be sufficient. Use moly-lithium grease.

OVERHAUL

Refer to Fig. AR1-1 for an exploded view of the spindle assembly. To remove a front spindle, proceed as follows:
1. Raise and support the side to be serviced.
2. Remove the wheel and tire as previously described.
3. Remove the retaining bolt (13–Fig. AR1-1), lockwasher and washer.
4. Remove the spindle.

5. Inspect components for damage.
6. Install the spindle by reversing the removal procedure. Tighten the spindle retaining bolt securely.

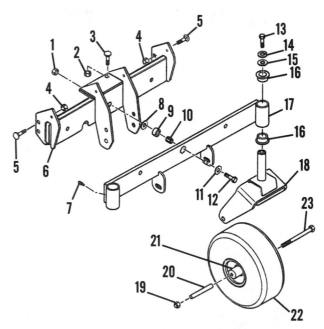

Fig. AR1-1–Exploded view of front axle assembly.

1. Nut	13. Bolt
2. Nut	14. Lockwasher
3. Bolt	15. Washer
4. Nut	16. Flange bushing
5. Bolt	17. Axle main member
6. Crossmember	18. Spindle
7. Grease fitting	19. Locknut
8. Washer	20. Bushing
9. Bushing	21. Bearings
10. Bushing	22. Wheel
11. Washer	23. Bolt
12. Bolt	

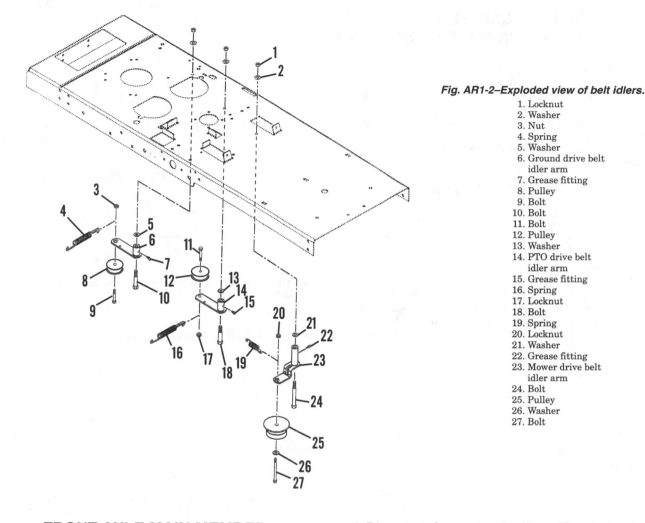

Fig. AR1-2–Exploded view of belt idlers.

1. Locknut
2. Washer
3. Nut
4. Spring
5. Washer
6. Ground drive belt
   idler arm
7. Grease fitting
8. Pulley
9. Bolt
10. Bolt
11. Bolt
12. Pulley
13. Washer
14. PTO drive belt
   idler arm
15. Grease fitting
16. Spring
17. Locknut
18. Bolt
19. Spring
20. Locknut
21. Washer
22. Grease fitting
23. Mower drive belt
   idler arm
24. Bolt
25. Pulley
26. Washer
27. Bolt

FRONT AXLE MAIN MEMBER OVERHAUL

The front axle main member is center-pivoted in the crossmember at the front of the chassis. Refer to the following procedure to remove and install the front axle main member.

1. Remove the mower deck as described in this section.
2. Raise and support the front end of the frame.
3. Remove the front spindles as previously described.
4. Support the axle main member.
5. Remove the axle bolt (12–Fig. AR1-1), then lower and remove the axle main member (17).
6. Inspect the bushings in the axle main member and replace if damaged.
7. Clean and inspect all parts. Replace damaged parts.
8. Install by reversing the removal procedure. Tighten the pivot bolt securely.

ENGINE

Refer to the appropriate engine section in this manual for tune-up specifications, engine overhaul procedures and engine maintenance.

REMOVAL AND INSTALLATION

1. Remove the engine cover.
2. Disconnect the spark plug wire.

3. Disconnect the negative battery cable.
4. Disconnect any interfering electrical wires from the engine.
5. Disconnect the throttle cable from the engine.
6. Disconnect the fuel line from the engine.
7. Detach the exhaust system from the engine.
8. Remove the belts from the engine pulley.
9. Remove the engine retaining bolts.
10. Remove the engine.
11. Install by reversing the removal procedure.

BELT IDLERS

Drive belt tension for the mower clutch drive belt and transaxle drive belt is maintained by spring-loaded idler arms. Refer to Fig. AR1-2.

LUBRICATION

Lubricate the idler arms after every 50 hours of operation. Inject grease into the idler arms through the grease fittings on each idler arm. One or two shots from a hand-held grease gun should be sufficient. Use moly-lithium grease.

REMOVAL AND INSTALLATION

Refer to Fig. AR1-2 when removing and installing the belt idler arms. Note the position of the pulley and pulley retaining bolt in Fig. AR1-2 when installing the pulley on the idler arm.

TRANSAXLE DRIVE BELT
REMOVAL AND INSTALLATION

1. Disconnect the battery negative lead.
2. Disconnect the engine spark plug lead.
3. Detach the spring from the transaxle belt idler (A—Fig. AR1-3).
4. Remove the transaxle drive belt (B) from the engine and transaxle pulleys.
5. Install the transaxle drive belt by reversing the removal procedure.

STEERING CONTROL LINKAGE

Each transaxle is independently controlled to permit zero-radius turning. Refer to Fig. AR1-4 for an exploded view of the steering control linkage.

LUBRICATION

Lubricate the control arms and flange bushings on both sides after every 50 hours of operation. Inject grease into the grease fittings (27 and 37–Fig. AR1-4) using moly-lithium grease. One or two shots from a hand-held grease gun should be sufficient.

NEUTRAL ADJUSTMENT

Note that the following adjustment procedure must be performed on both sides for each transaxle.

> **CAUTION: Be sure the unit is adequately supported and cannot move when performing the following procedure.**

1. Raise and support the rear of the unit. The rear wheels must be off the ground.
2. Remove the rear fenders.
3. Place the steering control levers in the NEUTRAL position.
4. Be sure the PTO switch is OFF.
5. Loosen the locknuts (A—Fig. AR1-5) securing the outer control arm (B).
6. Loosen the jam nuts on the steering control rod (C).
7. Adjust the length of the steering control rod (C) so the bearing (D) seats in the neutral bend (E) on the neutral detent bracket (F). Be sure the steering control hand lever is still in NEUTRAL.
8. Tighten the steering control rod (C) jam nuts.

> **NOTE: Place a weight in the operator's seat to activate the seat switch so the engine will run.**

9. Start the engine, then run it at half-throttle.
10. Move the outer control arm (B) so the rear wheel does not rotate. If it is not possible to stop wheel rotation by moving the outer control arm, adjust the transaxle linkage as described in the transaxle section.
11. Tighten the locknuts (A).
12. Repeat the procedure for the opposite side.
13. Operate the steering control levers and be sure the rear wheels do not rotate when the levers are in NEUTRAL.

HYDROSTATIC TRANSAXLE

The unit is equipped with two hydrostatic transaxles. Each transaxle drives a rear wheel, which allows

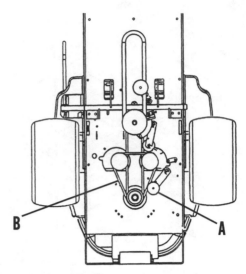

Fig. AG1-3–Refer to text for ground drive belt removal and installation procedure.

zero-turn-steering through independent operation of the transaxles.

LUBRICATION

Normal Operation

The oil level should be maintained at the FULL mark on the oil expansion tank (2–Fig. AR1-6). If necessary, add oil to the tank. Recommended oil is Mobil DTE-26.

Refill and Bleed Transaxle

To refill the hydrostatic transmission with oil and bleed air from the system after the transaxle has been serviced, proceed as follows.

> **CAUTION: Be sure the unit is adequately supported and cannot move when performing the following procedure.**

1. Fill the oil tank to the full line.
2. Raise and support the rear of the unit so the rear wheels are off the ground.
3. Remove the rear fenders, then remove the steering control linkage stops so the linkage can move full range.
4. Start the engine and run at idle speed for about three minutes.
5. Move the steering control lever from full forward to full reverse in 15-second intervals for three minutes.
6. Return the lever to NEUTRAL for five seconds.
7. Add oil to the oil tank as needed.
8. Repeat the procedure until the oil level stabilizes.
9. Install the steering control linkage stops and lower the unit.
10. Check operation. Repeat the procedure if the unit does not function normally.

NEUTRAL ADJUSTMENT

> **CAUTION: Be sure the unit is adequately supported and cannot move when performing the following procedure.**

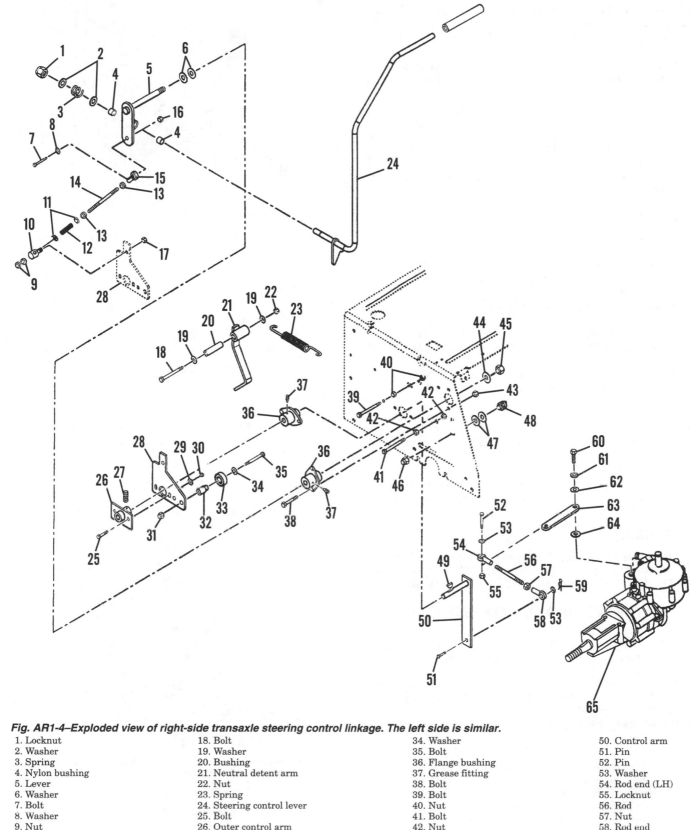

Fig. AR1-4–Exploded view of right-side transaxle steering control linkage. The left side is similar.

1. Locknut	18. Bolt	34. Washer
2. Washer	19. Washer	35. Bolt
3. Spring	20. Bushing	36. Flange bushing
4. Nylon bushing	21. Neutral detent arm	37. Grease fitting
5. Lever	22. Nut	38. Bolt
6. Washer	23. Spring	39. Bolt
7. Bolt	24. Steering control lever	40. Nut
8. Washer	25. Bolt	41. Bolt
9. Nut	26. Outer control arm	42. Nut
10. Pivot	27. Grease fitting	43. Locknut
11. Washer	28. Inner control arm	44. Washer
12. Spring	29. Washer	45. Locknut
13. Nut	30. Locknut	46. Nut
14. Rod	31. Locknut	47. Washer
15. Rod end	32. Hub	48. Neutral switch
16. Locknut	33. Bearing	49. Key
17. Locknut		

50. Control arm
51. Pin
52. Pin
53. Washer
54. Rod end (LH)
55. Locknut
56. Rod
57. Nut
58. Rod end
59. Hairpin
60. Bolt
61. Lockwasher
62. Washer
63. Shift control arm
64. Washer
65. Transaxle

1. Check and, if necessary, adjust the steering control linkage as previously described.
2. Loosen the jam nut (A–Fig. AR1-7) on the control rod (B).

NOTE: Place a weight in the operator's seat to activate the seat switch so the engine will run.

3. Start the engine, then run it at half-throttle.
4. Rotate the transaxle control rod (B) as needed so the rear wheel does not rotate.
5. Tighten the jam nut (A).
6. Stop the engine.
7. Perform the adjustment procedure for the opposite rear wheel.

REMOVAL AND INSTALLATION

The transaxles are mounted in a subframe, which requires that the subframe and transaxles be removed as an unit. Refer to Fig. AR1-8.
1. Disconnect the battery negative lead.
2. Disconnect the engine spark plug lead.
3. Raise and support the rear of the unit.
4. Remove the rear wheels.
5. Remove the transaxle drive belt as previously described.
6. Detach the PTO drive belt idler arm spring from the transaxle subframe.
7. Detach the control arm rod ends from both transaxles.
8. On the left transaxle, detach the parking brake linkage from the transaxle.
9. Disconnect the oil hose.
10. Support the transaxles.
11. Remove the three subframe retaining screws on each side and remove the transaxles and subframe.
12. Remove the transaxle from the subframe.
13. To install the transaxle, reverse the removal procedure. Fill the oil tank as needed, and if necessary, bleed air from the transaxle.

OVERHAUL

All models are equipped with two Eaton Model 778 hydrostatic transaxles. Refer to the HYDROSTATIC TRANSAXLE REPAIR section for service information.

PARKING BRAKE ADJUSTMENT

Pulling the parking brake knob fully forward engages the parking brake, while moving it backward disengages the brake.
1. Adjust the position of the jam nuts on the parking brake rod (1–Fig. AR1-8) so the rod cannot move backward when the brake is engaged
2. If the brake on both rear wheels is not engaged, proceed as follows:
   a. Remove the hairpin and clevis pin (3).
   b. Rotate the clevis (4) as needed so the braking action at both rear wheels is balanced. Note that the brake levers on the transaxles should be perpendicular to the axles in the disengaged position.
   c. Reinstall the clevis pin and hairpin.

PTO CLUTCH DRIVE BELT REMOVAL AND INSTALLATION

1. Remove the mower drive belt (D–Fig. AR1-9) as described in this section.

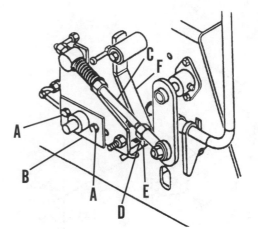

Fig. AR1-5–Refer to text for neutral adjustment procedure.

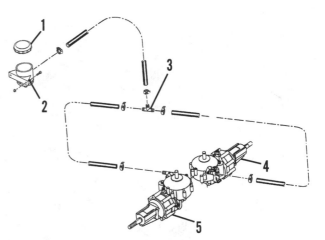

Fig. AR1-6–Drawing of transaxle oil reservoir and hoses.

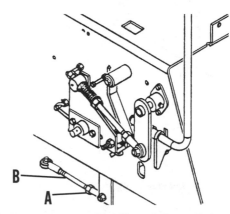

Fig. AR1-7–View of transaxle shift control rod. Refer to text for neutral adjustment procedure.

2. Remove the transaxle drive belt as described in this section.
3. Detach the spring from the clutch idler (A–Fig. AR1-9).
4. Disconnect the PTO clutch electrical lead.
5. Remove the PTO drive belt (B) from the engine and clutch pulleys.
6. Install the PTO drive belt by reversing the removal procedure.

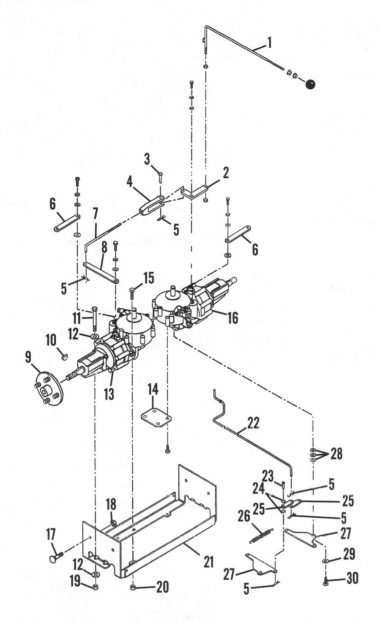

Fig. AR1-8–Exploded view of transaxle sub-frame and brake and dump valve linkage.

1. Parking brake control lever
2. Transaxle brake arm
3. Clevis pin
4. Clevis
5. Hairpin
6. Shift arm
7. Rod
8. Transaxle brake arm
9. Wheel hub
10. Key
11. Bolt
12. Washer
13. Transaxle (left)
14. Bracket
15. Bolt
16. Tranaxle (right)
17. Bolt
18. Locknut
19. Locknut
20. Locknut
21. Subframe
22. Dump valve lever
23. Clevis pin
24. Washer
25. Link
26. Spring
27. Plate
28. Washer
29. Washer
30. Scrcw

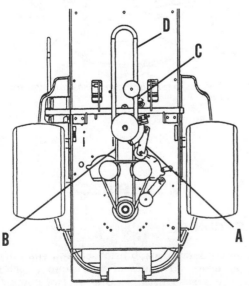

Fig. AR1-9–Refer to text for PTO drive belt removal and installation procedure.

ELECTRIC PTO CLUTCH

TESTING

Use the following procedure to locate the cause if the PTO clutch malfunctions.

1. Turn the ignition switch ON.

2. Actuate the PTO switch.

3. If the clutch does not engage, disconnect the wiring connector from the clutch.

4. Use a 12-volt test lamp to check continuity of the wire coming from the PTO switch.

5. If the lamp lights, the PTO is either defective or the wiring connector at the clutch field coil is faulty.

6. To check the PTO field coil, perform the following procedures:

   a. Clutch installed–Connect an ohmmeter to the clutch wire and ground. Ohmmeter should indicate the resistance specified in the following table.

Models	Coil resistance
915001, 915004, 915301, 915303	5.87-7.87 ohms
915002, 915003, 915005, 915006, 915007, 915302	1.98-3.98 ohms

b. Clutch removed—Ground the field coil frame and energize the coil lead wire with a known 12-volt source. Hold a piece of steel next to the coil. The coil should attract the steel.

7. If the pto clutch fails the preceding tests, replace the coil or entire clutch assembly.

NOTE: Ariens only supplies the complete clutch assembly. Note clutch manufacturer. It may be possible to obtain clutch parts from other parts suppliers.

REMOVAL AND INSTALLATION

1. Remove the mower drive belt as described in this section.
2. Disconnect the pto clutch electrical wire.
3. Remove the clutch retaining bolt.
4. Remove the clutch assembly from the jackshaft. Use a plastic hammer to tap and loosen the clutch from the jackshaft if necessary.
5. Reverse the removal procedure to install the pto clutch. Apply Loctite 271 to the clutch retaining bolt and tighten to 40 ft.-lb. (54 N•m).

PTO JACKSHAFT OVERHAUL

1. Remove the mower deck.
2. Disconnect the battery negative lead.
3. Disconnect the engine spark plug lead.
4. Raise and support the unit.
5. Remove the right, rear wheel.
6. Remove the transaxle drive belt and PTO clutch drive belt as described in this section.
7. Remove the four screws securing the jackshaft housing (11–Fig. AR1-10).
8. Remove the jackshaft assembly.
9. Remove the clutch retaining bolt.
10. Remove the clutch assembly from the jackshaft. Use a plastic hammer to tap and loosen the clutch from the jackshaft if necessary.
11. Refer to Fig. AR1-10 and disassemble the jackshaft as needed. Note that the bearings are pressed into the housing. Inspect the components for damage.
12. Reverse the disassembly procedure to reassemble the jackshaft. Note the following:
   a. Apply Loctite 271 to the upper jackshaft retaining bolt (17–Fig. AR1-10) and tighten to 40 ft.-lb. (54 N•m).
   b. Tighten the jackshaft housing retaining bolts to 25 ft.-lb. (34 N•m).

MOWER DRIVE BELT REMOVAL AND INSTALLATION

1. Detach the idler arm spring (C–Fig. AR1-9) from the frame.
2. Remove the mower drive belt (D) from the PTO clutch pulley.
3. Remove the mower drive belt from the mower drive pulley.

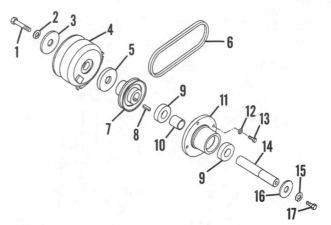

Fig. AR1-10–PTO clutch and jackshaft assembly.

1. Bolt
2. Lockwasher
3. Washer
4. PTO clutch
5. Spacer
6. Belt
7. Pulley
8. Key
9. Bearing
10. Spacer
11. Bearing housing
12. Washer
13. Bolt
14. Jackshaft
15. Washer
16. Lockwasher
17. Bolt

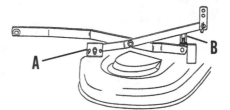

Fig. AR1-11A–Refer to the text for the mower deck adjustment procedure.

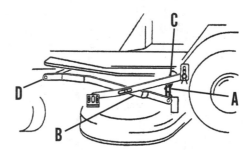

Fig. AR1-11B–Refer to text for mower deck removal and installation procedure.

4. Install the mower drive belt by reversing the removal procedure.

MOWER DECK

LUBRICATION

On 48-inch mower deck, lubricate the spindles and pivot arm after every 50 hours of operation. Inject grease through the grease fittings. One or two shots from a hand-held grease gun should be sufficient. Use moly-lithium grease.

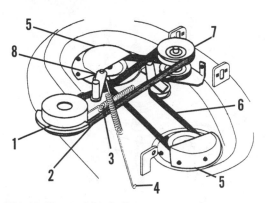

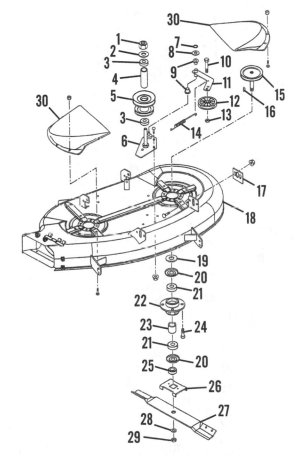

Fig. AR1-12–Mower drive belts.

1. Electric clutch
2. Mower drive belt
3. Mower idler spring
4. Main Idler spring
5. Sheave cover
6. Mower belt
7. Drive pulley
8. Idler

Fig. AR1-13–Exploded view of mower spindle used on 40-inch mower deck.

1. Nut
2. Washer
3. Bearing
4. Spacer
5. Drive pulley
6. Spindle plate
7. Snap ring
8. Washer
9. Bushing
10. Bolt
11. Idler arm
12. Idler pulley
13. Locknut
14. Spring
15. Spindle
16. Key
17. Adjustment tab
18. Mower deck
19. Bushing
20. Bearing slinger
21. Bearings
22. Bearing housing
23. Spacer
24. Bolt
25. Hub
26. Blade tray
27. Blade
28. Lockwasher
29. Nut
30. Cover

ADJUSTMENT

Before attempting any adjustment, the machine must be on level ground and tires must be properly inflated. Disconnect the spark plug wire and tie it out of the way.

BLADE HEIGHT

1. Move the mower height control to the highest deck position.
2. Measure the height of the blade tip above the ground. The blade tip height should be 4 inches (102 mm).
3. Adjust blade height by rotating the nut on the adjustment link (A–Fig. AR1-11A). Rotate the nut on the adjustment link on the opposite side an equal amount.

SIDE-TO-SIDE HEIGHT

1. Move the mower height control to the highest deck position.
2. Measure the height of the blade tip above the ground. The blade tip height should be 4 inches (102 mm) within $\frac{1}{8}$ inch (3.2 mm) of blade tip on opposite side.
3. Adjust blade side-to-side height by rotating the nut on one of the adjustment links (A–Fig. AR1-11A).
4. Recheck blade height.

FRONT-TO-REAR HEIGHT

1. Measure the height of the blade above the ground at the front and rear. Rear height should be $\frac{1}{8}$-$\frac{1}{4}$ inch (3.2-6.4 mm) higher.
2. Adjust front height of the mower by relocating the bolt in each adjusting tab (B–Fig. AR1-11A) on the front of the mower deck.

REMOVAL AND INSTALLATION

1. Position the unit on level ground and engage the parking brake.
2. Disconnect and ground the spark plug wire.
3. Move the mower deck to the lowest position.
4. Remove the mower drive belt as previously described.
5. Detach the height adjusters (A–Fig. AR1-11B) from lift arm (B).
6. Detach the rear hangers (C) from the frame.
7. Detach the front end of the lift arm (B) by removing the pin (D).
8. Remove the mower deck by sliding it out from the right side of the unit.
9. Reverse the removal procedure to install the mower deck.

MOWER DECK BELT REMOVAL AND INSTALLATION

1. Remove the mower drive belt (2–Fig. AR1-12) as previously described.
2. Remove the pulley covers (5).
3. Remove the idler arm spring (3).
4. Remove the mower drive belt (6) from the spindle pulleys.
5. Reverse the removal procedure to install the mower drive belt.

MOWER DECK SPINDLE OVERHAUL

40-INCH MOWER DECK

1. Remove the mower drive belt as previously described.
2. Remove the blade (27–Fig. AR1-13), blade tray (26), retainer hub (25) and key (16).

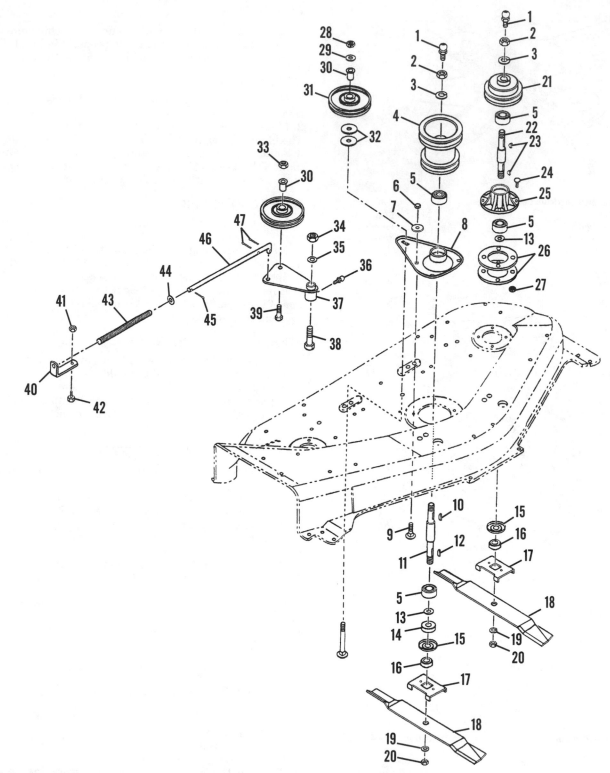

Fig. AR1-14—Exploded view of center and outer mower spindles used on 48-inch mower deck.

1. Grease fitting	13. Washer	25. Bearing housing	37. Idler arm
2. Nut	14. Spacer	26. Spacer	38. Bolt
3. Lockwasher	15. Bearing slinger	27. Nut	39. Bolt
4. Pulley (center)	16. Hub	28. Locknut	40. Bracket
5. Bearing	17. Blade tray	29. Washer	41. Locknut
6. Nut	18. Blade	30. Bushing	42. Bolt
7. Washer	19. Lockwasher	31. Idler pulley	43. Spring
8. Bearing housing	20. Nut	32. Washer	44. Washer
9. Bolt	21. Pulley (outer)	33. Locknut	45. Cotter pin
10. Key	22. Spindle (outer)	34. Locknut	46. Rod
11. Spindle (Center)	23. Key	35. Washer	47. Cotter pin
12. Key	24. Bolt	36. Grease fitting	

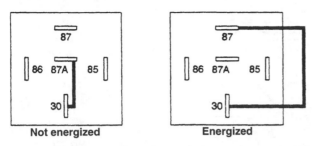

Fig. AR1-15–Refer to text for relay testing procedure.

ELECTRICAL

1. A neutral switch contacts each steering control lever. Both steering control levers must be in NEUTRAL for the engine to start.
2. The PTO switch must be in the OFF position for the engine to start.
3. The operator must be in the seat for the engine to start.
4. The engine should stop if the operator leaves the seat and the transmission is in gear or the mower is engaged.

DIODE TESTING

1. Remove the diode.
2. Connect an ohmmeter or diode tester to the diode.
3. Check for continuity, then reverse the tester leads and again check for continuity.
4. The ohmmeter or diode tester should indicate continuity in one direction, but not when the tester leads are reversed.

STARTER RELAY TESTING

Note the terminal identifying numbers on the bottom of the relay when performing the following test.
1. Using an ohmmeter or continuity tester, check for continuity between relay terminals (30 and 87a–Fig. AR1-15). The tester should indicate no continuity.
2. Connect a 12-volt battery to terminals 85 and 86.
3. The tester should indicate continuity between terminals 30 and 87a.

SEAT/PTO RELAY TESTING

Note the terminal identifying numbers on the bottom of the relay when performing the following test.
1. Using an ohmmeter or continuity tester, check for continuity between relay terminals (30 and 87–Fig. AR1-15). The tester should indicate no continuity.
2. Connect a 12-volt battery to terminals 85 and 86.
3. The tester should indicate continuity between terminals 30 and 87.

WIRING DIAGRAMS

Refer to AR1-16, AR1-17 and AR1-18 for wiring schematics.

3. Pull out the spindle and pulley assembly (15).

4. Remove the bearing housing retaining bolts (24), then remove the bearing housing.

5. If necessary, press the bearings (21) out of the bearing housing (22).

6. Inspect components for damage.

7. Install the spindle assembly by reversing the removal procedure.

48-INCH MOWER DECK

The service procedures for the center and outer spindles are similar. Refer to Fig. AR1-14 for an exploded view of the spindle components.

1. Remove the mower drive belt as previously described.

2. Remove the blade (18–Fig. AR1-14), blade tray (17), retainer hub (16) and key.

3. Unscrew the pulley retaining nut (2) and remove the pulley.

4. Remove the bearing housing retaining bolts, then remove the spindle and bearing housing assembly.

5. Disassemble the spindle assembly components as needed. Spindle and bearings must be pressed out of the housing.

6. Inspect components for damage.

7. Install the spindle assembly by reversing the removal procedure.

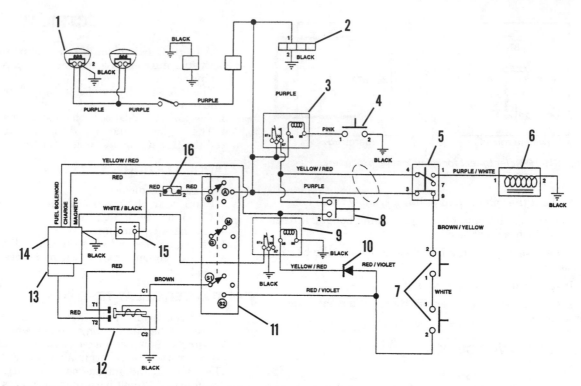

Fig. AR1-16–Typical wiring diagram for models equipped with a Briggs & Stratton engine.

1. Lights (optional)
2. Hour meter (optional)
3. Seat relay
4. Seat switch
5. PTO switch
6. PTO clutch
7. Neutral switches
8. Brake switch
9. Start relay
10. Diode
11. Key switch
12. Starter solenoid
13. Starter
14. Engine
15. Battery
16. Fuse

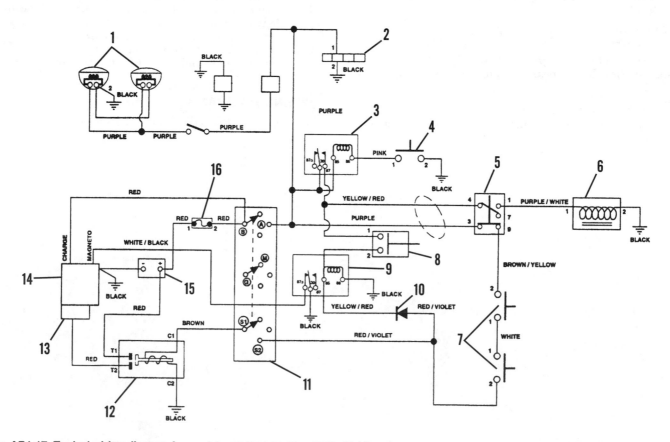

Fig. AR1-17–Typical wiring diagram for models equipped with a 15-hp Kohler engine. Refer to Fig. AR1-16 for parts identification.

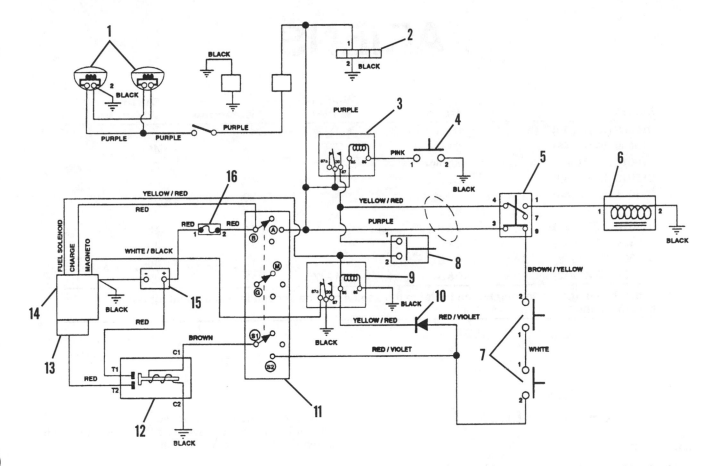

Fig. AR1-18–Typical wiring diagram for models equipped with a 16-hp Tecumseh engine. Refer to Fig. AR1-16 for parts identication.

ARIENS

Model	Make	Engine Model	Horsepower	Cutting Width, In.
915008 (EZR1540)	B&S	*	15	40
915009 (EZR1648)	B&S	*	16	48
915010 (EZR1540)	Kohler	*	15	40
915013 (EZR1742)	B&S	*	17	42
915014 (EZR2048)	B&S	*	20	48
915017 (EZR1542)	B&S	*	15	42
915018 (EZR1842)	B&S	*	18	42
915304 (EZR1540)	B&S	*	15	40
915305 (EZR1648)	B&S	*	16	48
915307 (EZR1742)	B&S	311777	17	42

*Note the engine model number and refer to the engine service section in this manual for engine specifications.

FRONT WHEELS

LUBRICATION

Each front wheel hub is equipped with a sealed bearing. Periodic lubrication is not required.

REMOVAL AND INSTALLATION

Each front wheel is equipped with a replaceable bearing. To remove the wheel and bearing, refer to Fig. AR2-1 and proceed as follows:
1. Support the front of the mower.
2. Remove the nut (19–Fig. AR2-1) and withdraw the axle bolt (23).
3. Remove the wheel with bearing.
4. Separate the bearing from the wheel.
5. Inspect the bearing for damage.
6. Inspect the wheel for damage to the rim and hub.
7. Reverse the removal steps to reassemble.

FRONT SPINDLES

MAINTENANCE

Lubricate the front wheel spindles after every 50 hours of operation. Inject grease to the spindles through the grease fitting (7–Fig. AR2-1) at each end of the axle. One or two shots from a hand-held grease gun should be sufficient. Use moly-lithium grease.

OVERHAUL

Refer to Fig. AR2-1 for an exploded view of the spindle assembly. To remove a front spindle, proceed as follows:
1. Raise and support the side to be serviced.
2. Remove the wheel and tire as previously described.
3. Remove the retaining bolt (13–Fig. AR2-1), lockwasher and washer.
4. Remove the spindle.

5. Inspect components for damage.
6. Install the spindle by reversing the removal procedure. Tighten the spindle retaining bolt securely.

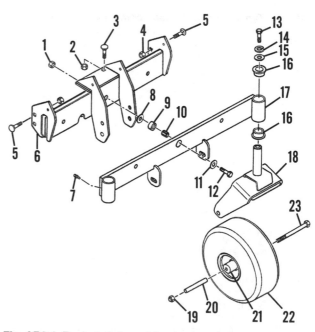

Fig. AR2-1–Exploded view of front axle member.

1. Nut	13. Bolt
2. Nut	14. Lockwasher
3. Bolt	15. Washer
4. Nut	16. Flange bushing
5. Bolt	17. Axle main member
6. Crossmember	18. Spindle
7. Grease fitting	19. Locknut
8. Washer	20. Bushing
9. Bushing	21. Bearings
10. Bushing	22. Wheel
11. Washer	23. Bolt
12. Bolt	

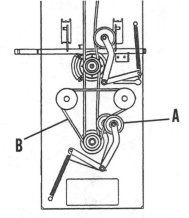

Fig. AG2-3–Refer to text for ground drive belt removal and installation procedure.

FRONT AXLE MAIN MEMBER OVERHAUL

The front axle main member is center-pivoted in the crossmember at the front of the chassis. Refer to the following procedure to remove and install the front axle main member.

1. Remove the mower deck as described in this section.
2. Raise and support the front end of the frame.
3. Remove the front spindles as previously described.
4. Support the axle main member.
5. Remove the axle bolt (12–Fig. AR2-1), then lower and remove the axle main member (17).
6. Inspect the bushings in the axle main member and replace if damaged.
7. Clean and inspect all parts. Replace damaged parts.
8. Install by reversing the removal procedure. Tighten the pivot bolt securely.

ENGINE

Refer to the appropriate engine section in this manual for tune-up specifications, engine overhaul procedures and engine maintenance.

Fig. AR2-2–Exploded view of belt idlers.

1. Locknut
2. Washer
3. Nut
4. Bolt
5. Spring
6. Grease fitting
7. Spacer
8. PTO drive belt idler arm
9. Bolt
10. Washer
11. Pulley
12. Bolt
13. Washer
14. Ground drive belt idler arm
15. Bolt
16. Bolt

REMOVAL AND INSTALLATION

1. Remove the engine cover.
2. Disconnect the spark plug wire.
3. Disconnect the negative battery cable.
4. Disconnect any interfering electrical wires from the engine.
5. Disconnect the throttle cable from the engine.
6. Disconnect the fuel line from the engine.
7. Detach the exhaust system from the engine.
8. Remove the belts from the engine pulley.
9. Remove the engine retaining bolts.
10. Remove the engine.
11. Install by reversing the removal procedure.

BELT IDLERS

Drive belt tension for the mower clutch drive belt and transaxle drive belt is maintained by spring-loaded idler arms. Refer to Fig. AR2-2.

LUBRICATION

Lubricate the idler arms after every 50 hours of operation. Inject grease into the idler arm through the grease fitting (6–Fig. AR2-2) on the idler arm. One or two shots from a hand-held grease gun should be sufficient. Use moly-lithium grease.

REMOVAL AND INSTALLATION

Refer to Fig. AR2-2 when removing and installing the belt idler arms. Note the position of the pulley (11) and pulley retaining bolt (12) in Fig. AR2-2 when installing the pulley on the idler arm.

TRANSAXLE DRIVE BELT REMOVAL AND INSTALLATION

1. Disconnect the battery negative lead.
2. Disconnect the engine spark plug lead.
3. Detach the spring from the transaxle belt idler (A–Fig. AR2-3).
4. Remove the transaxle drive belt (B) from the engine and transaxle pulleys.
5. Install the transaxle drive belt by reversing the removal procedure.

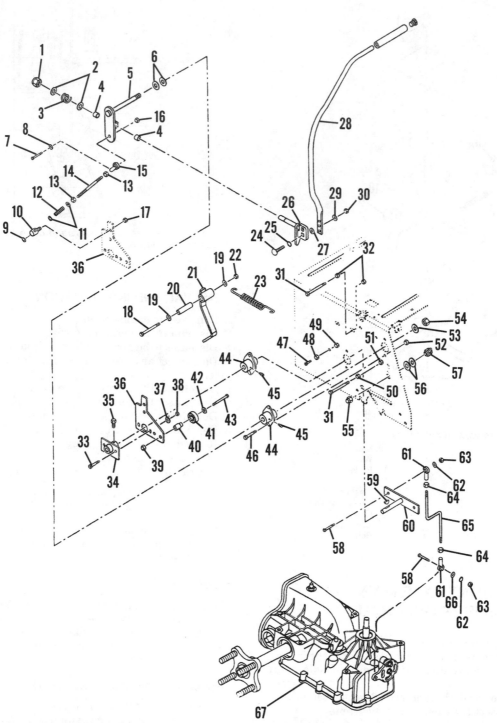

AR2-4–Exploded view of right-side transaxle steering control linkage. The left side is similar.

1. Locknut
2. Washer
3. Spring
4. Nylon bushing
5. Lever
6. Washer
7. Bolt
8. Washer
9. Washer
10. Pivot
11. Washer
12. Spring
13. Nut
14. Rod
15. Rod end
16. Locknut
17. Locknut

18. Bolt
19. Washer
20. Bushing
21. Neutral detent arm
22. Nut
23. Spring
24. Bolt
25. Lockwasher
26. Lever
27. Lockwasher
28. Steering control lever
29. Washer
30. Nut
31. Bolt
32. Nut
33. Bolt
34. Outer control arm

35. Grease fitting
36. Inner control arm
37. Washer
38. Locknut
39. Locknut
40. Hub
41. Bearing
42. Washer
43. Bolt
44. Flange bushing
45. Grease fitting
46. Bolt
47. Bolt
48. Nut
49. Locknut
50. Nut
51. Locknut

52. Locknut
53. Washer
54. Locknut
55. Nut
56. Washer
57. Neutral switch
58. Bolt
59. Key
60. Control arm
61. **Rod end**
62. **Washer**
63. **Locknut**
64. **Nut**
65. Rod
66. Washer
67. Transaxle

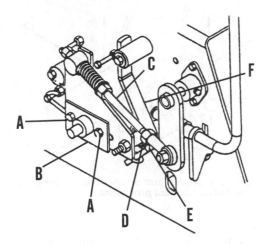

Fig. AR2-5–Refer to text for netural adjustment procedure.

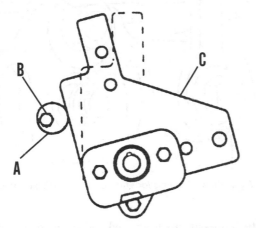

Fig. AR2-6–Rotate eccentric (B) as described in test to adjust tracking.

STEERING CONTROL LINKAGE

Each transaxle is independently controlled to permit zero-radius turning. Refer to Fig. AR2-4 for an exploded view of the steering control linkage.

LUBRICATION

Lubricate the control arms and flange bushings on both sides after every 50 hours of operation. Inject grease into the grease fittings (35 and 45–Fig. AR2-4) using moly-lithium grease. One or two shots from a hand-held grease gun should be sufficient.

NEUTRAL ADJUSTMENT

Note that the following adjustment procedure must be performed on both sides for each transaxle.

CAUTION: Be sure the unit is adequately supported and cannot move when performing the following procedure.

1. Raise and support the rear of the unit. The rear wheels must be off the ground.
2. Remove the rear fenders.
3. Place the steering control levers in NEUTRAL.

4. Be sure the PTO switch is OFF.
5. Loosen the locknuts (A–Fig. AR2-5) securing the outer control arm (B).
6. Loosen the jam nuts on the steering control rod (C).
7. Adjust the length of the steering control rod (C) so the bearing (D) seats in the neutral bend (E) on the neutral detent bracket (F). Be sure the steering control hand lever is still in NEUTRAL.
8. Tighten the steering control rod (C) jam nuts.

NOTE: Place a weight in the operator's seat to activate the seat switch so the engine will run.

9. Start the engine, then run it at half-throttle.
10. Move the outer control arm (B) so the rear wheel does not rotate. If it is not possible to stop wheel rotation by moving the outer control arm, adjust the transaxle linkage as described in the transaxle section.
11. Tighten the locknuts (A).
12. Repeat the procedure for the opposite side.
13. Operate the steering control levers and be sure the rear wheels do not rotate when the levers are in NEUTRAL.

TRACKING ADJUSTMENT

Later models are equipped with an eccentric (A–Fig. AR2-6) adjacent to the steering control arm. The eccentric may be adjusted to limit control arm travel, which affects steering tracking operation.

Because the rear wheels are powered by independent transaxles, the riding mower may not track straight if the transaxle control linkage is not properly synchronized.

NOTE: If the unit will not steer in a straight line, the problem may be incorrect tire pressure. Check and adjust tire pressure as needed.

1. To check the control linkage, push both steering control levers to the full forward position. If the lever travel is not equidistant, use the following adjustment procedure.
2. Remove the rear fenders.
3. Loosen, but do not remove, the bolt (B–Fig. AR2-6) retaining the eccentric (A).
4. Rotate the eccentric to adjust the steering control lever travel. Lever travel is least when the wide portion of the eccentric contacts the steering control arm (C).
5. Adjust both sides as needed to obtain equal steering control lever travel.
6. Be sure to tighten the eccentric retaining bolt (A).
7. Recheck lever travel, then reinstall the rear fenders.

HYDROSTATIC TRANSAXLE

The unit is equipped with two Hydro-Gear hydrostatic transaxles. Each transaxle drives a rear wheel, which allows zero-turn-steering through independent operation of the transaxles.

LUBRICATION

Normal Operation

To check the oil level, remove the oil fill plug on the transmission. The oil level should be 1.25-1.62 inches (32-41 mm) below the top of the housing. If necessary, add oil to the transaxle. Recommended oil is SAE 20W50 engine oil with a SH API service rating.

Refill and Bleed Transaxle

To refill the hydrostatic transaxle with oil and bleed air from the system after the transaxle has been serviced, proceed as follows.
1. Fill the transaxle with oil as described in previous section.
2. Pull out and engage the dump valve lever (Fig. AR2-7).

NOTE: The dump valve lever operates both transaxles.

3. Start and run the engine.
4. Move the steering control lever three times from full FORWARD to full REVERSE in 10-second intervals.
5. Disengage the dump valve lever.
6. Operate the unit while moving the steering control lever three times from full FORWARD to full REVERSE in 10-second intervals.
7. Recheck the transaxle oil level.
8. Repeat procedure if operation is not normal and oil level is satisfactory.

NEUTRAL ADJUSTMENT

CAUTION: Be sure the unit is adequately supported and cannot move when performing the following procedure.

1. Raise and support the rear of the unit. The rear wheels must be off the ground.
2. Remove the rear fenders.
3. Place the steering control levers in NEUTRAL.
4. Be sure the PTO switch is OFF.
5. Unscrew the rod end retaining bolt and detach the rod end (1-Fig. AR2-8) from the control arm (3).

NOTE: Place a weight in the operator's seat to activate the seat switch so the engine will run.

6. Start the engine, then run it at half-throttle.
7. Rotate the transaxle control arm (3) as needed so the rear wheel does not rotate.
8. Tighten the control arm locknut (2) to hold the control arm in the NEUTRAL position.
9. Stop the engine.
10. Be sure the operator steering control lever is in NEUTRAL.
11. Loosen the jam nuts on the control rod (1) and adjust the length of the control rod so the rod end fits onto the transaxle control arm (3).
12. Reattach the control rod end (1).
13. Loosen the control arm locknut (2).
14. Recheck the adjustment.
15. Perform the adjustment procedure for the opposite rear wheel.

REMOVAL AND INSTALLATION

The transaxles are mounted in a subframe, which requires the subframe and transaxles be removed as an unit. Refer to Fig. AR2-9.
1. Disconnect the battery negative lead.
2. Disconnect the engine spark plug lead.
3. Raise and support the rear of the unit.
4. Remove the rear wheel.
5. Remove the transaxle drive belt as previously described.

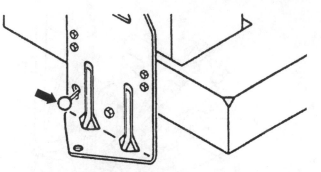

Fig. AR2-7–View of shift arm on Hydro-Gear transaxle. Refer to text for neutral adjustment procedure.

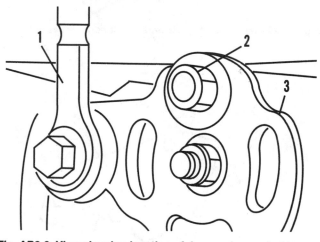

Fig. AR2-8–View showing location of dump valve control lever.

6. Detach the parking brake rod and spring on the top side of the unit's frame.
7. Tighten the shift arm friction locknut (2-Fig. AR2-8) on each transaxle to hold the transaxle in NEUTRAL.
8. Detach the shift rod end (1-Fig. AR2-8) from the shift arm (3) on each transaxle.
9. Support the transaxles and subframe.
10. Detach the subframe rear anchor strap.
11. Remove the subframe retaining bolts and lower the transaxle assembly from the unit.
12. Remove the transaxle from the subframe.
13. Reverse the removal procedure to install the transaxle while noting the following:
   a. Do not tighten the mounting fasteners until all fasteners are installed.
   b. Be sure to loosen the shift arm friction locknut (2-Fig. AR2-8) on each transaxle.

OVERHAUL

All models are equipped with Model 310-2400 Hydro-gear transaxles.
Refer to the HYDROSTATIC TRANSAXLE REPAIR section for service information.

PARKING BRAKE

Refer to Fig. AR2-10 for an exploded view of the parking brake. The brake linkage operates the brake mechanism on each transaxle. No adjustment is required.

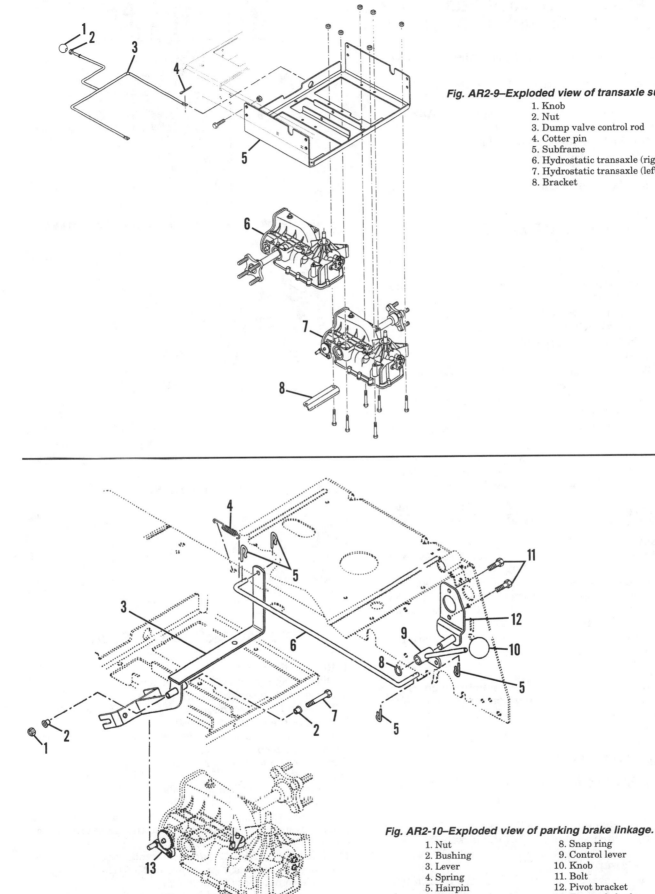

Fig. AR2-9–Exploded view of transaxle subframe.
1. Knob
2. Nut
3. Dump valve control rod
4. Cotter pin
5. Subframe
6. Hydrostatic transaxle (right)
7. Hydrostatic transaxle (left)
8. Bracket

Fig. AR2-10–Exploded view of parking brake linkage.

1. Nut	8. Snap ring
2. Bushing	9. Control lever
3. Lever	10. Knob
4. Spring	11. Bolt
5. Hairpin	12. Pivot bracket
6. Rod	13. Transaxle brake
7. Bolt	assy.

PTO CLUTCH DRIVE BELT
REMOVAL AND INSTALLATION

1. Remove the mower drive belt as described in this section.

2. Remove the transaxle drive belt as described in this section.

3. Detach the spring from the clutch idler (A–Fig. AR2-11).

4. Remove the PTO clutch anchor bolts.

5. Disconnect the PTO clutch electrical lead.

6. Remove the PTO drive belt (B) from the engine and clutch pulleys.

7. Install the PTO drive belt by reversing the removal procedure.

ELECTRIC PTO CLUTCH

TESTING

Use the following procedure to locate the cause if the PTO clutch malfunctions.

1. Turn the ignition switch ON.

2. Actuate the PTO switch.

3. If the clutch does not engage, disconnect the wiring connector at the clutch.

4. Use a 12-volt test lamp to check continuity of the wire coming from the PTO switch.

5. If the lamp lights, the PTO is either defective or the wiring connector at the clutch field coil is faulty.

6. To check the PTO field coil, perform the following procedures:

   a. Clutch installed—Connect an ohmmeter to the clutch wire and ground. The ohmmeter should indicate the resistance specified in the following table.

Models	Coil resistance
915008, 915013, 915015, 915304, 915307	5.87-7.87 ohms
915009, 915010, 915014, 915016, 915305, 915306	1.98-3.98 ohms

   b. Clutch removed—Ground the field coil frame and energize the coil lead wire with a known 12-volt source. Hold a piece of metal next to the coil. The coil should attract the metal.

7. If the PTO clutch fails the preceding tests, replace the coil or entire clutch assembly.

NOTE: Ariens only supplies the complete clutch assembly. Note the clutch manufacturer. It may be possible to obtain clutch parts from other parts suppliers.

REMOVAL AND INSTALLATION

1. Remove the mower drive belt as described in this section.

2. Disconnect the PTO clutch electrical wire.

3. Remove the clutch retaining bolt.

4. Remove the clutch assembly from the jackshaft. Use a plastic hammer to tap and loosen the clutch from the jackshaft if necessary.

5. Reverse the removal procedure to install the PTO clutch. Apply Loctite 271 to the clutch retaining bolt and tighten to 40 ft.-lb. (54 N•m).

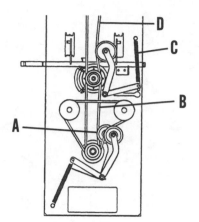

Fig. AR2-11–Refer to text for PTO drive belt removal and installation procedure.

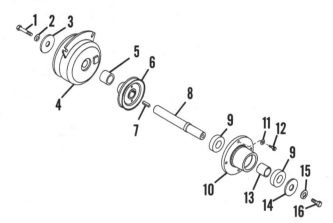

Fig. AR2-12–PTO clutch and jackshaft assembly.

1. Bolt	9. Bearing
2. Lockwasher	10. Bearing housing
3. Washer	11. Washer
4. PTO clutch	12. Bolt
5. Spacer	13. Spacer
6. Pulley	14. Washer
7. Key	15. Lockwasher
8. Jackshaft	16. Bolt

PTO JACKSHAFT OVERHAUL

1. Remove the mower deck.

2. Disconnect the battery negative lead.

3. Disconnect the engine spark plug lead.

4. Raise and support the unit.

5. Remove the right, rear wheel.

6. Remove the transaxle drive belt and PTO clutch drive belt as described in this section.

7. Remove the four screws securing the jackshaft housing (10–Fig. AR2-12).

8. Remove the jackshaft assembly.

9. Remove the clutch retaining bolt.

10. Remove the clutch assembly from the jackshaft. Use a plastic hammer to tap and loosen the clutch from the jackshaft if necessary.

11. Refer to Fig. AR2-12 and disassemble the jackshaft as needed. Note the bearings are pressed into the housing. Inspect the components for damage.

12. Reverse the disassembly procedure to reassemble the jackshaft. Note the following:

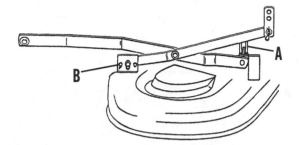

Fig. AR2-13–Refer to rext for mower deck adjustment procedure for 42-inch mower deck.

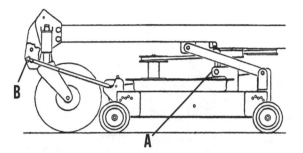

Fig. AR2-14–Refer to text for mower deck adjustment procedure for 48-inch mower decks.

a. Apply Loctite 271 to the jackshaft retaining bolt (16–Fig. AR2-12) and tighten to 40 ft.-lb. (54 N•m).

b. Tighten the jackshaft housing retaining bolts to 25 ft.-lb. (34 N•m).

MOWER DRIVE BELT REMOVAL AND INSTALLATION

1. Detach the idler arm spring (C–Fig. AR2-11) from the frame.
2. Remove the mower drive belt (D) from the pto clutch pulley.
3. Remove the mower drive belt from the mower drive pulley.
4. Install the mower drive belt by reversing the removal procedure.

MOWER DECK

LUBRICATION

On 48-inch mower deck, lubricate the spindles and pivot arm after every 50 hours of operation. Inject grease through grease fittings. One or two shots from a hand-held grease gun should be sufficient. Use moly-lithium grease.

ADJUSTMENT (40-INCH MOWER)

Before attempting any adjustment, the machine must be on level ground and tires must be properly inflated. Disconnect the spark plug wire and tie out of the way.

Blade Height

1. Move the mower height control to the highest deck position.

2. Measure the height of the blade tip above the ground. The blade tip height should be 4 inches (102 mm).
3. Adjust blade height by rotating the nut on the adjustment link (A-Fig. AR2-13). Rotate the nut on the adjustment link on the opposite side an equal amount.

Side-To-Side Height

1. Move the mower height control to the highest deck position.
2. Measure the height of the blade tip above the ground. The blade tip height should be 4 inches (102 mm) with $\frac{1}{8}$ inch (3.2 mm) of the blade tip on opposite side.
3. Adjust blade side-to-side height by rotating the nut on one of the adjustment links (A–Fig. AR2-13).
4. Recheck blade height.

Front-To-Rear Height

1. Measure the height of the blade above the ground at the front and rear. Rear height should be $\frac{1}{8}$-$\frac{1}{4}$ inch (3.2-6.4 mm) higher.
2. Adjust front height of the mower by relocating the bolt in each adjusting tabs (B–Fig. AR2-13) on the front of the mower deck.

ADJUSTMENT (42-INCH MOWER)

Before attempting any adjustment, the machine must be on level ground and tires must be properly inflated. Disconnect the spark plug wire and tie it out of the way.

Blade Height

1. Position the antiscalp rollers so they do not contact the ground.
2. Move the mower height control to the number three middle position.
3. Measure the height of the blade tip above the ground. Blade tip height should be $2\frac{3}{4}$ inch (70 mm).
4. Adjust the blade height by rotating the nut on the adjustment link (A—Fig. AR2-14). Rotate the nut on the adjustment link on the opposite side an equal amount.

Side-To-Side Height

1. Position the antiscalp rollers so they do not contact the ground.
2. Move the mower height control to the number three middle position.
3. Measure the height of the blade tip above the ground. Blade tip height should be $2\frac{3}{4}$ inch (70 mm) within $\frac{1}{8}$ inch (3.2 mm) of blade tip on the opposite side.
4. Adjust the blade side-to-side height by rotating the nut on one of the adjustment links (A–Fig. AR2-14).
5. Recheck the blade height.

Front-To-Rear Height

1. Measure the height of the blade above the ground at the front and rear. Rear height should be $\frac{1}{8}$-$\frac{1}{4}$ inch (3.2-6.4 mm) higher.
2. Adjust the front height of the mower by rotating the nut (B–Fig. AR2-14) on the rod link.

ADJUSTMENT (48-INCH MOWER)

Before attempting any adjustment, the machine must be on level ground and tires must be properly inflated. Disconnect the spark plug wire and tie it out of the way.

Blade Height

1. Position the antiscalp rollers so they do not contact the ground.
2. Move the mower height control to the number three middle position.
3. Measure the height of the blade tip above the ground. Blade tip height should be 2¾ inch (70 mm).
4. Adjust the blade height by loosening the jam nut (A–Fig. AR2-13) on each adjustment link.
5. Detach the adjustment link from the lift arm and rotate the link to obtain the desired height. Rotate the adjustment link on the opposite side an equal amount.
6. Reattach the adjustment link and tighten the jam nut.

Side-To-Side Height

1. Position the antiscalp rollers so they do not contact the ground.
2. Move the mower height control to the number three middle position.
3. Measure the height of the blade tip above the ground. Blade tip height should be 2¾ inch (70 mm) within ⅛ inch (3.2 mm) of blade tip on the opposite side.
4. Adjust the side-to-side blade height by loosening the jam nut (A–Fig. AR2-13) on the adjustment link.
5. Detach the adjustment link from the lift arm and rotate the link to obtain the desired height.
6. Reattach the adjustment link and tighten the jam nut.
7. Recheck the blade height.

Front-To-Rear Height

1. Measure the height of the blade above the ground at the front and rear. Rear height should be ⅛-¼ inch (3.2-6.4 mm) higher.
2. Loosen the locknuts (B–Fig. AR2-13) on the front hanger bracket on both sides of the deck.
3. Relocate the adjusting plate and tighten the locknuts.

REMOVAL AND INSTALLATION

40-inch Mower

1. Position the unit on level ground and engage the parking brake.
2. Move the mower deck to the lowest position.
3. Remove the mower drive belt as previously described.
4. Detach the height adjusters (A–Fig. AR2-15) from lift arm (B).
5. Detach the rear hangs (C) from the frame.
6. Detach the front end of the lift arm (B) by removing the pin (D).
7. Remove the mower deck by sliding it out from the right side of the unit.
8. Reverse the removal procedure to install the mower deck.

42-inch Mower Deck

1. Position the unit on level ground and engage the parking brake.
2. Move the mower deck to the lowest position.

> **WARNING: When the attachment lift lock lever is engaged the lift spring contains considerable spring force. Do not disengage the lock lever with the mower deck removed.**

3. Pull out the attachment lift lock lever and move to the locked down position as shown in Fig. AR2-16.

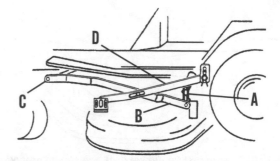

Fig. AR2-15–Refer to text for 42-inch mower deck removal and installation procedure.

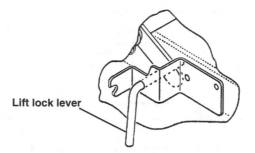

Lift lock lever

Fig. AR2-16–The lift lock lever is engaged in the down position.

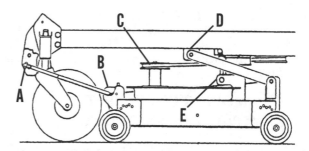

Fig. AR2-17–Refer to text for 42-inch mower deck removal and installation procedure.

4. Loosen, but do not remove, the rod link nut (A–Fig. AR2-17).

5. Detach the rod link from the rod link brackets (B) on the front of the mower deck.

6. Disengage the drive belt from the mower deck drive pulley (C).

7. Remove the hairpins and clevis pins (D) from the lift link and disengage the lift link.

8. Remove the hairpins and washers (E) from the deck lift and disengage the deck lift pin.

9. Rotate the right front wheel to obtain clearance while removing the mower deck.

10. Remove the mower deck by sliding it out from the unit's right side.

11. Reverse the removal procedure to install the mower deck.

48-inch Mower Deck

1. Position the unit on level ground and engage the parking brake.
2. Move the mower deck to the lowest position.

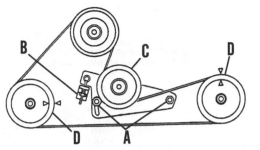

Fig. AG2-18–Diagram showing mower belt routing on 42-inch mower deck.

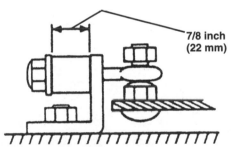

Fig. AG2-19–Drawing showing adjust bolt components on 42-inch mower deck.

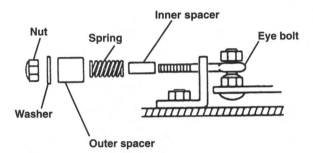

Fig. AG2-20–The distance between the adjuster bolt washer and bracket must be 7/8 inch (22 mm)

WARNING: When the attachment lift lock lever is engaged the lift spring contains considerable spring force. Do not disengage the lock lever with the mower deck removed.

3. Pull out the attachment lift lock lever and move to the locked down position as shown in Fig. AR2-16.

4. Remove the mower drive belt as previously described.

5. Detach the height adjusters (A–Fig. AR2-15) from the lift arm (B).

6. Detach the rear hangers (C) from frame.

7. Detach the front end of the lift arm (B) by removing the pin (D).

8. Remove the mower deck by sliding it out from the unit's right side.

9. Reverse the removal procedure to install the mower deck.

MOWER DECK DRIVE BELT REMOVAL AND INSTALLATION

40-INCH MOWER

1. Remove the mower deck as previously described.
2. Remove the pulley covers.
3. Remove the idler arm spring.
4. Remove the mower drive belt.
5. Reverse the removal procedure to install the mower drive belt.

42-INCH MOWER DECK

1. Remove the mower deck as previously described.
2. Remove the pulley covers.
3. Loosen the nuts (A–Fig. AR2-18) on the belt adjustment arm.
4. Loosen the nut (B) on the belt adjusting bolt sufficiently to allow belt removal.
5. Move the idler (C) away from the belt and remove the mower drive belt.
6. Before installing the mower belt, position the blade drive pulleys so the triangle arrow on the pulley aligns with the arrow on the mower deck (D).
7. Install the mower belt.
8. Push the idler (C) against the belt to remove belt slack. Be sure the pulley arrows (D) are aligned.
9. If removed, reinstall the adjuster bolt components (B) as shown in Fig. AR2-19.
10. Tighten the nut on the adjuster bolt so the outer spacer will barely rotate when turned by hand. The distance (Fig. AR2-20) between the washer and bracket must be ⅞ inch (22 mm). Do not overtighten.
11. Tighten the nuts (A–Fig. AR2-18) on the belt adjustment arm.
12. Install the pulley covers.
13. Install the mower deck as previously described.

48-INCH MOWER DECK

1. Remove the mower deck as previously described.
2. Remove the pulley covers.
3. Remove the idler arm spring.
4. Remove the mower drive belt.
5. Reverse the removal procedure to install the mower drive belt.

MOWER DECK SPINDLE OVERHAUL

40-INCH MOWER

1. Remove the mower drive belt as previously described.
2. Remove the blade (27–AR2-21), blade tray (26), retainer hub (25) and key (16).
3. Pull out the spindle and pulley assembly (15).
4. Remove the bearing housing retaining bolts (24), then remove the bearing housing.
5. If necessary, press the bearings (21) out of the bearing housing (22).
6. Inspect components for damage.
7. Install the spindle assembly by reversing the removal procedure.

42-INCH MOWER DECK

1. Remove mower drive belt as previously described.
2. Remove the blade (14–Fig. AR2-22), blade tray (13), retainer hub (12) and key (11).

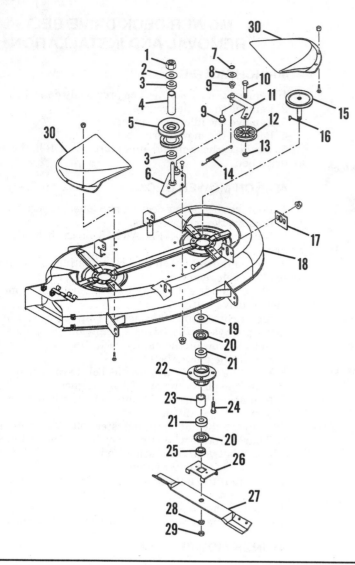

Fig. AR2-21–Exploded view of mower spindle used on 40-inch mower deck.

1. Nut
2. Washer
3. Bearing
4. Spacer
5. Drive pulley
6. Spindle plate
7. Snap ring
8. Washer
9. Bushing
10. Bolt
11. Idler arm
12. Idler pulley
13. Locknut
14. Spring
15. Spindle
16. Key
17. Adjustment tab
18. Mower deck
19. Washer
20. Bearing slinger
21. Bearings
22. Bearing housing
23. Spacer
24. Bolt
25. Hub
26. Blade tray
27. Blade
28. Lockwasher
29. Nut
30. Cover

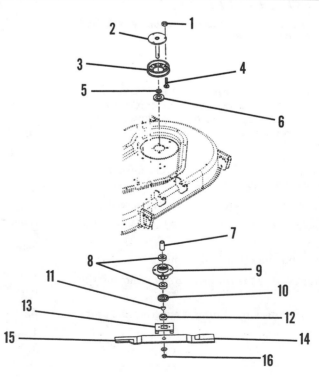

Fig. AR2-22–Exploded view of mower spindle used on 42-inch mower deck. Components 7 through 9 are available only as a unit assembly.

1. Nut
2. Spindle
3. Pulley
4. Bolt
5. Washer
6. Bearing slinger
7. Spacer
8. Bearings
9. Bearing housing
10. Bearing slinger
11. Key
12. Hub
13. Blade tray
14. Blade
15. Lockwasher
16. Nut

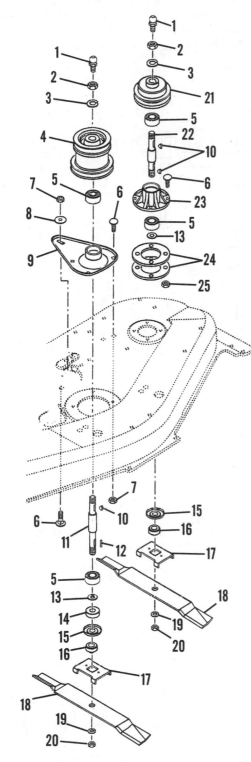

3. Pull out the spindle and pulley assembly.

4. Remove the bearing housing (9) retaining bolts, then remove the bearing housing.

5. Inspect components for damage. The bearing housing, bearings and spacer are available only as an unit assembly.

6. Install the spindle assembly by reversing the removal procedure.

48-INCH MOWER DECK

The service procedures for the center and outer spindles are similar. Refer to Fig. AR2-23 for an exploded view of the spindle components.

1. Remove the mower drive belt as previously described.

2. Remove the blade (18–Fig. AR2-23), blade tray (17), retainer hub (16) and key (12).

3. Unscrew the pulley retaining nut (2) and remove the pulley.

4. Remove the bearing housing retaining bolts (6), then remove the spindle and bearing housing assembly.

5. Disassemble spindle assembly components as needed. Spindle and bearings must be pressed out of the housing.

6. Inspect components for damage.

7. Install the spindle assembly by reversing the removal procedure.

ELECTRICAL

Refer to Fig. AR2-24 for wiring schematic. Note the following points:

1. A neutral switch contacts each steering control lever. Both steering control levers must be in NEUTRAL for the engine to start.

2. The PTO switch must be OFF for the engine to start.

3. The operator must be in seat for the engine to start.

4. The engine should stop if the transmission is in gear or the mower is engaged and the operator leaves the seat.

DIODE TESTING

1. Remove the diode.

2. Connect an ohmmeter or diode tester to the diode.

3. Check for continuity, then reverse the tester leads and again check for continuity.

4. The ohmmeter or diode tester should indicate continuity in one direction, but not when the tester leads are reversed.

STARTER RELAY TESTING

Note the terminal identifying numbers on the bottom of the relay when performing the following test.

1. Using an ohmmeter or continuity tester, check for continuity between relay terminals 30 and 87a. The tester should indicate no continuity.

2. Connect a 12-volt battery to terminals 85 and 86.

3. The tester should indicate continuity between terminals 30 and 87a.

SEAT/PTO RELAY TESTING

Note the terminal identifying numbers on the bottom of the relay when performing the following test.

1. Using an ohmmeter or continuity tester, check for continuity between relay terminals 30 and 87. The tester should indicate no continuity.

2. Connect a 12-volt battery to terminals 85 and 86.

3. The tester should indicate continuity between terminals 30 and 87.

Fig. AR2-23–Exploded view of center and outer mower spindles used on 48-inch mower deck.

1. Grease fitting	14. Spacer
2. Nut	15. Bearing slinger
3. Lockwasher	16. Hub
4. Pulley (center)	17. Battery tray
5. Bearing	18. Blade
6. Bolt	19. Lockwasher
7. Nut	20. Nut
8. Washer	21. Pulley (outer)
9. Bearing housing	22. Spindle (outer)
10. Key	23. Bearing housing
11. Spindle (center)	24. Spacer
12. Key	25. Nut
13. Washer	

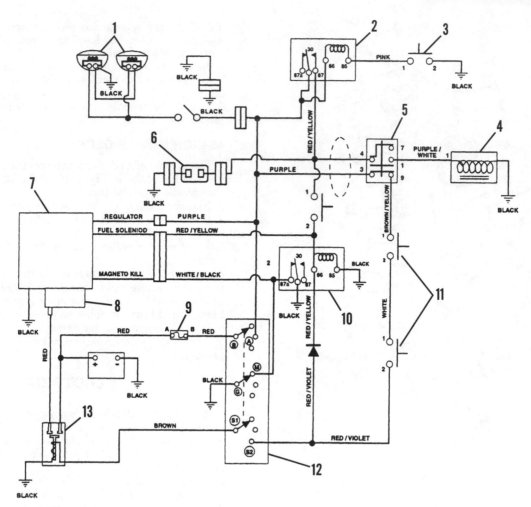

Fig. AR2-24–Typical wiring diagram.

1. Lights (optional)
2. Seat/PTO relay
3. Seat switch
4. PTO clutch
5. PTO switch
6. Hour meter
   (optional)
7. Engine
8. Starter
9. Fuse
10. Start relay
11. Neutral switches
12. Key switch
13. Starter solenoid

ARIENS

Model	Make	Engine Model	Horsepower	Cutting Width, In.
927037 (RM830E)	B&S	196707	8.5	30
927043 (RM1230E)	B&S	281707	12	30
927045 (RM828E)	B&S	195707	8	28
927046 (RM1028)	B&S	*	10	28
927048 (RM9028E)	B&S	28A707	9	28
927048 (RM8028)	B&S	28A707	9	28
927049 (RM9030E)	B&S	28B707	9	30
927049 (RM8530)	B&S	28B707	9	30
927052 (RM1330)	B&S	*	13	30
927053 (RM8028)	B&S	*	9	28
927054 (RM9030)	B&S	*	9	30
927056 (RM1330)	B&S	*	13	30
927301 (RM8028E)	B&S	195707	8	28
927302 (RM1228E)	B&S	283707	12	28
927304 (RM1328)	B&S	*	13	28
927306 (RM8028E)	B&S	*	9	28
927307 (RM1328)	B&S	*	13	28
927310 (RM1028)	B&S	*	10	28

*Note the engine model number and refer to the engine service section in this manual for engine specifications.

FRONT WHEELS

MAINTENANCE

Lubricate the front wheel bushings after every 25 hours of operation, or twice each season, whichever occurs first. Inject grease into each wheel hub through the grease fitting (Fig. AR3-1). One or two shots from a hand-held grease gun should be sufficient. Use multipurpose grease.

Fig. AR3-1–View of front wheel grease fitting.

REMOVAL AND INSTALLATION

The front wheels are equipped with replaceable bushings. To remove the wheel and bushings, proceed as follows:
1. Remove the hub cap (19–Fig. AR3-2).
2. Remove the cotter pin (20).
3. Remove the spindle cap (18).
4. Remove the wheel.
5. Inspect the inner washer and cotter pin. Replace if damaged.
6. Separate the bushings from the wheel.
7. Inspect the bushings for damage.
8. Inspect the wheel for rim and hub damage.
9. Reverse the removal steps to reassemble and install the wheel.

FRONT AXLE

MAINTENANCE

Lubricate the front wheel spindles and front axle pivot after every 25 hours of operation, or twice each season, whichever occurs first. Inject grease to spindles through the grease fitting at each end of the axle. One or two shots from a hand-held grease gun should be sufficient. Use multipurpose grease. Check for looseness and binding in the front axle components.

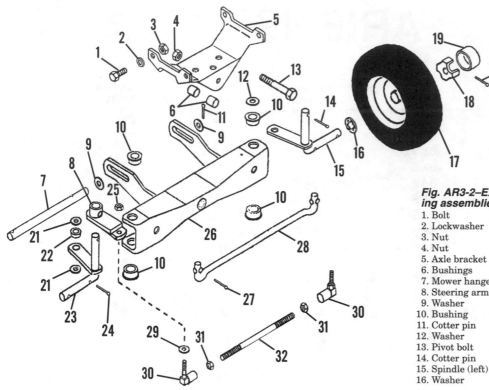

Fig. AR3-2–Exploded view of front axle and steering assemblies.

1. Bolt	17. Wheel
2. Lockwasher	18. Spindle cup
3. Nut	19. Hub cap
4. Nut	20. Cotter pin
5. Axle bracket	21. Washer
6. Bushings	22. Bushing
7. Mower hanger shaft	23. Spindle (right)
8. Steering arm	24. Cotter pin
9. Washer	25. Nut
10. Bushing	26. Axle main member
11. Cotter pin	27. Cotter pin
12. Washer	28. Tie rod
13. Pivot bolt	29. Washer
14. Cotter pin	30. Rod end
15. Spindle (left)	31. Jam nut
16. Washer	32. Steering link

OVERHAUL

Axle main member is center-pivoted in a channel at the front of the chassis. Refer to the following procedure to remove and reinstall the front axle.

1. Remove the mower deck as described in this section.
2. Raise and support the front end of the frame.
3. Remove the steering link (32–Fig. AR3-2).
4. Remove the front wheels.
5. Disconnect the tie rod (28) from the spindles.
6. Remove the cotter pins and washers, then lower the spindles (15 and 23) from the axle.
7. Support the front axle.
8. Remove the axle bolt (13), then lower and remove the front axle (26).
9. Inspect the bushings in the front axle and replace if damaged.
10. Clean and inspect all parts. Replace damaged parts.
11. Install by reversing the removal procedure. Tighten the axle pivot nut (19) to 35 ft.-lb. (48 N•m).

STEERING GEAR

ADJUSTMENT

Adjustment to compensate for wear of the pinion and steering gear teeth is possible without removing the steering gear assembly. To adjust, use the following procedure.

1. Loosen the nut (1–Fig. AR3-3 or Fig. AR3-4).
2. Tighten the nut (2) slightly.
3. Tighten the nut (1), then turn the steering to be sure that the steering does not bind anywhere in the operating range.
4. If binding occurs, loosen the nut (1), loosen the nut (2), retighten the nut (1), then recheck steering for smoothness.

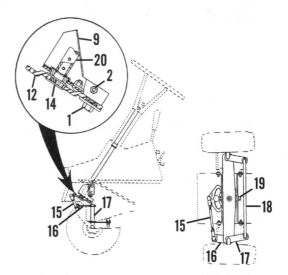

Fig. AR3-3–Views of typical steering system and front axle. Tighten axle pivot nut (19) to 35 ft.-lb. (48 N m).

1. Nut	16. Arm
2. Nut	17. Spindle
9. Bracket	18. Tie rod
12. Steering gear	19. Nut
14. Pinion	20. Steering shaft
15. Steering link	

OVERHAUL

CAUTION: Exercise care when the unit is raised to prevent the unit from accidentally falling during servicing.

1A. If equipped with a rear service bar, proceed as follows:

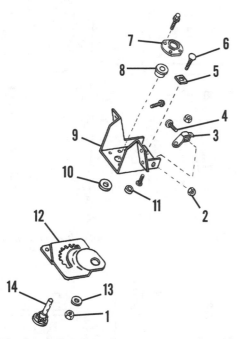

Fig. AR3-4–Exploded view of steering gear. Refer to AR3-3 for cross-sectional view.

1. Nut
2. Nut
3. Adjuster block
4. Screw
5. Pivot spacer
6. Screw
7. Retainer
8. Bushing
9. Bracket
10. Washer
11. Bushing
12. Steering gear
13. Washer
14. Pinion

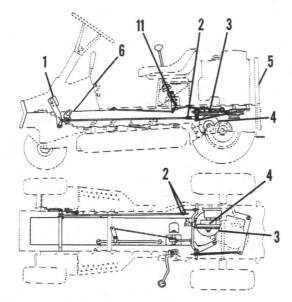

Fig. AR3-5–Drawing of clutch operating system. Refer to text for adjustment procedures.

1. Pedal
2. Adjusting nuts
3. Drive disc
4. Friction wheel
5. Rear service bar
6. Parking brake control
11. Link

a. Drain the fuel tank and operate the engine until all fuel is removed from the carburetor.

b. Disconnect the spark plug wire, remove the battery, air cleaner and rear grass catcher.

c. Raise the front enough to tip the unit back onto the service bar.

1B. If not equipped with service bar at the rear, proceed as follows:

a. Disconnect the spark plug wire.

b. Raise the unit using sufficient blocks or hoist to permit access to the steering gear from below. Be extremely careful to prevent the unit from falling over while servicing.

NOTE: If the unit is raised only at the front, remove fluids as described in Step 1A.

2. Detach the steering link (15—Fig. AR3-3) from the steering gear (12).
3. Detach the steering shaft (20) from the pinion (14).
4. Remove the steering gear assembly (Fig. AR3-4).
5. Reverse the removal procedure to install the steering gear. Adjust as previously outlined.

ENGINE

Refer to the appropriate engine section in this manual for tune-up specifications, engine overhaul procedures and engine maintenance.

REMOVAL AND INSTALLATION

1. Disconnect the spark plug wire.
2. On electric start models, disconnect and remove the battery.
3. Disconnect any interfering electrical wires from the engine.
4. Disconnect the throttle cable from the engine.
5. Remove the belts from the engine pulley.
6. Remove the engine.
7. Install by reversing the removal procedure.

TRACTION DRIVE BELT
REMOVAL AND INSTALLATION

1. Remove the mower drive belt, then remove the friction wheel as described in the FRICTION DRIVE section.
2. Remove the traction drive belt.
3. Position the new belt in the grooves of the engine pulley, drive disc and idler pulley. Make sure the belt is not twisted.
4. Install and adjust the friction wheel.
5. Install and adjust the mower drive belt as described in the MOWER DRIVE BELT section.

TRACTION DRIVE CLUTCH
ADJUSTMENT

Clutch action is accomplished by raising the drive disc (3—Fig. AR3-5) vertically away from the friction wheel (4). The clutch and brake are interactive. Depressing the brake pedal also causes the clutch to release. Depressing the brake pedal or depressing the clutch pedal past the clutch range engages the brake. Adjust the clutch linkage first, then check and, if necessary, adjust the brake controls.

To adjust the clutch and brake, use the following procedure.

1. Tip unit back onto the rear service bar (5–Fig. AR3-5) or raise the unit sufficiently to provide access from below.

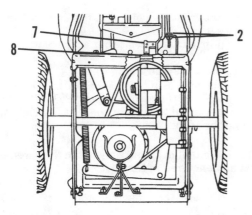

Fig. AR3-6–Refer to text for adjustment of traction drive clutch and friction drive. Linkage is interactive and must be adjusted correctly.

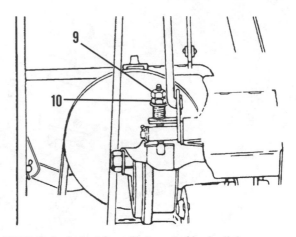

Fig. AR3-7–Refer to text for adjustment of brake linkage.

2. Move the speed control lever to NEUTRAL.

3. Depress the clutch pedal fully and engage the parking brake (6).

4. Turn nuts (2–Fig. AR3-6) until clearance between the neutral stop (7) and the carrier yoke (8) is $\frac{1}{8}$-$\frac{1}{4}$ inch.

5. Release the parking brake and rotate the rear wheels by hand. The wheels should rotate freely in NEUTRAL, but not in any other position.

6. Move the speed control to NEUTRAL.

7. Loosen nuts (9 and 10–Fig. AR3-7). Be careful not to distort the brake band when loosening the nuts.

8. Tighten nut (10) until the wheel just starts to bind, then loosen $1\frac{1}{2}$ turns and tighten the locknut (9).

9. Recheck brake action using the clutch pedal. The drive disc should just move away from the friction wheel when the clutch pedal is approximately $\frac{3}{4}$ inch (19 mm) from the travel limit. The final $\frac{3}{4}$ inch (19 mm) should be sufficient to engage the brake. Be sure the brake band is not twisted.

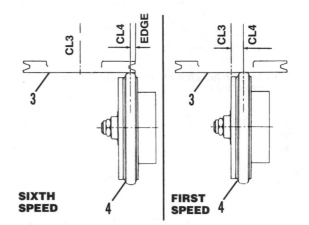

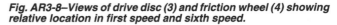

Fig. AR3-8–Views of drive disc (3) and friction wheel (4) showing relative location in first speed and sixth speed.

FRICTION DRIVE

OPERATION

Raising the drive disc (3–Fig. AR3-5) vertically away from the friction wheel (4) disengages the clutch. Refer to the preceding TRACTION DRIVE CLUTCH paragraphs for adjustment procedures.

The position of the drive disc (3) determines the ground speed of the lawnmower. Moving the drive disc (3) laterally across the friction surface of the friction wheel (4) changes the ground speed. When the center of the drive disc is directly over the friction wheel the speed control is in NEUTRAL.

ADJUSTMENT

To adjust the shift positions, proceed as follows.

1. Move the carrier yoke (8–Fig. AR3-6) until it is centered on the neutral stop (7).

2. Detach the link (11–Fig. AR3-5) from the speed control lever.

3. Change the length of the link (11) if necessary so it can be reattached with the shift lever in NEUTRAL and the carrier yoke centered.

4. Connect the link and shift to the sixth speed.

5. Check to be sure the rubber friction wheel (4–Fig. AR3-5) is still on the drive disc (3).

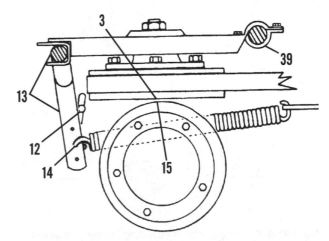

Fig. AR3-9–Refer to text for adjustment of friction drive.

6. Shift to FIRST and REVERSE speeds and check to be sure the carrier yoke (8–Fig. AR3-6) moves off center in both directions.

7. Distance between the centerline of the drive disc (CL3–Fig. AR3-8) and the centerline of the friction wheel (CL4) should be $\frac{11}{16}$-$\frac{3}{4}$ inch (17.5-19 mm) in the first speed.

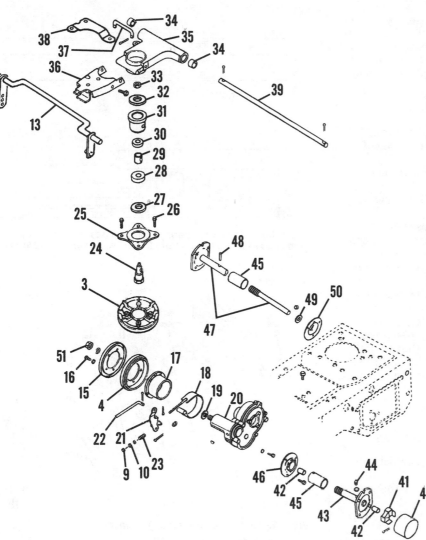

Fig. AR3-10–Exploded view of drive and die cast carrier control parts.

3. Drive disc	31. Housing
4. Friction wheel	32. Washer
9. Nut	33. Nut
10. Nut	34. Bushing
13. Clutch shaft	35. Carrier
15. Guard	36. Carrier yoke
16. Screws	37. Link
17. Hub	38. Bellcrank
18. Brake band	39. Transfer shaft
19. Washer	40. Hub cap
20. Gearcase	41. Retainer
21. Lever	42. Bushing
22. Link	43. Left axle
23. Spring	44. Grease fitting
24. Spindle	45. Spacers
25. Adapter	46. Seal
26. Scews	47. Right axle
27. Shim	48. Roll pin
28. Bearing	49. Washer
29. Sleeve	50. Seal
30. Bearing	51. Nut

DAMAGE ANALYSIS

The friction drive consists of the friction wheel (4–Fig. AR3-10), drive disc (3) and related parts of the spindle carrier (24-36).

If the friction wheel (4–Fig. AR3-10) is damaged, careful analysis may indicate the necessary repair. Refer to Fig. AR3-11 and the following types of damage.

View 1–Small scuff marks and localized flat spot which could be caused by the parking brake not releasing completely or by the drive disc contacting the friction wheel in NEUTRAL.

View 2–Large, chunked-out spot with cracks running around the friction surface which can be caused by the drive disc contacting the friction wheel in NEUTRAL.

View 3–Normal deterioration after long period of normal use. Too much pressure on the friction roller causes this to occur prematurely..

View 4–Shiny friction surface with surface cracks caused by not enough pressure or operator riding the clutch.

View 5–Split indicating friction surface seam failure.

View 6–Radical failure which is usually caused by slippage even though pressure is normal. Overloading the mower or operating on long inclines for extended time can also cause this damage.

View 7–Improper bond may result in missing rubber friction surface.

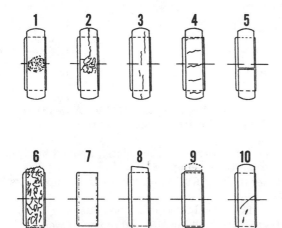

Fig. AH3-11–Drawings of some friction wheel failures. Refer to text for description of conditions shown.

8. Remove the friction wheel to measure the clearance between the guard (15–Fig. AR3-9) and the drive disc (3) when adjusting the stop position (12). Refer to the following OVERHAUL paragraphs for friction wheel and adjusting stop removal.

View 8—Friction surface worn at an angle caused by a bent or loose spindle or carrier frame (Fig. AR3-12).

View 9—Rubber friction surface may be prematurely worn and roughened if the drive disc surface is not smooth.

View 10—Cuts in the friction surface are usually caused by foreign objects caught in the drive assembly.

FRICTION WHEEL

1. Remove the battery and drain the fuel.
2. Raise the machine or tip it back onto the service bar, if so equipped.
3. Remove the attaching screws (16—Fig. AR3-10) and remove the guard (15) and friction wheel (4).
4. When reinstalling, assemble the guard (15) without the wheel (4).
5. Move the speed control to a FORWARD position.
6. Check the clearance between the drive disc (3) and guard (15).
7. Loosen the two nuts on the clutch shaft stop screw (12–Fig. AR3-9).
8. Reposition the stop screw in the slot so only a small amount of clearance exists between the guard (15) and disc (3).
9. Move the speed control back to NEUTRAL, then proceed with the friction wheel installation. Be sure that the friction wheel is correctly located over the shoulder of the hub and that all five retaining screws are tightened upon final assembly.

CARRIER ASSEMBLY AND DRIVE DISC

1. Remove the friction wheel (4–Fig. AR3-10) as described in the previous paragraph.
2. Remove the cotter pin from the link (37) and detach from the lever (38).
3. Disconnect the spring (14–Fig. AR3-9) from the shaft and lever (13).
4. Remove the snap rings and withdraw the shaft (39-Fig. 3-10).
5. Disengage the yoke from the clutch shaft (13) and withdraw the carrier assembly.
6. Remove the nut (33) and thrust washer (32).
7. Remove the drive disc (3), bearings (28 and 30) and sleeve (29) from the bearing housing (31).
8. Remove the screws attaching the adapter (25) to the drive disc and remove the adapter and spindle bolt (24).
9. Remove the screws attaching the yolk (36) to the carrier (35) and separate the yoke from the carrier.
10. Remove the screws attaching the bearing housing (31) to the carrier and remove the housing.
11. Reassemble by reversing the disassembly procedure. Adjust the bearings using shims (27). Tighten nut (33) to 45 ft.-lb. (60 N•m).

GEARCASE OVERHAUL

1. Support the rear of the lawnmower and remove the rear wheels.
2. Drive the roll pin (48–Fig. AR3-10) from the long right side axle, then withdraw the axle.
3. Remove the washer (49) from the inside bearing.
4. Remove the cotter pin, then detach the rod (22) from the lever (21).
5. Unbolt and remove the seal (46).
6. Remove the screws attaching the gearcase (20) to the frame, then withdraw the gearcase assembly.
7. Remove the nut (51), then slide the friction wheel (4), guard (15) and hub (17) from the shaft as an assembly.

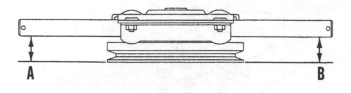

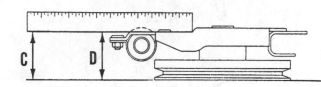

Fig. AR3-12—Check for bent parts by measuring as shown. Dimensions (A and B) and (C and D) should be within 1/32 inch (0.8 mm).

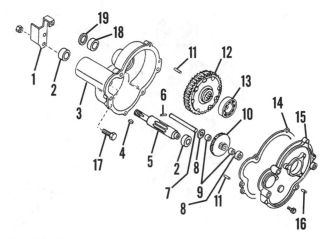

Fig. AR3-13—Exploded view of gearcase.

1. Brake bracket
2. Ball bearing
3. Housing
4. Woodruff key
5. Pinion shaft
6. Roll pin
7. Idler shaft
8. Washer
9. Needle bearings
10. Cluster gear
11. Groove pin
12. Differential assy.
13. Ball bearing
14. Gasket
15. Cover
16. Breather
17. Special screw
18. Bushing
19. Seal

8. Remove the Woodruff key (4–Fig. AR3-13) from the shaft. Remove the screws retaining the cover (15) to the housing (3).
9. Insert screwdrivers in the slots provided and pry the cover from the housing.
10. Refer to Fig. AR3-13 and remove the components from gearcase.
11. Pry the oil seal (19) out of the housing
12. Inspect the bushing (18) and replace if worn.
13. Inspect the breather (16) and clean or replace it.
14. Reassemble by reversing the disassembly procedure. If replacement is necessary, the pinion (5) and cluster gear (10) are available only as a matched set. Note the following:

   a. Install the breather by pressing in from the outside of the cover.

   b. Press the bushing (18) into the housing until bottomed against the shoulder in the bore.

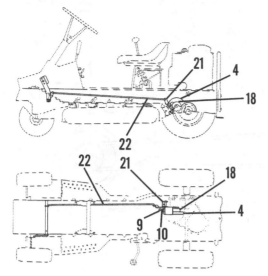

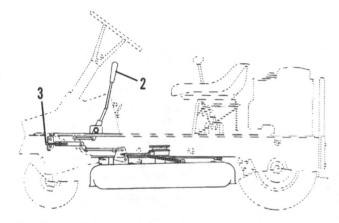

Fig. AR3-14–Views of brake controls. Refer to text for adjustment procedures.

4. Friction wheel	18. Brake band
9. Nut	21. Lever
10. Nut	22. Link

Fig. AR3-15–View of mower adjustment screw (3), mower lever (2) and associated controls on models with 28- or 30-inch mower.

c. Install the seal (19) flush with the face of the housing.

d. Install the numbered side of bearings (9) facing out and flush with the face of the gear.

e. Install the differential assembly (12) with small inside diameter spline towards the inside of the housing (3).

f. Press the special ribbed screws (17) into the housing to attach the brake bracket (1).

g. Fill the gearcase cavity with 8 ounces (237 mL) of multipurpose grease before installing the cover.

h. Tighten the nut (51–Fig. AR3-10) to 70 ft.-lb. (95 N•m).

i. Refer to the TRACTION DRIVE CLUTCH adjustment section and to FRICTION DRIVE section while installing and assembling the gearcase.

GROUND DRIVE BRAKE

ADJUSTMENT

Refer to Fig. AR3-14 for views of the brake controls. The clutch and brake are interactive and depressing the brake pedal causes the clutch to release. Adjust the clutch linkage first, then adjust the brake controls. Refer to the TRACTION DRIVE CLUTCH adjustment paragraphs for the procedures.

OVERHAUL

The brake band (18–Fig. AR3-10) operates by contracting around the hub (17). Refer to the GEARCASE section to remove the gearcase and disassemble the brake. When assembling, tighten the hub retaining nut (51) to 70 ft.-lb. (95 N•m). Adjust the brake as described in the TRACTION DRIVE CLUTCH adjustment paragraphs.

MOWER DRIVE BELT

ADJUSTMENT

During the first hours of operation, a new mower drive belt will stretch and will require adjustment as follows.

1. Set mower height in the middle notch.

2. Hold the mower clutch lever (2–Fig. AR3-15) so the lever's front edge is aligned with the rear edge of the forward detent notch of the quadrant as viewed through the slot on the cowl's left side.

3. Turn adjustment screw (3) with a ¾ inch socket. Press the socket against the spring clip when turning the screw (3). Be sure the wire spring clip engages the adjustment screw when released. The mower clutch lever will pull back slightly as tension is increased sufficiently. The mower clutch should begin to engage when the lever's front edge is aligned with the rear edge of the quadrant's forward notch and should be fully locked in when the lever is completely engaging the notch. Do not overtighten as the bearing and belt may fail prematurely due to increased wear.

4. If the mower is usually operated in the lowest cutting position, readjust the belt tension with the height set in the lowest position.

5. On models equipped with a belt finger retaining the belt in the idler pulley, belt slippage can also be caused by the finger adjusted against the belt. Correct adjustment is ⅛ inch (3 mm) clearance between the retaining finger and the back edge of the belt.

6. If loosened, tighten the blade attaching nut to 50-55 ft.-lb. (68-75 N•m).

REMOVAL AND INSTALLATION

CAUTION: Exercise care when the unit is raised to prevent the unit from accidentally falling during servicing.

1A. If equipped with a rear service bar, proceed as follows:

   a. Drain the fuel and operate the engine until all fuel is removed from the carburetor.

   b. Disconnect the spark plug wire and remove the battery.

   c. Raise the front enough to tip the unit back onto the service bar.

1B. If not equipped with service bar at rear, proceed as follows:

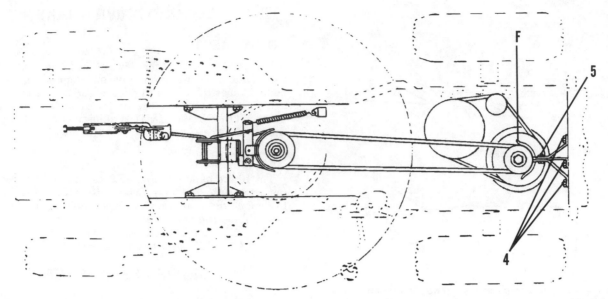

Fig. AR3-16–View of drive belt controls and belt guard (finger) for 28- or 30-inch mower drive. Refer to text.

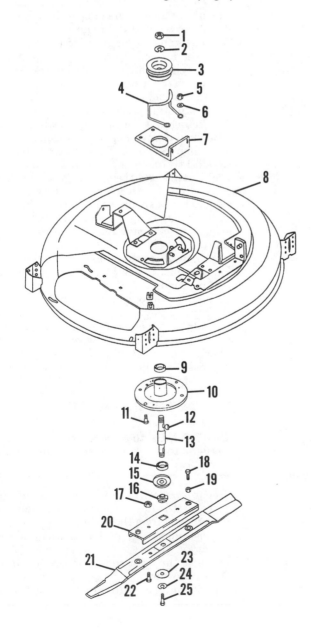

Fig. AR3-17–Exploded view of 28- or 30-inch mower deck, spindle and blade.

1. Nut
2. Lockwasher
3. Pulley
4. Belt finger
5. Nut
6. Washer
7. Plate
8. Mower deck
9. Bearing
10. Spindle housing
11. Bolt
12. Woodruff key
13. Spindle
14. Bearing
15. Bearing slinger
16. Retainer nut
17. Nut
18. Bolt
19. Nut
20. Blade tray
21. Blade
22. Bolt
23. Washer
24. Lockwasher
25. Bolt

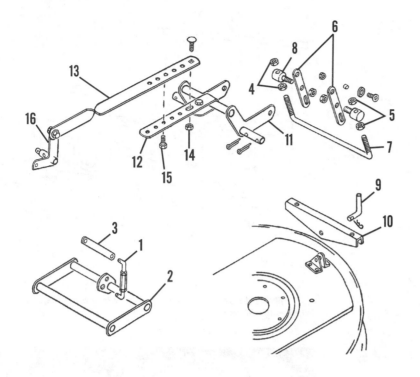

Fig. AR3-18–Views of mower linkage. Refer also to Figs. AR3-19 and AR3-20.

1. Link
2. Front lift arm
3. Strap
4. Nuts
5. Nuts
6. Link plates
7. Link
8. Blocks
9. Pin
10. Swivel bracket
11. Rear mower hanger
12. Adjusting strap
13. Lift strap
14. Nut
15. Cap screw
16. Lift arm

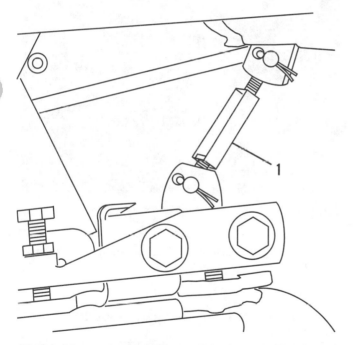

Fig. AR3-19–Adjust length of front link (1) to change height of front of mower deck.

a. Disconnect the spark plug wire.
b. Raise the unit using sufficient blocks or a hoist to permit access to the underside.

2. Move the mower clutch lever to the OUT disengaged position.

3. Loosen the three nuts (4—Fig. AR3-16) and move the rear finger out of the way.

4. Roll the belt out of the pulley groove.

5. Replace the drive belt.

6. Install in the reverse order of disassembly. When installing the rear finger nuts (4), tighten the top nuts first. Rear finger belt clearance should be $\frac{1}{16}$ inch (1.6 mm).

MOWER SPINDLE

LUBRICATION

Mower spindle bearings (9 and 14—Fig. AR3-17) should be packed with grease when assembling and should not require additional lubrication until disassembled for other service.

OVERHAUL

To remove the spindle (13—Fig. AR3-17), proceed as follows.

1. Remove the mower deck as outlined in the appropriate following paragraph.

2. Remove the blade retaining bolt (25), lockwasher (24), washer (23) and blade (21).

3. Remove the nut (1), lockwasher (2), pulley (3) and top Woodruff key (12).

4. Remove the hub (16), slinger (15) and lower Woodruff key.

5. Bump the spindle (13) out of the spindle housing (10).

6. Inspect the bearings and spindle. Replace if damaged.

7. Reverse the disassembly steps to reassemble. Tighten the blade retaining bolt (25) to 50-55 ft.-lb. (68-75 N•m).

MOWER DECK

ADJUSTMENT

Before attempting any adjustment, the machine must be on level ground and the tires must be properly inflated. Disconnect the spark plug wire and tie it out of the way. Check cutting height with the clutch engaged.

Front-to-rear height difference is determined by measuring the height of the blade above the ground at the front and rear. Rear height should be $\frac{1}{4}$-$\frac{3}{8}$ inch (6.4-9.5 mm) higher. Adjust the front height of the mower by adjusting the length of the link (1—Fig. AR3-18 or Fig. AR3-19). To change the link length, loosen the jam nut, and turn the link's center coupling. Adjust the mower's rear height by

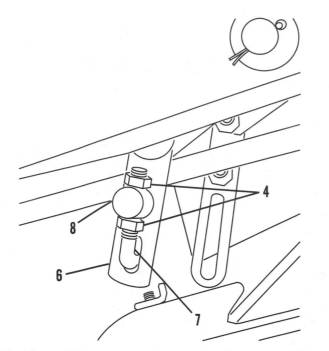

Fig.AR3-20–Refer to text for mower deck height adjustment by turning nuts (4) on rear links.

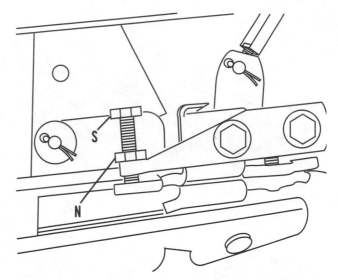

Fig, AR3-21–Loosen nut (N) and rotate screw (S) to alter side-to-side height.

turning the nuts (4 and 5-Fig. AR3-18 or Fig. AR3-20). If specified front-to-rear height dimension cannot be obtained using the preceding adjustment procedure, additional adjustment may be obtained by relocating the screw (15–Fig. AR3-18) in the lift straps. Moving the straps apart will decrease the rear mower height.

If mower deck side-to-side height is uneven, rotate the screw adjuster adjacent to the front mower hanger (Fig. AR3-21) so the deck height is level.

After the mower deck height has been adjusted, check the height of the antiscalping rollers (Fig. AR3-22). Height of the rollers should be at least ½ inch (13 mm) above the ground surface after adjusting the deck height, otherwise, set the roller height according to terrain and desired cut appearance.

REMOVAL AND INSTALLATION

1. Move the mower control lever to the disengaged position and lower the mower to its lowest setting.
2. Remove the belt finger attaching nuts (4–Fig. AR3-16) and remove the finger assembly.
3. Roll the blade drive belt out of the rear pulley.
4. Remove the clip from the pin (9–Fig. AR3-18).
5. Remove the pin (9) and lower the rear of the mower.
6. Remove the clips from the link (1).
7. Remove the link (1) and lower the front of the mower.
8. Install the mower deck by reversing the removal procedure. Be sure to check and adjust the mower drive belt ten-

Fig. AR3-22–View of anti-scalping rollers on mower deck.

sion, belt finger clearance and deck height as previously outlined.

ELECTRICAL

Refer to Fig. AR3-23 for wiring schematic. Note the following points:

1. The transmission must be in NEUTRAL, the mower must be disengaged and the operator must be in the seat for the engine to start.
2. The engine should stop if the transmission is in gear or the mower is engaged and the operator leaves the seat.

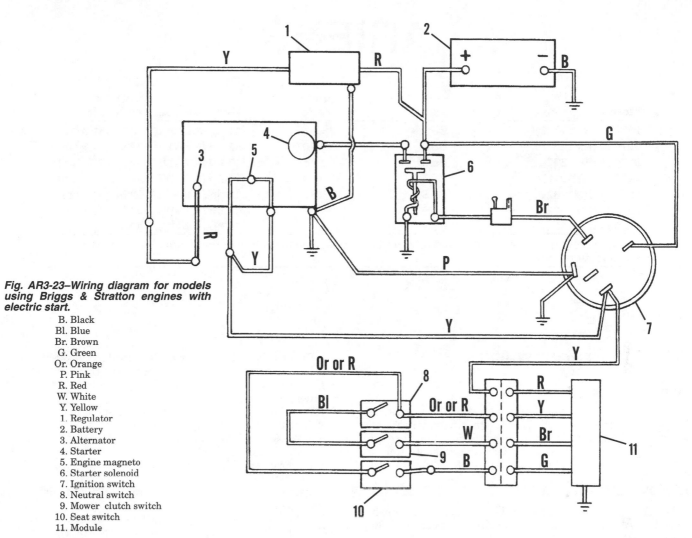

Fig. AR3-23–Wiring diagram for models using Briggs & Stratton engines with electric start.

B. Black
Bl. Blue
Br. Brown
G. Green
Or. Orange
P. Pink
R. Red
W. White
Y. Yellow
1. Regulator
2. Battery
3. Alternator
4. Starter
5. Engine magneto
6. Starter solenoid
7. Ignition switch
8. Neutral switch
9. Mower clutch switch
10. Seat switch
11. Module

ARIENS

Model	Make	Engine Model	Horsepower	Cutting Width, In.
927047 (RM1132E)	B&S	28D707	11 hp (8.6 kW)	32 in. (81.3 cm)
927050 (RM1232E)	B&S	283707	12 hp (9 kW)	32 in. (81.3 cm)
927051 (RM1332)	B&S	*	13 hp (9.7 kW)	32 in. (81.3 cm)
927055 (RM1332)	B&S	*	13 hp (9.7 kW)	32 in. (81.3 cm)
927303 (RM1232E)	B&S	283707	12 hp (9 kW)	32 in. (81.3 cm)
927305 (RM1332)	B&S	*	13 hp (9.7 kW)	32 in. (81.3 cm)
927308 (RM1332)	B&S	*	13 hp (9.7 kW)	32 in. (81.3 cm)

*Note the engine model number and refer to the engine service section in this manual for engine specifications.

FRONT WHEELS

MAINTENANCE

Lubricate the front wheel bushings after every 25 hours of operation, or twice each season, whichever occurs first. Inject multipurpose grease into each wheel hub through the grease fitting (Fig. AR4-1). One or two shots from a hand-held grease gun should be sufficient.

REMOVAL AND INSTALLATION

The front wheels are equipped with replaceable bushings. To remove the wheel and bushings, proceed as follows:

1. Remove the hub cap (19–Fig. AR4-2).
2. Remove the cotter pin (20).
3. Remove the spindle cap (18).
4. Remove the wheel.
5. Inspect the inner washer and cotter pin. Replace if damaged.
6. Separate the bushings from the wheel.
7. Inspect the bushings for damage.
8. Inspect the wheel for rim and hub damage.
9. Reverse the removal steps to reassemble and install the wheel.

FRONT AXLE

MAINTENANCE

Lubricate the front wheel spindles and front axle pivot after every 25 hours of operation, or twice each season, whichever occurs first. Inject multipurpose grease to the spindles through the grease fitting at each end of axle. One or two shots from a hand-held grease gun should be sufficient. Check for looseness and binding in front axle components.

OVERHAUL

Axle main member is center-pivoted in a channel at the front of the chassis. Refer to the following procedure to remove and install the front axle.

1. Remove the mower deck as described in this section.
2. Raise and support the front end of the frame.
3. Remove the steering link (32–Fig. AR4-2).
4. Remove the front wheels.
5. Disconnect the tie rod (28) from the spindles.
6. Remove the cotter pins and washers, then lower the spindles (15 and 23) from the axle.
7. Support the front axle.
8. Remove the axle bolt (13), then lower and remove the front axle (26).
9. Inspect the bushings in the front axle and replace if damaged.
10. Clean and inspect all parts. Replace damaged parts.
11. Install by reversing the removal procedure. Tighten the axle pivot bolt (13) to 35 ft.-lb. (48 N•m).

STEERING GEAR

ADJUSTMENT

Adjustment to compensate for wear of the pinion and steering gear teeth is possible without removing the steering gear assembly. To adjust, use the following procedure.

Fig. AR4-1–View of front wheel grease fitting.

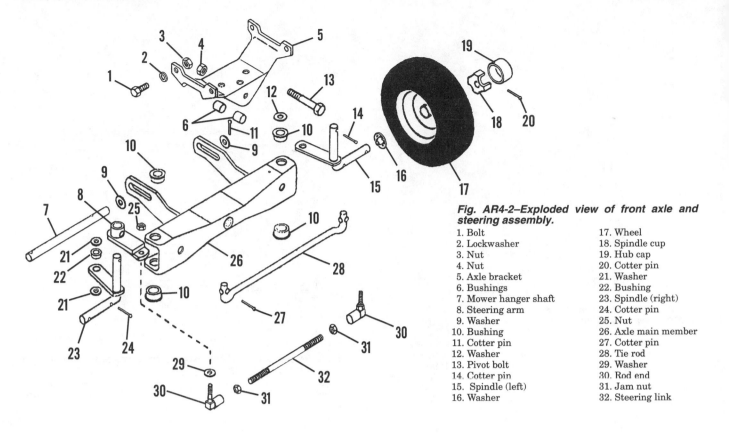

Fig. AR4-2–Exploded view of front axle and steering assembly.

1. Bolt	17. Wheel
2. Lockwasher	18. Spindle cup
3. Nut	19. Hub cap
4. Nut	20. Cotter pin
5. Axle bracket	21. Washer
6. Bushings	22. Bushing
7. Mower hanger shaft	23. Spindle (right)
8. Steering arm	24. Cotter pin
9. Washer	25. Nut
10. Bushing	26. Axle main member
11. Cotter pin	27. Cotter pin
12. Washer	28. Tie rod
13. Pivot bolt	29. Washer
14. Cotter pin	30. Rod end
15. Spindle (left)	31. Jam nut
16. Washer	32. Steering link

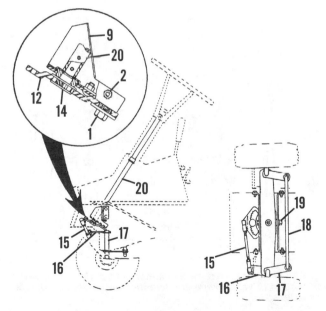

Fig. AR4-3–Exploded view of front axle and steering assemblies.

1. Nut	16. Arm
2. Nut	17. Spindle
9. Bracket	18. Tie rod
12. Steering gear	19. Nut
14. Pinion	20. Steering shaft
15. Steering link	

1. Loosen the nut (1–Fig. AR4-3 or Fig. AR4-4).

2. Tighten the nut (2) slightly.

3. Tighten the nut (1), then turn the steering to be sure that steering does not bind anywhere in the operating range.

4. If binding occurs, loosen the nuts (1 and 2), retighten the nut (1) and recheck steering for smoothness.

OVERHAUL

CAUTION: Exercise care when the unit is raised to prevent the unit from accidentally falling during servicing.

1A. If equipped with a rear service bar, proceed as follows:
   a. Drain the fuel tank and operate the engine until all fuel is removed from the carburetor.
   b. Disconnect the spark plug wire. Remove the battery, air cleaner and rear grass catcher.
   c. Raise the front enough to tip unit back onto the service bar.

1B. If not equipped with a service bar at the rear, proceed as follows:
   a. Disconnect the spark plug wire.
   b. Raise the unit using sufficient blocks or hoist to permit access to the steering gear from below. Be extremely careful to prevent the unit from falling over while servicing.

NOTE: If the unit is raised only at the front, remove fluids as described in Step 1A.

2. Detach the steering link (15–Fig. AR4-3) from the steering gear (12).

3. Detach the steering shaft (20) from the pinion (14).

4. Remove the steering gear assembly (Fig. AR4-4).

5. Replace the damaged parts.

6. Install by reversing the removal procedures.

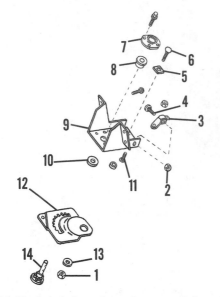

Fig. AR4-4–Exploded view of steering gear. Refer to Fig. AR4-3 for cross-sectional view.

1. Nut
2. Nut
3. Adjuster block
4. Screw
5. Pivot spacer
6. Screw
7. Retainer
8. Bushing
9. Bracket
10. Washer
11. Bushing
12. Steering gear
13. Washer
14. Pinion

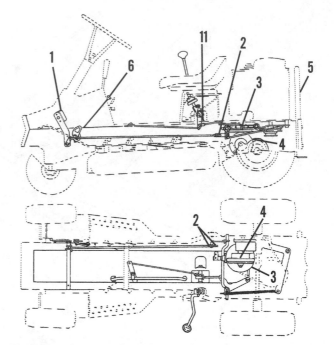

Fig. AR4-5–Drawing of clutch operating system. Refer to text for adjustment procedure.

1. Pedal
2. Adjusting nuts
3. Drive disc
4. Friction wheel
5. Rear service bar
6. Parking brake control
11. Link

ENGINE

Refer to the appropriate engine section in this manual for tune-up specifications, engine overhaul procedures and engine maintenance.

REMOVAL AND INSTALLATION

To remove the engine, proceed as follows.

1. Disconnect the spark plug wire.

2. On electric start models, disconnect and remove the battery.

3. Disconnect any interfering electrical wires from the engine.

4. Disconnect throttle cable from the engine.

5. Remove the belts from the engine pulley.

6. Remove the engine.

7. Install by reversing the removal procedure.

TRACTION DRIVE BELT REMOVAL AND INSTALLATION

1. Remove the mower drive belt, then remove the friction wheel as described in the FRICTION DRIVE section.

2. Remove the belt.

3. Position the new belt in the grooves of the engine pulley, drive disc and idler pulley. Make sure the belt is not twisted.

4. Install and adjust the friction wheel.

5. Install and adjust the mower drive belt as described in the MOWER DRIVE BELT section.

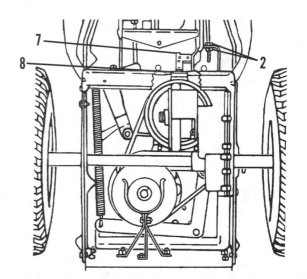

Fig. AR4-6–Refer to text for adjustment of traction drive clutch and friction drive. Linkage is interactive and must be adjusted correctly.

TRACTION DRIVE CLUTCH ADJUSTMENT

Clutch action is accomplished by raising the drive disc (3—Fig. AR4-5) vertically away from the friction wheel (4). The clutch and brake are interactive. Depressing the brake pedal also causes the clutch to release. Depressing the brake pedal or depressing the clutch pedal past the clutch range engages the brake. Adjust the clutch linkage first, then check and, if necessary, adjust the brake controls.

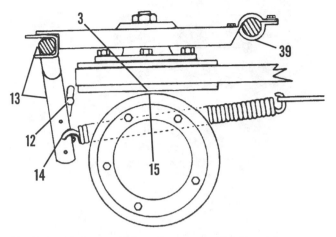

Fig. AR4-9–Refer to text for adjustment of friction drive.

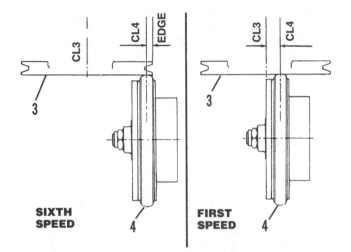

Fig. AR4-7–Refer to text for adjustment of brake linkage.

Fig. AR4-8–Views of drive disc (3) and friction wheel (4) showing relative location in first speed and sixth speed.

To adjust the clutch and brake, use the following procedure.

1. Tip the unit back onto the rear service bar (5—Fig. AR4-5) or raise the unit sufficiently to provide access from below.
2. Move the speed control lever to NEUTRAL.
3. Depress the clutch pedal fully and engage the parking brake (6).
4. Turn the nuts (2–Fig. AR4-6) until the clearance between the neutral stop (7) and the carrier yoke (8) is $\frac{1}{8}$-$\frac{1}{4}$ inch.
5. Release the parking brake and rotate the rear wheels by hand. The wheels should rotate freely in NEUTRAL, but not in any other position.
6. Move the speed control to NEUTRAL.
7. Loosen the nuts (9 and 10–Fig. AR4-7). Be careful not to distort the brake band when loosening the nuts.
8. Tighten the nut (10) until the wheel just starts to bind, then loosen 1½ turns and tighten locknut (9).
9. Recheck brake action using the clutch pedal. The drive disc should just move away from the friction wheel when the clutch pedal is approximately $\frac{3}{4}$ inch (19 mm) from the limit of travel. The final $\frac{3}{4}$ inch (19 mm) should be suffi-

cient to engage the brake. Be sure the brake band is not twisted.

FRICTION DRIVE

OPERATION

Raising the drive disc (3–Fig. AR4-5) vertically away from the friction wheel (4) disengages the clutch. Refer to the preceding TRACTION DRIVE CLUTCH paragraphs for adjustment procedures.

The position of the drive disc (3) determines the ground speed of the lawnmower. Moving the drive disc (3) laterally across the friction surface of the friction wheel (4) changes the ground speed. When the center of the drive disc is directly over the friction wheel the speed control is in NEUTRAL.

ADJUSTMENT

To adjust the shift positions, proceed as follows.

1. Move the carrier yoke (8–Fig. AR4-6) until it is centered on the neutral stop (7).
2. Detach the link (11–Fig. AR4-5) from the speed control lever.
3. Change the length of the link (11) if necessary so it can be reattached with the shift lever in NEUTRAL and carrier yoke centered.
4. Connect the link and shift to sixth speed.
5. Check to be sure that the rubber friction wheel (4–Fig. AR4-5) is still on the drive disc (3).
6. Shift to first and reverse speeds and check to be sure the carrier yoke (8—Fig. AR4-6) moves off center in both directions.
7. Distance between the drive disc centerline (CL3–Fig. AR4-8) and the friction wheel centerline (CL4) should be $\frac{11}{16}$-$\frac{3}{4}$ inch (17.5-19 mm) in first speed.
8. Remove the friction wheel to measure the clearance between the guard (15–Fig. AR4-9) and drive disc (3) when adjusting the position of the stop (12). Refer to the following OVERHAUL paragraphs for friction wheel and adjusting stop removal.

DAMAGE ANALYSIS

The friction drive consists of the friction wheel (4–Fig. AR4-10), drive disc (3) and related parts of the spindle carrier (24-36).

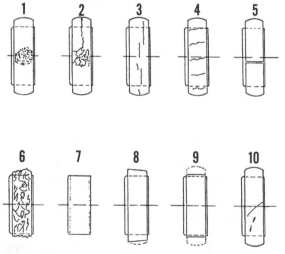

Fig. AR4-10–Exploded view of drive and die cast carrier control parts.

3. Drive disc	31. Housing
4. Friction wheel	32. Washer
9. Nut	33. Nut
10. Nut	34. Bushings
13. Clutch shaft	35. Carrier
15. Guard	36. Carrier yoke
16. Screws	37. Link
17. Hub	38. Bellecrank
18. Brake band	39. Transfer shaft
19. Washer	40. Hub cap
20. Gearcase	41. Retainer
21. Lever	42. Bushing
22. Link	43. Left axle
23. Spring	44. Grease fitting
24. Spindle	45. Spacers
25. Adapter	46. Seal
26. Screws	47. Right axle
27. Shim	48. Roll pin
28. Bearing	49. Washer
29. Sleeve	50. Seal
30. Bearing	51. Nut

If the friction wheel (4–Fig. AR4-10) is damaged, careful analysis may indicate the necessary repair. Refer to Fig. AR4-11 and the following types of damage.

View 1–Small scuff marks and localized flat spot which could be caused by the parking brake not releasing completely or by the drive disc contacting the friction wheel in NEUTRAL.

View 2–Large, chunked-out spot with cracks running around the friction surface which can be caused by the drive disc contacting the friction wheel in NEUTRAL.

View 3–Normal deterioration after long period of normal use. Too much pressure on the friction roller causes this to occur prematurely.

View 4–Shiny friction surface with surface cracks caused by not enough pressure or the operator riding the clutch.

View 5–Split indicating failure of the friction surface seam.

View 6–Radical failure which is usually caused by slippage even though pressure is normal. Overloading the mower or operating on long inclines for extended time can also cause this damage.

View 7–Improper bond may result in missing rubber friction surface.

View 8–Friction surface worn at angle caused by a bent or loose spindle or carrier frame (Fig. AR4-12).

View 9–Rubber friction surface may be prematurely worn and roughened if the drive disc surface is not smooth.

View 10–Cuts in the friction surface are usually caused by foreign objects caught in drive assembly.

Fig. AR 4-11–Drawings of some friction wheel failures. Refer to text for descirption of conditions shown.

FRICTION WHEEL AND DRIVE DISC

1. Remove the battery and drain the fuel. Raise the machine or tip the machine back onto the service bar, if so equipped.

2. Remove the attaching screws (16–Fig. AR4-10), remove the guard (15) and friction wheel (4).

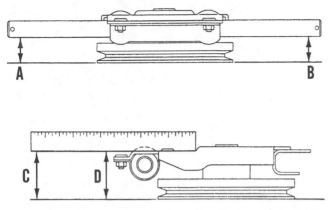

Fig. AR4-12–Check for bent parts by measuring as shown. Dimensions (A and B) and (C and D) should be within 1/32 inch (0.8 mm).

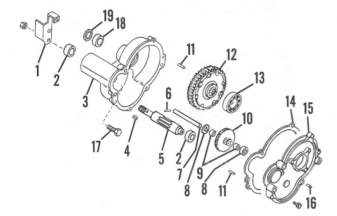

Fig. AR4-13–Exploded view of gearcase.

1. Brake bracket	11. Groove pin
2. Ball bearing	12. Differential assy.
3. Housing	13. Ball bearing
4. Woodruff key	14. Gasket
5. Pinion shaft	15. Cover
6. Roll pin	16. Breather
7. Idler shaft	17. Special screw
8. Washer	18. Bushing
9. Needle bearing	19. Seal
10. Cluster gear	

3. When reinstalling, assemble the guard (15) without the wheel (4).

4. Move the speed control to a forward position.

5. Check the clearance between the drive disc (3) and guard (15).

6. Loosen the two nuts on the clutch shaft stop screw (12–Fig AR4-9).

7. Reposition the stop screw in the slot so only a small amount of clearance exists between the guard (15) and disc (3).

8. Move the speed control back to NEUTRAL, then proceed with the friction wheel installation. Be sure the friction wheel is correctly located over the shoulder of the hub and all five retaining screws are tightened upon final assembly.

CARRIER ASSEMBLY AND DRIVE DISC

1. Remove the friction wheel (4–Fig. AR4-10) as described in the previous paragraph.

2. Remove the cotter pin from link (37) and detach from lever (38).

3. Disconnect the spring (14–Fig. AR4-9) from the shaft and lever (13).

4. Remove the snap rings and withdraw the shaft (39–Fig. AR4-10).

5. Disengage the yoke from the clutch shaft (13) and withdraw the carrier assembly.

6. Remove the nut (33) and thrust washer (32).

7. Remove the drive disc (3), bearing (28 and 30) and sleeve (29) from the bearing housing (31).

8. Remove the screws attaching the adapters (25) to the drive disc and remove the adapter and spindle bolt (24).

9. Remove the screws attaching the yoke (36) to the carrier (35) and separate the yoke from the carrier.

10. Remove the screws attaching the bearing housing (31) to the carrier and remove the housing.

11. Reassemble by reversing the disassembly procedure. Adjust the bearings using shims (27). Tighten the nut (33) to 45 ft.-lb. (60 N•m).

GEARCASE OVERHAUL

1. Support the rear of the lawnmower and remove the rear wheels.

2. Drive the roll pin (48–Fig. AR4-10) from the long right side axle, then withdraw the axle.

3. Remove the washer (49) from the inside bearing.

4. Remove the cotter pin, then detach the rod (22) from the lever (21).

5. Unbolt and remove the seal (46).

6. Remove the screws attaching the gearcase (20) to the frame, then withdraw the gearcase assembly.

7. Remove the nut (51), then slide the friction wheel (4), guard (15) and hub (17) from the shaft as an assembly.

8. Remove the Woodruff key (4–Fig. AR4-13) from the shaft. Remove the screws retaining the cover (15) to the housing (3).

9. Insert screwdrivers in the slots provided and pry the cover from the housing.

10. Refer to Fig. AR4-13 and remove components from the gearcase.

11. Pry the seal (19) from the housing.

12. Inspect the bushing (18) and replace if worn or damaged.

13. Inspect the breather (16) and clean or replace it.

14. Reassemble by reversing the disassembly procedure. If replacement is necessary, pinion (5) and cluster gear (10) are available only as a matched set. Note the following:

   a. Install the breather by pressing in from the outside of the cover.

   b. Press the bushing (18) into the housing until bottomed against the shoulder in the bore.

   c. Install the seal (19) flush with the face of the housing.

   d. Install the numbered side of bearings (9) facing out and flush with the gear face.

   e. Install the differential assembly (12) with small inside diameter spline towards the inside of the housing (3).

   f. Press the special ribbed screws (17) into the housing to attach the brake bracket (1).

   g. Fill the gearcase cavity with 8 ounces (237 mL) of multipurpose grease before installing the cover.

   h. Tighten the nut (51–Fig. AR4-10) to 70 ft.-lb. (95 N•m).

   i. Refer to the TRACTION DRIVE CLUTCH adjustment section and to the FRICTION DRIVE section while installing and assembling gearcase.

GROUND DRIVE BRAKE

ADJUSTMENT

Refer to Fig. AR4-14 for brake control views. The clutch and brake are interactive and depressing the brake pedal causes the clutch to release. Adjust the clutch linkage first, then adjust the brake controls. Refer to the TRACTION DRIVE CLUTCH adjustment paragraphs for procedures.

OVERHAUL

The brake band (18–Fig. AR4-10) operates by contracting around the hub (17). Refer to the GEARCASE section to remove the gearcase and disassemble the brake. When assembling, tighten the hub retaining nut (51) to 70 ft.-lb. (95 N•m). Adjust the brake as described in the TRACTION DRIVE CLUTCH adjustment paragraphs.

MOWER DRIVE BELT

ADJUSTMENT

During the first hours of operation, a new mower drive belt will stretch and will require adjustment as follows.
1. Rotate the clutch spring adjusting nut (A–Fig. AR4-15) so the spring length (B) is 5¼ to 5⅜ inches (133.3-136.5 mm) with the belt engaged.
2. Hold the mower clutch lever so the lever's front edge is aligned with the rear edge of the forward detent notch of the quadrant as viewed through the slot in the left side of the cowl. The mower clutch lever will pull back slightly as tension is increased sufficiently. The mower clutch should begin to engage when the front edge of lever is aligned with the rear edge of the forward notch in the quadrant and should be fully locked in when the lever is completely engaging the notch.

REMOVAL AND INSTALLATION

> CAUTION: Exercise care when unit is raised to prevent the unit from accidentally falling during servicing.

1A. If equipped with a rear service bar, proceed as follows:
   a. Drain the fuel and operate the engine until all fuel is removed from the carburetor.
   b. Disconnect the spark plug wire and remove the battery.
   c. Raise the front enough to tip the unit back onto the service bar.
1B. If not equipped with a service bar at the rear, proceed as follows:
   a. Disconnect the spark plug wire.
   b. Raise the unit using sufficient blocks or hoist to permit access to the underside.
2. Move the mower clutch lever to the OUT disengaged position.
3. Loosen the three nuts (A–Fig. AR4-16) and move the rear finger out of the way.
4. Remove the mower belt finger (C–Fig. AR4-15).
5. Loosen the fixed idler (D) bolt and clutch idler (E) bolt sufficiently so there is increased clearance between the idlers and belt fingers.
6. Remove the old drive belt.
7. Install the new drive belt in the reverse order of disassembly. Note the following:

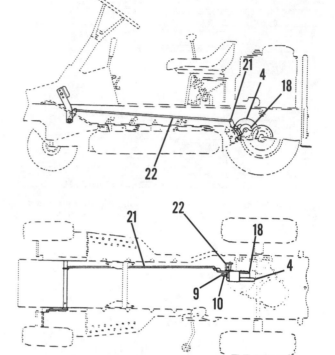

Fig. AR4-14–Views of brake controls. Refer to text for adjustment procedure.

4. Friction wheel	18. Brake band
9. Nut	21. Lever
10. Nut	22. Link

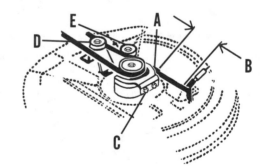

Fig. AR4-15–View of mower clutch adjustment screw (3), mower lever (2) and associated controls on models with 28- or 30-inch mower.

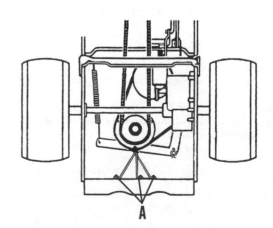

Fig. AR4-16–Remove nuts (A) to move or remove rear belt finger.

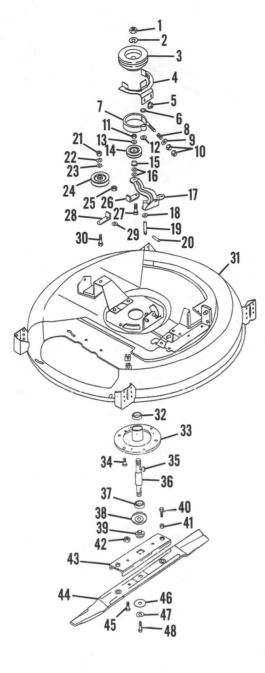

Fig. AR4-17–Exploded view of 32-inch mower deck, spindle and blade.

1. Nut
2. Lockwasher
3. Pulley
4. Belt finger
5. Nut
6. Washer
7. Brake band
8. Spring
9. Washer
10. Nuts
11. Nut
12. Washer
13. Washer
14. Clutch idler
15. Bushing
16. Washers
17. Clutch arm
18. Washer
19. Pin
20. Roll pin
21. Nut
22. Lockwasher
23. Washer
24. Fixed idler
25. Nut
26. Belt finger
27. Bolt
28. Belt finger
29. Washer
30. Bolt
31. Mower deck
32. Bearing
33. Spindle housing
34. Bolt
35. Woodruff key
36. Spindle
37. Bearing
38. Bearing slinger
39. Retainer hub
40. Bolt
41. Nut
42. Nut
43. Blade tray
44. Blade
45. Bolt
46. Washer
47. Lockwasher
48. Bolt

a. When installing the rear finger nuts (A–Fig. AR4-16), tighten the top nuts first. The rear finger belt clearance should be $\frac{1}{16}$ inch (1.6 mm).

b. Tighten the clutch idler (E–Fig. AR4-15) bolt. Finger clearance should be $\frac{1}{8}$ inch (3.2 mm).

c. Tighten the fixed idler (D) bolt. Be sure the tab on the mount engages the belt finger hole.

d. Bend the mower belt finger (C) as required so belt clearance is $\frac{1}{16}$ inch (1.6 mm).

MOWER SPINDLE OVERHAUL

1. Remove the mower deck from the rider as described in this section.

2. Remove the belt finger (4–Fig. AR4-17)

3. Remove the retaining nut (1) and pulley (3).

4. Remove the nuts (10) and spring (8) from the brake band.

5. Remove the fastener (6) from the top of the brake band (7) and remove the brake band.

6. Remove the nut (11) attaching the idler (14) to the idler arm (17). Remove the idler, spacer (15), washer (16) and belt finger (26).

7. Remove the idler arm from the mower deck.

8. Remove the bolt (48) retaining the blade (44) to the spindle (36). Remove the blade and tray (43).

9. Remove the retainer hub (39), slinger (38) and Woodruff keys from the spindle.

10. Remove the cap screws attaching the spindle housing (33) to the mower deck. Remove the spindle assembly from the deck.

11. Press the spindle shaft (36) from the housing and remove the bearings (32 and 37).

12. Replace damaged parts.

13. Reverse the disassembly procedure to reassemble. Tighten the spindle nut (1) and retainer hub to 50-55 ft.-lb. (37-40 N•m).

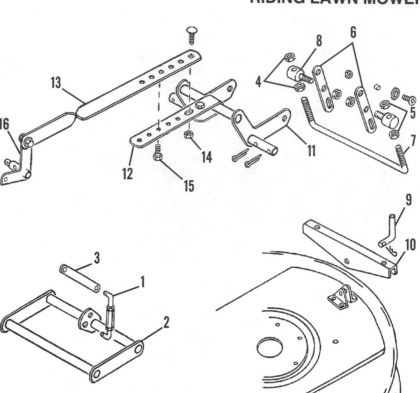

Fig. AG4-18–Views of mower linkage. Refer also to AR4-19 and AR4-20.

1. Link
2. Front lift arm
3. Strap
4. Nuts
5. Nuts
6. Link plates
7. Link
8. Blocks
9. Pin
10. Swivel bracket
11. Rear mower hanger
12. Adjusting strap
13. Lift strap
14. Nut
15. Cap screw
16. Lift arm

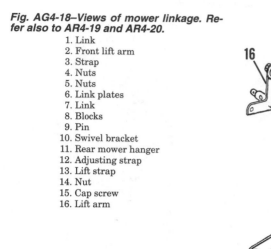

Fig. AR4-19–Adjust length of front link (1) to change height of front of mower deck.

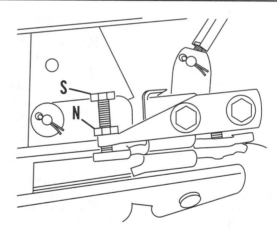

Fig. AR4-21–Loosen nut (N) and rotate screws (S) to alter side-to-side height.

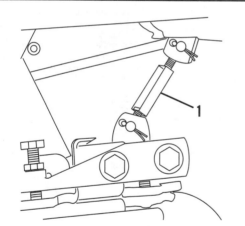

Fig. AR4-20–Refer to text for adjustment of rear links by turning nuts (4) on rear links.

Fig. AR4-22–View of anti-scalping rollers on mower deck.

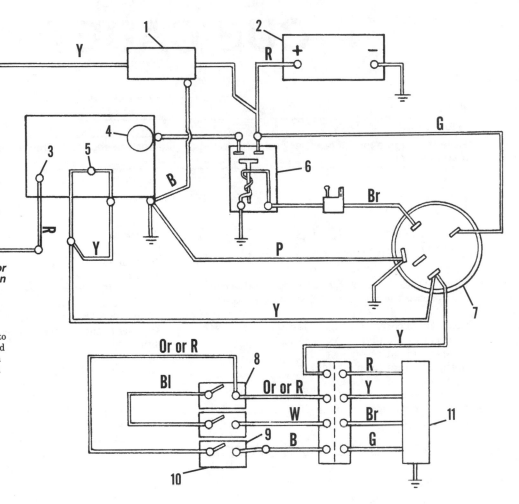

Fig. AR4-23–Wiring diagram for models using Briggs & Stratton engines with electric start

B. Black
Bl. Blue
Br. Brown
G. Green
Or. Orange
P. Pink
R. Red
W. White
Y. Yellow
1. Regulator
2. Battery
3. Alternator
4. Starter
5. Engine magneto
6. Starter solenoid
7. Ignition switch
8. Neutral switch
9. Mower clutch switch
10. Seat switch
11. Module

MOWER DECK

ADJUSTMENT

Before attempting any adjustment, the machine must be on level ground and the tires must be properly inflated. Disconnect the spark plug wire and tie it out of the way. Check the cutting height with the clutch engaged.

Front-to-rear height difference is determined by measuring the height of the blade above the ground at the front and rear. Rear height should be ¼-⅜ inch (6.4-9.5 mm) higher. Adjust front height of the mower by adjusting the length of the link (1–Fig. AR4-18 or Fig. AR4-19). To change the link length, loosen the jam nut and turn the center coupling of the link. Adjust rear height of the mower by turning the nuts (4 and 5–Fig. AR4-18 or Fig. AR4-20). If specified front-to-rear height dimension cannot be obtained using the preceding adjustment procedure, additional adjustment may be obtained by relocating the screw (15—Fig. AR4-18) in the lift straps. Moving the straps apart will decrease the rear mower height.

If the mower deck side-to-side height is uneven, rotate the screw adjuster adjacent to the front mower hanger (Fig. AR4-21) so the deck height is level.

After the mower deck height has been adjusted, check the height of the antiscalping rollers (Fig. AR4-22). The height of rollers should be at least ½ inch (13 mm) above the ground surface after adjusting the deck height, other-

wise, set roller height according to terrain and desired cut appearance.

REMOVAL AND INSTALLATION

1. Move the mower control lever to the disengaged position and lower the mower to the lowest setting.
2. Remove the belt finger attaching nuts (A–Fig. AR4-16) and remove the finger assembly.
3. Roll the blade drive belt out of the rear pulley.
4. Disconnect the clutch rod at the front.
5. Remove the clip from the pin (9–Fig. AR4-18).
6. Remove the pin (9) and lower the rear of the mower.
7. Remove the clips from the link (1).
8. Remove the link (1) and lower the front of the mower.
9. Install the mower deck by reversing the removal procedure. Be sure to check and adjust the mower drive belt tension, belt finger clearance and deck height as previously outlined.

ELECTRICAL

Refer to Fig. AR4-23 for wiring schematic. Note the following points:
1. The transmission must be in NEUTRAL, the mower must be disengaged and the operator must be in seat for engine to start.
2. The engine should stop if the transmission is in gear or the mower is engaged and the operator leaves the seat.

CUB CADET

Model	Make	Engine Model	Horsepower
1030	*	*	*

*Note the engine model number and refer to the engine service section in this manual for engine specifications.

FRONT WHEELS REMOVAL AND INSTALLATION

The front wheels are equipped with replaceable sealed bearings. To remove the wheel and bearings, proceed as follows:
1. Remove the wheel cover (33–Fig. CC1-1).
2. Remove the cotter pin (34).
3. Remove the wheel with bearings.
4. Separate the bearings from the wheel.
5. Inspect the bearings for damage.
6. Inspect the wheel for damage to the rim and hub.
7. Reverse the removal steps to reassemble and install the wheel and bearings.

FRONT AXLE AND STEERING SYSTEM

TOE-IN SETTING

Adjustable tie rods are used on all models. Proceed as follows to check and adjust toe-in.
1. Be sure the tires are properly inflated.
2. Position the machine on a flat, smooth surface.
3. Position the front wheels in the straight-ahead position.
4. Measure the distance at the spindle height between the center of the tires on the rear side.
5. Locate the same tire centerline points on the front side of the tires and measure the front distance.
6. The distance on the front side should be ⅛ inch (3.2 mm) shorter (toed-in) than the measured distance on the rear side.
7. To adjust the toe-in, detach the tie rod ends (32–Fig. CC1-1) from the sector gear.
8. Rotate the tie rod ends to change the tie rod length as necessary and reattach to the sector gear.
9. Recheck the toe-in measurement.

OVERHAUL

Refer to the exploded view in Fig. CC1-1 when performing the following procedure.
1. Remove the mower deck.
2. Remove the steering wheel cap, retaining nut and washer.
3. Lift off the steering wheel.
4. Remove the sleeve (6–Fig. CC1-1).
5. Remove the cover (21).
6. Unscrew the nut at the lower end of the steering shaft and remove the gear (18).
7. Remove the bolt (9) and remove the steering shafts.
8. Disconnect the tie rods from the spindles.

9. Detach the steering support plate (15) and sector gear (20).
10. Support the frame and remove the front wheels.
11. Remove the cotter pins and washers, then lower the spindles (37) from the axle.
12. Detach the front axle support (14) from the frame.
13. Remove the axle main member (25).
14. Clean and inspect all parts and replace any that are damaged.
15. Reassemble by reversing the disassembly procedure while noting the following:
   a. Lubricate bushings and all pivot points with SAE 30 oil.
   b. Operate the steering through a full range of movement and check for binding.
   c. Adjust front wheel toe-in as previously described.

ENGINE

Refer to the appropriate engine section in this manual for tune-up specifications, engine overhaul procedures and engine maintenance.

REMOVAL AND INSTALLATION

1. Disconnect the spark plug wire and remove the engine cover.
2. Electric start models–Disconnect and remove the battery.
3. Disconnect any interfering electrical wires from the engine.
4. Disconnect the throttle cable from the engine.
5. Detach the exhaust pipe.
6. Remove the mower as outlined in the MOWER DECK section.
7. Remove the traction drive belt from the engine pulley as outlined in the TRACTION DRIVE CLUTCH AND DRIVE BELTS section.
8. Detach the pulleys from the engine crankshaft.
9. Remove the engine mounting fasteners.
10. Remove the engine.
11. Install the engine by reversing the removal procedure.

TRACTION DRIVE CLUTCH AND DRIVE BELTS

All models are equipped with a drive system using two drive belts and a variable speed pulley to transfer power from the engine to the transaxle. The primary drive belt connects the engine to the variable speed pulley (23–Fig. CC1-2). The secondary drive belt connects the variable speed pulley to the transaxle.

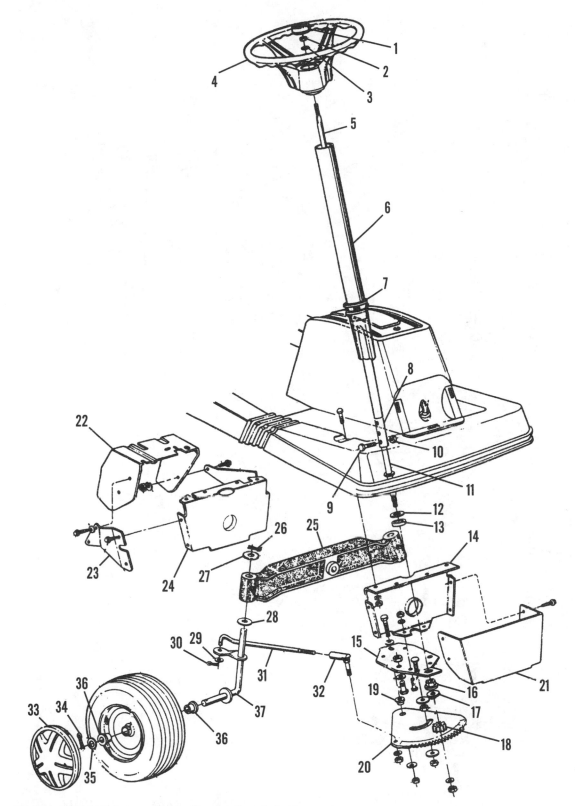

Fig CC1-1–Exploded view of typical front axle and steering system.

1. Cap
2. Nut
3. Washer
4. Steering wheel
5. Steering shaft
6. Steering column
7. Bearing assy.
8. Coupler
9. Bolt
10. Nut
11. Lower shaft
12. Washer
13. Spacer
14. Axle support
15. Steering plate
16. Bushing
17. Washer
18. Steering gear
19. Bushing
20. Sector gear
21. Brackct
22. Bracket
23. Plate
24. Axle support
25. Axle main member
26. Cotter pin
27. Washer
28. Washer
29. Washer
30. Cotter pin
31. Tie rod
32. Tie rod end
33. Wheel cover
34. Cotter pin
35. Washer
36. Bushing
37. Spindle

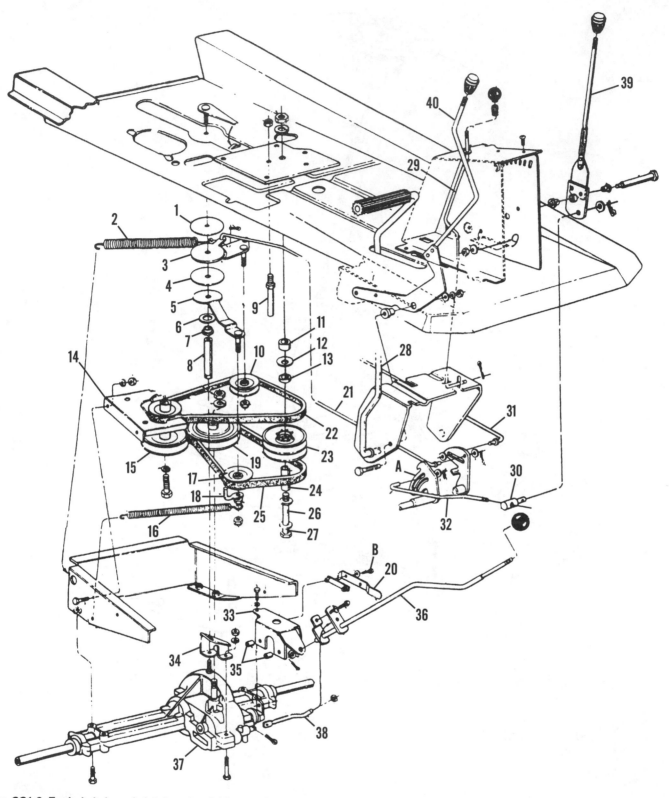

Fig. CC1-2–Exploded view of clutch and variable speed assembly.

1. Thrust washer
2. Spring
3. Idler arm
4. Thrust washer
5. Idler arm
6. Washer
7. Bushing
8. Torque rod
9. Belt guide
10. Idler
11. Spacer
12. Belleville washer
13. Thrust washer
14. Belt guard
15. Engine pulley
16. Spring
17. Idler
18. Belt guide
19. Transaxle pulley
20. Spring switch
21. Clutch rod
22. Upper drive belt
23. Variable speed pulley
24. Spacer
25. Thrust washer
26. Washer
27. Cap screw
28. Pedal rod
29. Park brake rod
30. Ferrule
31. Brake rod
32. Speed control rod
33. Bracket
34. Bracket
35. Spacers
36. Shift lever
37. Transaxle
38. Shift rod
39. Speed control lever
40. Mower engagement lever

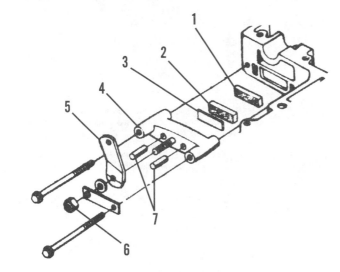

Fig. CC1-3–Exploded view of caliper brake.

1. Brake pad (inner)
2. Brake pad (outer)
3. Backup plate
4. Carrier
5. Cam lever
6. Adjusting nut
7. Actuating pins

The diameters of the pulley grooves are determined by belt tension, which is regulated by the position of the idlers (10 and 17). The idlers move when the speed control lever is operated. The ground speed changes when the pulley diameters change on the variable speed pulley.

ADJUSTMENT

The speed control lever and gear shift lever must be synchronized with the positions of the belt idlers. Proceed as follows.

1. Start and run the engine.
2. Be sure the gear shift lever is in NEUTRAL.
3. Place the speed control lever in the high speed position.
4. Release, then slowly depress fully the clutch/brake pedal and hold down the pedal.
5. Stop the engine, then release the pedal when the engine stops.
6. Move the speed control lever to the second speed position.
7. Detach the bent end of the lower speed control rod (32–Fig. CC1-2).
8. Turn the rod so the end of the rod will just enter the forward end of the slot (A).
9. Reattach the rod.
10. Move the gear shift lever to the NEUTRAL slot on the gear indicator panel.
11. If the machine does not move freely forward and backward thereby indicating the transaxle is in NEUTRAL, proceed as follows:
   a. Loosen the screw (B–Fig. CC1-2).
   b. Move the shift lever (36) as needed so the transaxle is in NEUTRAL and the shift lever is in the center of the neutral slot on the control panel.
   c. Retighten the screw (B) to 13 ft.-lb. (18 N•m).

DRIVE BELTS

Lower Belt

1. Disconnect the spark plug wire and remove the battery.
2. Remove the mower as outlined in the MOWER DECK section.
3. Disconnect the idler spring (16–Fig. CC1-2).

4. Detach the torque rod bracket (34) from the transaxle and the torque rod (8).
5. Remove the bracket.
6. Separate the belt from the pulleys and remove the belt.
7. Install the lower belt by reversing the removal procedure.

Upper Belt

1. Remove the lower belt as described in the previous section.
2. Detach the engine pulley belt guide (14–Fig. CC1-2).
3. Unscrew the retaining nut and the remove the idler (10).
4. Remove the upper belt.
5. Install the upper belt by reversing the removal procedure. Be sure the hub side of the idler (10) is next to the idler arm (3). Install the belt and idler simultaneously so the belt is inside the belt guide (9).

VARIABLE SPEED PULLEY OVERHAUL

The variable speed pulley is accessible after removing the drive belts as previously described. The variable speed pulley is available only as a unit assembly; individual components are not available.

TRANSAXLE

REMOVAL AND INSTALLATION

1. Remove the drive belts as previously described.
2. Disconnect the brake linkage and the shift linkage.
3. Support the rear of the machine.
4. Remove the transaxle mounting bolts.
5. Raise the rear of the machine and roll the transaxle assembly from under the machine.
6. Install by reversing the removal procedure.

OVERHAUL

All models are equipped with a MTD Model 618 transaxle. Refer to the TRANSAXLE REPAIR section for service information.

GROUND DRIVE BRAKE

ADJUSTMENT

Check brake operation by pushing the brake pedal and attempting to move the machine. If the brake does not hold the machine with the pedal fully depressed, adjust the brake. To adjust the brake, release the brake and turn the nut (6–Fig. CC1-3) on the cam lever until desired brake operation is obtained.

OVERHAUL

1. Disconnect the brake spring and the brake rod from the actuating lever.
2. Unbolt and remove the brake pad carrier (4–Fig. CC1-3).
3. Slide the brake disc off the transaxle shaft.
4. Remove the inner brake pad from the slot in the transaxle housing.
5. Clean and inspect all parts for damage.
6. Reassemble by reversing the disassembly procedure.

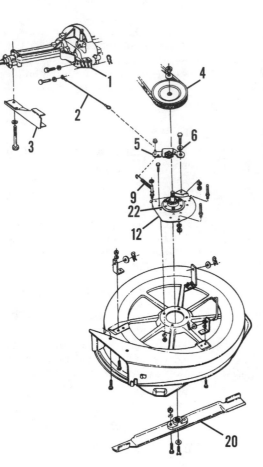

1. Bracket
2. Blade brake cable
3. Bracket
4. Pulley
5. Blade brake
6. Spacer
9. Spring
12. Spindle mounting plate
20. Blade
22. Bearing and spindle assy.

MOWER DRIVE BELT REMOVAL AND INSTALLATION

Refer to Fig. CC1-4 when performing the following procedure.
1. Disconnect the spark plug wire.
2. Place the blade engagement lever in the disengaged position.
3. Locate the outside engine belt guard at the right rear side of machine and remove one retaining bolt while loosening the other bolt.
4. Pivot the belt guard out and away from the engine pulley.
5. Disconnect the blade brake cable from the belt guard and remove the belt guard.
6. Disconnect the mower deck links and remove the belt guides on the deck.
7. Remove the belt.
8. Install the mower belt by reversing the removal procedure.

MOWER DECK

HEIGHT ADJUSTMENT

The front of the mower blade should be ¼-⅜ inch (6.4-9.5 mm) lower than the rear of the blade. The mower deck should be level from side to side. Adjust the hanger lengths as needed to obtain the desired height.

REMOVAL AND INSTALLATION

Refer to Fig. CC1-4 when performing the following procedure.

Fig. CC1-5–Attach end of blade brake cable as described in text.

1. Disconnect the spark plug wire.

2. Move the mower deck to the lowest position.

3. Place the blade engagement lever in the disengaged position.

4. Locate the outside engine belt guard at the right rear side of the machine and remove one retaining bolt while loosening the other bolt.

5. Pivot the belt guard out and away from the engine pulley.

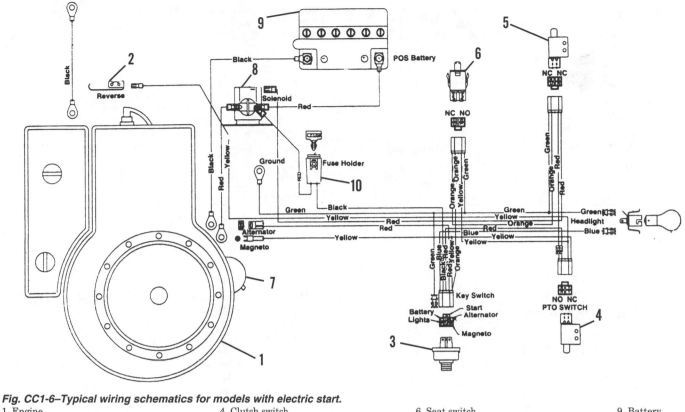

Fig. CC1-6–Typical wiring schematics for models with electric start.

1. Engine
2. Reverse gear switch
3. Ignition switch
4. Clutch switch
5. Blade engagement switch
6. Seat switch
7. Starter
8. Starter solenoid
9. Battery
10. Fuse holder

6. Disconnect the blade brake cable from the belt guard and remove the belt guard.

7. Separate the drive belt from the engine pulley.

8. Disconnect the safety switch wire on models so equipped.

9. Detach the lift linkage from the mower deck and remove the mower deck.

10. Install by reversing removal procedure. Adjust the blade brake cable as outlined in the BLADE BRAKE section.

BLADE BRAKE ADJUSTMENT

1. Place the mower deck in the lowest position.

2. Move the blade engagement lever to the disengaged position.

3. Attach the cable (C–Fig. CC1-5) end to the rearmost hole in the bracket (B) so the cable has the least amount of slack but no tension.

MOWER SPINDLE OVERHAUL

Refer to Fig. CC1-4 when performing the following procedure.

1. Remove the mower deck as previously described.
2. Remove the mower blade (20).
3. Unbolt and remove the spindle assembly (22). The spindle assembly is available only as a unit assembly.

ELECTRICAL

Refer to Fig. CC1-6 for a typical wiring schematic. All switches must be in good operating condition for the machine to operate properly.

JOHN DEERE

Model	Make	Engine Model	Horsepower
GX70, GX75	Kawasaki	FC290V	9
GX85	B&S	28M707	13
GX95	Kawasaki	FB460V	12.5
SRX75	Kawasaki	FC290V	9
SRX95	Kawasaki	FB460V	12.5
SX85	B&S	28M707	13

FRONT WHEELS REMOVAL AND INSTALLATION

The front wheels are equipped with replaceable sealed bearings. To remove the wheel and bearings, proceed as follows:
1. Remove the hub cap.
2. Remove the retaining ring.
3. Remove the wheel with bearings.
4. Separate the bearings from the wheel.
5. Inspect the bearings for damage.
6. Inspect the wheel for rim and hub damage.
7. Reverse the removal steps to reassemble and install the wheel and bearings.

FRONT SPINDLE

MAINTENANCE

Lubricate the front wheel spindles after every 10 hours of operation. Inject No. 2 multipurpose grease into the front axle main member through the grease fitting (Fig. JD1-1) at each end. One or two shots from a hand-held grease gun should be sufficient. Check for looseness and binding in the front axle components.

OVERHAUL

Refer to Fig. JD1-2 when performing the following procedure.
To remove a front spindle, proceed as follows:
1. Raise and support the side to be serviced.
2. Remove the wheel and tire.
3. Disconnect the tie rod end and drag link end, if necessary, from the spindle.
4. Detach the snap ring (Fig. JD1-3) securing the top of the spindle, then withdraw the spindle from the axle.
5. Reverse the removal steps to install the front spindle. Tighten the drag link and tie rod retaining nuts to 22 ft.-lb. (30 N•m).

FRONT AXLE OVERHAUL

To remove the axle main member, proceed as follows:
1. Remove the mower deck, then raise and support the front of the machine.

2. Disconnect the drag link end (19–Fig. JD1-2) from the steering sector arm (11).
3. Use a jack to support the axle assembly.
4. Unscrew the pivot pin nut (18), withdraw the pivot pin (17) and lower the axle assembly.
5. Reverse the removal steps to install the axle main member while noting the following:
   a. Before assembly, lubricate the pivot pin with multipurpose grease.
   b. Do not overtighten the pivot pin nut (18) during assembly; the axle must pivot freely.

STEERING SECTOR AND SHAFT OVERHAUL

1. Detach the steering wheel by removing the retaining bolt, then install a pin in the steering shaft hole to hold the shaft in position.
2. Raise and support the front of the machine.
3. Remove the tie rod (20–Fig. JD1-2) and disconnect the drag link (19) from the steering sector arm (11).
4. Remove the pin from the steering shaft's upper end and remove the steering shaft (9) with the steering sector (11).
5. Inspect components and replace if damaged.
6. Reassemble the steering components by reversing the disassembly procedure. Tighten the drag link and tie rod retaining nuts to 22 ft.-lb. (30 N•m).

Fig. JD1-1–Lubricate spindles by injecting grease into fittings on front axle.

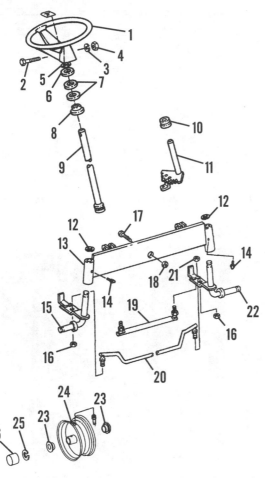

Fig. JD1-3—Detach snap ring to release spindle for removal.

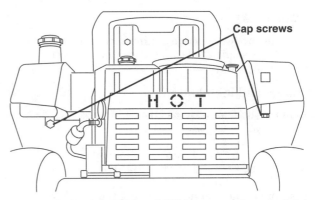

Fig. JD1-4—On Models GX85 and GX95, remove shroud retaining cap screws.

Fig. JD1-2—Exploded view of front axle and steering mechanism.

1. Steering wheel
2. Screw
3. Lockwasher
4. Nut
5. Washer
6. Washer
7. Washer
8. Bushing
9. Steering shaft
10. Bushing
11. Sector gear
12. Snap ring
13. Axle main member
14. Grease fitting
15. Spindle (right)
16. Nut
17. Pivot pin
18. Nut
19. Drag link
20. Tie rod
21. Nut
22. Spindle
23. Bearings
24. Wheel
25. Retaining ring
26. Cap

ENGINE

MODELS GX70, GX75 AND SRX75

Refer to the appropriate engine section in this manual for tune-up specifications, engine overhaul procedures and engine maintenance.

Removal and Installation

1. Remove the transaxle as outlined in the TRANSAXLE section.
2. Remove the engine shroud on Model SRX75 using the procedure outlined in the engine removal section for Model SRX95.
3. Close the fuel valve and disconnect the fuel line.
4. Remove the muffler heat shield.
5. Disconnect the throttle cable.
6. Unscrew the nut and screws securing the engine.

7. Move the engine for access to the red and white wires and disconnect the wires.
8. If equipped with an electric starter, disconnect the starter cable.
9. Remove the engine.
10. To install the engine, reverse the disassembly procedure. Note the following:
   a. If the engine pulley was removed, apply antiseize compound to the crankshaft before installing the pulley.
   b. Tighten the pulley retaining screw to 54 ft.-lb. (73 N•m).
   c. Tighten the engine mounting screws and nut to 80 in.-lb. (9 N•m).

MODEL GX85

Refer to the appropriate engine section in this manual for tune-up specifications, engine overhaul procedures and engine maintenance.

Removal and Installation

1. Remove the transaxle as outlined in the TRANSAXLE section.
2. Lift up the seat.
3. Remove the left- and right-side control panels.
4. Remove the rear cap screws (Fig. JD1-4).
5. Turn the fuel valve OFF.
6. Disconnect the fuel hose and the plug openings.
7. Loosen the nuts (Fig. JD1-5).
8. Remove the engine shroud along with the fuel tank.
9. Remove the muffler heat shield and muffler.

10. Disconnect the throttle cable.

11. Disconnect the engine fuel lines.

12. Disconnect the wires leading to the engine, including the starter cable.

13. Remove the screws securing the engine, then remove engine.

14. To install the engine, reverse the disassembly procedure while noting the following:

   a. If the engine pulley was removed, apply antiseize compound to the crankshaft before installing the pulley.

   b. Tighten the pulley retaining screw to 54 ft.-lb. (73 N•m).

   c. Be sure to reconnect the ground cable when installing the engine mounting screws.

   d. Tighten the engine mounting screws to 30 ft.-lb. (42.5 N•m).

MODEL GX95

Refer to the appropriate engine section in this manual for tune-up specifications, engine overhaul procedures and engine maintenance.

Removal and Installation

1. Remove the transaxle as outlined in the TRANSAXLE section.

2. Lift up the seat.

3. Remove the left- and right-side control panels.

4. Remove the rear cap screws (Fig. JD1-4).

5. Turn the fuel valve OFF.

6. Disconnect the fuel hose and plug the openings.

7. Loosen the nuts (Fig. JD1-5).

8. Remove the engine shroud along with the fuel tank.

9. Remove the muffler heat shield and muffler.

10. Disconnect the throttle cable.

11. Disconnect the wire from the fuel control solenoid.

12. Disconnect the engine fuel lines.

13. Disconnect the wires leading to the engine, including the starter cable.

14. Remove the screws securing engine, then remove the engine.

15. To install the engine, reverse the disassembly procedure while noting the following:

   a. If the engine pulley was removed, apply antiseize compound to the crankshaft before installing pulley.

   b. Tighten the pulley retaining screw to 54 ft.-lb. (73 N•m).

   c. Tighten the engine mounting screws to 80 in.-lb. (9 N•m).

MODEL SRX95

Refer to appropriate the engine section in this manual for tune-up specifications, engine overhaul procedures and engine maintenance.

Removal and Installation

1. Remove the transaxle as outlined in the TRANSAXLE section.

2. Lift up the seat and remove the right-side control panel.

3. Unscrew the engine shroud mounting nuts so the shroud can be moved to allow removal of the seat pivot rod and seat.

4. Detach the throttle and mower control knobs.

5. Push the shift lever and mower control lever forward.

6. Close the fuel valve and detach the fuel hose from the valve.

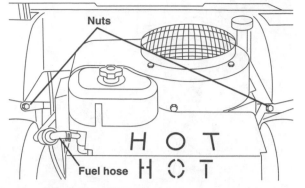

Fig. JD1-5–On Models GX85 and GX95, remove shroud retaining nuts.

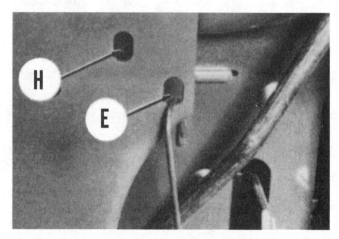

Fig. JD1-6–On Model GX70, GX75, GX85 and GX95 increase spring tension by relocating the spring end (E) to outermost hole (H).

7. Unscrew any remaining engine shroud mounting nuts and remove the engine shroud and fuel tank.

8. Remove the muffler heat shield and muffler.

9. Disconnect the throttle cable.

10. Disconnect the fuel solenoid wire and disconnect the fuel line.

11. Disconnect the wires leading to the engine.

12. Remove the screws securing the engine, then remove the engine.

13. To install the engine, reverse the disassembly procedure while noting the following:

   a. If the engine pulley was removed, apply antiseize compound to the crankshaft before installing the pulley.

   b. Tighten the pulley retaining screw to 54 ft.-lb. (73 N•m).

   c. Tighten the engine mounting screws to 80 in.-lb. (9 N•m).

MODEL SX85

Refer to the appropriate engine section in this manual for tune-up specifications, engine overhaul procedures and engine maintenance.

Removal and Installation

1. Remove the transaxle as outlined in the TRANSAXLE section.

2. Lift up the seat and remove the right-side control panel.

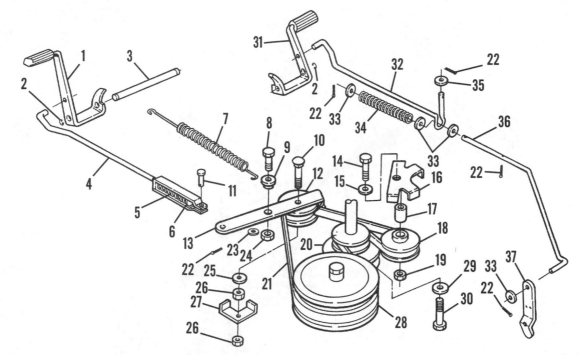

Fig. JD1-7–Exploded view of traction drive, brake and control components used on Models GX70, GX75, GX85 and GX95.

1. Clutch pedal
2. Snap ring
3. Shaft
4. Clutch rod
5. Spring
6. Washer
7. Spring
8. Bolt
9. Bushing
10. Spindle bolt
11. Clevis pin
12. Tension pulley
13. Clutch lever
14. Bolt
15. Washer
16. Belt guide
17. Spacer
18. Idler
19. Nut
20. Engine pulley
21. Belt
22. Cotter pin
23. Washer
24. Nut
25. Washer
26. Nut
27. Belt guide
28. Transaxle pulley
29. Washer
30. Screw
31. Brake pedal
32. Brake rod
33. Washer
34. Spring
35. Washer
36. Brake rod
37. Brake lever

3. Unscrew the engine shroud mounting nuts so the shroud can be moved to allow the removal of the seat pivot rod and seat.

4. Detach the throttle and mower control knobs.

5. Push the shift lever and mower control lever forward.

6. Close the fuel valve and detach the fuel hose from the valve.

7. Unscrew any remaining engine shroud mounting nuts and remove the engine shroud and fuel tank.

8. Remove the muffler heat shield and muffler.

9. Disconnect the throttle cable.

10. Disconnect the engine fuel lines.

11. Disconnect the wires leading to the engine, including the starter cable.

12. Remove the screws securing the engine, then remove the engine.

13. To install the engine, reverse the disassembly procedure while noting the following:

   a. If the engine pulley was removed, apply an antiseize compound to the crankshaft before installing the pulley.

   b. Tighten the pulley retaining screw to 54 ft.-lb. (73 N•m).

   c. Be sure to reconnect the ground cable when installing the engine mounting screws.

   d. Tighten the engine mounting screws to 30 ft.-lb. (42.5 N•m).

TRACTION DRIVE
CLUTCH AND DRIVE BELT
(MODELS GX70, GX75, GX85 AND GX95)

The traction drive clutch is a spring-tensioned, belt idler operated by the clutch pedal. When the clutch pedal is depressed, belt tension is removed, allowing the engine drive pulley to rotate freely within the drive belt. When the brake pedal is depressed, the clutch pedal is also actuated so the drive train is disengaged when the brake is operated. Spring tension on the clutch pulley may be increased by relocating the spring end (E–Fig. JD1-6) to the outermost hole (H). No other adjustment is available. If the belt is worn or stretched so slippage occurs, replace the belt.

DRIVE BELT

1. Disconnect the spark plug wire and, if so equipped, remove the battery.

2. Place the shift lever in NEUTRAL and the mower deck in the lowest position.

3. Raise and support the rear of the machine.

4. Loosen the nuts securing the transaxle.

5. Remove the belt guide from the transaxle and remove the mower belt from the engine pulley.

6. Disconnect the spring (7–Fig. JD1-7), remove the belt guide (27) and loosen the idler pulley retaining nut (19).

7. Remove the drive belt.

8. Reverse the removal procedure to install the drive belt. Note the following:

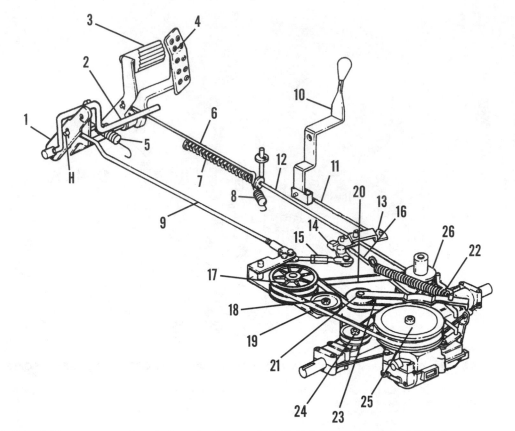

Fig. JD1-8–Drawing of drive system and control mechanism used on Models SRX75, SRX95 and SX85.

1. Speed control lever
2. Brake interlock rod
3. Brake pedal
4. Speed control pedal
5. Spring
6. Brake rod
7. Spring
8. Spring
9. Speed control rod
10. Shift control lever
11. Shift rod
12. Brake rod
13. Shift lever
14. Interlock
15. Adjuster
16. Shift rod
17. Variator
18. Primary belt idler
19. Secondary belt
20. Primary belt
21. Secondary belt idler
22. Spring
23. Secondary belt idler arm
24. Primary belt fixed idler
25. Transaxle pulley
26. Engine pulley

a. Tighten the transaxle retaining nuts to 80 in.-lb. (9 N•m).

b. Position the belt guide (16) so it does not interfere with the belt.

c. Install the belt guide (27) so it contacts the clutch arm (13) near the pivot screw (8).

VARIATOR AND DRIVE BELTS (MODELS SRX75, SRX95 AND SX85)

Models SRX75, SRX95 and SX85 are equipped with a drive system using two drive belts and a variable diameter pulley (variator) to transfer power from the engine to the transaxle. The lower primary drive belt (20–Fig. JD1-8) connects the engine to the variator (17).

The diameters of the variator pulley grooves are determined by the primary belt tension. Primary belt tension changes according to the pressure applied to the speed control pedal (4). Depressing the pedal increases primary belt tension and decreases the diameter of the lower pulley on the variator (17). When the lower variator pulley diameter decreases, the upper pulley diameter increases thereby increasing the ground speed. Releasing the pedal decreases the primary belt tension and the ground speed decreases.

When the pedal is in the full UP position, the primary belt idler (18) moves away from the belt and the drive train is in NEUTRAL. The upper secondary drive belt (19) con-

nects the variator (17) to the transaxle pulley (25). A spring-loaded pulley (21) maintains the secondary belt tension.

An interlock (14) prevents depression of the speed control pedal when the transaxle is in NEUTRAL or movement of the gear shift lever when the pedal is depressed.

BELT GUIDES

Position the belt guides so there is a clearance of 0.064-0.128 inch (1.63-3.25 mm) at engine pulley and 0.04-0.08 inch (1.0-2.0 mm) at the variator.

ADJUSTMENT

1. Be sure the speed control pedal is in full UP position.
2. Engage the park brake.
3. Loosen the locknut on the adjuster (15–Fig. JD1-8).
4. Rotate the adjuster so the clearance between the interlock (14) and the lever (13) is ¼ inch (6.4 mm).
5. Detach the pin from the front end of the control rod (9) and detach the rod end from the arm (1).
6. Rotate the rod (9) so the primary belt idler (18) just touches the belt, but the variator is not loaded, and insert the rod end in the upper hole on the arm (1).
7. Install the pin in the rod end.
8. Move the interlock rear (14) towards the engine pulley so the play in the linkage is removed.

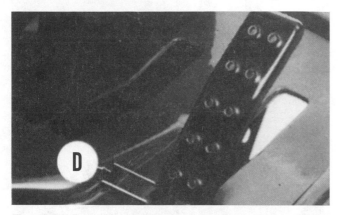

Fig. JD1-9–Depress speed control pedal on Models SRX75, SRX95 and SX85 so pedal free play is just removed. If distance (D) between bottom of speed control pedal and opening in floor is more than 1-1/2 inches (38.1 mm), adjust drive mechanism as outlined in text.

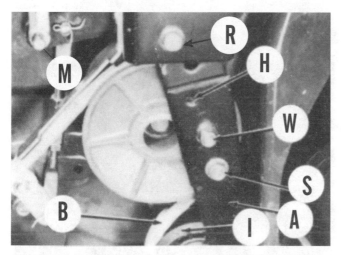

Fig. JD1-10–Relocate screw (S) on Models SRX75, SRX95 and SX85 to adjust drive mechanism as outlined in text.

A. Arm	M. Arm
B. Primary belt	R. Screw
H. Hole	S. Screw
I. Idler	W. Screw

9. Turn the adjuster so clearance between the interlock (14) and the lever (13) is 0.030-0.060 inch (0.76-1.52 mm).
10. Retighten the locknut on the adjuster.

Control Rod

Adjust the control rod (9–Fig. JD1-8) to a slightly longer length if the machine does not stop moving when the speed control pedal is released, if the drive is jerky when engaged, or if the operator desires a slower maximum ground speed. If the operator desires a faster maximum ground speed, adjust the control rod to a slightly longer length, but be sure the machine will stop when the speed control pedal is released.

Speed control pedal pressure may be reduced and maximum ground speed may be reduced if the control rod (9–Fig. JD1-8) is inserted in the lower hole (H) in the arm (1).

Primary Belt Idler Arm

Additional adjustment is possible by relocating the position of the primary belt idler arm.

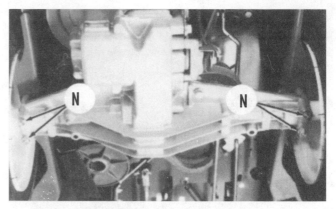

Fig. JD1-11–Tighten transaxle outer retaining nuts (N) on all models to 80 in.-lb. (9 N m).

Prior to adjustment, move the shift lever to the forward position and measure the distance (D–Fig. JD1-9) between the bottom of the speed control pedal and the opening in the floor. Depress the pedal so free play is just removed. If distance (D) is not at least 1½ inches (38.1 mm), this adjustment procedure must not be performed as there is not sufficient free play in the components. To perform the adjustment, proceed as follows.

1. Remove the screw (S–Fig. JD1-10) and loosen the screw (W).
2. Push the idler (I) towards the belt (B) and install the screw in the hole (H).
3. Tighten the screws and check operation. If the machine does not stop when the speed control pedal is released, return the screw and arm to the original positions.

DRIVE BELTS

Primary Belt

1. Disconnect the spark plug wire.
2. Remove the battery.
3. Place the shift lever in NEUTRAL and the mower deck in the lowest position.
4. Raise and support the rear of the machine.
5. Loosen the innermost belt guide and remove the outermost belt guide adjacent to the engine pulley.
6. Detach the upper secondary belt idler spring (22–Fig. JD1-8).
7. Remove the mower drive belt from the engine pulley.
8. Loosen the retaining nut for the belt guide at the variator (17) and push back the belt guide.
9. Loosen the retaining nut on the bottom of the transaxle securing the fixed idler (24).
10. Remove the belt.
11. Install the primary belt by reversing the removal procedure. Adjust the belt guides as previously outlined.

Secondary Belt

1. Remove the lower primary belt as described in the previous section.
2. Loosen, but do not totally unscrew, the four nuts (N–Fig. JD1-11) retaining the transaxle so the belt can pass over the transaxle pulley.
3. Remove the secondary belt.
4. Install the secondary belt by reversing the removal procedure. Tighten the transaxle retaining nuts to 80 in.-lb. (9 N•m).

Fig. JD1-12–Drive out pin (P) before removing variator.

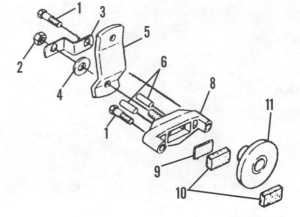

Fig. JD1-13–Exploded view of disc brake assembly used on Models SRX75, SRX95 and SX85.

1. Screw	6. Dowel pins
2. Nut	8. Caliper half
3. Brace	9. Half
4. Washer	10. Brake pads
5. Brake lever	11. Brake disc

OVERHAUL VARIATOR

The variator must be serviced as a unit assembly except for the bushing, which is available separately.

To remove variator, perform the following.

1. Disconnect the spark plug wire.
2. Remove the battery.
3. Place the shift lever in NEUTRAL and the mower deck in the lowest position.
4. Raise and support the rear of the machine.
5. Disconnect the links from the variator arm (M–Fig. JD1-10).
6. Unscrew the idler arm screw (R) and move the arm away from the variator bracket.
7. Remove the lower primary belt from the variator.
8. Move the upper spring-loaded secondary belt idler back and remove the secondary belt from the variator.
9. Drive out the pin (P–Fig. JD1-12).
10. Remove the variator.
11. To remove the bushing in the variator hub, force the bushing towards the top of the variator. Install the bushing so it bottoms against the step in the variator.
12. Install the variator by reversing the disassembly procedure.

GROUND DRIVE BRAKE

All models are equipped with a disc brake mounted on the transaxle. Refer to Figs. JD1-7 and JD1-8 for views of the brake operating components. No adjustment is required.

OVERHAUL

Models GX70, GX75, GX85 and GX95

The transaxle must be disassembled for access to the brake on Models GX70, GX75, GX85 and GX95. Refer to the TRANSMISSION REPAIR section for service information.

Models SRX75, SRX95 and SX85

Refer to Fig. JD1-13 and proceed as follows.

1. Detach the operating rod.
2. Unscrew the lever retaining nut (2).
3. Unscrew the caliper mounting screws (1).

Fig. JD1-14–The tranaxle on Models GX70, GX75 and GX95 is equipped with grease fittings (G) at outer ends.

4. Disassemble the brake components.
5. Inspect the brake components for damage. Brake pad wear limit is $\frac{1}{4}$ inch (6.4 mm).
6. Reverse the disassembly steps to reassemble the brake. Note the following:
   a. Coat the transmission brake shaft with Lubriplate.
   b. Apply Lubriplate to the ends of the dowel pins (6) and rubbing surfaces of the brake lever and washer (4).
   c. Tighten the caliper screws (1) to 95 in.-lb. (10.7 N•m).

TRANSAXLE
(MODELS GX70, GX75, GX85 AND GX95)

LUBRICATION

The outer ends of the transaxle are equipped with grease fittings (G–Fig. JD1-14). Inject No. 2 multipurpose grease into the grease fittings after every 25 hours of operation. One or two shots from a hand-held grease gun should be sufficient. Refer to the repair section for internal lubrication information.

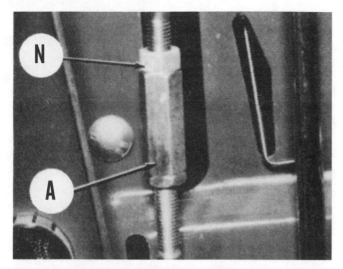

Fig. JD1-15–On Models GX70, GX75, GX85 and GX95 loosen locknut (N) and rotate adjuster (A) to synchronize shift control lever and marks on control panel.

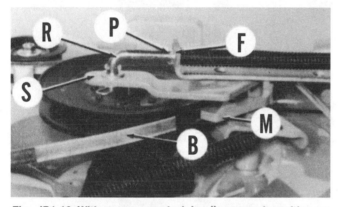

Fig. JD1-16–With mower control in disengaged position on Models SRX75, SRX95 and SX85, control rod (R) should not contact either end of slot (L) and brake arm (M) should contact mower belt. Refer to text for adjustment.

B. Belt
F. Flange
M. Blade brake arm

P. Projections
R. Control rod
S. Slot

NEUTRAL ADJUSTMENT

Adjust the shift linkage so the neutral positions in the transaxle and at the shift lever are synchronized. Use the following procedure.

1. Raise and support the rear of the machine.
2. Move the shift lever so the transaxle is in NEUTRAL, then loosen the locknut (N–Fig. JD1-15) and rotate the adjuster (A) so the shift lever is aligned with the neutral mark on the shift control panel.
3. Retighten the locknut and check adjustment.

REMOVAL AND INSTALLATION

To remove the transaxle, proceed as follows.
1. Raise and support the rear of the machine.
2. Remove the rear wheels.
3. Remove the drive belt.
4. Disconnect the shift linkage.
5. Disconnect the brake link.
6. Detach the wiring harness clamp and disconnect the neutral switch wire from the switch on the transaxle.

7. Detach the upper transaxle mount.
8. Support the transaxle.
9. Unscrew the outer retaining nuts (N–Fig. JD1-11), then lower the transaxle away from the machine towards the rear so the pulleys clear.
10. Install the transaxle by reversing the removal procedure. Tighten the transaxle retaining nuts to 80 in.-lb. (9 N•m).

OVERHAUL

Models GX70, GX75, GX85 and GX95 are equipped with a Peerless transaxle. Refer to the repair section in this manual for service information.

TRANSAXLE
(MODELS SRX75, SRX95 AND SX85)

ADJUSTMENT

No adjustment is required, however, if faulty shifting is encountered, inspect the shift linkage for wear and damage.

The drive system uses an interlock (14–Fig. JD1-8) preventing depression of the speed control pedal when the transaxle is in NEUTRAL or movement of the gear shift lever when the pedal is depressed. Adjust the clearance between the interlock and shift lever (13) as outlined in the VARIATOR AND DRIVE BELTS section.

REMOVAL AND INSTALLATION

1. Raise and support the rear of the machine.
2. Remove the rear wheels.
3. Remove the drive belts.
4. Disconnect the shift linkage.
5. Disconnect the brake link.
6. Disconnect the neutral switch wire from the switch on the transaxle.
7. Detach the rear and side transaxle mounts.
8. Support the transaxle.
9. Unscrew the outer retaining nuts (N–Fig. JD1-11), then lower the transaxle away from the machine towards the rear so the pulleys clear.
10. Install the transaxle by reversing the removal procedure. Tighten the transaxle retaining nuts to 80 in.-lb. (9 N•m).

OVERHAUL

Models SRX75, SRX95 and SX85 are equipped with a Peerless transaxle. Refer to the TRANSMISSION REPAIR section for service information.

MOWER CONTROL
LINKAGE ADJUSTMENT

All mower control linkage must be in good operating condition.
1. With the engine stopped and the machine parked on a level surface, place mower in the lowest position.
2. With the mower control in disengaged position, check the position of the control rod (R–Fig. JD1-16 or JD1-17). The control rod should not contact either end of the slot (S) and the brake arm (M) should contact the mower belt.
3A. Models GX70, GX75, GX85, SRX75 and SX85–With the mower control in the engaged position, check the positon of the flange (F—Fig. JD1-16). The flange should

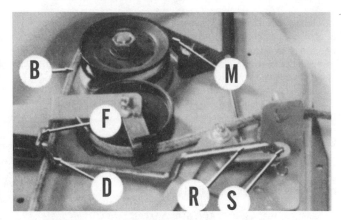

Fig. JD1-17–WIth mower control in disengaged position on Models SRX75, SRX95 and SX85, control rod (R) should not contact either end of slot (L) and brake arm (M) should contact mower belt. Refer to text for adjustment.

B. Belt	M. Blade brake arm
D. Bend in rod	R. Control rod
F. Flange	S. Slot

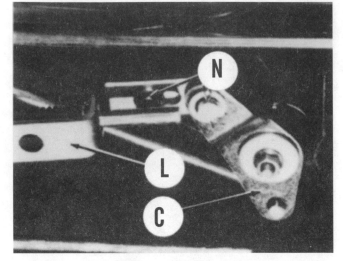

Fig. JD1-18–To adjust mower control mechanism, loosen nut (N) and relocate link (L).

be pulled away from the projections (P) on the rod and the brake arm (M) should not contact the belt.

3B. Models GX95 and SRX95–With the mower control in the engaged position, the bend (D–Fig. JD1-17) in the rod should be pulled away from the flange (F) and the brake arm (M) should not contact the belt.

4. Place the mower in the highest position and repeat the checking procedure. If components are out-of-position, loosen the nut (N–Fig. JD1-18) and relocate the link (L) as needed. Retighten the nut and recheck the adjustment.

MOWER DECK

MODELS GX95 AND SRX95

Refer to Fig. JD1-19 for a drawing of the mower deck components. The blades rotate when the actuation of the mower control lever forces the belt tension pulley (10) against the belt to remove the belt slack. When the blades are not engaged, the spring-loaded blade brake arms (4) contact the belt to prevent blade rotation. The control mechanism pushes the brake arms away from the belt when blade rotation is selected.

Height Adjustment

1. Position the machine on a level surface.
2. Disconnect the spark plug wire.
3. Measure the distance from the ground to the blades from side to side. Maximum difference should be $\frac{1}{8}$ inch (3.2 mm).
4. To adjust the side-to-side dimension, perform the following:
    a. Loosen the front (F–Fig. JD1-20) and rear (R) nuts retaining the left front draft link to the mower deck; do not loosen the middle nut (M).
    b. Rotate the eccentric (E) so the desired dimension is obtained.
    c. Retighten the front nut (F) first and then retighten the rear nut (R).
5. Measure the distance from the ground to the blades from the front to the rear. The front of the blades should be $\frac{1}{8}$-$\frac{3}{8}$ inch (3.2-9.5 mm) lower than the rear of the blades. To adjust the front-to-rear dimension, proceed as follows:
    a. Loosen the nuts (N–Fig. JD1-21).

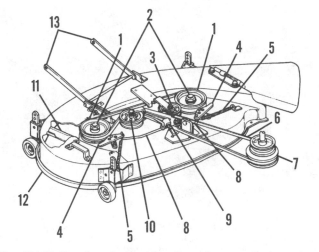

Fig. JD1-19–Drawing showing location of mower deck components on Model GX95 and SRX95.

1. Drive pulley	8. Brake rods
2. Pulley spindles	9. Engagement lever
3. Fixed idler	10. Belt tension pulley
4. Blade brake arm	11. Blade
5. Spring	12. Mower deck
6. Belt	13. Front draft link
7. Engine pulley	14. Bracket

    b. Loosen the nut (T) on the eccentric (E).
    c. Rotate the eccentric (E) so the desired dimension is obtained. Additional height adjustment is available by turning the nuts (U) on the lift link (L).
    d. Retighten the nuts.

Removal and Installation

1. Move the mower engagement lever to the full rear position.
2. Place the mower in the highest position.
3. Loosen the nut (N–Fig. JD1-22) and move the belt guide (G) away from the engine pulley.
4. Unscrew the nut (T) and remove the belt guide (D).
5. Separate the belt from the engine pulley.
6. Place the mower in the lowest position.
7. Remove the pin (P–Fig. JD1-23) and separate the rear draft link (L) from the mower bracket.

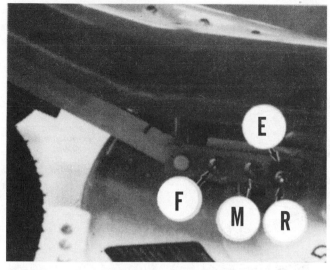

Fig. JD1-20–Refer to text for side-to-side blade adjustment procedure. Do not loosen center nut (M).

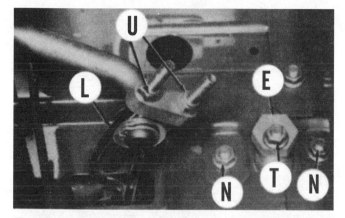

Fig. JD1-21–Refer to text for front-to-rear blade adjustment procedure. Additional adjustment is available by turning nuts (U) on lift link (L).

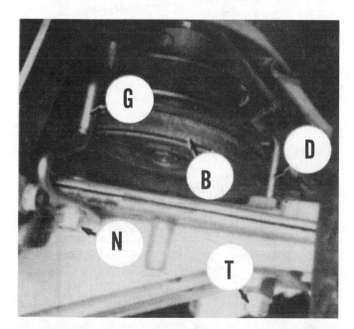

Fig. JD1-22–Refer to text to disengage belts from engine pulley.

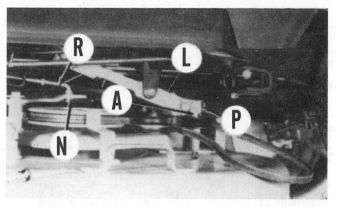

Fig. JD1-23–When removing mower doeck on Models GX95 and SRX95 control rod (R) and rear draft link (L) must be detached. See text.

8. Remove the pin (N) and detach the rod (R).
9. Detach the front draft links (13–Fig. JD1-19) from the front axle main member (13–Fig. JD1-2) and remove the mower from the left side of the machine.
10. Reverse the removal procedure to install the mower deck. Position the engine pulley belt guides so there is a clearance of 0.064-0.128 inch (1.63-3.25 mm).

ALL OTHER MODELS

Refer to Fig. JD1-24 for a drawing of the mower deck components. The blade rotates when actuation of the mower control lever forces the belt tension pulley (10) against the belt to remove belt slack. When the blade is not engaged, spring-loaded blade brake arm (4) contacts the belt to prevent blade rotation. The control mechanism pushes the brake arm away from the belt when blade rotation is selected.

Height Adjustment

Follow the procedure previously outlined for Models GX95 and SRX95.

Removal and Installation

1. Move the mower engagement lever to the full rear position.
2. Place the mower in the highest position.
3. Loosen the nut (N–Fig. JD1-22) and move the belt guide (G) away from the engine pulley.
4. Unscrew the nut (T) and remove the belt guide (D).
5. Separate the belt from the engine pulley.
6. Place the mower in the lowest position.
7. Remove the pin (P–Fig. JD1-25) and separate the rear draft link (L) from the mower bracket.
8. Remove the pin and detach the rod (R–Fig. JD1-26).
9. Detach the front draft links (13–Fig. JD1-24) from the front axle main member (13—Fig. JD1-2) and remove the mower from the left side of the machine.
10. Reverse the removal procedure to install the mower deck. Position the engine pulley belt guides so there is a clearance of 0.064-0.128 inch (1.63-3.25 mm).

MOWER BELT

REMOVAL AND INSTALLATION

Models GX95 and SRX95

1. Remove the mower deck as previously described.
2. Remove the belt shield.

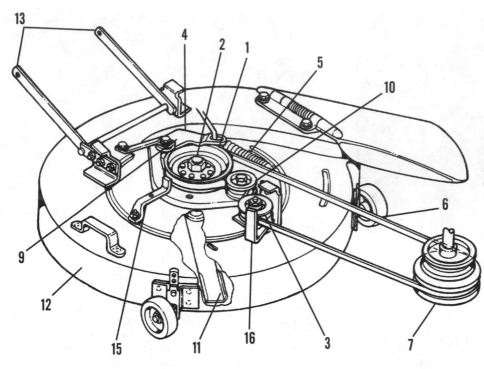

Fig. JD1-24—Drawing showing location of mower deck components on Models GX70, GX75, GX85, SRX75 and SX85. Refer to Fig. JD1-19 for parts identification except for: 15 and 16. Belt guides.

3. Loosen the spindle nut or bolt on the idler (3–Fig. JD1-19) and the tension pulley (10).

4. Reposition the belt guides, push back the brake arms (4) and remove the belt.

5. Reverse the removal procedure to install the mower belt. Note the following:

  a. Note belt routing in Fig. JD1-19.

  b. Push the belt guide on the tension pulley (10) against the bracket (14) after installing the belt.

  c. After installing the belt and positioning the belt guides, tighten the spindle nut or bolt on the idler (3) and tension pulley (10).

All Other Models

1. Remove the mower deck as previously outlined.

2. Loosen the spindle nut on the idler (3–Fig. JD1-24) and move the belt guide (16) away from the belt.

3. Loosen the retaining screw of the front belt guide (15) and move the guide.

4. Push back the brake arm (4) and remove the belt.

5. Reverse the removal procedure to install the mower belt. Position the belt guides (15 and 16) $\frac{1}{16}$ inch (1.6 mm) from the belt and tighten the fasteners.

MOWER SPINDLE

LUBRICATION

Models GX95 And SRX95

Each mower spindle should be lubricated after every 10 hours of operation. Apply No. 2 multipurpose grease to the mower spindles through grease fitting (9–Fig. JD1-27) in each spindle housing (7). One or two shots from a hand-held grease gun should be sufficient.

All Other Models

The mower spindles are equipped with sealed bearings and periodic lubrication of the spindle is not required.

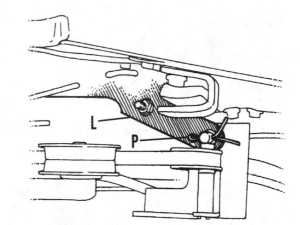

Fig. JD1-25—When removing mower deck on Models GX70, GX75, GX85, SRX75 and SX85, remove pin (P) and detach rear draft link (L). See text.

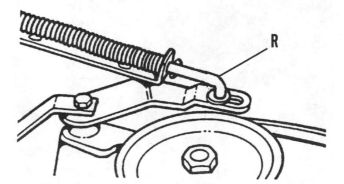

Fig. JD1-26—When removing mower deck on Modesl GX70, GX75, GX85, SRX75 and SX85, detach control rod (R). See text.

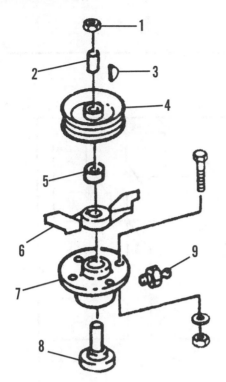

Fig. JD1-27–Exploded view of mower spindle assembly used on Models GX95 and SRX95.

1. Nut
2. Spacer
3. Key
4. Pulley
5. Bearing

6. Fan
7. Housing
8. Blade adapter
9. Grease fitting

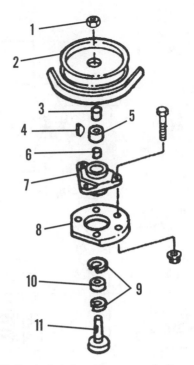

Fig. JD1-28–Exploded view of mower spindle assembly used on Models GX70, GX75, GX85, SRX75 and SX85.

1. Nut
2. Pulley
3. Spacer
4. Key
5. Bearing
6. Spacer

7. Housing
8. Plate
9. Snap ring
10. Bearing
11. Blade adapter

OVERHAUL

Models GX95 And SRX95

1. Remove the mower deck and blade.
2. Disengage the belt from the spindle pulley.
3. Unscrew the bolts securing the spindle housing (7–Fig. JD1-27) and remove the spindle assembly.
4. Unscrew the spindle nut (1) and disassemble the spindle assembly components as needed.
5. Inspect components for damage.
6. Reassemble by reversing the disassembly steps. Note the following:
    a. Tighten the spindle nut (1) to 103 ft.-lb. (140 N•m).
    b. Tighten the mower blade retaining screw to 55 ft.-lb. (75 N•m).

All Other Models

1. Remove the mower deck and blade.
2. Disengage the belt from the spindle pulley.
3. Unscrew the pulley retaining nut (1–Fig. JD1-28) and remove the pulley (2).
4. Unscrew the bolts securing the plate (8) and spindle housing (7) and remove the spindle assembly.
5. Disassemble the spindle assembly components as needed. Spindle and bearings must be pressed out of the housing.
6. Inspect components for damage.

7. Reassemble by reversing the disassembly steps. Note the following:
    a. Fill the spindle housing a little over half full with multipurpose grease.
    b. Press the upper bearing (5) in until flush with the top of the spindle housing (7).
    c. Install the inner snap ring (9) and spacer (5) and press the lower bearing (10) in until bottomed against the spacer.
    d. Install the outer snap ring (9) and press the spindle into the bearings until it bottoms.
    e. Tighten the spindle housing mounting bolts to 222 in.-lb. (25 N•m).
    f. Tighten the spindle nut (1) to 103 ft.-lb. (140 N•m).
    g. Tighten the mower blade retaining screw to 55 ft.-lb. (75 N•m).

ELECTRICAL

Refer to Figs. JD1-29, JD1-30, JD1-31 and JD1-32 for wiring schematics. Note the following points:
1. The transmission must be in NEUTRAL, the mower must be disengaged and the operator must be in seat for engine to start.
2. The engine should stop if the transmission is in gear or the mower is engaged and the operator leaves the seat.
3. Models GX95 and SRX95 are equipped with a fuel shut-off solenoid that is closed if the operator is not in the seat.

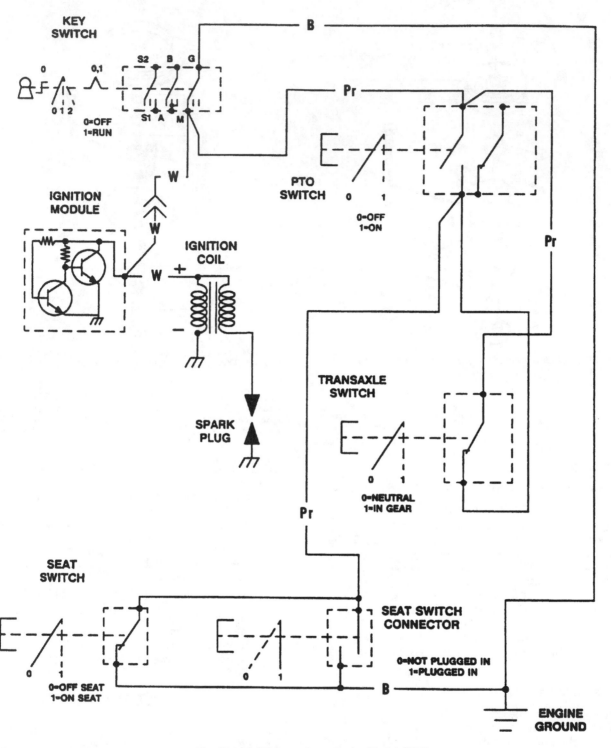

Fig. JD1-29–Wiring schematic for Model GX70.

B. Black
Pr. Purple
W. White

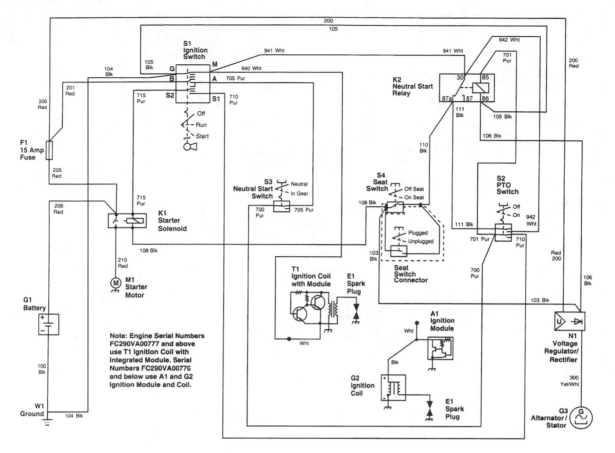

Fig. JD1-30–Wiring schematic for Models GX75 and SRX75.

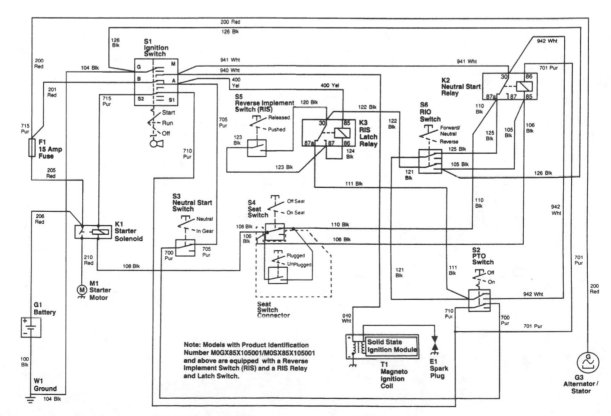

Fig. JD1-31–Wiring schematic for Models GX85 and SX85.

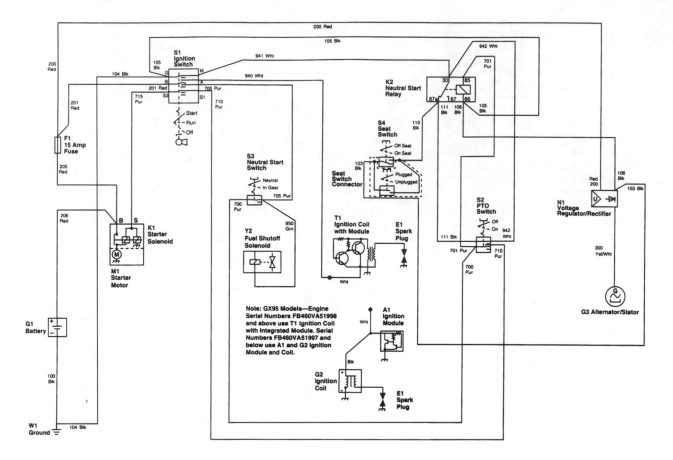

Fig. JD1-32—Wiring schematic for Models GX95 and SRX95.

HONDA

Model	Make	Engine Model	Horsepower
H1011HS	Honda	GXV340	11
H1011R	Honda	GXV340	11
H1011S	Honda	GXV340	11

NOTE: Special Honda tools may be required for some procedures and are indicated in the text. Read the text completely before attempting the procedure.

NOTE: Both metric and US fasteners are used on the models in this section. Be sure to install the correct fastener.

FRONT WHEELS

The front wheels are equipped with replaceable sealed bearings. To remove the wheel and bearings, proceed as follows:
1. Remove the hub cap (14–Fig. HN1-1).
2. Remove the snap ring (13) and washer (12).
3. Remove the wheel with bearings.
4. Separate the bearings from the wheel.
5. Inspect the bearings for damage.
6. Inspect the wheel for rim and hub damage.
7. Reverse the removal steps to reassemble and install the wheel and bearings. Do not reuse a removed snap ring; in-

stall a new snap ring. When installing the snap ring, be sure the flat side of the snap ring is toward the end of the axle as shown in Figure HN1-2.

FRONT SPINDLE

MAINTENANCE

Lubricate the front wheel spindles after every 50 hours of operation or every six months, whichever occurs first. Inject multipurpose grease into the front axle main member through the grease fitting (Fig. HN1-3) at each end. One shot from a hand-held grease gun should be sufficient. Check for looseness and binding in the front axle components.

OVERHAUL

Refer to Fig. HN1-1 when performing the following procedures. To remove a front spindle, proceed as follows:
1. Raise and support the side to be serviced.
2. Remove the wheel and tire.
3. Disconnect the tie rod end (Fig. HN1-4) from the spindle.
4. Detach the snap ring (2–Fig. HN1-1) securing the top of the spindle and remove the washer (3).
5. Withdraw the spindle from the axle.
6. Reverse the removal steps to install the front spindle. Tighten the tie rod retaining nut to 40 N•m (29 ft.-lb.).

FRONT AXLE

OVERHAUL

To remove the axle main member, proceed as follows:
1. Remove the mower deck, then raise and support the front of the machine.

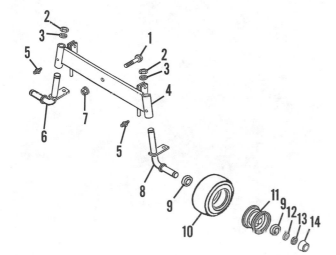

Fig. HN1-1–Exploded view of front axle.

1. Pivot bolt
2. Snap ring
3. Washer
4. Axle main member
5. Grease fitting
6. Spindle (right)
7. Nut

8. Spindle (left)
9. Bearing
10. Tire
11. Wheel
12. Washer
13. Snap ring
14. Hub cap

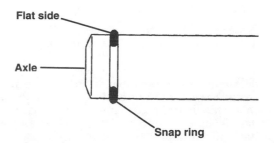

Fig. HN1-2–Install snap ring on spindle axle so flat side is toward end of axle.

2. Disconnect the tie rod end (Fig. HN1-4) from each spindle.

3. Use a jack to support the axle assembly.

4. Unscrew the pivot bolt nut (Fig. HN1-5), withdraw the pivot bolt and lower the axle assembly.

5. Reverse the removal steps to install the axle main member. Do not overtighten the pivot bolt nut (Fig. HN1-5) during assembly. Tighten the nut until 26-40 lb. (12-18 kg) vertical force at a wheel is required to pivot the axle.

FRONT SUBFRAME

The front subframe is attached to the main frame and supports the steering gears and pedal pivot assemblies. The subframe may be removed as an assembly so service can be performed on components attached to the subframe.

REMOVAL

Proceed as follows to remove the subframe.

1. Remove the mower deck.

2. Remove the mower body as described in this chapter.

3. Remove the front axle main member as previously described.

4. Raise and support the mower so it is at least 39 inches (1 meter) above the ground.

5. Be sure the parking brake is released.

6. Detach the pedal return springs.

7A. Model H1011HS–Identify the transaxle neutral return rod connecting the brake pedal to the transaxle control lever. Detach the return rod from the transaxle control lever.

7B. Models H1011R and H1011S–Disconnect the clutch rod adjusting turnbuckle (Fig. HN1-6).

NOTE: The brake control rod will remain on the brake arm in the next step. Do not detach the control rod from the brake arm.

8A. Model H1011HS–Remove the brake arm retaining nut (A–Fig. HN1-7) and washer. Remove the brake arm (B) from the transaxle brake shaft, then reinstall the nut and washer onto the brake shaft to retain the brake pins in place.

8B. Models H1011R and H1011S–Loosen the brake relay arm pivot bolt (Fig. HN1-6), then detach the front brake control rod from the relay arm.

9. Remove the pedal pivot shaft cotter pin, then remove the pedal pivot shaft.

10. Remove the bolts and carriage bolts securing the front subframe to the front of the main frame.

11. Support the front subframe, then remove the carriage bolts securing the subframe sides to the side of the main frame.

12. Carefully lower the subframe and steering assembly away from the main frame.

INSTALLATION

Proceed as follows to install the subframe.

1. Prior to assembly lubricate all moving parts including the steering and pedal assemblies.

2. Use tape or other means to hold the control rods and pedal components in position during assembly.

3. Install the subframe by holding the rear of the subframe higher while inserting the steering column into the main frame. When the subframe is in place, install a couple of bolts to hold it in place.

4. Be sure tangs on the pedal levers (Fig. HN1-8) properly engage slots in the adjacent levers.

Fig. HN1-3–To lubricate spindles, inject grease into grease fitting at each end of axle semiannually or after every 50 hours of operation.

Fig. HN1-4–Unscrew the nut to detach the tie rod end from the spindle.

Fig. HN1-5–Unscrew pivot bolt nut and remove pivot bolt to remove axle main member.

5. Install the pedal pivot shaft, then install the cotter pin in the shaft end. Be sure the pedal assemblies operate properly.

6. Be sure the indexing lug on the upper steering shaft bushing fits into the slot in the steering bracket on the frame (Fig. HN1-9).

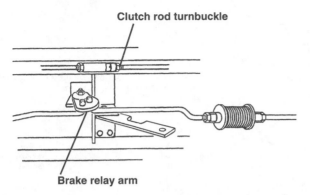

Fig, HN1-6–Refer to text for brake and clutch adjustment procedure.

Fig. HN1-7–Remove the nut (A) and washer for access to the brake arm (B).

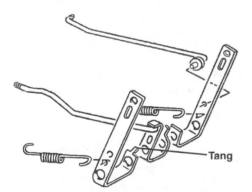

Fig. HN1-8–Tang on pedal lever must engage hole in adjacent lever.

7. Be sure the control rods are in the proper position and move freely.

8. Install the subframe retaining fasteners and tighten to 21.5 N•m (16 ft.-lb.).

9A. Model H1011HS–Remove the brake arm retaining nut and washer (A–Figure HN1-7). Install the brake arm (B) onto the transaxle brake shaft, then reinstall the nut and washer.

9B. Models H1011R and H1011S–Attach the front brake control rod to the relay arm. Tighten the brake relay arm pivot bolt (Figure HN1-6).

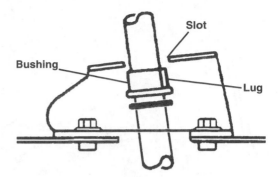

Fig. HN1-9–The lug on the steering shaft bushing must fit into the slot on the supporting bracket.

10A. Model H1011HS–Attach the transaxle neutral return rod to the transaxle control lever.

10B. Models H1011R and H1011S–Reconnect the clutch rod adjusting turnbuckle (Fig. HN1-6).

11. Reattach the pedal return springs.

12. Install the front axle main member.

13. Install the mower body as described in this chapter.

14. Adjust clutch and brake free play as described in this chapter.

15. Install the mower deck.

STEERING SYSTEM
REMOVAL AND INSTALLATION

To service the steering system, proceed as follows. Refer to Fig. HN1-10 for an exploded view of the steering system.

1. Remove the subframe as previously described.

2. Detach the cotter pin from the upper end of the sector shaft (Fig. HN1-11) and remove the washer.

3. Detach the cotter pin from the lower end of the steering shaft (Fig. HN1-11) and remove the washer.

4. Remove the sector shaft and bushing.

5. Remove the pinion and pinion pin from the steering shaft, then lift the steering shaft up and out of the subframe.

6. If necessary, remove the bushing from the subframe.

7. Reverse the removal steps to install the steering system components while noting the following:

   a. Install the bushings so the lug on the bushing aligns with the locating slot in the subframe.

   b. When installing the pinion, position the steering shaft so the pinion pin is parallel to the front of the subframe. Install the pinion and mark the gear root that points to the rear of the subframe. See Fig. HN1-12. Install the sector shaft so the centermost gear tooth engages the marked gear root on the pinion.

BODY
REMOVAL AND INSTALLATION

To remove the mower body, proceed as follows.

1. Raise the seat and disconnect the seat switch connector.

2. Remove the seat pivot assembly, then remove the seat.

3. Disconnect the negative battery cable, then disconnect the positive battery cable.

4. Remove the battery.

5. Position the shift lever in first gear, then remove the shift knob by twisting and pulling up.

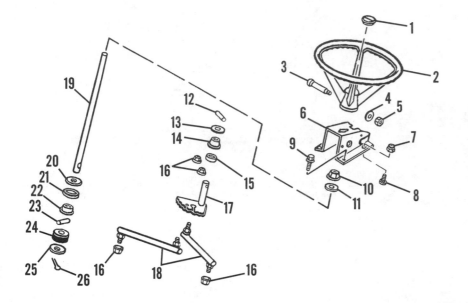

1. Cap		14. Bushing	
2. Steering wheel		15. Collar	
3. Bolt		16. Nuts	
4. Washer		17. Sector shaft	
5. Nut		18. Tie rods	
6. Bracket		19. Steering shaft	
7. Nut		20. Washer	
8. Bolt		21. Collar	
9. Bolt		22. Bushing	
10. Nut		23. Pin	
11. Washer		24. Pinion	
12. Cotter pin		25. Washer	
13. Washer		26. Cotter pin	

6. Place the mower deck height lever in the highest position.

7. Position the throttle lever in the choke position. Unscrew and remove the throttle lever knob, being careful not to lose the nut and spacer.

8. Remove the ignition switch retaining nut and washer.

9. On Model H1011HS, disconnect the neutral switch.

10. Place the PTO lever in the on position, then remove the lever.

11. Be sure the parking brake is off, then remove the clutch and brake pedals.

12. Loosen the steering wheel retaining bolt nut. Hold the steering wheel, then tap on the nut to dislodge the bolt. Remove the nut, then remove the bolt and steering wheel.

13. Remove seven body retaining screws located in the following positions:
   a. Two screws adjacent to the steering column, one on each side.
   b. One screw in each footpan area.
   c. Three screws located in the seat mounting area.

14. Remove the fuel cap and rubber grommet from the fuel filler neck.

NOTE: The body should be at room temperature to lessen the possibility of cracking.

15. Grasp the body near the battery box opening and the steering column. Carefully flex the body while lifting up and remove the body. Move the body as needed to disengage the body from the control levers and body supports. The shift lever may move as the body is removed.

16. Reinstall the fuel cap to prevent contamination.

17. Reverse the removal procedure to install the body while noting the following:
   a. Position the control levers in the following positions:
   • Throttle control in the choke position.
   • Shift lever in first gear. The shift lever will move as the body moves down into place.
   • Parking brake lever in the OFF position.
   • PTO lever in the ON position.
   • Mower height lever in the highest position.
   b. The index peg on the underside of the body near the battery box must fit into a hole in the frame. All screw holes should align.

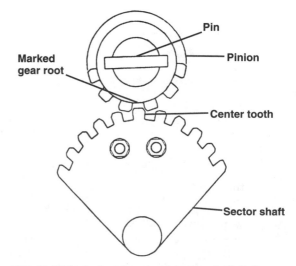

Fig. HN1-11–Drawing of steering assembly.

Fig. HN1-12–Refer to text for steering gear installation procedure.

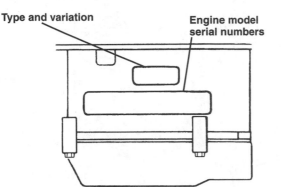

Fig. HN1-13–Engine model information is located on engine as shown.

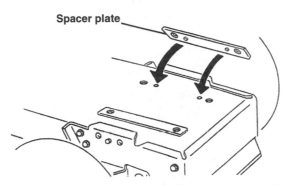

Fig. HN1-14–Install engine spacer plate so dimples on underside of plate fit into indentations in frame.

c. On Models H1011R and H1011S, verify that the shift lever is in the neutral detent when the transaxle is in NEUTRAL. If necessary, adjust the shift lever as described in this chapter.

ENGINE

All models are equipped with a four-stroke, overhead valve, single-cylinder, air-cooled engine with a vertical crankshaft.

Engine model information appears on the side of the crankcase as shown in Fig. HN1-13.

REMOVAL AND INSTALLATION

Proceed as follows to remove and install the engine.
1. Remove the body as previously described.
2. Remove the drive belt as described in this chapter.
3. On Models H1011HS and H1011S, disconnect electrical wires from the electric starter motor.
4. Remove the muffler support bolts.
5. Remove the carburetor vent hose from the hole in the frame.
6. Detach the throttle cable from the carburetor.
7. Unscrew the engine pulley retaining bolt, then remove the pulley.
8. Remove the engine fasteners.
9. Remove the engine.
10. Reverse the removal procedure to install the engine while noting the following:
    a. Spacer plates are located between the engine and frame. Be sure the locating dimples on the spacer plates fit into the locating holes in the frame (Fig. HN1-14).

b. A carriage bolt secures the left, front of the engine.
c. Insert the carriage bolt and right, rear bolt first to properly align the engine in the frame. The engine must not contact the heat shield on the frame.
d. Tighten the engine mounting fasteners to 21.5 N•m (16 ft.-lb.).
e. Tighten the engine pulley retaining bolt to 49 N•m (36 ft.-lb.).

ENGINE MAINTENANCE

Air Cleaner

Engine is equipped with a dry air filter which should be cleaned and inspected after every 50 hours of operation. Proceed as follows.
1. Remove the foam and paper air filter elements from the air filter housing.
2. Wash the foam element in a mild detergent and water solution.
3. Rinse the foam element in clean water and allow to air dry.
4. Soak the foam element in clean engine oil. Squeeze out excess oil.
5. Clean the paper element by directing a low pressure compressed air stream from inside the filter toward the outside.
6. Replace the elements if damage is evident.
7. Reinstall the elements.

Lubrication

Engine oil level should be checked prior to operating the engine. Check the oil level with the oil cap not screwed in, but just touching the first threads.

Oil should be changed after the first 20 hours of engine operation and every 100 hours thereafter. A drain valve is located below the oil fill tube. Open the valve four turns. Do not open the valve more than six turns to prevent damage to the valve seals.

Manufacturer recommends oil with an API service classification SF or SG. Use SAE 10W-30 oil or use SAE 30 if ambient temperature is above 80° F (27° C).

Crankcase capacity is 1.1 L (1.16 qt.) for all models.

Spark Plug

Spark plug should be removed, cleaned and inspected after every 100 hours of use.

Recommended spark plug is a NGK BPR5ES or ND W16EPR-U. The spark plug electrode gap should be 0.7-0.8 mm (0.028-0.031 in.) for all models.

When installing the spark plug, manufacturer recommends installing the spark plug fingertight, then for a new plug, tighten an additional $\frac{1}{2}$ turn. For a used plug, tighten an additional $\frac{1}{8}$ to $\frac{1}{4}$ turn after the spark plug seats.

Carburetor

All models are equipped with a Keihin float carburetor with a fixed main fuel jet and an adjustable low speed fuel mixture needle.

Initial Adjustment

Initial adjustment of the low speed fuel mixture screw (A—Fig. HN1-15) from a lightly seated position is $2\frac{1}{2}$ turns open.

Throttle Cable and Idle Adjustment

To adjust the throttle cable, proceed as follows.

Fig. HN1-15–Adjust low speed mixture screw (A) and throttle stop screw (B) as outlined in text.

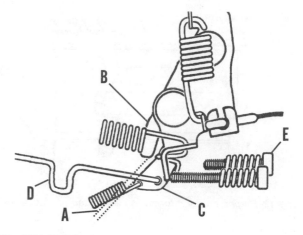

Fig. HN1-16–When throttle is in wide open position, gap (A) between control lever (B) and choke lever (C) must be 0-0.5 mm (0.0-0.2 in.). Refer to text for adjustment

1. Disconnect the spark plug wire and remove the fuel tank.

2. With the throttle in wide open position, measure the gap (A–Fig. HN1-16) between the control lever (B) and the choke lever (C). The gap must be 0-0.5 mm (0.0-0.2 in.).

3. To obtain the correct gap, loosen the locknut (N–Fig. HN1-17) and rotate the adjuster (A) in the throttle cable.

4. The choke plate in the carburetor should be closed when the throttle lever is in the START position. If not, bend the choke rod at the U-section (D–Fig. HN1-16) as needed.

5. With the choke closed, rotate the screw (E–Fig. HN1-16) so it just touches the choke lever (C).

6. Before final adjustment run the engine so it is at operating temperature.

7. Operate the engine at idle speed and adjust the low speed mixture screw (A–Fig. HN1-15) to obtain a smooth idle and satisfactory acceleration.

8. Adjust the idle speed by turning the throttle stop screw (B–Fig. HN1-15). Recommended idle speed is 1750-1950 rpm.

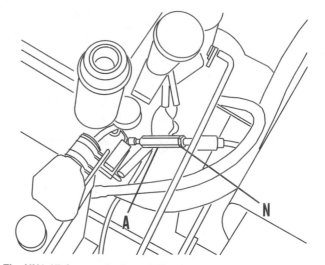

Fig. HN1-17–Loosen locknut (N) and rotate adjuster (A) in throttle cable to obtain correct gap (A–Fig. HN1-16). See text.

Overhaul

Note the following when overhauling the carburetor.

1. To check the float level, remove the fuel bowl and invert the carburetor. Measure from the top edge of the float to the fuel bowl mating edge of carburetor body. Measurement should be 11.9-14.5 mm (0.47-57 in.). Replace the float if the float height is incorrect.

2. Standard main jet is #88.

3. When reinstalling the carburetor, install the small gasket next to the cylinder head and install the insulator block next to the gasket. The gasket and insulator block must be installed in the correct direction to align properly with the intake passage. Install the large gasket between the carburetor and insulator block.

Governor

The mechanical flyweight governor is located inside the engine crankcase. To adjust the external linkage, proceed as follows.

1. Remove the fuel tank and make certain all linkage is in good condition and the tension spring (A–Fig. HN1-18) is not stretched or damaged.

2. Loosen the clamp bolt (B) and move the governor lever (C) so the throttle is completely open.

3. Hold the governor lever in this position and rotate the governor shaft (D) in the same direction until it stops.

4. Tighten the clamp bolt.

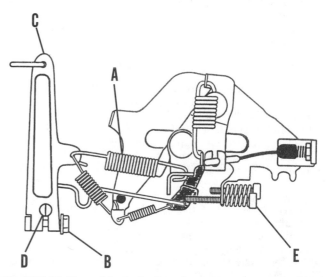

Fig. HN1-18–View of typical external governor linkage used on all models.

A. Tension spring
B. Clamp bolt
C. Governor lever
D. Governor shaft
E. Maximum speed screw

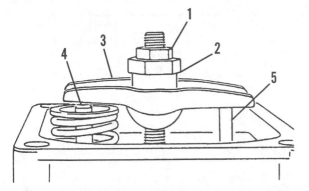

Fig. HN1-19–Loosen rocker arm jam nut (1) and turn adjusting nut (2) to obtain desired valve clearance.

1. Jam nut
2. Adjustment nut
3. Rocker arm
4. Valve stem clearance
5. Push rod

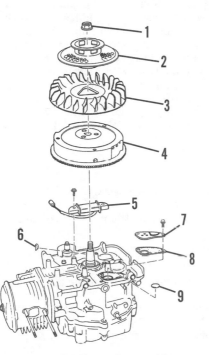

Fig. HN1-20–Exploded view of flywheel assembly.

1. Nut
2. Starter pulley
3. Cooling fan
4. Flywheel
5. Charge coil
6. Key
7. Breather cover
8. Gasket
9. Breather valve disc

5. Start the engine and operate at an idle until operating temperature has been reached.

6. Attach a tachometer to the engine and move the throttle so the engine is operating at maximum speed. Maximum speed should be 3200-3300 rpm.

7. Adjust the maximum speed by rotating the throttle stop screw (E). Turn the screw clockwise to decrease maximum speed.

Ignition System

The breakerless ignition system requires no regular maintenance. Ignition coil unit is mounted outside the flywheel. Air gap between flywheel and coil should be 0.2-0.6 mm (0.008-0.024 in.).

To check the ignition coil primary side, connect one ohmmeter lead to the primary (black) coil lead and touch the iron coil laminations with the remaining lead. Ohmmeter should register 0.7-0.9 ohm.

To check the ignition coil secondary side, connect one ohmmeter lead to the spark plug lead wire and the remaining lead to the iron core laminations. Ohmmeter should read 6.3k-7.7k ohms. If ohmmeter readings are not as specified, replace the ignition coil.

Valve Adjustment

Valve-to-rocker arm clearance should be checked and adjusted after three years or after every 300 hours of operation.

To adjust valve clearance, refer to Fig. HN1-19 and proceed as follows.

1. Remove the rocker arm cover.
2. Rotate the crankshaft so the piston is at top dead center (TDC) on compression stroke.
3. Insert a feeler gauge between the rocker arm (3) and the end of the valve stem.
4. Loosen the rocker arm jam nut (1) and turn the adjusting nut (2) to obtain the desired clearance. Specified clearance is 0.13-0.17 mm (0.005-0.007 in.) for intake and 0.18-0.22 mm (0.007-0.009 in.) for exhaust.
5. Tighten the jam nut and recheck the clearance.
6. Install the rocker arm cover.

ENGINE REPAIRS

Tightening Torques

Recommended tightening torque specifications are as follows:

Connecting rod	14 N•m (124 in.-lb.)
Cylinder head	35 N•m (26 ft.-lb.)
Flywheel nut	115 N•m (85 ft.-lb.)
Oil pan	24 N•m (212 in.-lb.)
Rocker arm cover	8.5 N•m (75 in.-lb.)
Rocker arm jam nut	10 N•m (88 in.-lb.)
Rocker arm pivot stud	24 N•m (212 in.-lb.)

Flywheel
Removal and Installation

1. Disconnect the spark plug lead.
2. Remove the blower shroud.
3. Prevent flywheel rotation by inserting a screwdriver through the holes in the starter pulley (2–Fig. HN1-20).
4. Unscrew the flywheel nut (1).
5. Remove the starter pulley (2) and cooling fan (3).

CAUTION: Do not strike or pry against the flywheel. Doing so may damage the flywheel, which may fly apart while the engine operates.

6. Attach a suitable flywheel puller or Honda tool 07935-8050003 to the flywheel, and remove the flywheel.
7. Inspect the flywheel, crankshaft, key and cooling fan for damage. Clean any foreign objects from the flywheel.

8. Install the flywheel by reversing the removal procedure. Note the following:

   a. Be sure the lugs on the cooling fan fit into the holes in the flywheel.

   b Align the hole in the starter pulley with the cooling fan lug.

   c. Tighten the flywheel nut to 115 N•m (85 ft.-lb.).

Crankcase Breather

The engine is equipped with a disc crankcase breather (9–Fig. HN1-20). The breather is mounted on the top of the crankcase below the flywheel.

When installing the breather cover (7), position the cover with the lug down toward the crankcase.

Cylinder Head

Removal and Installation

To remove the cylinder head, proceed as follows.

1. Remove the cooling shroud and fuel tank.
2. Disconnect and remove the carburetor linkage and carburetor.
3. Remove the muffler.
4. Remove the rocker arm cover and the four head bolts.
5. Remove the cylinder head. Use care not to lose the push rods.
6. Remove the rocker arms, compress the valve springs and remove the valve retainers. Note that the exhaust valve is equipped with a valve rotator on the valve stem.
7. Remove the valves and springs.
8. Remove the push rod guide plate if necessary.
9. Reverse the removal procedure to install the cylinder head. Note the following:

   a. When assembling the valve system, note that the intake and exhaust valve spring retainers are different. The exhaust valve spring retainer has a larger indentation than the intake valve spring retainer to accommodate the exhaust valve rotator.

   b. Tighten the head bolts to 35 N•m (26 ft.-lb.) in a crossing pattern. Adjust the valves as outlined in the VALVE ADJUSTMENT section.

Overhaul

Note the following specifications when servicing the cylinder head components:

Valve face angle	45°
Valve seat angle	45°
Standard valve seat width	1.1 mm
	(0.043 in.)
Maximum allowable valve seat width	2.0 mm
	(0.079)
Standard valve spring free length	39.0 mm
	(1.54 in.)
Minimum valve spring free length	37.5 mm
	(1.48 in.).
Standard valve guide inside diameter	6.60 mm
	(0.260 in.)
Maximum valve guide inside diameter	6.66 mm
	(0.262 in.).
Valve stem-to-guide clearance	
Intake valve	0.010-0.037 mm
	(0.0004-0.0015 in.)
Maximum	0.10 mm
	(0.004 in.)
Exhaust valve	0.050-0.077 mm
	(0.002-0.003 in.)
Maximum	0.12 mm
	(0.005 in.)

Fig. HN1-21–Drive in the valve guides so the top of the intake valve stands 9.0 mm (0.35 in.) above the cylinder head boss (D) and the exhaust valve guide stands 7.0 mm (0.28 in.) above the cylinder head boss.

To replace valve guides, heat the entire cylinder head to 150° C (300° F) and use valve guide driver 07942-6570100 to remove and install the guides. DO NOT heat the head above the recommended temperature as the valve seats may loosen. Drive the guides out toward the rocker arm end of head. Chill the valve guides in a freezer for approximately one hour prior to installation. Drive in the valve guides so the top of the intake valve guide stands 9.0 mm (0.35 in.) above the cylinder head boss (D–Fig. HN1-21) and the exhaust valve guide stands 7.0 mm (0.28 in.) above the cylinder head boss (D). Ream the valve guides after installation.

Oil Pump

The engine is equipped with a rotor oil pump located in the oil pan and driven by the camshaft. The oil pump is accessible by removing the pump cover on the outside of the oil pan.

When servicing the oil pump, refer to the following specifications:

Inner rotor-to-outer rotor clearance	0.18 mm
	(0.007 in.)
Maximum	0.30 mm
	(0.012 in.)
Outer rotor-to-bore clearance	0.15-0.20 mm
	(0.006-0.008 in.)
Maximum	0.26 mm
	(0.010 in.)
Outer rotor height (min.)	7.45 mm
	(0.293 in.)
Pump bore depth (max.)	7.56 mm
	(0.298 in.)
Rotor-to-body side clearance	0.02-0.09 mm
	(0.0008-0.0040 in.)
Maximum	0.11 mm
	(0.004 in.)
Pump bore (max.)	29.21 mm
	(1.150 in.)

Camshaft

Removal and Installation

Camshaft and camshaft gear are an integral casting equipped with a compression release mechanism (Fig. HN1-22). Proceed as follows to remove the camshaft.

1. Drain the oil and remove the engine as previously outlined.
2. Clean the crankshaft and remove any rust or burrs.

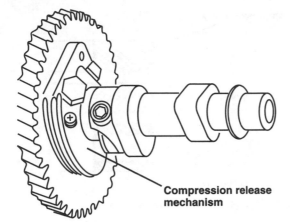

Fig. HN1-22–Compression release spring and weight are installed on camshaft gear.

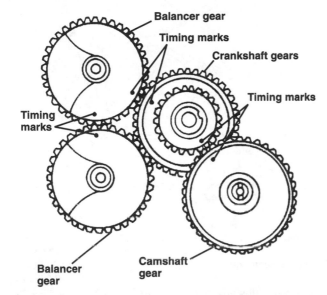

Fig. HN1-23–Drawing showing correct alignment of timing marks on crankshaft, camshaft and balancer shaft gears.

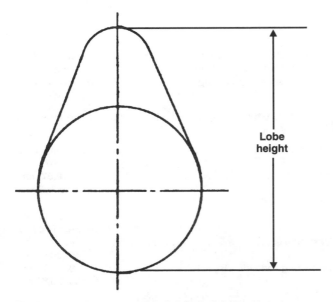

Fig. HN1-24–Measure camshaft lobe height as shown.

3. Unscrew the oil pan retaining screws and remove the oil pan.

4. Withdraw the camshaft assembly and remove the cam followers from the cylinder block.

5. When installing the camshaft, note the following:

   a. Make certain the camshaft and crankshaft gear timing marks are aligned as shown in Fig. HN1-23.

   b. Be sure the slot in the end of the camshaft aligns with the oil pump rotor when installing the oil pan.

   c. Tighten the oil pan screws to 24 N•m (212 in.-lb.).

Inspection

Refer to the following specifications when inspecting the camshaft:

Camshaft bearing journal diameter

Standard	15.984 mm
	(0.6293 in.)
Minimum	15.916 mm
	(0.6266 in.)

Camshaft lobe height (Fig. HN1-24)

Intake	33.00 mm
	(1.299 in.)
Minimum.	32.75 mm
	(1.289 in.)
Exhaust	32.60 mm
	(1.283 in.)
Minimum.	32.35 mm
	(1.274 in.)

Inspect the compression release mechanism for damage. The spring must pull the weight tightly against the camshaft so the decompressor lobe holds the exhaust valve slightly open. The weight overcomes the spring tension and moves the decompressor lobe away from the cam lobe to release the exhaust valve.

Balancer Shafts

The engine is equipped with two balancer shafts that are accessible after removing the oil pan. See previous section for oil pan removal procedure. Each balancer shaft rides in ball bearings at both ends that are a press fit in the crankcase and oil pan. Replace the oil pan if the ball bearing is loose in the bore. Align the timing marks as shown in Fig. HN1-23 during installation of shafts.

Piston, Pin and Rings

Piston and connecting rod are removed as an assembly. Refer to Fig. HN1-25 when performing the following procedure. To remove the piston and connecting rod, proceed as follows.

1. Drain the oil and remove engine as previously described.

2. Remove the cylinder head as previously described.

3. Clean the crankshaft and remove any rust or burrs.

4. Unscrew the oil pan retaining screws and remove the oil pan.

5. Withdraw the camshaft assembly and remove the cam followers from the cylinder block.

6. Remove the balancer shafts.

7. Remove the connecting rod cap screws and cap.

8. Push the connecting rod and piston assembly out of the cylinder.

9. Remove the piston pin retaining rings and separate the piston from the connecting rod.

10. Reverse the removal procedure when installing the piston and connecting rod. Note the following during assembly:

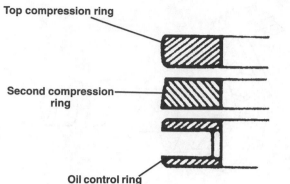

Fig. HN1-25–Long side of connecting rod and arrowhead (triangle) on top of piston must be on same side and facing pushrod side of engine after installation. Refer to text.

A. Arrowhead
1. Top
2. Second ring
3. Oil control ring
4. Retaining ring
5. Piston ring
6. Piston
7. Connecting rod
8. Rod cap

a. Install the piston rings as shown in Fig. HN1-26. The top compression ring is chrome plated. Install the piston rings so the marked side is toward the piston crown. Stagger the ring end gaps equally around the piston.

b. When reassembling the piston on the connecting rod, position the long side (LS–Fig. HN1-27) of the connecting rod and the arrowhead on the piston crown (Fig. HN1-25) on the same side.

c. Install the piston and connecting rod assembly in the cylinder so the arrowhead on the piston crown is on the push rod side of the engine.

d. Align the connecting rod cap and connecting rod match marks (AM–Fig. HN1-27).

e. Tighten the connecting rod screws to 14 N•m (124 in.-lb.).

Inspection

Refer to the following specifications. Oversize pistons and piston rings are available. Measure the piston diameter at the lower edge of the piston skirt and 90° from the piston pin.

Piston diameter .... 81.985 mm
(3.2277 in.)
   Minimum .... 81.85 mm
(3.222 in.)
Piston pin bore diameter .... 20.002 mm
(0.7875 in.)
   Maximum .... 20.042 mm
(0.7890 in.)
Piston pin diameter .... 20.000 mm
(0.7874 in.)
   Minimum .... 19.95 mm
(0.7854 in.)
Piston pin clearance .... 0.002-0.014 mm
(0.0001-0.0006 in.)

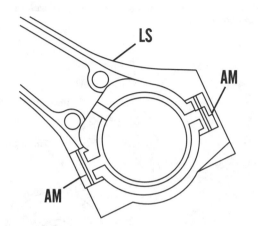

Fig. HN1-26–Install piston rings as shown.

Fig. HN1-27–View of connecting rod. Match marks (AM) on rod and cap must be aligned.

   Maximum .... 0.08 mm
(0.003 in.)
Ring side clearance .... 0.030-0.060 mm
(0.0012-0.0024 in.)
Compression ring end gap .... 0.2-0.4 mm
(0.008-0.016 in.)
   Maximum .... 1.0 mm
(0.040 in.)

Connecting Rod

The aluminum alloy connecting rod rides directly on the crankpin journal. To remove and install the connecting rod, refer to the preceding section and follow the procedure to remove and install the piston and connecting rod.

Refer to the following specifications when inspecting the connecting rod:

Piston pin bore diameter .... 20.005 mm
(0.7876 in.)
   Maximum .... 20.07 mm
(0.790 in.)
Connecting rod bearing
   bore-to-crankpin clearance .... 0.040-0.066 mm
(0.0015-0.0026 in.)
   Maximum .... 0.12 mm
(0.0047 in.)
Connecting rod side play .... 0.1-0.7 mm
(0.004-0.028 in.)
   Maximum .... 1.1 mm
(0.043 in.)

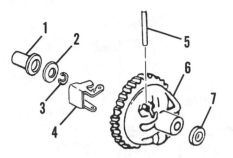

Fig. HN1-28–Exploded view of governor gear assembly.

1. Thrust sleeve
2. Washer
3. Clip
4. Flyweight
5. Pin
6. Governor gear
7. Washer

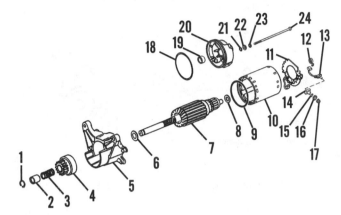

Fig. HN1-29–Exploded view of electric starter motor.

1. Clip
2. Pinion stopper
3. Spring
4. Pinion gear/clutch
5. Drive housing
6. Washer
7. Armature
8. Washer
9. O-ring
10. Frame
11. Brush plate
12. Brush spring
13. Brush (positive)
14. Insulator
15. Washer
16. Insulating washer
17. Nut
18. O-ring
19. Bushing
20. End cover
21. O-ring
22. Washer
23. Lockwasher
24. Through-bolt

If the crankpin is excessively worn, the crankshaft may be machined so an undersize connecting rod may be installed. The connecting rod large end of undersize rod is 0.25 mm (0.010 in.) undersize.

Crankshaft, Main Bearings and Seals

The crankshaft is supported at each end in ball bearing type main bearings. The crankshaft may be removed after removing the flywheel and piston as previously described. Note the following when removing and installing the crankshaft assembly.

1. The timing gears are a press fit on the crankshaft. Prior to removal of the timing gears, mark the gear's position on the crankshaft using the timing marks on the gears as a reference point. Transfer marks to the new timing gears so they can be installed in same position as old gears.
2. Ball bearing main bearings are a press fit on the flywheel end of the crankshaft and in the bearing bore of the oil pan. Replace bearings if damaged. Replace the oil pan when the bearing bore is excessively worn.
3. Press seals into the seal bore until the outer edge of the seal is flush with the seal bore.

4. When installing the crankshaft, make certain timing marks on the crankshaft gear, camshaft gear and balancer gears are aligned as shown in Fig. HN1-23.
5. Note the following specifications when inspecting the crankshaft:

Standard crankpin journal diameter	**35.985 mm**
	(1.4167 in)
Minimum	**35.93 mm**
	(1.4146 in.)

Cylinder and Crankcase

Cylinder and crankcase are an integral casting. Refer to the following table for standard cylinder bore size:

Cylinder bore	**82.000 mm**
	(3.2283 in.)
Wear limit	**82.17 mm**
	(3.235 in.)

Rebore or replace the cylinder if the cylinder diameter exceeds the wear limit. Oversize pistons and piston rings are available.

Governor

The centrifugal flyweight type governor located in the oil pan controls engine rpm via external linkage. Refer to the GOVERNOR paragraphs in the MAINTENANCE section for the adjustment procedure.

To remove the governor, refer to Fig. HN1-28 and proceed as follows.

1. Drain the oil and remove the engine as previously outlined.
2. Clean the crankshaft and remove any rust or burrs.
3. Unscrew the oil pan retaining screws and remove the oil pan.
4. Remove the thrust sleeve and thrust washer.
5. Remove the clip.
6. Remove the governor gear and flyweight assembly.
7. Reinstall the governor assembly by reversing the removal procedure. Note the following:
   a. Be sure the flyweights move freely.
   b. Adjust the external linkage as described under GOVERNOR in the MAINTENANCE section.

ELECTRIC STARTER

The starter motor produces a very high torque but only for a brief period of time, due to heat buildup. Never operate the starter motor continously for more than 5 seconds. Let the motor cool for at least 15 seconds before operating it again.

If the starter motor does not operate, check the battery, starter relay (see ELECTRICAL section) and all connecting wiring for loose corroded connections. If this does not solve the problem, refer to the wiring diagram in this chapter and test the components in the electric starter circuit.

REMOVAL AND INSTALLATION

1. Disconnect the negative terminal wire from the battery.
2. Remove the flywheel as previously described.
3. Disconnect the electrical wires from the starter.
4. Remove the starter retaining screws and remove the starter.
5. Reverse the removal procedure to reinstall the starter. Be sure to install the locating dowel pins in the starter legs and the engine.

DISASSEMBLY

Refer to Fig. HN1-29 for this procedure.

1. Mark the end cover, frame and drive housing to aid during assembly.
2. Loosen and remove the two through-bolts (24—Fig. HN1-29), noting the washers and O-rings used on the bolts for reassembly.
3. Remove the end cover (20) and brush plate from the frame.

NOTE: Two different thrust washers are used on the starter motor. Mark each washer as it is removed so it can be installed in its original position.

4. Remove the thrust washer (8) positioned on the armature shaft next to the commutator.
5. Slide the armature out of the frame.
6. The pinion gear assembly consists of the pinion gear return spring, pinion stopper and clip. To remove the pinion gear assembly:
   a. Support the drive housing in a vise so the armature is positioned vertically.

WARNING: The clip (1—Fig. HN1-29) securing the pinion gear assembly is difficult to remove. Likewise, the clip is difficult to control once it has been released from the armature shaft groove and may fly off when released from the shaft. Wear safety eyewear when removing and installing the clip.

   b. See Fig. HN1-30. Place a wrench over the pinion stopper and lightly tap the wrench downward to uncover the clip.
   c. Hold the clip with locking pliers as shown in Fig. HN1-31. Then pry the clip open with a screwdriver.
   d. Remove the clip, pinion stopper (2—Fig. HN1-29), spring (3) and pinion gear (4) from the armature.
   e. Remove the thrust washer (6).
7. Slide the drive housing (5) off the armature.
8. Inspect the starter assembly and perform the electrical test procedures as described under INSPECTION in this chapter.

CLEANING

Improper cleaning can damage the starter assembly. Clean the individual starter components as follows:
1. The starter clutch/pinion gear and armature must **not** be soaked in cleaning solvent. Clean these parts with a dry, lint-free cloth.
2. Clean the brushes with a clean, lint-free cloth.
3. Clean the brush holder with a solvent-soaked rag. Dry with compressed air.
4. Clean the commutator with electrical contact cleaner.
5. Clean the cover bushings with a clean rag. Do not clean the bushings with a grease dissolving cleaner.

INSPECTION

Refer to Fig. HN1-29 when performing the following procedures.
1. Clean the starter components as described in the previous section.
2. Check the bushings for damage. If a bushing is worn, it will be necessary to replace the drive housing or end cover.
3. Check all O-rings for damage.
4. Check the metal thrust washers for damage. Replace if necessary.
5. Wipe the brushes and brush springs with a dry, lint-free cloth. Inspect the brushes and springs as follows:

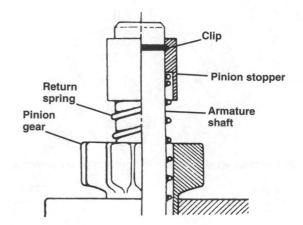

Fig. HN1-30—Disassemble and assemble pinion stopper assembly as described in text.

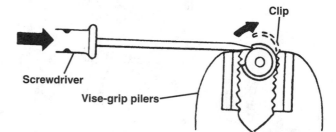

Fig. HN1-31—Remove the pinion stopper clip as described in text.

   a. Visually inspect both brushes for damage. The brushes should show the same wear curvature where they ride against the commutator. If the wear curvature is different, check for weak or damaged brush springs.
   b. Inspect the positive brush assembly (13—Fig. HN1-29) for frayed or damaged insulation and loose wire connections. Inspect the O-ring on the brush terminal for cracks or damage.
   c. Inspect the negative brush assembly on the brush plate (11) for loose wire connections or other damage.
   d. Install each brush into its holder. The brushes should have free movement in their holder. The spring should provide adequate spring tension.
   e. Measure the length of each brush. If any brush length is less than 8.5 mm (0.34 in.), replace the brushes as a set.
6. Inspect the commutator copper bars for discoloration. If a pair of bars are discolored, grounded armature coils are indicated.
7. Inspect the commutator. The mica in a good commutator should be 0.20 mm (0.01 in.) below the surface of the copper bars. On a worn commutator, the mica and copper bars may be worn to the same level (Fig. HN1-32). If the mica depth is less than specified, the segments may be undercut. Use a hacksaw blade or other cutting tool to undercut the mica. The width of the cutting tool should be slightly less than the distance between the copper bars. Burrs resulting from undercutting should be removed with a strip of fine sandpaper. Clean the commutator to remove all copper dust.
8. Check commutator runout with a set of V-blocks and a dial indicator. If commutator out-of-round exceeds 0.40 mm (0.016 in.) the commutator should be turned on a lathe.

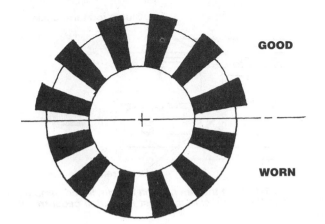

Fig. HN1-32–Note difference between good and worn commutator bars.

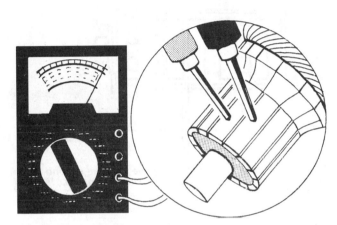

Fig. HN1-33–Use an ohmmeter and check for continuity between the commutator bars. Refer to text.

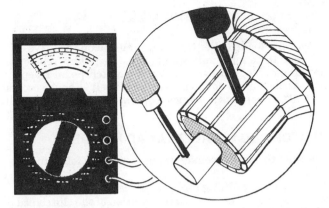

Fig. HN1-34–Check for continuity between the commutator bars and the shaft. Refer to text.

9. Check the frame field magnets for damage. Blow clean with compressed air.

10. Check the through-bolts for corrosion, bending or thread damage.

11. Inspect the pinion gear for excessively worn or damaged gear teeth.

12. Slide the pinion gear/starter clutch onto the armature engaging the splines on both parts. Slide the gear up and down the shaft, checking for binding and tight spots; the gear must slide freely for the pinion gear to engage and disengage properly. If the gear does not slide freely, check the gear and shaft for excessively worn or damaged splines.

13. Slide the pinion gear/starter clutch assembly onto the armature. Try to turn the starter clutch clockwise and then counterclockwise. The starter clutch should only turn clockwise. If the starter clutch slips or turns counterclockwise, replace the pinion gear/starter clutch assembly.

14. Check the pinion gear stopper and spring for damage.

> **NOTE:An ohmmeter is required to perform the following checks.**

15. Use an ohmmeter and check for continuity between the commutator bars (Fig. HN1-33); there should be continuity between pairs of bars. Also check for continuity between the commutator bars and the shaft (Fig. HN1-34);

there should be no continuity. If the unit fails either of these tests, replace the armature.

16. With an ohmmeter set on $R \times 1$, measure the resistance between the insulated brush holder and the brush plate; there should be no continuity. If continuity exists, replace the brush plate.

ASSEMBLY

Refer to Fig. HN1-29 when assembling the starter motor.

1. Lubricate the bushings with engine oil.

2. Apply G.E. Versilube G341M or equivalent to the armature splines, starter clutch/pinion gear splines and bushing.

3. To install the pinion gear/starter clutch assembly:
   a. Install the thrust washer (6–Fig. HN1-29) onto the armature shaft.
   b. Slide the armature into the drive housing.
   c. Secure the drive housing in a vise.
   d. Install the pinion gear/starter clutch (4) onto the armature, aligning the splines on the parts.
   e. Install the spring.
   f. Install the pinion stopper.
   g. Compress the spring and install a new clip into the groove in the armature. See Fig. HN1-30.
   h. Compress the spring and check that the clip seats in the groove completely.

4. Install a new ring onto the drive housing.

5. Install the frame over the armature, aligning the index marks on the frame and the drive housing.

6. Install the thrust washer (8–Fig. HN1-29) and seat it next to the commutator.

7. To assemble the brushes and install the brush plate:
   a. Install the positive brush (13) into its brush holder on the brush plate.
   b. Install the negative brush into its holder on the brush plate (11).
   c. The brush springs must apply tension against the backs of both brushes.
   d. Compress the brushes and install the brush holder over the commutator, aligning the notch in the brush plate with the locating tab in frame.

8. Install the O-ring into the groove on the end cover (20).

9. Insert the positive brush terminal through the hole in the end cover and install the end cover. Align the index marks on the cover and frame.

10. Install the through-bolts and tighten securely.

DRIVE BELT

A spring-loaded idler maintains tension on the drive belt between the engine pulley and transaxle pulley. Tension is not adjustable, however, adjust the clutch pedal freeplay as described in the following section. If belt slippage occurs and all components are in good operating condition, install a new belt.

CLUTCH PEDAL FREEPLAY ADJUSTMENT

Adjust the clutch pedal freeplay using the following procedure.

1. Be sure the parking brake is released.
2. On the mower body mark the location of the clutch pedal lever in the released position.
3. Press on the clutch pedal until freeplay is removed and mark the location of the clutch pedal lever.
4. Measure the distance from the released clutch pedal position to the position where freeplay is removed. The distance should be 25-27 mm (1 to 1$\frac{1}{16}$ in.). If the distance is less than 17 mm ($\frac{11}{16}$ in.), adjust pedal freeplay.
5. To adjust the pedal freeplay, lower the mower deck.
6. Locate the clutch pedal actuating rod and the turnbuckle in the rod (Fig. HN1-35).
7. Loosen the jam nuts on the turnbuckle, then rotate the turnbuckle to adjust the clutch pedal freeplay.
8. Retighten the jam nuts, then recheck clutch pedal freeplay.
9. If correct freeplay cannot be obtained, replace the drive belt.

DRIVE BELT REMOVAL AND INSTALLATION

1. Position the mower on level ground with the parking brake engaged and the transaxle in NEUTRAL.
2. Disconnect and ground the spark plug lead.
3. Remove the rear cover.
4. Remove the mower drive belt as described in this chapter.
5A. Model H1011HS—Detach the idler tension spring from the rear of the mower frame.
5B. Models H1011R and H1011S—Remove the frame access port cover. Unfasten the rear belt guide and remove it.
6. Remove the drive belt.
7. Reverse the removal procedure to install the drive belt. On Models H1011R and H1011S, position the belt guides so there is 1-3 mm (0.039-0.120 in.) clearance between the belt and guide with the clutch engaged.

GROUND DRIVE BRAKE

BRAKE ADJUSTMENT

Model H1011HS

1. Raise and support the rear of the mower.
2. Be sure the parking brake is disengaged.
3. Using a feeler gauge, measure the clearance between the first and second brake plates as shown in Fig. HN1-36. The clearance should be 0.40-0.60 mm (0.016-0.024 in.).
4. If brake plate clearance is incorrect, loosen the locknut on the brake arm shaft and rotate the brake arm retaining nut. Retighten the locknut.
5. Recheck the brake adjustment.

Models H1011R And H1011S

1. Be sure the parking brake is released.

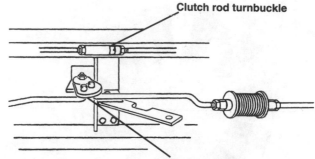

Fig. HN1-35—Loosen the jam nuts on the clutch rod turnbuckle, then rotate the turnbuckle to adjust the clutch pedal freeplay. Refer to text.

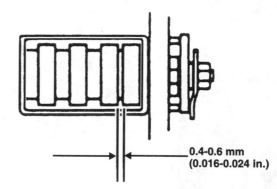

Fig. HN1-36—The clearance between the first and second brake plates on Model H1011HS should be 0.40-0.60 mm (0.016-0.024 in.). Refer to text.

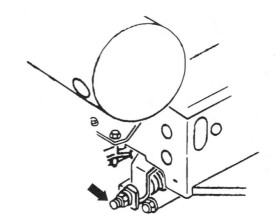

Fig. HN1-37—To adjust the brake on Models H1011R and H1011S, rotate the adjustment nut at the end of the brake actuating rod.

2. On the mower body mark the location of the brake pedal lever in the released position.
3. Push the clutch pedal all the way down.
4. Press on the brake pedal until freeplay is removed and the brake is applied. Mark the location of the brake pedal lever.
5. Measure the distance from the released brake pedal position to the position where freeplay is removed. The distance should be 57-63 mm (2$\frac{1}{4}$ to 2$\frac{1}{2}$ in.). If the distance is more than 70 mm (2$\frac{3}{4}$ in.), adjust the brake.
6. To adjust the brake, rotate the adjustment nut at the end of the brake actuating rod (Fig. HN1-37).
7. Recheck the brake adjustment.

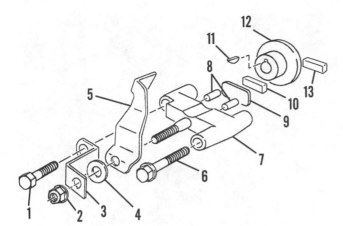

Fig. HN1-38–Exploded view of brake assembly used on Models H1011R and H1011S.

1. Bolt
2. Nut
3. Bracket
4. Washer
5. Brake arm
6. Bolt
7. Caliper
8. Pins
9. Spacer
10. Brake pad (thick)
11. Key
12. Brake disc
13. Brake pad (thin)

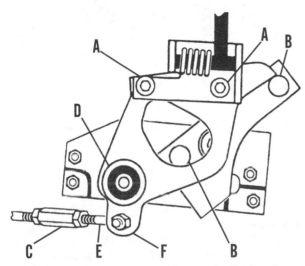

Fig. HN1-39–Refer to text for speed control adjustment procedure on Model H1011HS.

BRAKE OVERHAUL

Model H1011HS

The brake assembly is contained in the transaxle and is not serviceable.

Models H1011R And H1011S

All models are equipped with a disc brake mounted on the transaxle.

To determine brake pad wear, measure the distance on the brake rod (Fig. HN1-37) between the painted band on the rod and the face of the adjusting nut. Replace the brake pads if the distance is greater than 1.5 mm (0.06 in.).

To service brake components, refer to Fig. HN1-38 and proceed as follows.
1. Detach the operating rod.
2. Tighten the brake lever retaining nut so the brake pads contact the brake disc.

3. Measure and record the distance from the face of the nut (Fig. HN1-37) to the brake wear indicator ring on the brake rod.
4. Unscrew the lever retaining nut.
5. Unscrew the caliper mounting screws.
6. Disassemble the brake components.
7. Inspect the brake components for damage.
8. Reverse the disassembly steps to reassemble the brake. Note the following:
   a. Coat the transaxle brake shaft with Lubriplate.
   b. Apply Lubriplate to the ends of the dowel pins and the rubbing surfaces of the brake lever.
   c. Install the thinner brake pad (13–Fig. HN1-38) into the recess of the transaxle case.
   d. Tighten the caliper retaining screws to 18-22 N•m (160-195 in.-lb.).
   e. If installing original pads, tighten the brake lever retaining nut so the brake pads contact the brake disc. Back off the nut to the previously measured distance from the brake indicator ring on the brake rod.
   f. If installing new pads, tighten the brake lever retaining nut so the brake pads contact the brake disc. Back off the nut ¾ turn. Install a new brake indicator ring so it contacts the nut.

HYDROSTATIC TRANSAXLE (MODEL H1011HS)

OPERATION

The hydrostatic transaxle provides infinitely variable selection of forward and reverse speed from stopped to full speed.

A control lever on the side of the transaxle determines transaxle operation thereby setting machine speed.

Internal transaxle components are constructed to close tolerances and clean oil is a requirement to obtain a long service life.

LUBRICATION

Transaxle oil level should be checked periodically. Remove the oil breather on the front of the transaxle to check the transaxle oil level. The oil level should be 1¾ to 2 inches (44.5-51 mm) from the top of the opening. Recommended oil is SAE 20W-50 oil with API grade SG/CD.

SHIFT CONTROL LINKAGE

To adjust the shift control linkage, proceed as follows.
1. Raise the rear of the mower and support the mower so the rear wheels are off the ground.
2. Loosen the change lever retaining bolts (A–Fig. HN1-39).
3. Push down the brake pedal so the pins (B) on the return arm touch the change arm.
4. Loosen the jam nuts, then rotate the turnbuckle so there is a 2-5 mm (0.079-0.197 in.) gap between the brake pedal lever and the slot end in the mower body (Fig. HN1-40).
5. While holding the change arm so it cannot move, tighten the change lever retaining bolts (A–Fig. HN1-39).
6. Remove the brake arm retaining nut and washer (A–Fig. HN1-41). Remove the brake arm from the transaxle brake shaft, then reinstall the nut and washer onto the brake shaft to retain the brake pins in place.
7. Engage the parking brake.
8. Start the engine and set the throttle to slow position.
9. Loosen the jam nuts on the shift control rod turnbuckle (C–Fig. HN1-39).

Fig. HN1-40—With the brake pedal depressed on Model H1011HS there should be a 2-5 mm (0.079-0.197 in.) gap between the brake pedal lever and the slot end in the mower body.

Fig. HN1-41—Remove nut (A) and washer for access to the brake arm (B).

10. Rotate the turnbuckle until the rear wheels just begin to rotate.

11. While noting the number of turns, rotate the turnbuckle in the opposite direction until the rear wheels just begin to rotate in the opposite direction. Stop the engine.

12. Divide the number of turns of the turnbuckle by two, then rotate the turnbuckle to the midpoint position. Hold the turnbuckle and tighten the jam nuts.

13. Reinstall the brake arm, then check brake pedal freeplay as previously described.

14. Set the mower back onto the ground. Check mower operation. The mower should begin to move at equidistant points on the shift lever panel in either forward or reverse. If not, recheck the linkage adjustment.

15. If the shift lever will not stay in a set position, replace the washers on the pivot bolt (D–Fig. HN1-39). Refer to Fig. HN1-42. Install the tab washer (5) so the Teflon side is toward the nut. Install the Belleville washers (6) so the inner diameters contact the washer (7). Tighten the nut to 39 N•m (29 ft.-lb.).

REMOVAL AND INSTALLATION

1. Position the shift control lever in NEUTRAL. Using a bolt, secure the control arm in position.

2. Remove the drive belt as previously described.

3. Raise the rear of the mower and support the mower so the rear wheels are at least 8 inches off the ground.

4. Remove the brake arm retaining nut and washer (A–Fig. HN1-41). Remove the brake arm from the transaxle brake shaft, then reinstall the nut and washer onto the brake shaft to retain the brake pins in place.

5. Detach the shift control rod (E–Fig. HN1-39) from the change arm (F).

6. Remove the transaxle mounting bolt at the left, rear of the frame (Fig. HN1-43).

7. Support the transaxle. Remove the transaxle mounting bolts on each side (Fig. HN1-44).

8. Carefully lower the transaxle while guiding the transaxle disengagement control rod through the rear frame panel. Be careful not to snag the brake or shift control rods.

9. Reverse the removal steps to install the transaxle while noting the following:

   a. Tighten the transaxle mounting bolts to 21.5 N•m (16 ft.-lb.).

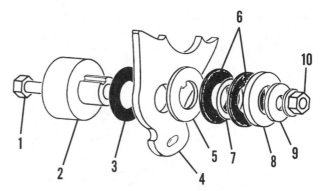

Fig. HN1-42—Exploded view of pivot bolt assembly.

1. Bolt	6. Belleville washers
2. Shaft	7. Washer
3. Washer	8. Washer
4. Change arm	9. Washer
5. Tab washer	10. Nut

   b. Be sure to remove the temporary bolt installed to secure the control arm in NEUTRAL.

   c. Adjust the shift control linkage as previously described.

   d. Adjust the brake freeplay as previously described.

OVERHAUL

Repair parts are not available. If faulty, replace the transaxle as a unit assembly.

GEAR TRANSAXLE
(MODELS H1011R AND H1011S)

LUBRICATION

The outer ends of the transaxle are equipped with grease fittings. Inject No. 2 multipurpose grease into the grease fittings after every 50 hours of operation or every six months, whichever occurs first. One or two shots from a hand-held grease gun should be sufficient. Refer to the TRANSMISSION REPAIR section for internal lubrication information.

REMOVAL AND INSTALLATION

1. Remove the drive belt as previously described.

Fig. HN1-43–View showing location of transaxle mounting bolt on Model H1011HS.

Fig. HN1-44–View showing location of transaxle mounting bolts on Model H1011HS. The transaxle mounting bolts on Model H1011R and H1011S are in the same position.

2. Raise the rear of the mower and support the mower so the rear wheels are at least 8 inches off the ground.

3. Refer to the BRAKE OVERHAUL section and remove the brake components from the transaxle.

4. Disconnect the electrical connector from the neutral switch on top of the transaxle.

5. Remove the shift arm from the transaxle.

6. Remove the transaxle mounting bolt securing the transaxle to the frame (Fig. HN1-44).

7. Support the transaxle. Remove the rear transaxle mounting bolts on each side.

8. Carefully lower the transaxle. Be careful not to snag the brake or shift control rods.

9. Reverse the removal steps to install the transaxle while noting the following:

   a. Tighten the transaxle mounting bolts to 21.5 N•m (16 ft.-lb.).
   b. When installing the shift arm on the transaxle, install the large washer beneath the shift arm and the small washer on top of the shift arm.
   c. Install the brake components as previously described.
   d. Adjust the clutch and brake freeplay as previously described.

OVERHAUL

Repair parts are not available from Honda, although parts may be available from lawn equipment parts companies.

1. Clean the exterior of the transaxle.

2. Remove the drive pulley and Woodruff key from the input shaft.

3. Remove the capscrews from the brake holder (64–Fig. HN1-45) and remove the disc brake assembly.

4. Place the shift fork in NEUTRAL.

5. Remove the two setscrews (2) from the case, then turn the transmission over and catch the detent springs and balls (3).

6. With the transmission upside down, remove the screws attaching the case halves together, then lift the lower half straight up to separate the case halves.

7. Lift the intermediate shaft (21) with the gears and the drive shaft (43) with gears as an assembly from the case.

8. Remove the chain (22) from the sprockets. All parts on the intermediate shaft and drive shaft are a slip fit.

NOTE: Keep parts in the proper sequence when disassembling to aid reassembly.

9. Lift out the idler shaft (37) and gear (35) assembly.

10. Push the axles (53 and 59) toward the center of the differential and lift the assembly from the case.

11. Remove the retaining ring (15) and press the input shaft (13) out of the housing.

12. Press out the needle bearings (10), being careful not to damage the bore of the housing.

13. Clean and inspect all parts and replace any showing damage.

14. To reassemble, reverse the disassembly procedure while noting the following:

   a. Before installing the input shaft assembly, pack the needle bearings (10) with grease.
   b. Install the input shaft using the original shim washers (9 and 12), then check shaft end play. Add or remove shim washers (9 and 12) as necessary to obtain recommended shaft end play of 0.13-0.38 mm (0.005-0.015 in.) and bevel gear-to-pinion gear backlash of 0.13-0.38 mm (0.005-0.015 in.).
   c. Intermediate shaft and drive shaft end play should be 0.0-0.38 mm (0-0.015 in.). Adjust by changing the thickness of the shims (17 and 42).
   d. Gear (35) end play on the idler shaft (37) should be 0.33-0.66 mm (0.013-0.026 in.). Adjust the gear end play by changing the thickness of shim (36).

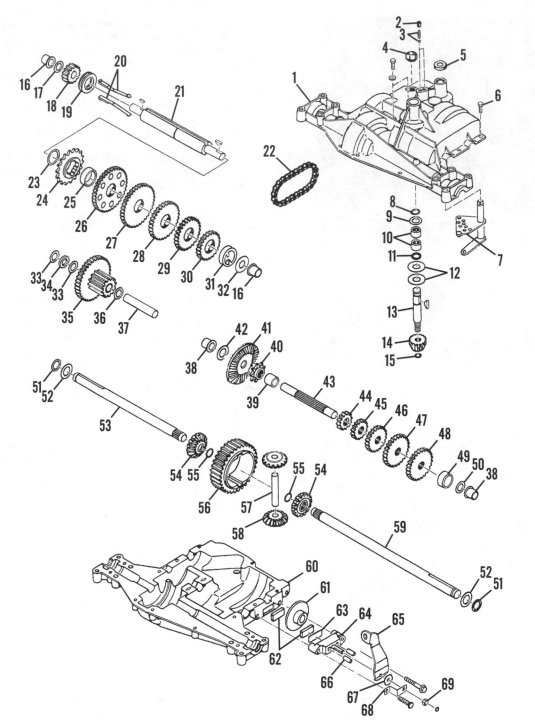

Fig. HN1-45–Exploded view of gear transaxle.

1. Upper housing
2. Setscrew
3. Detent spring & ball
4. Neutral switch
5. Seal
6. Bolt
7. Shifter
8. Snap ring
9. Shim
10. Needle bearings
11. O-ring
12. Washers
13. Input shaft
14. Bevel pinion
15. Snap ring
16. Flange bearing
17. Shim
18. Gear (14T)
19. Shift collar
20. Shift keys
21. Intermediate shaft
22. Chain
23. Snap ring
24. Sprocket
25. Spacer
26. Gear
27. Gear
28. Gear
29. Gear
30. Gear
31. Spacer
32. Washer
33. Washers
34. Spacer
35. Gear assy.
36. Shim
37. Idler shaft
38. Flange bearing
39. Spacer
40. Sprocket
41. Bevel gear
42. Shim washer
43. Drive shaft
44. Gear
45. Gear
46. Gear
47. Gear
48. Gear
49. Spacer
50. Washer
51. Felt seal
52. Shim washer
53. Axle L.H.
54. Axle gear
55. Retaining rings
56. Differential gear
57. Cross shaft
58. Differential pinion
59. Axle R.H.
60. Lower housing
61. Brake disc
62. Brake pads
63. Backup plate
64. Brake holder
65. Brake lever
66. Actuating pins
67. Washer
68. Bracket
69. Adjusting nut

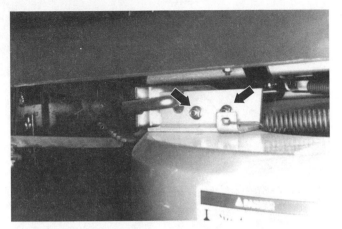

Fig. HN1-46–To adjust blade height, loosen the plate retaining nuts on the left side of the mower deck. Refer to text.

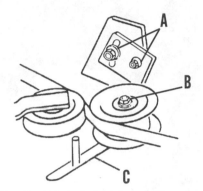

Fig. HN1-47–To adjust blade height, loosen the nuts (A) that secure the adjustment plate on the mower deck. Refer to text.

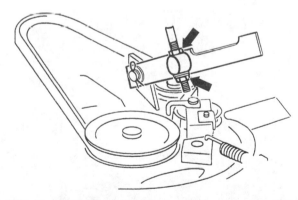

Fig. HN1-48–Adjust mowing height by rotating adjustment nuts on hanger rods as needed.

e. Gear (54) side clearance in the housing should be 0.18-0.38 mm (0.007-0.015 in.). Adjust by changing the thickness of shims (52).

f. The tab on bushings (16 and 38) must fit into the notch in the case.

g. Apply RTV sealant to the mating surfaces of the cases.

h. Pack the housing with 15 ounces (445 mL) of Unirex N-3 grease.

i. Mate the upper and lower case halves and tighten mounting bolts evenly to 9-10 N•m (80-90 in.-lb.).

j. Tighten the brake holder mounting bolts to 18-22 N•m (160-195 in.-lb.).

MOWER

MOWER HEIGHT

All mower control linkage must be in good operating condition and the tires properly inflated. The mower blade must be straight. Park the machine on a level surface with the engine stopped and the spark plug wire disconnected.

Side-to-side Adjustment

1. Place the mower height control lever in the number 2 position.
2. Position the mower blade parallel to the front axle.
3. Measure the blade height on both sides.
4. To adjust the blade height, loosen the plate retaining nuts on the left side of the mower deck (Fig. HN1-46). Move the plate back to raise the left side of the mower deck.
5. Retighten the plate retaining nuts and recheck the blade height.

Front-to-rear Adjustment

1. Place the mower height control lever in the number 2 position.
2. Position the mower blade perpendicular to the front axle.
3. Measure the blade height at both ends. The front blade tip should be 6-9 mm ($\frac{1}{4}$ - $\frac{3}{8}$ in.) lower than the rear tip.
4. To adjust the blade height, loosen the nuts (A–Fig. HN1-47) securing the adjustment plate on the mower deck.
5. Adjust the mower deck position, then retighten the nuts.
6. Recheck blade height.

Mowing Height Adjustment

1. Place the mower height control lever in the number 2 position, which should result in a cut-grass height of 2 inches.
2. Position the mower blade perpendicular to the front axle.
3. Measure the blade height at the front blade tip. The front blade tip should be 48-54 mm ($1\frac{7}{8}$ to $2\frac{1}{8}$ in.) above ground level.
4. Adjust mowing height by rotating the adjustment nuts (Fig. HN1-48) on the mower hanger rods as needed.

MOWER LEVER
FREEPLAY ADJUSTMENT

1. Place the mower control lever in the OFF position.
2. Raise the mower to the highest position.
3. Check the tension of the mower idler arm spring (A–Fig. HN1-49). There should be no free play at the spring end. If free play exists, proceed to Step 4.
4. To adjust the spring tension, loosen the spring plate mounting bolts (B).
5. Rotate the spring plate (C) to apply tension to the spring, then tighten the mounting bolts (B).

MOWER BELT

Adjust Belt Tension

1. Check and, if necessary, adjust the mower lever freeplay as previously described.
2. Position the steering wheel so the front wheels are pointing straight ahead.
3. Place the mower control lever in the ON position.

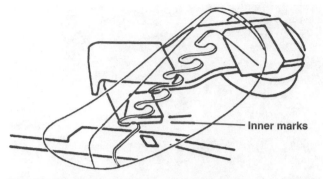

Fig. HN1-49–Check the tension of the mower idler arm spring (A). There should be no free play at the spring end. Refer to text.

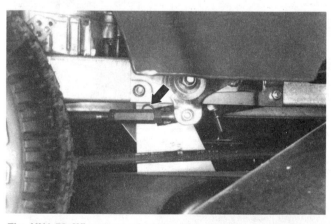

Fig. HN1-50–When checking mower belt tension, the edge of the idler arm should be positioned between the two inner marks on the mower deck. Refer to text.

4. Lower the mower to the lowest position.

5. Check the position of the mower idler arm by looking down into the mower control lever slot. The edge of the idler arm should be positioned between the two inner marks on the mower deck. See Fig. HN1-50. If not, proceed to Step 6.

6. Loosen the spindle bolt (B–Fig. HN1-47) on the fixed idler pulley.

7. Move the fixed idler pulley in the slot (C) in the mower deck so the idler arm edge is between the two marks on the mower deck. If alignment is not possible, the mower belt may be excessively worn.

8. Retighten the spindle bolt securely.

Removal and Installation

1. Remove the mower deck as described in this chapter.

2. Remove the belt guide adjacent to the blade drive pulley.

3. Loosen the bolt that retains the idler arm belt guide, but do not remove the belt guide.

> NOTE: The idler arm is under spring tension. Use care when moving the idler arm.

4. Push in the idler arm and work the belt off the pulleys.

5. Reverse the removal procedure to install the mower belt. Position the belt guides so there is 1-3 mm (0.039-0.118 in.) clearance between the guide and the fully seated belt.

MOWER DECK
REMOVAL AND INSTALLATION

1. Engage the parking brake.

2. Position the shift lever in NEUTRAL.

3. Place the mower control lever in the OFF position.

4. Disconnect the spark plug wire.

5. If installed, remove the lower chute from the mower deck.

6. Be sure the front wheels point straight ahead.

7. Place the mower deck at its lowest position.

8. Remove the engine pulley belt guide. Note that the guide lip fits around the mower.

9. Support the front of the mower deck.

10. Detach the clip from the end of the mower deck support rod. Withdraw the support rod (Fig. HN1-51), then lower the mower deck.

11. Detach the clip and remove the washer from the height adjustment link (Fig. HN1-52), then disengage the link pin from the mower deck.

12. Position the mower height control lever to the highest position.

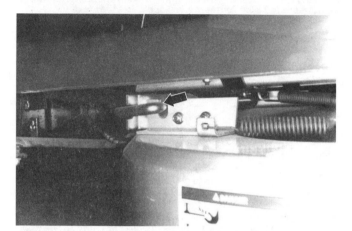

Fig. HN1-51–To remove mower deck, refer to text and withdraw the support.

Fig. HN1-52–When removing the mower deck, detach the clip and remove the washer from the height adjustment link. Disengage the link pin from the mower deck.

13. Position the mower control lever to the ON position.

14. Move the mower deck forward so the clutch lever falls out of the way.

15. Move the mower deck back so the front link falls out of the way.

16. Rotate the steering wheel fully to the right.

17. Remove the mower deck from the left side of the frame.

18. Reverse the removal steps to install the mower deck. After installation, perform the following:

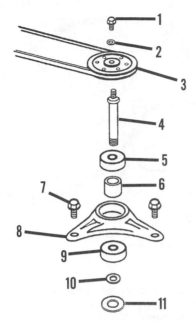

Fig. HN1-53–Exploded view of mower spindle assembly.

1. Bolt
2. Washer
3. Pulley
4. Spindle
5. Bearing
6. Spacer
7. Bolt
8. Housing
9. Bearing
10. Washer
11. Washer

	IGN	GND	BAT	LO	ST1	ST2
OFF	●—————●					
RUN			●————●			
START			●————●		●————●	

Fig. HN1-55–Table showing terminal connections on ignition switch. Not all terminals may be used. Refer to wiring diagram for specific model.

2. Remove the mower deck as previously described.
3. Remove the blade.
4. Refer to Fig. HN1-53, remove the spindle housing retaining bolts, then remove the spindle assembly.
5. Disassemble the spindle assembly.
6. Reverse the removal steps to install the spindle assembly. Using a multipurpose grease, lubricate sliding and rotating components.

ELECTRICAL

INTERLOCK SWITCHES

The interlock switches are designed to prevent unsafe operation of the mower. The switches must be closed to either start the engine or operate the mower, depending on the specific action. The mower is equipped with the following switches:

Transaxle neutral switch (closed in NEUTRAL)
Mower control switch (closed in the OFF position)
Seat switch (closed with weight on the seat)
Parking brake switch (closed in the engaged position)

Testing

To test an interlock switch, remove the switch lead. Using an ohmmeter check for continuity between the contacts on the switch.

INTERLOCK RELAY TESTING (MODELS H1011HS AND H1011S)

Refer to Fig. HN1-54 when performing the following test.
1. Using an ohmmeter or continuity tester, check for continuity between relay terminals 30 and 87a. The tester should indicate continuity.
2. Connect a 12-volt battery to terminals 85 and 86.
3. The tester should indicate no continuity between terminals 30 and 87a.

INTERLOCK DIODE TESTING (MODELS H1011HS AND H1011S)

1. Remove the diode.
2. Connect an ohmmeter or diode tester to the diode.
3. Check for continuity, then reverse the tester leads and again check for continuity.
4. The ohmmeter or diode tester should indicate continuity in one direction, but not when the tester leads are reversed.

IGNITION SWITCH TESTING

Refer to Fig. HN1-55 when testing the ignition switch. Also refer to the wiring diagrams in this chapter. Use an ohmmeter or continuity tester to check for continuity be-

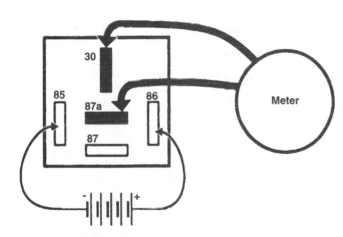

Fig. HN1-54–Refer to diagram and text to text the interlock relay on Models H1011HS and H1011S.

a. Adjust mower control freeplay.
b. Adjust blade belt tension.

MOWER BLADE
REMOVAL AND INSTALLATION

Disconnect the spark plug wire. Remove the blade retaining bolts to remove the blade.

When installing the blade, install the washer so the INSIDE mark on the washer is toward the blade. Tighten the center blade retaining bolt to 49 N•m (36 ft.-lb.) and the outer retaining bolts to 83 N•m (61 ft.-lb.).

MOWER DECK SPINDLE
REMOVAL AND INSTALLATION

1. Remove the mower drive belt as previously described.

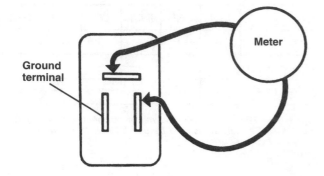

Fig. HN1-56–Refer to diagram and text to test the rectifer on Models H1011HS and H1011S.

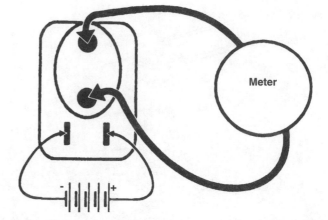

Fig. HN1-57–Refer to diagram and text to test the starter relay on Models H1011HS and H1011S.

tween the switch terminals shown in Fig. HN1-58 with the switch turned to the indicated position.

RECTIFIER TESTING (MODELS H1011HS AND H1011S)

1. Remove the rectifier.
2. Connect an ohmmeter to the rectifier terminals shown in Fig. HN1-56.
3. Check for continuity, then reverse the ohmmeter leads and again check for continuity.
4. The ohmmeter should indicate continuity in one direction, but not when the tester leads are reversed.
5. Connect the ohmmeter leads to the ground terminal and any other terminal. There should be no continuity.

STARTER RELAY TESTING (MODELS H1011HS AND H1011S)

Refer to Fig. HN1-57 when performing the following test.

1. Using an ohmmeter or continuity tester, check for continuity between the two large relay terminals. The tester should indicate no continuity.
2. Connect a 12-volt battery to the two small terminals.
3. The tester should indicate continuity between the two large terminals.

ENGINE CONTROL UNIT (MODEL H1011R)

Testing of the engine control unit is not possible without specialized testing equipment. Check all other electrical components, including electrical wiring, before replacing the engine control unit.

WIRING DIAGRAMS

Refer to Figs. HN1-58, HN1-59 and HN1-60 for a wiring diagram.

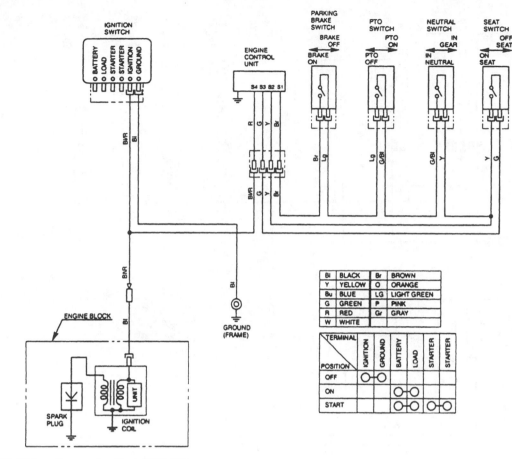

Fig. HN1-58–Wiring diagram for Model H1011R.

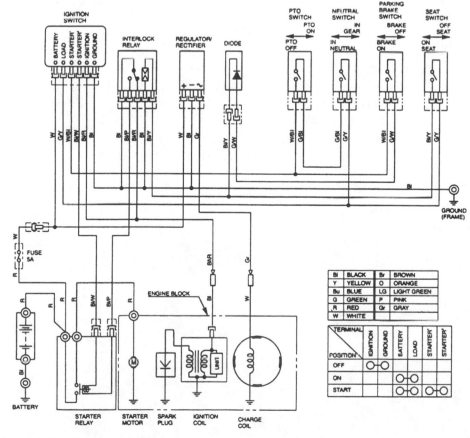

Fig. HN1-59–Wiring diagram for Model H1011S.

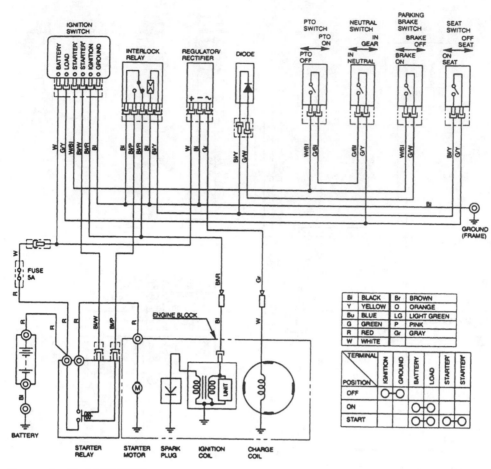

Fig. HN1-60–Wiring diagram for Model H1011HS.

MASSEY FERGUSON

Model	Make	Engine Model	Horsepower
1692489	*	*	8.5
1692491	B&S	*	13
1692823	B&S	*	11
1693048	B&S	*	11
1693050	Kohler	*	14

*Note the engine model number and refer to the engine service section in this manual for engine specifications.

FRONT WHEELS

LUBRICATION

Each front wheel hub is equipped with a grease fitting. The front wheels should be injected with multipurpose lithium grease after every 25 hours of operation. Lubricate the front wheels more frequently when ambient temperature exceeds 85° F (39° C) or when operating in dusty conditions.

REMOVAL AND INSTALLATION

The front wheels are equipped with replaceable bushings. To remove the wheel and bushings, proceed as follows:

1. Remove the wheel cover (8–Fig. MF1-1).
2. Remove the retaining ring (7).
3. Remove the wheel with the bushings.
4. Separate the bushings from the wheel.
5. Inspect the bushings and axle for damage.
6. Inspect the wheel for rim and hub damage.

7. Reverse the removal steps to reassemble and install the wheel and bushings. Lubricate the busings after assembly

FRONT SPINDLE

LUBRICATION

Lubricate the front wheel spindles after every 25 hours of operation. Inject multipurpose grease into the front axle main member through grease fitting (A–Fig. MF1-2) at each end.

OVERHAUL

1. Raise and support the side to be serviced.
2. Remove the wheel and tire.
3. Disconnect the tie rod end and drag link end, if necessary, from the spindle.
4. Detach the snap ring (B–Fig. MF1-2) securing the top of the spindle, then withdraw the spindle from the axle.
5. Reverse the removal steps to reinstall the front spindle. Lubricate the spindle after assembly.

FRONT AXLE MAIN MEMBER REMOVAL AND INSTALLATION

1. Remove the mower deck, then raise and support the front of the machine.
2. Remove the steering link (C–Fig. MF1-2).
3. Remove the spindles.

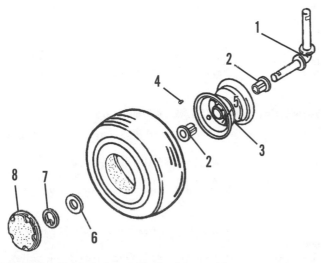

Fig. MF1-1–Exploded view of wheel assembly.
1. Spindle
2. Bushing
3. Wheel
4. Grease fitting
5. Tire
6. Washer
7. Snap ring
8. Wheel cover

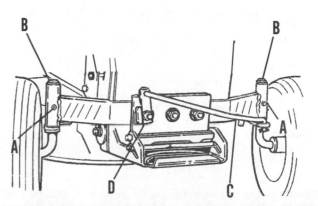

Fig. MF1-2–Inject grease into front axle main member through grease fittings (A). The spindles are retained by snap rings (B).

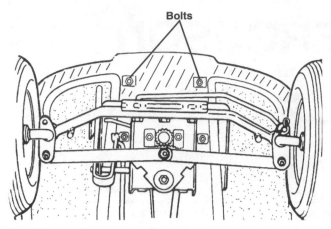

Fig. MF1-3–Adjust gear backlash by loosening the bolts and moving the steering shaft. Refer to text.

4. While noting the parts arrangement for the steering pivot (D), remove the three bolts securing the axle main member.

5. Remove the axle main member.

6. Reinstall the axle main member by reversing the removal procedure.

STEERING SECTOR AND SHAFT

LUBRICATION

Lubricate the steering gears with multipurpose grease after 25 hours of operation, or more frequently when operated in a dusty environment.

ADJUSTMENT

Adjust steering gear backlash by loosening the bolts (Fig. MF1-3) and moving the steering shaft. Be sure the steering gears move smoothly without binding after adjustment.

OVERHAUL

1. Remove the mower deck as described in this section.

2. Remove the steering wheel cap (1–Fig. MF1-4).

3. Drive out the roll pin (3).

4. Remove the steering wheel.

5. Remove the shaft cover (4).

6. Remove the shaft retaining pin (5).

7. Remove the washers (6).

8. Raise and support the front of the machine.

9. Remove the steering shaft from the bottom of the machine.

10. Detach the tie rods from the sector gear.

11. Remove the sector gear pivot bolt (27) and remove the sector gear.

12. Inspect components and replace if damaged.

13. Reassemble steering components by reversing the disassembly procedure. Check steering gear backlash after installation and if necessary, adjust as previously described.

ENGINE

Refer to the appropriate engine section in this manual for tune-up specifications, engine overhaul procedures and engine maintenance.

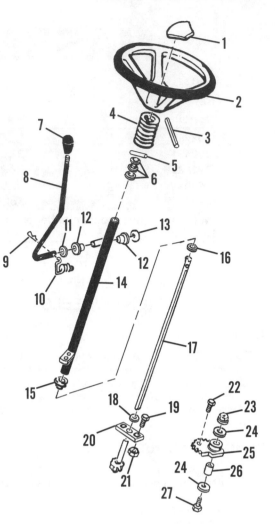

Fig. MF1-4–Exploded view of steering shaft assembly.

1. Cap	15. Bushing
2. Steering wheel	16. Washer
3. Pin	17. Steering shaft
4. Cover	18. Washer
5. Pin	19. Bolt
6. Washers	20. Plate
7. Knob	21. Plate
8. Shift lever	22. Bolt
9. Pin	23. Nut
10. Spring	24. Washer
11. Washer	25. Sector gear
12. Bushing	26. Spacer
13. Washer	27. Bolt
14. Shift tube	

REMOVAL AND INSTALLATION

1. Remove the engine cover and disconnect the spark plug wire.

2. Electric start models–Disconnect and remove the battery.

3. Disconnect any interfering electrical wires from the engine.

4. Disconnect the throttle cable from the engine.

5. Remove the mower as outlined in the MOWER DECK section.

6. Remove the traction drive belt from the engine pulley.

7. Detach the pulley from the engine crankshaft.

8. Remove the engine mounting fasteners.

9. Remove the engine.

10. Install the engine by reversing the removal procedure.

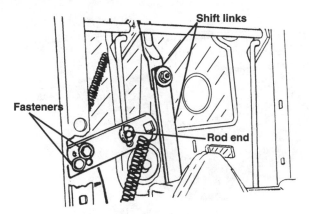

Fig. MF1-5—Refer to text for clutch adjustment procedure on models equipped with a gear transaxle.

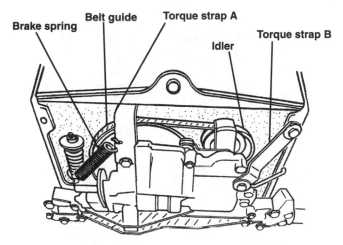

Fig. MF1-6—Refer to text for drive belt removal procedure on models equipped with a gear transaxle.

TRACTION DRIVE CLUTCH AND DRIVE BELT

MODELS WITH GEAR TRANSAXLE

Adjustment

If the rear wheels continue to drive the machine when the clutch/brake pedal is depressed, adjust the clutch idler position as follows.

1. Disconnect the spark plug wire.
2. Loosen the fasteners on the idler arm (Fig. MF1-5).
3. Engage the parking brake.
4. Move the idler arm against spring tension and retighten the fasteners.
5. Check operation. If the clutch rod end is against the slot end in the idler arm and belt slippage occurs, replace the belt. Also inspect components for wear that may allow belt slippage.

REMOVAL AND INSTALLATION

Refer to Fig. MF1-6 when performing the following procedure.

1. Remove the mower deck as described in this section.
2. Raise and support the rear of the machine.
3. Detach the brake spring.

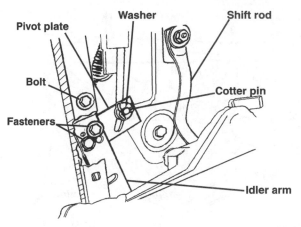

Fig. MF1-7—Refer to text for clutch adjustment procedure on models equipped with a hydrostatic transaxle.

4. Remove the torque strap A.
5. Remove the belt guide.
6. Remove the torque strap B.
7. Loosen the transaxle mounting bolts.
8. Loosen the idler axle sufficiently so the belt can pass between the idler and belt guide.
9. Disconnect the shift links (Fig. MF1-5).
10. Disconnect the PTO clutch electrical wire.
11. Remove the drive belt.
12. Reverse the removal procedure to install the drive belt. Position the idler belt guide so it is 1/8 inch (3.2 mm) from the idler. Perform the transaxle neutral adjustment procedure described in this section.

MODELS WITH HYDROSTATIC TRANSAXLE

Adjustment

If the rear wheels continue to drive the machine when the clutch/brake pedal is depressed, adjust the clutch idler position as follows.

1. Disconnect the spark plug wire.
2. Loosen the fasteners on the pivot plate (Fig. MF1-7).
3. Move the pivot plate so the washer's forward edge on the control rod aligns with the end of the slot in the plate.
4. Tighten the fasteners.
5. Check operation. The drive belt should not rotate when the parking brake is engaged and the engine is running.

Removal and Installation

Refer to Fig. MF1-8 when performing the following procedure.

1. Remove the mower deck as described in this section.
2. Raise and support the rear of the machine.
3. Loosen the fasteners retaining the belt guides.
4. Loosen the fasteners retaining torque strap A.
5. Loosen the fasteners retaining torque strap B.
6. Loosen the transaxle mounting bolts.
7. Detach the idler spring from the frame.
8. Refer to Fig. MF1-7. Remove the cotter pin and washer from the control rod end, then separate the rod from the pivot plate.
9. Remove the idler arm attaching bolt (Fig. MF1-7) and spacer. The idler may now rest against the belt.
10. Note the position of the belt guide on the idler.
11. Disconnect the upper and lower shift rods.
12. Loosen the transaxle control link (Fig. MF1-8).

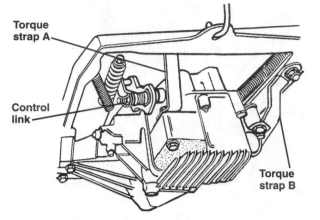

Fig. MF1-8–Refer to text for drive belt removal procedure on models equipped with a hydrostatic transaxle.

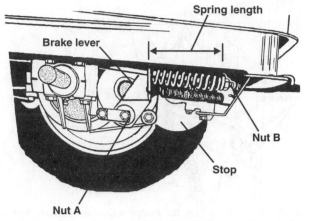

Fig. MF1-9–Rotate nut A to adjust brake on models equipped with a gear transaxle.

13. Disconnect the PTO clutch electrical wire.
14. Remove the drive belt.
15. Reverse the removal procedure to install the drive belt. Perform the transaxle neutral adjustment and the return-to-neutral adjustment procedures described in this section.

GROUND DRIVE BRAKE ADJUSTMENT

MODELS WITH GEAR TRANSAXLE

Refer to Fig. MF1-9 when performing the following procedure.
1. Remove the left rear wheel.
2. Push the brake lever forward and measure the gap between the lever and stop. The gap should be ⅛ inch (3.2 mm).
3. Rotate nut A to obtain the specified gap.
4. Engage the parking brake. Measure the spring length. Specified spring length is 2⁹⁄₁₆ to 2⅝ inches (65-66.6 mm).
5. Rotate nut B to obtain specified spring length.

MODELS WITH HYDROSTATIC TRANSAXLE

These models are equipped with a Hydro-Gear hydrostatic transaxle equipped with brake discs inside the transaxle housing. Check for correct brake adjustment using the following procedure.
1. Insert a feeler gauge between two brake discs through opening on the underside of the housing (Fig. MF1-10).
2. Measure the gap between the brake discs. The gap should be 0.025-0.030 inch (0.64-0.76 mm).
3. Rotate the brake lever retaining nut A to obtain the specified gap.
4. Engage the parking brake. Measure the spring length. Specified spring length is 2¹¹⁄₁₆ to 2²³⁄₃₂ inches (68.3-69.1 mm).
5. Rotate nut B to obtain the specified spring length.

TRANSAXLE

MODELS WITH GEAR TRANSAXLE
Lubrication

The outer ends of the transaxle are equipped with grease fittings (Fig. MF1-11). Inject multipurpose grease into the grease fittings after every 25 hours of operation. One or

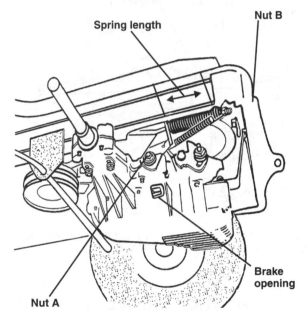

Fig. MF1-10–Insert a feeler gauge through the brake opening in the tranaxle housing to measure brake disc clearance. Refer to text.

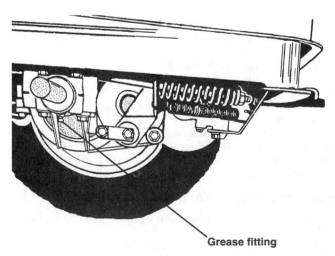

Fig. MF1-11–On gear transaxle, inject grease into fittings on each end of axle housing.

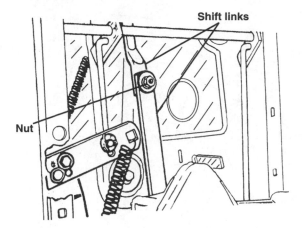

Fig. MF1-12–Loosen nut and reposition shift links as described in text for neutral adjustment.

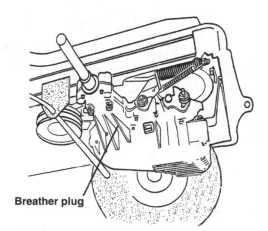

Fig. MF1-13–Drawing showing location of breather plug on hydrostatic transaxle.

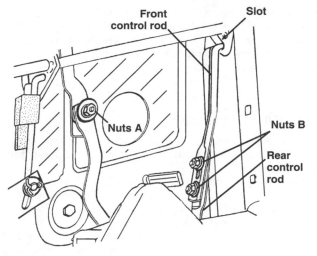

Fig. MF1-14–Refer to text for neutral adjustment procedure on models equipped with a hydrostatic transaxle.

8. Detach the torque straps (Fig. MF1-6).
9. Support the transaxle.
10. Remove the transaxle mounting bolts.
11. Remove the transaxle.
12. Install the transaxle by reversing the removal procedure.

Overhaul

Models equipped with a gear transaxle use a Peerless 915 transaxle. Refer to the repair section in this manual for overhaul information.

MODELS WITH HYDROSTATIC TRANSAXLE

Lubrication

The recommended oil is SAE 20W50 with an API rating of SG. To check or fill the transaxle, clean the area around the breather plug (Fig. MF1-13), then unscrew the breather plug. To check the oil level, measure from the boss surface to the oil. The oil level should be 1.75-2.00 inches (44-51 mm).

Neutral Adjustment

Adjust the shift linkage so neutral positions in the transaxle and at the shift lever are synchronized. Refer to Fig. MF1-14 when performing the following procedure.

NOTE: Operate the machine in Step 1 to verify that the transaxle is in NEUTRAL.

1. Move the shift lever so the transaxle is in NEUTRAL.
2. Raise and support the rear of the machine.
3. Loosen nut A securing the shift rods together so the rods can move independently.
4. Move the shift control lever to the neutral position indicated on the control panel.
5. Retighten the nut to 17 ft.-lb. (23 N•m) and check adjustment.

NOTE: Be sure the forward control rod is not binding in the frame slot before proceeding. If needed, lubricate the rod.

two shots from a hand-held grease gun should be sufficient. Refer to the repair section for internal lubrication information.

Neutral Adjustment

Adjust the shift linkage so neutral positions in the transaxle and at the shift lever are synchronized. Refer to Fig. MF1-12 when performing the following procedure.
1. Raise and support the rear of the machine.
2. Move the shift lever so the transaxle is in NEUTRAL.
3. Loosen the nut securing the shift links.
4. Move the shift control lever to the neutral position indicated on the control panel.
5. Retighten the nut to 17 ft.-lb. (23 N•m) and check adjustment.

Removal and Installation

To remove the transaxle, proceed as follows.
1. Remove the mower deck.
2. Raise and support the rear of the machine.
3. Remove the rear wheels.
4. Remove the drive belt.
5. Disconnect the shift linkage.
6. Disconnect the brake link.
7. Disconnect the neutral switch wire from the switch on the transaxle.

6. Loosen the nuts (B) securing the front and rear control rods so the rods can move independently.

7. Move the speed control lever to the full forward position.

8. Push the forward control rod fully back until it contacts the rear of the slot.

9. Tighten the nuts (B).

10. Check operation.

Purge Air In Transaxle

Air trapped inside the transaxle during overhaul or service must be purged for proper operation and to prevent internal damage.

1. Position the machine on a level surface.

2. Pull the pressure release lever located under the right, rear frame corner back to the PUSH position.

3. Run the engine at slow idle speed.

4. Move the speed control lever alternately to the full FORWARD and full REVERSE positions three times. Keep the lever in the FORWARD or REVERSE position for five seconds each time.

5. Move the speed control lever to the neutral position.

6. Push the pressure release lever forward to the DRIVE position.

7. Run the engine at full speed and operate the speed control lever so the machine moves forward and reverse alternately at least five feet in each direction. The speed control lever must be at the maximum speed position. Operate the machine three times in each direction.

8. Repeat the purging procedure as needed until the machine operates smoothly.

Removal and Installation

To remove the transaxle, proceed as follows.

1. Remove the mower deck.

2. Raise and support the rear of the machine.

3. Remove the rear wheels.

4. Remove the drive belt.

5. Disconnect the brake link and detach the brake return spring.

6. Disconnect the shift linkage.

7. Detach the torque straps (Fig. MF1-8).

8. Support the transaxle.

9. Remove the transaxle mounting bolts.

10. Remove the transaxle.

11. Install the transaxle by reversing the removal procedure.

Overhaul

Models equipped with a hydrostatic transaxle use a Hydro-Gear 310-0500 transaxle. Refer to the repair section in this manual for overhaul information.

ELECTRIC PTO CLUTCH

TESTING

Use the following procedure to locate the cause if the PTO clutch malfunctions.

1. Turn the ignition switch ON.

2. Actuate the PTO switch.

3. If the clutch does not engage, disconnect the wiring connector at the clutch.

4. Use a 12-volt test lamp to check continuity of the wire coming from the PTO switch.

5. If the lamp lights, the PTO is either defective or the wiring connector at the clutch field coil is faulty.

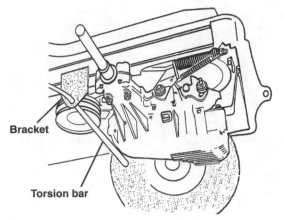

Fig. MF1-15–Drawing showing location of torsion bar and brackets.

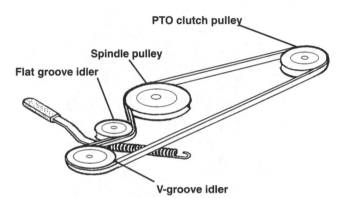

Fig. MF1-16–Mower belt routing diagram for 30-inch mower deck.

6. To check the PTO field coil, perform the following procedures:

    a. Clutch installed—Connect an ohmmeter to the terminals on the clutch. The ohmmeter should indicate a resistance of 6.59-7.29 ohms.

    b. Clutch removed—Apply a 12-volt source to the clutch terminals. Hold a piece of steel next to the coil. The coil should attract the metal. There should be an audible click when the clutch engages.

7. If the PTO clutch fails the preceding tests, replace the coil or entire clutch assembly.

REMOVAL AND INSTALLATION

1. Remove the mower deck as described in this section.

2. Raise and support the rear of the machine.

3. Remove the torsion bar bracket and torsion bar (Fig. MF1-15).

4. Disconnect the PTO clutch electrical wire.

5. Hold the spacer below the clutch by placing a wrench on the two flats on the spacer.

6. Remove the clutch retaining bolts.

7. Remove the clutch assembly from the crankshaft.

8. Reverse the removal procedure to install the PTO clutch. Apply antiseize compound to the engine crankshaft. Tighten the clutch retaining bolts to 45-50 ft.-lb. (63-68 N•m).

9. If installing a new clutch or components, run the engine at full speed and engage the clutch several times after mower is installed to burnish the clutch surfaces.

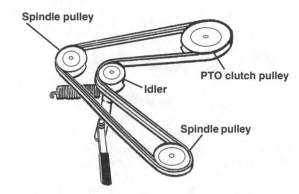

Fig. MF1-17—Mower belt routing diagram for 34-inch mower deck.

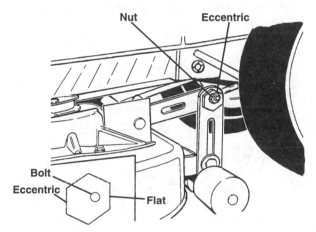

Fig. MF1-18—Rotate the eccentric as described in text to adjust mower side-to-side height. The left side is shown.

MOWER DRIVE BELT REMOVAL AND INSTALLATION

30-INCH MOWER DECK

Refer to Fig. MF1-16 when performing the following procedure.

1. Place the mower height control lever in the lowest position.

2. Move the moveable idler away from the belt and remove the belt from the PTO pulley and mower spindle pulley.

3. Remove the mower drive belt.

4. Reverse the removal procedure to install the belt.

34-INCH MOWER DECK

Refer to Fig. MF1-17 when performing the following procedure.

1. Place the mower height control lever in the lowest position.

2. Move the moveable idler away from the belt and remove the belt from the PTO pulley and idler.

3. Remove the cover over the left mower spindle pulley.

4. Remove the mower drive belt.

5. Reverse the removal procedure to install the belt. The flat side of the belt must contact the idler.

MOWER DECK

LUBRICATION

Lubricate the spindles and idler arm after every 25 hours of operation. Inject multipurpose grease through the grease fittings. One or two shots from a hand-held grease gun should be sufficient. Apply clean engine oil to the contact surface of all moving parts.

Lubricate more frequently when the ambient temperature exceeds 85° F (39° C) or when operating in dusty conditions.

ADJUSTMENT

Before attempting any adjustment, the machine must be on level ground and the tires must be properly inflated. Disconnect the spark plug wire and tie out of way.

Side-To-Side Height

1. Position the mower deck in the down position at mid-height.

2. Loosen the rear mower deck hanger links so the deck rests on the rear rollers.

> NOTE: The deck must rest on the rollers. If not adjust the roller position, then readjust roller position after performing the leveling adjustment.

3. Measure the height of the blade tip above the ground. Measurement should be within $\frac{1}{8}$ inch (3.2 mm) of blade tip on opposite side.

4. Note the position of the eccentric (Fig. MF1-18) on the left side of the deck. The flat on the eccentric near the bolt must be toward the rear of the deck. If not, reposition the eccentric and tighten the nut to 30 ft.-lb. (41 N•m).

5. Adjust the blade side-to-side height by rotating the eccentric on the right side of the deck.

6. Recheck the blade height.

7. Tighten the rear hanger link fasteners and reposition the rear rollers, if moved.

Front-To-Rear Height

1. Measure the distance from the ground to the blade from front to rear.

2A. 30-inch Mower Deck— The front of the blade should be level with the rear of the blade or up to $\frac{1}{8}$ inch (3.2 mm) higher.

2B. 34-inch Mower Deck— The front of the blade should be level with the rear of the blade or up to $\frac{1}{4}$ inch (6.4 mm) higher.

3. To adjust the front-to-rear dimension, adjust the position of the nuts (Fig. MF1-19) on the height adjustment rod.

TRANSPORT HEIGHT ADJUSTMENT

When the mower lift lever is in the transport position, the rollers on the rear of the mower deck should be $\frac{1}{8}$-$\frac{1}{4}$ inch (3.2-6.4 mm) above the ground. Refer to Fig. MF1-20 and use the following procedure to adjust the transport height.

1. Adjust the mower height to 3 inches (76 mm) on 30-inch mower deck or $2\frac{3}{4}$ inches (70 mm) on 34-inch mower deck.

2. Loosen the nut and move the spacer against the trailing arm. Retighten the nut. Perform the adjustment on both sides of the mower deck.

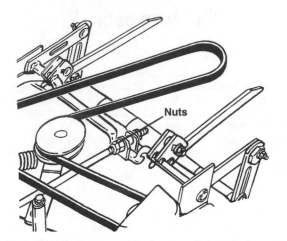

Fig. MF1-19–Rotate nuts to adjust mower height. Refer to text.

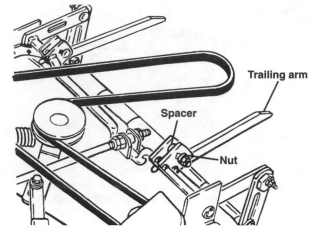

Fig. MF1-20–Refer to text for roller height adjustment procedure.

3. Check the roller height. If incorrect, repeat the procedure.

REMOVAL AND INSTALLATION

1. Turn the front wheels fully to the left.
2. Move the mower deck to the lowest position.
3. Push the idler arm and remove the mower belt from the mower pulleys.
4. Support the front of the mower deck with a block of wood.
5. Detach the lift cable hook from the mower deck eye.
6. Pull out the hitch lever (Fig. MF1-21), disengage the hitch and place it out of the way.
7. Remove the mower deck by moving it out from the right side of the machine.
8. Reverse the removal procedure to install the mower deck. Be sure the open portion of the hook on the lift cable is toward the rear of the machine. The trailing arms (Fig. MF1-20) must be above the torsion bar.

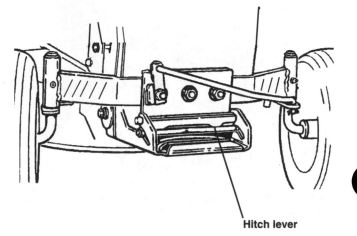

Fig. MF1-21–Pull the hitch lever to detach the hitch.

MOWER DECK SPINDLE

Two spindle configurations have been used. Early spindles are identified by the use of a bolt to secure the pulley. Later spindles are equipped with a nut to hold the pulley on the spindle.

OVERHAUL

Early Models

Refer to Fig. MF1-22 when performing the following procedure.
1. Remove the mower deck as previously described.
2. Remove the blade.
3. Note the position of the belt guides attached to the spindle housing, then unscrew the spindle housing mounting screws and remove the spindle assembly.
4. Secure the blade adapter (15) in a vise.
5. Remove the bolt (1), lockwasher (2), washer (3), pulley (4) and shield (5).
6. Free the unit from the vise, then remove the collar (16) from the blade adapter.
7. Remove the blade adapter (15), shield (14) and shim (13).
8. Separate the spindle housings by prying apart.
9. Press the bearings off the spindle.

10. Assemble the spindle by reversing the disassembly procedure. Note the following:
   a. If a foam gasket is not available, apply RTV sealant to mating surfaces of the upper and lower spindle housings.
   b. Fill the lower spindle housing with lithium-based grease.
   c. Install the pulley so the long end of the hub is toward the housing.
   d. Tighten the pulley retaining screw to 50-70 ft.-lb. (68-95 N•m).
   e. Maximum spindle end play is 1/8 inch (3.2 mm).
   f. Install the long spindle housing screws at the belt guide location.

Later Models

Refer to Fig. MF1-23 when performing the following procedure.
1. Remove the mower deck as previously described.
2. Remove the blade.
3. Unscrew the spindle housing mounting screws and remove the spindle assembly.
4. Secure the spindle in a vise.
5. Remove the nut (1), Belleville washers (2), pulley (3) and spacer (4).
6. Separate the spindle housings by prying apart.

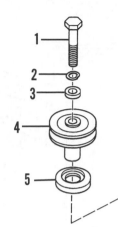

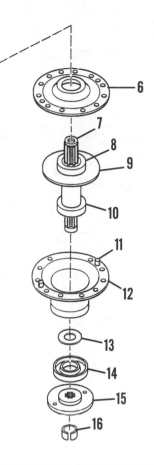

Fig. MF1-22–Exploded view of a mower spindle used on a 30-inch mower deck.

1. Bolt
2. Lockwasher
3. Washer
4. Pulley
5. Shield
6. Upper spindle housing
7. Spindle
8. Bearing
9. Foam gasket
10. Bearing
11. Pin
12. Lower spindle housing
13. Shim
14. Shield
15. Adapter
16. Collar

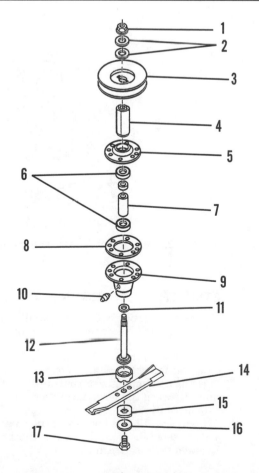

Fig. MF1-23–Exploded view of a mower spindle used on a 34-inch mower deck.

1. Nut
2. Belleville washer
3. Pulley
4. Spacer
5. Upper spindle housing
6. Bearing
7. Spacer
8. Foam gasket
9. Lower spindle housing
10. Grease fitting
11. Bearing
12. Spindle
13. Collar
14. Blade
15. Washer
16. Lockwasher
17. Bolt

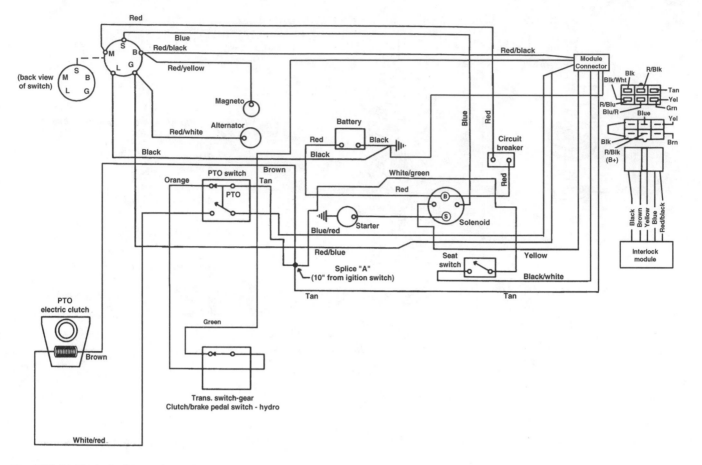

Fig. MF1-24–Typical wiring schematic.

7. Disassemble the remainder of the spindle housing components.

8. Inspect the components for damage.

9. Install the washer (11) onto the shaft with the concave side toward the flange on the spindle.

10. Install the bearings and spacer (7) into the lower spindle housing.

11. Install the spindle into the lower spindle housing and bearings.

12. Install the foam gasket. If a foam gasket is not available, apply RTV sealant to upper and lower spindle mating surfaces.

13. Fill the lower spindle housing with lithium based grease.

14. Install the remainder of the components while noting the following:

    a. Tighten the pulley retaining screw to 50-70 ft.-lb. (68-95 N•m).

    b. Maximum spindle end play is ⅛ inch (3.2 mm).

ELECTRICAL

Refer to Fig. MF1-24 for a wiring schematic. Note the following points:

1. The transaxle must be in NEUTRAL, the mower must be disengaged and the operator must be in the seat for the engine to start.

2. The engine should stop if the transaxle is in gear or the mower is engaged and the operator leaves the seat.

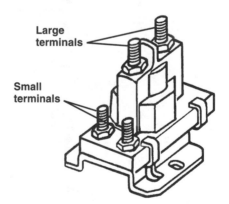

Fig. MF1-25–Refer to text for starter relay testing procedure.

STARTER RELAY TESTING

Note the location of the small and large terminals on the relay (Fig. MF1-25) when performing the following test.

1. Using an ohmmeter or continuity tester, check for continuity between the small terminals. The tester should indicate continuity less than 10 ohms.

2. Using an ohmmeter or continuity tester, check for continuity between the large terminals. The tester should indicate no continuity.

3. Connect a 12-volt battery to the small terminals.

4. The tester should indicate continuity less than 10 ohms between the large terminals.

MASSEY FERGUSON

ZT SERIES

Model	Make	Engine Model	Horsepower
1692910	Kohler	CV14S	14
1692911	Kohler	CV16S	16
1693234	B&S	*	18
1693300	Kohler	CV14S	14
1693302	Kohler	CV16S	16
1693471	Kohler	CV14S	14
1693477	B&S	*	16

*Note the engine model number and refer to the engine service section in this manual for engine specifications.

FRONT WHEELS

LUBRICATION

Each front wheel hub is equipped with a grease fitting. Front wheels should be injected with multipurpose grease after every 25 hours of operation. Lubricate the front wheels more frequently when ambient temperature exceeds 85° F. (30° C.) or when operating in dusty conditions.

REMOVAL AND INSTALLATION

The front wheels are equipped with replaceable bushings. To remove the wheel and bushings, proceed as follows:
1. Remove the hub cap (8—Fig. MF2-1).
2. Remove the retaining ring (7).
3. Remove the wheel with the bushings.
4. Separate the bushings from the wheel.
5. Inspect the bushings and axle for damage.

6. Inspect the wheel for rim and hub damage.
7. Reverse the removal steps to reassemble and install the wheel and bushings. Lubricate the bushings after assembly.

FRONT SPINDLES

MAINTENANCE

Lubricate the front wheel spindles after every 25 hours of operation. Inject multipurpose grease into the grease fitting on the spindle housing. Lubricate the spindles more frequently when ambient temperature exceeds 85° F (30° C) or when operating in dusty conditions.

OVERHAUL

Refer to Fig. MF2-2 for an exploded view of the spindle assembly. To remove a front spindle, proceed as follows.
1. Raise and support the side to be serviced.
2. Remove the wheel and tire as previously described.
3. Remove the snap ring (1–Fig. MF2-2) from the top of the spindle.
4. Remove the spindle (6).

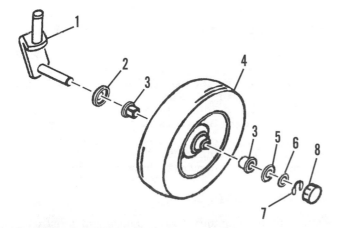

Fig. MF2-1–Exploded view of wheel assembly.

1. Spindle
2. Cup washer
3. Bushing
4. Wheel
5. Large washer
6. Small washer
7. E-ring
8. Hub cap

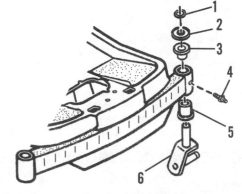

Fig. MF2-2–Exploded view of spindle assembly.

1. E-ring
2. Washer
3. Bushing
4. Grease fitting
5. Bushing
6. Spindle

5. Inspect the components for damage.

6. Install the spindle by reversing the removal procedure. Lubricate the spindle after assembly.

ENGINE

Refer to the appropriate engine section in this manual for tune-up specifications, engine overhaul procedures and engine maintenance.

REMOVAL AND INSTALLATION

1. Remove the engine cover and disconnect the spark plug wire.

2. Electric start models—Disconnect and remove the battery.

3. Disconnect any interfering electrical wires from the engine.

4. Disconnect the throttle cable from the engine.

5. Remove the mower as outlined in the MOWER DECK section.

6. Remove the traction drive belt from the engine pulley.

7. Detach the pulley from the engine crankshaft.

8. Remove the engine mounting fasteners.

9. Remove the engine.

10. Install the engine by reversing the removal procedure.

TRANSAXLE DRIVE BELT

Early models use five wire-type belt guides (A–Fig. MF2-3A) to hold the belt in place. Later models use three wire-type belt guides (A and D–Fig. MF2-3B).

REMOVAL AND INSTALLATION

Early Models

1. Remove the engine cover and disconnect the spark plug wire.

2. Remove the mower deck.

3. Remove the PTO clutch (P-Fig. MF2-3A) as described in this section.

4. Push down the clutch pedal.

5. Remove the drive belt (B–Fig. MF2-3A) by sliding the belt between the pulleys and the belt guides.

6. Install the belt by reversing the removal procedure. Adjust the belt guides as needed so there is $\frac{1}{8}$ inch (3.2 mm) clearance between the belt and guides.

Later Models

1. Remove the engine cover and disconnect the spark plug wire.

2. Remove the mower deck.

3. Remove the PTO clutch as described in this section.

4. Remove the carrier assembly as described in this section.

5. Remove the wire belt guide (D–Fig. MF2-2-3B) from the transmission pulleys.

6. Remove the drive belt (B–Fig MF2-3B) by sliding the belt between the pulleys and the belt guides.

7. Install the drive belt by reversing the removal procedure. Adjust the belt guides as needed so there is $\frac{1}{8}$ inch (3.2 mm) clearance between the belt and the guides.

STEERING CONTROL LINKAGE

LUBRICATION

Periodically lubricate all rubbing contact surfaces with engine oil. Apply oil more frequently when the machine is operated in dusty conditions.

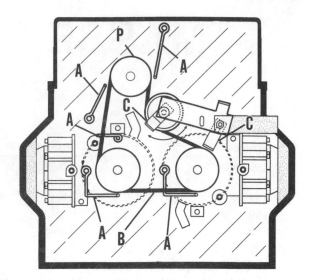

Fig. MF2-3A–Drawing of traction drive belt components on early models. Five belt guides (A) are used on early models.

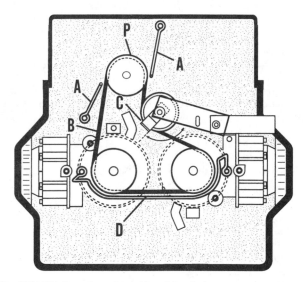

Fig. MF2-3B–Drawing of traction drive belt components on later models. Three belt guides (A and D) are used on later models.

RUNNING ADJUSTMENT

Each transaxle is independently controlled to permit zero-radius turning. If the machine tracks slightly off course while running, the top speed of each transaxle may be controlled by turning the appropriate adjustment knob (Fig. MF2-4). Minor adjustment may be necessary while running because the transaxles may not operate equally.

If the operating levers are not parallel within $\frac{3}{8}$ inch (3.2 mm) when the machine is traveling straight ahead, perform the linkage adjustment as described in this section.

LINKAGE ADJUSTMENT

Before performing the following adjustment, be sure the machine is situated on level ground and the tires are properly inflated.

1. Rotate the adjustment knobs (Fig. MF2-4) fully counterclockwise.

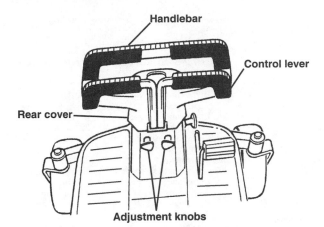

Fig. MF2-4–Refer to the text for the steering linkage adjustment procedure.

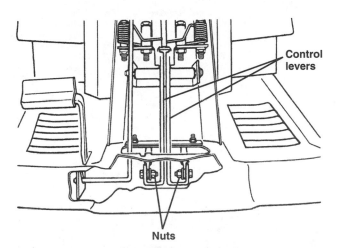

Fig. MF2-5A–Steering linkage (early models).

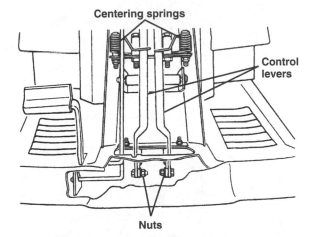

Fig.MF2-5B–Steering linkage (later models).

NOTE: The front shroud is shown removed in the following drawings for clarity. Front shroud removal is not necessary to perform the adjustment.

2. Loosen the adjustment nuts shown in Figs. MF2-5A or MF2-5B.

3. Move the bolts to the bottom of the slots in the control levers.

4. Tighten the nuts and check operation. If the machine does not track properly, proceed to Step 5.

5. Loosen the adjusment nut in one of the control levers and move the bolt in the control lever slot. Retighten the nut and check machine operation.

NOTE: Perfectly straight tracking is not necessary when performing Step 6. See Step 7.

6. After noting the directional change caused by Step 5, relocate the bolts in the control lever slots to obtain tracking as straight as possible.

7. Turn the adjustment knobs shown in Fig. MF2-4 as needed to obtain straight tracking.

CONTROL LEVER POSITION ADJUSTMENT

When the machine is in NEUTRAL, the distance from each control lever (Fig. MF2-4) to the handlebar should be $2\frac{1}{4}$ to $2\frac{3}{8}$ inches (57-60 mm). If incorrect, perform the following adjustment procedure.

1. Remove the mower deck as described in this section.

2. Remove the rear handlebar cover (Fig. MF2-4).

3. If so equipped, disconnect the wires from the headlight switch.

4. Remove the front handlebar cover (4–Fig. MF2-6).

5. If so equipped, remove the headlight.

6. Remove the covers from the top of the front control tower cover (39–Fig. MF2-6) and the screws underneath the frame. Remove the front control tower cover.

7. Loosen the fastener (A–Fig. MF2-7) on each transaxle control rod.

NOTE: To assist in obtaining an equidistant space, attach a suitably sized board to the control levers.

8. Loosen the bolt in each centering spring (Fig. MF2-5B). Move the bolt in the slot to obtain the desired distance from each control lever to the handlebar, then retighten the bolt.

9. Reassemble the covers.

10. Perform the neutral adjustment as described in this section.

REAR CARRIER

The transaxles and transaxle drive belt idler are mounted on a carrier at the rear of the machine. The carrier permits the rear of the machine to pivot independently during operation. Use the following procedure to remove the carrier for service to the carrier or if removing both transaxles.

REMOVAL AND INSTALLATION

1. Disconnect the engine spark plug lead.

2. Remove any weights attached to the carrier.

3. Remove the mower deck.

4. Raise and support the rear of the machine.

5. Remove the rear wheels.

6. Remove the PTO clutch as described in this section.

7. Disconnect the electrical lead from the clutch/brake switch on the clutch rod.

8. Disconnect the transaxle control rods (B–Fig. MF2-7).

9. Disconnect the brake rod (C) from the linkage inside the carrier.

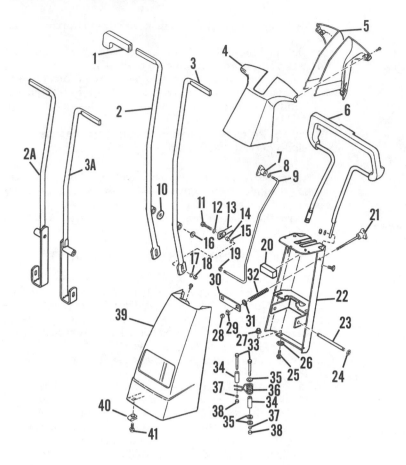

Fig. MF2-6–Exploded view of control tower assembly.

1. Grip	19. Nut
2. Right control lever (later models)	20. Pad
	21. Speed adjustment knob
2A. Right control lever (early models)	22. Control tower
3. Left control lever (later model)	23. Shaft
	24. E-ring
3A. Left control lever (early models)	25. Screw
	26. Washer
4. Front cover	27. Nut
5. Rear cover	28. Locknut
6. Handlebar	29. Nut
7. Parking brake knob	30. Stop bar
8. Washer	31. Washer
9. Parking brake rod	32. Spring
10. Washer	33. Bolt
11. Bolt	34. Spacer
12. Washer	35. Washer
13. Transaxle control rod	36. Spring
	37. Lockwasher
14. Spacer	38. Nut
15. Washer	39. Front shroud
16. Washer	40. Nut plate
17. Washer	41. Screw
18. Nut	

10. Detach the oil reservoirs (Fig. MF2-8) from the mainframe.

11. Support the carrier assembly with a jack.

12. Remove the carrier retaining bolts, then lower the carrier assembly out of the mainframe.

13. Refer to Fig. MF2-9 if disassembling carrier components.

14. Reverse the removal procedure to install the carrier assembly. Tighten the carrier retaining bolts to 75 ft.-lb. (102 N•m).

HYDROSTATIC TRANSAXLE

The machine is equipped with two hydrostatic transaxles. Each transaxle drives a rear wheel, which allows zero-turn-steering through independent operation of the transaxles.

LUBRICATION

Normal Operation

The oil level should be at maintained at the FULL mark on the oil reservoirs (Fig. MF2-8). If necessary, add oil to the tanks. Recommended oil is Simplicity Multipurpose Hydro Oil, Mobil DTE-26 or equivalent.

Refill and Bleed Transaxle

To refill the hydrostatic transaxle with oil and bleed air from the system after the transaxle has been serviced, proceed as follows.

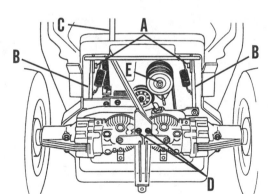

Fig. MF2-7–Drawing of transaxle carrier underside.

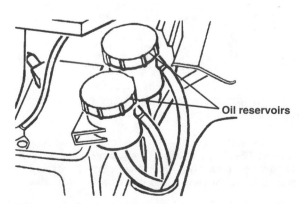

Fig. MF2-8–Drawing showing transaxle oil reservoirs used on later models. On early models, only a single hose connects the oil reservoir to the transaxle.

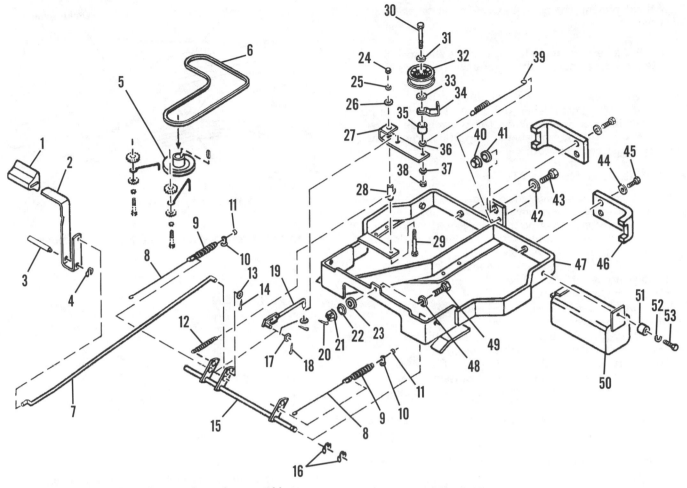

Fig. MF2-9–Exploded view of transaxle carrier assembly.

1. Pedal pad
2. Clutch/brake pedal
3. Shaft
4. Clip
5. Engine pulley
6. Drive belt
7. Clutch/brake rod
8. Brake rod
9. Spring
10. Trunnion pin
11. Locknut
12. Spring
13. Washer
14. Cotter pin
15. Pivot shaft
16. Clips
17. Washer
18. Cotter pin
19. Clutch rod
20. Cotter pin
21. Locknut
22. Belleville washer
23. Busing
24. Nut
25. Lockwasher
26. Washer
27. Idler arm
28. Pivot spacer
29. Bolt
30. Bolt
31. Washer
32. Pulley
33. Washer
34. Belt guide
35. Spacer
36. Spacer
37. Lockwasher
38. Nut
39. Spring
40. Locknut
41. Bushing
42. Washer
43. Bolt
44. Washer
45. Bolt
46. Weight (18 hp models)
47. Carrier
48. Washer
49. Bolt
50. Weight
51. Spacer
52. Lockwasher
53. Bolt

CAUTION: Be sure the machine is adequately supported and cannot move when performing the following procedure.

1. Fill the oil reservoirs to the full line.
2. Raise and support the rear of the machine so the rear wheels are off the ground.
3. Start the engine and run at idle speed for about three minutes.
4. Move the steering control levers from full forward to full reverse in 15-second intervals for three minutes.
5. Return the levers to neutral for five seconds.
6. Add oil to the oil reservoirs as needed.
7. Repeat the procedure until the oil level stabilizes.
8. Check operation. Repeat the procedure if the machine does not function normally.

NEUTRAL ADJUSTMENT

When released the control levers should return to the NEUTRAL position. Check, and if necessary, adjust the control lever positions as described in this section.

CAUTION: Be sure the unit is adequately supported and cannot move when performing the following procedure.

1. Position the machine on level ground with the parking brake disengaged.
2. Raise and support the rear of the machine.
3. Loosen the fastener (A–Fig. MF2-7) on each transaxle control rod so the rods can move freely.
4. Move each transaxle control rod (B) until it engages the positive neutral detent in the transaxle.

5. Without moving the rods, tighten the fastener (A) on each rod.

NOTE: Place a weight in the operator's seat to activate the seat switch so the engine will run.

6. Start the engine, then run it at half-throttle.
7. Operate each control lever and check the operation of the respective rear wheel. When the control lever is released, rear wheel rotation should stop. If not, repeat the neutral adjustment procedure.

REMOVAL AND INSTALLATION

The transaxles are mounted in a carrier. The following procedure describes the removal procedure for an individual transaxle. If servicing both transaxles, it may be advantageous to remove the carrier assembly with both transaxles as previously described.

1. Disconnect the engine spark plug lead.
2. Remove any weights attached to the carrier.
3. Remove the mower deck.
4. Raise and support the rear of the machine.
5. Remove the rear wheel.
6. Push down the clutch pedal and remove the transaxle drive belt from the transaxle drive pulley.
7. Disconnect the transaxle control rod (B–Fig. MF2-7).
8. Disconnect the brake rod from the transaxle lever.
9. Disconnect the transaxle oil reservoir hose and plug the openings.
10. Detach the pressure relief dump valve arm (D) from the transaxle.
11. Support the transaxle.
12. Remove the transaxle mounting bolts and remove the transaxle.
13. Install the transaxle by reversing the removal procedure. Note the following:
   a. Perform the neutral adjustment procedure as described in this section.
   b. Perform the brake adjustment procedure as described in this section.

OVERHAUL

All models are equipped with two Eaton Model 778 hydrostatic transaxles. Refer to the HYDROSTATIC TRANSAXLE REPAIR section for service information.

BRAKE ADJUSTMENT

Refer to Fig. MF2-10 when performing the following procedure.
1. Raise the seat.
2. Push the brake lever on the transaxle forward as far as possible.
3. Pull the brake rod to the rear.
4. Measure the gap between the nut on the brake rod and the pivot.
5. Rotate the nut so the gap is ⅛ inch (3.2 mm).
6. Repeat the procedure on the opposite transaxle.

ELECTRIC PTO CLUTCH

Early and late models have been equipped with different PTO clutch units. The clutch unit may be identified by the color of the electrical wires. The electrical wires connected to early units are colored brown and white/red. Late model

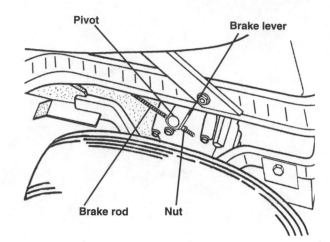

Fig. MF2-10–Refer to text for brake adjustment procedure.

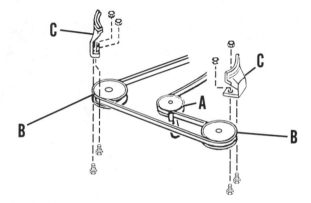

Fig. MF2-11–Drawing showing mower drive belt on 38-inch mower deck.

A. Idler pulley
B. Mower spindle pulley
C. Belt guide

clutches are connected to wires colored orange and black/white.

TESTING

Use the following procedure to locate the cause if the PTO clutch malfunctions.
1. Turn the ignition switch ON.
2. Actuate the PTO switch.
3. If the clutch does not engage, disconnect the wiring connector from the clutch.
4. Use a 12-volt test lamp to check wire continuity coming from the PTO switch.
5. If the lamp lights, the PTO is either defective or the wiring connector at the clutch field coil is faulty.
6. To check the PTO field coil, perform the following procedures:
   a. Clutch installed—Connect an ohmmeter to the clutch terminals. The ohmmeter should indicate a resistance of 6.59-7.29 ohms on early units or 2.74-3.02 ohms on late units.
   b. Clutch removed—Apply a 12-volt source to the clutch terminals. Hold a piece of steel next to the coil. The coil should attract the metal. There should be an audible click when the clutch engages.
7. If the PTO clutch fails the preceding tests, replace the coil or entire clutch assembly.

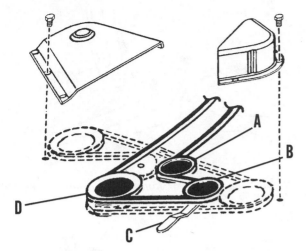

Fig. MF2-12–Drawing showing mower drive belt on 38-inch mower deck.

A. Idler pulley
B. Idler pulley

C. Lever
D. Center mower spindle pulley

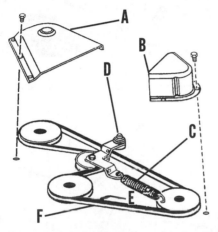

Fig. MF2-13–Mower spindle drive belt routing for 44-inch and 50-inch mower decks.

REMOVAL AND INSTALLATION

1. Remove the mower deck as described in this section.
2. Raise and support the rear of the machine.
3. Disconnect the PTO clutch electrical wire.
4. Remove the clutch retaining bolt (E–Fig. MF2-7).
5. Remove the clutch assembly from the crankshaft.
6. Reverse the removal procedure to reinstall the PTO clutch. Apply antiseize compound to the engine crankshaft. Tighten the clutch retaining bolt to 35 ft.-lb. (47.6 N•m).
7. If installing a new clutch or components, engage clutch several times after mower is installed to burnish the clutch surfaces.

MOWER DECK DRIVE BELT

REMOVAL AND INSTALLATION

38-inch Mower Deck

Refer to Fig. MF2-11 when performing the following procedure.
1. Remove the mower deck as described in this section.

2. Loosen the idler (A) bolt and relocate the belt guide.
3. Loosen and move the belt guides (C) adjacent to the mower spindle pulleys (B).
4. Remove the belt.
5. Install the belt, then move the belt guides into proper position.
6. Install the mower deck.

44-inch and 50-inch Mower Deck

Refer to Fig. MF2-12 when performing the following procedure.
1. Place the mower height control lever in the lowest position.
2. Move the moveable idler (B) away from the belt using the lever (C) attached to the idler.
3. Remove the belt from the PTO pulley, then remove the mower drive belt.
4. Reverse the removal procedure to install the belt.

MOWER SPINDLE DRIVE BELT REPLACEMENT (44-INCH AND 50-INCH MOWER DECK)

Refer to Fig. MF2-13 when performing the following procedure.
1. Remove the mower deck as described in this section.
2. Remove the mower deck drive belt as described in this section.
3. Remove the belt covers (A and B).
4. Detach the spring (C) from the idler arm.
5. Loosen the idler arm bolt (D).
6. Remove the spring (E).
7. Remove the spindle drive belt (F) from the deck pulleys.
8. Reverse the removal procedure to install the belt.

MOWER DECK

LUBRICATION

Lubricate the spindles and idler arm after every 25 hours of operation. Inject multipurpose grease through the grease fittings. One or two shots from a hand-held grease gun should be sufficient. Apply clean engine oil to the contact surface of all moving parts.

Lubricate more frequently when ambient temperature exceeds 85° F (39° C) or when operating in dusty conditions.

ADJUSTMENT

Before attempting any adjustment, the machine must be on level ground and the tires must be properly inflated. Disconnect the spark plug wire and tie it out of the way.

Side-To-Side Height

1. Position the mower deck in the highest cutting position.
2. Position the blades so they are perpendicular to the machine centerline.
3. Measure the height of the blade tips above the ground. Measurement should be within 1/8 inch (3.2 mm) from side-to-side. If the dimension is incorrect, proceed to Step 4.
4. Loosen the nut (Fig. MF2-14) adjacent to the eccentric.
5. Loosen the screw.
6. Adjust the blade side-to-side height by rotating the eccentric.
7. Retighten the nut and screw.
8. Recheck the blade height.

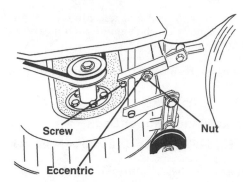

MF2-14–Mower side-to-side adjustment for all models

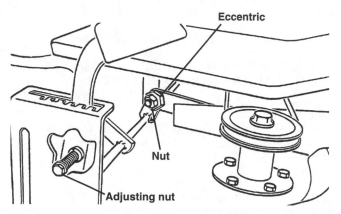

Fig. MF2-15–Refer to text for front-to-rear height adjustment procedure on 38-inch and 44-inch mower decks.

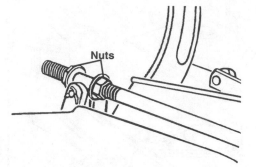

Fig. MF2-16–Refer to text for front-to-rear height adjustment procedure on 50-inch mower deck.

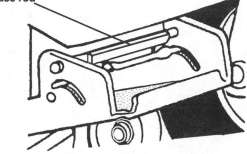

Fig. MF2-17–Pull the hitch release rod to detach the hitch.

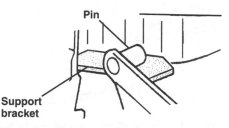

Fig. MF2-18–Mower hitch components.

Front-To-Rear Height

38-inch and 44-inch Mower Deck

1. Measure the distance from the ground to the blade from front to rear.
2A. 38-inch Mower Deck–The front of the blade should be level with the rear of the blade or up to 1/8 inch (3.2 mm) higher.
2B. 44-inch Mower Deck–The front of the blade should be 1/8-1/4 inch (3.2-6.4 mm) higher then the rear.
3. To adjust front-to-rear dimension, loosen the nut on the eccentric (Fig. MF2-15) and rotate the eccentric.
4. Tighten the nut and recheck the blade heights.
5. If the mower height control lever drops out of the quadrant, rotate the spring adjusting nut (Fig. MF2-15) clockwise to increase spring tension. Do not totally compress the spring.

50-inch Mower Deck

1. Measure the distance from the ground to the blade from front to rear.
2. The front of the blade should be 1/8-1/4 inch (3.2-6.4 mm) higher then the rear.
3. To adjust front-to-rear dimension, rotate the nuts on the height control rod (Fig. MF2-16).
4. Tighten the nuts against the bracket and recheck blade height.

REMOVAL AND INSTALLATION

38-inch and 44-inch Mower Deck

1. Turn the front wheels fully sideways.
2. Move the mower deck to the lowest position.

3. Push the idler arm lever and remove the mower belt from the PTO clutch pulley.
4. Pull out the hitch release rod (Fig, MF2-17) and disengage the front mower deck hitch.
5. Slide the mower deck forward so the support pins on each side disengage from the support brackets.
6. Remove the mower deck by moving it out from the right side of the machine.
7. Reverse the removal procedure to install the mower deck.

50-inch Mower Deck

1. Turn the front wheels fully sideways.
2. Set the mower height control to the middle height position.
3. Push the idler arm lever and remove the mower belt from the PTO clutch pulley.
4. Pull out the hitch release rod (Fig. MF2-19) and disengage the front mower deck hitch.
5. Remove the hitch rod pin (Fig. MF2-19), then remove the hitch rod and disengage the hitch from the mower deck.
6. Slide the mower deck forward so the support pins (Fig. MF2-18) on each side disengage from the support brackets.

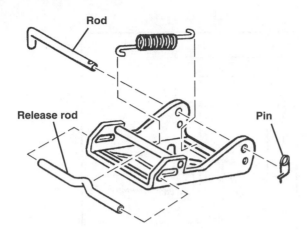

Fig. MF2-19–Remove the pin and rod to detach the hitch from the 50-inch mower deck.

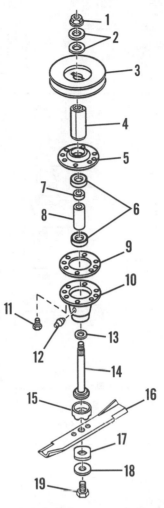

Fig. MF2-21–Exploded view of mower spindle assembly used on 44- and 50-inch decks..

1. Nut
2. Belleville washer
3. Pulley
4. Spacer
5. Upper spindle housing
6. Bearing
7. Spacer
8. Spacer
9. Foam gasket
10. Lower spindle housing
11. Bolt
12. Grease fitting
13. Washer
14. Spindle
15. Collar
16. Blade
17. Washer
18. Spring washer
19. Bolt

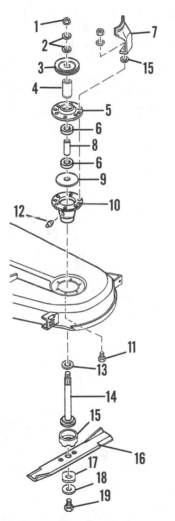

Fig. MF2-20–Exploded view of spindle assembly used on 38-inch mower decks.

1. Nut
2. Belleville washers
3. Pulley
4. Spacer
5. Spindle upper housing
6. Bearings
7. Belt stop
8. Spacer
9. Foam gasket
10. Spindle lower housing
11. Screw
12. Grease fitting
13. Washer
14. Spindle
15. Grass shield
16. Mower blade
17. Washer
18. Spring washer
19. Screw

7. Remove the mower deck by moving it out from the right side of the machine.

8. Reverse the removal procedure to install the mower deck.

MOWER DECK SPINDLE OVERHAUL

Refer to Fig. MF2-20 for 38-inch mower or Fig. MF2-21 for 44-inch and 50-inch mower decks when performing the following procedure.

1. Remove the mower deck as previously described.

2. Remove the blade.

3. Unscrew the spindle housing mounting screws and remove the spindle assembly.

4. Secure the spindle in a vise.

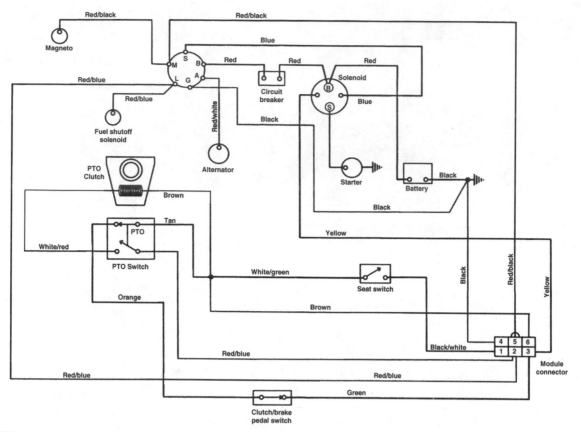

Fig. MF2-22–Wiring diagram for early models. Early models are equipped with an interlock module.

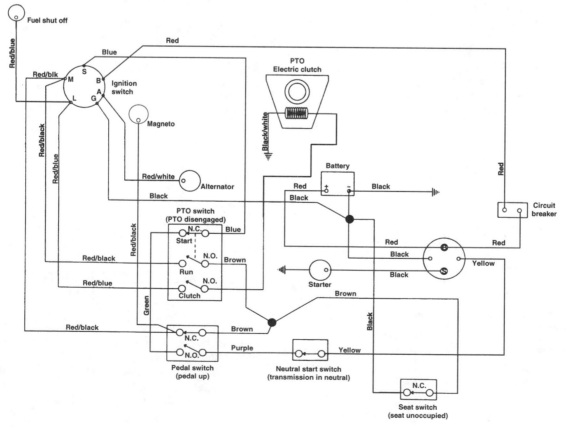

Fig. MF2-23–Wiring diagram for later models.

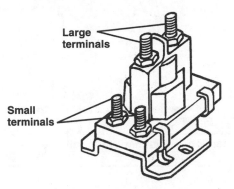

Fig. MF2-24–Refer to text for starter relay testing procedure.

5. Remove the nut (1), Belleville washers (2), pulley (3) and spacer (4).

6. Pry apart the spindle housings.

7. Disassemble the remainder of the spindle housing components.

8. Inspect the components for damage.

9. Install the washer (13) onto the shaft with the concave side toward the flange on the spindle.

10. Install the bearings and spacer (8) into the lower spindle housing.

11. Install the spindle into the lower spindle housing and bearings.

12. Install the foam gasket. If a foam gasket is not available, apply RTV sealant to mating surfaces of the upper and lower spindle housings.

13. Fill the lower spindle housing with multipurpose grease.

14. Install the remainder of the components while noting the following:

   a. Tighten the pulley retaining screw to 50-70 ft.-lb. (68-95 N•m).

   b. Maximum spindle end play is ⅛ inch (3.2 mm).

   c. Tighten the blade retaining screw to 45-55 ft.-lb. (61-74 N•m).

ELECTRICAL

Refer to Fig. MF2-22 or MF2-23 for a wiring schematic. Early models are equipped with a safety interlock module. The module grounds the engine ignition if the PTO is operated when the operator is out of the seat, or if the brake pedal is up when the operator is out of the seat.

Note the following points:

1. The transaxle must be in NEUTRAL, the mower must be disengaged and the operator must be in the seat for the engine to start.

2. The engine should stop if the transaxle is in gear or the mower is engaged and the operator leaves the seat.

STARTER RELAY TESTING

Note the location of the small and large terminals on the relay (Fig. MF2-24) when performing the following test.

1. Using an ohmmeter or continuity tester, check for continuity between the small terminals. The tester should indicate a continuity of less than 10 ohms.

2. Using an ohmmeter or continuity tester, check for continuity between the large terminals. The tester should indicate no continuity.

3. Connect a 12-volt battery to the small terminals.

4. The tester should indicate a continuity of less than 10 ohms between the large terminals.

INTERLOCK MODULE TESTING (EARLY MODELS)

The interlock module should be considered faulty only after all other wiring and devices have been tested or checked. An accurate testing procedure is not available. Replace the unit with a new or good unit and recheck operation.

MTD

Model	Make	Engine Model	Horsepower	Cutting Width, In.
560, 561	*	*	*	30

*Note the engine model number and refer to the engine service section in this manual for engine specifications.

FRONT WHEELS
REMOVAL AND INSTALLATION

The front wheels are equipped with replaceable sealed bearings. To remove the wheel and bearings, proceed as follows:
1. Remove hub cap (37–Fig. MT1-1).
2. Remove cotter pin (38).
3. Remove wheel with bearings.
4. Separate the bearings from the wheel.
5. Inspect the bearings for damage.
6. Inspect the wheel for rim and hub damage.
7. Reverse the removal steps to reassemble and install the wheel and bearings.

FRONT AXLE AND STEERING SYSTEM

TOE-IN SETTING

Adjustable tie rods are used on all models. Proceed as follows to check and adjust front wheel toe-in.
1. Be sure the tires are properly inflated.
2. Position the machine on a flat, smooth surface.
3. Position the front wheels in the straight-ahead position.
4. Measure the distance at spindle height between the center of the tires on the rear side.
5. Locate the same tire centerline points on the front side of the tires and measure the front distance.
6. The distance on the front side should be ⅛ inch (3.2 mm) shorter (toed-in) than the measured distance on the rear side.
7. To adjust the toe-in, detach the tie rod ends (36–Fig. MT1-1).
8. Rotate the tie rod ends to lengthen or shorten the tie rods as needed and reattach to the sector gear.
9. Recheck the toe-in measurement.

OVERHAUL

Refer to the exploded view in Fig. MT1-1 when performing the following procedure.
1. Remove the mower deck.
2. Remove the steering wheel cap, retaining nut and washer.
3. Lift off the steering wheel.
4. Model 560—Remove the sleeve (6–Fig. MT1-1).
5. Remove the cover (25).
6. Unscrew the nut at the lower end of the steering shaft and remove the gear (22).
7. Remove the bolt (13) and remove the steering shafts.
8. Disconnect the tie rods from the spindles.

9. Detach the steering support plate (19) and sector gear (24).
10. Support the frame and remove the front wheels.
11. Remove the cotter pins and washers, then the lower spindles (41) from the axle.
12. Detach the front axle support (18) from the frame.
13. Remove the axle main member (29).
14. Clean and inspect all parts and replace any that are damaged.
15. Reassemble by reversing the disassembly procedure while noting the following:
   a. Lubricate bushings and all pivot points with SAE 30 oil.
   b. Operate the steering through full range of movement and check for binding.
   c. Adjust the front wheel toe-in as previously described.

ENGINE

Refer to the appropriate engine section in this manual for tune-up specifications, engine overhaul procedures and engine maintenance.

REMOVAL AND INSTALLATION

1. Disconnect the spark plug wire and remove the engine cover.
2. Electric start models—Disconnect and remove the battery.
3. Disconnect any interfering electrical wires from the engine.
4. Disconnect the throttle cable from the engine.
5. Detach the exhaust pipe.
6. Remove the mower as outlined in the MOWER DECK section.
7. Remove the traction drive belt from the engine pulley as outlined in the TRACTION DRIVE CLUTCH AND DRIVE BELTS section.
8. Detach the pulleys from the engine crankshaft.
9. Remove the engine mounting fasteners.
10. Remove the engine.
11. Install the engine by reversing the removal procedure.

TRACTION DRIVE CLUTCH
AND DRIVE BELT

All models are equipped with a drive system using two drive belts and a variable speed pulley to transfer power from the engine to the transaxle. The upper primary drive belt connects the engine to the variable speed pulley

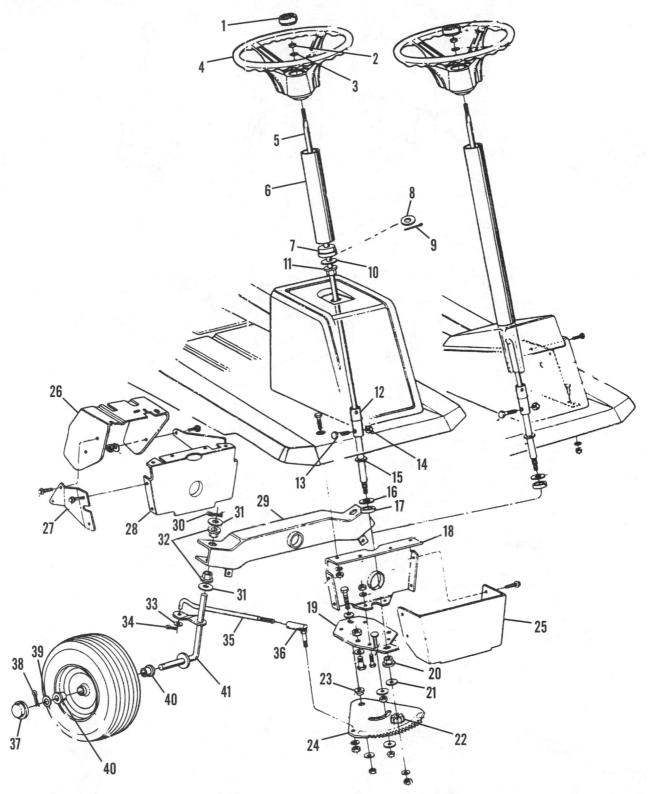

Fig. MT1-1–Exploded view of typical front axle and steering system. Model 561 steering shaft assembly is shown on right.

1. Cap
2. Nut
3. Washer
4. Steering wheel
5. Steering shaft
6. Steering column
7. Spacer
8. Washer
9. Cotter pin
10. Washer
11. Bushing

12. Coupler
13. Bolt
14. Nut
15. Lower shaft
16. Washer
17. Spacer
18. Axle support
19. Steering plate
20. Bushing
21. Washer

22. Steering gear
23. Bushing
24. Sector gear
25. Bracket
26. Bracket
27. Plate
28. Axle support
29. Axle main member
30. Cotter pin
31. Washer

32. Bushing
33. Washer
34. Cotter pin
35. Tie rod
36. Tie rod end
37. Hub cap
38. Cotter pin
39. Washer
40. Bushing
41. Spindle

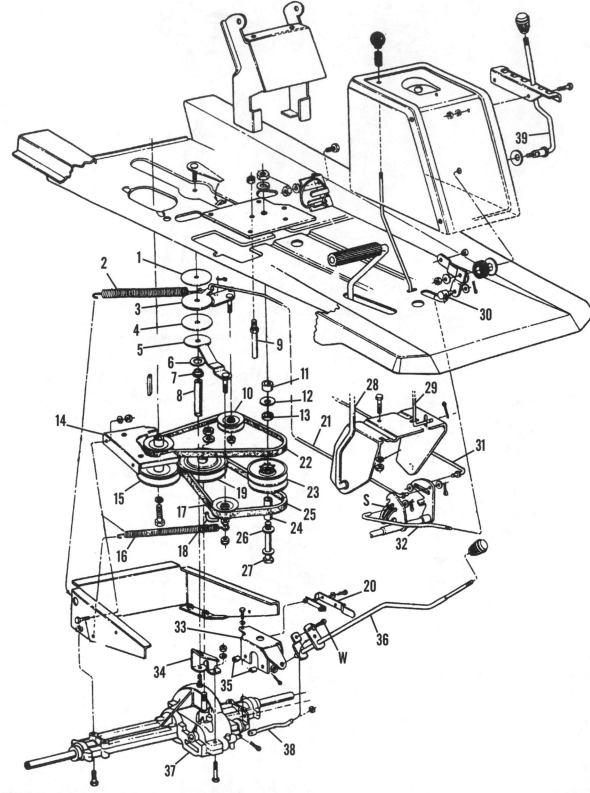

Fig. MT1-2–Exploded view of clutch and variable speed assembly.

1. Thrust washer
2. Spring
3. Idler arm
4. Thrust washer
5. Idler arm
6. Washer
7. Bushing
8. Torque rod
9. Belt guide
10. Idler
11. Spacer
12. Belleville washer
13. Thrust washer
14. Belt guard
15. Engine pulley
16. Spring
17. Idler
18. Belt guide
19. Transaxle pulley
20. Spring switch
21. Clutch rod
22. Upper drive belt
23. Variable speed pulley
24. Spacer
25. Lower drive belt
26. Thrust washer
27. Cap screw
28. Pedal rod
29. Park brake rod
30. Ferrule
31. Brake rod
32. Speed control rod
33. Bracket
34. Bracket
35. Spacers
36. Shift lever
37. Transaxle
38. Shift rod
39. Speed control lever

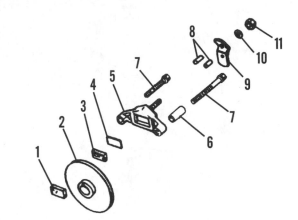

Fig. MT1-3–Exploded view of caliper brake.

1. Brake pad (inner)
2. Brake disc
3. Brake pad (outer)
4. Back up plate
5. Carrier
6. Spacer

7. Cap screws
8. Actuating pins
9. Cam lever
10. Washer
11. Adjusting nut

(23–Fig. MT1-2). The lower drive belt connects the variable speed pulley to the transaxle.

The diameters of the pulley grooves are determined by belt tension, which is regulated by the position of idlers (10 and 17). The idlers move when the speed control lever is operated. The ground speed changes when the pulley diameters change on the variable speed pulley.

ADJUSTMENT

The speed control lever and gear shift lever must be synchronized with the positions of the belt idlers. Proceed as follows.
1. Start and run the engine.
2. Be sure the gear shift lever is in NEUTRAL.
3. Place the speed control lever in the high speed position.
4. Release, then slowly depress fully the clutch/brake pedal and hold down the pedal.
5. Stop the engine, then release the pedal when the engine stops.
6. Move the speed control lever to the second speed position.
7. Detach the bent end of the lower speed control rod (32–Fig. MT1-2).
8. Turn the rod so the end of the rod will just enter the forward end of the slot (S).
9. Reattach the rod.
10. Move the gear shift lever to the neutral slot on the gear indicator panel.
11. If the machine does not move freely forward and backward thereby indicating the transaxle is in NEUTRAL, proceed as follows:
   a. Loosen the screw (W–Fig. MT1-2).
   b. Move the shift lever (36) as needed so the transaxle is in NEUTRAL and the shift lever is in the center of the neutral slot on the control panel.
   c. Retighten the screw (W) to 13 ft. lb. (18 N·m).

DRIVE BELTS

Lower Belt

1. Disconnect the spark plug wire and remove the battery.
2. Remove the mower as outlined in the MOWER DECK section.
3. Disconnect the idler spring (16–Fig. MT1-2).

4. Detach the torque rod bracket (34) from the transaxle and the torque rod (8).
5. Remove the bracket.
6. Separate the belt from the pulleys and remove the belt.
7. Install the lower belt by reversing the removal procedure.

Upper Belt

1. Remove the lower belt as described in the previous section.
2. Detach the engine pulley belt guide (14–Fig. MT1-2).
3. Unscrew the retaining nut and the remove the idler (10).
4. Remove the upper belt.
5. Install the upper belt by reversing the removal procedure. Be sure the hub side of idler (10) is next to the idler arm (3). Install the belt and idler simultaneously so the belt is inside the belt guide (9).

VARIABLE SPEED PULLEY OVERHAUL

The variable speed pulley is accessible after removing the drive belts as previously described. The variable speed pulley is available only as a unit assembly; individual components are not available.

TRANSAXLE

REMOVAL AND INSTALLATION

1. Remove the drive belts as previously described.
2. Disconnect the brake linkage and the shift linkage.
3. Support the rear of the machine.
4. Remove the transaxle mounting bolts.
5. Raise the rear of the machine and roll the transaxle assembly from under the machine.
6. Install by reversing the removal procedure.

OVERHAUL

All models are equipped with a MTD Model 618 transaxle. Refer to the TRANSAXLE REPAIR section for service information.

GROUND DRIVE BRAKE

ADJUSTMENT

Check brake operation by pushing the brake pedal and attempting to move the machine. If the brake does not hold the machine with the pedal fully depressed, adjust the brake.

To adjust the brake, release the brake and turn the nut (11–Fig. MT1-3) on the cam lever until the desired brake operation is obtained.

OVERHAUL

1. Disconnect the brake spring and the brake rod from the actuating lever.
2. Unbolt and remove the brake pad carrier (5–Fig. MT1-3).
3. Slide the brake disc off the transaxle shaft.
4. Remove the inner brake pad from the slot in the transaxle housing.
5. Clean and inspect all parts for damage.
6. Reassemble by reversing the disassembly procedure.

MOWER DRIVE BELT
REMOVAL AND INSTALLATION

Refer to Fig. MT1-4 when performing the following procedure.

1. Disconnect the spark plug wire.

2. Place the blade engagement lever in disengaged position.

3. Locate the outside engine belt guard at the machine's right rear side and remove one retaining bolt while loosening the other bolt.

4. Pivot the belt guard out and away from the engine pulley.

5. Disconnect the blade brake cable from the belt guard and remove the belt guard.

6. Disconnect the mower deck links and remove the belt guides on the deck.

7. Remove the belt.

8. Install the mower belt by reversing the removal procedure.

MOWER DECK

HEIGHT ADJUSTMENT

The front of the mower blade should be ¼-⅜ inch (6.4-9.5 mm) lower than the rear of the blade. The mower deck should be level from side to side. Adjust the hanger lengths as needed to obtain the desired height.

REMOVAL AND INSTALLATION

Refer to Fig. MT1-4 when performing the following procedure.

1. Disconnect the spark plug wire.

2. Move the mower deck to the lowest position.

3. Place the blade engagement lever in the disengaged position.

4. Locate the outside engine belt guard at the machine's right rear side and remove one retaining bolt while loosening the other bolt.

5. Pivot the belt guard out and away from the engine pulley.

6. Disconnect the blade brake cable from the belt guard and remove the belt guard.

7. Separate the drive belt from the engine pulley.

8. Disconnect the safety switch wire on models so equipped.

9. Detach the lift linkage from the mower deck and remove the mower deck.

10. Install by reversing the removal procedure. Adjust the blade brake cable as outlined in the BLADE BRAKE section.

BLADE BRAKE
ADJUSTMENT

1. Place the mower deck in the lowest position.

2. Move the blade engagement lever to the disengaged position.

3. Attach the cable (C–Fig. MT1-5) end to the rearmost hole in the bracket (B) so the cable has the least amount of slack but no tension.

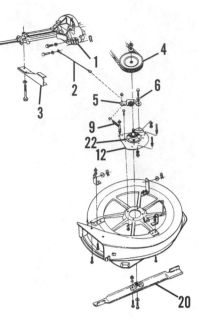

Fig. MT1-4–Exploded view of mower deck. Spindle components are available only as a unit assembly

1. Bracket
2. Blade brake cable
3. Bracket
4. Pulley
5. Blade brake
6. Spacer
9. Spring
12. Spindle mounting plate
20. Blade
22. Bearing & spindle assy.

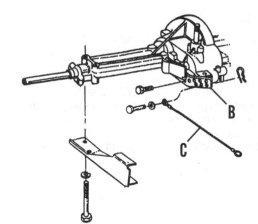

Fig. MT1-5–Attach end of blade brake cable as described in text.

MOWER SPINDLE
OVERHAUL

Refer to Fig. MT1-4 when performing the following procedure.

1. Remove the mower deck as previously described.

2. Remove the mower blade.

3. Unbolt and remove the spindle assembly. The spindle assembly is available only as a unit assembly.

ELECTRICAL

Refer to Figs. MT1-6 and MT1-7 for a typical wiring schematic. All switches must be in good operating condition for machine to operate properly.

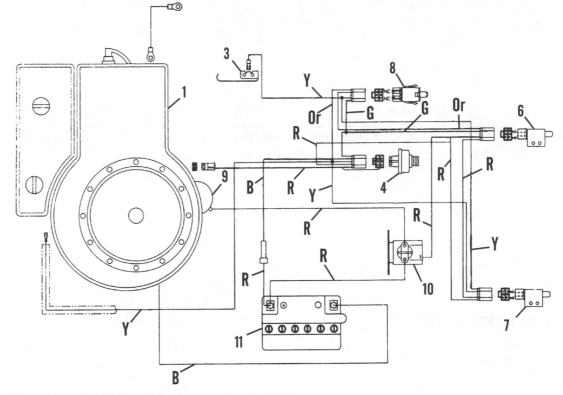

Fig. MT1-6–Typical wiring schematic models with electric start. Prior to 1997.

B. Black	Y. Yellow	6. Clutch switch	9. Starter
G. Green	1. Engine	7. Blade engagement switch	10. Starter solenoid
Or. Orange	3. Reverse gear switch	8. Seat switch	11. Battery
R. Red	4. Ignition switch		

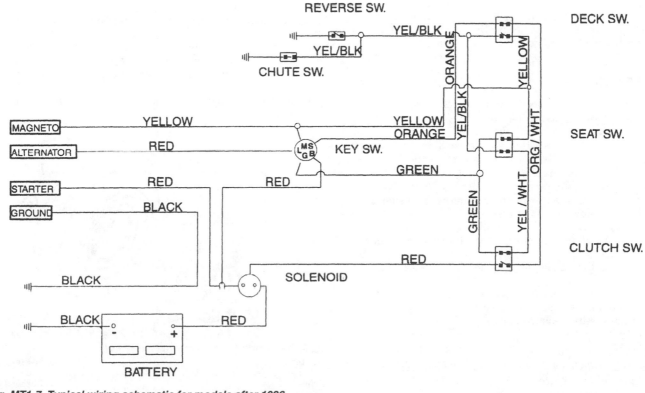

Fig. MT1-7–Typical wiring schematic for models after 1996.

MTD

Model	Make	Engine Model	Horsepower	Cutting Width, In.
320, 325 Yardbug	*	*	*	30

*Note the engine model number and refer to the engine service section in this manual for engine specifications.

FRONT WHEELS

MAINTENANCE

Lubricate the front wheel bearings annually by injecting multipurpose grease into the grease fitting in each wheel hub.

REMOVAL AND INSTALLATION

1. Remove the hub cap.
2. Remove the cotter pin (1–Fig. MT2-1).
3. Remove the wheel with bearings.
4. Separate the bearings from the wheel.
5. Inspect the bearings for damage.
6. Inspect the wheel for rim and hub damage.
7. Reverse the removal steps to reassemble and install the wheel and bearings. Lubricate the bearings after assembly.

FRONT AXLE AND STEERING SYSTEM

MAINTENANCE

Lubricate the steering shaft with light oil annually. After 25 hours of operation or annually, whichever occurs first, lubricate the steering gear teeth with a multipurpose grease.

TOE-IN SETTING

Adjustable tie rods are used on all models. Proceed as follows to check and adjust front wheel toe-in.
1. Be sure the tires are properly inflated.
2. Position the machine on a flat, smooth surface.
3. Position the front wheels in the straight-ahead position.
4. Measure the distance at the spindle height between the center of the tires on the rear side.
5. Locate the same tire centerline points on the front side of the tires and measure the front distance.
6. The distance on the front side should be should be $\frac{1}{16}$-$\frac{5}{16}$ inch (1.6-7.9 mm) shorter (toed-in) than the measured distance on the rear side.
7. To adjust the toe-in, detach the tie rod ends (23–Fig. MT2-2).
8. Rotate the tie rod ends to shorten or lengthen the tie rods as needed and reattach to the sector gear.
9. Recheck the toe-in measurement.

OVERHAUL

Refer to the exploded view in Fig. MT2-2 when performing the following procedure.
1. Remove the mower deck.

2. Remove the steering wheel cover, retaining bolt and washer.
3. Lift off the steering wheel.
4. Remove the control knobs on the steering column housing.
5. Remove the steering column housing.
6. Unscrew the nut (14–Fig. MT2-2) at the lower end of the steering shaft and remove the steering gear (12).
7. Remove the steering shafts.
8. Disconnect the tie rods from the spindles.
9. Detach the steering support plate (7) and sector gear (17).
10. Support the frame and remove the front wheels.
11. Remove the cotter pins and washers, then lower the spindles from the axle.
12. Remove the pedals and the pedal shaft.
13. Remove the cotter pin (24) and washer (25) from the pivot pin (5).
14. Remove the pivot pin.
15. Remove the axle main member (26).
16. Clean and inspect all parts and replace any that are damaged.
17. Reassemble by reversing the disassembly procedure while noting the following:
   a. Lubricate bushings and all pivot points with SAE 30 oil.
   b. Operate the steering through the full range of movement and check for binding.
   c. Adjust the front wheel toe-in as previously described.
   d. Install the Belleville washer (2) so the concave side is down.

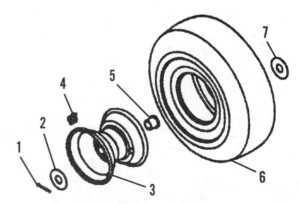

Fig. MT2-1–Exploded view of wheel assembly.

1. Cotter pin	5. Bearing
2. Washer	6. Tire
3. Wheel	7. Washer
4. Grease fitting	

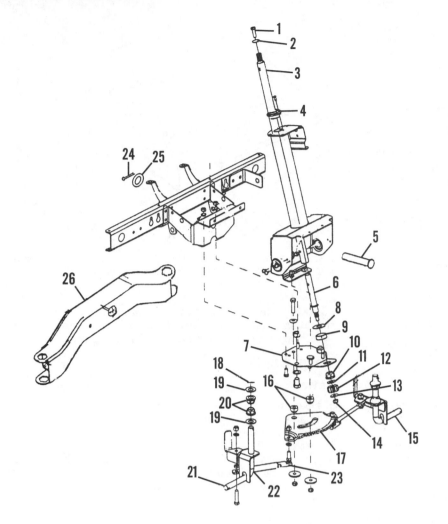

Fig. MT2-2–Exploded view of the front axle and steering system.

1. Bolt
2. Washer
3. Steering shaft
4. Bearing
5. Pin
6. Lower shaft
7. Steering plate
8. Washer
9. Spacer
10. Bushing
11. Washer
12. Steering gear
13. Washer
14. Nut
15. Spindle (left)
16. Spacer
17. Sector gear
18. Cotter pin
19. Washer
20. Bushing
21. Spindle (right)
22. Tie rod
23. Tie rod end
24. Cotter pin
25. Washer
26. Axle main member

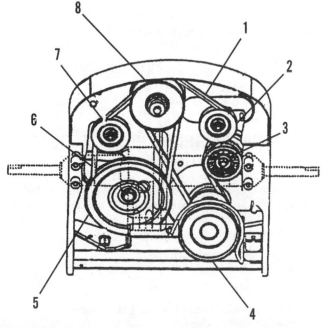

Fig. MT2-3–Drawing showing the location of the drive system components.

1. Upper drive belt	5. Transaxle pulley
2. Moveable idler pulley	6. Lower drive belt
3. Fixed idler pulley	7. Moveable idler pulley
4. Engine pulley	8. Variable speed pulley

ENGINE

Refer to the appropriate engine section in this manual for tune-up specifications, engine overhaul procedures and engine maintenance.

REMOVAL AND INSTALLATION

1. Raise the seat deck.
2. Disconnect the spark plug wire.
3. Disconnect and remove the battery.
4. Remove the fuel tank.
5. Disconnect any interfering electrical wires from the engine.
6. Disconnect the throttle cable from the engine.
7. Remove the upper traction drive belt as outlined in the TRACTION DRIVE CLUTCH AND DRIVE BELTS section.
8. Remove the engine mounting fasteners.
9. Remove the engine.
10. Install the engine by reversing the removal procedure.

TRACTION DRIVE CLUTCH AND DRIVE BELT

All models are equipped with a drive system using two drive belts and a variable speed pulley to transfer power from the engine to the transaxle. The upper primary drive belt (1–Fig. MT2-3) connects the engine to the variable speed pulley (8). The diameters of the pulley grooves are determined by belt tension, which is regulated by the position of idlers (2 and 7). The idlers move when the speed control lever is operated. The ground speed changes when the pulley diameters change on the variable speed pulley.

ADJUSTMENT

Static Adjustment

The following adjustment procedure may be used with the engine stopped if the unit is equipped with new drive belts.

1. Engage the parking brake.
2. Disconnect the spark plug wire.
3. Loosen the drive control cable jam nuts (A–Fig. MT2-4) on both sides of the frame support.
4. Rotate the jam nuts as needed so the length (B) of the exposed threads on the cable housing is $\frac{3}{4}$-$\frac{7}{8}$ inch (19-21 mm), measured from the face of the jam nut.
5. Tighten the jam nuts.
6. Disengage the parking brake.
7. Attach a spring scale to the speed control pedal and apply 10 pounds (44 N) of force to the pedal.
8. Lift the seat cover and locate the opening (A–Fig. MT2-5) on the rear frame.
9. Note the welded pin (B) on the idler arm.
10. With the spring scale pulling the pedal as described in Step 7, measure the distance from the welded pin on the idler arm to the outer edge of the frame opening. The distance should be 1.60-1.65 inches (40.6-41.9 mm).
11. If it is not possible to obtain the desired measurement, refer to the adjustment procedure described in the RUNNING ADJUSTMENT section.

Running Adjustment

The following adjustment procedure is performed while operating the transmission with the engine running.

> **CAUTION: Be sure the unit is adequately supported and cannot move when performing the following procedure.**

1. Raise and support the rear of the unit. The rear wheels must be off the ground.
2. Disengage the parking brake.
3. Loosen the jam nuts (A–Fig. MT2-4) on the drive control cable.
4. Apply a reference mark on the rear jam nut and the cable housing.
5. Rotate the rear jam nut one turn clockwise.

> **NOTE: Place a weight in the operator's seat to activate the seat switch so the engine will run.**

6. Start the engine and move the shift lever to the FORWARD position.
7. Be sure the speed control pedal is fully released.
8. Observe the rear tires. If there is no motion, repeat Steps 5 through 7. If the tires move, stop the engine and proceed to Step 9.
9. Rotate the rear jam nut two turns counterclockwise.
10. Hand tighten the front jam nut.
11. Tighten both jam nuts.
12. Start the engine and check operation by depressing and releasing the speed control pedal several times.

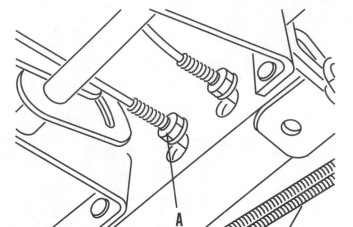

Fig. MT2-4–Loosen jam nut (A) on both sides of the frame support and adjust drive control cable as described in text.

13. If the wheels move with the pedal fully released, stop the engine. Rotate the rear jam nut one turn counterclockwise, retighten the jam nuts and recheck operation.

DRIVE BELTS

Lower Belt

1. Disconnect the spark plug wire.
2. Push the idler (7–Fig. MT2-3) inward.
3. Disengage the lower drive belt (6) from the idler and transaxle pulley.
4. Unscrew the variable pulley (8) retaining bolt, then lower the variable pulley sufficiently to remove the belt.
5. Install the lower belt by reversing the removal procedure.

Upper Belt

1. Remove the lower belt as described in the previous section.
2. Push the idler (2–Fig. MT2-3) inward.
3. Disengage the upper drive belt (1) from the idlers and variable pulley.
4. Unscrew the engine pulley (4) retaining bolt, then remove the pulley and upper drive belt.
5. Install the upper belt by reversing the removal procedure.

VARIABLE SPEED PULLEY OVERHAUL

The variable speed pulley (6–Fig. MT2-5) is accessible after removing the drive belts as previously described. The variable speed pulley is available only as a unit assembly; individual components are not available.

TRANSAXLE

REMOVAL AND INSTALLATION

1. Remove the drive belts as previously described.
2. Disconnect the brake linkage and the shift linkage.
3. Support the rear of the machine.
4. Remove the transaxle mounting bolts.
5. Raise the rear of the machine and roll the transaxle assembly from under the machine.
6. Install by reversing removal procedure.

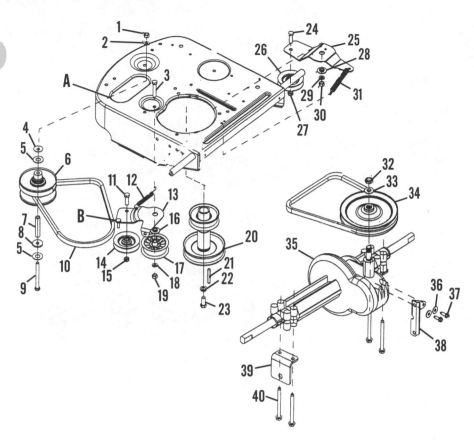

Fig. MT2-5–Exploded view of drive system components.

1. Nut	21. Key
2. Lockwasher	22. Lockwasher
3. Bolt	23. Bolt
4. Bell washer	24. Bolt
5. Thrust washer	25. Idler arm
6. Variable drive pulley	26. Idler
7. Spacer	27. Locknut
8. Washer	28. Shoulder spacer
9. Bolt	29. Lockwasher
10. Drive belt	30. Nut
11. Bolt	31. Spring
12. Spring	32. Nut
13. Idler arm	33. Belleville washer
14. Idler	34. Transaxle pulley
15. Locknut	35. Transaxle
16. Shoulder spacer	36. Washer
17. Idler	37. Bolt
18. Lockwasher	38. Bracket
19. Nut	39. Plate
20. Engine pulley	40. Bolts

Fig. MT2-6–Loosen jam nut (A) on both sides of the frame support and adjust brake control cable as described in text.

OVERHAUL

All models are equipped with a MTD Model 618 transaxle. Refer to the TRANSAXLE REPAIR section for service information.

GROUND DRIVE BRAKE

ADJUSTMENT

Check brake operation by pushing the brake pedal and attempting to move the machine. If the brake does not hold the machine with the pedal fully depressed, adjust the brake.

1. Disconnect the spark plug wire.

2. Be sure the parking brake is disengaged.

3. Loosen the brake control cable jam nuts (A–Fig. MT2-6) on both sides of the frame support.

4. Rotate the jam nuts as needed so the brake operates properly.

5. Tighten the jam nuts.

6. If proper brake operation cannot be obtained by adjusting the jam nuts, brake adjustment on the transaxle is necessary. Proceed to Step 7.

7. Loosen the control cable jam nuts (A–Fig. MT2-6) and position them so the maximum number of threads (B) on the control cable housing are exposed.

8. Tighten the jam nuts.

9. Insert a 0.011-inch (.28 mm) feeler gauge between the brake pad (9–Fig. MT2-7) and the brake disc (10).

10. Rotate the brake adjusting nut (2) so there is a slight pull when removing the feeler gauge.

11. Check the brake operation.

OVERHAUL

1. Disconnect the brake control cable from the actuating lever.

2. Unbolt and remove the brake pad carrier (7–Fig. MT2-7).

3. Slide the brake disc off the transaxle shaft.

4. Remove the inner brake pad from the slot in the transaxle housing.

5. Clean and inspect all parts for damage.

6. Reassemble by reversing the disassembly procedure.

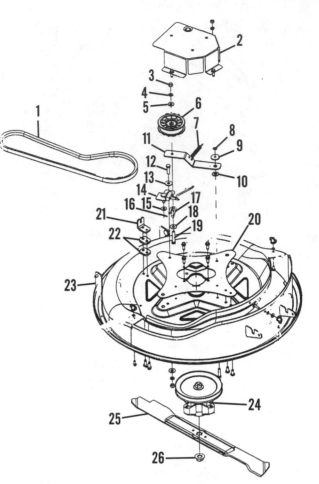

Fig. MT2-7–Exploded view of caliper brake.

1. Bolts	6. Pin
2. Adjusting nut	7. Carrier
3. Bracket	8. Backup plate
4. Washer	9. Brake pads
5. Cam lever	10. Brake disc

BLADE ENGAGEMENT PEDAL

Depressing the blade engagement pedal operates the mower deck blade. Releasing the pedal causes the blade brake to stop blade rotation.

ADJUSTMENT

Blade engagement should begin when the pedal is depressed ¾ inch as measured at the lever base.
1. Place the mower deck in the lowest height position.
2. Remove the grass catcher.
3. Disconnect the spark plug wire.
4. Depress the blade engagement pedal so the pedal lever travels ¾ inch (19 mm) as measured from the end of the lever slot in the floor.
5. Attempt to pull the mower drive belt through the blade pulley. If the belt slips, proceed to Step 6.
6. Release the blade engagement pedal.
7. Adjust the position of the blade control cable by rotating the jam nuts on either side of the cable bracket (21–Fig. MT2-8) on the mower deck.
8. Check belt deflection with the blade control pedal fully depressed. Belt deflection should not exceed ½ inch (13 mm), otherwise, replace the belt.

MOWER DRIVE BELT
REMOVAL AND INSTALLATION

1. Disconnect the spark plug wire.
2. Remove the grasscatcher.
3. Place the mower deck in the lowest height position.
4. At the rear of the mower deck, remove the belt guard.
5. Move the belt guard out of the way.
6. Remove the belt cover on the mower deck.
7. Remove the belt guard around the engine pulley.
8. Loosen the idler pulley retaining nut.
9. Remove the belt.
10. Install the mower belt by reversing the removal procedure.

MOWER DECK

HEIGHT ADJUSTMENT

The front of the mower blade should be ¼-⅜ inch (6.4-9.5 mm) lower than the rear of the blade. The mower deck

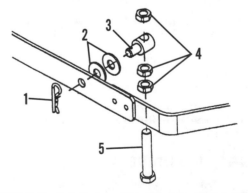

Fig. MT2-8–Exploded view of mower deck.

1. Drive belt	14. Blade brake
2. Cover	15. Washer
3. Nut	16. Cotter pin
4. Lockwasher	17. Belt guide
5. Washer	18. Washer
6. Idler	19. Bolt
7. Spring	20. Plate
8. Speed nut	21. Cable bracket
9. Washer	22. Spacer
10. Bushing	23. Mower deck
11. Idler arm	24. Spindle assembly
12. Bolt	25. Blade
13. Washer	26. Nut

Fig. MT2-9–Exploded view of front mower deck hanger assembly. Rotate the nuts on the bolt to adjust deck height. Refer to text.

1. Hairpin	4. Nuts
2. Washer	5. Bolt
3. Ferrule	

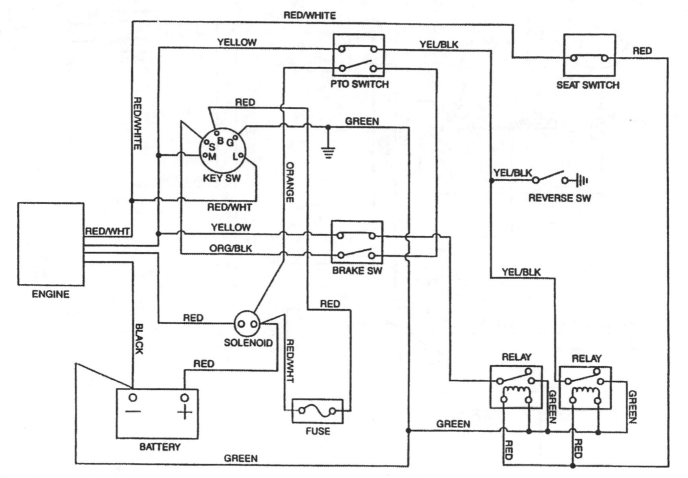

Fig. MT2-10–Wiring schematic of early models. Note presence of relays and two-wire seat switch.

should be level from side to side. Adjust the hanger lengths by rotating the nuts (4–Fig. MT2-9) as needed to obtain the desired height.

REMOVAL AND INSTALLATION

1. Remove the mower drive belt as previously described.
2. Move the mower deck to the lowest position.
3. Detach the blade brake cable from the mower deck bracket and the brake arm.
4. Remove the hairpins and washers from the hanger pins.
5. Detach the mower deck from the hanger pins and remove the mower deck.
6. Reinstall by reversing the removal procedure. Adjust the blade brake cable as outlined in the BLADE BRAKE section.

BLADE BRAKE

The mower is equipped with a blade brake (14–Fig. MT2-8) that stops the blade pulley when the blade control

pedal is released. Perform the blade control pedal adjustment procedure as previously described.

MOWER SPINDLE OVERHAUL

Refer to Fig. MT2-8 when performing the following procedure.
1. Remove the mower deck as previously described.
2. Remove the mower blade.
3. Remove the mower drive pulley.
4. Unbolt and remove the spindle assembly (24). The spindle assembly is available only as a unit assembly.

ELECTRICAL

Refer to Figs. MT2-10 and MT2-11 for a typical wiring schematic. All switches must be in good operating condition for the machine to operate properly.

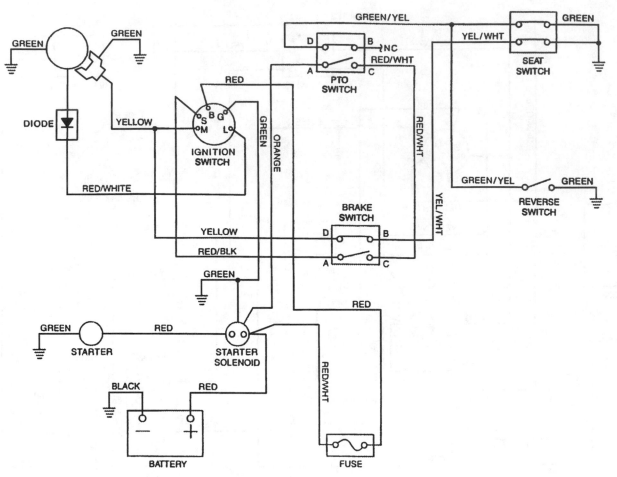

Fig. MT2-11–Wiring schematic of later models. Note absence of relays and use of a four-wire seat switch.

SIMPLICITY
CORONET SERIES

Model	Make	Engine Model	Horsepower
1692129	B&S	*	12.5
1692130	Tecumseh	*	12.5
1692168	*	*	8.5
1692380	*	*	8.5
1692382	B&S	*	12.5
1692385	B&S	*	13
1692387	*	*	8.5
1692389	B&S	*	12.5
1692392	B&S	*	13
1692515	Tecumseh	*	12.5
1692517	*	*	12
1692748	B&S	*	11
1692750	B&S	*	13
1693030	B&S	*	11
1693034	B&S	*	13
1693038	Kohler	*	14

*Note the engine model number and refer to the engine service section in this manual for engine specifications.

FRONT WHEELS

LUBRICATION

Each front wheel hub is equipped with a grease fitting. Front wheels should be injected with multipurpose grease after every 25 hours of operation. Lubricate the front wheels more frequently when ambient temperature exceeds 85° F (30° C) or when operating in dusty conditions.

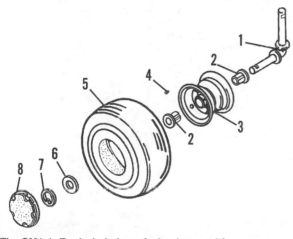

Fig. SM1-1–Exploded view of wheel assembly.

1. Spindle
2. Bushing
3. Wheel
4. Grease fitting
5. Tire
6. Washer
7. Snap ring
8. Wheel cover

REMOVAL AND INSTALLATION

The front wheels are equipped with replaceable bushings. To remove the wheel and bushings, proceed as follows:
1. Remove the wheel cover (8–Fig. SM1-1).
2. Remove the retaining ring (7).
3. Remove the wheel with the bushings.
4. Separate the bushings from the wheel.
5. Inspect the bushings and axle for damage.
6. Inspect the wheel for rim and hub damage.
7. Reverse the removal steps to reassemble and install the wheel and bushings. Lubricate the bushings after assembly.

FRONT SPINDLE

LUBRICATION

Lubricate the front wheel spindles after every 25 hours of operation. Inject multipurpose grease into the front axle main member through the grease fitting (A–Fig. SM1-2) at each end.

OVERHAUL

1. Raise and support the side to be serviced.
2. Remove the wheel and tire.
3. Disconnect the tie rod end and drag link end, if necessary, from the spindle.
4. Detach the snap ring (B–Fig. SM1-2) securing the top of the spindle, then withdraw the spindle from the axle.

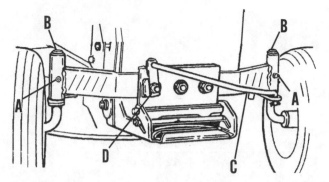

Fig. SM1-2–Inject grease into front axle main member through grease fittings (A). The spindles are retained by snap rings (B).

5. Reverse the removal steps to install the front spindle. Lubricate the spindle after assembly.

FRONT AXLE MAIN MEMBER REMOVAL AND INSTALLATION

1. Disconnect the spark plug cable.
2. Remove the mower deck, then raise and support the front of the machine.
3. Remove the steering link (C–Fig. SM1-2).
4. Remove the spindles.
5. While noting the parts arrangement for the steering pivot (D), remove the three bolts securing the axle main member.
6. Remove the axle main member.
7. Install the axle main member by reversing the removal procedure.

STEERING SECTOR AND SHAFT

LUBRICATION

Lubricate the steering gears with multipurpose grease after 25 hours of operation, or more frequently when operated in a dusty environment.

ADJUSTMENT

Adjust steering gear backlash by loosening the bolts (Fig. SM1-3) and moving the steering shaft. Be sure the steering gears move smoothly without binding after adjustment.

OVERHAUL.

1. Remove the mower deck as described in this section.
2. Remove the steering wheel cap (1–Fig. SM1-4).
3. Drive out the roll pin (3).
4. Remove the steering wheel.
5. Remove the shaft cover (4).
6. Remove the shaft retaining pin (5).
7. Remove the washers (6).
8. Raise and support the front of the machine.
9. Remove the steering shaft from the bottom of the machine.
10. Detach the tie rods from the sector gear.
11. Remove the sector gear pivot bolt (27) and remove the sector gear.
12. Inspect components and replace if damaged.
13. Reassemble steering components by reversing the disassembly procedure. Check steering gear backlash after

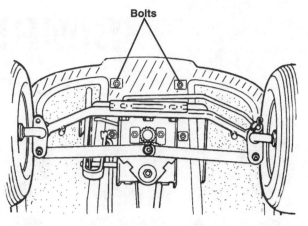

Bolts

Fig. SM1-3–Adjust gear backlash by loosening the bolts and moving the steering shaft. Refer to text.

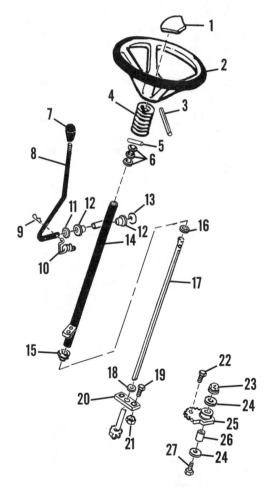

Fig. SM1-4–Exploded view of steering shaft assembly.

1. Cap	15. Bushing
2. Steering wheel	16. Waher
3. Pin	17. Steering shaft
4. Cover	18. Washer
5. Pin	19. Bolt
6. Washer	20. Plate
7. Knob	21. Nut
8. Shift lever	22. Bolt
9. Pin	23. Nut
10. Spring	24. Washer
11. Washer	25. Sector gear
12. Bushings	26. Spacer
13. Washer	27. Bolt
14. Shift tube	

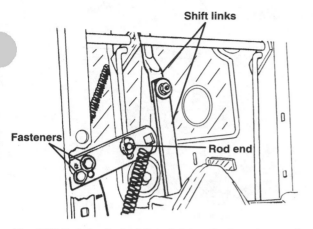

Fig. SM1-5–Refer to text for clutch adjustment procedure on models equipped with a gear transaxle.

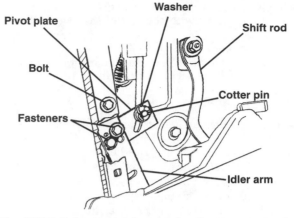

Fig. SM1-7–Refer to text for clutch adjustment procedure on models equipped with a hydrostatic transaxle.

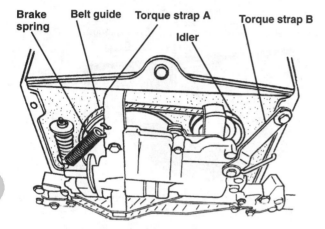

Fig. SM1-6–Refer to text for drive belt removal procedure on models equipped with a gear transaxle.

installation and if necessary, adjust as previously described.

ENGINE

Refer to the appropriate engine section in this manual for tune-up specifications, engine overhaul procedures and engine maintenance.

REMOVAL AND INSTALLATION

1. Remove the engine cover and disconnect the spark plug wire.

2. Electric start models–Disconnect and remove battery.

3. Disconnect any interfering electrical wires from the engine.

4. Disconnect the throttle cable from the engine.

5. Remove the mower as outlined in the MOWER DECK section.

6. Remove the traction drive belt from the engine pulley.

7. Detach the pulley from the engine crankshaft.

8. Remove the engine mounting fasteners.

9. Remove the engine.

10. Install the engine by reversing the removal procedure.

TRACTION DRIVE CLUTCH AND DRIVE BELT

MODELS WITH GEAR TRANSAXLE

Adjustment

If the rear wheels continue to drive the machine when the clutch/brake pedal is depressed, adjust the clutch idler position as follows.

1. Disconnect the spark plug wire.
2. Loosen the fasteners on the idler arm (Fig. SM1-5).
3. Engage the parking brake.
4. Move the idler arm against spring tension and retighten the fasteners.
5. Check operation. If the clutch rod end is against the slot end in the idler arm and belt slippage occurs, replace the belt. Also inspect components for excessive wear that may allow belt slippage.

Removal and Installation

Refer to Fig. SM1-6 when performing the following procedure.

1. Remove the mower deck as described in this section.
2. Raise and support the rear of the machine.
3. Detach the brake spring.
4. Remove the torque strap (A).
5. Remove the belt guide.
6. Remove the torque strap (B).
7. Loosen transaxle mounting bolts.
8. Loosen the idler axle sufficiently so the belt can pass between the idler and belt guide.
9. Disconnect the shift links (Fig. SM1-5).
10. Disconnect the PTO clutch electrical wire.
11. Remove the drive belt.
12. Reverse the removal procedure to install the drive belt. Position the idler belt guide so it is $\frac{1}{8}$ inch (3.2 mm) from the idler. Perform the transaxle neutral adjustment procedure described in this section.

MODELS WITH HYDROSTATIC TRANSAXLE

Adjustment

If the rear wheels continue to drive the machine when the clutch/brake pedal is depressed, adjust the clutch idler position as follows.

1. Disconnect the spark plug wire.
2. Loosen the fasteners on the pivot plate (Fig. SM1-7).

3. Move the pivot plate so the forward edge of the washer on the control rod aligns with the end of the slot in the plate.

4. Tighten the fasteners.

5. Check operation. The drive belt should not rotate when the parking brake is engaged and the engine is running.

Removal and Installation

Refer to Fig. SM1-8 when performing the following procedure.

1. Remove the mower deck as described in this section.

2. Raise and support the rear of the machine.

3. Loosen the fasteners retaining the belt guides.

4. Loosen the fasteners retaining torque strap (A).

5. Loosen the fasteners retaining torque strap (B).

6. Loosen the transaxle mounting bolts.

7. Detach the idler spring from the frame.

8. Refer to Fig. SM1-7. Remove the cotter pin and washer from the control rod end, then separate the rod from the pivot plate.

9. Remove the idler arm attaching bolt (Fig. SM1-7) and spacer. The idler may now rest against the belt.

10. Note the position of the belt guide on the idler.

11. Disconnect the upper and lower shift rods.

12. Loosen the transaxle control link (Fig. SM1-8).

13. Disconnect the PTO clutch electrical wire.

14. Remove the drive belt.

15. Reverse the removal procedure to install the drive belt. Perform the transaxle neutral adjustment and the return-to-neutral adjustment procedures described in this section.

GROUND DRIVE BRAKE ADJUSTMENT

MODELS WITH GEAR TRANSAXLE

Refer to Fig. SM1-9 when performing the following procedure.

1. Remove the left rear wheel.

2. Push the brake lever forward and measure the gap between the lever and stop. The gap should be ⅛ inch (3.2 mm).

3. Rotate nut (A) to obtain the specified gap.

4. Engage the parking brake. Measure the spring length. Specified spring length is $2\frac{9}{16}$ to $2\frac{5}{8}$ inches (65-66.6 mm).

5. Rotate nut (B) to obtain the specified spring length.

MODELS WITH HYDROSTATIC TRANSAXLE

These models are equipped with a Hydro-Gear hydrostatic transaxle equipped with brake discs inside the transaxle housing. Check for correct brake adjustment using the following procedure.

1. Insert a feeler gauge between two brake discs through an opening on the underside of the housing (Fig. SM1-10).

2. Measure the gap between the brake discs. The gap should be 0.025-0.030 inch (0.64-0.76 mm).

3. Rotate the brake lever retaining nut (A) to obtain the specified gap.

4. Engage the parking brake. Measure the spring length. Specified spring length is $2\frac{11}{16}$ to $2\frac{23}{32}$ inches (68.3-69.1 mm).

5. Rotate nut (B) to obtain the specified spring length.

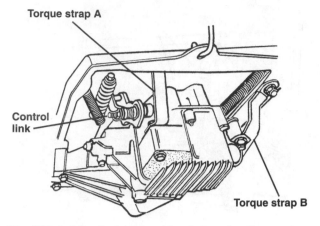

Fig. SM1-8–Refer to text for drive belt removal procedure on models equipped with a hydrostatic transaxle.

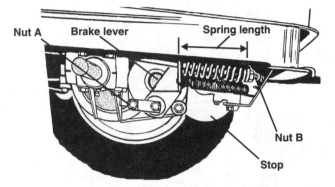

Fig. SM1-9–Rotate nut A to adjust brake on models equipped with a gear transaxle.

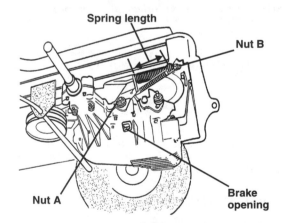

Fig. SM1-10–Insert a feeler gauge through the brake opening in the transaxle housing to measure brake disc clearance. Refer to text.

TRANSAXLE

MODELS WITH GEAR TRANSAXLE

Lubrication

The outer ends of the transaxle are equipped with grease fittings (Fig. SM1-11). Inject multipurpose grease into the grease fittings after every 25 hours of operation. One or two shots from a hand-held grease gun should be suffi-

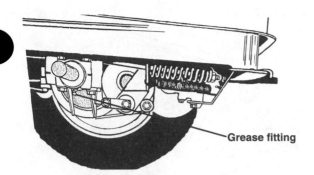

Fig. SM1-11–On gear transaxle, inject grease into fittings on each end of axle housing.

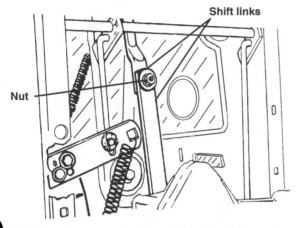

Fig. SM1-12–Loosen nut and reposition shift links as described in text for neutral adjustment.

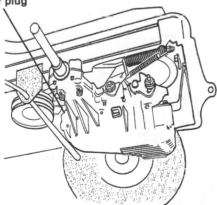

Fig. SM1-13–Drawing showing location of breather plug on hydrostatic transaxle.

cient. Refer to the repair section for internal lubrication information.

Neutral Adjustment

Adjust the shift linkage so neutral positions in the transaxle and at shift lever are synchronized. Refer to Fig. SM1-12 when performing the following procedure.
1. Raise and support the rear of the machine.
2. Move the shift lever so the transaxle is in NEUTRAL.
3. Loosen the nut securing the shift links.

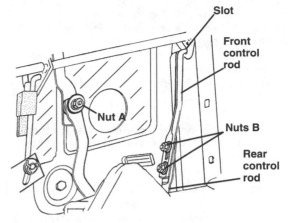

Fig. SM1-14–Refer to text for neutral adjustment procedure on models equipped with a hydrostatic transaxle.

4. Move the shift control lever to the neutral position indicated on the control panel.
5. Retighten the nut to 17 ft.-lb. (23 N•m) and check adjustment.

Removal and Installation

To remove the transaxle, proceed as follows.
1. Remove the mower deck.
2. Raise and support the rear of the machine.
3. Remove the rear wheels.
4. Remove the drive belt.
5. Disconnect the shift linkage.
6. Disconnect the brake link.
7. Disconnect neutral switch wire from switch on transaxle.
8. Detach the torque straps (Fig. SM1-6).
9. Support the transaxle.
10. Remove the transaxle mounting bolts.
11. Remove the transaxle.
12. Install the transaxle by reversing the removal procedure.

Overhaul

Models equipped with a gear transaxle use a Peerless 915 transaxle. Refer to the repair section in this manual for overhaul information.

MODELS WITH HYDROSTATIC TRANSAXLE

Lubrication

Recommended oil is SAE 20W50 with an API rating of SG. To check or fill the transaxle, clean the area around the breather plug (Fig. SM1-13), then unscrew the breather plug. To check the oil level, measure from the boss surface to the oil. The oil level should be 1.75-2.00 inches (44-51 mm).

Neutral Adjustment

Adjust the shift linkage so neutral positions in transaxle and at shift lever are synchronized. Refer to Fig. SM1-14 when performing the following procedure.

NOTE: Operate the machine in Step 1 to verify that the transaxle is in NEUTRAL.

1. Move the shift lever so the transaxle is in NEUTRAL.

2. Raise and support the rear of the machine.

3. Loosen nut (A) securing the shift rods together so the rods can move independently.

4. Move the shift control lever to the neutral position indicated on the control panel.

5. Retighten the nut to 17 ft.-lb. (23 N•m) and check adjustment.

> **NOTE: Be sure the forward control rod is not binding in the frame slot before proceeding. If needed, lubricate the rod.**

6. Loosen the nuts (B) securing the front and rear control rods so the rods can move independently.

7. Move the speed control lever to the full forward position.

8. Push the forward control rod fully back until it contacts the rear of the slot.

9. Tighten the nuts (B).

10. Check operation.

Purge Air In Transaxle

Air trapped inside the transaxle during overhaul or service must be purged for proper operation and to prevent internal damage.

1. Position the machine on a level surface.

2. Pull the pressure release lever located under the right, rear frame corner back to the PUSH position.

3. Run the engine at slow idle speed.

4. Move the speed control lever alternately to the full forward and full reverse positions three times. Keep the lever in the forward or reverse position for five seconds each time.

5. Move the speed control lever to NEUTRAL.

6. Push the pressure release lever forward to DRIVE.

7. Run the engine at full speed and operate the speed control lever so the machine moves forward and reverse alternately at least five feet in each direction. The speed control lever must be at the maximum speed position. Operate the machine three times in each direction.

8. Repeat the purging procedure as needed until the machine operates smoothly.

Removal and Installation

To remove the transaxle, proceed as follows.

1. Remove the mower deck.

2. Raise and support the rear of the machine.

3. Remove the rear wheels.

4. Remove the drive belt.

5. Disconnect the brake link and detach the brake return spring.

6. Disconnect the shift linkage.

7. Detach the torque straps (Fig. SM1-8).

8. Support the transaxle.

9. Remove the transaxle mounting bolts.

10. Remove the transaxle.

11. Install the transaxle by reversing the removal procedure.

Overhaul

Models equipped with a hydrostatic transaxle use a Hydro-Gear 310-0500 transaxle. Refer to the repair section in this manual for overhaul information.

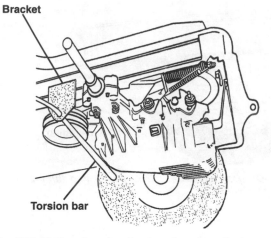

Fig. SM1-15–Drawing showing location of torsion bar and brackets.

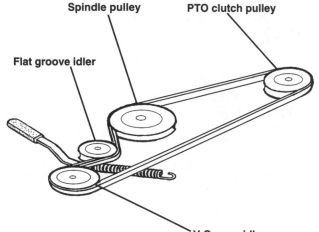

Fig. SM1-16–Mower belt rouitng diagram for 30-inch mower deck.

ELECTRIC PTO CLUTCH

TESTING

Use the following procedure to locate the cause if the PTO clutch malfunctions.

1. Turn the ignition switch ON.

2. Actuate the PTO switch.

3. If the clutch does not engage, disconnect the wiring connector at the clutch.

4. Use a 12-volt test lamp to check continuity of the wire coming from the PTO switch.

5. If the lamp lights, the PTO is either defective or the wiring connector at the clutch field coil is faulty.

6. To check the PTO field coil, perform the following procedures:

   a. Clutch installed–Connect an ohmmeter to the clutch terminals. The ohmmeter should indicate a resistance of 6.59-7.29 ohms.

   b. Clutch removed–Apply a 12-volt source to the clutch terminals. Hold a piece of steel next to coil. The coil should attract the metal. There should be an audible click when the clutch engages.

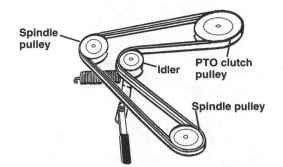

Fig. SM1-17–Mower belt routing diagram for 34-inch mower deck.

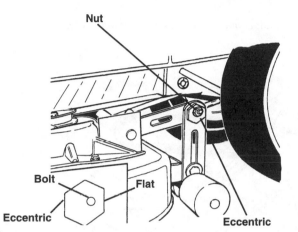

Fig. SM1-18–Rotate the eccentric as described in text to adjust mower side-to-side height. The left side is shown.

7. If the PTO clutch fails the preceding tests, replace the coil or entire clutch assembly.

REMOVAL AND INSTALLATION

1. Remove the mower deck as described in this section.
2. Raise and support the rear of the machine.
3. Remove the torsion bar bracket and torsion bar (Fig. SM1-15).
4. Disconnect the PTO clutch electrical wire.
5. Hold the spacer below the clutch by placing a wrench on the two flats on the spacer.
6. Remove the clutch retaining bolts.
7. Remove the clutch assembly from the crankshaft.
8. Reverse the removal procedure to install the PTO clutch. Apply antisieze compound to the engine crankshaft. Tighten the clutch retaining bolts to 45-50 ft.-lb. (63-68 N•m).
9. If installing a new clutch or components, run the engine at full speed and engage the clutch several times after the mower is installed to burnish the clutch surfaces.

MOWER DRIVE BELT REMOVAL AND INSTALLATION

30-inch Mower Deck

Refer to Fig. SM1-16 when performing the following procedure.
1. Place the mower height control lever in the lowest position.

2. Move the moveable idler away from the belt and remove the belt from the PTO pulley and mower spindle pulley.
3. Remove the mower drive belt.
4. Reverse the removal procedure to install the belt.

34-inch Mower Deck

Refer to Fig. SM1-17 when performing the following procedure.
1. Place the mower height control lever in the lowest position.
2. Move the moveable idler away from the belt and remove the belt from the PTO pulley and idler.
3. Remove the cover over the left mower spindle pulley.
4. Remove the mower drive belt.
5. Reverse the removal procedure to install the belt. The flat side of the belt must contact the idler.

MOWER DECK

LUBRICATION

Lubricate the spindles and idler arm after every 25 hours of operation. Inject multipurpose grease through the grease fittings. One or two shots from a hand-held grease gun should be sufficient. Apply clean engine oil to the contact surface of all moving parts.

Lubricate more frequently when ambient temperature exceeds 85° F (39° C) or when operating in dusty conditions.

ADJUSTMENT

Before attempting any adjustment, the machine must be on level ground and the tires must be properly inflated. Disconnect the spark plug wire and tie it out of the way.

Side-to-Side Height

1. Position the mower deck in the down position at mid-height.
2. Loosen the rear mower deck hanger links so the deck rests on the rear rollers.

NOTE: The deck must rest on the rollers. If not, adjust the roller position, then readjust the roller position after performing leveling adjustment.

3. Measure the height of the blade tip above the ground. Measurement should be within ⅛ inch (3.2 mm) of blade tip on opposite side.
4. Note the position of the eccentric (Fig. SM1-18) on the left side of the deck. The flat on the eccentric near the bolt must be toward the rear of the deck. If not, reposition the eccentric and tighten the nut to 30 ft.-lb. (41 N•m).
5. Adjust the blade side-to-side height by rotating the eccentric on the right side of the deck.
6. Recheck the blade height.
7. Tighten the rear hanger link fasteners and reposition the rear rollers, if moved.

Front-to-Rear Height

1. Measure the distance from the ground to the blade from front to rear.
2A. 30-inch Mower Deck–The front of the blade should be level with the rear of the blade or up to ⅛ inch (3.2 mm) higher.

2B. 34-inch Mower Deck–The front of the blade should be level with the rear of the blade or up to ¼ inch (6.4 mm) higher.

3. To adjust the front-to-rear dimension, adjust the position of the nuts (Fig. SM1-19) on the height adjustment rod.

Transport Height Adjustment

When the mower lift lever is in the transport position, the rollers on the rear of the mower deck should be ⅛-¼ inch (3.2-6.4 mm) above the ground. Refer to Fig. SM1-20 and use the following procedure to adjust the transport height.

1. Adjust the mower height to 3 inches (76 mm) on 30-inch mower deck or 2¾4 inches (70 mm) on 34-inch mower deck.

2. Loosen the nut and move the spacer against the trailing arm. Retighten the nut. Perform on both sides of the mower deck.

3. Check the roller height. If incorrect, repeat the procedure.

REMOVAL AND INSTALLATION

1. Turn the front wheels fully to the left.
2. Move the mower deck to the lowest position.
3. Push the idler arm and remove the mower belt from the mower pulleys.
4. Support the front of the mower deck with a block of wood.
5. Detach the lift cable hook from the mower deck eye.
6. Pull out the hitch lever (Fig. SM1-21), disengage the hitch and place it out of the way.
7. Remove the mower deck by moving it out from the right side of the machine.
8. Reverse the removal procedure to install the mower deck. Be sure the open portion of the hook on the lift cable is toward the rear of the machine. The trailing arms (Fig. SM1-20) must be above the torsion bar.

MOWER DECK SPINDLE

Two spindle configurations have been used. Early spindles are identified by the use of a bolt to secure the pulley. Later spindles are equipped with a nut to hold the pulley on the spindle.

OVERHAUL

Early Models (Fig. SM1-22)

1. Remove the mower deck as previously described.
2. Remove the blade.
3. Note the position of the belt guides attached to the spindle housing, then unscrew the spindle housing mounting screws and remove the spindle assembly.
4. Secure the blade adapter (15) in a vise.
5. Remove the bolt (1), lockwasher (2), washer (3), pulley (4) and shield (5).
6. Free the unit from the vise, then remove the collar (16) from the blade adapter.
7. Remove the blade adapter (15), shield (14) and shim (13).
8. Separate the spindle housings by prying apart.
9. Press the bearings off the spindle.
10. Assemble the spindle by reversing the disassembly procedure. Note the following:
   a. If a foam gasket is not available, apply RTV sealant to the upper and lower spindle housing mating surfaces.

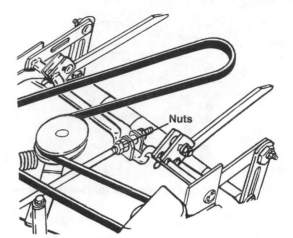

Fig. SM1-19–Rotate nuts to adjust mower height. Refer to text.

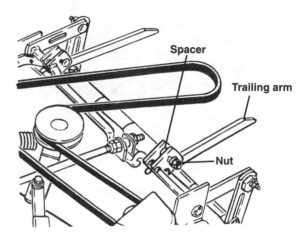

Fig. SM1-20–Refer to text for roller height adjustment procedure.

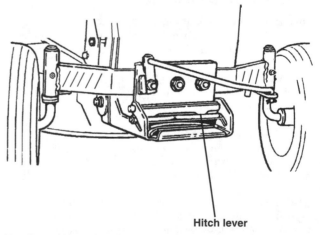

Fig. SM1-21–Pull the hitch lever to detach the hitch.

   b. Fill the lower spindle housing with multipurpose grease.
   c. Install the pulley so the long end of the hub is toward the housing.
   d. Tighten the pulley retaining screw to 50-70 ft.-lb. (68-95 N•m).
   e. Maximum spindle end play is ⅛ inch (3.2 mm).

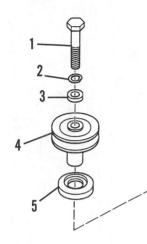

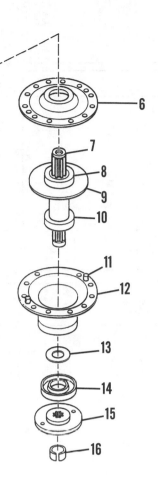

Fig. SM1-22–Exploded view of a mower spindle used on a 30-inch mower deck.

1. Bolt
2. Lockwasher
3. Washer
4. Pulley
5. Shield
6. Upper spindle housing
7. Spindle
8. Bearing
9. Foam gasket
10. Bearing
11. Pin
12. Lower spindle housing
13. Shim
14. Shield
15. Adapter
16. Collar

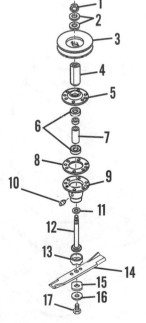

Fig. SM1-23–Exploded view of a mower spindle used on a 34-inch mower deck.

1. Nut
2. Belleville washer
3. Pulley
4. Spacer
5. Upper spindle housing
6. Bearing
7. Spacer
8. Foam gasket
9. Lower spindle housing
10. Grease fitting
11. Bearing
12. Spindle
13. Collar
14. Blade
15. Washer
16. Lockwasher
17. Bolt

f. Install the long spindle housing screws at the belt guide location.

Later Models (Fig. SM1-23)

1. Remove the mower deck as previously described.

2. Remove the blade.

3. Unscrew the spindle housing mounting screws and remove the spindle assembly.

4. Secure the spindle in a vise.

5. Remove the nut (1), Belleville washers (2), pulley (3) and spacer (4).

6. Separate the spindle housings by prying apart.

7. Disassemble the remainder of the spindle housing components.

8. Inspect the components for damage.

9. Install the washer (11) onto the shaft with the concave side toward the flange on the spindle.

10. Install the bearings and spacer (7) into the lower spindle housing.

11. Install the spindle into the lower spindle housing and bearings.

12. Install the foam gasket. If a foam gasket is not available, apply RTV sealant to the upper and lower spindle housing mating surfaces.

13. Fill lower spindle housing with multipurpose grease.

14. Install the remainder of the components while noting the following:

a. Tighten the pulley retaining screw to 50-70 ft.-lb. (68-95 N•m).

b. Maximum spindle end play is ⅛ inch (3.2 mm).

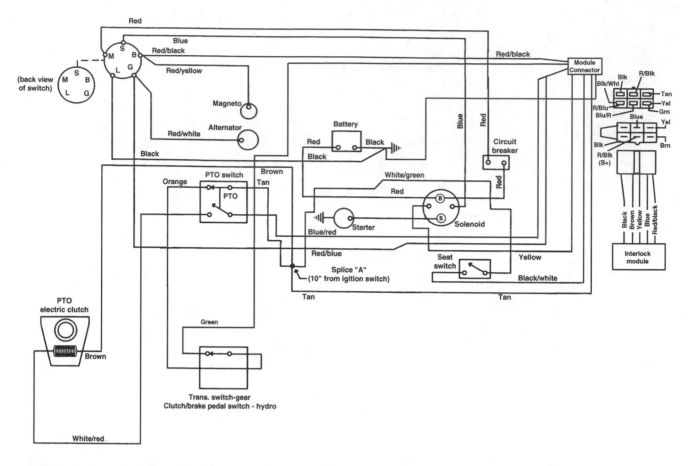

Fig. SM1-24–Typical wiring schematic.

ELECTRICAL

Refer to Fig. SM1-24 for a wiring schematic. Note the following points:

1. The transaxle must be in NEUTRAL, the mower must be disengaged and the operator must be in the seat for the engine to start.

2. The engine should stop if the transaxle is in gear or the mower is engaged and the operator leaves the seat.

STARTER RELAY TESTING

Note the location of the small and large terminals on the relay (Fig. SM1-25) when performing the following test.

1. Using an ohmmeter or continuity tester, check for continuity between the small terminals. The tester should indicate a continuity of less than 10 ohms.

2. Using an ohmmeter or continuity tester, check for continuity between the large terminals. The tester should indicate no continuity.

3. Connect a 12-volt battery to the small terminals.

4. The tester should indicate a continuity of less than 10 ohms between the large terminals.

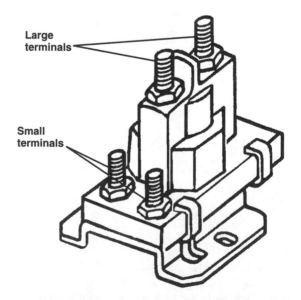

Fig. SM1-25–Refer to text for starter relay testing procedure.

SIMPLICITY

ZT SERIES

Model	Make	Engine Model	Horsepower
1692905	Kohler	CV14S	14
1692906	Kohler	CV16S	16
1693230	B&S	*	18
1693286	Kohler	CV14S	14
1693288	Kohler	CV16S	16
1693467	Kohler	CV14S	14
1693473	B&S	*	16

*Note the engine model number and refer to the engine service section in this manual for engine specifications.

FRONT WHEELS

LUBRICATION

Each front wheel hub is equipped with a grease fitting. Front wheels should be injected with multipurpose grease after every 25 hours of operation. Lubricate the front wheels more frequently if ambient temperature exceeds 85° F (30° C) or if operating in dusty conditions.

REMOVAL AND INSTALLATION

The front wheels are equipped with replaceable bushings. To remove the wheel and bushings, proceed as follows:
1. Remove the hub cap (8–Fig. SM2-1).
2. Remove the retaining ring (7).
3. Remove the wheel with the bushings.
4. Separate the bushings from the wheel.
5. Inspect the bushings and axle for damage.
6. Inspect the wheel for rim and hub damage.

7. Reverse the removal steps to reassemble and install the wheel and bushings. Lubricate the bushings after assembly.

FRONT SPINDLES

MAINTENANCE

Lubricate the front wheel spindles after every 25 hours of operation. Inject multipurpose grease into the grease fitting on the spindle housing. Lubricate the spindles more frequently when ambient temperature exceeds 85° F. (30° C.) or when operating in dusty conditions.

OVERHAUL

Refer to Fig. SM2-2 for an exploded view of the spindle assembly. To remove a front spindle, proceed as follows.
1. Raise and support the side to be serviced.
2. Remove the wheel and tire as previously described.
3. Remove the snap ring (1–Fig. SM2-2) from the top of the spindle.
4. Remove the spindle (6).

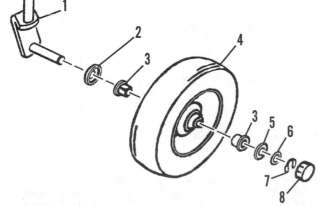

Fig. SM2-1–Exploded view of wheel assembly.

1. Spindle
2. Cup washer
3. Bushing
4. Wheel
5. Large washer
6. Small washer
7. E-ring
8. Hub cap

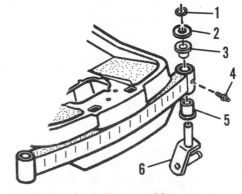

Fig. SM2-2–Exploded view of spindle assembly.

1. E-ring
2. Washer
3. Bushing
4. Grease fitting
5. Bushing
6. Spindle

5. Inspect the components for damage.

6. Install the spindle by reversing the removal procedure. Lubricate the spindle after assembly.

ENGINE

Refer to the appropriate engine section in this manual for tune-up specifications, engine overhaul procedures and engine maintenance.

REMOVAL AND INSTALLATION

1. Remove the engine cover and disconnect the spark plug wire.

2. Electric start models–Disconnect and remove the battery.

3. Disconnect any interfering electrical wires from the engine.

4. Disconnect the throttle cable from the engine.

5. Remove the mower as outlined in the MOWER DECK section.

6. Remove the traction drive belt from the engine pulley.

7. Detach the pulley from the engine crankshaft.

8. Remove the engine mounting fasteners.

9. Remove the engine.

10. Install the engine by reversing the removal procedure.

TRANSAXLE DRIVE BELT

Early models use five wire-type belt guides (A–Fig. SM2-3A) to hold the belt in place. Later models use three wire-type belt guides (A and D–Fig. SM2-3B).

REMOVAL AND INSTALLATION

Early Models

1. Remove the engine cover and disconnect the spark plug wire.

2. Remove the mower deck.

3. Remove the PTO clutch (P–Fig. SM2-3A) as described in this section.

4. Push down the clutch pedal.

5. Remove the drive belt (B–Fig. SM2-3A) by sliding the belt between the pulleys and the belt guides.

6. Install the belt by reversing the removal procedure. Adjust the belt guides as needed so there is 1/8 inch (3.2 mm) clearance between the belt and the guides.

Later Models

1. Remove the engine cover and disconnect the spark plug wire.

2. Remove the mower deck.

3. Remove the PTO clutch as described in this section.

4. Remove the carrier assembly as described in this section.

5. Remove the wire belt guide (D–Fig. SM2-3B) from the transmission pulleys.

6. Remove the drive belt (B–Fig. SM2-3B) by sliding the belt between the pulleys and the belt guides.

7. Install the drive belt by reversing the removal procedure. Adjust the belt guides as needed so there is 1/8 inch (3.2 mm) clearance between the belt and the guides.

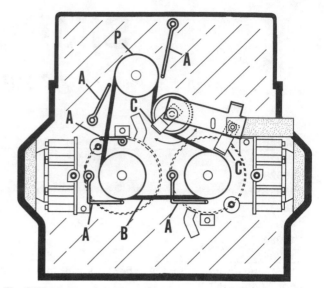

Fig. SM2-3A–Drawing of traction drive belt components on early models. Five belt guides (A) are used on early models.

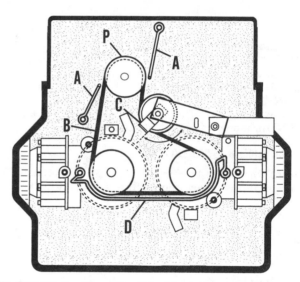

Fig. SM2-3B–Drawing of traction drive belt components on later models. Three belt guides (A and D) are used on later models.

STEERING CONTROL LINKAGE

LUBRICATION

Periodically lubricate all rubbing contact surfaces with engine oil. Apply oil more frequently when the machine is operated in dusty conditions.

RUNNING ADJUSTMENT

Each transaxle is independently controlled to permit zero-radius turning. If the machine tracks slightly off course while running, the top speed of each transaxle may be controlled by turning the appropriate adjustment knob (Fig. SM2-4). Minor adjustment may be necessary while running because the transaxles may not operate equally.

If the operating levers are not parallel within 3/8 inch (3.2 mm) when the machine is traveling straight ahead, perform the linkage adjustment as described in this section.

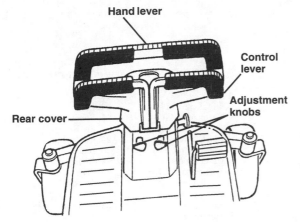

Fig. SM2-4–Refer to text for steering linkage adjustment procedure.

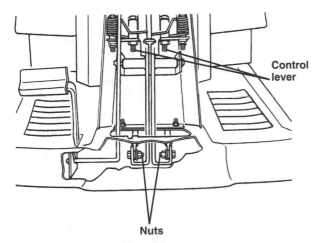

Fig. SM2-5A–Steering linkage (early models).

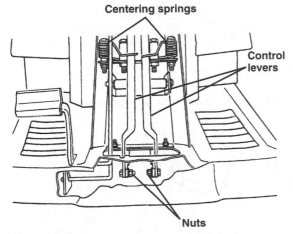

Fig, SM2-5B–Steering linkage (later models).

LINKAGE ADJUSTMENT

Before performing the following adjustment, be sure the machine is situated on level ground and the tires are properly inflated.

1. Rotate the adjustment knobs (Fig. SM2-4) fully counterclockwise.

NOTE: The front shroud is shown removed in the following drawings for clarity. Front shroud removal is not necessary to perform the adjustment.

2. Loosen the adjustment nuts shown in Figs. SM2-5A or SM2-5B.

3. Move the bolts to the bottom of the slots in the control levers.

4. Tighten the nuts and check operation. If the machine does not track properly, proceed to Step 5.

5. Loosen the adjusment nut in one of the control levers and move the bolt in the control lever slot. Retighten the nut and check machine operation.

NOTE: Perfectly straight tracking is not necessary when performing Step 6. See Step 7.

6. After noting the directional change caused by Step 5, relocate the bolts in the control lever slots to obtain tracking as straight as possible.

7. Turn the adjustment knobs shown in Fig. SM2-4 as needed to obtain straight tracking.

CONTROL LEVER POSITION ADJUSTMENT

When the machine is in NEUTRAL, the distance from each control lever (Fig. SM2-4) to the handlebar should be $2\frac{1}{4}$ to $2\frac{3}{8}$ inches (57-60 mm). If incorrect, perform the following adjustment procedure.

1. Remove the mower deck as described in this section.

2. Remove the rear handlebar cover (Fig. SM2-4).

3. If so equipped, disconnect the wires from the headlight switch.

4. Remove the front handlebar cover (4–Fig. SM2-6).

5. If so equipped, remove the headlight.

6. Remove the covers from the top of the front control tower cover (39–Fig. SM2-6) and the screws underneath the frame. Remove the front control tower cover.

7. Loosen the fastener (A–Fig. SM2-7) on each transaxle control rod.

NOTE: To assist in obtaining an equidistant space, attach a suitably sized board to the control levers.

8. Loosen the bolt in each centering spring (Fig. SM2-5B). Move the bolt in the slot to obtain the desired distance from each control lever to the handlebar, then retighten the bolt.

9. Reassemble the covers.

10. Perform the neutral adjustment as described in this section.

REAR CARRIER

The transaxles and transaxle drive belt idler are mounted on a carrier at the rear of the machine. The carrier permits the rear of the machine to pivot independently during operation. Use the following procedure to remove the carrier for service to the carrier or if removing both transaxles.

REMOVAL AND INSTALLATION

1. Disconnect the engine spark plug lead.

2. Remove any weights attached to the carrier.

3. Remove the mower deck.

4. Raise and support the rear of the machine.

5. Remove the rear wheels.

6. Remove the PTO clutch as described in this section.

7. Disconnect the electrical lead from the clutch/brake switch on the clutch rod.

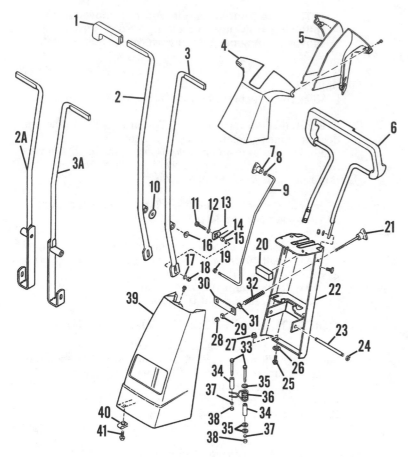

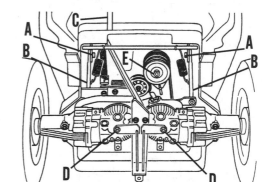

Fig. SM2-6–Exploded view of control tower assembly.

1. Grip	19. Nut
2. Right control lever (later models)	20. Pad
2A. Right control lever (early models)	21. Speed adjustment knob
3. Left control lever (later models0	22. Control tower
3A. Left control lever (early models)	23. Shaft
4. Front cover	24. E-ring
5. Rear cover	25. Screw
6. Handlebar	26. Washer
7. Parking brake knob	27. Nut
8. Washer	28. Locknut
9. Parking brake rod	29. Nut
10. Washer	30. Stop bar
11. Bolt	31. Washer
12. Wasther	32. Spring
13. Transaxle control rod	33. Bolt
14. Spacer	34. Spacer
15. Washer	35. Washer
16. Washer	36. Spring
17. Washer	37. Lockwasher
18. Nut	38. Nut
	39. Front shroud
	40. Nutplate
	41. Screw

8. Disconnect the transaxle control rods (B–Fig. SM2-7).

9. Disconnect the brake rod (C) from the linkage inside the carrier.

10. Detach the oil reservoirs (Fig. SM2-8) from the mainframe.

11. Support the carrier assembly with a jack.

12. Remove the carrier retaining bolts, then lower the carrier assembly out of the mainframe.

13. Refer to Fig. SM2-9 if disassembling carrier components.

14. Reverse the removal procedure to install the carrier assembly. Tighten the carrier retaining bolts to 75 ft.-lb. (102 N•m).

HYDROSTATIC TRANSAXLE

The machine is equipped with two hydrostatic transaxles. Each transaxle drives a rear wheel, which allows zero-turn-steering through independent operation of the transaxles.

LUBRICATION

Normal Operation

The oil level should be at maintained at the FULL mark on the oil reservoirs (Fig. SM2-8). If necessary, add oil to the tanks. The recommended oil is Simplicity Multipurpose Hydro Oil, Mobil DTE-26.

Refill and Bleed Transaxle

To refill the hydrostatic transaxle with oil and bleed air from the system after the transaxle has been serviced, proceed as follows.

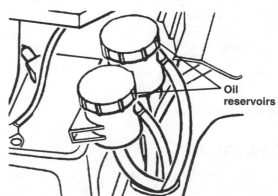

Fig. SM2-7–Drawing of transaxle carrier underside.

Oil reservoirs

Fig. SM2-8–Drawing showing transaxle oil reservoirs used on later models. On early models, only a single hose connects the oil reservoir to the transaxle.

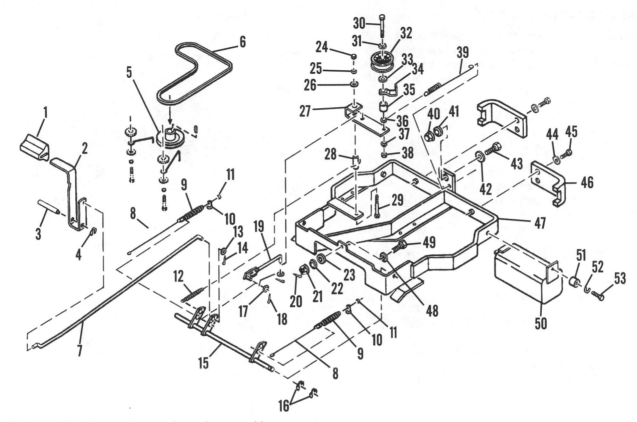

Fig. SM2-9–Exploded view of transaxle carrier assembly.

1. Pedal pad	15. Pivot shaft	29. Bolt	42. Washer
2. Clutch/brake pedal	16. Clips	30. Bolt	43. Bolt
3. Shaft	17. Washer	31. Washer	44. Washer
4. Clip	18. Cotter pin	32. Pulley	45. Bolt
5. Engine pulley	19. Clutch rod	33. Washer	46. Weight (18 hp
6. Drive belt	20. Cotter pin	34. Belt guide	models)
7. Clutch/brake rod	21. Locknut	35. Spacer	47. Carrier
8. Brake rod	22. Belleville washer	36. Spacer	48. Washer
9. Spring	23. Bushing	37. Lockwasher	49. Bolt
10. Trunnion pin	24. Nut	38. Nut	50. Weight
11. Locknut	25. Lockwasher	39. Nut	51. Spacer
12. Spring	26. Washer	40. Locknut	52. Lockwasher
13. Washer	27. Idler arm	41. Bushing	53. Bolt
14. Cotter pin	28. Pivot spacer		

CAUTION: Be sure the machine is adequately supported and cannot move when performing the following procedure.

1. Fill the oil reservoirs to the full line.
2. Raise and support the rear of the machine so the rear wheels are off the ground.
3. Start the engine and run at idle speed for about three minutes.
4. Move the steering control levers from full forward to full reverse in 15-second intervals for three minutes.
5. Return the levers to NEUTRAL for five seconds.
6. Add oil to the oil reservoirs as needed.
7. Repeat the procedure until the oil level stabilizes.
8. Check operation. Repeat the procedure if the machine does not function normally.

NEUTRAL ADJUSTMENT

When released the control levers should return to the NEUTRAL position. Check, and if necessary, adjust the control lever positions as described in this section.

CAUTION: Be sure the unit is adequately supported and cannot move when performing the following procedure.

1. Position the machine on level ground with the parking brake disengaged.
2. Raise and support the rear of the machine.
3. Loosen the fastener (A–Fig. SM2-7) on each transaxle control rod so the rods can move freely.
4. Move each transaxle control rod (B) until it engages the positive neutral detent in the transaxle.
5. Without moving the rods, tighten the fastener (A) on each rod.

NOTE: Place a weight in the operator's seat to activate the seat switch so the engine will run.

6. Start the engine, then run it at half-throttle.
7. Operate each control lever and check the operation of the respective rear wheel. When the control lever is released, rear wheel rotation should stop. If not, repeat the neutral adjustment procedure.

REMOVAL AND INSTALLATION

The transaxles are mounted in a carrier. The following procedure describes the removal procedure for an individual transaxle. If servicing both transaxles, it may be advantageous to remove the carrier assembly with both transaxles as previously described.

1. Disconnect the engine spark plug lead.
2. Remove any weights attached to the carrier.
3. Remove the mower deck.
4. Raise and support the rear of the machine.
5. Remove the rear wheel.
6. Push down the clutch pedal and remove the transaxle drive belt from the transaxle drive pulley.
7. Disconnect the transaxle control rod (B–Fig. SM2-7).
8. Disconnect the brake rod from the transaxle lever.
9. Disconnect the transaxle oil reservoir hose and plug the openings.
10. Detach the pressure relief dump valve arm (D) from the transaxle.
11. Support the transaxle.
12. Remove the transaxle mounting bolts and remove the transaxle.
13. Install the transaxle by reversing the removal procedure. Note the following:
    a. Perform the neutral adjustment procedure as described in this section.
    b. Perform the brake adjustment procedure as described in this section.

OVERHAUL

All models are equipped with two Eaton Model 778 hydrostatic transaxles. Refer to the HYDROSTATIC TRANSAXLE REPAIR section for service information.

BRAKE ADJUSTMENT

Refer to Fig. SM2-10 when performing the following procedure.
1. Raise the seat.
2. Push the brake lever on the transaxle forward as far as possible.
3. Pull the brake rod to the rear.
4. Measure the gap between the nut on the brake rod and the pivot.
5. Rotate the nut so the gap is ⅛ inch (3.2 mm).
6. Repeat the procedure on the opposite transaxle.

ELECTRIC PTO CLUTCH

Early and late models have been equipped with different PTO clutch units. The clutch unit may be identified by the color of the electrical wires. The electrical wires connected to early units are colored brown and white/red. Late model clutches are connected to wires colored orange and black/white.

TESTING

Use the following procedure to locate the cause if the PTO clutch malfunctions.
1. Turn the ignition switch ON.
2. Actuate the PTO switch.
3. If the clutch does not engage, disconnect the wiring connector at the clutch.
4. Use a 12-volt test lamp to check continuity of the wire coming from the PTO switch.

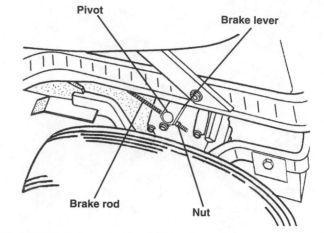

Fig. SM2-10–Refer to text for brake adjustment procedure.

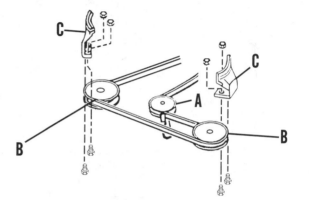

Fig. SM2-11–Drawing showing mower drive belt on 38-inch mower deck.
A. Idler pulley   C. Belt guide
B. Mower spindle pulley

5. If the lamp lights, the PTO is either defective or the wiring connector at the clutch field coil is faulty.
6. To check the PTO field coil, perform the following procedures:
    a. Clutch installed–Connect an ohmmeter to the clutch terminals. The ohmmeter should indicate a resistance of 6.59-7.29 ohms on early units or 2.74-3.02 ohms on late units.
    b. Clutch removed–Apply a 12-volt source to the clutch terminals. Hold a piece of steel next to the coil. The coil should attract the metal. There should be an audible click when the clutch engages.
7. If the PTO clutch fails the preceding tests, replace the coil or entire clutch assembly.

REMOVAL AND INSTALLATION

1. Remove the mower deck as described in this section.
2. Raise and support the rear of the machine.
3. Disconnect the PTO clutch electrical wire.
4. Remove the clutch retaining bolt (E—Fig. SM2-7).
5. Remove the clutch assembly from the crankshaft.
6. Reverse the removal procedure to install the PTO clutch. Apply antiseize compound to the engine crankshaft. Tighten the clutch retaining bolt to 35 ft.-lb. (47.6 N•m).
7. If installing a new clutch or components, run the engine at full speed and engage the clutch several times after the mower is installed to burnish the clutch surfaces.

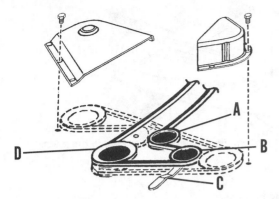

Fig. SM2-12–Drawing showing mower drive belt on 44- and 50-inch mower decks.

A. Idler pulley
B. Idler pulley

C. Lever
D. Center mower spindle pulley

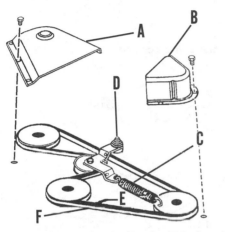

SN2-13–Mower spindle drive belt routing for 44-inch and 50-inch mower decks.

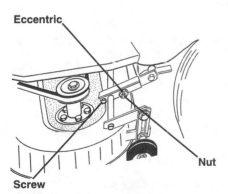

Fig. SM2-14–Mower side-to-side adjustment for all models.

MOWER DECK DRIVE BELT

REMOVAL AND INSTALLATION

38-inch Mower Deck

Refer to Fig. SM2-11 when performing the following procedure.
1. Remove the mower deck as outlined in this section.
2. Loosen the idler (A) bolt and relocate the belt guide.

3. Loosen and move the belt guides (C) adjacent to the mower spindle pulleys (B).
4. Remove the belt.
5. Install the belt, then move the belt guides into proper position.
6. Install the mower deck.

44-inch and 50-inch Mower Deck

Refer to Fig. SM2-12 when performing the following procedure.
1. Place the mower height control lever in the lowest position.
2. Move the moveable idler (B) away from the belt using the lever (C) attached to the idler.
3. Remove the belt from the PTO pulley, then remove the mower drive belt.
4. Reverse the removal procedure to install the belt.

MOWER SPINDLE DRIVE BELT REPLACEMENT (44-INCH AND 50-INCH MOWER DECK)

Refer to Fig SM2-13 when performing the following procedure.
1. Remove the mower deck as described in this section.
2. Remove the mower deck drive belt as described in this section.
3. Remove the belt covers (A and B).
4. Detach the spring (C) from the idler arm
5. Loosen the idler arm bolt (D).
6. Remove the spring (E).
7. Remove the spindle drive belt (F) from the deck pulleys.
8. Reverse the removal procedure to install the belt.

MOWER DECK

LUBRICATION

Lubricate the spindles and idler arm after every 25 hours of operation. Inject multipurpose grease through the grease fittings. One or two shots from a hand-held grease gun should be sufficient. Apply clean engine oil to the contact surface of all moving parts.

Lubricate more frequently when the ambient temperature exceeds 85° F (39° C) or when operating in dusty conditions.

ADJUSTMENT

Before attempting any adjustment, the machine must be on level ground and the tires must be properly inflated. Disconnect the spark plug wire and tie it out of the way.

Side-To-Side Height

1. Position the mower deck in the highest cutting position.
2. Position the blades so they are perpendicular to the machine centerline.
3. Measure the height of the blade tips above the ground. Measurement should be within ⅛ inch (3.2 mm) from side-to-side. If the dimension is incorrect, proceed to Step 4.
4. Loosen the nut (Fig. SM2-14) adjacent to the eccentric.
5. Loosen the screw.
6. Adjust the blade side-to-side height by rotating the eccentric.
7. Retighten the nut and screw.
8. Recheck the blade height.

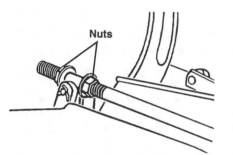

Fig. SM2-15–Refer to text for front-to-rear height adjustment procedure on 38-inch and 44-inch mower decks.

Fig. SM2-17–Pull the hitch release rod to detach the hitch.

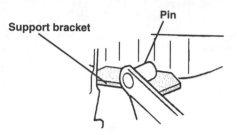

Fig. SM2-18–Mower hitch components.

Fig. SM2-16–Refer to text for front-to-rear height adjustment procedure on 50-inch mowers.

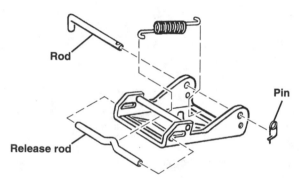

Fig. SM2-19–Remove the pin and rod to detach the hitch from the 50-inch mower deck.

Front-To-Rear Height

38-inch and 44-inch Mower Deck

1. Measure the distance from the ground to the blade from front to rear.

2A. 38-inch Mower Deck–The front of the blade should be level with the rear of the blade or up to $\frac{1}{8}$ inch (3.2 mm) higher.

2B. 44-inch Mower Deck–The front of the blade should be $\frac{1}{8}$-$\frac{1}{4}$ inch (3.2-6.4 mm) higher then the rear.

3. To adjust front-to-rear dimension, loosen the nut on the eccentric (Fig. SM2-15) and rotate the eccentric.

4. Tighten the nut and recheck the blade heights.

5. If the mower height control lever drops out of the quadrant, rotate the spring adjusting nut (Fig. SM2-15) clockwise to increase spring tension. Do not totally compress the spring.

50-inch Mower Deck

1. Measure the distance from the ground to the blade from front to rear.

2. The front of the blade should be $\frac{1}{8}$-$\frac{1}{4}$ inch (3.2-6.4 mm) higher then the rear.

3. To adjust front-to-rear dimension, rotate the nuts on the height control rod (Fig. SM2-16).

4. Tighten the nuts against the bracket and recheck blade height.

REMOVAL AND INSTALLATION

38-inch and 44-inch Mower Deck

1. Turn the front wheels fully sideways.

2. Move the mower deck to the lowest position.

3. Push the idler arm lever and remove the mower belt from the PTO clutch pulley.

4. Pull out the hitch release rod (Fig. SM2-17) and disengage the front mower deck hitch.

5. Slide the mower deck forward so the support pins (Fig. SM2-18) on each side disengage from the support brackets.

6. Remove the mower deck by moving it out from the right side of the machine.

7. Reverse the removal procedure to install the mower deck.

50-inch Mower Deck

1. Turn the front wheels fully sideways.

2. Set the mower height control to the middle height position.

3. Push the idler arm lever and remove the mower belt from the PTO clutch pulley.

4. Pull out the hitch release rod (Fig. SM2-17) and disengage the front mower deck hitch.

5. Remove the hitch rod pin (Fig. SM2-19), then remove the hitch rod and disengage the hitch from the mower deck.

6. Slide the mower deck forward so the support pins (Fig. SM2-18) on each side disengage from the support brackets.

7. Remove the mower deck by moving it out from the right side of the machine.

8. Reverse the removal procedure to install the mower deck.

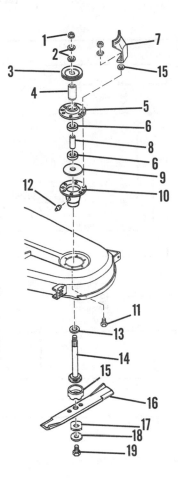

Fig. SM2-20–Exploded view of spindle assembly used on 38-inch mower decks.

1. Nut
2. Belleville washers
3. Pulley
4. Spacer
5. Spindle upper housing
6. Bearings
7. Belt stop
8. Spacer
9. Foam gasket
10. Spindle lower housing
11. Screw
12. Grease fitting
13. Washer
14. Spindle
15. Grass shield
16. Mower blade
17. Washer
18. Spring washer
19. Screw

MOWER DECK SPINDLE OVERHAUL

Refer to Fig. SM2-20 for 38-inch mower deck or Fig. SM2-21 for 44-inch and 50-inch mower decks when performing the following procedure.

1. Remove the mower deck as previously described.
2. Remove the blade.
3. Unscrew the spindle housing mounting screws and remove the spindle assembly.
4. Secure the spindle in a vise.
5. Remove the nut (1), Belleville washers (2), pulley (3) and spacer (4).
6. Separate the spindle housings by prying them apart.
7. Disassemble the remainder of the spindle housing components.
8. Inspect the components for damage.
9. Install the washer (13) onto the shaft with the concave side toward the flange on the spindle.
10. Install the bearings and spacer (8) into the lower spindle housing.
11. Install the spindle into the lower spindle housing and bearings.
12. Install the foam gasket. If a foam gasket is not available, apply RTV sealant to the upper and lower spindle housing mating surfaces.
13. Fill the lower spindle housing with lithium based grease.
14. Install the remainder of the components while noting the following:
   a. Tighten the pulley retaining screw to 50-70 ft.-lb. (68-95 N•m).
   b. Maximum spindle end play is 1/8 inch (3.2 mm).

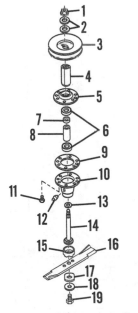

Fig. SM2-21–Exploded view of mower spindle assembly used on 44- and 50-inch decks.

1. Nut
2. Belleville washers
3. Pulley
4. Spacer
5. Upper spindle housing
6. Bearing
7. Spacer
8. Spacer
9. Foam gasket
10. Lower spindle housing
11. Bolt
12. Grease fitting
13. Washer
14. Spindle
15. Collar
16. Blade
17. Washer
18. Spring washer
19. Bolt

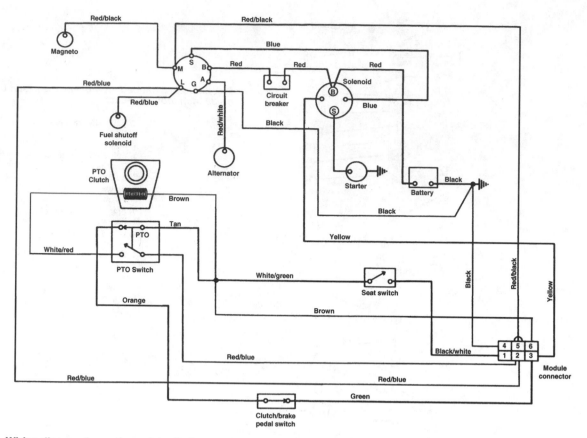

Fig. SM2-22–Wiring diagram for early models. Early models are equipped with an interlock module.

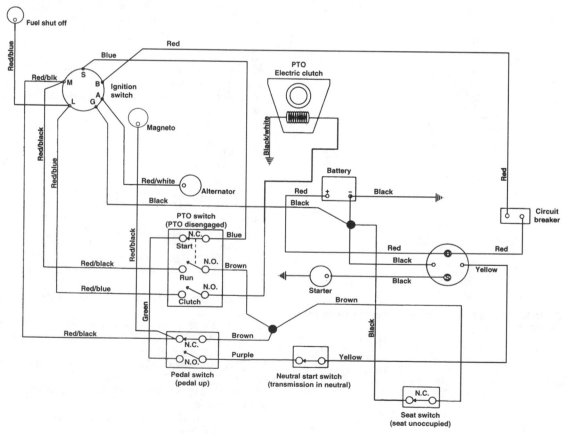

Fig. SM2-23–Wiring diagram for later models.

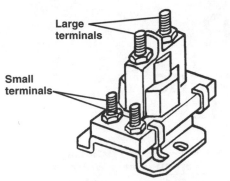

Fig. SM2-24–Refer to text for starter relay testing procedure.

c. Tighten the blade retaining screw to 45-55 ft.-lb. (61-74 N•m).

ELECTRICAL

Refer to Fig. SM2-22 or SM2-23 for a wiring schematic. Early models are equipped with a safety interlock module. The module grounds the engine ignition if the PTO is operated when the operator is out of the seat, or if the brake pedal is up when the operator is out of the seat.

Note the following points:
1. The transaxle must be in NEUTRAL, the mower must be disengaged and the operator must be in the seat for the engine to start.
2. The engine should stop if the transaxle is in gear or the mower is engaged and the operator leaves the seat.

STARTER RELAY TESTING

Note the location of the small and large terminals on the relay (Fig. SM2-24) when performing the following test.
1. Using an ohmmeter or continuity tester, check for continuity between the small terminals. The tester should indicate a continuity of less than 10 ohms.
2. Using an ohmmeter or continuity tester, check for continuity between the large terminals. The tester should indicate no continuity.
3. Connect a 12-volt battery to the small terminals.
4. The tester should indicate a continuity of less than 10 ohms between the large terminals.

INTERLOCK MODULE TESTING (EARLY MODELS)

The interlock module should be considered faulty only after all other wiring and devices have been tested or checked. An accurate testing procedure is not available. Replace the unit with a new or good unit and recheck operation.

SNAPPER

FRONT-STEER MOWERS
SERIES 10 AND 12

Model	Make	Engine Model	Horsepower	Cutting Width, In.
250610T	Tecumseh	*	6	25
250612T	Tecumseh	*	6	25
280812BE	B&S	195707	8	28
300812B	B&S	*	8	30
300812BE	B&S	*	8	30

*Note the engine model number and refer to the engine service section in this manual for engine specifications.

NOTE: Some operations may be performed more easily if the machine is standing upright. Observe the following safety recommendations when raising the machine to the upright position:

1. Drain the fuel tank or make certain that the fuel level is low enough so the fuel will not drain out.
2. Close the fuel shut-off valve if so equipped.
3. Remove the battery if so equipped.
4. Disconnect the spark plug wire and tie it out of way.
5. Although not absolutely essential, on models with spark plug at the rear of the machine, the engine oil should be drained to prevent flooding the combustion chamber with oil when the engine is tilted.
6. Secure the mower from tipping by lashing the machine to a post or overhead beam.

MODEL IDENTIFICATION

Snapper models are categorized by series numbers that indicate design differences. The series number of a particular model is the last two numerals in the model number. For instance, Model 280812BE is a Series 12 model. Some service procedures in this section are directed to models of a specific series.

FRONT WHEELS

LUBRICATION

Each front wheel hub is equipped with a grease fitting. Front wheels should be injected with multipurpose grease after every 25 hours of operation. Five shots should be sufficient, however, ten shots may be required if the hub assembly is clean and new bearings are installed.

REMOVAL AND INSTALLATION

The front wheels are equipped with replaceable bearings. To remove the wheel and bearings, proceed as follows:
1. Remove the hub cap (38–Fig. SN1-1).
2. Remove the cotter pin (36–Fig. SN1-1).

3. Remove the wheel with bearings.
4. Separate the bearings from the wheel.
5. Inspect the bearings and spindle for damage.
6. Inspect the wheel for rim and hub damage.
7. Reverse the removal steps to reassemble. Pack the wheel bearings with grease before installation.

FRONT SPINDLES
OVERHAUL

Refer to Fig. SN1-1 for an exploded view of the spindle assembly. To remove a front spindle, proceed as follows.
1. Raise and support the side to be serviced.
2. Remove the hub cap, cotter pin, wheel and tire.
3. Disconnect the tie rod from the spindle.
4. Detach the snap ring and remove the spindle.
5. Inspect components for damage.
6. Install the spindle by reversing the removal procedure.

STEERING SYSTEM
OVERHAUL

1. Raise the front of the machine.
2. Detach the tie rods from the steering arm.
3. Unscrew the handlebar (1–Fig. SN1-1) from the upper end of the steering shaft and clamp (7).
4. Withdraw the steering shaft from the bottom of the machine.
5. Reassemble the steering shaft by reversing the disassembly procedure. Note the following:
   a. The bolt (4–Fig. SN1-2) has a tapered head. Tighten the bolt until the head is a distance (D) of $\frac{1}{8}$ inch (3.2 mm) from shaft.
   b. Position the clamp (7–Fig. SN1-2) so the clamp gap (G) is aligned with the tube slot (S). The bottom of the clamp must be a distance (H) of $\frac{1}{4}$ inch (6.4 mm) from the bottom of the tube.

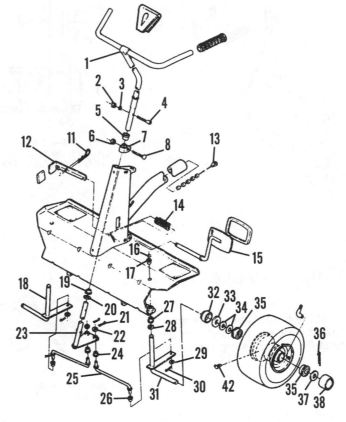

Fig. SN1-1–Exploded view of front steering system.

1. Handlebar	12. Parking brake clutch	21. Cotter pin	30. Cotter pin
2. Nut	13. Clutch/brake cable	22. Washer	31. Spindle (left)
3. Lockwasher	14. Parking brake spring	23. Steering arm	32. Boot
4. Tapered screw	15. Clutch/brake pedal	24. Bushing	33. Felt seal
5. Bushing	16. Snap ring	25. Tie rod	34. Washers
6. Nut	17. Bushing	26. Bushing	35. Bearing
7. Clamp	18. Spindle (right)	27. Bushing	36. Cotter pin
8. Carriage bolt	19. Bushing	28. Washer	37. Washer
11. Spring clip	20. Washer	29. Washer	38. Hub cap

Fig. SN1-2–Tighten bolt (4) so tapered head is a distance (D) of 1/8 inch (3.2 mm) from shaft. Piston clamp (7) so clamp gap (G) is aligned with tube slot (S) and bottom of clamp is a distance (H) of 1/4 inch (6.4 mm) from bottom of tube.

ENGINE

Refer to appropriate the engine section in this manual for tune-up specifications, engine overhaul procedures and engine maintenance.

REMOVAL AND INSTALLATION

1. Disconnect the spark plug wire.

2. If the engine is equipped with an electric starter, disconnect the cable from the starter motor.

3. Shift the mower drive control lever to the OUT position.

4. Unbolt and remove the spindle cover from the mower deck.

5. Relieve tension from the idler, then slip the belt off the mower spindle pulley(s).

6. Remove the belt from the driving disc hub pulley.

7. Disconnect the fuel hose from the engine.

8. Detach the throttle cable from the carburetor.

9. Disconnect all interfering wiring from the engine.

10. Remove the engine mounting screws and remove the engine.

11. Install engine by reversing the removal procedure.

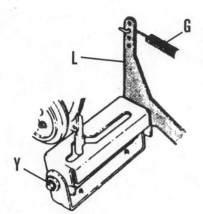

Fig. SN1-3–Clutch lever (L) is bolted to lift yolk (Y). Relocating spring (G) end in holes in clutch lever changes clutch traction. See text.

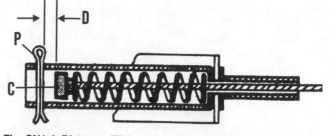

Fig. SN1-4–Distance (D) from cotter pin (P) to rear end of cable (C) should be 3/16-7/16 in ch (4.8-11.1 mm). Rotate nuts (N–Fig. SN1-5) to obtain desired distance.

CLUTCH/BRAKE CABLE

NOTE: If the location of the frame tube is changed, for instance, to adjust the mower belt tension, always check the clutch/brake operating cable for proper adjustment.

OPERATION

All models are equipped with a cable-operated clutch. The cable extends from a keyhole slot in the clutch/brake pedal through the main frame tube to the lever arm portion of the lift yoke (Y–Fig. SN1-3). Pulling the lift yoke by depressing the clutch/brake pedal moves the chaincase and driven disc away from the drive disc attached to the engine.

ADJUSTMENT

1. Fully depress the clutch/brake pedal and engage the parking brake.
2. Place the shift control lever in the REVERSE position.
3. Measure the gap between the drive disc and driven disc. The gap should be $\frac{1}{16}$-$\frac{1}{8}$ inch (1.6-3.2 mm). If the gap is not correct, proceed to Step 4.
4. Disengage the parking brake and relocate the front end of the clutch/brake cable in the control arm slot so another ferrule on the cable is engaged.
5. Recheck the gap between the discs.
6. Fully depress the clutch/brake pedal and engage the parking brake.
7. Measure the distance (D–Fig. SN1-4) from the cotter pin (P) to the rear end of the cable (C). Distance should be $\frac{3}{16}$-$\frac{7}{16}$ inch (4.8-11.1 mm). Rotate the nuts (N–Fig. SN1-5) to obtain desired distance.

TRACTION DRIVE CLUTCH

ADJUSTMENT

For normal setting, position the spring (G–Fig. SN1-3) end in the second hole from the end of the clutch lever (L). If the unit stutters or hops during clutch engagement, move the spring end to an inner hole. If traction is insufficient, move the spring end to the outermost hole in the lever.

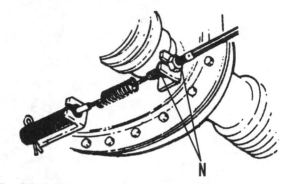

Fig. SN1-5–Rotate nuts (N) to obain desired distance (D–Fig. SN1-4) at cable end.

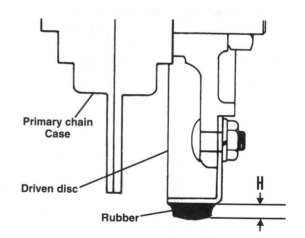

Fig. SN1-6–If height (H) of rubber ring on driven disc is 1/16 inch (1.6 mm) or less, disc must be replaced.

DISCS
INSPECTION AND ADJUSTMENT

Replace the driven disc if it is worn to less than $\frac{1}{16}$ inch (1.6 mm) as shown in Fig. SN1-6. To check disc contact, proceed as follows.

1. Install a driven disc that has half the rubber ring removed so the metal is showing. If modification of an old driven disc is not possible, a test disc may be fabricated using the dimensions of the metal portion of the existing driven disc.
2. Position the shift control lever in any forward gear.
3. With the clutch pedal released, measure the clearance (C–Fig. SN1-7) between the metal on the driven disc gauge (N) and the drive disc (D). The clearance should be 0.005-0.010 inch (0.13-0.25 mm).

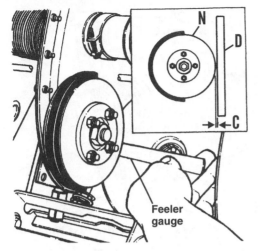

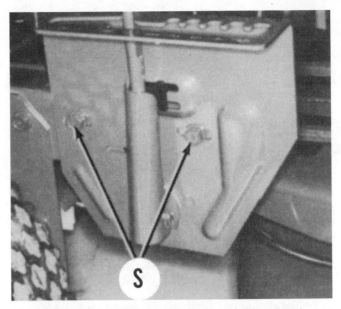

Fig. SN1-7–With the clutch pedal released and the shift control lever in any forward gear, clearance (C) between metal of driven disc gauge (N) and drive disc (D) should be 0.005-0.010 inch (0.13-0.25 mm).

Fig. SN1-10–To synchronize shift lever and drive disc, loosen mouting screws (S) and relocate shift quadrant.

4. To obtain desired clearance, adjust the position of the drive disc on the engine crankshaft.

SHIFT CONTROL LINKAGE

LUBRICATION

The shift lever grease fitting (F–Fig. SN1-8) should be injected with good quality multipurpose grease after every 25 hours of operation. Two shots should be sufficient.

ADJUSTMENT

The shift lever should be synchronized with the position of the driven disc against the drive disc. Refer to Fig. SN1-9 and note the driven disc position against the drive disc at the related ground speed. Note the first speed position of the driven disc is approximately 1/16 inch (1.6 mm) from the outer diameter of the hole in the drive disc.

Loosen the mounting screws (S–Fig. SN1-10) and relocate the shift quadrant as needed so the shift lever and driven disc positions are synchronized.

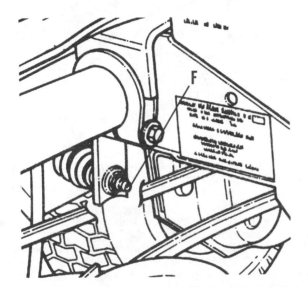

Fig. SN1-8–The shift lever grease fitting (F) should be injected with mulitpurpose grease after every 25 hours of operation.

FRICTION DRIVE TRANSMISSION AND FINAL DRIVE

OPERATION

Power for the machine is transmitted through two discs, a drive disc and a driven disc. The drive disc is attached to the engine's crankshaft while the driven disc is attached to the primary chain case input shaft. As the primary chain case is moved from side-to-side through the shift mechanism, the driven friction disc contacts a different spot on the drive disc to change ground speed. Moving the driven disc to the opposite side of the drive disc reverses direction. The final drive case contains the reduction gear, differential and axle assemblies.

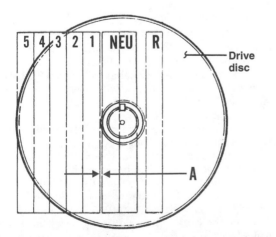

Fig. SN1-9–The driven disc should be positioned against drive disc (D) as shown for transmission speed shown. Distance (A) from outer diameter of center hole in drive disc to first speed position is 1/16 inch (1.6 mm).

LUBRICATION

Position the machine so it is upright as previously described. Annually fill the final drive case so the grease level in the case is even with the plug opening (P–Fig. SN1-11). The recommended lubricant is Snapper 0 grease.

Annually add 1 ounce (30 mL) of Snapper 0 grease to the primary chaincase; but do not overfill. Primary chaincase capacity is 2 ounces (60 mL).

Inject multipurpose grease into the left, rear axle grease fitting (F–Fig. SN1-12) after every 25 hours of operation. Two shots should be sufficient.

Periodically lubricate the lift yoke pivot points.

INSPECTION AND TROUBLESHOOTING

If a malfunction in the drive system is suspected, proceed as follows.

1. Raise the machine so it is upright as previously described.
2. Check for leaks at the primary chaincase flanges, final drive case and shaft seals.
3. Disengage the mower deck drive and roll the rear wheels by hand with the clutch both depressed and released and with the shift control lever in NEUTRAL and also when shifted into drive.
4. Loosen the clamps on the drive tube boots and pull back so the rotation of the hex drive tube can be observed.
5. Check for normal action of the differential pinions.
6. Jamming, locking or noise in the final drive case can be caused by damaged differential parts or a broken drive chain. Undue noise or abnormal operation in the final drive case or in the primary chaincase will determine which assemblies should be removed for inspection and/or repair. Refer to Table 1 DRIVE SYSTEM TROUBLESHOOTING GUIDE for additional service information.

OVERHAUL

Refer to the appropriate following section for service information on the assembly requiring service.

Driven Disc

The driven disc rubber ring must not be worn to less than $\frac{1}{32}$-$\frac{1}{16}$ inch (0.8-1.6 mm), otherwise, replace the driven disc (see Fig. SN1-6). If the driven disc is damaged and requires service, proceed as follows.

1. Place the machine in an upright position on the rear stand as previously described.
2. Unscrew disc retaining nuts and remove disc (20–Fig. SN1-13).
3. When installing disc on models equipped with a fiber thrust washer (21), be sure the fiber washer is centered on the hub (19) and is free-floating.

Drive Disc

Maximum allowable drive disc warpage is 0.020 inch (0.51 mm). To remove the drive disc, proceed as follows.
1. Remove the driven disc as previously described as well as the driven disc hub (19–Fig. SN1-13).
2. Separate the mower drive belt from the idler and remove the mower drive belt from the drive disc pulley.
3. Place the shift control lever in the fifth speed position.

NOTE: The drive disc on Series 12 units may be retained by a bolt in the end of the engine crankshaft rather than the setscrews shown in Fig. SN1-14.

4. Unscrew the setscrews (S–Fig. SN1-14) and carefully pull the drive disc off the crankshaft. It may be necessary to move the lift yoke aside during removal.

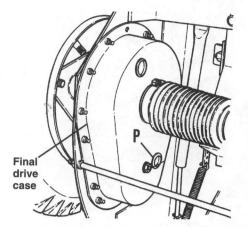

Fig. SN1-11–Level of grease in final drive case should be even with opening for plug (P).

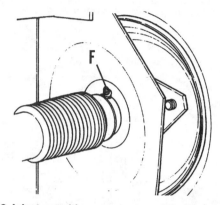

Fig. SN1-12–Inject a multipurpose grease into the left rear axle grease fitting (F) after every 25 hours of operation.

5. To separate the disc from the hub, secure the hub in a vise and unscrew the disc from the hub.
6. Install the drive disc by reversing the removal procedure. See the TRACTION DRIVE CLUTCH section for the procedure to position the drive disc on the engine crankshaft.

Left Side (Primary Chaincase)

1. Place the machine in an upright position on the rear stand as previously described.
2. Remove the left rear wheel.
3. Unscrew the hub retaining screw and remove the hub using Snapper tool 60237 or other suitable puller.
4. Remove the dust shield from the axle.
5. Series 10—remove the lock collar (33–Fig. SN1-13) by rotating in a clockwise direction after loosening the setscrew.
6. Detach the boot (29).
7. Unscrew the tie rod (34) nut.
8. Unscrew the fasteners securing the left fender plate (32) and remove the left fender plate.
9. Disconnect the shift link from the chaincase half (8).
10. Detach the boot from the chaincase half (8).
11. Separate the chaincase rod from the lift yoke and slide the chaincase off the hex tube.
12. Secure the driven disc hub (19).
13. Unscrew the brake lever retaining screw and remove the brake lever (35).
14. Remove the driven disc and hub assembly.
15. Unscrew the chaincase bolts and separate the chaincase halves (8 and 18).

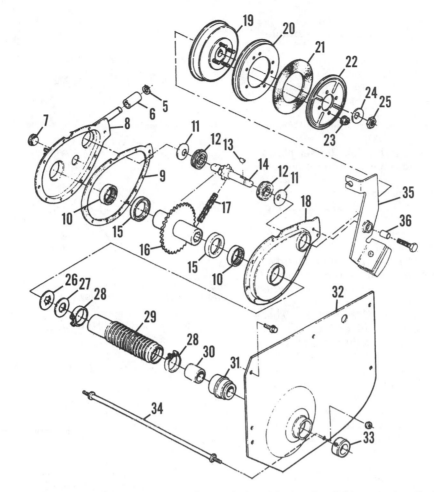

Fig. SN1-13–Exploded view of primary chaincase assembly. Spacer (30) and lock collar (33) are used on Series 10 models.

5. Snap ring	13. Key	21. Fiber washer	29. Boot
6. Roller	14. Sprocket shaft	22. Plate	30. Spacer
7. Plug	15. Thrust washer	23. Locknut	31. Bearing
8. Chaincase half	16. Sprocket & hub	24. Belleville washer	32. Fender plate (left)
9. Gasket	17. Chain	25. Locknut	33. Lock collar
10. Needle bearing	18. Chaincase half	26. Hex thrust washer	34. Tie rod
11. Belleville washer	19. Driven disc hub	27. Nylon thrust washer	35. Brake arm
12. Bearing	20. Driven disc	28. Clamp	36. Bushing

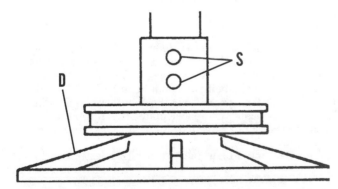

Fig. SN1-14–Remove setscrews (S) to remove drive disc (D). On Series 12 units, a bolt may secure the drive disc to the engine crankshaft instead of the setscrews shown.

16. Remove, clean and inspect the chaincase components.

17. Remove the needle bearings (10) and ball bearings (12) by pressing to the inside of the case half.

18. Reassemble the primary chaincase by reversing the disassembly procedure. Note the following:

a. Press the ball bearings (12) into the case halves until the locating ring around the outside of the bearing seats against the case.

b. Press against the lettered side of the needle bearings (10) so the lettered side is to the inside of the case half and the bearing is flush with the inner surface of the case half.

c. The cup side of the Belleville washers (11) must be away from the bearings (12).

d. After assembly, check end play between the hex tube (T–Fig. SN1-15) and bearing (B). Desired end play is $3/32$ inch (2.4 mm). Adjust end play by installing the nylon split shims (S) between the tube and bearing.

e. Fill the primary chaincase with 2 ounces (60 mL) of Snapper 0 grease. Install a new plug (7–Fig. SN1-13).

Right Side (Final Drive Case)

Place the machine in an upright position on the rear stand as previously outlined then proceed as follows.

1. Remove the rear wheels.

2. Unscrew the hub retaining screws and remove both wheel hubs using Snapper tool 60237 or other suitable puller.

3. Remove the dust shields from the axles.

4. Series 10—remove the lock collars (33–Fig. SN1-13) from each axle by loosening the setscrew and rotating the collar in the direction opposite to the forward wheel rotation.

5. Unscrew the tie rod nut.

6. Detach the boot (30–Fig SN1-16) from the final drive case.

7. Unscrew the fasteners securing the right fender plate (5–Fig. SN1-16) to the frame and remove the right fender plate with the final drive case.

8. Place the assembly on a workbench so the axle protrudes downward through a hole in the workbench and the fender plate is on top.

9. Unscrew the fender plate retaining screws and nuts and remove the fender plate from the final drive case.

10. Prevent the hex shaft (33) from moving and withdraw the final drive gear (16) and axle assembly from the case.

11. Remove the idler and sprocket components (17 through 26).

12. Remove the hex tube components (32 through 35). The bushings in the hex tube (33) are not replaceable.

13. To disassemble and reassemble the differential, proceed as follows:

   a. Unscrew the capscrews securing the differential plate (9). Discard capscrews–the screw's threads lose their locking capability when unscrewed.

   b. Disassemble the differential components.

   c. Replace the nylon spacer (12) if worn. Bushings in the short axle (11) are not replaceable. Be sure the nylon spacer (12) fits over the weld on the long axle (15).

   d. Assemble the pinions (14), spacers (13) and short axle as shown in Fig. SN1-17.

   e. Lubricate the bushings in the short axle before assembly.

   f. Install the differential plate (9–Fig. SN1-16) using new capscrews (Snapper part 1-2333).

14. Reassemble the final drive assembly and fender plate by reversing the disassembly procedure while noting the following:

   a. Be sure the thrust washers (32 and 34) are installed; the absence of thrust washers will cause rapid wear.

   b. Install the nylon hex washer (35) with lip towards the sprocket on the hex tube.

   c. Lubricate the bushings in the hex tube (33) prior to assembly. Make sure the lubrication hole in the idler (19) is open.

   d. Install the Belleville washers (18 and 24) so the cupped side is towards the O-rings (17 and 26).

   e. Idler, sprocket, hex tube and chain must be installed as a unit.

   f. Lubricate the outside of the short axle (11).

   g. After placing the fender plate on the final drive case, tighten the case retaining screws and nuts, then tighten the idler bolt retaining locknut (N) to 18-20 ft.-lb. (25-27 N•m). The locknut must be tightened properly as loosening of the nut may allow the chain to jump from the sprockets due to sprocket misalignment.

   h. Lubricate the outside of the hex tube (33) before inserting in the primary chaincase.

   i. Series 10–rotate the lock collars in the same direction as the forward wheel rotation.

   j. Fill the final drive case with Snapper 0 grease so the grease level in the case is even with the plug opening

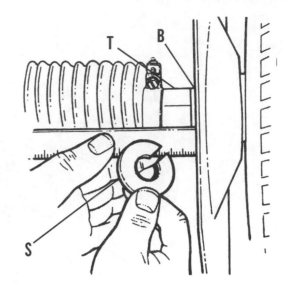

Fig. SN1-15–End play between hex tube (T) and bearing (B) should be 3/32 inch (2.4 mm).

(P–Fig. SN1-11). New plugs (28 and 31–Fig. SN1-16) should be installed.

GROUND DRIVE BRAKE

NOTE: If the location of the frame tube is changed, for instance, to adjust the mower belt tension, always check the brake operating cable for proper adjustment.

All models are equipped with a combination clutch/brake pedal on the machine's left side. The brake is applied when the clutch/brake pedal is pressed down to its limit. At this point, brake lever (35–Fig. SN1-13) rotates so its lined shoe contacts the inner rim of the driven hub (19). Pressure on the upper end of the brake lever is exerted by the lift yoke when actuated by tension on the clutch/brake cable.

To adjust brake, refer to the CLUTCH/BRAKE CABLE section.

MOWER BELT

ADJUSTMENT

Mower drive belt tension is determined by measuring the distance between the opposite runs of the belt at the closest point with the mower engaged. See Fig. SN1-18. Distance between the belt runs should be 1 inch (25 mm).

To adjust belt tension, remove the shoulder bolt (B–Fig. SN1-19) and relocate the spacer plates (R) in front or behind the bracket (T) as needed. Reinstall and tighten the shoulder bolt.

Belt guides should be at least 1/8 inch (3.2 mm) from the belt.

REMOVAL AND INSTALLATION

1. Detach the mower deck cover.

2. Loosen the belt idler and move the idler away from the belt to increase belt slack.

3. Place the machine in an upright position on the rear stand as previously described.

4. Move the clutch lift yoke so the driven disc is moved away from the drive disc and a gap exists.

5. Separate the mower drive belt from the engine pulley.

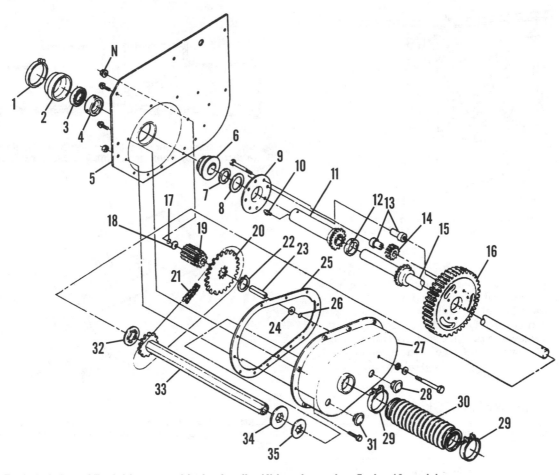

Fig. SN1-16—Exploded view of final drive assembly. Lock collar (4) is only used on Series 10 models.

1. Clamp	10. Grease fitting	19. Gear	28. Plug
2. Dust cover	11. Short axle	20. Sprocket	29. Clamp
3. Seal	12. Nylon spacer	21. Chain	30. Boot
4. Lock collar	13. Pinion spacers	22. Snap ring	31. Plug
5. Fender plate (right)	14. Pinions	23. Spacer	32. Thrust washer
6. Bearing	15. Long axle	24. Belleville washer	33. Hex drive tube
7. Spacer	16. Final drive gear	25. Gasket	34. Nylon thrust washer
8. Thrust washer	17. O-ring	26. O-ring	35. Hex thrust washer
9. Plate	18. Belleville washer	27. Case	

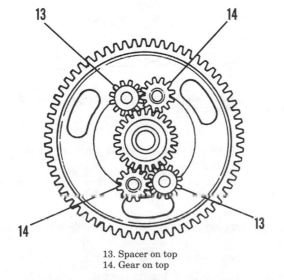

Fig. SN1-17—When installing pinion spacers and pinions on final drive gear, alternate top positions of pinion spacers (13) and pinions (14) so they appear as shown.

13. Spacer on top
14. Gear on top

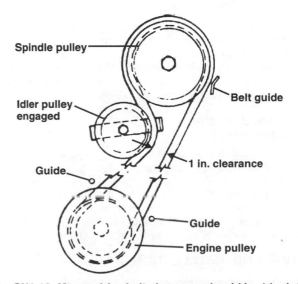

Fig. SN1-18—Mower drive belt clearance should be 1 inch (25 mm) at idler pulley as shown. Refer to text for adjustment procedure.

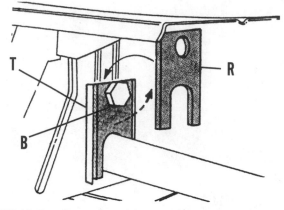

Fig. SN1-19—To adjust mower drive belt tension, remove bolt (B) and relocate spacer plates (R) next to bracket (T) to extend or withdraw main frame tube.

6. Remove the mower belt by passing the belt through the gap between the driven and drive discs.

7. Install the mower drive belt by reversing the removal procedure. The belt can be forced around the drive disc by the moving shift control lever to the fifth speed position thereby forcing the belt out towards the edge of the drive disc. Adjust the belt tension as outlined in the ADJUSTMENT section.

MOWER DECK

HEIGHT ADJUSTMENT

All mower control linkage must be in good operating condition and the tires properly inflated. Park the machine on a level surface with the engine stopped and the spark plug wire disconnected.

Blade Height

The blade adapter bar on some models is equipped with adjusting screws to aid blade alignment. Distance (D—Fig. SN1-20) from the mower deck to the blade tip should be $\frac{5}{16}$ inch (7.9 mm). Be sure all fasteners are secure.

Front-To-Rear Adjustment

Front-to-rear height difference is determined by measuring the height of the blade above ground at the front and rear. Rear height should be $\frac{5}{8}$ inch (15.9 mm) higher than the front on all models except Hi-Vac mowers, which should have a zero height difference. To adjust the height, relocate the ferrules on the hanger cables.

Side-To-Side Adjustment
(30-inch Mowers)

Side-to-side height is adjustable on 30-inch mower decks. Maximum difference side-to-side should be $\frac{1}{8}$ inch (3.2 mm). To adjust side-to-side height, loosen the capscrew and rotate the eccentric (E—Fig. SN1-21) on the left front lift arm so the desired dimension is obtained and retighten the nuts. Rotate the eccentric counterclockwise to raise the right side of the deck or clockwise to raise the left side of the deck.

REMOVAL AND INSTALLATION

1. Detach the mower deck cover.
2. Loosen the belt idler and move the idler away from the belt to increase belt slack.

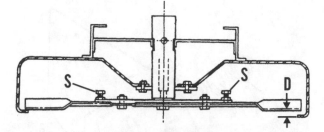
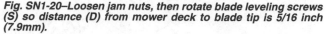

Fig. SN1-20—Loosen jam nuts, then rotate blade leveling screws (S) so distance (D) from mower deck to blade tip is 5/16 inch (7.9mm).

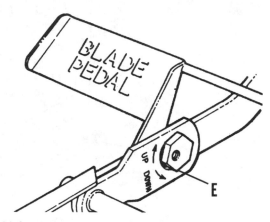

Fig. SN1-21—Loosen capscrew and rotate eccentric (E) on left front lift arm to adjust side-to-side dimension on 30-inch mower deck.

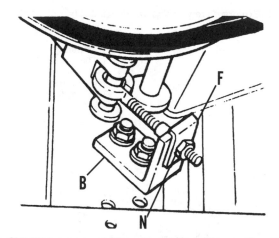

Fig. SN1-22—Loosen nut (N) and rotate nut (F) as outlined in the text to adjust blade brake.

3. Place the machine in an upright position on the rear stand as previously described.

4. Move the clutch lift yoke so the driven disc is moved away from the drive disc and a gap exists.

5. Separate the mower drive belt from the engine pulley and feed it through the gap between the driven and drive discs.

6. Place the machine on all four wheels.

7. Disconnect the interlock switch wire.

8. Detach the front and rear lift arms and links and remove the mower deck.

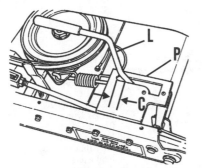

Fig. SN1-23—The mower engagement lever (L) should be 1/4 inch (6.4 mm) from rear edge of latch plate (P) when blade brake is properly adjusted. See text.

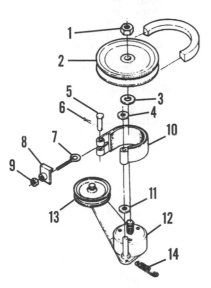

Fig. SN1-24—Exploded view of blade brake mechanism.

1. Nut	8. Flange nut
2. Pulley	9. Jam nut
3. Washer	10. Brake band
4. Washer	11. Spacer
5. Clevis pin	12. Brake drum
6. Cotter pin	13. Idler
7. Eye-bolt	14. Spring

9. Install the mower deck by reversing the removal procedure.

BLADE BRAKE

The mower is equipped with a band brake that stops rotation of the blade spindle within 3 seconds. The mower engagement lever is held in position by pedals. When either pedal is released, the mower engagement lever snaps into disengaged position and the blade brake is actuated.

ADJUSTMENT

1. Remove the mower deck cover so the spindle pulley is visible.
2. Run the mower so the blade is rotating at normal speed, then release the blade stop pedal. If time required for blade to stop is not satisfactory, proceed to Step 3 and adjust the blade brake.
3. Lower the mower deck and remove the belt cover.
4. While holding the mower engagement lever to the rear, loosen the jam nut (N–Fig. SN1-22).

5. Move the mower engagement lever to the ON position and turn the flange nut (F) clockwise to increase the brake band tension. Be sure the flange fits over the bracket (B).
6. Release the blade stop pedal.
7. Move the mower engagement lever to the OFF position, then depress the blade stop pedal.
8. Rotate the flange nut (F) so clearance (C–Fig. SN1-23) between the mower engagement lever (L) and the rear edge of the latch plate (P) is ¼ inch (6.4 mm).
9. Tighten the jam nut (N–Fig. SN1-22) and recheck the blade brake operation. If the blade brake engagement time is unsatisfactory, replacement of the brake components may be necessary.

OVERHAUL

Blade brake components (see Fig. SN1-24) are accessible after removing the mower belt and spindle pulley. Replace the brake band if excessively worn or contaminated by oil or grease. Be sure all components are in good operating condition. Adjust the blade brake as outlined in the previous section.

MOWER SPINDLE

LUBRICATION

The mower spindle should be lubricated annually. Apply multipurpose grease to the mower spindle through the grease fitting on the underside of the spindle housing. Two shots should be sufficient.

OVERHAUL

Refer to Fig. SN1-25 for an exploded view of the spindle assembly and proceed as follows.
1. Remove the blade.
2. Remove the spindle pulley.
3. Remove the blade brake components.
4. Unscrew the spindle housing and remove from the deck. Note the location of any spacers during disassembly and mark them so they can be installed in the original position.
5. Unscrew the blade adapter.
6. Drive or press the spindle with the lower bearing out of the bottom of the spindle housing.
7. Detach the snap ring in the upper end of the spindle housing and press or drive out the upper bearing.
8. Reassemble by reversing the disassembly procedure. When installing the spindle housing on the deck, position the mounting bolts so there is not a bolt in front of the grease fitting.

ELECTRICAL

Refer to Fig. SN1-26 for a wiring diagram. The shift control lever must be in PARK and the mower must be disengaged for the engine to start.

The shift detent switch prevents engine starting unless the shift control lever is in PARK position. To adjust detent switch engagement, loosen the screws (S–Fig. SN1-10) and reposition the shift quadrant so the switch is fully engaged with the shift control lever in PARK.

The interlock module should be considered faulty only after all other wiring and devices have been tested or checked. The interlock module may malfunction when subjected to heat and function normally when cold. Modules are designed for operation with specific engine brands and must not be interchanged. Use of improper module may result in unsafe operation.

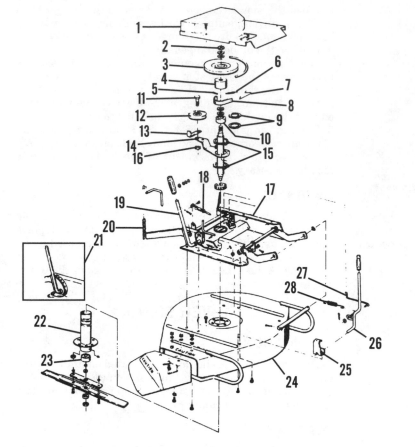

Fig. SN1-25–Exploded view of typical single-blade mower deck assembly.

1. Spindle cover
2. Locknut
3. Driven pulley
4. Brake drum
5. Cotter pin
6. Return spring
7. Wire link
8. Brake assy.
9. Snap rings
10. Upper spindle bearing
11. Idler shaft bolt
12. Idler pulley
13. Keeper
14. Idler arm
15. Retainer ring
16. Spindle shaft
17. Deck rail assy.
18. Timing link & rod
19. Lift handle
20. Suspension chain (2)
21. Height indicator
22. Spindle housing
23. Bearing
24. Deck
25. Handle mount
26. Blade control handle
27. Idler control rod
28. Idler spring

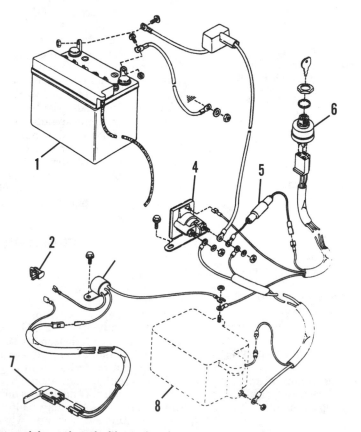

Fig. SN1-26–Wiring diagram for models equipped with an electric starter.

1. Battery
2. Shift detent switch
3. Interlock module
4. Solenoid
5. Fuse (10 amp)
6. Key switch
7. Deck switch
8. Engine

Table 1. DRIVE SYSTEM TROUBLESHOOTING GUIDE

PROBLEM	POSSIBLE CAUSE	CORRECTIVE ACTION
No drive—mower will not move in either direction.	Oil or grease on drive or driven grease.	Clean with solvent and wipe dry.
	Excessive clearance between drive and driven discs.	Check clutch adjustment. Check speed selector lever linkage and lift yoke for jamming or damage. Repair or replace.
	Rubber tread of driven disc damaged or worn out.	Replace driven disc.
	Breakage in primary chaincase or final drive case.	Use check procedure to locate trouble. Disassemble and repair
Selector hard to move when shifting through speed range.	Hex shaft dry-galled or burred.	Remove burrs, polish hex surface lightly, check shifting action.
	Jammed or damaged control linkage.	Disassemble linkage only, clean, lube and replace parts as needed.
Noisy drive.	Damaged driven chain or bearings.	Use check procedure to locate problem. Repair as needed.
Overheating of final drive case or primary chaincase.	Insufficient lubrication.	Lubricate as required.
	Grease leaks from case.	Disassemble leaking case and replace gasket. Check for other possible damage

SNAPPER

FRONT-STEER MOWERS
SERIES 11, 13, 14, 15, 16, 17,
18 AND 19 (Except 42-inch Mower)

Model	Make	Engine Model	Horsepower	Cutting Width, In.
250814B	B&S	195702	8	25
250814BE	B&S	195707	8	25
250815B	B&S	195702	8	25
250815BE	B&S	195707	8	25
250816B	B&S	195702	8	25
250816BE	B&S	195707	8	25
280914BE	B&S	28A707	9	28
280915BE	B&S	28A707	9	28
281011BE	B&S	*	10	28
281013BE	B&S	*	10	28
281014BE	B&S	28A707	10	28
281016BE	B&S	28A707	10	28
281318BE	B&S	*	13	28
300914BE	B&S	28A707	9	30
300915BE	B&S	28A707	9	30
301011BE	B&S	*	10	30
301013BE	B&S	*	10	30
301014BE	B&S	28A707	10	30
301016BE	B&S	28A707	10	30
301213BE	B&S	*	12	30
301214BE	B&S	*	12	30
301215BE	B&S	*	12	30
301216BE	B&S	*	12	30
301318BE	B&S	*	13	30
301413KVE	Kohler	*	14	30
3312511BE	B&S	*	12.5	33
3312513BE	B&S	*	12.5	33
331314BE	B&S	28M707	13	33
331413KVE	Kohler	CV14ST	14	33
331414KVE	Kohler	CV14ST	14	33
331415BVE	B&S	287707	14	33
331415KVE	Kohler	CV14ST	14	33
331416BVE	B&S	287707	14	33
331416KVE	Kohler	CV14ST	14	33
3314518BVE	B&S	*	14.5	33
331518KVE	Kohler	*	15	33
M250819BE	B&S	*	8	25
M280817B	B&S	*	8	28
M280917B	B&S	28B702	9	28
M280919B	B&S	*	9	28
M281019BE	B&S	*	10	28
M281019BE	B&S	*	10	28
M300919B	B&S	*	9	30
M301019BE	B&S	*	10	30

(Continued)

Model	Make	Engine Model	Horsepower	Cutting Width, In.
N250816B	B&S	195702	8	25
N250816BE	B&S	195707	8	25
N281016BE	B&S	28A707	10	28
R281213BE	B&S	*	12	28
R3312513BE	B&S	*	12.5	33

*Note the engine model number and refer to the engine service section in this manual for engine specifications.

NOTE: Some operations may be performed more easily if the machine is standing upright. Observe the following safety recommendations when raising the machine to the upright position:

1. Drain the fuel tank or make certain the fuel level is low enough so that fuel will not drain out.
2. Close the fuel shut-off valve if so equipped.
3. Remove the battery if so equipped.
4. Disconnect the spark plug wire and tie it out of way.
5. Although not absolutely essential, on models with the spark plug at the rear of the machine, the engine oil should be drained to prevent flooding the combustion chamber with oil when the engine is tilted.
6. Secure the mower from tipping by lashing the machine to a post or overhead beam.

MODEL IDENTIFICATION

Snapper models are categorized by series numbers that indicate design differences. The series number of a particular model is the last two numerals in the model number. For instance, Model 281014BE is a Series 14 model and Model 301216BE is a Series 16 model. Some service procedures in this section are directed to models of a specific series.

FRONT WHEELS

LUBRICATION

Each front wheel hub is equipped with a grease fitting. Front wheels should be injected with multipurpose grease after every 25 hours of operation. Five shots should be sufficient, however, ten shots may be required if the hub assembly is clean and new bearings are installed.

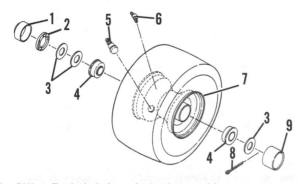

Fig. SN2-1—Exploded view of wheel assembly.

1. Boot
2. Felt seal
3. Washers
4. Bearing
5. Air valve
6. Grease fitting
7. Wheel
8. Cotter pin
9. Hub cap

REMOVAL AND INSTALLATION

The front wheels are equipped with replaceable bearings. To remove the wheel and bearings, proceed as follows:
1. Remove the hub cap (9–Fig. SN2-1).
2. Remove the cotter pin (8–Fig. SN2-1).
3. Remove the wheel with bearings.
4. Separate the bearings from the wheel.
5. Inspect the bearings for damage.
6. Inspect the wheel for rim and hub damage.
7. Reverse the removal steps to reassemble. Pack the wheel bearings with grease before installation.

OVERHAUL

Refer to Fig. SN2-2 or SN2-3 for an exploded view of the spindle assembly. To remove a front spindle, proceed as follows.
1. Raise and support the side to be serviced.
2. Remove the hub cap, cotter pin, wheel and tire.
3. Disconnect the tie rod from the spindle.
4. Detach the snap ring from the upper end of the spindle and lower the spindle from the axle.
5. Inspect components for damage.
6. Install the spindle by reversing the removal procedure.

STEERING SYSTEM

TOE-IN SETTING

Toe-in setting on all models except Series 11 models is not adjustable. Adjustable tie rods are used on Series 11 models. Proceed as follows to check and adjust toe-in on Series 11 models.
1. Be sure the tires are properly inflated.
2. Position the machine on a flat, smooth surface.
3. Position the front wheels in the straight-ahead position.
4. Measure the distance at spindle height between the center of the tires on the rear side.
5. Locate the same tire centerline points on the front side of the tires and measure the front distance.
6. The distance on the front side should be ⅜-½ inch (9.5-12.7 mm) shorter (toed-in) than the measured distance on the rear side.
7. To adjust the toe-in, detach the tie rod end (7–Fig. SN2-3).
8. Loosen the jam nut (6) and turn the tie rod end to shorten or lengthen the tie rod as needed to obtain the specified toe-in.
9. Retighten the jam nut after completing the adjustment.

OVERHAUL

1. Raise the front of the machine.
2. Detach the tie rods from the steering arm (20–Fig. SN2-2).
3. Drive out the pin (2) and remove the steering wheel.
4. Remove the foam sleeve (3) and washer (4).

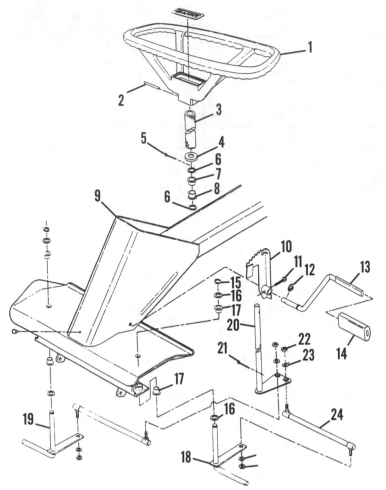

Fig. SN2-2–Exploded view of front steering system.

1. Steering wheel
2. Pin
3. Sleeve
4. Washer
5. Cotter pin
6. Washer
7. Bushing
8. Bushing
9. Front frame
10. Clutch/brake arm
11. Screw
12. Snap ring
13. Clutch/brake pedal
14. Pad
15. Snap ring
16. Washer
17. Bushing
18. Spindle (left)
19. Spindle (right)
20. Steering shaft
21. Cotter pin
22. Nut
23. Washer
24. Tie rod

5. Remove the cotter pin (5) and washer (6).

6. Withdraw the steering shaft from the bottom of the machine.

7. Reassemble the steering shaft by reversing the disassembly procedure.

ENGINE

Refer to the appropriate engine section in this manual for tune-up specifications, engine overhaul procedures and engine maintenance.

REMOVAL AND INSTALLATION

1. Disconnect the spark plug wire.

2. If the engine is equipped with an electric starter, disconnect the cable from the starter motor.

3. Shift the mower drive control lever to the OUT position.

4. Unbolt and remove the spindle cover from the mower deck.

5. Relieve tension from the idler, then slip the belt off the mower spindle pulley(s).

6. Remove the belt from the driving disc hub pulley.

7. Disconnect the fuel hose from the engine.

8. Detach the throttle cable from the carburetor.

9. Disconnect all interfering wiring from the engine.

10. Remove the engine mounting screws and remove the engine.

11. Install the engine by reversing the removal procedure.

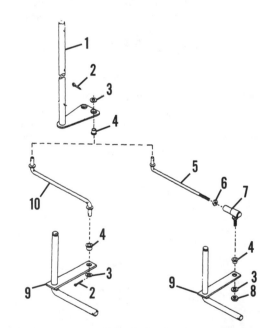

Fig. SN2-3–Exploded view of adjustable tie rod used on Series 11 models and non-adjustable tie rod used on some Series 13 models.

1. Steering shaft
2. Cotter pin
3. Washer
4. Bushing
5. Tie rod (Series 11)
6. Jam nut
7. Tie rod end
8. Nut
9. Spindle (left)
10. Tie rod (Series 13)

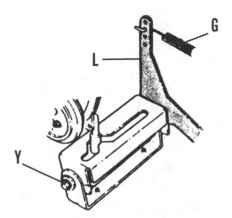

Fig. SN2-4–Clutch lever (L) is bolted to lift yoke (Y). Relocating spring (G) end in holes in clutch lever changes clutch traction. See text.

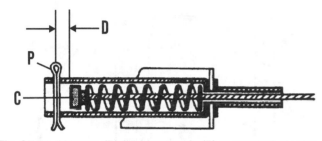

Fig. SN2-5–Distance (D) from cotter pin (P) to rear end of cable (C) should be 1/2-3/4 inch (13-19 mm). Rotate nuts (N–Fig. SN2-6) to obtain desired distance.

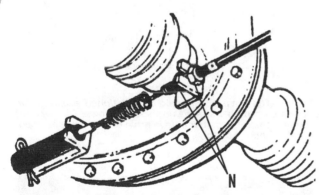

Fig. SN2-6–Rotate nuts (N) to obtain desired distance (D–Fig. SN2-5) at cable end.

CLUTCH/BRAKE CABLE

NOTE: If the location of the frame tube is changed, for instance, to adjust mower belt tension, always check the clutch/brake operating cable for proper adjustment.

OPERATION

All models are equipped with a cable-operated clutch. The cable extends from a keyhole slot in the clutch/brake pedal arm (10–Fig. SN2-2) through the main frame tube to the lever arm portion of the lift yoke (Y–Fig. SN2-4). Pulling the lift yoke by depressing the clutch/brake pedal moves the chaincase and driven disc away from the drive disc attached to the engine.

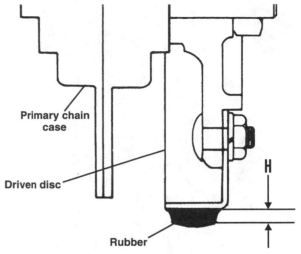

Fig. SN2-7–If height (H) of rubber ring on driven disc is 1/16 inch (1.6 mm) or less, disc must be replaced.

ADJUSTMENT

1. Fully depress the clutch/brake pedal and engage the parking brake.
2. Place the shift control lever in the REVERSE position.
3. Measure the gap between the drive disc and driven disc. The gap should be $\frac{1}{16}$-$\frac{1}{8}$ inch (1.6-3.2 mm). If the gap is not correct, proceed to Step 4.
4. Disengage the parking brake and relocate the front end of the clutch/brake cable in the control arm slot so another ferrule on the cable is engaged.
5. Recheck the gap between the discs.
6. Fully depress the clutch/brake pedal and engage the parking brake.
7. Measure the distance (D–Fig. SN2-5) from the cotter pin (P) to the rear end of the cable (C). Distance should be $\frac{1}{2}$-$\frac{3}{4}$ inch (13-19 mm). Rotate the nuts (N–Fig. SN2-6) to obtain the desired distance.

TRACTION DRIVE CLUTCH

ADJUSTMENT

For normal setting, position the spring (G–Fig. SN2-4) end in the second hole from the end of the clutch lever (L). If the unit stutters or hops during clutch engagement, move the spring end to an inner hole. If the traction is insufficient, move the spring end to the outermost hole in the lever.

DISCS INSPECTION AND ADJUSTMENT

Replace the driven disc if it is worn to less than $\frac{1}{16}$ inch (1.6 mm) as shown in Fig. SN2-7. To check disc contact, proceed as follows.

1. Install a driven disc that has half the rubber ring removed so the metal is showing. If modification of an old driven disc is not possible, a test disc may be fabricated using the dimensions of the metal portion of the existing driven disc.
2. Position the shift control lever in any forward gear.
3. With the clutch pedal released, measure the clearance (C–Fig. SN2-8) between the metal on the driven disc gauge (N) and the drive disc (D). The clearance should be 0.005-0.010 inch (0.13-0.25 mm).

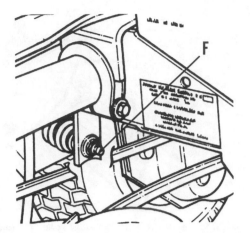

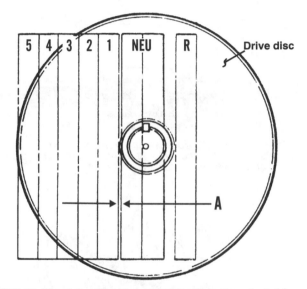

Fig. SN2-9–The shift lever grease fitting (F) should be injected with multipurpose grease after every 25 hours of operation.

Fig. SN2-8–With the clutch pedal released and the shift control lever in any forward gear, clearance (C) between metal of drive disc (D) should be 0.005-0.010 inch (0.13-0.25 mm).

4. To obtain desired clearance, adjust the position of the drive disc on the engine crankshaft.

SHIFT CONTROL LINKAGE

LUBRICATION

The shift lever grease fitting (F–Fig. SN2-9) should be injected with multipurpose grease after every 25 hours of operation. Two shots should be sufficient.

ADJUSTMENT

The shift lever should be synchronized with the position of the driven disc against the drive disc. Refer to Fig. SN2-10 and note the position of the driven disc against the drive disc at related ground speed. Note the first speed position of the driven disc is approximately $\frac{1}{16}$ inch (1.6 mm) from the outer diameter of the hole in the drive disc.

Loosen the mounting screws (S–Fig. SN2-11) and relocate the shift quadrant as needed so the shift lever and driven disc positions are synchronized.

FRICTION DRIVE TRANSMISSION AND FINAL DRIVE

OPERATION

Power for the machine is transmitted through two discs, a drive disc and a driven disc. The drive disc is attached to the engine's crankshaft while the driven disc is attached to the primary chain case input shaft. As the primary chain case is moved from side-to-side through the shift mechanism, the driven friction disc contacts a different spot on the drive disc to change the ground speed. Moving the driven disc to the opposite side of the drive disc reverses the direction. The final drive case contains the reduction gear, differential and axle assemblies.

LUBRICATION

Position the machine so it is upright as previously described. Annually fill the final drive case so the grease level in the case is even with the plug's opening (P–Fig.

Fig. SN2-10–The drive disc should be positioned against drive disc (D) as shown for transmission speed shown. Distance (A) from outer diameter of center hole in drive disc to first speed position is 1/16 inch (1.6mm).

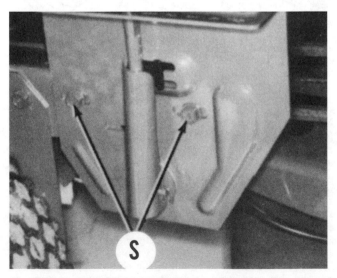

Fig. SN2-11–To synchronize shift lever and drive disc, loosen mounting screw (S) and related shift quadrant.

190

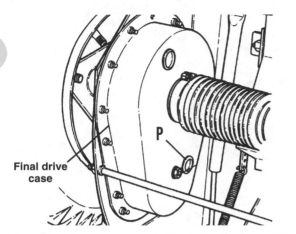

Fig. SN2-12–Lever of grease in final drive case should be even with opening for plug (P).

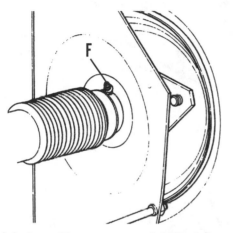

Fig. SN2-13–Inject a multipurpose grease into the left rear axle grease fitting (F) after ever 25 hours of operation.

SN2-12). The recommended lubricant is Snapper 0 grease or equivalent.

Annually add 1 ounce (30 mL) of Snapper 0 grease to the primary chaincase; but do not overfill. Primary chaincase capacity is 2 ounces (60 mL).

Inject multipurpose grease into the left, rear axle grease fitting (F–Fig. SN2-13) after every 25 hours of operation. Two shots should be sufficient.

Periodically lubricate lift yoke pivot points.

INSPECTION AND TROUBLESHOOTING

If a malfunction in the drive system is suspected, proceed as follows.

1. Raise the machine so it is upright as previously described.
2. Check for leaks at the primary chaincase flanges, final drive case and shaft seals.
3. Disengage the mower deck drive and roll the rear wheels by hand with the clutch both depressed and released and with the shift control lever in NEUTRAL and when shifted into DRIVE.
4. Loosen the drive tube boot clamps and pull back so rotation of the hex drive tube can be observed.
5. Check for normal action of the differential pinions.
6. Jamming, locking or noise in final drive case can be caused by damaged differential parts or a broken drive chain. Undue noise or abnormal operation in the final drive

case or in the primary chaincase will determine which assemblies should be removed for inspection and/or repair. Refer to Table 1 DRIVE SYSTEM TROUBLESHOOTING GUIDE for additional service information.

OVERHAUL

Refer to the appropriate following section for service information on assembly requiring service.

Driven Disc

Driven disc rubber ring must not be worn to less than $\frac{1}{32}$-$\frac{1}{16}$ inch (0.8-1.6 mm), otherwise, replace the driven disc (see Fig. SN2-7). If the driven disc is damaged and requires service, proceed as follows.

1. Place the machine in an upright position on the rear stand as previously described.
2. Unscrew the disc retaining nuts and remove the disc (20–Fig. SN2-14).
3. When installing the disc on models equipped with the fiber thrust washer (21), be sure the fiber washer is centered on the hub (19) and is free-floating.

Drive Disc

The maximum allowable drive disc warpage is 0.020 inch (0.51 mm). To remove the drive disc, proceed as follows.

1. Remove the driven disc as previously described as well as the driven disc hub (19–Fig. SN2-14).
2. Separate the mower drive belt from the idler and remove the mower drive belt from the drive disc pulley.
3. Place the shift control lever in the fifth speed position.
4. Unscrew the setscrews (S–Fig. SN2-15) and carefully pull the drive disc off the crankshaft. It may be necessary to move the lift yoke aside during removal.
5. To separate the disc from the hub, secure hub in a vise and unscrew the disc from the hub.
6. Install the drive disc by reversing the removal procedure. See the TRACTION DRIVE CLUTCH section for procedure to position the drive disc on the engine crankshaft.

Left Side (Primary Chaincase)

1. Place the machine in an upright position on the rear stand as previously described.
2. Remove the left rear wheel.
3. Unscrew the hub retaining screw and remove the hub using Snapper tool 60237 or other suitable puller.
4. Remove the dust shield from the axle.
5. 12- and 14-hp Models–remove the lock collar (33–Fig. SN2-14) by rotating in a clockwise direction after loosening the setscrew.
6. Detach the boot (29).
7. Unscrew the tie rod (34) nut.
8. Unscrew the fasteners securing the left fender plate (32) and remove the left fender plate.
9. Disconnect the shift link from the chaincase half (8).
10. Detach the boot from the chaincase half (8).
11. Separate the chaincase rod from the lift yoke and slide the chaincase off the hex tube.
12. Secure the driven disc hub (19).
13. Unscrew the brake lever retaining screw and remove the brake lever (35).
14. Remove the driven disc and hub assembly.
15. Unscrew the chaincase bolts and separate the chaincase halves (8 and 18).

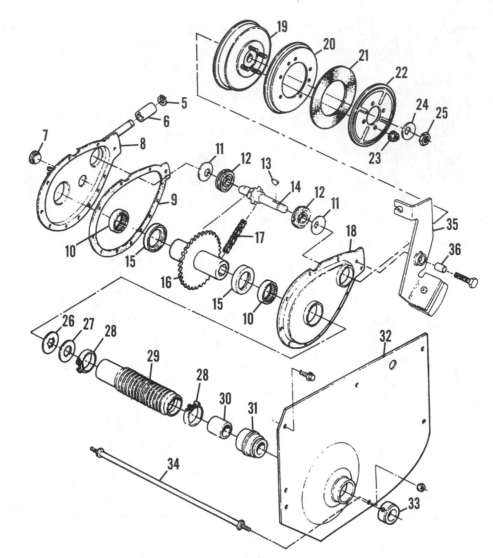

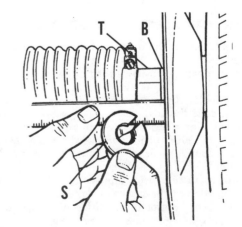

Fig. SN2-14—Exploded view of primary chaincase assembly. Spacer (30) and lock collar (33) are used only on 12- and 14-hp models.

5. Snap ring	13. Key	21. Fiber washer	29. Boot
6. Roller	14. Sprocket shaft	22. Plate	30. Spacer
7. Plug	15. Thrust washer	23. Locknut	31. Bearing
8. Chaincase half	16. Sprocket & hub	24. Belleville washer	32. Fender plate (left)
9. Gasket	17. Chain	25. Locknut	33. Lock collar
10. Needle bearing	18. Chaincase half	26. Hex thrust washer	34. Tie rod
11. Belleville washer	19. Driven disc hub	27. Nylon thrust washer	35. Brake lever
12. Bearing	20. Driven disc	28. Clamp	36. Bushing

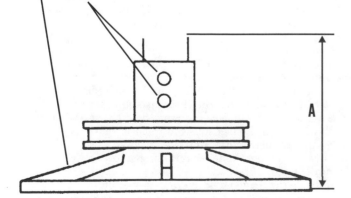

Fig. SN2-15—Remove setscrews (S) to remove drive disc (D).

Fig. SN2-16—End play between hex tube (T) and bearing (B) should be 3/32 inch (2.4 mm).

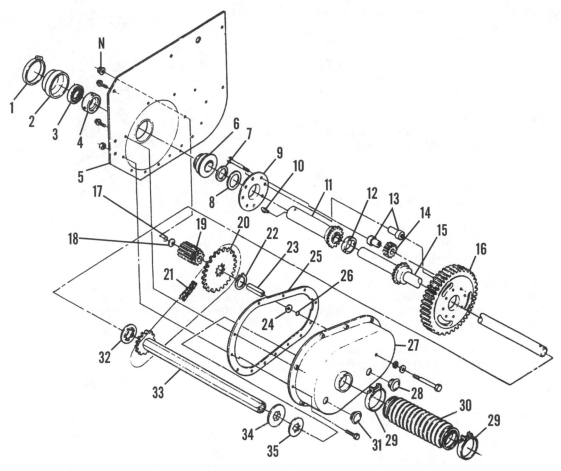

Fig. SN2-17—Exploded view of final drive assembly. Lock collar (4) is used on 12-and 14-hp models.

1. Clamp
2. Dust cover
3. Seal
4. Lock collar
5. Fender plate (right)
6. Baring
7. Spacer
8. Thrust washer
9. Plate
10. Grease fitting
11. Short axle
12. Nylon spacer
13. Pinion spacers
14. Pinions
15. Long axle
16. Final drive gear
17. O-ring
18. Belleville washer
19. Gear
20. Sprocket
21. Chain
22. Snap ring
23. Spacer
24. Belleville washer
25. Gasket
26. O-ring
27. Case
28. Plug
29. Clamp
30. Boot
31. Plug
32. Thrust washer
33. Hex drive tube
34. Nylon thrust washer
35. Hex thrust washer

16. Remove, clean and inspect the chaincase components.

17. Remove the needle bearings (10) and ball bearings (12) by pressing to the inside of the case half.

18. Reassemble the primary chaincase by reversing the disassembly procedure. Note the following:

   a. Press the ball bearings (12) into the case halves until the locating ring around the outside of the bearing seats against the case.

   b. Press against the lettered side of the needle bearings (10) so the lettered side is to the inside of the case half and the bearing is flush with the inner surface of the case half.

   c. The cup side of the Belleville washers (11) must be away from the bearings (12).

   d. After assembly, check end play between the hex tube (T–Fig. SN2-16) and bearing (B). Desired end play is $\frac{3}{32}$ inch (2.4 mm). Adjust end play by installing the nylon split shims (S) between the tube and bearing.

   e. Fill the primary chaincase with 2 ounces (60 mL) of Snapper 0 grease. A new plug (7–Fig. SN2-14) should be installed.

Right Side (Final Drive Case)

Place the machine in an upright position on the rear stand as previously outlined then proceed as follows.

1. Remove the rear wheels.

2. Unscrew the hub retaining screws and remove both wheel hubs using Snapper tool 60237 or other suitable puller.

3. Remove the dust shields from the axles.

4. 12- and 14-hp Models—Remove the lock collars (33–Fig. SN2-14) from each axle by loosening the setscrew and rotating the collar in the direction opposite to forward wheel rotation.

5. Unscrew the tie rod nut.

6. Detach the boot (30–Fig. SN2-17) from the final drive case.

7. Unscrew the fasteners securing the right fender plate (5–Fig. SN2-17) to the frame and remove the right fender plate with the final drive case.

8. Place the assembly on a workbench so the axle protrudes down through a hole in the workbench and the fender plate is on top.

9. Unscrew the fender plate retaining screws and nuts and remove the fender plate from the final drive case.

10. Prevent the hex shaft (33) from moving and withdraw the final drive gear (16) and axle assembly from the case.

11. Remove the idler and sprocket components (17 through 26).

12. Remove the hex tube components (32 through 35). The bushings in the hex tube (33) are not replaceable.

13. To disassemble and reassemble the differential, proceed as follows:

   a. Unscrew the capscrews securing the differential plate (9). Discard the capscrews–the screw threads lose their locking capability when unscrewed.

   b. Disassemble the differential components.

   c. Replace the nylon spacer (12) if worn. Bushings in the short axle (11) are not replaceable. Be sure the nylon spacer (12) fits over the weld on the long axle (15).

   d. Assemble the pinions (14), spacers (13) and short axle as shown in Figs. SN2-18 or SN2-19.

   e. Lubricate the bushings in the short axle before assembly.

   f. Install the differential plate (9–Fig. SN2-17) using new capscrews (Snapper part 1-2333).

14. Reassemble the final drive assembly and fender plate by reversing the disassembly procedure while noting the following:

   a. Be sure the thrust washers (32 and 34) are installed. The absence of thrust washers will cause rapid wear.

   b. Install a nylon hex washer (35) with the lip towards the sprocket on the hex tube.

   c. Lubricate the bushings in the hex tube (33) prior to assembly. Make sure the lubrication hole in the idler (19) is open.

   d. Install the Belleville washers (18 and 24) so the cupped side is towards the O-rings (17 and 26).

   e. The idler, sprocket, hex tube and chain must be installed as a unit.

   f. Lubricate the outside of the short axle (11).

   g. After placing the fender plate on the final drive case, tighten the case retaining screws and nuts, then tighten the idler bolt retaining locknut (N) to 18-20 ft.-lb. (25-27 N•m). The locknut must be tightened properly as loosening the nut may allow the chain to jump from the sprockets due to sprocket misalignment.

   h. Lubricate the outside of the hex tube (33) before inserting it in the primary chaincase.

   i. 12- and 14-hp Models—rotate the lock collars in the same direction as the forward wheel rotation.

   j. Fill the final drive case with Snapper 0 grease so the grease level in the case is even with the plug opening (P–Fig. SN2-12). New plugs (28 and 31–Fig. SN2-17) should be installed.

GROUND DRIVE BRAKE

NOTE: If the frame tube location is changed, for instance, to adjust mower belt tension, always check the brake operating cable for proper adjustment.

All models are equipped with a combination clutch/brake pedal on the machine's left side. The brake is applied when the clutch/brake pedal is pressed down to its limit. At this point, the brake lever (35–Fig. SN2-14) rotates so its lined shoe contacts the inner rim of the driven hub (19). Pressure on the upper end of the brake lever is exerted by the lift yoke when actuated by tension on the clutch/brake cable.

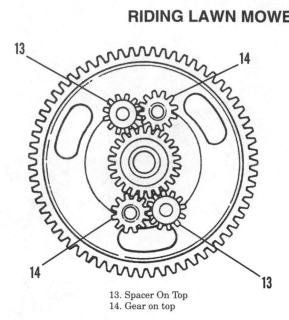

13. Spacer On Top
14. Gear on top

Fig. SN2-18–When installing pinion spacers and pinions on final drive gear on all except 12- and 14- hp models, alternate top positions of pinion spacers (13) and pinions (14) so they appear as shown.

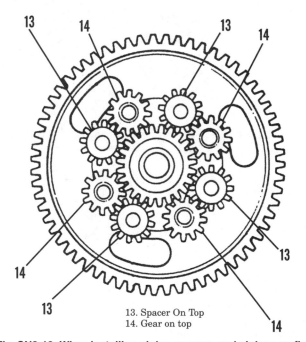

13. Spacer On Top
14. Gear on top

Fig. SN2-19–When installing pinion spacers and pinions on final drive gear of 12- and 14-hp models, alternate top position of pinions spacers (13) and pinions (14) so they appear as shown.

To adjust the brake, refer to the CLUTCH/BRAKE CABLE section.

MOWER BELT

ADJUSTMENT

Series 11, 13 and 14

Mower drive belt tension is determined by measuring the distance between the opposite runs of the belt at the closest point with the mower engaged. See Fig. SN2-20.

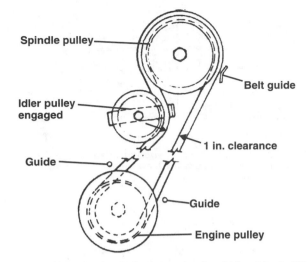

Fig. SN2-20–Mower drive belt clearance should be 1 inch (25 mm) at idler pulley as shown. Refer to text for adjustment procedure.

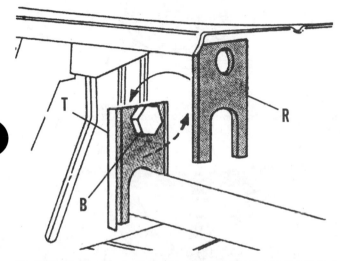

Fig. SN2-21–To adjust mower drive belt tension on Series 11 and 13, remove bolt (B) and relocated spacer plates (R) next to bracket (T) to extend or withdraw main frame tube.

The distance between the belt runs should be 1 inch (25 mm).

To adjust belt tension, remove the shoulder bolt (B—Fig. SN2-21) and relocate the spacer plates (R) in front or behind the bracket (T) as needed. Reinstall and tighten the shoulder bolt.

Belt guides should be at least ⅛ inch (3.2 mm) from the belt.

Series 14

Mower drive belt tension is determined by measuring the distance between the opposite runs of the belt at the closest point with the mower engaged. See Fig. SN2-20. The distance between the belt runs should be 1 inch (25 mm).

To adjust belt tension, remove the hairpin (Fig. SN2-22) and washers. Pull the front frame forward as needed to obtain the desired distance (Fig. SN2-20). Install the spacer plates behind the bracket as needed. Reinstall the washers and hairpin.

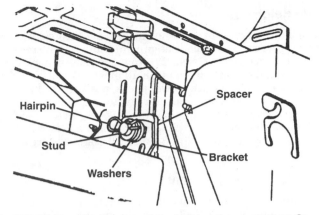

Fig. SN2-22–To adjust mower drive belt tension, except on Series 11 and 13 models, remove hairpin and washers, then insert spacer plates as needed.

Belt guides should be at least ¹⁄₁₆ inch (1.6 mm) from belt.

Series 15, 16, 17, 18 and 19

25-inch Mower

Mower drive belt tension is determined by measuring the distance between the opposite runs of the belt at the closest point with the mower engaged. See Fig. SN2-20. The distance between the belt runs should be 1 inch (25 mm).

To adjust belt tension, remove the hairpin (Fig. SN2-22) and washers. Pull the front frame forward as needed to obtain the desired distance (Fig. SN2-20). Install the spacer plates behind the bracket as needed. Reinstall the washers and hairpin.

Belt guides should be at least ¹⁄₁₆ inch (1.6 mm) from belt.

28-, 30- and 33-inch Mowers

Mower belt adjustment is not necessary. If belt slippage occurs, install a new belt.

REMOVAL AND INSTALLATION

1. Detach the mower deck cover.
2. Loosen the belt idler and move the idler away from the belt to increase belt slack.
3. Place the machine in an upright position on the rear stand as previously described.
4. Move the clutch lift yoke so the driven disc is moved away from the drive disc and a gap exists.
5. Separate the mower drive belt from the engine pulley.
6. Remove the mower belt by passing the belt through the gap between the driven and drive discs.
7. Install the mower drive belt by reversing the removal procedure. The belt can be forced around the drive disc by moving the shift control lever to fifth speed position thereby forcing the belt out towards the edge of the drive disc. Adjust the belt tension as outlined in the ADJUSTMENT section.

MOWER DECK

HEIGHT ADJUSTMENT

All mower control linkage must be in good operating condition and tires properly inflated. Park the machine on a level surface with the engine stopped and the spark plug wire disconnected.

Blade Height

The blade adapter bar on some models is equipped with adjusting screws to aid blade alignment. Adjust the screws so the distance (D–Fig. SN2-23) from the mower deck to the blade tip is $\frac{3}{8}$ inch (9.5 mm) on all mower decks except 30-inch decks. On 30-inch mower decks, position the blade so it is aligned with the front-to-rear unit centerline. Adjust the screws so the front of the blade is $\frac{1}{8}$-$\frac{1}{4}$ inch (3.2-6.4 mm) above the deck lip and the rear of the blade is $\frac{3}{8}$ inch (9.5 mm) above the deck lip. Be sure all fasteners are secure.

Front-To-Rear Adjustment

Front-to-rear height difference is determined by measuring the height of the blade above the ground at the front and rear. On 30-inch mower decks, the rear height should be level or $\frac{1}{8}$ inch (3.2 mm) higher than the front. On all other models, the rear height should be level or $\frac{1}{8}$ inch (3.2 mm) lower than the front. To adjust the height, relocate the ferrules on the hanger cables.

Side-to-side Adjustment

Models So Equipped

Side-to-side height is adjustable on mower decks equipped with a leveling eccentric (E–Fig. SN2-24). Maximum difference side-to-side should be $\frac{1}{8}$ inch (3.2 mm). To adjust side-to-side height, loosen the capscrew and rotate the eccentric (E–Fig. SN2-24) on the left front lift arm so the desired dimension is obtained and retighten the nuts. Rotate the eccentric counterclockwise to raise the deck's right side or clockwise to raise the deck's left side.

REMOVAL AND INSTALLATION

1. Detach the mower deck cover.
2. Loosen the belt idler and move the idler away from the belt to increase belt slack.
3. Place the machine in an upright position on the rear stand as previously described.
4. Move the clutch lift yoke so the driven disc is moved away from the drive disc and a gap exists.
5. Separate the mower drive belt from the engine pulley and feed through the gap between the driven and drive discs.
6. Place the machine on all four wheels.
7. Disconnect the interlock switch wire.
8. Detach the front and rear lift arms and links and remove the mower deck.
9. Install the mower deck by reversing the removal procedure.

BLADE BRAKE

The mower is equipped with a band brake stopping rotation of the blade spindle within 3 seconds. The mower engagement lever is held in position by pedals. When either pedal is released, the mower engagement lever snaps into the disengaged position and the blade brake is actuated.

ADJUSTMENT

Series 11, 13 and 14

1. Remove the mower deck cover so the spindle pulley is visible.
2. Run the mower so the blade is rotating at normal speed, then release the blade stop pedal. If the time required for

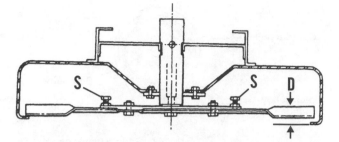
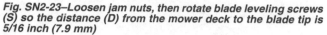

Fig. SN2-23–Loosen jam nuts, then rotate blade leveling screws (S) so the distance (D) from the mower deck to the blade tip is 5/16 inch (7.9 mm)

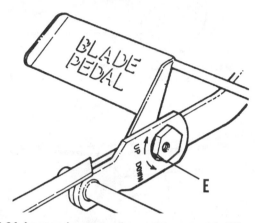

Fig. SN2-24–Loosen jam nuts, then rotate eccentric (E) on left front lift arm to adjust side-to-side dimension on 30-inch mower decks.

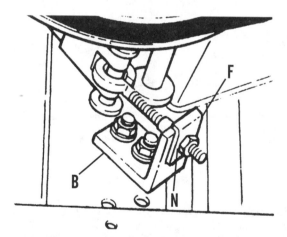

Fig. SN2-25–Loosen nut (N) and rotate flange nut (F) as outlined in text to adjust blade brake on Series 11, 13 and 14.

the blade to stop is not satisfactory, proceed to Step 3 and adjust the blade brake.

3. Lower the mower deck and remove the belt cover.

4. While holding the mower engagement lever to the rear, loosen the jam nut (N—Fig. SN2-25).

5. Move the mower engagement lever to the ON position and turn the flange nut (F) clockwise to increase the brake band tension. Be sure the flange fits over the bracket (B).

6. Release the blade stop pedal.

7. Move the mower engagement lever to the OFF position, then depress the blade stop pedal.

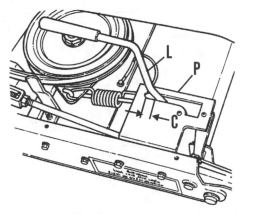

Fig. SN2-26–The mower engagement lever (L) should be 1/4 inch (6.4 mm) from rear edge of latch plate (P) when blade brake is properly adjusted. See text.

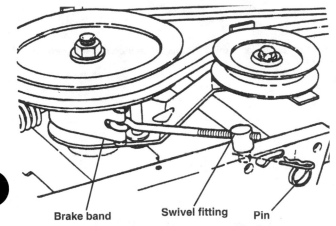

Brake band   Swivel fitting   Pin

Fig. SN2-27–Rotate swivel fitting to adjust blade brake on Series 15 models. Refer to text.

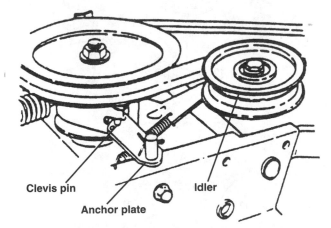

Clevis pin   Idler

Anchor plate

Fig. SN2-28–Relocated clevis pin in anchor plate to adjust blade brake on Series 16, 17 and 19 models. Refer to text.

8. Rotate the flange nut (F) so clearance (C–Fig. SN2-26) between the mower engagement lever (L) and the rear edge of the latch plate (P) is ¼ inch (6.4 mm).

9. Tighten the jam nut (N–Fig. SN2-25) and recheck the blade brake operation. If the blade brake engagement time is unsatisfactory, replacement of brake components may be necessary.

Series 15

1. Remove the mower deck cover so the spindle pulley is visible.

2. Run the mower so blade is rotating at normal speed, then release the blade stop pedal. If the time required for the blade to stop is not satisfactory, proceed to Step 3 and adjust the blade brake.

3. Lower the mower deck and remove the belt cover.

4. Detach the retaining pin (Fig. SN2-27), then dislodge the swivel fitting.

5. Rotate the swivel fitting several turns clockwise.

6. Reinstall the swivel fitting and pin.

7. Move the mower engagement lever to the OFF position, then depress the blade stop pedal.

8. Measure the clearance (C–Fig. SN2-26) between the mower engagement lever (L) and the rear edge of the latch plate (P). Clearance should be ¼ inch (6.4 mm).

9. Adjust the swivel fitting position as needed to obtain the desired clearance.

10. Recheck blade brake operation. If blade brake engagement time is unsatisfactory, replacement of brake components may be necessary.

Series 16 and 17

1. Remove the mower deck cover so the spindle pulley is visible.

2. Run the mower so the blade is rotating at normal speed, then release the blade stop pedal. The belt idler (Fig. SN2-28) should move at least ½ inch (13 mm) from the disengaged position to the engaged position. If the idler movement is inadequate and if the time required for the blade to stop is not satisfactory, proceed to Step 3 and adjust the blade brake.

3. Lower the mower deck and remove the belt cover.

4. Detach the cotter pin and remove the washer from the brake band clevis pin (Fig. SN2-28).

NOTE: The idler arm spring and cable should not be tensioned when the mower control lever is in the disengaged position.

5. To adjust the brake band movement, withdraw the clevis pin and relocate it into another hole in the anchor plate. Relocating the clevis pin into the front hole decreases blade brake tension.

Series 18 and 19

1. Remove the mower deck cover so the spindle pulley is visible.

2. Run the mower so the blade is rotating at normal speed, then release the blade stop pedal. If the time required for the blade to stop is not satisfactory, proceed to Step 3 and adjust the blade brake.

3. Lower the mower deck and remove the belt cover.

4. While holding the mower engagement lever to the rear, loosen the locknut (Fig. SN2-29).

5. Move the mower engagement lever to the ON position and turn the locknut clockwise to increase the brake band tension.

6. Release the blade stop pedal.

7. Move the mower engagement lever to the OFF position, then depress the blade stop pedal.

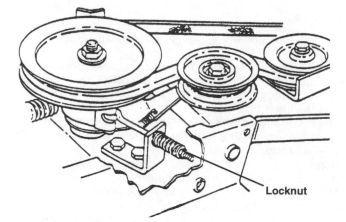

Fig. SN2-29–Rotate locknut as outlined in text to adjust blade brake on Series 18 and 19.

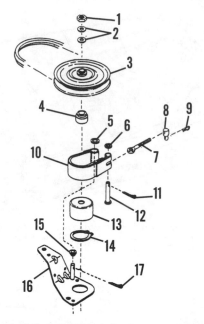

Fig. SN2-31–Exploded view of blade brake mechanism used on Series 15 models.

1. Nut	10. Brake band
2. Washer	11. Cotter pin
3. Pulley	12. Clevis pin
4. Hub	13. Brake drum
5. Washer	14. Snap ring
6. Washer	15. Spacer
7. Eye-bolt	16. Idler arm
8. Swivel fitting	17. Cotter pin
9. hairpin	

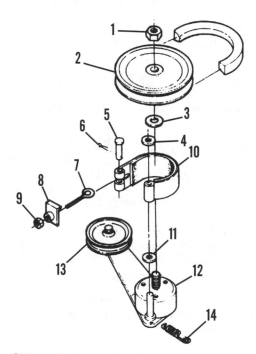

Fig. SN2-30–Exploded view of blade brake mechanism used on Series 11, 13 and 14.

1. Nut	8. Flange nut
2. Pulley	9. Jam nut
3. Washer	10. Brake band
4. Washer	11. Spacer
5. Clevis pin	12. Brake drum
6. Cotter pin	13. Idler
7. Eye-bolt	14. Spring

8. Rotate the locknut so clearance (C–Fig. SN2-26) between the mower engagement lever (L) and the rear edge of the latch plate (P) is ¼ inch (6.4 mm).

9. Recheck the blade brake operation. If blade brake engagement time is unsatisfactory, replacement of brake components may be necessary.

OVERHAUL

Blade brake components (see Figs. SN2-30, SN2-31, SN2-32 and SN2-33) are accessible after removing mower belt and spindle pulley. Replace the brake band if excessively worn or contaminated by oil or grease. Be sure all

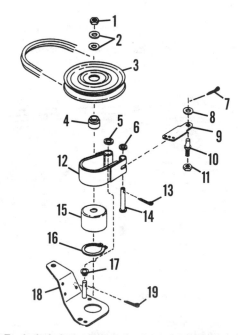

Fig. SN2-32–Exploded view of blade brake mechanism used on Series 16 and 17 models.

1. Nut	11. Nut
2. Washer	12. Brake band
3. Pulley	13. Cotter pin
4. Hub	14. Clevis pin
5. Washer	15. Brake drum
6. Washer	16. Snap ring
7. Cotter pin	17. Spacer
8. Washer	18. Idler arm
9. Anchor plate	19. Cotter pin
10. Stud	

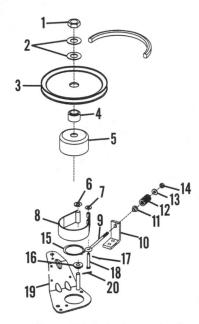

Fig. SN2-33–Exploded view of blade brake mechanism used on Series 18 and 19 models.

1. Nut	11. Bushing
2. Washer	12. Spring
3. Pulley	13. Washer
4. Hub	14. Locknut
5. Brake drum	15. Snap ring
6. Washer	16. Spacer
7. Washer	17. Cotter pin
8. Brake band	18. Clevis pin
9. Eye-bolt	19. Idler arm
10. Bracket	20. Cotter pin

components are in good operating condition. Adjust the blade brake as outlined in the previous section.

MOWER SPINDLE

LUBRICATION

The mower spindle should be lubricated annually. Apply grease to the mower spindle through the grease fitting on the underside of the spindle housing. Two shots should be sufficient. Use multipurpose grease.

OVERHAUL

Refer to Fig. SN2-34 for an exploded view of the spindle assembly and proceed as follows.

1. Remove the blade.
2. Remove the spindle pulley.
3. Remove the blade brake components.
4. Unscrew the bolts retaining the spindle housing and remove it from the deck. Note the location of any spacers during disassembly and mark them so they can be installed in their original position.
5. Unscrew the blade adapter.
6. Drive or press the spindle with the lower bearing out of the bottom of the spindle housing.

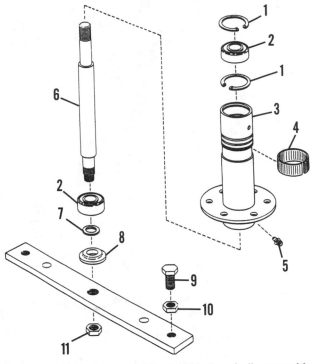

Fig. SN2-34–Exploded view of typical blade spindle assembly.

1. Snap ring	7. Washer
2. Bearing	8. Washer
3. Spindle housing	9. Locknut
4. Tolerance ring	10. Nut
5. Grease fitting	11. Nut
6. Spindle	

7. Detach the snap ring in the upper end of the spindle housing and press or drive out the upper bearing.
8. Reassemble by reversing the disassembly procedure. When installing the spindle housing on the deck, position mounting bolts so there is not a bolt in front of the grease fitting.

ELECTRICAL

Refer to the wiring diagrams (Fig. SN2-35 -Fig. SN2-42) at the end of this chapter. The shift control lever must be in PARK and the mower must be disengaged for the engine to start.

On Series 14 models, the shift detent switch prevents the engine from starting unless the shift control lever is in PARK position. To adjust detent switch engagement, loosen the screws (S–Fig. SN2-11) and reposition the shift quadrant so the switch is fully engaged with the shift control lever in PARK.

The interlock module should be considered faulty only after all other wiring and devices have been tested or checked. The interlock module may malfunction when subjected to heat and function normally when cold. Modules are designed for operation with specific engine brands and must not be interchanged. Use of an improper module may result in unsafe operation.

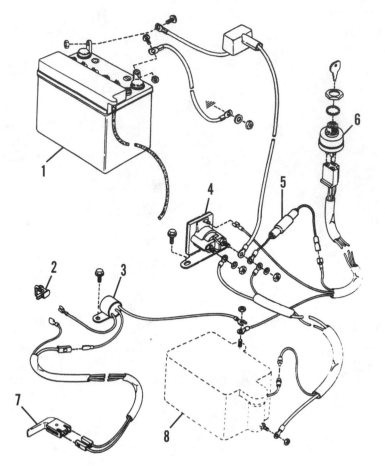

Fig. SN2-35–WIring diagram for Series 11, 13 and 14 models equipped with an electric starter.

1. Battery
2. Shift detent switch
3. Interlock module
4. Interlock solenoid
5. Fuse (10 amp)
6. Ignition switch
7. Deck switch
8. Engine and starter

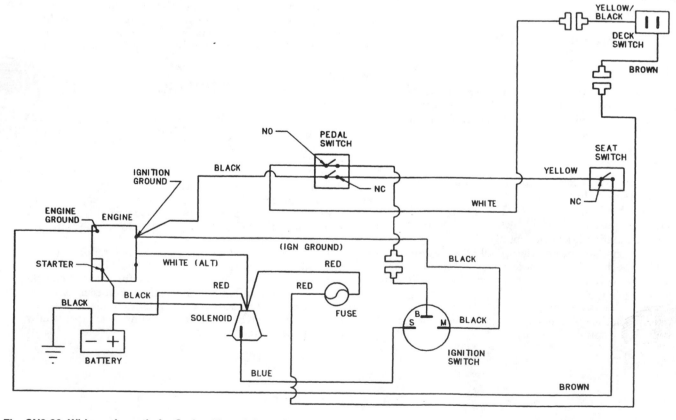

Fig. SN2-36–Wiring schematic for Series 15 models equipped with 8hp Briggs & Stratton engine with an electric starter.

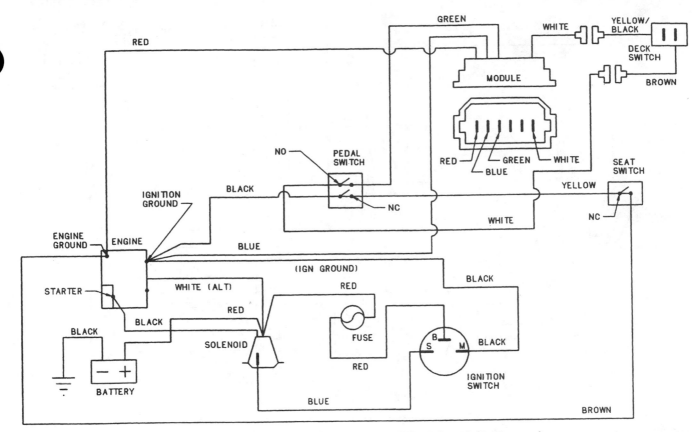

Fig. SN2-37–Wiring schematic for Series 15 models equipped with 9, 12 and 14 hp Briggs & Stratton engines.

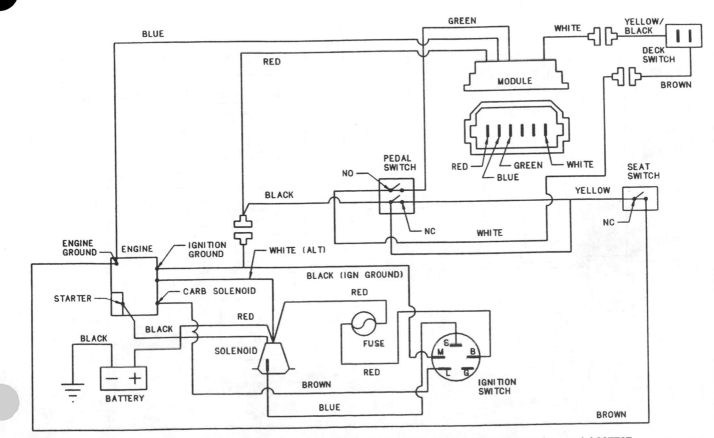

Fig. SN2-38–Wiring schematic for Series 15 and 16 models equipped with 14 hp Briggs & Stratton engine model 287707.

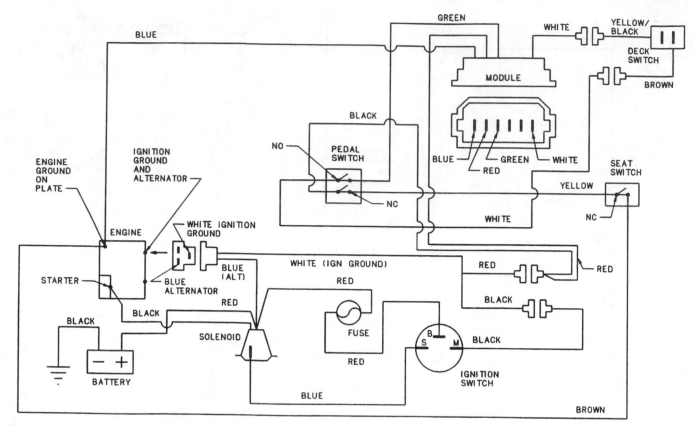

Fig. SN2-39—Wiring schematic for Series 15, 16 and 18 models equipped with a Kohler engine.

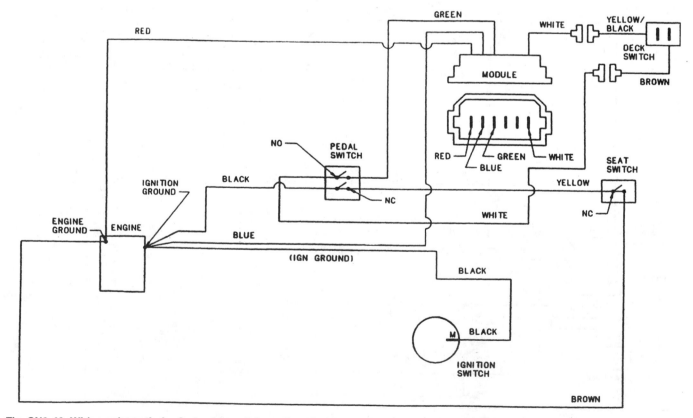

Fig. SN2-40—Wiring schematic for Series 16 models equipped with 8 hp Briggs & Stratton engines with no electric starter.

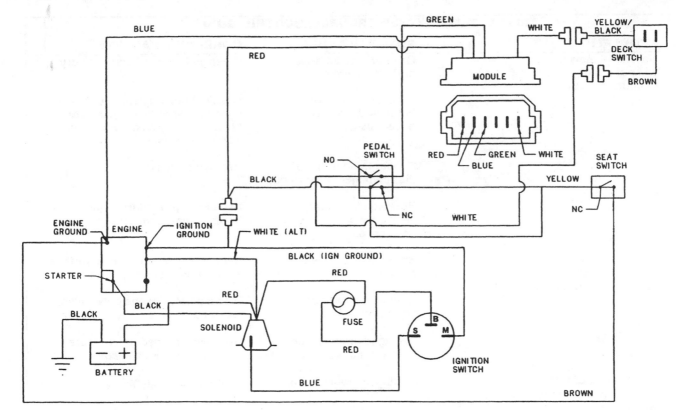

Fig. SN2-41—Wiring schematic for Series 16, 17, 18 and 19 models equipped with 8, 10 and 12 hp Briggs & Stratton engines equipped with an electric starter.

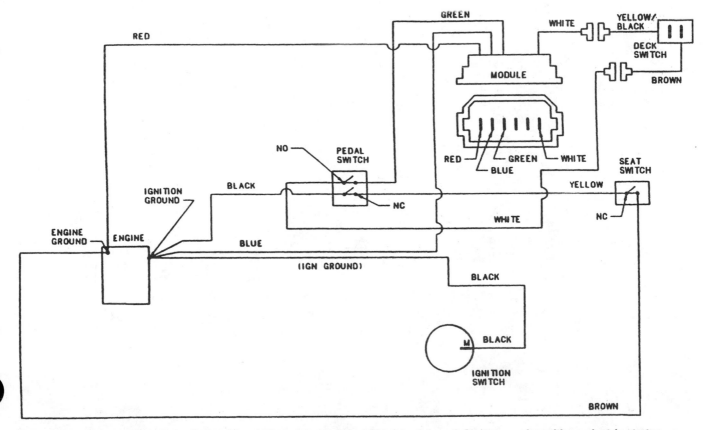

Fig. SN2-42—Wiring schematic for Series 17 and 19 models equipped with 9 hp Briggs & Stratton engine with no electric starter.

Table 1. DRIVE SYSTEM TROUBLESHOOTING GUIDE

PROBLEM	POSSIBLE CAUSE	CORRECTIVE ACTION
No drive—mower will not move in either direction.	Oil or grease on drive or driven grease.	Clean with solvent and wipe dry.
	Excessive clearance between drive and driven discs.	Check clutch adjustment. Check speed selector lever linkage and lift yoke for jamming or damage. Repair or replace.
	Rubber tread of driven disc damaged or worn out.	Replace driven disc.
	Breakage in primary chaincase or final drive case.	Use check procedure to locate trouble. Disassemble and repair
Selector hard to move when shifting through speed range.	Hex shaft dry-galled or burred.	Remove burrs, polish hex surface lightly, check shifting action.
	Jammed or damaged control linkage.	Disassemble linkage only, clean, lube and replace parts as needed.
Noisy drive.	Damaged driven chain or bearings.	Use check procedure to locate problem. Repair as needed.
Overheating of final drive case or primary chaincase.	Insufficient lubrication.	Lubricate as required.
	Grease leaks from case.	Disassemble leaking case and replace gasket. Check for other possible damage.

SNAPPER

FRONT-STEER MOWERS SERIES 13, 14, 15, 16, 17 AND 18 (With 42-inch Mower)

Model	Make	Engine Model	Horsepower	Cutting Width, In.
421613BVE	B&S	*	16	42
421614BVE	B&S	303777	16	42
421615BVE	B&S	*	16	42
421616BVE	B&S	303777	16	42
421618BVE	B&S	*	18	42

*Note the engine model number and refer to the engine service section in this manual for engine specifications.

NOTE: Some operations may be performed more easily if the machine is standing upright. Observe the following safety recommendations when raising the machine to the upright position:

1. Drain the fuel tank or make certain the fuel level is low enough so fuel will not drain out.
2. Close the fuel shut-off valve if so equipped.
3. Remove the battery if so equipped.
4. Disconnect the spark plug wire and tie it out of the way.
5. Although not absolutely essential, on models with the spark plug at the rear of the machine, the engine oil should be drained to prevent flooding the combustion chamber with oil when the engine is tilted.
6. Secure the mower from tipping by lashing the machine to a post or overhead beam.

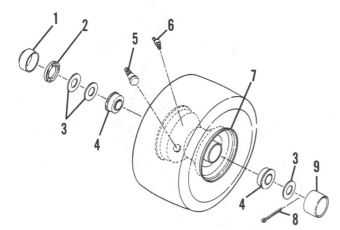

Fig. SN3-1–Exploded view of wheel assembly.

1. Boot
2. Felt seal
3. Washers
4. Bearing
5. Air valve
6. Grease fitting
7. Wheel
8. Cotter pin
9. Hub cap

MODEL IDENTIFICATION

Snapper models are categorized by series numbers that indicate design differences. The series number of a particular model is the last two numerals in the model number. For instance, Model 421615BVE is a Series 15 model and Model 421618BVE is a Series 18 model. Some service procedures in this section are directed to models of a specific series.

FRONT WHEELS

LUBRICATION

Each front wheel hub is equipped with a grease fitting. Front wheels should be injected with multipurpose grease after every 25 hours of operation. Five shots should be sufficient, however, ten shots may be required if the hub assembly is clean and new bearings are installed.

REMOVAL AND INSTALLATION

The front wheels are equipped with replaceable bearings. To remove the wheel and bearings, proceed as follows:
1. Remove the hub cap (9–Fig. SN3-1).
2. Remove the cotter pin (8–Fig. SN3-1).
3. Remove the wheel with bearings.
4. Separate the bearings from the wheel.
5. Inspect the bearings for damage.
6. Inspect the wheel for rim and hub damage.
7. Reverse the removal steps to reassemble. Pack the wheel bearings with grease before installation.

OVERHAUL

Refer to Fig. SN3-2 for an exploded view of the spindle assembly. To remove a front spindle, proceed as follows:
1. Raise and support the side to be serviced.
2. Remove the hub cap, cotter pin, wheel and tire.
3. Disconnect the tie rod from the spindle.

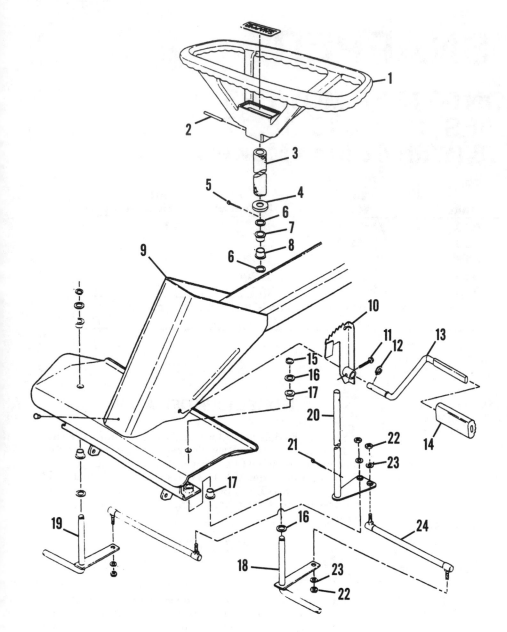

Fig. SN3-2—Exploded view of front
steering system.

1. Steering wheel
2. Pin
3. Sleeve
4. Washer
5. Cotter pin
6. Washer
7. Bushing
8. Bushing
9. Front frame
10. Clutch/brake arm
11. Screw
12. Snap ring
13. Clutch/brake pedal
14. Pad
15. Snap ring
16. Washer
17. Bushing
18. Spindle (left)
19. Spindle (right)
20. Steering shaft
21. Cotter pin
22. Nut
23. Washer
24. Tie rod

4. Detach the snap ring from the upper end of the spindle
and lower the spindle from the axle.

5. Inspect the components for damage.

6. Install the spindle by reversing the removal procedure.

STEERING SYSTEM
OVERHAUL

1. Raise the front of the machine.

2. Detach the tie rods from the steering arm (20–Fig.
SN3-2).

3. Drive out the pin (2) and remove the steering wheel.

4. Remove the foam sleeve (3) and washer (4).

5. Remove the cotter pin (5) and washer (6).

6. Withdraw the steering shaft from the bottom of the machine.

7. Reassemble the steering shaft by reversing the disassembly procedure.

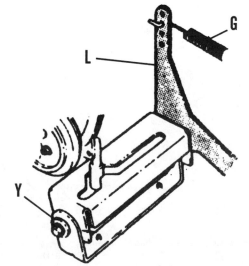

Fig. SN3-3—Clutch lever (L) is bolted to lift yoke (Y). Relocating
spring (G) end in holes in clutch lever changes clutch traction.
See text.

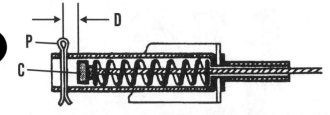

Fig. SN3-4–Distance (D) from cotter pin (P) to rear end of cable (C) should be 1/2-3/4 inch (13-19 mm). Rotate nuts (N–Fig. SN3-5) to obtain desired distance.

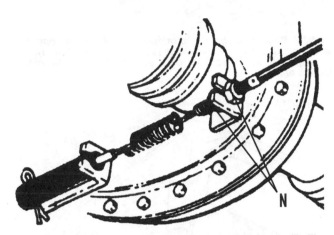

Fig. SN3-5–Rotate nuts (N) to obtain desired distance (D–Fig. SN3-4) at cable end.

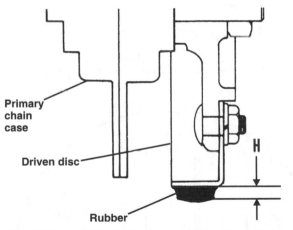

Fig. SN3-6–If height (H) of rubber ring on drive disc is 1/16 inch (1.6 mm) or less, disc must be replaced.

ENGINE

Refer to the appropriate engine section in this manual for tune-up specifications, engine overhaul procedures and engine maintenance.

REMOVAL AND INSTALLATION

1. Disconnect the spark plug wire.
2. Disconnect the cable from the starter motor.
3. Shift the mower drive control lever to the OUT position.
4. Unbolt and remove the spindle cover from the mower deck.

5. Relieve the tension from the idler, then slip the belt off the mower spindle pulley(s).
6. Remove the belt from the driving disc hub pulley.
7. Disconnect the fuel hose from the engine.
8. Detach the throttle cable from the carburetor.
9. Disconnect all interfering wiring from the engine.
10. Remove the engine mounting screws and remove the engine.
11. Reinstall the engine by reversing the removal procedure.

CLUTCH/BRAKE CABLE

NOTE: If the location of the frame tube is changed, for instance, to adjust the mower belt tension, always check the clutch/brake operating cable for proper adjustment.

OPERATION

All models are equipped with a cable-operated clutch. The cable extends from a keyhole slot in the clutch/brake pedal arm (10–Fig. SN3-2) through the main frame tube to the lever arm portion of the lift yoke (Y–Fig. SN3-3). Pulling the lift yoke by depressing the clutch/brake pedal moves the chaincase and driven disc away from the drive disc attached to the engine.

ADJUSTMENT

1. Fully depress the clutch/brake pedal and engage the parking brake.
2. Place the shift control lever in the REVERSE position.
3. Measure the gap between the drive disc and driven disc. Gap should be $\frac{1}{16}$-$\frac{1}{8}$ inch (1.6-3.2 mm). If the gap is not correct, proceed to Step 4.
4. Disengage the parking brake and relocate the front end of the clutch/brake cable in the control arm slot so another ferrule on the cable is engaged.
5. Recheck the gap between the discs.
6. Fully depress the clutch/brake pedal and engage the parking brake.
7. Measure the distance (D–Fig. SN3-4) from cotter pin (P) to the rear end of the cable (C). Distance should be $\frac{1}{2}$-$\frac{3}{4}$ inch (13-19 mm). Rotate the nuts (N–Fig. SN3-5) to obtain the desired distance.

TRACTION DRIVE CLUTCH

ADJUSTMENT

For normal setting, position the spring (G–Fig. SN3-3) end in the second hole from the end of the clutch lever (L). If the unit stutters or hops during clutch engagement, move the spring end to an inner hole. If traction is insufficient, move the spring end to the outermost hole in the lever.

DISCS INSPECTION AND ADJUSTMENT

Replace the driven disc if it is worn to less than $\frac{1}{16}$ inch (1.6 mm) as shown in Fig. SN3-6. To check disc contact, proceed as follows.
1. Install a driven disc that has half the rubber ring removed so the metal is showing. If modification of an old driven disc is not possible, a test disc may be fabricated using the dimensions of the metal portion of the existing driven disc.

2. Position the shift control lever in any forward gear.

3. With the clutch pedal released, measure the clearance (C–Fig. SN3-7) between the metal on the driven disc gauge (N) and the drive disc (D). The clearance should be 0.005-0.010 inch (0.13-0.25 mm).

4. To obtain desired clearance, adjust the position of the drive disc on the engine crankshaft.

SHIFT CONTROL LINKAGE

LUBRICATION

The shift lever grease fitting (F–Fig. SN3-8) should be injected with good quality multipurpose grease after every 25 hours of operation. Two shots should be sufficient.

ADJUSTMENT

The shift lever should be synchronized with the position of the driven disc against the drive disc. Refer to Fig. SN3-9 and note the position of the driven disc against the drive disc at related ground speed. Note the first speed position of the driven disc is approximately $\frac{1}{16}$ inch (1.6 mm) from the outer diameter of the hole in the drive disc.

Loosen the mounting screws (S–Fig. SN3-10) and relocate the shift quadrant as needed so the shift lever and driven disc positions are synchronized.

FRICTION DRIVE TRANSMISSION AND FINAL DRIVE

OPERATION

Power for the machine is transmitted through two discs, a drive disc and a driven disc. The drive disc is attached to the engine's crankshaft while the driven disc is attached to the primary chain case input shaft. As the primary chain case is moved from side-to-side through the shift mechanism, the driven friction disc contacts a different spot on the drive disc to change the ground speed. Moving the driven disc to the opposite side of the drive disc reverses the direction. The final drive case contains the reduction gear, differential and axle assemblies.

LUBRICATION

Position the machine so it is upright as previously described. Annually fill the final drive case so the level of grease in the case is even with the opening for plug (P–Fig. SN3-11). Recommended lubricant is Snapper 0 grease.

Annually add 1 ounce (30 mL) of Snapper 0 grease to the primary chain case; but do not overfill. Primary chain case capacity is 2 ounces (60 mL).

Inject multipurpose grease into the left, rear axle grease fitting (F–Fig. SN3-12) after every 25 hours of operation. Two shots should be sufficient.

Periodically lubricate the lift yoke pivot points.

INSPECTION AND TROUBLESHOOTING

If a malfunction in the drive system is suspected, proceed as follows.

1. Raise the machine so it is upright as previously described.

2. Check for leaks at the primary chain case flanges, final drive case and shaft seals.

3. Disengage the mower deck drive and roll the rear wheels by hand with the clutch both depressed and released and

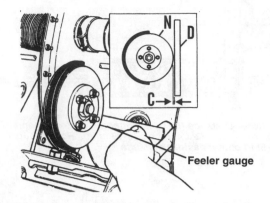

Fig. SN3-7–With the clutch pedal released and the shift control lever in any forward gear, clearance (C) between metal of drive disc gauge (N) and drive disc (D) should be 0.005-0.010 inch (0.13-0.25 mm).

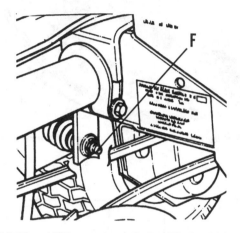

Fig. SN3-8–The shift lever grease fitting (F) should be injected with mulitpurpose grease after every 25 hours of operation.

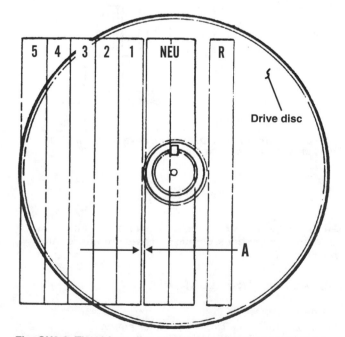

Fig. SN3-9–The driven disc should be positioned against drive disc (D) as shown for transmission speed shown. Distance (A) from outer diameter of center hole in drive disc to first speed position is 1/16 inch (1.6 mm).

Fig. SN3-10–To synchronize shift lever and driven disc, loosen mounting screws (S) and relocated shift quadrant.

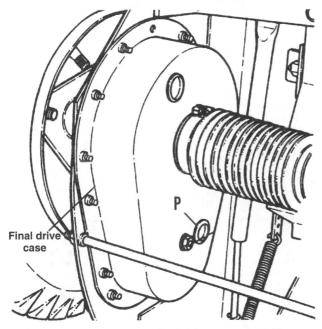

Fig. SN3-11–Level of grease in final drive case should be even with opening for plug (P).

with the shift control lever in NEUTRAL and also when shifted into DRIVE.

4. Loosen the clamps on the drive tube boots and pull back so the rotation of the hex drive tube can be observed.

5. Check for normal action of the differential pinions.

6. Jamming, locking or noise in the final drive case can be caused by damaged differential parts or a broken drive chain. Undue noise or abnormal operation in the final drive case or in the primary chain case will determine which assemblies should be remove for inspection and/or repair. Refer to Table 1 DRIVE SYSTEM TROUBLESHOOTING GUIDE for additional service information.

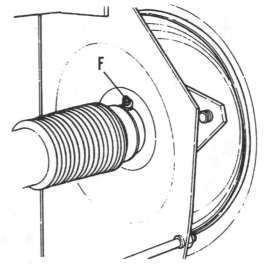

Fig. SN3-12–Inject a multipurpose grease into the left rear axle grease fitting (F) after every 25 hours of operation.

OVERHAUL

Refer to the appropriate following section for service information on assembly requiring service.

Driven Disc

Driven disc rubber ring must not be worn to less than $\frac{1}{32}$-$\frac{1}{16}$ inch (0.8-1.6 mm), otherwise, replace the driven disc (see Fig. SN3-6). If the driven disc is damaged and requires service, proceed as follows.

1. Place the machine in upright position on the rear stand as previously described.

2. Unscrew the disc retaining nuts and remove the disc (20–Fig. SN3-13).

3. When installing the disc on models equipped with a fiber thrust washer (21), be sure the fiber washer is centered on the hub (19) and is free-floating.

Drive Disc

Maximum allowable drive disc warpage is 0.020 inch (0.51 mm). To remove the drive disc, proceed as follows.

1. Remove the driven disc as previously described as well as the driven disc hub (19–Fig. SN3-13).

2. Separate the mower drive belt from the idler and remove the mower drive belt from the drive disc pulley.

3. Place the shift control lever in fifth speed position.

4. Unscrew the setscrews (S–Fig. SN3-14) and carefully pull the drive disc off the crankshaft. It may be necessary to move the lift yoke aside during removal.

5. To separate the disc from the hub, secure hub in a vise and unscrew the disc from the hub.

6. Install the drive disc by reversing the removal procedure. See the TRACTION DRIVE CLUTCH section for the procedure to position the drive disc on the engine crankshaft.

Left Side (Primary Chaincase)

1. Place the machine in an upright position on the rear stand as previously described.

2. Remove the left rear wheel.

3. Unscrew the hub retaining screw and remove the hub using Snapper tool 60237 or other suitable puller.

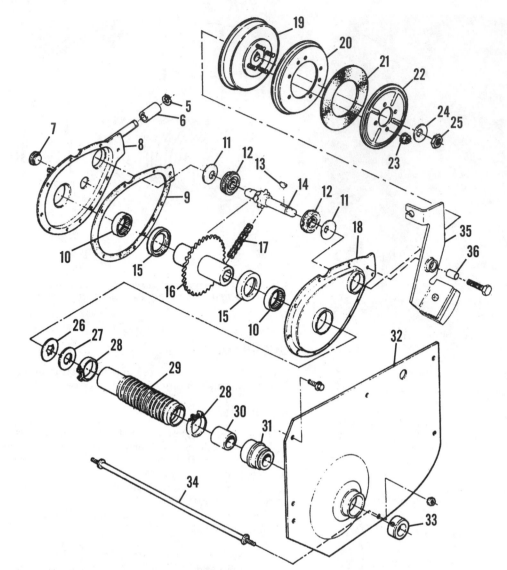

Fig. SN3-13–Exploded view of primary chaincase assembly.

5. Snap ring	13. Key	21. Fiber washer	29. Boot
6. Roller	14. Sprocket washer	22. Plate	30. Spacer
7. Plug	15. Thrust washer	23. Locknut	31. Bearing
8. Chaincase half	16. Sprocket & hub	24. Belleville washer	32. Fender plate (left)
9. Gasket	17. Chain	25. Locknut	33. Lock collar
10. Needle bearing	18. Chaincase half	26. Hex thrust washer	34. Tie rod
11. Belleville washer	19. Driven disc hub	27. Nylon thrust washer	35. Brake lever
12. Bearing	20. Drive disc	28. Clamp	36. Bushing

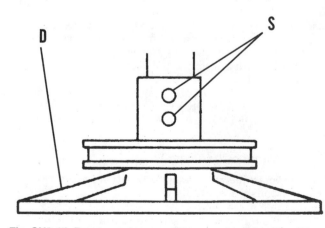

Fig. SN3-14–Remove setscrews (S) to remove drive disc (D).

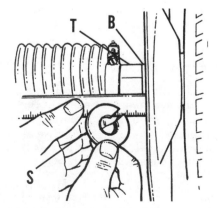

Fig. SN3-15–End play between hex tube (T) and bearing (B) should be 3/32 inch (2.4 mm).

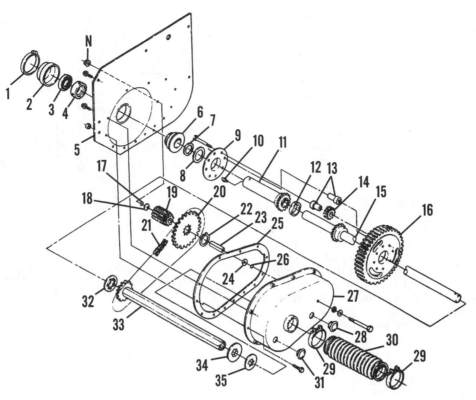

Fig. SN3-16–Exploded view of final drive assembly.

1. Clamp	10. Grease fitting	19. Gear	28. Plug
2. Dust cover	11. Short axle	20. Sprocket	29. Clamp
3. Seal	12. Nylon spacer	21. Chain	30. Boot
4. Lock collar	13. Pinion spacers	22. Snap ring	31. Plug
5. Fender plate (right)	14. Pinions	23. Spacer	32. Thrust washer
6. Bearing	15. Long axle	24. Belleville washer	33. Hex drive tube
7. Spacer	16. Final drive gear	25. Gasket	34. Nylon thrust washer
8. Thrust washer	17. O-ring	26. O-ring	35. Hex thrust washer
9. Plate	18. Belleville washer	27. Case	

4. Remove the dust shield from the axle.

5. Remove the lock collar (33–Fig. SN3-13) by rotating in a clockwise direction after loosening the setscrew.

6. Detach the boot (29).

7. Unscrew the tie rod (34) nut.

8. Unscrew the fasteners securing the left fender plate (32) and remove the left fender plate.

9. Disconnect the shift link from the chain case half (8).

10. Detach the boot from the chain case half (8).

11. Separate the chain case rod from the lift yoke and slide the chain case off the hex tube.

12. Secure the driven disc hub (19).

13. Unscrew the brake lever retaining screw and remove the brake lever (35).

14. Remove the driven disc and hub assembly.

15. Unscrew the chain case bolts and separate the chain case halves (8 and 18).

16. Remove, clean and inspect the chain case components.

17. Remove the needle bearings (10) and ball bearings (12) by pressing to the inside of the case half.

18. Reassemble the primary chaincase by reversing the disassembly procedure. Note the following:

   a. Press the ball bearings (12) into the case halves until locating the ring around the outside of the bearing seats against the case.

   b. Press against the lettered side of the needle bearings (10) so the lettered side is to the inside of the case

half and the bearing is flush with the inner surface of the case half.

   c. The cup side of the Belleville washers (11) must be away from the bearings (12).

   d. After assembly, check end play between the hex tube (T–Fig. SN3-15) and bearing (B). Desired end play is 3/32 inch (2.4 mm). Adjust the end play by installing nylon split shims (S) between the tube and bearing.

   e. Fill the primary chain case with 2 ounces (60 mL) of Snapper 0 grease. A new plug (7–Fig. SN3-13) should be installed.

Right Side (Final Drive Case)

Place machine in an upright position on the rear stand as previously outlined then proceed as follows.

1. Remove the rear wheels.

2. Unscrew the hub retaining screws and remove both wheel hubs using Snapper tool 60237 or other suitable puller.

3. Remove the dust shields from the axles.

4. Remove the lock collars (33–Fig. SN3-13) from each axle by loosening the setscrew and rotating the collar in the direction opposite to forward wheel rotation.

5. Unscrew the tie rod nut.

6. Detach the boot (30–Fig. SN3-16) from the final drive case.

7. Unscrew the fasteners securing the right fender plate (5–Fig. SN3-16) to the frame and remove the right fender plate with final drive case.

8. Place the assembly on a workbench so the axle protrudes down through a hole in the workbench and the fender plate is on top.

9. Unscrew the fender plate retaining screws and nuts and remove the fender plate from the final drive case.

10. Prevent the hex shaft (33) from moving and withdraw the final drive gear (16) and axle assembly from the case.

11. Remove the idler and sprocket components (17 through 26).

12. Remove the hex tube components (32 through 35). The bushings in the hex tube (33) are not replaceable.

13. To disassemble and reassemble the differential, proceed as follows:

   a. Unscrew the capscrews securing the differential plate (9). Discard the capscrews–the screw threads lose their locking capability when unscrewed.

   b. Disassemble the differential components.

   c. Replace the nylon spacer (12) if worn. Bushings in the short axle (11) are not replaceable. Be sure the nylon spacer (12) fits over the weld on the long axle (15).

   d. Assemble the pinions (14), spacers (13) and short axle as shown in Fig. SN3-17.

   e. Lubricate the bushings in the short axle before assembly.

   f. Install the differential plate (9–Fig. SN3-16) using new capscrews (Snapper part 1-2333).

14. Reassemble the final drive assembly and fender plate by reversing the disassembly procedure while noting the following:

   a. Be sure the thrust washers (32 and 34) are installed. The absence of thrust washers will cause rapid wear.

   b. Install the nylon hex washer (35) with the lip towards the sprocket on the hex tube.

   c. Lubricate the bushings in the hex tube (33) prior to assembly. Make sure the lubrication hole in the idler (19) is open.

   d. Install the Belleville washers (18 and 24) so the cupped side is towards the O-rings (17 and 26).

   e. The idler, sprocket, hex tube and chain must be installed as a unit.

   f. Lubricate the outside of the short axle (11).

   g. After placing the fender plate on the final drive case, tighten the case retaining screws and nuts, then tighten the idler bolt retaining locknut (N) to 18-20 ft.-lb. (25-27 N•m). The locknut must be tightened properly because loosening the nut may allow the chain to jump from the sprockets due to sprocket misalignment.

   h. Lubricate the outside of the hex tube (33) before inserting it in the primary chaincase.

   i. Rotate the lock collars in the same direction as the forward wheel rotation.

   j. Fill the final drive case with Snapper 0 grease so the grease level in the case is even with the plug opening (P–Fig. SN3-11). New plugs (28 and 31–Fig. SN3-16) should be installed.

GROUND DRIVE BRAKE

NOTE: If the location of the frame tube is changed, for instance, to adjust the mower belt tension, always check the brake operating cable for proper adjustment.

All models are equipped with a combination clutch/brake pedal on the left side of the machine. The

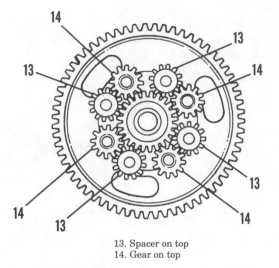

13. Spacer on top
14. Gear on top

Fig. SN3-17–When installing pinion spacers and pinions on final drive gear, alternate top positions of pinion spacers (13) and pinions (14) so they appear as shown.

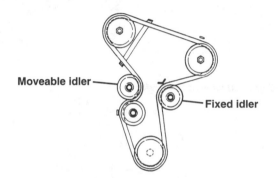

Fig. SN3-18–Remove the fixed idler and moveable idler, then remove the mower driver belt as described in text.

Moveable idler

Fixed idler

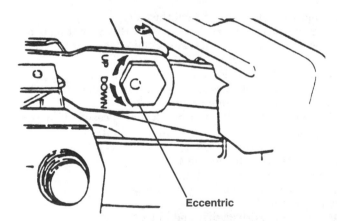

Eccentric

Fig. SN3-19–Loosen the capscrew and rotate the eccentric on the left front lift arm to adjust side-to-side dimension.

brake is applied when the clutch/brake pedal is pressed down to its limit. At this point, the brake lever (35—Fig. SN3-13) rotates so its lined shoe contacts the inner rim of the driven hub (19). Pressure on the brake lever;s upper end is exerted by the lift yoke when actuated by the tension on the clutch/brake cable.

To adjust the brake, refer to the CLUTCH/BRAKE CABLE section.

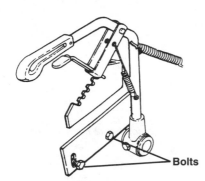

Fig. SN3-20–Loosen the height lever bracket retaining bolts and relocate the bracket to adjust the mower height range.

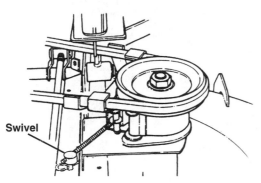

Fig. SN3-21–Detach, then rotate the swivel fitting to adjust the blade brake. Refer to text.

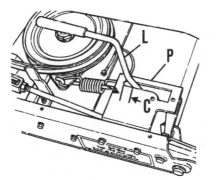

Fig. SN3-22–The mower engagement lever (L) should be 1/16-1/8 inch (1.6 mm) from rear edge of latch plate (P) when blade brake is properly adjusted.

MOWER BELT

ADJUSTMENT

Mower belt adjustment is not necessary. If belt slippage occurs, install a new belt.

REMOVAL AND INSTALLATION

1. Detach the mower deck cover.
2. Remove the fixed and moveable idlers (Fig. SN3-18).
3. Place the machine in an upright position on the rear stand as previously described.
4. Move the clutch lift yoke so the driven disc is moved away from the drive disc and a gap exists.
5. Separate the mower drive belt from the engine pulley.
6. Remove the mower belt by passing the belt through a gap between driven and drive discs.

7. Install the mower drive belt by reversing the removal procedure while noting the following:
   a. Refer to Fig. SN3-18 for belt routing diagram.
   b. The belt can be forced around the drive disc by moving the shift control lever to fifth speed position thereby forcing the belt out toward the edge of the drive disc.
   c. Adjust the position of the belt guides so the gap between the guide and belt is $\frac{1}{16}$ inch (1.6 mm).

MOWER DECK

HEIGHT ADJUSTMENT

All mower control linkage must be in good operating condition and the tires properly inflated. Park the machine on a level surface with the engine stopped and the spark plug wire disconnected.

Front-To-Rear Adjustment

Front-to-rear height difference is determined by measuring the height of the blade above the ground at the front and rear. Rear height should be level or $\frac{1}{8}$ inch (3.2 mm) lower than the front. To adjust the height, relocate the ferrules on the hanger cables.

Side-To-Side Adjustment

The maximum side-to-side difference should be $\frac{1}{8}$ inch (3.2 mm). To adjust the side-to-side height, loosen the capscrew and rotate the eccentric (Fig. SN3-19) on the left front lift arm so the desired dimension is obtained and retighten the nuts. Rotate the eccentric counterclockwise to raise the right side of the deck or clockwise to raise the left side of the deck.

Height Range

If the height range of the mower deck is not adequate, relocate the height lever bracket. Loosen the bracket retaining bolts (Fig. SN3-20), then move the bracket.

REMOVAL AND INSTALLATION

1. Remove the mower drive belt as previously described.
2. Place the machine on all four wheels.
3. Disconnect the interlock switch wire.
4. Detach the front and rear lift arms and links and remove the mower deck.
5. Install the mower deck by reversing the removal procedure.

BLADE BRAKE

The mower is equipped with a band brake stopping rotation of the blade spindle within 3 seconds. The mower engagement lever is held in position by pedals. When either pedal is released, the mower engagement lever snaps into the disengaged position and the blade brake is actuated.

ADJUSTMENT

1. Remove the mower deck cover so the spindle pulley is visible.
2. Run the mower so the blade is rotating at normal speed, then release the blade stop pedal. If the time required for the blade to stop is not satisfactory, proceed to Step 3 and adjust the blade brake.
3. Lower the mower deck and remove the belt cover.
4. Remove the cotter pin from the swivel (Fig. SN3-21).

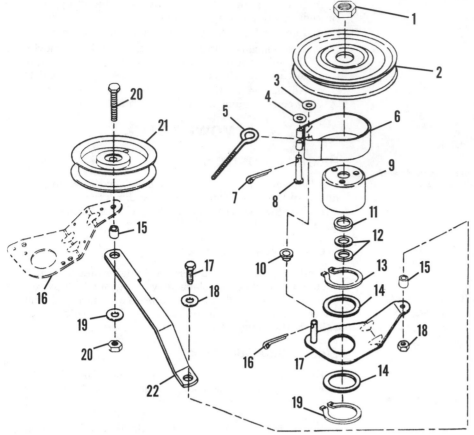

20
21
5
3
4
6
7
8
9
11
12
10
13
15
14
15
16
17
18
19
20
16
17
18
14
19
22
1
2

Fig. SN3-23–Exploded view of typical blade brake mechanism.

1. Nut
2. Pulley
3. Washer
4. Washer
5. Eyebolt
6. Brake bank
7. Cotter pin
8. Clevis pin
9. Brake drum
10. Spacer
11. Spacer
12. Spacer
13. Snap ring
14. Nylon washer
15. Spacer
16. Cotter pin
17. Brake arm
18. Locknut
19. Snap ring
20. Bolt
21. Idler
22. Link

5. Rotate the swivel so the clearance (C–Fig. SN3-22) between the mower engagement lever (L) and the rear edge of the latch plate (P) is 1/16-1/8 inch (1.5-3.2 mm).

6. Recheck the blade brake operation. If blade brake engagement time is unsatisfactory, replacement of brake components may be necessary.

OVERHAUL

Blade brake components (see Fig. SN3-23) are accessible after removing the mower belt and spindle pulley. Replace the brake band if excessively worn or contaminated by oil or grease. Be sure all components are in good operating condition. Adjust blade brake as outlined in the previous section.

MOWER SPINDLE

LUBRICATION

The mower spindle should be lubricated annually. Apply multipurpose grease to the mower spindle through the grease fitting on the underside of the spindle housing. Two shots should be sufficient.

OVERHAUL

Refer to Fig. SN3-24 for an exploded view of the spindle assembly and proceed as follows.

1. Remove the blade.
2. Remove the spindle pulley.
3. Remove the blade brake components.
4. Unscrew the bolts retaining the spindle housing and remove it from the deck. Note the location of any spacers dur-

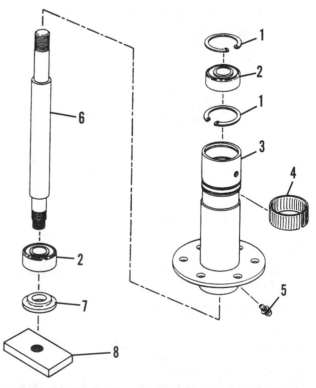

Fig. SN3-24–Exploded view of typical blade spindle assembly.

1. Snap ring
2. Bearing
3. Spindle housing
4. Tolerance ring
5. Grease fitting
6. Spindle
7. Washer
8. Blade adapter

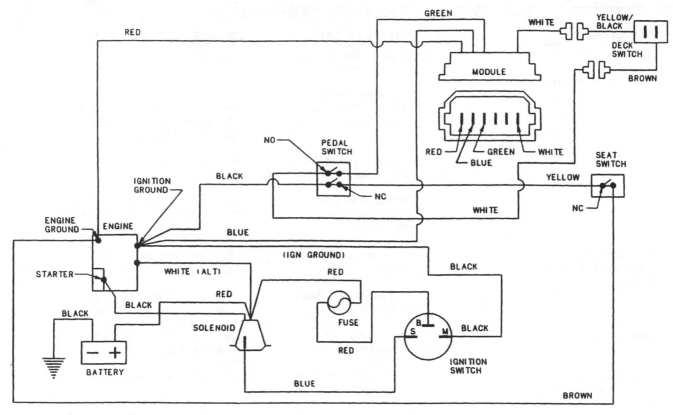

Fig. SN3-25–Typical wiring diagram.

ing disassembly and mark them so they can be installed in their original position.

5. Unscrew the blade adapter.

6. Drive or press the spindle with the lower bearing out of the bottom of the spindle housing.

7. Detach the snap ring in the upper end of the spindle housing and press or drive out the upper bearing.

8. Reassemble by reversing the disassembly procedure. When installing the spindle housing on the deck, position the mounting bolts so there is not a bolt in front of the grease fitting.

ELECTRICAL

Refer to the wiring diagram (Fig. 3-25) at the end of this chapter. The shift control lever must be in PARK and the mower must be disengaged for engine to start.

The interlock module should be considered faulty only after all other wiring and devices have been tested or checked. The interlock module may malfunction when subjected to heat and function normally when cold. Modules are designed for operation with specific engine brands and must not be interchanged. Use of an improper module may result in unsafe operation.

Table 1. DRIVE SYSTEM TROUBLESHOOTING GUIDE

PROBLEM	POSSIBLE CAUSE	CORRECTIVE ACTION
No drive—mower will not move in either direction.	Oil or grease on drive or driven grease.	Clean with solvent and wipe dry.
	Excessive clearance between drive and driven discs.	Check clutch adjustment. Check speed selector lever linkage and lift yoke for jamming or damage. Repair or replace.
	Rubber tread of driven disc damaged or worn out.	Replace driven disc.
	Breakage in primary chaincase or final drive case.	Use check procedure to locate trouble. Disassemble and repair
Selector hard to move when shifting through speed range.	Hex shaft dry-galled or burred.	Remove burrs, polish hex surface lightly, check shifting action.
	Jammed or damaged control linkage.	Disassemble linkage only, clean, lube and replace parts as needed.
Noisy drive.	Damaged driven chain or bearings.	Use check procedure to locate problem. Repair as needed.
Overheating of final drive case or primary chain case.	Insufficient lubrication.	Lubricate as required.
	Grease leaks from case.	Disassemble leaking case and replace gasket. Check for other possible damage.

SNAPPER
ZERO-TURN MOWERS
SERIES 0, 1 AND 2

Model	Make	Engine Model	Horsepower	Cutting Width, In.
HZ14330BVE	B&S	287707	14	30
HZ14380BVE	B&S	287707	14	38
HZ15420KVE	Kohler	CV15	15	42
HZS14330BVE	B&S	287707	14	33
HZS14331BVE	B&S	287707	14	33
HZS14380BVE	B&S	287707	14	38
HZS14381BVE	B&S	287707	14	38
HZS15420KVE	Kohler	CV15	15	42
HZS15421KVE	Kohler	CV15	15	42
HZS15422KVE	Kohler	CV15	15	42
HZS18482BVE	B&S	350707	18	48
YZ13331BE	B&S	*	13	33
YZ13381BE	B&S	*	13	38

*Note the engine model number and refer to the engine service section in this manual for engine specifications.

NOTE: Some operations may be performed more easily if the machine is standing upright. Observe the following safety recommendations when raising the machine to the upright position:

1. Drain the fuel tank or make certain the fuel level is low enough so fuel will not drain out.

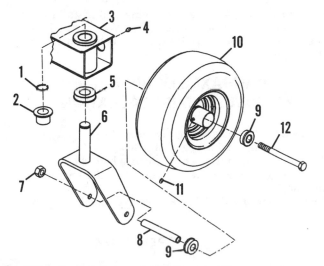

Fig. SN4-1–Exploded view of spindle assembly.

1. Snap ring
2. Bushing
3. Frame
4. Grease fitting
5. Bushing
6. Spindle
7. Nut
8. Spacer
9. Bushing
10. Wheel assy.
11. Grease fitting
12. Bolt

2. Close the fuel shut-off valve if so equipped.
3. Remove the battery if so equipped.
4. Disconnect the spark plug wire and tie it out of way.
5. Although not absolutely essential, on models with a spark plug at the rear of the machine, the engine oil should be drained to prevent flooding the combustion chamber with oil when the engine is tilted.
6. Secure the mower from tipping by lashing the machine to a post or overhead beam.

MODEL IDENTIFICATION

Snapper models are categorized by series numbers indicating design differences. The series number of a particular model is the last numeral in the model number. For instance, Model YZ13331BE is a Series 1 model. Some service procedures in this section may be directed to models of a specific series.

FRONT WHEELS

LUBRICATION

Each front wheel hub is equipped with a grease fitting. Front wheels should be injected with multipurpose grease after every 25 hours of operation or annually, whichever occurs first. Five shots from a hand-held grease gun should be sufficient.

REMOVAL AND INSTALLATION

Each front wheel is equipped with replaceable bearings. To remove the wheel and bearings, refer to Fig. SN4-1 and proceed as follows:

1. Support the front of the mower.
2. Remove the nut (7–Fig. SN4-1) and withdraw the axle bolt (12).
3. Remove the wheel.
4. Separate the bearings from the wheel.
5. Inspect the bearings for damage.
6. Inspect the wheel for rim and hub damage.
7. Reverse the removal steps to reassemble.

FRONT SPINDLES

MAINTENANCE

Lubricate the front wheel spindles after every 25 hours of operation or annually, whichever occurs first. Inject multipurpose grease to the spindles through the grease fitting at each end of the frame. The grease fitting is accessible through the hole (A–Fig. SN4-2) in the frame. One or two shots from a hand-held grease gun should be sufficient.

OVERHAUL

Refer to Fig. SN4-1 for an exploded view of the spindle assembly. To remove a front spindle, proceed as follows.
1. Raise and support the side to be serviced.
2. Remove the wheel and tire as previously described.
3. Remove the snap ring (B–Fig. SN4-2) from the top of the spindle.
4. Lower the spindle from the front axle.
5. Inspect the components for damage.
6. Install the spindle by reversing the removal procedure.

FRONT FRAME

The front frame (1 and 2–Fig. SN4-3) supports the mower deck, spindles and bodywork. The front frame tube fits into grommets (7) in the main frame. Slots in the front frame bracket allow the front frame to pivot on the tube so the mower deck can more easily follow the ground contour. Two bolts in the pivot slots limit the pivot travel and secure the front frame bracket to the main frame.

REMOVAL AND INSTALLATION

1. Remove the mower deck.
2. Support the main frame so it cannot tip forward or back.
3. HZ series—remove the fiberglass floorpan from the front frame.
4. Remove the pivot screws (3–Fig. SN4-3), washers and spacers.
5. Separate the front frame tube from the main frame, then roll the front frame assembly away from the main frame.
6. Inspect the grommets in the main frame and the front frame for damage.
7. Reassemble by reversing the removal procedure.

ENGINE

Refer to the appropriate engine section in this manual for tune-up specifications, engine overhaul procedures and engine maintenance.

REMOVAL AND INSTALLATION

1. On models so equipped, remove the bodywork surrounding the engine.
2. Disconnect the spark plug wire.
3. Disconnect the negative battery cable.

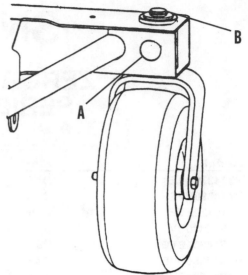

Fig. SN4-2–The spindle grease fitting is accessible through the hole (A) in the frame. Snap ring (B) retains the spindle.

4. Disconnect any interfering electrical wires from the engine.
5. Disconnect the throttle cable from the engine.
6. Disconnect the fuel line.
7. Remove the engine drive belt.
8. Detach the exhaust system from the engine.
9. Remove the engine retaining bolts.
10. Remove the engine.
11. Install by reversing the removal procedure.

BELT IDLERS

Drive belt tension for the mower clutch drive belt and transaxle drive belt is maintained by spring-loaded idler arms. Refer to Fig. SN4-4.

REMOVAL AND INSTALLATION

Refer to Fig. SN4-4 when removing and installing the belt idler arms. Note the position of the V-groove pulley (6) and flat-groove pulley (14). Be sure the belt properly contacts the pulley.

TRANSAXLE DRIVE BELT
REMOVAL AND INSTALLATION

1. Disconnect the battery negative lead.
2. Disconnect the engine spark plug lead.
3. Detach the spring from the transaxle belt idler.
4. Remove the transaxle drive belt from the engine and transaxle pulleys.
5. Install the transaxle drive belt by reversing the removal procedure.

STEERING CONTROL LINKAGE

Each transaxle is independently controlled to permit zero-radius turning. A joystick controls forward, reverse and turning motion. The joystick is connected by cables to the control lever on each hydrostatic transaxle (Fig. SN4-5). Refer to Fig. SN4-6 for an exploded view of the joystick assembly.

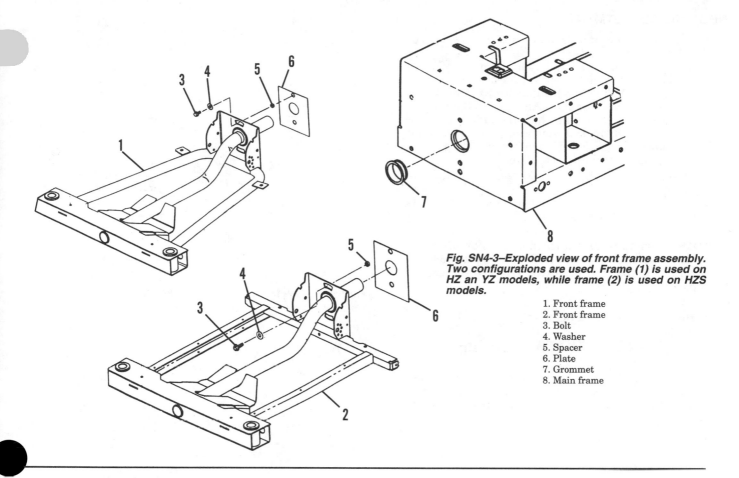

Fig. SN4-3–Exploded view of front frame assembly. Two configurations are used. Frame (1) is used on HZ an YZ models, while frame (2) is used on HZS models.

1. Front frame
2. Front frame
3. Bolt
4. Washer
5. Spacer
6. Plate
7. Grommet
8. Main frame

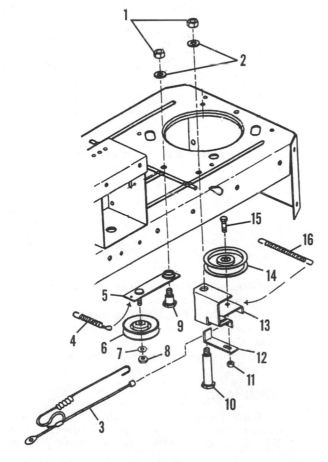

Fig. SN4-4–Exploded view of belt idlers.

1. Nut
2. Washer
3. Cable
4. Spring
5. Idler arm
6. V-pulley
7. Washer
8. Locknut
9. Pivot bolt
10. Pivot bolt
11. Locknut
12. Belt guide
13. Bracket
14. Flat pulley
15. Bolt
16. Spring

NEUTRAL ADJUSTMENT

When the joystick control is centered, the unit should be in NEUTRAL and not move.

If the unit does not track straight, perform the following adjustment procedure. Refer to Fig. SN4-5.

1. Determine which direction the unit tracks toward.

2. Adjust the location of the transaxle cable on the side corresponding to the direction in which the unit tracks. For instance, if the unit tracks to the right, adjust the right transaxle cable. Use the following procedure:

    a. Loosen the bottom nut on the cable.

    b. Rotate the top nut ⅛-turn clockwise, then recheck operation.

    c. Continue to turn the top nut in ⅛-turn increments until the unit tracks straight.

NOTE: If there are not sufficient threads on the cable end, perform the neutral adjustment procedure described in the HYDROSTATIC TRANSAXLE section.

    d. Hold the top nut and tighten the lower nut.

HYDROSTATIC TRANSAXLE

The unit is equipped with two hydrostatic transaxles. Each transaxle drives a rear wheel, which allows zero-turn-steering through independent operation of the transaxles.

LUBRICATION

Normal Operation

The oil level should be maintained at the FULL level on the transaxle oil expansion tank . If necessary, add oil to the tank. Recommended oil is Mobil DTE-26 or equivalent.

Refill and Bleed Transaxle

To refill the hydrostatic transmission with oil and bleed air from the system after the transaxle has been serviced, proceed as follows.

CAUTION: Be sure the unit is adequately supported and cannot move when performing the following procedure.

1. Fill the oil tank to the full line.

2. Raise and support the rear of the unit so the rear wheels are off the ground.

3. Start the engine and run at idle speed for about three minutes.

4. Move the steering control joystick from full forward to full reverse in 15-second intervals for three minutes.

5. Return the lever to NEUTRAL for five seconds.

6. Add oil to the oil tank as needed.

7. Repeat the procedure until the oil level stabilizes.

8. Check operation. Repeat the procedure if the unit does not function normally.

REMOVAL AND INSTALLATION

1. Remove the rear wheels.

2. Remove the transaxle drive belt.

3. Detach the parking brake rod from the transaxle lever.

4. Disconnect the speed control cable from the transaxle lever.

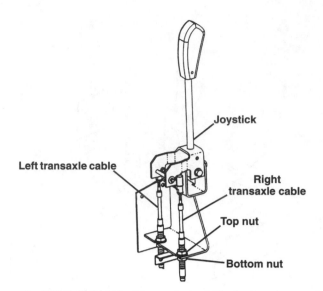

Fig. SN4-5—Refer to text for control cable adjustment procedure.

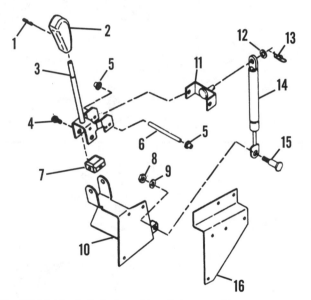

Fig. SN4-6—Exploded view of joystick assembly.

1. Pin	9. Lockwasher
2. Knob	10. Bracket
3. Lever	11. Bracket
4. Shoulder bolt	12. Washer
5. Push nut	13. Cotter pin
6. Pin	14. Cylinder
7. Pivot	15. Shoulder bolt
8. Nut	16. Bracket

5. Disconnect the transaxle pressure relief cable.

6. Support the transaxle.

7. Remove the transaxle mounting brackets.

8. Unscrew the transaxle mounting bolts and remove the transaxle.

9. Reverse the removal procedure to reinstall the transaxle.

OVERHAUL

All models are equipped with two Eaton Model 778 hydrostatic transaxles. Refer to the HYDROSTATIC TRANSAXLE REPAIR section for service information.

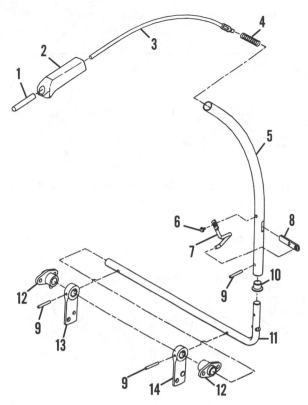

Fig. SN4-7—Exploded view of parking brake lever assembly.

1. Button pin	8. Arm
2. Handle	9. Pin
3. Rod	10. Bushing
4. Spring	11. Rod
5. Tube	12. Pivot
6. Screw	13. Lever
7. Pivot rod	14. Lever

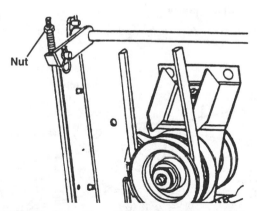

Fig. SN4-8—Refer to text for adjustment of parking brake rod nut.

PARKING BRAKE

The parking brake lever applies the parking brake on each transaxle. The button on the brake handle must be depressed before moving the brake lever. Refer to Fig. SN4-7 for an exploded view of the brake lever assembly.

ADJUSTMENT

Rotate the nut (Fig. SN4-8) on the end of each parking brake rod to adjust the parking brake. Rotate the nut

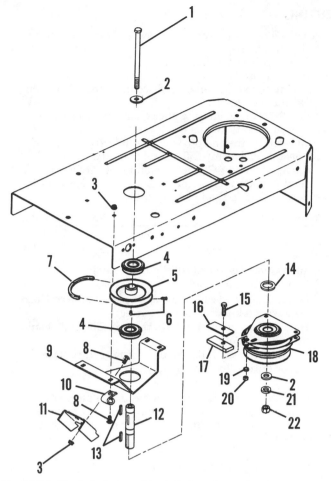

Fig. SN4-9—Exploded view of jackshaft and pto clutch.

1. Bolt	12. Jackshaft
2. Washer	13. Key
3. Nut	14. Washer
4. Bearing	15. Bolt
5. Pulley	16. Washer
6. Setscrews	17. Bumper
7. Drive belt	18. Pto clutch
8. Bolt	19. Lockwasher
9. Bracket	20. Nut
10. Wire clamp	21. Lockwasher
11. Bracket	22. Nut

clockwise to increase braking action. Be sure to adjust the parking brake rod on both transaxles.

PTO CLUTCH DRIVE BELT REMOVAL AND INSTALLATION

1. Remove the pto clutch as described in this section.
2. Remove the jackshaft bracket (9–Fig. SN4-9).
3. Remove the pto drive belt from the engine and jackshaft pulleys.
4. Install the pto drive belt by reversing the removal procedure.

ELECTRIC PTO CLUTCH

The unit may be equipped with an Ogura or Warner electric pto clutch. Pulling up the pto switch routes current to the pto clutch. When the clutch engages, power is transferred to the mower drive belt.

TESTING

Use the following procedure to locate the cause if the pto clutch malfunctions.

1. Turn the ignition switch ON.
2. Actuate the pto switch.
3. If the clutch does not engage, disconnect the wiring connector at the clutch.
4. Use a 12-volt test lamp to check continuity of the wire coming from the pto switch.
5. If the lamp lights, the pto is either defective or the wiring connector at the clutch field coil is faulty.
6A. Clutch Installed—Connect an ohmmeter to the clutch wire and the ground. The ohmmeter should indicate the resistance specified in the following table.

Pto clutch	Coil resistance
Ogura	3.0 ohms
Warner	3.5 ohms

6B. Clutch removed—perform the following procedures:
   a. Remove the pto clutch.
   b. Ground the field coil frame and energize the coil lead wire with a known 12-volt source.
   c. Hold a piece of steel next to the coil. The coil should attract the metal.
   d. If the pto clutch fails the preceding test, replace the coil or entire clutch assembly.

NOTE: Snapper only supplies the complete clutch assembly. Note the clutch manufacturer. It may be possible to obtain clutch parts from other parts suppliers.

REMOVAL AND INSTALLATION

1. Remove the mower drive belt as described in this section.
2. Disconnect the pto clutch electrical wire.
3. Remove the clutch retaining bolt.
4. Remove the clutch assembly from the jackshaft. Use a plastic hammer to tap and loosen the clutch from the jackshaft if necessary.
5. Reverse the removal procedure to install the pto clutch. Apply Loctite 271 to the jackshaft bolt threads and tighten the clutch retaining nut securely.

PTO JACKSHAFT OVERHAUL

1. Remove the pto clutch drive belt as previously described.
2. Remove the jackshaft (12–Fig. SN4-9) and pulley (5).
3. Remove the bearings (4).
4. If necessary, loosen the setscrews (6) and separate the pulley from the jackshaft.
5. Inspect the jackshaft, pulley, keys, keyways and bearings for damage.
6. Reverse the disassembly procedure to reassemble the jackshaft.

MOWER DRIVE BELT REMOVAL AND INSTALLATION

Refer to Figs. SN4-10, SN4-11 and SN4-12 for belt routing diagrams.
1. Remove the floorpan over the mower deck for access to the mower drive belt.

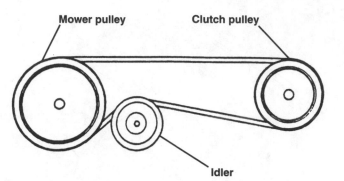

Fig. SN4-10–Mower drive belt routing diagram for 33-inch mower deck.

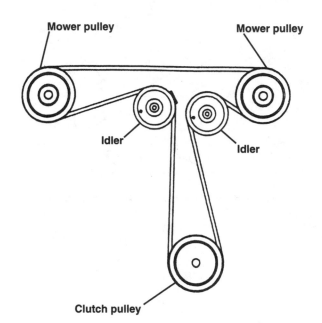

Fig. SN4-11–Mower drive belt routing diagram for 38- and 42-inch mower deck.

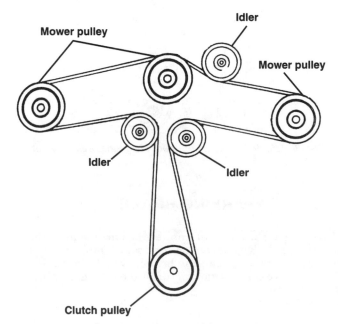

Fig. SN4-12–Mower drive belt routing diagram for 48-inch mower deck.

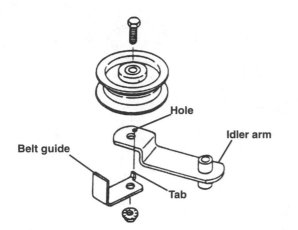

Fig. SN4-13–Insert the tab on the belt guide into the hole in the idler arm.

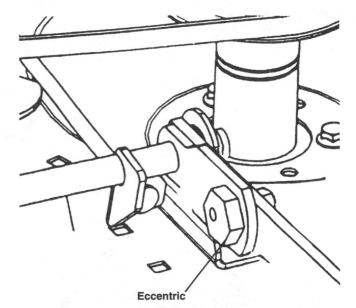

Fig. SN4-15–Side-to-side height is adjustable on mower decks equipped with a leveling eccentric.

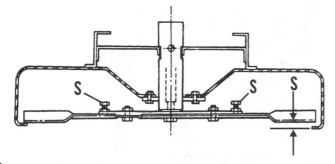

Fig. SN4-14–Loosen jam nuts, then rotate blade leveling screws (S) so distance (D) from mower deck to blade tip is 3/8 inch (9.5 mm)

2. Disengage the idler spring.
3. Where necessary, loosen or remove the idler bolt so the belt guide may be relocated for belt removal from the idler.
4. Remove the mower drive belt.
5. Install the mower drive belt by reversing the removal procedure. When installing the belt on the idler, be sure the tab on the belt guide fits into the hole in the idler arm (Fig. SN4-13).

MOWER DECK

HEIGHT ADJUSTMENT

All mower control linkage must be in good operating condition and tires properly inflated. Park the machine on a level surface with the engine stopped and the spark plug wire disconnected.

Blade Height

The blade adapter bar on models with a 33-inch mower deck is equipped with adjusting screws to aid blade alignment. Adjust the screws so the distance (D–Fig. SN4-14) from the mower deck to the blade tip is ⅜ inch (9.5 mm). Adjust the screws so the front of the blade is ⅛-¼ inch (3.2-6.4 mm) above the deck lip and the rear of the blade is ⅜ inch (9.5 mm) above the deck lip. Be sure all fasteners are secure.

Front-To-Rear Adjustment

Front-to-rear height difference is determined by measuring the height of the blade above the ground at the front and rear. The rear height should be level or ¼ inch (6.4

mm) lower than the front. To adjust height on 48-inch mower decks, detach the rear link rods and rotate the rods. On all other mower decks, relocate the ferrules on the hanger cables.

Side-To-Side Adjustment

Side-to-side height is adjustable on mower decks equipped with a leveling eccentric (Fig. SN4-15). Maximum side-to-side difference should be ⅛ inch (3.2 mm). To adjust side-to-side height, loosen the capscrew and rotate the eccentric on the left front lift arm so the desired dimension is obtained and retighten the nuts. Rotate the eccentric counterclockwise to raise the deck's right side or clockwise to raise the deck's left side.

REMOVAL AND INSTALLATION

Refer to Figs. SN4-16, SN4-17, SN4-18 and SN4-19 for an exploded view of the mower deck.
1. Remove the mower drive belt as previously described.
2. Disconnect the interlock switch wire.
3. Detach the front and rear lift arms and links and remove the mower deck.
4. Install mower deck by reversing the removal procedure.

MOWER SPINDLE

LUBRICATION

Some mowers are equipped with a grease fitting allowing injection of grease into the spindle housing. On models so equipped, the mower spindle should be lubricated annually. Apply multipurpose grease to the mower spindle through the grease fitting on the spindle housing. Two shots should be sufficient.

OVERHAUL

Refer to Fig. SN4-20, SN4-21, SN4-22 or SN4-23 for an exploded view of the spindle assembly. When servicing the spindle, note the following:

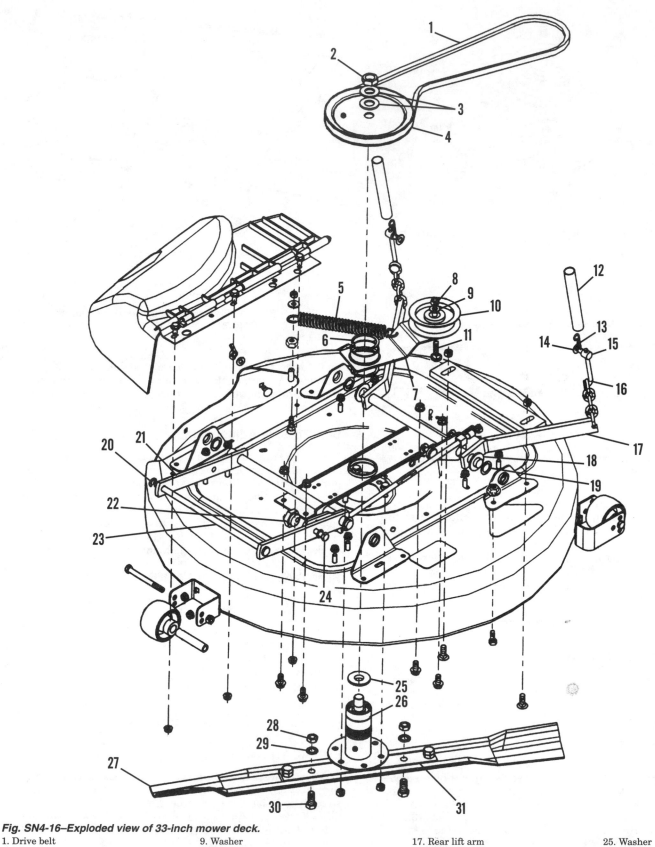

Fig. SN4-16—Exploded view of 33-inch mower deck.

1. Drive belt
2. Nut
3. Washer
4. Pulley
5. Spring
6. Snap ring
7. Idler arm
8. Locknut
9. Washer
10. Idler
11. Bolt
12. Cover
13. Pin
14. Washer
15. Swivel pin
16. Hanger rod
17. Rear lift arm
18. Washer
19. Washer
20. Snap ring
21. Front lift arm
22. Eccentric
23. Rod
24. Bolt
25. Washer
26. Spindle assy.
27. Blade
28. Nut
29. Lockwasher
30. Bolt
31. Blade support

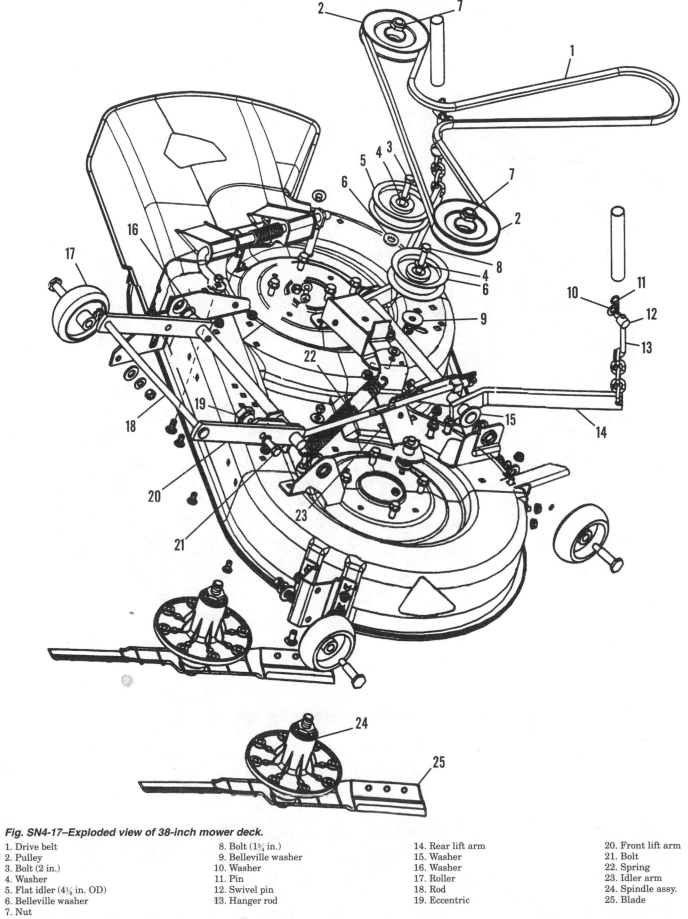

Fig. SN4-17–Exploded view of 38-inch mower deck.

1. Drive belt
2. Pulley
3. Bolt (2 in.)
4. Washer
5. Flat idler (4⅛ in. OD)
6. Belleville washer
7. Nut
8. Bolt (1¾ in.)
9. Belleville washer
10. Washer
11. Pin
12. Swivel pin
13. Hanger rod
14. Rear lift arm
15. Washer
16. Washer
17. Roller
18. Rod
19. Eccentric
20. Front lift arm
21. Bolt
22. Spring
23. Idler arm
24. Spindle assy.
25. Blade

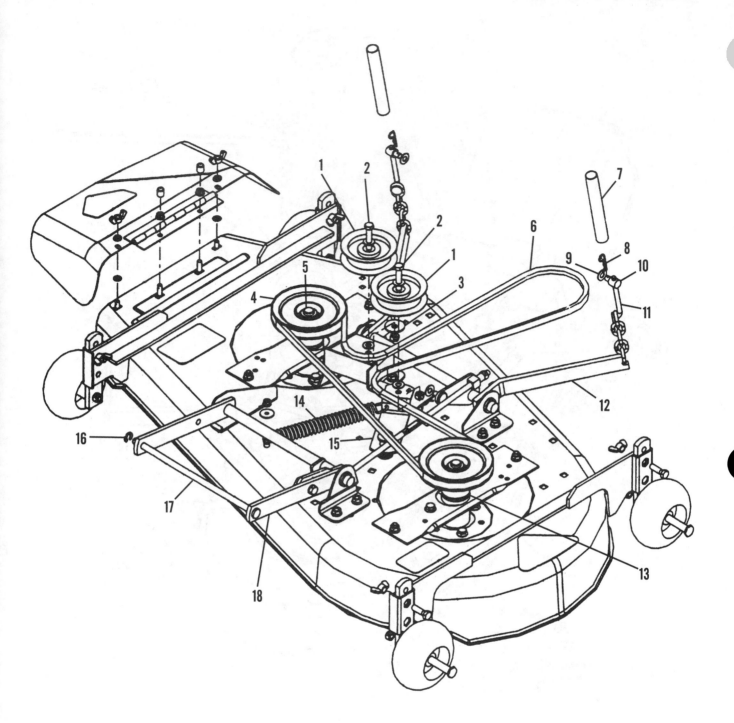

Fig. SN4–18–Exploded view of 42-inch mower deck.

1. Idler
2. Bolt
3. Washer
4. Pulley
5. Locknut
6. Drive belt
7. Cover
8. Pin
9. Washer
10. Swivel pin
11. Hanger rod
12. Rear lift arm
13. Spindle assy.
14. Spring
15. Idler arm
16. Snap ring
17. Rod
18. Front lift arm

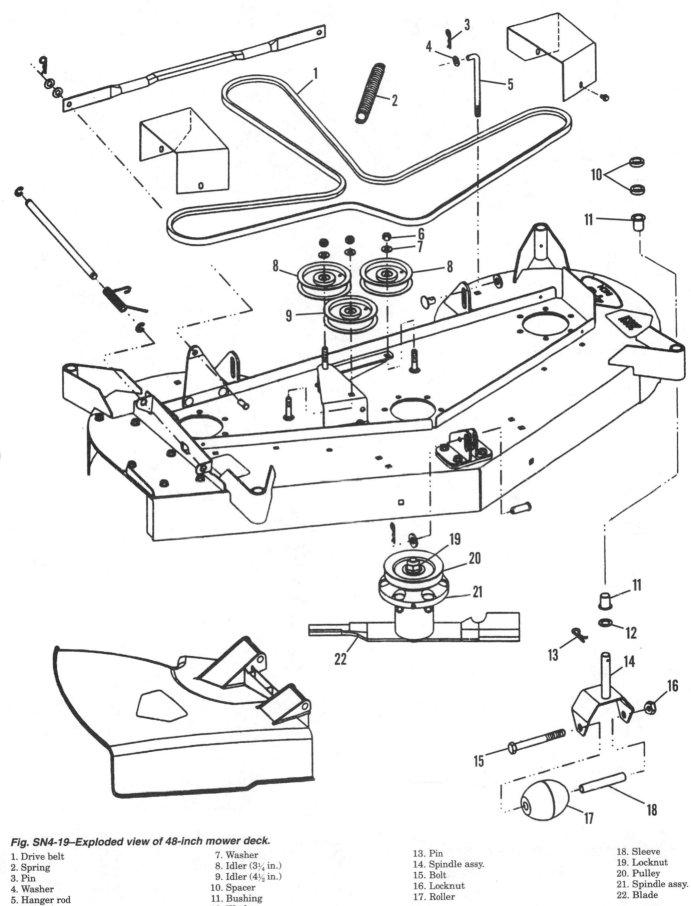

Fig. SN4-19–Exploded view of 48-inch mower deck.

1. Drive belt
2. Spring
3. Pin
4. Washer
5. Hanger rod
6. Locknut
7. Washer
8. Idler (3¼ in.)
9. Idler (4½ in.)
10. Spacer
11. Bushing
12. Washer
13. Pin
14. Spindle assy.
15. Bolt
16. Locknut
17. Roller
18. Sleeve
19. Locknut
20. Pulley
21. Spindle assy.
22. Blade

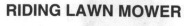

Fig. SN4-20–Exploded view of blade spindle assembly used on 33-inch mower deck.

1. Tolerance ring
2. Spindle housing
3. Grease fitting
4. Bearing
5. Washer
6. Screw
7. Nut
8. Blade holder
9. Locknut
10. Snap ring
11. Spindle

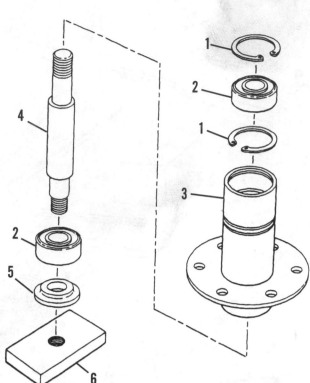

Fig. SN4-22–Exploded view of blade spindle assembly used on 42-inch mower deck.

1. Snap ring
2. Bearing
3. Spindle housing
4. Spindle
5. Washer
6. Blade holder

Fig. SN4-21–Exploded view of blade spindle assembly used on 38-inch mower deck.

1. Spindle
2. Bearing
3. Spacer
4. Spindle housing
5. Spacer
6. Belleville washer
7. Nut

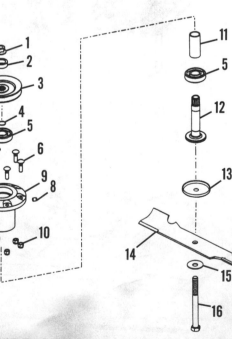

Fig. SN4-23–Exploded view of blade spindle assembly used on 48-inch mower deck.

1. Locknut
2. Washer
3. Pulley
4. Snap ring
5. Bearing
6. Ribbed bolt
7. Grease fitting
8. Vent
9. Spindle housing
10. Nyloc nut
11. Spacer
12. Spindle
13. Cover
14. Balde
15. Belleville washer
16. Bolt

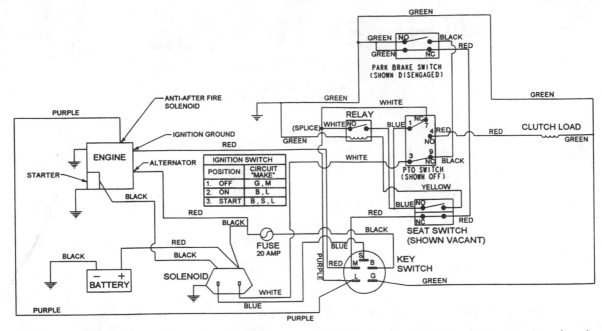

Fig. SN4-24–Wiring schematic for models equipped with a Briggs & Stratton engine. Some engines are not equipped with an anti-afterfire solenoid.

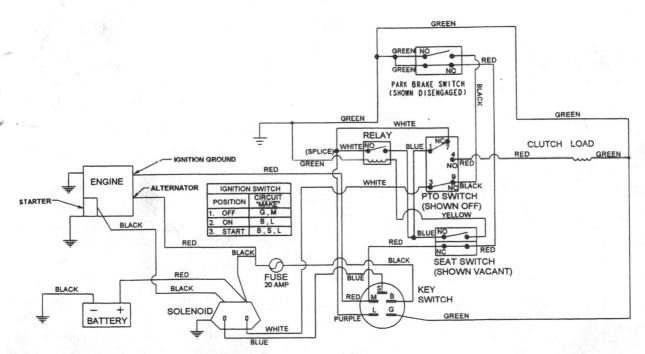

Fig. SN4-25–Wiring schematic for models equipped with a Kohler engine.

1. Remove all components from both ends of the spindle.

2. Remove the spindle and housing from the mower deck.

NOTE: Note the orientation of the bearings markings and closed or open sides so they can be installed in their original direction.

3. Drive or press the spindle with the lower bearing out the bottom of the spindle housing.

4. On models so equipped, detach the snap ring in the upper end of the spindle housing and press or drive out the upper bearing.

5. Reassemble by reversing the disassembly procedure.

ELECTRICAL

Refer to the wiring diagrams (Fig. SN4-24 and Fig. SN4-25). The parking brake must be engaged, the mower must be disengaged and the operator must be in the seat for the engine to start.

WHEEL HORSE (TORO)

Model	Make	Engine Model	Horsepower
70040	B&S	195707	8
70041	B&S	195707	8
70044	B&S	195707	8
70060	B&S	195707	8
70122	B&S	195707	8

NOTE: Some operations may be performed more easily if the machine is standing upright. Observe the following safety recommendations when raising the machine to an upright position:

1. Drain the fuel tank or make certain the fuel level is low enough so fuel will not drain out.
2. Close the fuel shut-off valve if so equipped.
3. Remove the battery if so equipped.
4. Disconnect the spark plug wire and tie it out of the way.
5. Although not absolutely essential, on models with the spark plug at the rear of the machine, engine oil should be drained to prevent flooding the combustion chamber with oil when the engine is tilted.
6. Secure the mower from tipping by lashing the machine to a post or overhead beam.

FRONT WHEELS

MAINTENANCE

Lubricate the front wheel bushings after every 25 hours of operation or annually, whichever occurs first. Using a hand-held grease gun, inject multipurpose grease into the grease fitting on each front wheel.

REMOVAL AND INSTALLATION

The front wheels are equipped with replaceable bushings. To remove the wheel, proceed as follows:
1. Remove the hub cap (9–Fig. WH1-1).
2. Remove the cotter pin (10).
3. Remove the washer (11).
4. Remove the wheel.
5. Inspect the washer and cotter pin. Replace if damaged.
6. Separate the bushings from the wheel.
7. Inspect the bushings and spindles for damage.
8. Inspect the wheel for rim and hub damage.
9. Reverse the removal steps to reassemble and install the wheel.

FRONT SPINDLE

LUBRICATION

Lubricate the front wheel spindles after every 25 hours of operation or annually, whichever occurs first. Inject mul-

tipurpose grease into the front axle main member through the grease fitting (22–Fig. WH1-1) at each end.

OVERHAUL

1. Raise and support the side to be serviced.
2. Remove the wheel and tire.
3. Disconnect the tie rod end (20–Fig. WH1-1) from the spindle.
4. Detach the snap ring (14–Fig. WH1-1) securing the top of the spindle, then withdraw the spindle from the axle.
5. Inspect the axle main member and spindle and replace if necessary.
6. Reverse the removal steps to install the front spindle.

STEERING SYSTEM OVERHAUL

1. Remove the mower deck as described in this section.
2. Drive out the roll pin (3–Fig. WH1-1) and remove the steering wheel.
3. Support the front of the machine. The machine must be raised sufficiently to allow the removal of the steering shaft out the bottom of the machine.
4. Detach the tie rod ends from the steering shaft flange (21).
5. Remove the spacer (4), roll pin (5) and washer (6).
6. Remove the steering shaft (21) out the bottom of the machine.
7. Inspect the bushings (7) in the steering column and replace if necessary.
7. Reverse the removal procedure to install the steering shaft. Check steering operation after assembly.

FRONT AXLE MAIN MEMBER OVERHAUL

The axle main member is center-pivoted at the front of the chassis. Refer to the following procedure to remove and install the front axle.
1. Remove the mower deck as described in this section.
2. Remove the front spindles.
3. Remove the axle pivot shaft nut, then remove the axle main member.
4. Install by reversing the removal procedure.

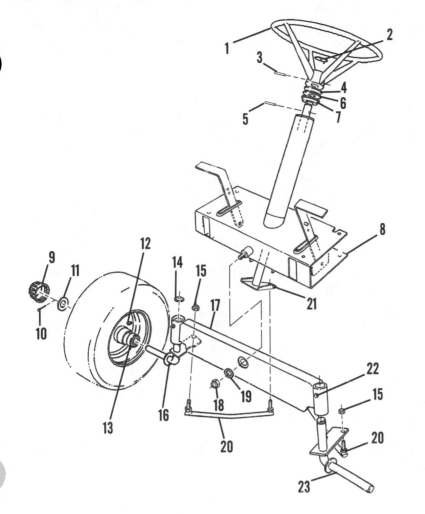

Fig. WH1-1—Exploded view of front axle and steering system.

1. Steering wheel
2. Cap
3. Roll pin
4. Spacer
5. Roll pin
6. Washer
7. Bushing
8. Subframe
9. Hub cap
10. Cotter pin
11. Washer
12. Grease fitting
13. Bearing
14. Snap ring
15. Locknut
16. Spindle
17. Axle main member
18. Locknut
19. Washer
20. Tie rod
21. Steering shaft
22. Grease fitting
23. Spindle

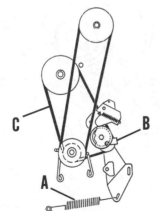

Fig. WH1-2—Refer to the text for the traction drive belt removal procedure.

ENGINE

Refer to the appropriate engine section in this manual for tune-up specifications, engine overhaul procedures and engine maintenance.

REMOVAL AND INSTALLATION

1. Remove the mower deck as described in this section.

2. Raise the seat assembly and disconnect the spark plug wire.

3. Electric start models—Disconnect and remove the battery.

4. Disconnect any interfering electrical wires from the engine.

5. Disconnect the throttle cable from the engine.

6. Disconnect the fuel line, and if necessary, remove the fuel tank.

7. Remove the traction drive belt from the engine pulley as described in this section.

8. Remove the engine mounting fasteners.

9. Remove the engine.

10. Install the engine by reversing the removal procedure.

TRACTION DRIVE CLUTCH AND DRIVE BELT

The traction drive clutch is a spring-tensioned, belt idler operated by the clutch pedal. When the clutch pedal is depressed, belt tension is removed, allowing the engine drive pulley to rotate freely within the drive belt. If the belt is worn or stretched so slippage occurs, replace the belt.

DRIVE BELT

1. Disconnect the spark plug wire.

2. Remove the mower drive belt as described in this section.

3. Detach the idler spring (A—Fig. WH1-2).

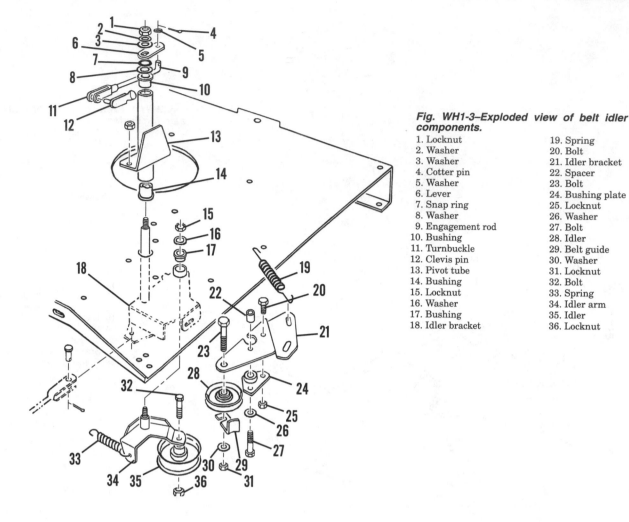

Fig. WH1-3–Exploded view of belt idler components.

1. Locknut	19. Spring
2. Washer	20. Bolt
3. Washer	21. Idler bracket
4. Cotter pin	22. Spacer
5. Washer	23. Bolt
6. Lever	24. Bushing plate
7. Snap ring	25. Locknut
8. Washer	26. Washer
9. Engagement rod	27. Bolt
10. Bushing	28. Idler
11. Turnbuckle	29. Belt guide
12. Clevis pin	30. Washer
13. Pivot tube	31. Locknut
14. Bushing	32. Bolt
15. Locknut	33. Spring
16. Washer	34. Idler arm
17. Bushing	35. Idler
18. Idler bracket	36. Locknut

4. Loosen the idler pulley bolt and relocate the belt guide (B) so the belt can be removed from the pulley.

5. Relocate the belt guides as needed.

6. Remove the traction drive belt (C). Refer to Fig. WH1-3 for an exploded view of the drive belt components.

7. Reverse the removal procedure to install the drive belt.

GROUND DRIVE BRAKE

ADJUSTMENT

If the brake does not prevent movement when engaged, rotate the nut (Fig. WH1-4) on the transaxle brake lever clockwise. Check operation. The machine must move freely when the brake is disengaged. If not, rotate the nut counterclockwise.

OVERHAUL

Refer to Fig. WH1-5 and proceed as follows.

1. Detach the operating rod.

2. Unscrew the lever retaining nut (9).

3. Unscrew the caliper mounting screws (10).

4. Disassemble the brake components.

5. Inspect the brake components for damage. Brake pad wear limit is ¼ inch (6.4 mm).

6. Reverse the disassembly steps to reassemble the brake. Note the following:

    a. Coat the transaxle brake shaft with Lubriplate.

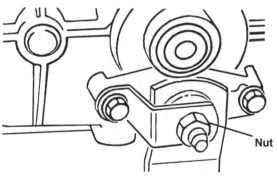

Fig. WH1-4–Adjust the brake by rotating the adjuster nut as described in text.

    b. Apply Lubriplate to the ends of the dowel pins (5) and the rubbing surfaces of the brake lever (6) and washer (7).

    c. Tighten the caliper screws (10) to 95 in.-lb. (10.7 N•m).

TRANSMISSION

REMOVAL AND INSTALLATION

Refer to Fig. WH1-6 for an exploded view of the transmission and related components.

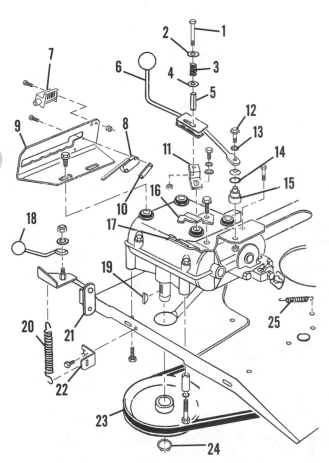

Fig. WH1-5–Exploded view of disc brake assembly.

1. Brake pads	6. Brake lever
2. Brake disc	7. Washer
3. Plate	8. Brace
4. Caliper	9. Nut
5. Dowel pins	10. Screw

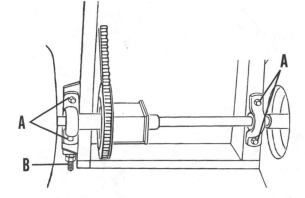

Fig. WH1-7–Refer to text for drive chain adjustment procedure.

1. Remove body components as needed for access to the transmission.
2. Disconnect wiring to the transmission safety switch.
3. Remove the master link from the drive chain and disconnect the chain.
4. Remove the mower deck as described in this section.
5. Remove the drive belt from the transmission pulley.
6. Remove the snap ring (24–Fig. WH1-6) from the transmission input shaft and separate the pulley from the input shaft.
7. Detach the brake return spring (25).
8. Disconnect the brake control rod from the transmission brake lever.
9. Detach the mower control lever spring (20).
10. Remove the mower control lever brackets (16 and 17).
11. Unbolt and remove the transmission.
12. Reverse the removal procedure to install the transmission. Adjust the drive chain and drive belt as needed.

OVERHAUL

All models are equipped with a Peerless 700 transmission. Refer to the Peerless transmission repair section in this manual for overhaul information.

DRIVE CHAIN

ADJUSTMENT

1. Disconnect the spark plug wire.
2. Remove the chain cover.
3. Check chain deflection by moving the bottom chain up and down at the midpoint between the chain sprockets. Total chain deflection should be 1/8 inch (3.2 mm). If chain deflection is incorrect, proceed to Step 4.
4. Raise and support the rear of the machine.

NOTE: Some models may be equipped with a single locknut in place of the jam nuts identified in the following steps.

5. Loosen the nuts (A–Fig. WH1-7) securing the axle pillow blocks.
6. Loosen the rear jam nut (B–Fig. WH1-7) on the chain adjuster.
7. Rotate the inner nut as needed to obtain the desired chain deflection.
8. Retighten the nuts on the pillow blocks.
9. Check the location of the axle as described in this section.

Fig. WH1-6–Exploded view of transmission related components.

1. Bolt	14. Belleville washer
2. Washer	15. Pivot spacer
3. Spring	16. Bracket
4. Washer	17. Bracket
5. Spacer	18. Mower engagement
6. Shift lever	lever
7. Switch	19. Key
8. Switch	20. Spring
9. Shift gate	21. Engagement lever
10. Nut plate	22. Bracket
11. Shift lever	23. Pulley
12. Bolt	24. Snap ring
13. Washer	25. Spring

WHEEL HORSE (TORO)

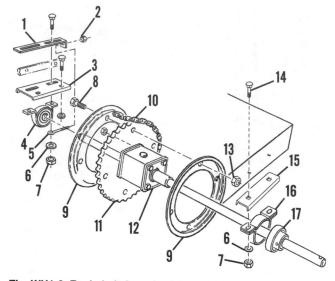

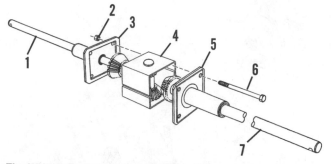

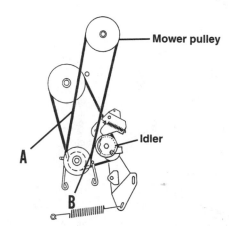

Fig. WH1-8—Exploded view of axle assembly.

1. Chain adjuster plate	
2. Locknut	10. Drive chain
3. Support plate	11. Sprocket
4. Pillow block	12. Differential
5. Cotter pin	13. Locknut
6. Washer	14. Bolt
7. Locknut	15. Support plate
8. Bolt	16. Bearing holder
9. Chain guide	17. Bearing

Fig. WH1-9—Exploded view of differential.

1. Axle (right)	5. End cap (left)
2. Locknut	6. Bolt
3. End cap (right)	7. Axle (left)
4. Case	

REMOVAL AND INSTALLATION

1. Raise and support the rear of the machine.
2. Remove the chain cover.
3. Rotate the axle sprocket and locate the master link in the chain.
4. Disconnect the master link and remove the chain.
5. Inspect the chain and sprockets and replace if necessary.
6. Install the chain and lubricate with a light coat of engine oil.

DIFFERENTIAL AND AXLES

ADJUSTMENT

The axles must be perpendicular to the frame. Proceed as follows to check and align the axle position.
1. Disconnect the spark plug wire.
2. Raise and support the rear of the machine.
3. Measure the distance of both axles to the rear of the frame. The distances should be equal to within 1/8 inch (3.2 mm). If distances are unequal, proceed to Step 4.
4. Loosen the retaining nuts (A–Fig. WH1-7) on the axle pillow blocks.
5. Relocate the pillow blocks as needed, then tighten the retaining nuts.
6. Recheck the axle locations.
7. Adjust chain slack as described in this section.

REMOVAL AND INSTALLATION

Refer to Fig. WH1-8 when performing the following procedure.
1. Remove the drive chain as described in this section.
2. Remove the rear wheels.
3. Support the differential and rear axle assembly.

Fig. WH1-10—Refer to the text for the mower drive belt adjustment procedure.

4. Remove the retaining nuts (A–Fig. WH1-7) from the axle pillow blocks and remove the differential and axle assembly.
5. Install by reversing the removal procedure. Perform the axle adjustment procedure as previously described.

OVERHAUL

Refer to Figs. WH1-8 and WH1-9 when performing the following procedure.
1. Mark the orientation and location of the bearings (17–Fig. WH1-8) before disassembly.
2. Unscrew the setscrew in each bearing and remove the bearings from the axles.
3. Remove the chain guides (9) and sprocket (11) from the differential.
4. Remove the bolts securing the end caps (3 and 5–Fig. WH1-9) to the differential housing.
5. Separate the end caps from the differential housing.
6. Clean and inspect all parts. Replace parts that are damaged.
7. Reassemble by reversing the disassembly procedure. Fill differential with 3/4 to1 1/4 ounces (0.02-0.04 kg) of multipurpose EP grease.

MOWER DRIVE BELT

ADJUSTMENT

1. Place the mower control lever in the engaged position.

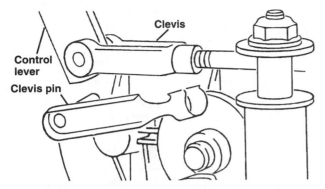

Fig. WH1-11–To disconnect the clevis from the control lever, disengage the clip and clevis pin from the clevis.

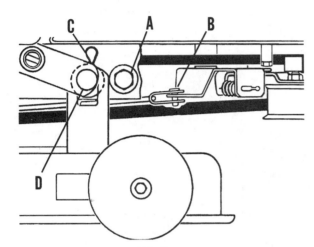

Fig. WH1-12–Refer to text for mower removal procedure.

2. Push the mower drive belt outward (A–Fig. WH1-10) to remove all slack.

3. Measure the gap between the outside of the drive belt and the inside of the idler (B). The gap should be ⅛ inch (3.2 mm). If the measurement is incorrect, proceed to Step 4.

4. Remove the clevis pin (Fig. WH1-11 or 12–Fig. WH1-3) from the clevis on the mower control rod.

NOTE: The clevis pin is attached to a flange and clip that fits around the clevis.

5. Separate the clevis from the control lever (Fig. WH1-11 or 21–Fig. WH1-6).

6. Rotate the clevis, then reattach it and remeasure the gap. Repeat as needed.

REMOVAL AND INSTALLATION

1. Place the machine in an upright position on the rear stand as previously described.

2. Remove the bolts (A–Fig. WH1-12) holding the deck stops to the mower deck.

3. Slide the mower deck back to decrease mower drive belt tension.

4. Place the mower height control in the lowest deck position.

5. Loosen and move the belt guides adjacent to the engine pulley.

6. Place the mower control lever in the engaged position.

7. Remove the belt guide on the mower deck.

8. Remove the mower drive belt.

9. Install the mower drive belt by reversing the removal procedure. Position the belt guides ⅛ inch (3.2 mm) from the belt or pulley. Adjust the drive belt as previously described.

MOWER DECK REMOVAL AND INSTALLATION

1. Remove the mower drive belt as previously described.

2. Remove the clevis pin (B–Fig. WH1-12) connecting the blade brake rod end to the idler bracket.

3. Remove the cotter pins (C) in the mounting pins on both sides of the mower deck.

4. Disengage the mounting pins and move the deck forward for removal.

5. Reverse the removal procedure to install the mower deck.

MOWER SPINDLE

LUBRICATION

Periodically lubricate the contact surfaces of rubbing components with engine oil. Periodic lubrication of the mower spindle is not required.

OVERHAUL

Refer to Fig. WH1-13 when performing the following procedure.

1. Remove the mower deck.

2. Disengage the belt from the spindle pulley.

3. Remove the pulley retaining nut and the pulley.

4. Remove the blade.

5. Unscrew the bolts securing the spindle housing (14–Fig. WH1-13) and remove the spindle assembly.

6. Disassemble the spindle assembly components as needed.

7. Inspect components for damage.

8. Reassemble by reversing the disassembly steps. Note the following:

   a. Tighten the spindle nut securely.

   b. Tighten the mower blade retaining screw to 55 ft.-lb. (75 N•m).

BLADE BRAKE

The mower is equipped with a pad brake stopping rotation of the blade spindle within 3 seconds. Rotate the adjustment nut (10–Fig. WH1-13) as needed for proper brake operation. Be sure the brake pad does not contact the spindle pulley during normal cutting.

ELECTRICAL

Refer to Fig. WH1-14 for a wiring schematic. Note the following points:

1. The transaxle must be in NEUTRAL, the mower must be disengaged and the operator must be in the seat for the engine to start.

2. The engine should stop if the transaxle is in gear or the mower is engaged and the operator leaves the seat.

3. The engine will stop if the transaxle is shifted into REVERSE while the mower is engaged.

4. The Key Choice switch allows operation of the mower with the transaxle in reverse. A red indicator light is on when the machine is in REVERSE while the mower is operating.

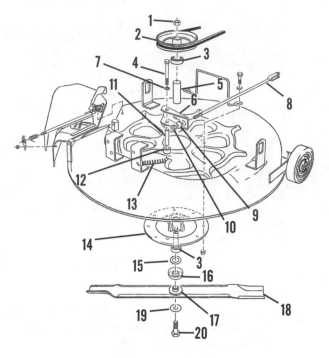

Fig. WH1-13–Exploded view of mower deck.
1. Nut
2. Pulley
3. Bearing
4. Bolt
5. Spacer
6. Blade brake
7. Washer
8. Brake rod
9. Swivel ball
10. Locknut
11. Post
12. Spacer
13. Spring
14. Spindle housing
15. Spacer
16. Bearing shield
17. Spindle
18. Blade
19. Belleville washer
20. Bolt

Diagram Key

Connectors

Ground

Frame ground

Connection

No connection

NMIR module

Over ride lamp

Color Code
B	Black
R	Red
G	Green
Br	Brown
W	White
Y	Yellow
L	Blue
Gy	Gray
O	Orange
P	Pink
T	Tan
V	Violet

Ignition switch

Neutral switch

Seat switch

Parking brake switch

PTO switch

Over ride switch

Reverse switch

Engine stop switch

Fuse 7.5A

Fuse 7.5A

Magneto

Alternator

Starter relay

Starter motor

Battery

Fig. WH1-14–Wiring schematic.

WHEEL HORSE
(TORO)

Model	Make	Engine Model	Horsepower
70042	B&S	195707*	8
70080	B&S	28B707	10
70081	B&S	28D707	11.5
70082	B&S	28M707	12.5
70084	B&S	28M707	12.5
70089	B&S	28M707	12.5
70120	B&S	286707*	12
70131	B&S	28M707	13
70140	B&S	257707	12.5
70141	B&S	283707	12
70142	B&S	283707*	12
70171	B&S	28M707	12.5
70183	B&S	28M707	13

*May be equipped with an engine model other than that listed. Check the model number on the engine.

FRONT WHEELS

MAINTENANCE

Lubricate the front wheel bushings after every 25 hours of operation or annually, whichever occurs first. Using a hand-held grease gun, inject multipurpose grease into the grease fitting on each front wheel.

REMOVAL AND INSTALLATION

The front wheels are equipped with replaceable bushings. To remove the wheel, proceed as follows:
1. Remove the hub cap (1–Fig. WH2-1).
2. Remove the cotter pin (2).
3. Remove the washer (3).
4. Remove the wheel.
5. Inspect the inner washer and cotter pin. Replace if damaged.
6. Separate the bushings from the wheel.
7. Inspect the bushings and spindle for damage.
8. Inspect the wheel for rim and hub damage.
9. Reverse the removal steps to reassemble and install the wheel.

FRONT SPINDLE

LUBRICATION

Lubricate the front wheel spindles after every 25 hours of operation or annually, whichever occurs first. Inject multipurpose grease into the front axle main member through the grease fitting (29–Fig. WH2-1) at each end.

OVERHAUL

1. Raise and support the side to be serviced.
2. Remove the wheel and tire.

3. Disconnect the tie rod end from the spindle.
4. Detach the snap ring (8–Fig. WH2-1) securing the top of the spindle, then withdraw the spindle from the axle.
5. Inspect the bushings (26) in the axle main member and replace if necessary.
6. Reverse the removal steps to install the front spindle.

STEERING SYSTEM

LUBRICATION

Lubricate the steering gears with engine oil after 25 hours of operation, or more frequently when operated in a dusty environment.

TOE-IN SETTING

Proceed as follows to check and adjust toe-in on Series 11 models.
1. Be sure the tires are properly inflated.
2. Position the machine on a flat, smooth surface.
3. Position the front wheels in the straight-ahead position.
4. Measure the distance at spindle height between the center of the tires on the rear side.
5. Locate the same tire centerline points on the front side of the tires and measure the front distance.
6. The distance on the front side should be should be $\frac{1}{16}$-$\frac{1}{4}$ inch (1.5-6.4 mm) shorter (toed-in) than the measured distance on the rear side.
7. To adjust toe-in, adjust the lengths of both tie rods equally.
8. Detach the tie rod end (9–Fig. WH2-1).
9. Loosen the jam nut (11) and turn the tie rod end.
10. Retighten the jam nut after completing the adjustment.

OVERHAUL

1. Remove the mower deck as described in this section.

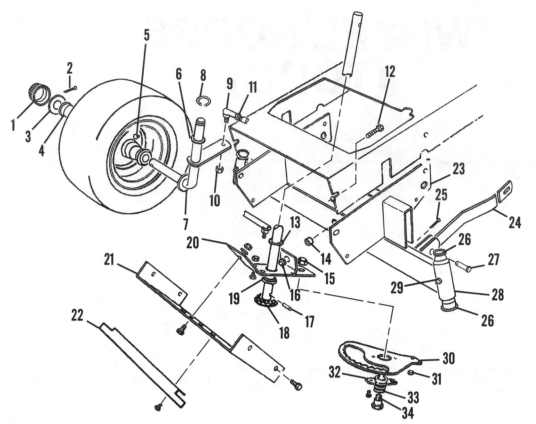

Fig. WH2-1–Exploded view of front axle and steering system.

1. Hub cap	10. Locknut	19. Bushing	27. Clevis pin
2. Cotter pin	11. Jam nut	20. Steering shaft plate	28. Axle main member
3. Washer	12. Pivot bolt	21. Front cover	29. Grease fitting
4. Bearing	13. Thrust washer	22. Front guard	30. Sector gear
5. Grease fitting	14. Bushing	23. Subframe	31. Locknut
6. Thrust washer	15. Locknut	24. Front suspension	32. Bushing
7. Spindle	16. Locknut	arm	33. Thrust washers
8. Snap ring	17. Roll pin	25. Cotter pin	34. Pivot bolt
9. Outer tie rod end	18. Steering shaft	26. Bushing	

2. Support the front of the machine. The machine must be raised sufficiently to allow the removal of the steering shaft out the bottom of the machine.

3. Remove the steering wheel from the steering shaft.

4. Remove the front cover (21–Fig. WH2-1).

5. Remove the steering shaft and gear (18) out the bottom of the machine.

6. Detach the tie rod ends from the sector gear (30).

7. Remove the sector gear pivot bolt (34), then remove the sector gear.

8. If necessary, remove the bushing (32) retaining screws and separate the bushing from the sector gear.

9. Inspect the components for damage. Replace as needed.

10. Reverse the removal procedure to reinstall the shaft and gears. Check steering operation after assembly.

FRONT AXLE MAIN MEMBER OVERHAUL

The axle main member is center-pivoted in a channel at the front of the chassis. Refer to the following procedure to remove and install the front axle.

1. Remove the mower deck as described in this section.

2. Remove the front wheels.

3. Remove the steering shaft and gears as described in this section.

4. Remove the cotter pin (25–Fig. WH2-1) and clevis pin (27), then separate the front suspension arms (24) from the axle main member.

5. Remove the axle pivot bolt nut and steering shaft plate retaining bolts.

6. Remove the steering shaft plate (20).

7. Remove the axle pivot bolt (12), then lower the axle main member out of the frame.

8. Clean and inspect all parts. Replace damaged parts.

9. Install by reversing the removal procedure.

ENGINE

Refer to the appropriate engine section in this manual for tune-up specifications, engine overhaul procedures and engine maintenance.

REMOVAL AND INSTALLATION

1. Disconnect the spark plug wire and remove engine cover.

2. Electric start models—disconnect and remove the battery.

3. Disconnect any interfering electrical wires from the engine.

4. Disconnect the throttle cable from the engine.

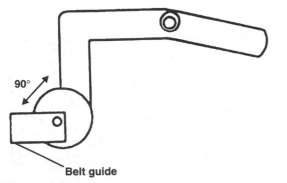

Fig. WH2-2–Position the belt guide on the idler pulley so it is 90° from the idler braket.

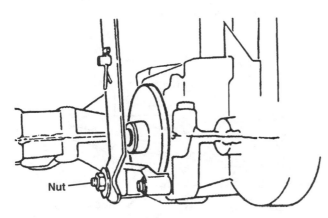

Fig. WH2-3–Adjust the brake by rotating the adjuster nut as described in text.

5. Disconnect the fuel line, and if necessary, remove the fuel tank.
6. Remove the traction drive belt from the engine pulley as described in this section.
7. Remove the engine mounting fasteners.
8. Remove the engine.
9. Install the engine by reversing the removal procedure.

TRACTION DRIVE CLUTCH AND DRIVE BELT

The traction drive clutch is a spring-tensioned, belt idler operated by the clutch pedal. When the clutch pedal is depressed, belt tension is removed, allowing the engine drive pulley to rotate freely within the drive belt. If the belt is worn or stretched so slippage occurs, replace the belt.

DRIVE BELT

1. Disconnect the spark plug wire.
2. Remove the mower deck as described in this section.
3. Raise and support the rear of the machine.
4. Remove the belt guides adjacent to the transaxle pulley.
5. Loosen the belt guides adjacent to the engine drive pulley and move them out of the way.
6. Fully depress the clutch pedal.
7. Remove the drive belt.
8. Reverse the removal procedure to install the drive belt. Position the belt guide on the idler pulley so it is 90° from the idler bracket as shown in Fig. WH2-2.

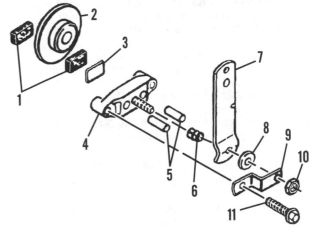

Fig. WH2-4–Exploded view of disc brake assembly.

1. Brake pads	7. Brake lever
2. Brake disc	8. Washer
3. Plate	9. Brace
4. Caliper	10. Nut
5. Dowel pins	11. Screw
6. Spring	

GROUND DRIVE BRAKE

ADJUSTMENT

If the brake does not prevent movement when engaged, rotate the nut (Fig. WH2-3) on the transaxle brake lever clockwise. Check operation. The machine must move freely when the brake is disengaged. If not, rotate the nut counterclockwise.

OVERHAUL

Refer to Fig. WH2-4 and proceed as follows.
1. Detach the operating rod.
2. Unscrew the lever retaining nut (10).
3. Unscrew the caliper mounting screws (11).
4. Disassemble the brake components.
5. Inspect the brake components for damage. Brake pad wear limit is ¼ inch (6.4 mm).
6. Reverse the disassembly steps to reassemble the brake. Note the following:
   a. Coat the transaxle brake shaft with Lubriplate.
   b. Apply Lubriplate to the ends of the dowel pins (5) and the rubbing surfaces of the brake lever and washer (8).
   c. Tighten the caliper screws (11) to 95 in.-lb. (10.7 N•m).

TRANSAXLE

LUBRICATION

The outer ends of the transaxle are equipped with grease fittings. Inject No. 2 multipurpose grease into the grease fittings after every 25 hours of operation. One or two shots from a hand-held grease gun should be sufficient. Refer to the repair section for internal lubrication information.

NEUTRAL ADJUSTMENT

Adjust the shift linkage so NEUTRAL positions in the transaxle and at the shift lever are synchronized. If the

WHEEL HORSE (TORO)

rear wheels are locked when the gearshift lever is in NEUTRAL, perform the following adjustment procedure.

Refer to Fig. WH2-5 when performing the following procedure.

1. Raise and support the rear of the machine.
2. Remove the cotter pin and detach the shift rod from the transaxle shift lever.
3. Move the shift control lever to the NEUTRAL position indicated on the control panel.
4. Move the transaxle shift lever to the NEUTRAL position. The rear wheels should turn freely.

NOTE: Do not move the shift control lever or transaxle shift lever while performing Step 5.

5. Rotate the shift rod as needed so it will fit easily into the hole in the transaxle shift lever. Reinstall the cotter pin.
6. Check operation.

REMOVAL AND INSTALLATION

To remove the transaxle, proceed as follows.
1. Remove the mower deck.
2. Raise and support the rear of the machine.
3. Remove the rear wheels.
4. Remove the drive belt.
5. Disconnect the shift linkage.
6. Disconnect the brake link.
7. Support the transaxle.
8. Remove the transaxle mounting bolts.
9. Remove the transaxle.
10. Install the transaxle by reversing the removal procedure.

NOTE: If removed, install the shift lever on the transaxle so the "T" mark is up.

OVERHAUL

All models are equipped with a Peerless 915 transaxle. Refer to the repair section in this manual for overhaul information.

MOWER DRIVE BELT

ADJUSTMENT

1. Place the mower height control lever in the lowest height position.
2. Place the mower control lever in the engaged position.
3. The gap (G–Fig. WH2-6) between the front of the pin and the front of the slot should be 0.060 inch (1.5 mm) or less. If the measurement is incorrect, proceed to Step 4.
4. Remove the cotter pin and detach the rod end from the lever.

NOTE: The adjustment rod has left-hand threads.

5. Rotate the rod, then reattach it and remeasure the gap. Repeat as needed.

REMOVAL AND INSTALLATION

1. Remove the mower deck as described in this section.
2. Loosen the belt guides adjacent to the engine drive pulley and move them out of the way.
3. Remove the mower drive belt.

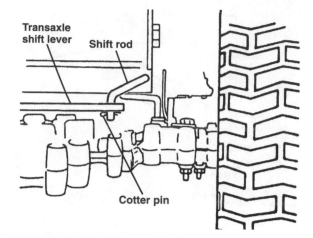

Fig. WH2-5–Refer to text for neutral alignment procedure.

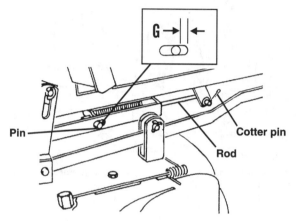

Fig. WH2-6–Measure the position of the pin in the slot as shown for mower drive belt adjustment. Refer to text.

4. Install the mower drive belt by reversing the removal procedure.

MOWER DECK

HEIGHT ADJUSTMENT

1. Position the machine on a level surface.
2. Disconnect the spark plug wire.
3. Position the blade so it is perpendicular to the machine centerline. Measure the distance from the ground to the blade from side to side. Maximum difference should be 1/8 inch (3.2 mm).
4. To adjust side-to-side dimension, loosen the support bracket bolts (Fig. WH2-7) and relocate the support bracket.
5. Recheck the blade height, and adjust as needed.

REMOVAL AND INSTALLATION

1. Position the machine on a level surface.
2. Disconnect the spark plug wire.
3. Turn the front wheels fully to one direction.
4. Place the mower height control to the lowest deck height position.
5. Loosen the belt guides adjacent to the engine drive pulley and move them out of the way.
6. Remove the mower drive belt from the engine pulley.

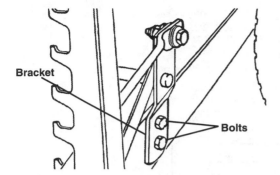

Fig. WH2-7–To adjust side-to-side blade, height, loosen the support bracket bolts and relocate the support bracket.

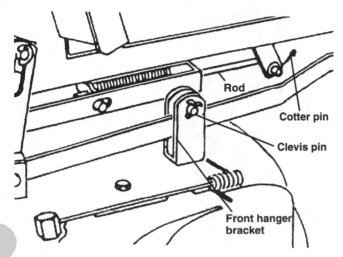

Fig. WH2-8–Refer to text for mower deck removal procedure.

7. Remove the cotter pin (Fig. WH2-8) and detach the rod end from the lever.

8. Remove the cotter pins from the clevis pins in the front hanger brackets.

9. Support the front of the mower deck, remove the clevis pins from the front hanger brackets, then lower the front of the mower deck.

10. Move the rear hanger brackets off the rear pins on the rear suspension arms.

11. Place the mower height control to the highest deck height position.

12. Remove the mower deck.

13. Reverse the removal procedure to install the mower deck.

MOWER SPINDLE

LUBRICATION

Periodically lubricate the contact surfaces of rubbing components with engine oil. Periodic lubrication of the mower spindle is not required.

OVERHAUL

Refer to Fig. WH2-9 when performing the following procedure.

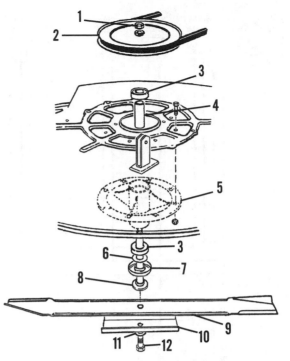

Fig. WH2-9–Exploded view of spindle assembly.

1. Nut	7. Bearing shield
2. Pulley	8. Spindle
3. Bearing	9. Blade
4. Spacer	10. Blade holder
5. Spindle housing	11. Belleville washer
6. Spacer	12. Bolt

1. Remove the mower deck.

2. Disengage the belt from the spindle pulley.

3. Remove the pulley retaining nut and pulley.

4. Remove the blade and blade holder.

5. Unscrew the bolts securing the spindle housing (5–Fig. WH2-9) and remove the spindle assembly.

6. Disassemble the spindle assembly components as needed.

7. Inspect components for damage.

8. Reassemble by reversing the disassembly steps. Note the following:

    a. Tighten the spindle nut securely.

    b. Tighten the mower blade retaining screw to 55 ft.-lb. (75 N•m).

ELECTRICAL

Refer to Fig. WH2-10 for a wiring schematic. Note the following points:

1. The transaxle must be in NEUTRAL, the mower must be disengaged and the operator must be in the seat for the engine to start.

2. The engine should stop if the transaxle is in gear or the mower is engaged and the operator leaves the seat.

3. The engine will stop if the transaxle is shifted into REVERSE while the mower is engaged.

4. The Key Choice switch allows operation of the mower with the transaxle in REVERSE. A red indicator light is on when the machine is in reverse while the mower is operating.

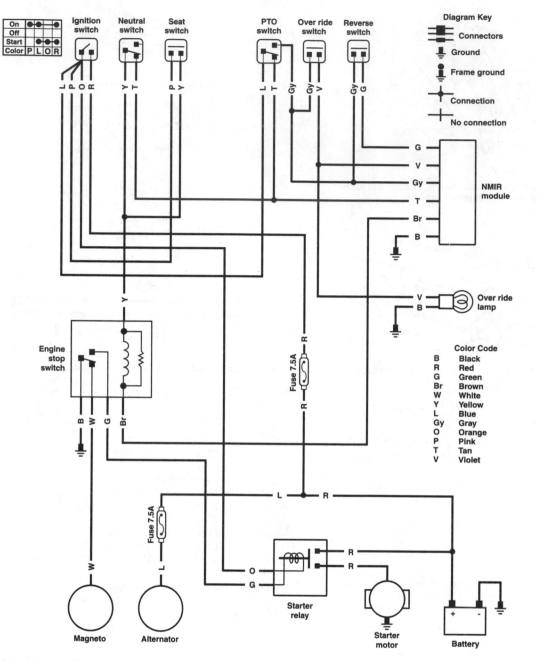

Fig. WH2-10–Wiring schematic.

WHITE

Model	Make	Engine Model	Horsepower	Cutting Width, In.
R-10	*	*	*	30

*Note the engine model number and refer to the engine service section in this manual for engine specifications.

FRONT WHEELS

REMOVAL AND INSTALLATION

The front wheels are equipped with replaceable sealed bearings. To remove the wheel and bearings, proceed as follows:
1. Remove the hub cap (31–Fig. WT1-1).
2. Remove the cotter pin (32).
3. Remove the wheel with bearings.
4. Separate the bearings from the wheel.
5. Inspect the bearings for damage.
6. Inspect the wheel for rim and hub damage.
7. Reverse the removal steps to reassemble and install the wheel and bearings.

FRONT AXLE AND STEERING SYSTEM

TOE-IN SETTING

Adjustable tie rods are used on all models. Proceed as follows to check and adjust toe-in.
1. Be sure the tires are properly inflated.
2. Position the machine on a flat, smooth surface.
3. Position the front wheels in the straight-ahead position.
4. Measure the distance at spindle height between the center of the tires on the rear side.
5. Locate the same tire centerline points on the front side of the tires and measure the front distance.
6. The distance on the front side should be should be ⅛ inch (3.2 mm) shorter (toed-in) than the measured distance on the rear side.
7. To adjust the toe-in, detach the tie rod ends (30–Fig. WT1-1).
8. Rotate the tie rod ends to lengthen or shorten the tie rod as needed and reattach to the sector gear.
9. Recheck the toe-in measurement.

OVERHAUL

Refer to the exploded view in Fig. WT1-1 when performing the following procedure.
1. Remove the mower deck.
2. Remove the steering wheel cap, retaining nut and washer.
3. Lift off the steering wheel.
4. Remove the cover (19–WT1-1).
5. Unscrew the nut at the lower end of the steering shaft and remove the gear (16).
6. Remove the bolt (7) and remove the steering shafts.
7. Disconnect the tie rods from the spindles.
8. Detach the steering support plate (13) and sector gear (18).

9. Support the frame and remove the front wheels.
10. Remove the cotter pins and washers, then lower the spindles (35) from the axle.
11. Detach the front axle support (12) from the frame.
12. Remove the axle main member (23).
13. Clean and inspect all parts and replace any that are damaged.
14. Reassemble by reversing the disassembly procedure while noting the following:
   a. Lubricate the bushings and all pivot points with SAE 30 oil.
   b. Operate the steering through the full range of movement and check for binding.
   c. Adjust the front wheel toe-in as previously described.

ENGINE

Refer to the appropriate engine section in this manual for tune-up specifications, engine overhaul procedures and engine maintenance.

REMOVAL AND INSTALLATION

1. Disconnect the spark plug wire and remove the engine cover.
2. Electric start models–disconnect and remove the battery.
3. Disconnect any interfering electrical wires from the engine.
4. Disconnect the throttle cable from the engine.
5. Detach the exhaust pipe.
6. Remove the mower as outlined in the MOWER DECK section.
7. Remove the traction drive belt from the engine pulley as outlined in the TRACTION DRIVE CLUTCH AND DRIVE BELTS section.
8. Detach the pulleys from the engine crankshaft.
9. Remove the engine mounting fasteners.
10. Remove the engine.
11. Install the engine by reversing the removal procedure.

TRACTION DRIVE CLUTCH AND DRIVE BELT

All models are equipped with a drive system using two drive belts and a variable speed pulley to transfer power from the engine to the transaxle. The lower primary drive belt connects the engine to the variable speed pulley (23–Fig. WT1-2).

The diameters of the pulley grooves are determined by belt tension, which is regulated by the position of idlers (10

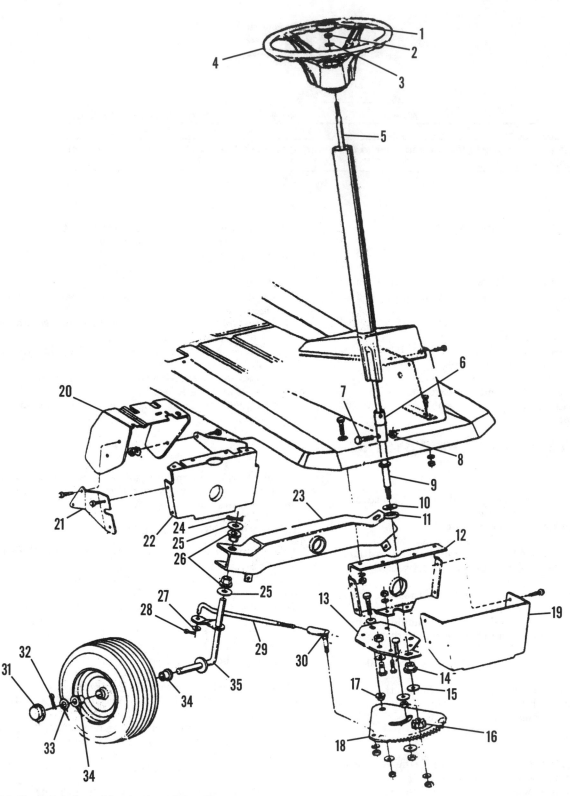

Fig. WT1-1–Exploded view of front axle and steering system.

1. Cap	10. Washer	19. Cover	28. Cotter pin
2. Nut	11. Spacer	20. Bracket	29. Tie rod
3. Washer	12. Axle support	21. Plate	30. Tie rod end
4. Steering wheel	13. Steering plate	22. Axle support	31. Hub cap
5. Steering shaft	14. Bushing	23. Axle main member	32. Cotter pin
6. Coupler	15. Washer	24. Cotter pin	33. Washer
7. Bolt	16. Steering gear	25. Washer	34. Bushing
8. Nut	17. Bushing	26. Bushing	35. Spindle
9. Lower shaft	18. Sector gear	27. Washer	

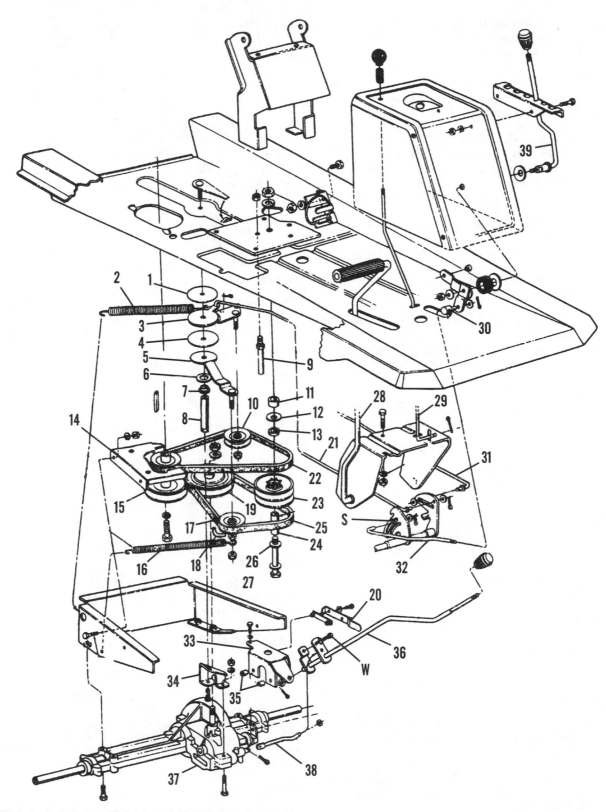

Fig. WH1-2–Exploded view of clutch and variable speed assembly.

1. Thrust washer	11. Spacer	21. Clutch rod	31. Brake rod
2. Spring	12. Belleville washer	22. Upper drive belt	32. Speed control rod
3. Idler arm	13. Thrust washer	23. Variable speed pulley	33. Bracket
4. Thrust washer	14. Belt guard	24. Spacer	34. Bracket
5. Idler arm	15. Engine pulley	25. Lower drive belt	35. Spacer
6. Washer	16. Spring	26. Thrust washer	36. Shift lever
7. Bushing	17. Idler	27. Cap screw	37. Transaxle
8. Torque rod	18. Belt guide	28. Pedal rod	38. Shift rod
9. Belt guide	19. Transaxle pulley	29. Park brake rod	39. Speed control lever
10. Idler	20. Spring switch	30. Ferrule	

and 17). The idlers move when the speed control lever is operated. Ground speed changes when the pulley diameters change on the variable speed pulley.

ADJUSTMENT

The speed control lever and gear shift lever must be synchronized with the belt idler positions. Proceed as follows.

1. Start and run the engine.
2. Be sure the gear shift lever is in NEUTRAL.
3. Place the speed control lever in the high speed position.
4. Release, then slowly depress fully the clutch/brake pedal and hold down the pedal.
5. Stop the engine, then release the pedal when the engine stops.
6. Move the speed control lever to the second speed position.
7. Detach the bent end of the lower speed control rod (32–Fig. WT1-2).
8. Turn the rod so the end of the rod will just enter the forward end of the slot (S).
9. Reattach the rod.
10. Move the gear shift lever to the NEUTRAL slot on the gear indicator panel.
11. If the machine does not move freely forward and backward thereby indicating the transaxle is in NEUTRAL, proceed as follows:
   a. Loosen the screw (W–Fig. WT1-2).
   b. Move the shift lever (36) as needed so the transaxle is in NEUTRAL and the shift lever is in the center of the neutral slot on the control panel.
   c. Retighten the screw (W) to 13 ft.-lb. (18 N•m).

DRIVE BELTS

Lower Belt

1. Disconnect the spark plug wire and remove the battery.
2. Remove the mower as outlined in the MOWER DECK section.
3. Disconnect the idler spring (16–Fig. WT1-2).
4. Detach the torque rod bracket (34) from the transaxle and the torque rod (8).
5. Remove the bracket.
6. Separate the belt from the pulleys and remove the belt.
7. Install the lower belt by reversing the removal procedure.

Upper Belt

1. Remove the lower belt as described in the previous section.
2. Detach the engine pulley belt guide (14–Fig. WT1-2).
3. Unscrew the retaining nut and the remove the idler (10).
4. Remove the upper belt.
5. Install the upper belt by reversing the removal procedure. Be sure the hub side of idler (10) is next to the idler arm (3). Install the belt and idler simultaneously so the belt is inside the belt guide (9).

VARIABLE SPEED PULLEY

OVERHAUL

The variable speed pulley is accessible after removing the drive belts as previously described. The variable speed pulley is available only as a unit assembly; individual components are not available.

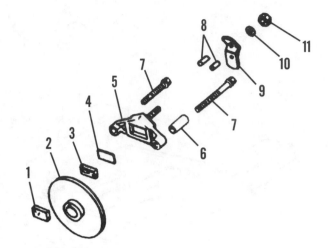

Fig. WT1-3–Exploded view of caliper brake.

1. Brake pad (inner)
2. Brake disc
3. Brake pad (outer)
4. Backup plate
5. Carrier
6. Spacer
7. Cap screws
8. Actuating pins
9. Cam lever
10. Washer
11. Adjusting nut

TRANSAXLE

REMOVAL AND INSTALLATION

1. Remove the drive belts as previously described.
2. Disconnect the brake linkage and the shift linkage.
3. Support the rear of the machine.
4. Remove the transaxle mounting bolts.
5. Raise the rear of the machine and roll the transaxle assembly from under the machine.
6. Install by reversing the removal procedure.

OVERHAUL

All models are equipped with a MTD Model 618 transaxle. Refer to the TRANSAXLE REPAIR section for service information.

GROUND DRIVE BRAKE

ADJUSTMENT

Check brake operation by pushing the brake pedal and attempting to move the machine. If the brake does not hold the machine with the pedal fully depressed, adjust the brake. To adjust the brake, release the brake and turn the nut (11—Fig. WT1-3) on the cam lever until desired brake operation is obtained.

OVERHAUL

1. Disconnect the brake spring and the brake rod from the actuating lever.
2. Unbolt and remove the brake pad carrier (5–Fig. WT1-3).
3. Slide the brake disc off the transaxle shaft.
4. Remove the inner brake pad from the slot in the transaxle housing.
5. Clean and inspect all parts for damage.
6. Reassemble by reversing the disassembly procedure.

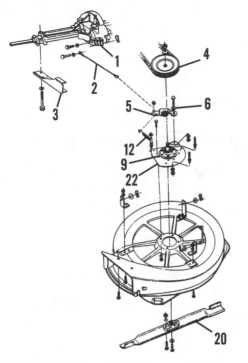

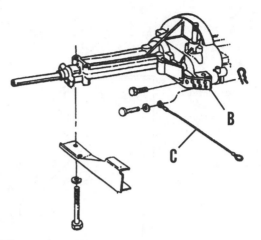

Fig. WT1-5–Attach end of blade brake cable as described in text.

Fig. WT1-4–Exploded view of 30-inch mower deck. Spindle components are available only as a unit assembly.

1. Bracket	6. Spacer
2. Blade brake cable	9. Spring
3. Bracket	12. Spindle mounting plate
4. Pulley	20. Blade
5. Blade brake.	22. Bearing & spindle assy.

MOWER DRIVE BELT

REMOVAL AND INSTALLATION

Refer to Fig. WT1-4 when performing the following procedure.

1. Disconnect the spark plug wire.
2. Place the blade engagement lever in the disengaged position.
3. Locate the outside engine belt guard at the right rear side of the machine and remove one retaining bolt while loosening the other bolt.
4. Pivot the belt guard out and away from the engine pulley.
5. Disconnect the blade brake cable from the belt guard and remove the belt guard.
6. Disconnect the mower deck links and remove the belt guides on the deck.
7. Remove the belt.
8. Install the mower belt by reversing the removal procedure.

MOWER DECK

HEIGHT ADJUSTMENT

The front of the mower blade should be $\frac{1}{4}$-$\frac{3}{8}$ inch (6.4-9.5 mm) lower than the rear of the blade. The mower deck should be level from side to side. Adjust the hanger lengths as needed to obtain the desired height.

REMOVAL AND INSTALLATION

Refer to Fig. WT1-4 when performing the following procedure.

1. Disconnect the spark plug wire.
2. Move the mower deck to the lowest position.
3. Place the blade engagement lever in the disengaged position.
4. Locate the outside engine belt guard at the right rear side of the machine and remove one retaining bolt while loosening the other bolt.
5. Pivot the belt guard out and away from the engine pulley.
6. Disconnect the blade brake cable from the belt guard and remove the belt guard.
7. Separate the drive belt from the engine pulley.
8. Disconnect the safety switch wire on models so equipped.
9. Detach the lift linkage from the mower deck and remove the mower deck.
10. Install by reversing the removal procedure. Adjust the blade brake cable as outlined in the BLADE BRAKE section.

BLADE BRAKE

ADJUSTMENT

1. Place the mower deck in the lowest position.
2. Move the blade engagement lever to the disengaged position.
3. Attach the cable (C–Fig. WT1-5) end to the rearmost hole in the bracket (B) so the cable has the least amount of slack but no tension.

MOWER SPINDLE

OVERHAUL

Refer to Fig. WT1-4 when performing the following procedure.

1. Remove the mower deck as previously described.
2. Remove the mower blade
3. Unbolt and remove the spindle assembly. The spindle assembly is available only as a unit assembly.

ELECTRICAL

Refer to Fig. WT1-6 for a typical wiring schematic. All switches must be in good operating condition for machine to operate properly.

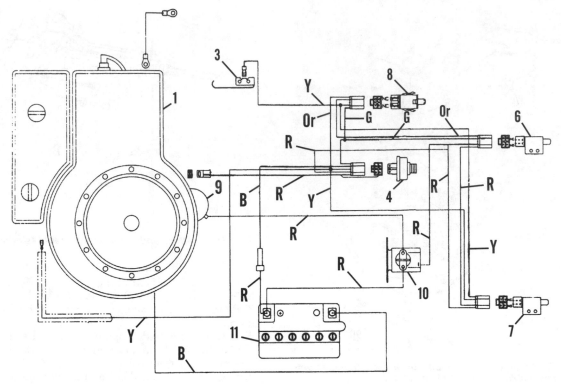

Fig. WT1-6–Typical wiring diagrams.

B. Black	Y. Yellow	6. Clutch switch	9. Starter
G. Green	1. Engine	7. Blade engagement switch	10. Starter solenoid
Or. Orange	3. Reverse gear switch	8. Seat switch	11. Battery
R. Red	4. Ignition switch		

ENGINE REPAIR
BRIGGS & STRATTON
SINGLE-CYLINDER OHV ENGINES

Model Series	No. Cyls.	Bore	Stroke	Displacement	Power Rating
287700	1	3.438 in. (87.3 mm)	3.06 in. (77.7 mm)	28.4 cu. in. (465 cc)	14.0 hp (10.4 kW)
28E700, 28N700, 28P700, 28Q700, 28S700, 28U700, 28W700	1	3.438 in. (87.3 mm)	3.06 in. (77.7 mm)	28.4 cu. in. (465 cc)	See text
310700, 311700, 312700	1	3.562 in. (90.6 mm)	3.06 in. (77.7 mm)	31.0 cu. in. (508 cc)	See text

NOTE: Power ratings vary between 14.0 to 16.0 horsepower (10.4-11.9 kW) due to differences in carburetor and camshaft design. Power rating is identified on the blower housing of each model.

Engines in this section are four-stroke, single-cylinder, overhead valve engines with a vertical crankshaft. All engines are constructed of aluminum.

The connecting rod on all models rides directly on the crankpin journal. An oil slinger wheel located on the governor gear provides splash lubrication.

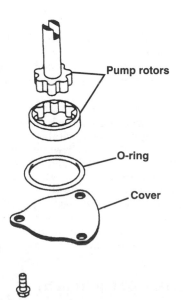

Fig. B400–An oil pump is used on some models to circulate engine oil through an oil filter.

All engines are equipped with a breakerless (Magnetron) ignition system. A float carburetor is used on all models.

Refer to BRIGGS & STRATTON ENGINE IDENTIFICATION INFORMATION section for engine identification. Engine model number as well as type and code numbers are necessary when ordering parts.

MAINTENANCE

LUBRICATION

An oil slinger located on the governor gear provides splash lubrication.

Series 31x700 and some 28x700 engines have a pressurized oil filtration system. A gerotor-style pump (Fig. B400) mounted in the engine's sump constantly circulates reservoir oil through the filter, then back into the sump to help keep the oil clean. The pump does not supply pressurized oil to any engine bearings; the engine is still splash lubricated.

A machined tab on the bottom of the camshaft drives the oil pump. Oil pump can be accessed for service from outside bottom of the engine; engine disassembly is not required. Inspect pump components when performing major engine repairs. The pump is serviced as an assembly. Tighten the pump cover screws to 80 in.-lb. (9.0 N•m). Replace filter at every oil change (50 hours).

Engine oil should be changed after first eight hours of operation and after every 50 hours of operation or at least once each operating season. If equipment undergoes severe usage, change oil weekly or after every 25 hours of operation. Drain the oil while the engine is warm. The oil will flow freely and carry away more impurities.

Manufacturer recommends using oil with an API service classification of SH or SJ, or any classification formulated to supercede SH or SJ. Use SAE 30 oil for temperatures above 40° F (4° C); use SAE 10W-30 oil for temperatures between 0° F (−18° C) and 40° F (4° C); below 0° F (−18° C) use petroleum-based SAE 5W-20 or a suitable synthetic oil. Do not use 10W-40 oil.

Crankcase oil capacity is approximately 3 pints (1.4 L).

SPARK PLUG

Replace the spark plug if electrodes are burned away or if the porcelain is cracked or fouled. Recommended spark plug is Champion RC12YC. Specified spark plug electrode gap is 0.030 inch (0.76 mm).

> **CAUTION: Briggs & Stratton does not recommend using abrasive blasting to clean spark plugs as this may introduce some abrasive material into the engine that could cause extensive damage.**

CARBURETOR

The Walbro LMT carburetor is equipped with a fixed main jet and an adjustable idle mixture screw. Carburetor adjustments must be made with the air cleaner installed and engine at operating temperature.

For initial setting of idle mixture screw (12–Fig. B401), turn the screw in (clockwise) until the head of the screw just contacts the spring. Start the engine and place the speed control lever in "SLOW" position. Adjust idle speed screw (11) so engine idles at 1750 rpm. With engine running at idle speed, turn idle mixture screw clockwise until engine speed just starts to drop. Note the screw position. Turn the idle mixture screw counterclockwise until engine speed just starts to drop again. Note the screw position, and turn the screw to the midpoint between the noted screw positions. Install the limiter cap (13) with the flat facing up. If the engine will not accelerate cleanly, slightly enrich the mixture by turning the idle mixture needle counterclockwise. If necessary, readjust idle speed screw to obtain idle speed specified by equipment manufacturer.

An optional main jet calibrated to compensate for high altitude operation is available.

To disassemble carburetor, remove fuel solenoid (22–Fig. B401) and float bowl (20). Remove the hinge pin (19), float (18) and fuel inlet valve (16). To remove fuel inlet seat (15), thread a ¼-20 tap or self-tapping screw into the seat and pull it from carburetor body. Remove the main jet (14), then unscrew jet nozzle (1) from the body using a suitable screwdriver. A ⁵⁄₁₆-inch diameter pin punch ground flat at the end makes a suitable tool for removing Welch plug (2). Remove limiter cap (13) and idle mixture screw (12). Remove throttle plate (5), shaft (6), seal (4) and bushing (3). Remove choke plate (8) and shaft (9).

Clean fuel passages with commercial carburetor cleaner and compressed air. Inspect components and discard any parts that are damaged or excessively worn. Fuel solenoid operation can be checked using a 9-volt battery. Plunger needle should snap into solenoid body when energized.

When reassembling carburetor, note the following: Do not deform Welch plug (2) during installation; it should be flat. Seal outer edges of plug with fingernail polish or a non-hardening sealer. When installing choke shaft (9), note that small hook in return spring (10) engages the shaft and large hook engages boss on carburetor body. Guide the detent spring (7) into the slot in choke shaft. Install choke plate (8) with single notch on edge towards fuel inlet side of body. Install throttle shaft seal (4) with sealing lip down until flush with top of body. Install throttle plate so numbers are facing outward and toward the idle mix-

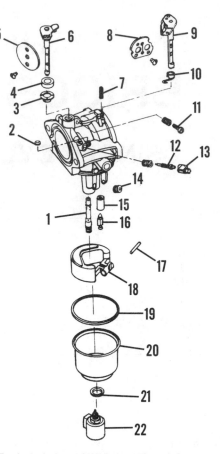

Fig. B401–Exploded view of Walbro LMT carburetor used on all models.

1. Nozzle	12. Idle mixture screw
2. Welch plug	13. Limiter cap
3. Bushing	14. Main jet
4. Seal	15. Valve seat
5. Throttle plate	16. Fuel inlet valve
6. Throttle shaft	17. Hinge pin
7. Spring	18. Float
8. Choke shaft	19. Gasket
9. Choke shaft	20. Float bowl
10. Return spring	21. Gasket
11. Idle speed screw	22. Fuel solenoid

ture screw side of body when plate is in closed position. After installing jet nozzle (1), use compressed air to blow out any debris that may have been loosened during installing of the nozzle. Install the main jet (14) after installing the nozzle.

Install fuel inlet seat using B&S driver 19135 or other suitable tool. Press seat in until flush with surface of fuel inlet boss. Float height is not adjustable. If float is not approximately parallel with the body when the carburetor is inverted, replace the float, fuel inlet valve and/or valve seat. Install idle mixture screw (12) with spring and turn in until head of screw just contacts the spring.

Install carburetor with new gasket. Long edge side of gasket should be opposite fuel inlet. Attach governor and choke links. Tighten carburetor mounting nuts to 65 in.-lbs. (7.3 N•m). Adjust carburetor as previously outlined.

REMOTE CONTROL ADJUSTMENT

With throttle control in "Fast" position, hole in governor control lever (3–Fig. B402) must align with hole in control

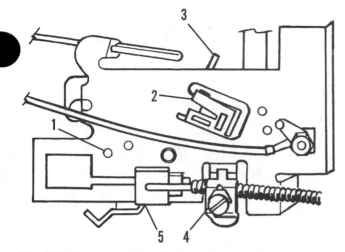

Fig. B402–Refer to text to adjust remote control.
1. Governor control plate hole
2. Stop switch
3. Governor control lever
4. Clamp screw
5. Governor control rack

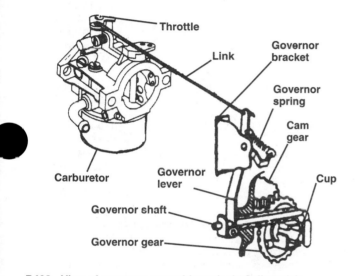

B403—View of governor assembly typical of all models.

plate (1). If it does not, loosen the throttle cable clamp screw and move the governor control rack (5) until holes are aligned. Tighten cable clamp screw.

FUEL PUMP

A fuel pump is available as optional equipment on some models. Refer to BRIGGS & STRATTON ACCESSORIES section for service information.

GOVERNOR

All engines are equipped with a gear-driven mechanical-type governor attached to the oil pan. The camshaft gear drives the governor. Governor and linkage must operate properly to prevent "hunting" or unsteady operation. The carburetor must be properly adjusted before performing governor adjustments.

To adjust governor linkage, loosen clamp bolt attaching governor lever to governor shaft (Fig. B403). Move governor lever so carburetor throttle plate is in wide-open posi-

tion and hold in this position. Rotate governor shaft clockwise as far as possible and tighten clamp bolt.

> **IMPORTANT: Running an engine at a maximum speed other than the speed specified by the equipment manufacturer can be dangerous to the operator, harmful to the equipment and inefficient. Adjust governed engine speed to specification stipulated by equipment manufacturer.**

To set maximum no-load speed, start engine and move remote speed control to maximum speed position. Insert a suitable tool between the governor control cover and engine casting and bend governor spring anchor tang to obtain desired maximum no-load speed.

IGNITION SYSTEM

All models are equipped with a Magnetron breakerless ignition system. The system does not require periodic maintenance. Flywheel removal is not necessary except to check or service keyway or crankshaft key.

To check spark, remove spark plug, connect spark plug cable to B&S tester 19051 and ground remaining tester lead on engine cylinder head. Rotate engine at 350 rpm or more. If spark jumps the 0.166 inch (4.2 mm) tester gap, system is functioning properly.

Air gap between armature legs and flywheel magnets should be 0.010-0.014 inch (0.25-0.36 mm). Ignition timing is not adjustable on these models.

VALVE ADJUSTMENT

Valve adjustment should be performed with the engine cold, using the following recommended procedure:

Remove spark plug and valve cover. Rotate crankshaft in normal direction (clockwise at flywheel) so the piston is at top dead center on compression stroke (both valves closed). Insert a narrow scale into the spark plug hole, then continue to rotate crankshaft so piston is ¼ inch (6.4 mm) down from top dead center. This position places the tappet away from the compression release device on the cam lobe.

Using feeler gauges, measure the clearance between rocker arms and valve stem caps. Refer to table below for specified valve clearance dimensions.

VALVE CLEARANCE

Series 28E700, 28N700, 28P700, 28Q700, 287700
Intake . . . . 0.003-0.005 in.
(0.08-0.13 mm)
Exhaust . . . . 0.005-0.007 in.
(0.13-0.18 mm)

Series 28S700, 28U700, 28W700, 310700, 311700, 312700
Intake . . . . 0.003-0.005 in.
(0.08-0.13 mm)
Exhaust . . . . 0.003-0.005 in.
(0.08-0.13 mm)

To adjust, loosen set screw inside rocker arm adjusting ball-nut, and adjust ball-nut to obtain proper clearance. While holding ball-nut, tighten rocker arm set screw to 60 in.-lb. (5.7 N•m) for Series 287700 and 28E700-28Q700 engines; 45 in.-lb. (5.0 N•m) for Series 28S700-28W700 and 310700-312700 engines.

Install valve cover with a new gasket. Tighten valve cover screws following the sequence shown in Fig. B404 to 55-60 in.-lb. (6.0-6.8 N•m.)

CRANKCASE BREATHER

A crankcase breather is located on the side of the cylinder block. A vent tube connects the breather to the carburetor air inlet tube. A partial vacuum must exist in crankcase to prevent oil seepage past oil seals, gaskets, breaker point plunger or piston rings. Air can flow out of crankcase through the breather, but a one-way valve blocks return flow, maintaining necessary vacuum.

Make certain the fiber disc valve in the breather is not stuck or binding. The two oil drain holes in the breather housing must be open. Breather mounting holes are offset one way.

CYLINDER HEAD

After 100 to 300 hours of engine operation, the cylinder head should be removed and any carbon or deposits should be removed.

COMPRESSION PRESSURE

Briggs & Stratton does not publish compression pressure specifications.

An alternate method of determining internal engine condition and wear is by using a cylinder leak-down tester. The tester is available commercially or through Briggs & Stratton (part No. 19413). The tester uses compressed air to pressurize the combustion chamber, then gauges the amount of leakage past the piston rings and valves. Instructions are included with the tester.

REPAIRS

TIGHTENING TORQUE

Recommended tightening torque specifications are as follows:

Alternator stator . . . . 18-24 in.-lb.
(2.0-2.7 N•m)
Blower housing . . . . 75-95 in.-lb.
(8.5-10.7 N•m)
Breather screws. . . . . 20-30 in.-lb.
(2.3-3.4 N•m)
Carburetor mounting screws . . . . 65-75 in.-lb.
(7.3-8.5 N•m)
Connecting rod. . . . . See Text
Crankcase cover. . . . . See Text
Cylinder head . . . . 220 in.-lb.
(24.9 N•m)
Electric starter . . . . 130-150 in.-lb.
(14.7-17.0 N•m)
Fan retainer . . . . 130-150 in.-lb.
(14.7-17.0 N•m)
Flywheel nut . . . . 95-105 ft.-lb.
(129-142 N•m)
Fuel pump . . . . 40-50 in.-lb.
(4.5-5.7 N•m)
Governor lever bolt . . . . 35-45 in.-lb.
(3.9-5.1 N•m)
Ignition module . . . . 20-28 in.-lb.
(2.3-3.2 N•m)
Intake manifold . . . . 95-105 in.-lb.
(10.7-11.9 N•m)

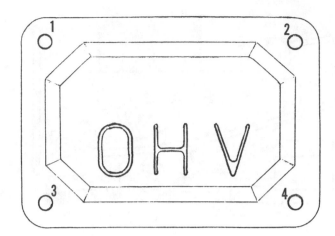

Fig. B404–Tighten valve cover screws in sequence shown.

Oil fill tube . . . . 20-24 in.-lb.
(2.3-2.7 N•m)
Oil filter adapter . . . . 110-140 in.-lb.
(12.4-15.8 N•m)
Oil pump cover . . . . 65-95 in.-lb.
(7.3-10.7 N•m)
Rocker arm screw . . . . 40-50 in.-lb.
(4.5-5.7 N•m)
Rocker arm stud . . . . 85 in.-lb.
(10.7-11.9 N•m)
Rocker cover . . . . 50-60 in.-lb.
(5.7-6.8 N•m)
Spark plug . . . . 140-200 in.-lb.
(15.8-22.6 N•m)
Starter gear cover . . . . 20-24 in.-lb.
(2.3-2.7 N•m)
Solenoid ground wire . . . . 40-50 in.-lb.
(4.5-5.7 N•m)

CYLINDER HEAD AND VALVE SYSTEM

Prior to removing cylinder head, relax tension on valve springs by removing spark plug and rotating crankshaft so piston is approximately $\frac{1}{4}$ in. (6 mm) down from TDC on power stroke. Remove external parts such as air cleaner, carburetor, intake manifold, muffler, fuel tank, oil fill tube and blower housing with rewind starter for access to the cylinder head.

When removing cylinder head, note positions of push rods: Exhaust push rod on 28x700 and 31x700 engines is steel, hollow and identified with a band of red paint, intake push rod is aluminum. Remove rocker cover, cylinder head screws, push rods, cylinder head and gasket.

To disassemble valve components, remove rocker arm ball-nuts (9–Fig. B405), and rocker arms (10), studs (11) and push rod guide (12). Remove valve cap (1). Push down on the spring retainer (3) to compress the valve spring until the large end of the slot in the retainer can be slipped off the valve stem. Remove spring retainer, spring and valve. Remove intake valve seal (5) if used.

Inspect valve seats and valves for damage or wear. Valve seats are not replaceable. If valve seats cannot be reconditioned, cylinder head must be replaced.

Valve seat and head dimensions are shown in Fig. B406. If excessive valve stem wear is evident or if valve head wear exceeds dimensions shown in Fig. B406, replace the valve

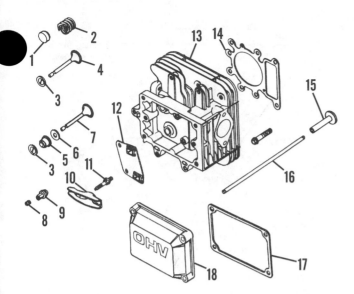

Fig. B405–Exploded view of cylinder head and valve components.

1. Cap	10. Rocker arm
2. Spring	11. Stud
3. Retainer	12. Guide plate
4. Exhaust valve	13. Cylinder head
5. Seal	14. Head gasket
6. Washer	15. Tappet
7. Intake valve	16. Push rod
8. Adjusting screw	17. Gasket
9. Ball-nut	18. Valve cover

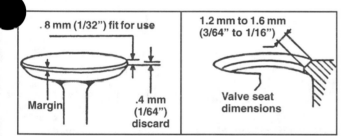

Fig. B406–Valve and valve seat dimensions.

Valve face angle is 45° for both intake and exhaust; seats should be cut at 46°. Valve lapping is recommended for a good final valve-to-seat seal.

Check valve guides for wear using plug gauge No. 19381. If flat end of gauge can be inserted into guide ¼ inch (6.35 mm) or more, guide is worn beyond limits. If gauge is not available, valve guide reject dimension is 0.240 inch (6.09 mm) for intake and exhaust. Valve guides are not available for service; replace cylinder head if guides are worn beyond limits.

To reassemble, install push rod guide with TOP stamping on guide facing up and toward flywheel side of head. Apply Loctite 270 or equivalent to threads of rocker arm studs. Insert studs through holes in push rod guide and tighten to 85 in.-lb. (9.6 N•m). Lightly coat valve stems with B&S lubricant 93963, Led-Plate or equivalent, then insert valves into guides. Be careful not to get any lubricant on valve seat, valve face or valve stem tip. If a sealing washer is used under the valve seal, place washer over intake valve guide. Lubricate valve stem seal with engine oil and press seal over intake guide. Install valve springs and retainers.

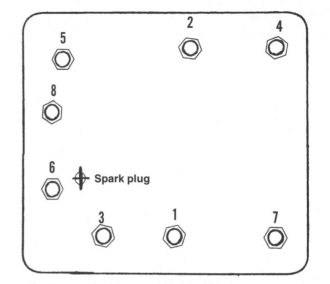

Fig. B407–Tighten cylinder head screws in sequence shown. Refer to text.

Always install a new cylinder head gasket. Do not apply sealer to head gasket. Apply lubricant to threads of cylinder head bolts. Tighten cylinder head bolts, using the sequence shown in Fig. B407, in 75 in.-lb. (8.5 N•m) increments to final torque of 220 in.-lb. (24.9 N•m).

Insert push rods through push rod guide plate, insuring that they properly seat into valve tappets. Exhaust valve push rod is steel, has a red paint band for identification, and is mounted in the upper position. Make sure valve caps and valve stem ends are dry, then insert caps onto stems. Install rocker arms. Thread rocker arm ball-nuts onto push rod studs finger-tight, seating rocker arm against push rod and cap. Rotate crankshaft two revolutions (clockwise, viewed from flywheel) to verify proper rocker arm operation. Position the piston ¼ inch (6 mm) down from TDC on power stroke, and adjust valve clearance as outlined in MAINTENANCE section.

CRANKCASE COVER/OIL PAN

Tighten crankcase cover/oil pan retaining screws evenly to 200 in.-lb. (22.6 N•m) following the fastener sequence shown in Fig. B408. On engines with a code number of 971120xx or lower, it is recommended that retaining screws be replaced with current style part No. 94624 screws.

CAMSHAFT

The camshaft is supported at both ends in bearing bores machined in crankcase and crankcase cover/oil pan. The camshaft gear is an integral part of camshaft.

Camshaft should be replaced if either journal is worn to a diameter of 0.498 inch (12.66 mm) or less, or if cam lobes are worn or damaged. Refer to the table below for cam lobe reject dimensions.

Cam Lobe Reject Sizes

Series	Reject Dimension
28S700, 28U700, 28W700, 287700	1.184 in. (30.07 mm)
28E700, 28N700, 28P700, 28Q700	1.221 in. (31.02 mm)
310700, 311700, 312700	1.184 in. (30.07 mm)

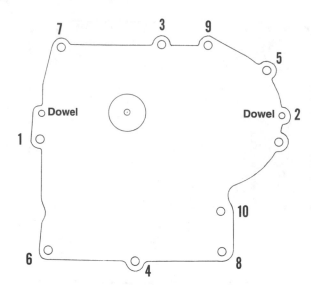

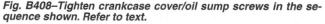

Fig. B408–Tighten crankcase cover/oil sump screws in the sequence shown. Refer to text.

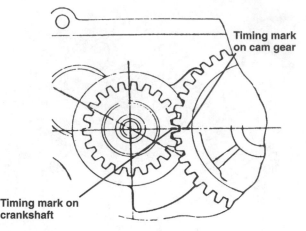

Fig. B409–Align timing marks on cam gear and crankshaft gear.

Crankcase or crankcase cover/oil pan must be replaced if bearing bores are 0.506 inch (12.85 mm) or larger, or if tool 19164 enters bearing bore ¼ inch (6.4 mm) or more.

Compression release mechanism on camshaft gear holds the exhaust valve slightly open at very low engine rpm as a starting aid. Mechanism should work freely and spring should hold actuator cam against pin. Compression release lobe reject dimension is 0.010 inch (0.25 mm).

When installing the camshaft, align timing marks on camshaft and crankshaft gears as shown in Fig. B409.

PISTON, PIN AND RINGS

Connecting rod and piston are removed from cylinder head end of block as an assembly. To remove, first remove cylinder head as previously outlined. Remove crankcase cover/oil sump and connecting rod cap. Remove any carbon or wear ridge at top of the cylinder to prevent damage to rings or piston during removal. Push the connecting rod and piston out through top of cylinder.

To remove piston pin and connecting rod, rotate piston pin retainer until open end is located in notch in piston pin bore. Grasp end of the retainer with needle nose pliers and pull in and up to remove the retainer. Push the piston pin out of the piston and rod.

Remove the rings from the piston and thoroughly clean combustion deposits from piston ring grooves and piston crown. Be careful not to damage or enlarge the piston ring grooves.

Reject piston showing visible signs of wear, scoring or scuffing. If, after cleaning carbon from top ring groove, a new top ring has a side clearance of 0.006 inch (0.15 mm) or more, reject the piston. Reject piston or hone piston pin hole to 0.005 inch (0.13 mm) oversize if pin hole is 0.0005 inch (0.013 mm) or more out-of-round, or is worn to a diameter of 0.801 inch (20.34 mm) or more.

If the piston pin is 0.0005 inch (0.013 mm) or more out-of-round, or is worn to a diameter of 0.799 inch (20.30 mm) or smaller, reject pin.

Pistons and rings are available in several oversizes as well as standard. Refer to Fig. B410 for correct installation of piston rings. Assemble connecting rod and piston as shown in Fig. B411. Install piston and rod in engine so notch (N) or arrow is toward flywheel side of engine.

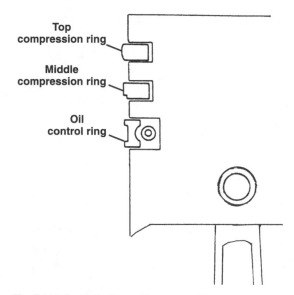

Fig. B410–Refer to illustration above for proper arrangement of piston rings.

Tighten connecting rod cap screws to torque listed in CONNECTING ROD paragraph.

CONNECTING ROD

Connecting rod and piston are removed from cylinder head end of block as an assembly. The aluminum alloy connecting rod rides directly on an induction hardened crankshaft crankpin journal. Rod should be rejected if big end of rod is scored or out-of-round more than 0.0007 inch (0.018 mm) or if piston pin bore is scored or out-of-round more than 0.0005 inch (0.013 mm). Replace the connecting rod if either crankpin bore or piston pin bore is worn to, or larger than, sizes given in table.

Reject Sizes For Connecting Rod

Series	Crankpin Bore	Pin Bore*
310700, 311700, 312700	1.502 in. (38.15 mm)	0.802 in. (20.37 mm)

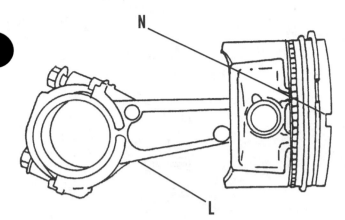

Fig. B411–If piston crown has a notch (N) or arrow, assemble connecting rod and piston as shown while noting relation of long side of rod (L) and notch or arrow on piston crown.

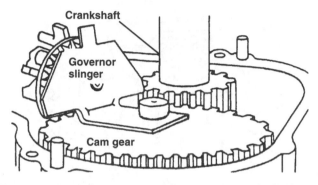

Fig. B412–View of governor weight assembly and oil slinger used on all engines.

All other models	1.252 in.	0.802 in.
	(31.8 mm)	(20.37 mm)

*Piston pins that are 0.005 inch (0.13 mm) oversize are available for service. Piston pin bore in rod can be reamed to this size if crankpin bore is within specifications.

Assemble connecting rod to piston as shown in Fig. B411. Install piston and rod in engine so notch (N) or arrow on piston crown is toward flywheel side of engine. Install rod cap with match marks on rod and cap aligned.

Tighten the connecting rod cap screws to torque listed in the table below:

Series	Torque
28x000 with equal size rod bolts.	185 in.-lb.
	(20.9 N•m)
28x000 with two rod bolt sizes—	
Small bolt.	130 in.-lb.
	(14.7 N•m)
Large bolt	260 in.-lb.
	(29.4 N•m)
310700, 311700, 312700	160 in.-lb.
	(18.0 N•m)

GOVERNOR

Governor gear and weight unit can be removed when engine is disassembled. The governor weight unit along with the oil slinger rides on the end of the camshaft as shown in Fig. B412.

Remove governor lever, cotter pin and washer from outer end of governor lever shaft. Slide governor lever out of bushing toward inside of engine. Governor gear and weight unit can now be removed. Replace governor lever shaft bushing in crankcase, if necessary, and ream new bushing after installation to 0.2385-0.2390 inch (6.058-6.071 mm). Briggs & Stratton tool 19333 can be used to ream bushing.

Replace governor lever seal if leaking. Use care not to damage seal lip when installing the seal. Wrap the governor lever shaft with thin plastic or cellophane tape before sliding seal over shaft.

CRANKSHAFT AND MAIN BEARINGS

The crankshaft is supported by bearing surfaces that are an integral part of crankcase and crankcase cover/oil sump.

The crankshaft should be replaced or reground if main bearing journals exceed service limits specified in following table.

Crankshaft Reject Sizes

Series	Magneto End Journal	PTO End Journal
All models	1.376 in.	1.376 in.
	(34.95 mm)	(34.95 mm)

Crankshaft for all models should be replaced or reground if connecting rod crankpin journal diameter exceeds service limit listed in following table.

Crankshaft Reject Sizes

Series	Crankpin Journal
310700, 311700, 312700	1.497 in.
	(38.02 mm)
All other models	1.247 in.
	(31.67 mm)

A connecting rod with undersize big end diameter is available to fit crankshaft that has had crankpin journal reground to 0.020 inch (0.51 mm) undersize.

On models equipped with integral main bearings, crankcase or cover/oil sump must be replaced or reamed to accept service bushings if service limits in following table are exceeded.

Main Bearing Reject Sizes

Model	Magneto End Bearing	PTO End Bearing
310700, 311700, 312700	1.504 in.	1.504 in.
	(38.20 mm)	(38.20 mm)
All other models	1.383 in.	1.383 in.
	(35.13 mm)	(35.13 mm)

Install the DU-type bushing with oil hole in line with oil hole in crankcase or crankcase cover/sump. If bushing does not have an oil hole, locate split in the bushing so it is not aligned with an oil notch in bearing boss. Stake bushing at oil notches in crankcase or sump. Bushing should be 7/64 inch (2.8 mm) below face of crankcase bore and 1/8 inch (3.2 mm) below face of crankcase cover/oil sump.

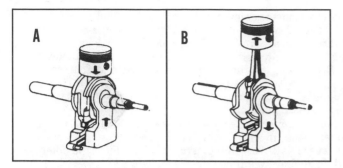

Fig. B413—View showing operating principles of oscillating balancer assembly. Counterweight oscillates in opposite direction of piston.

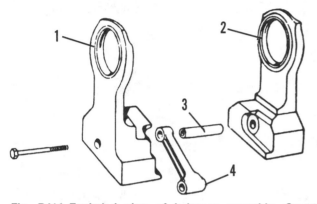

Fig. B414—Exploded view of balancer assembly. Counterweights ride on eccentric journals on crankshaft.
1. PTO side counterweight
2. Magneto side counterweight
3. Dowel pin
4. Link

Crankshaft end play is 0.002-0.023 inch (0.05-0.58 mm) for Series 287700 engines. For all other models, end play is 0.002-0.030 inch (0.05-0.76 mm). At least one 0.015-inch crankcase gasket must be in place when measuring end play. Additional gaskets in several sizes are available to adjust end play as needed. If end play is excessive, replace the crankcase cover/oil sump.

When installing crankshaft, make certain timing marks are aligned (Fig. B409).

CYLINDER

If cylinder bore wear is 0.003 inch (0.08 mm) or more or is 0.0025 inch (0.06 mm) or more out-of-round, cylinder must be replaced or bored to next larger oversize.

Standard cylinder bore diameter is 3.5620-3.5630 inches (90.474-90.500 mm) for 310700, 311700 and 312700 models. Standard cylinder bore diameter is 3.4365-3.4375 inches (87.287-87.313 mm) for all models.

OSCILLATING COUNTERBALANCE SYSTEM

All engines are equipped with an oscillating counterbalance system. A balance weight assembly rides on eccentric journals on the crankshaft and moves in opposite direction of piston (Fig. B413).

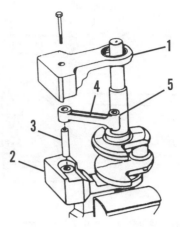

Fig. B415—Assemble balancer on crankshaft as shown. Install link (4) with rounded edge toward PTO end of crankshaft.

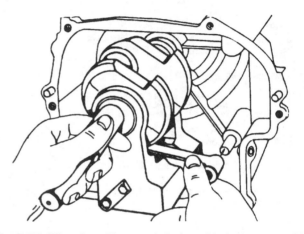

Fig. B416—When installing crankshaft and balancer assembly, place free end of link on anchor pin in crankcase.

To disassemble balancer unit, first remove flywheel, oil pan, cam gear, cylinder head, and connecting rod and piston assembly. Carefully pry off crankshaft gear and key. Remove the cap screw holding halves of counterweight together. Separate weights (1 and 2—Fig. B414) and remove link (4) and dowel pin (3). Slide weights from crankshaft.

Inspect the crankshaft eccentrics and counterweight bearings for wear or damage. Eccentric wear limit is 2.202 inches (55.93). Bearing wear limit is 2.212 inches (56.18 mm).

To reassemble, install magneto side weight on magneto end of crankshaft. Place crankshaft (PTO end up) in a vise (Fig. B415). Install dowel pin (3) and place link (4) on pin with rounded edge (5) on free end of link facing up. Install PTO side weight (1) and cap screw. Tighten cap screw to 115 in.-lbs. (13 N•m). Install key and crankshaft gear with chamfer on inside of gear facing shoulder on crankshaft.

Install crankshaft and balancer assembly in crankcase, sliding free end of link on anchor pin as shown in Fig. B416. Reassemble engine.

BRIGGS & STRATTON

BRIGGS & STRATTON CORPORATION
Milwaukee, Wisconsin 53201

SINGLE-CYLINDER L-HEAD ENGINES

Model Series	No. Cyls.	Bore	Stroke	Displacement	Power Rating
170000, 171000, 176400	1	3.00 in. (76.2 mm)	2.375 in. (60.3 mm)	16.8 cu. in. (275 cc)	7 hp (5.2 kW)
190400, 190700, 191700, 192400, 192700, 193000, 194400, 194700, 195400, 195700, 196400, 196700, 197400, 19A400, 19B400, 19C400, 19E400, 19F400, 19G400	1	3.00 in. (76.2 mm)	2.750 in. (69.85 mm)	19.44 cu. in. (318 cc)	8 hp (6 kW)
220700, 221400, 222400, 226400	1	3.438 in. (87.3 mm)	2.375 in. (60.3 mm)	22.04 cu. in. (361 cc)	10 hp (7.5 kW)
250400, 251000, 252400, 252700, 253400, 253700, 254400, 254700, 255400, 255700, 256400, 256700, 257000, 258700, 259700	1	3.438 in. (87.3 mm)	2.625 in. (66.68 mm)	24.36 cu. in. (399 cc)	11 hp (8.2 kW)
280700, 281700, 282700, 283000, 284700, 28A700, 28B700, 28C700, 28D700	1	3.438 in. (87.3 mm)	3.06 in. (77.7 mm)	28.4 cu. in. (465 cc)	12 hp (9 kW)
285000, 286000, 289700	1	3.438 in. (87.3 mm)	3.06 in. (77.7 mm)	28.4 cu. in. (465 cc)	12.5 hp (9.4 kW)
28M700	1	3.438 in. (87.3 mm)	3.06 in. (77.7 mm)	28.4 cu. in. (465 cc)	13.0 hp (9.7 kW)
28R700	1	3.438 in. (87.3 mm)	3.06 in. (77.7 mm)	28.4 cu. in. (465 cc)	15.5 hp (11.5 kW)
28T700, 28V700	1	3.438 in. (87.3 mm)	3.06 in. (77.7 mm)	28.4 cu. in. (465 cc)	See Note

NOTE: Power ratings vary between 14 to 16 horsepower (10.4-11.9 kW) for these models due to differences in carburetor and camshaft design. Power rating is identified on the blower housing of each engine.

GENERAL INFORMATION

Engines in this section are four-stroke, single-cylinder engines with either a horizontal or vertical crankshaft. The crankshaft may be supported by main bearings that are an integral part of crankcase and crankcase cover/oil pan or by ball bearings pressed on the crankshaft. All engines are constructed of aluminum. Cylinder bore may be either aluminum or a cast iron sleeve that is cast in the aluminum.

The connecting rod on all models rides directly on the crankpin journal. All models are splashed lubricated.

Early models are equipped with a magneto-type ignition system with points and condenser located underneath the flywheel. Later models are equipped with a breakerless (Magnetron) ignition system.

A float-type carburetor is used on all models. A fuel pump is available as optional equipment for some models.

Refer to BRIGGS & STRATTON ENGINE IDENTIFICATION INFORMATION section for engine identification. Engine model number as well as type and code numbers are necessary when ordering parts.

MAINTENANCE

LUBRICATION

An oil dipper attached to the connecting rod provides splash lubrication for horizontal crankshaft engines. An oil slinger wheel on governor gear that is driven by the camshaft gear provides a splash lubrication system for vertical crankshaft engines.

Engine oil should be changed after first eight hours of operation and after every 50 hours of operation or at least once each operating season. If equipment undergoes severe usage, change oil weekly or after every 25 hours of operation. Drain the oil while the engine is warm. The oil will flow freely and carry away more impurities.

Manufacturer recommends using oil with an API service classification of SH or SJ, or any classification formulated to supercede SH or SJ. Use SAE 30 oil for temperatures above 40° F (4° C); use SAE 10W-30 oil for temperatures between 0° F (−18° C) and 40° F (4° C); below 0° F (−18° C) use petroleum based SAE 5W-20 or a suitable synthetic oil. DO NOT use SAE 10W-40 oil.

Crankcase oil capacity for 16.8 and 19.44 cubic inch engines is 2 pints (1.1 L) for vertical crankshaft models and 2 pints (1.3 L) for horizontal crankshaft models.

Crankcase oil capacity for 22.04, 24.36 and 28.4 cubic inch engines is 3 pints (1.4 L) for vertical crankshaft models and 2 pints (1.2 L) for horizontal crankshaft models.

SPARK PLUG

The original spark plug may be either 1½ inches or 2 inches long. Recommended spark plug is either Champion or Autolite.

If a Champion spark plug is used and spark plug is 1½ inches long, recommended spark plug is Champion CJ-8 or J-19LM. Install Champion RCJ-8, RJ-12 or RJ-19LM if a resistor-type spark plug is required. If spark plug is 2 inches long, recommended spark plug is Champion J-19LM or J-8C. Install Champion RJ-19LM or RJ-8C if a resistor-type spark plug is required. Engines with Magnetron ignition should be equipped with resistor plugs.

If an Autolite spark plug is used and spark plug is 1½ inches long, recommended spark plug is 235. Install Autolite 245 if a resistor-type spark plug is required. If spark plug is 2 inches long, recommended spark plug is 295. Install Autolite 306 if a resistor-type spark plug is required.

Specified spark plug electrode gap is 0.030 inch (0.76 mm).

CAUTION: Briggs & Stratton does not recommend using abrasive blasting to clean spark plugs as this may introduce some abrasive material into the engine that could cause extensive damage.

AIR CLEANER

Engines may be equipped with cartridge type, dual element or oil foam air cleaner. The air cleaner should be inspected and cleaned after every 25 operating hours or once a season, whichever comes first. Refer to appropriate paragraph for filter type being serviced.

NOTE: When servicing the air filter on Series 280000 engines with a welded two-piece air filter

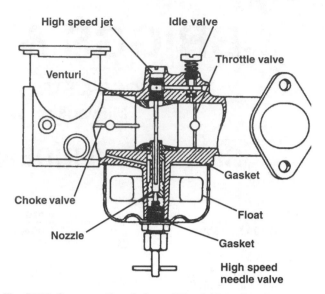

Fig. B500—Cross-sectional view of Flo-Jet I carburetor.

base, inspect the base carefully before reusing. Impact damage or improper service procedures can cause the base to warp or bend between the two metal pieces, allowing unfiltered air to enter the engine. There are two remedies available if damage is evident: Apply a flexible RTV sealant to the filter base at the separated area; or preferably, replace the filter base with newer style one-piece nonmetallic base.

Cartridge Air Cleaner

Thoroughly clean the area surrounding the air cleaner prior to removal. Remove the wing nut and cover, then carefully remove the cartridge to prevent dirt from entering the carburetor.

Clean the cartridge filter element by tapping gently on a flat surface. Do not use cleaning fluids or soap and water to clean the cartridge. Inspect the cartridge for tears or cracks, and replace it if damaged or restricted. Inspect the air cleaner mounting gaskets and replace them if damaged or worn.

Dual Element Air Cleaner

The dual element air cleaner consists of a foam precleaner and a paper cartridge filter element. Carefully remove the filter cover and filter assembly to prevent dirt from entering the carburetor.

Wash the foam precleaner in warm soapy water. Thoroughly dry the element, then saturate the foam with clean engine oil. Squeeze it to remove excess oil. DO NOT apply oil to foam precleaners labeled "DO NOT OIL."

Do not use cleaning fluids or soap and water to clean the paper filter cartridge. Tap the cartridge gently on a flat surface to dislodge debris from surface of the filter. Replace the filter if it is damaged or restricted.

Oil Foam Air Cleaner

Thoroughly clean the area surrounding the air cleaner to prevent dirt from entering the carburetor. Remove the air cleaner cover and withdraw foam filter from air cleaner body.

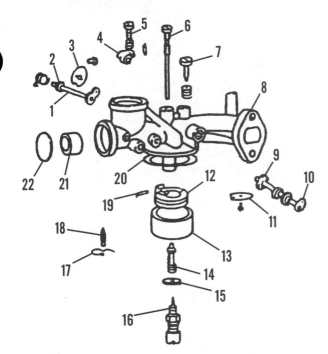

Fig. B501–Exploded view of typical Flo-Jet I carburetor.

1. Choke shaft
2. Seal
3. Choke plate
4. Throttle stop
5. Idle speed stop screw
6. High-speed jet
7. Idle mixture needle
8. Carburetor body
9. Seal
10. Throttle shaft
11. Throttle plate
12. Float
13. Float bowl
14. Nozzle
15. Gasket
16. High-speed mixture screw & packing nut
17. Clip
18. Fuel inlet needle
19. Pin
20. Gasket
21. Venturi
22. Welch plug

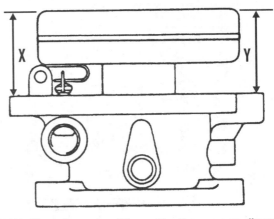

Fig. B502–Float dimension (Y) must be the same as dimension (X) plus or minus 1/32 inch (0.8 mm).

Clean the foam filter with a solution of warm water and liquid detergent. Squeeze out water and allow to air dry. Soak the foam element in clean engine oil. Squeeze out excess oil.

CARBURETOR

Engines in this section may be equipped with one of three different Flo-Jet carburetors as well as a Walbro carburetor. The Flo-Jet carburetors are identified as Flo-Jet I, Flo-Jet II or Cross-Over Flo-Jet. Refer to appropriate service section for model being serviced.

Flo-Jet I Carburetor

A cross-sectional view of a Flo-Jet I carburetor is shown in Fig. B500. Initial setting of idle mixture screw is one turn out and high-speed needle valve is 1½ turns out.

With engine at normal operating temperature and equipment control lever in SLOW position, adjust idle speed screw so engine idles at 1750 rpm. With engine running at idle speed, turn idle mixture screw clockwise until engine speed just starts to drop. Note screw position. Turn idle mixture screw counterclockwise until engine speed increases then just starts to drop again and note screw position. Then turn screw to midpoint between the lean and rich screw positions.

Adjust high-speed needle valve with control set to FAST using same procedure. If engine will not accelerate cleanly, slightly enrich mixture by turning idle mixture needle

valve counterclockwise. If necessary, readjust idle speed screw.

To disassemble carburetor, remove high-speed jet (6–Fig. B501) and idle mixture screw (7). Remove high-speed needle valve assembly (16) and float bowl (13). Remove pivot pin (19), float (12) and fuel inlet needle (18). Unscrew and remove nozzle (14). Remove choke shaft (1) and plate (3). Drive Welch plug (22) from carburetor body, then extract the venturi (21). On some carburetors there is a choke plate stop pin that must be removed before removing the venturi. Press or drive the pin into the bore.

Clean all parts with aerosol carburetor cleaner, then use compressed air to blow out passages and dry the carburetor. Inspect all parts for wear or damage. Wear between throttle shaft (10) and bushings should not exceed 0.010 inch (0.25 mm). Replacement throttle shaft bushings are available for some carburetors. Inspect the tip of idle mixture and high-speed mixture needles and replace if tip is bent or grooved. Carburetor assembly must be replaced if the needle seats are damaged. Inspect fuel inlet valve and replace it if tip is grooved. Fuel inlet valve seat may be either threaded or pressed into the carburetor body. Use a 1/4-inch tap or screw extractor to pull pressed-in seat from the carburetor. Install new seat flush with carburetor body.

Note the following special instructions when assembling carburetor. Install the venturi with the groove towards the fuel bowl. Install the nozzle and discharge tube or high-speed mixture screw to hold the venturi in place. Drive in the retaining pin if used. Install choke plate so cutout is down and concave side of dimple is towards intake end of carburetor.

To check float level, invert carburetor body and float assembly. Refer to Fig. B502 for proper float level dimensions. Adjust by bending float lever tang that contacts inlet valve. Be very careful when bending the float lever not to force the fuel inlet needle onto its seat as the tip of the needle is easily damaged.

Flo-Jet II Carburetor

A cross-sectional view of a Flo-Jet II carburetor is shown in Fig. B503 Initial setting of idle mixture screw is 1¼ turns out and high-speed needle valve is 1½ turns out. With engine at normal operating temperature and equipment control lever in SLOW position, adjust idle speed screw so engine idles at 1750 rpm.

With engine running at idle speed, turn idle mixture screw clockwise until engine speed just starts to drop. Note

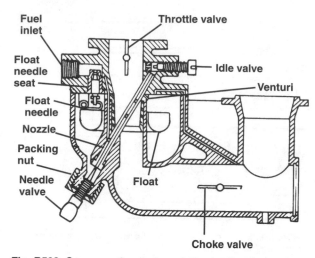

Fig. B503–Cross-sectional view of Flo-Jet II carburetor. Before separating upper and lower body secions, remove packing nut and power needle valve as a unit and use special screwdriver (tool 19062) to remove nozzle.

screw position. Turn idle mixture screw counterclockwise until engine speed increases then just starts to drop again and note screw position. Then turn screw to midpoint between the lean and rich screw positions.

Adjust high-speed needle valve with control set to FAST using same procedure. If engine will not accelerate cleanly, slightly enrich mixture by turning idle mixture needle valve counterclockwise. If necessary, readjust idle speed screw.

When disassembling the carburetor, note that the nozzle is angled between the body and cover (Fig. B503). The high-speed needle valve (17–Fig. B504), packing nut (15) and nozzle (13) must be removed before the cover (3) is removed, otherwise, the nozzle will be damaged. Withdraw the float pin (10) and remove float (11) and fuel inlet valve (8). Remove idle mixture needle (4).

Clean all parts with aerosol carburetor cleaner, then use compressed air to blow out passages and dry the carburetor. Inspect all parts for wear or damage. Check upper body for distortion using a 0.002 inch (0.05 mm) feeler gauge as shown in Fig. B505. Upper body must be replaced if warped more than 0.002 inch (0.05 mm). Wear between throttle shaft (1–Fig. B504) and bushings should not exceed 0.010 inch (0.25 mm). Replacement throttle shaft bushings are available for some carburetors. Inspect the tip of idle mixture and high-speed mixture needles and replace if tip is bent or grooved. Carburetor assembly must be replaced if the needle seats are damaged. Inspect fuel inlet valve (8) and replace it if tip is grooved. Fuel inlet valve seat may be either threaded or pressed into the carburetor body. Use a screwdriver to remove threaded type seat. Use a ¼-inch tap or screw extractor to pull pressed-in seat from the carburetor. Install new seat flush with carburetor body.

To check float level, invert carburetor body and float assembly. Refer to Fig. B502 for proper float level dimensions. Adjust by bending float lever tang that contacts inlet valve.

The float, part No. 99333, used in carburetors for 17 and 19-cubic inch engines has been redesigned to allow the float to 'drop' farther in the float bowl during engine operation. This helps prevent the engine from 'running out of gas' while there still appears to be gasoline in the tank.

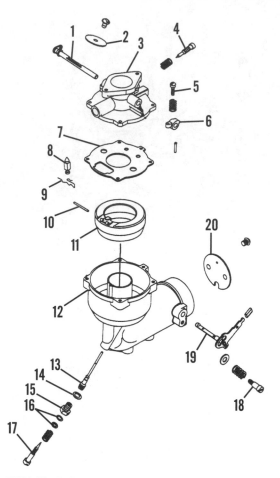

Fig. B504–Exploded view of typical Flo-Jet II carburetor.

1. Throttle shaft
2. Throttle plate
3. Upper body
4. Idle mixture needle
5. Idle speed stop screw
6. Throttle stop
7. Gasket
8. Fuel inlet valve
9. Clip
10. Pin
11. Float
12. Lower body
13. Nozzle
14. Gasket
15. Packing nut
16. Packing
17. High-speed mixture needle
18. Shoulder bolt
19. Choke shaft
20. Choke plate

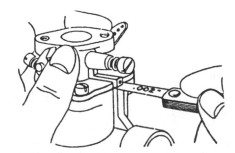

Fig. B505–Check upper body of Flo-Jet II carburetor for distortion as outlined in text.

This problem occurs mainly on engines with an engine-mounted tank opposite the carburetor.

Internal fuel leakage can result in the engine flooding and fuel running out of the drain hole in the bottom of carburetor air horn. This internal leakage problem may be caused by corrosion or an improper seal between the ta-

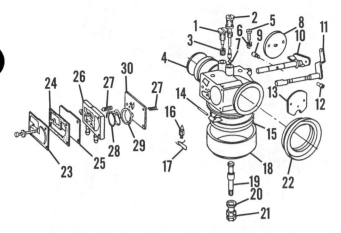

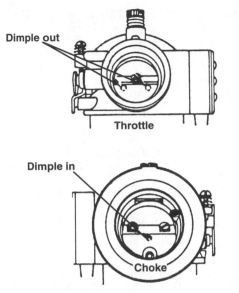

Fig. B506–Exploded view of Cross-Over Flo-Jet carburetor used on some models.

1. Idle mixture needle
2. High-speed mixture needle
3. Spring
4. O-ring
5. Idle speed screw
6. Spring
7. Packing
8. Throttle plate
9. Screw
10. Throttle shaft
11. Choke shaft
12. Screw
13. Choke plate
14. Pin
15. Float
16. Fuel inlet valve
17. Clip
18. Fuel bowl
19. Nozzle
20. Washer
21. Screw
22. Gasket
23. Fuel pump cover
24. Diaphragm
25. Fuel pump body
26.
27. Spring
28. Spring
29. Spring cup
30. Diaphragm

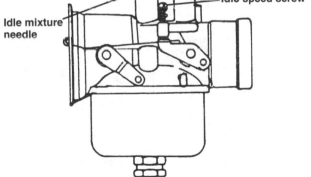

Fig. B507–View of alignment screws on Cross-Over Flo-Jet carburetor.

Fig. B508–Install throttle and choke plates on Cross-Over Flo-Jet carburetor so dimples are located as shown above when plates are closed.

3. Replace carburetor lower body and nozzle.

Cross-Over Flo-Jet Carburetor

The Cross-Over Flo-Jet carburetor (Fig. B506) is equipped with an integral diaphragm-type fuel pump.

Initial setting of idle mixture needle (Fig. B507) is 1 turn out and high-speed mixture needle is 1½ turns out. With engine at normal operating temperature and throttle lever in SLOW position, adjust idle speed screw so engine idles at 1750 rpm. With engine running at idle speed, turn idle mixture needle clockwise until engine speed just starts to drop. Note needle position. Turn idle mixture needle counterclockwise until engine speed increases then just starts to drop again and note needle position. Then turn needle to midpoint between the noted lean and rich needle positions.

If equipped with high-speed mixture needle, set control to FAST and adjust high-speed needle using same procedure. If engine will not accelerate cleanly, slightly enrich low-speed mixture by turning idle mixture needle counterclockwise. If necessary, readjust idle speed screw.

To disassemble carburetor, remove fuel pump cover fasteners and separate fuel pump components (23 through 27–Fig. B506). Remove idle mixture needle (1) and high-speed mixture needle (2). Remove the screw (21) retaining the fuel bowl (18). Remove float pin (14), float (15) and fuel inlet needle valve (16). Unscrew nozzle (19) from carburetor body.

Clean the carburetor with aerosol cleaner, then use compressed air to blow out passages and dry the carburetor. Inspect components and discard any parts that are damaged or excessively worn. Replace the fuel inlet valve needle if the tip is grooved. If fuel inlet valve seat replacement is required, thread a self-tapping screw or a screw extractor into the seat and pull seat from the body. Inspect the tip of idle mixture needle and replace if it is bent or grooved. Check for excessive play between throttle shaft and body. Carburetor must be replaced if throttle shaft bore is excessively worn, as bushings are not available.

When reassembling carburetor, note the following: Install throttle plate so indentations on the plate face outward as shown in Fig. B508. Install choke plate so dimple

pered seat on the main nozzle and its mating surface inside the lower carburetor body. Three solutions to this problem are:

1. Make a tool by filing or grinding the threads off a new nozzle so it slides easily into and out of the carburetor. Place a light coating of fine-grit lapping compound on the tapered face of the nozzle. Using a screwdriver in the nozzle end slot, lap the nozzle against the seat. Be very careful not to damage the threads in the carburetor body when rotating the screwdriver. Thoroughly clean all lapping compound from the carburetor. Install a new nozzle.

2. Force a Teflon washer from B&S repair kit No. 391413 over the end of the nozzle and against the nozzle shoulder to serve as a gasket.

on face of plate faces inward (Fig. B508). Install fuel inlet valve seat so it is flush with carburetor body surface. To check float level, invert carburetor body and float assembly. Float should be parallel to carburetor body as shown in Fig. B502. Adjust float level by bending float lever tang that contacts inlet valve. When assembling fuel pump, install springs (27–Fig. B509) on pegs (P) on pump body and carburetor body.

Walbro Carburetor

The Walbro carburetor may be equipped with a fixed main jet or the adjustable high-speed mixture needle shown in Fig. B510.

Initial setting of idle mixture needle (10) is 1 turn out and high-speed mixture needle (23), if so equipped, is 1½ turns out. With engine at normal operating temperature and equipment control lever in SLOW position, adjust idle speed screw (8) so engine idles at 1750 rpm.

With engine running at idle speed, turn idle mixture needle clockwise until engine speed just starts to drop. Note needle position. Turn idle mixture needle counterclockwise until engine speed increases then just starts to drop again and note needle position. Then turn needle to midpoint between the noted lean and rich needle positions.

If equipped with high-speed mixture needle, set control to FAST and adjust high-speed needle using same procedure. If engine will not accelerate cleanly, slightly enrich low-speed mixture by turning idle mixture needle counterclockwise. If necessary, readjust idle speed screw. If engine does not run properly at high altitude, remove main air jet (13) and adjust mixture for smooth operation.

NOTE: Main air jet (13–Fig. B510) is not removable on carburetors equipped with adjuster needle limiter caps. If limiter caps are removed, new caps MUST be installed on carburetors originally equipped with caps.

To disassemble carburetor, remove bowl retainer (20–Fig. B510) and fuel bowl (18). Remove float pin (15), float (16) and fuel inlet valve needle (14). Remove idle mixture needle (10). A 5⁄32-inch punch ground flat at the end makes a suitable tool for removing Welch plug (9).

Clean the carburetor with aerosol cleaner, then use compressed air to blow out passages and dry the carburetor. Inspect components and discard any parts that are damaged or excessively worn. Replace the fuel inlet valve needle if the tip is grooved. Pull the fuel inlet valve seat from carburetor body if seat is worn or damaged. Inspect the tip of idle mixture needle and replace if it is bent or grooved. Check for excessive play between throttle shaft and body. Carburetor must be replaced if throttle shaft bore is excessively worn, as bushings are not available.

Some carburetors are equipped with a replaceable Viton-tipped fuel inlet valve and a non-replaceable brass valve seat. Carburetor body must be replaced if seat is damaged or worn.

On carburetors equipped with a replaceable fuel inlet valve seat, a green-colored seat is used on older style gravity-feed fuel systems and a black-colored seat is used on later style gravity-feed systems. The green-colored seats were prone to leak, and they can be replaced with the newer style black seat. A brown-colored seat is used on engines equipped with a fuel pump.

When reassembling carburetor, note the following: Apply a fuel-resistant sealer such as fingernail polish to outer edge of Welch plug (9–Fig. B510). Do not deform the Welch

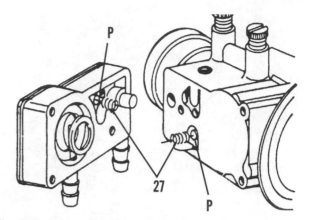

Fig. B509–When assembling fuel pump on Cross-Over Flo-Jet carburetor, install springs (27) onto pegs (P) on pump body and carburetor body.

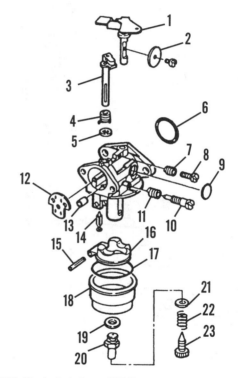

Fig. B510–Exploded view of Walbro-type carburetor.

1. Throttle shaft	13. Air jet
2. Throttle plate	14. Fuel inlet valve
3. Choke shaft	15. Float pin
4. Spring	16. Float
5. Seal	17. Gasket
6. Gasket	18. Fuel bowl
7. Spring	19. Washer
8. Idle speed stop screw	20. Bowl retainer
9. Welch plug	21. O-ring
10. Idle mixture needle	22. Spring
11. Spring	23. Main fuel
12. Choke plate	mixture needle

plug during installation; it should be flat. Install choke and throttle plates so numbers are on outer face when choke or throttle plate is in closed position. If fuel inlet seat is replaceable, install new seat using B&S driver 19057 or a suitable tool so grooved face of seat is down (Fig. B511). Float height is not adjustable. Tighten fuel bowl retaining nut to 50 in.-lbs. (5.6 N•m). Tighten carburetor mounting nuts to 90 in.-lbs. (10.2 N•m).

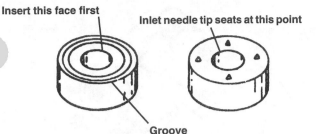

Fig. B511—Install fuel inlet valve seat with the grooved side downward.

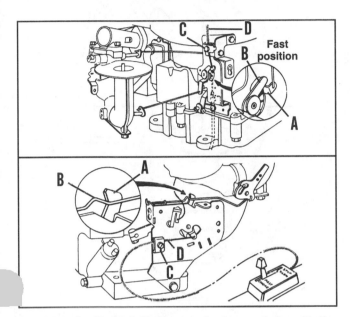

Fig. B512—On Choke-A-Matic controls shown, choke actuating lever (A) should just contact choke link or shaft (B) when control is at "FAST" position. If not, loosen screw (C) and move control wire housing (D) as required.

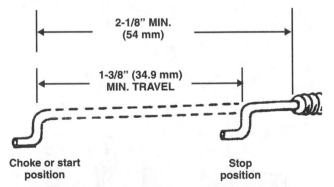

Fig. B513—For proper operation of Choke-A-Matic controls, remove control wire must extend to dimension shown and have a minimum travel of 1-3/8 inches (35 mm).

CHOKE-A-MATIC CARBURETOR CONTROLS

Engines may be equipped with a control unit that operates the carburetor choke, throttle and magneto grounding switch from a single lever (Choke A Matic carburetors).

To check operation of Choke-A-Matic controls, move control lever to CHOKE position; carburetor choke slide or plate must be completely closed. Move control lever to

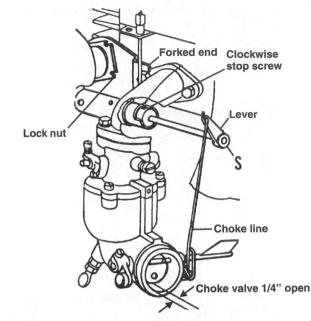

Fig. B514—Automatic choke used on some models equipped with Flo-Jet II carburetor showing unit in "HOT" position.

STOP position; magneto grounding switch should be making contact. With control in RUN, FAST or SLOW position, carburetor choke should be completely open. On units with remote controls, synchronize movement of remote lever to carburetor control lever by loosening screw (C–Fig. B512) and moving control wire housing (D) as required. Tighten screw to clamp housing securely. Refer to Fig. B513 to check remote control wire movement.

AUTOMATIC CHOKE (THERMOSTAT-TYPE)

A thermostat-operated choke is used on some models equipped with Flo-Jet II carburetor. To adjust choke linkage, hold choke shaft so thermostat lever is free. At room temperature, stop screw in thermostat collar should be located midway between thermostat stops. If not, loosen stop screw, adjust collar and tighten stop screw. Loosen set screw (S–Fig. B514) on thermostat lever. Slide lever on shaft to ensure free movement of choke unit. Turn thermostat shaft clockwise until stop screw contacts thermostat stop.

While holding shaft in this position, move shaft lever until choke is open exactly inch (3 mm) and tighten lever set screw. Turn thermostat shaft counterclockwise until stop screw contacts thermostat stop as shown in Fig. B515. Manually open choke valve until it stops against top of choke link opening. At this time, choke should be open at least $\frac{3}{32}$ inch (2.4 mm), but not more than $\frac{5}{32}$ inch (4 mm). Hold choke valve in wide-open position and check position of counterweight lever. Lever should be in a horizontal position with free end toward right.

FUEL TANK OUTLET

Some models are equipped with a fuel tank outlet as shown in Fig. B516. Other models may be equipped with a fuel sediment bowl that is part of the fuel tank outlet shown in Fig. B517.

Clean any debris or dirt from tank outlet screens with a brush. Varnish or other gasoline deposits can be removed using a suitable solvent. Tighten packing nut or remove

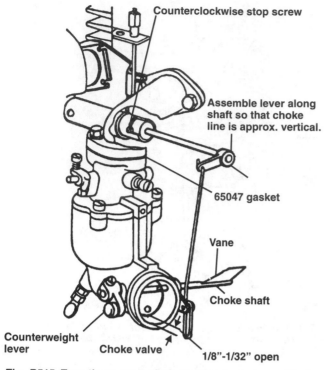

Fig. B515–Turn thermostat shaft counterclockwise until stop screw contacts thermostat stop as shown.

nut and shutoff valve, then replace the packing if leakage occurs around shutoff valve stem.

FUEL PUMP

A fuel pump is available as optional equipment on some models. Refer to BRIGGS & STRATTON ACCESSORIES section for service information.

GOVERNOR

All engines are equipped with a gear-driven mechanical-type governor attached to the crankcase cover or oil pan. The camshaft gear drives the governor. Governor and linkage must operate properly to prevent "hunting" or unsteady operation. The carburetor must be properly adjusted before performing governor adjustments.

To adjust governor linkage, loosen clamp bolt on governor lever shown in Figs. B518 or B519. Move link end of governor lever so carburetor throttle plate is in wide-open position. Using a screwdriver, rotate governor lever shaft clockwise as far as possible and tighten clamp bolt.

On models equipped with governed idle screw (I–Fig. B520), set remote control to idle position, then adjust idle speed screw on carburetor so engine idles at 1550 rpm. Place remote control so engine idles at 1750 rpm, then rotate governed idle screw (I) so screw just contacts remote control lever.

On models equipped with a governed idle stop (P–Fig. B521), set remote control to idle position, then adjust idle speed screw on carburetor so engine idles at 1550 rpm. Loosen governed idle stop screw (W). Place remote control so engine idles at 1750 rpm, then position stop (P) so it contacts remote control lever and tighten screw (W).

On Models 253400 and 255400, set remote control to idle position, then adjust idle speed screw on carburetor so engine idles at 1550 rpm. Bend tang (G–Fig. B522) so engine idles at 1750 rpm.

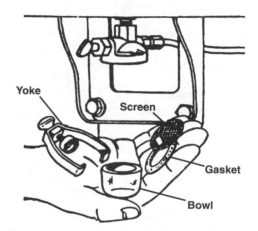

Fig. B516–Fuel tank outlet used on some models includes a filter screen.

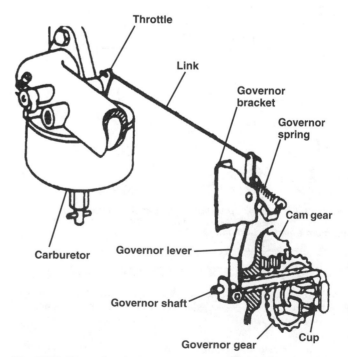

Fig. B517–Fuel sediment bowl and tank outlet used on some models.

Fig. B518–View of typical governor assembly used on engines with vertical crankshaft.

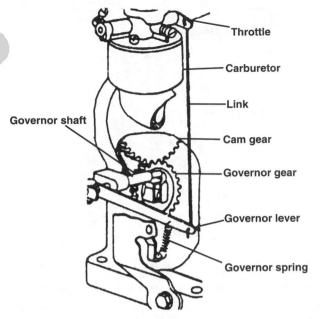

Fig. B519–View of typical governor assembly used on engines with horizontal crankshafts.

Throttle

Carburetor

Link

Governor shaft

Cam gear

Governor gear

Governor lever

Governor spring

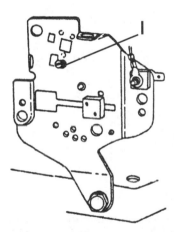

Fig. B520–On engines equipped with a governed idle adjustment screw (I), refer to text for adjustment procedure.

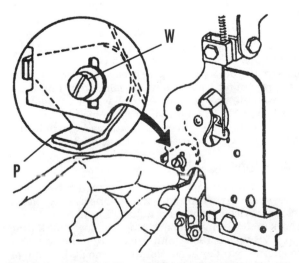

Fig. B521–On models equipped with a governed idle stop (P), refer to GOVERNOR section to adjust governed idle speed.

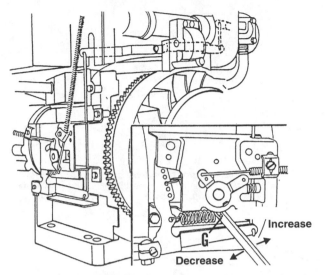

Fig. B522–On Series 253400 and 255400 engines, bend spring anchor tang (G) to adjust governed idle speed.

IMPORTANT: Running an engine at a maximum speed higher than the speed specified by the equipment manufacturer can be dangerous to the operator, harmful to the equipment and inefficient. Adjust governed engine speed to specification stipulated by equipment manufacturer.

To set maximum no-load speed on all models except 253400 and 255400, move remote speed control to maximum speed position. With engine running, bend governor spring anchor tang (T–Fig. B523) to obtain desired maximum no-load speed.

To set maximum no-load speed on Models 253400 and 255400, move remote speed control to maximum speed position. With engine running, turn screw (S–Fig. B524) to obtain desired maximum no-load speed.

Some models are equipped with a top speed screw (T–Fig. B525) that determines maximum no-load speed according to which hole the screw occupies. There may be one, two, three or four numbered holes. If a screw is not installed in one of the numbered holes, the maximum speed determined by adjusting the governor spring anchor tang will determine maximum no-load engine speed. If a screw is installed in a numbered hole, the maximum speed will be reduced. Installing the top speed screw (T) in a higher numbered hole will reduce top engine speed the most. For instance, installing the screw in hole 2 will reduce engine speed to 3300 rpm while installing the screw in hole 4 will reduce engine speed to 2400 rpm. An accurate tachometer should be used to determine engine speed for specific holes.

On Series 176400, 19A400, 19B400, 19C400, 19E400, 19F400, 19G400, 226400 and 250400 engines with dual-spring governor control (Fig. B526), adjust as follows: Remove the load from engine. Run engine until normal operating temperature is reached. Connect a tachometer to engine. Move the speed control lever (4) to put slack in main governor spring (3). Hold the throttle lever against the idle speed stop screw, and adjust screw to obtain 1750 rpm. While holding throttle lever against idle speed screw, adjust idle mixture screw to midpoint between too lean and too rich. Adjust idle speed stop screw to obtain 1200 rpm. Release the throttle lever, then bend the idle spring tang (1) to obtain idle speed of 1750 rpm. Back out the

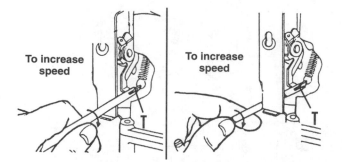

Fig. B523—Insert a suitable tool between cover and engine (left view) or through hole in cover (right view) and bend governor spring anchor tank (T) to adjust maximum governered speed.

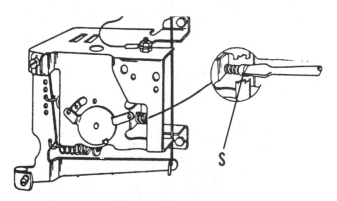

Fig. B524—On Series 253400 and 255400 engines, rotate screw (S) to adjust maximum governed speed.

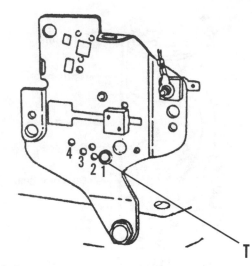

Fig. B525—Some engines may be equipped with a maximum governed speed limit screw (T). Location of screw in one of the numbered holes determines maximum governed speed. Refer to text.

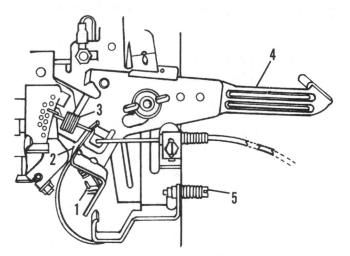

Fig. B526—Drawing of dual-spring governor control linkage used on some 176400, 19x226400, 226400 and 250400 series engines. Single-spring linkage is similar. Refer to text for adjustment procedure.

1. Idle speed tang
2. Governor main spring tang
3. Governor main spring

4. Throttle lever
5. High-speed stop screw

high-speed stop screw and move the speed control lever handle to the FAST position. Determine maximum no-load rpm specification, then bend main governor spring tang (2) until engine speed is 100-150 rpm over maximum no-load speed. Turn high-speed stop screw to bring maximum no-load rpm to specification.

IGNITION SYSTEM

Early models are equipped with a magneto ignition system; later models are equipped with a Magnetron breakerless ignition system. Refer to appropriate section for model being serviced.

Magneto Ignition

All models are equipped with breaker points and condenser located under the flywheel.

One of two different types of ignition points, as shown in Figs. B527 and B528, are used. Breaker point gap is 0.020 inch (0.51 mm) for all models with magneto ignition.

On each type, a plunger that rides against a cam on engine crankshaft actuates the breaker contact arm. The plunger operates in a bore in engine crankcase. The plunger can be removed after removing the breaker points. Replace the plunger if worn to a length of 0.870 inch (22.10 mm) or less.

If breaker point plunger bore in crankcase is worn, oil will leak past plunger. Check bore with B&S gauge 19055. If plug gauge will enter bore ¼ inch (6.4 mm) or more, bore should be reamed and a bushing installed. Refer to Fig. B529. To ream bore and install bushing it will be necessary to remove breaker points, armature, ignition coil and

crankshaft. Refer to Fig. B530 for steps in reaming bore and installation of bushing.

Plunger must be installed with groove toward top (Fig. B531) to prevent oil contamination in breaker point box.

To reassemble, set armature-to-flywheel air gap at 0.010-0.014 inch (0.25-0.36 mm) for two-leg armature or 0.012-0.016 inch (0.30-0.41 mm) for three-leg armature. Ignition timing is not adjustable on these models.

Magnetron Ignition

The Magnetron ignition is a self-contained breakerless ignition system. Flywheel removal is not necessary except to check or service keyway or crankshaft key.

To check spark, remove spark plug, connect spark plug cable to B&S tester 19051 and ground remaining tester lead on engine cylinder head. Rotate engine at 350 rpm or more. If spark jumps the 0.166 inch (4.2 mm) tester gap, system is functioning properly.

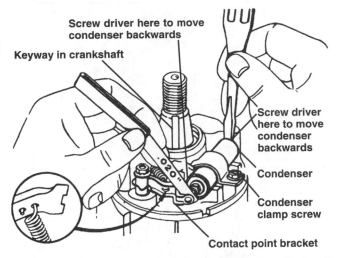

Fig. B527–Drawing showing breaker point adjustment onmodels with breaker points that are integral with condenser. Move condenser to adjust point gap.

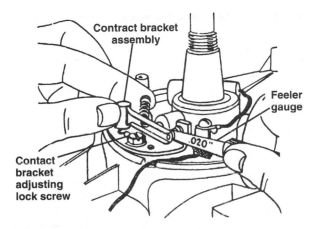

Fig. B528–Drawing showing adjustment of breaker points that are separate from condenser.

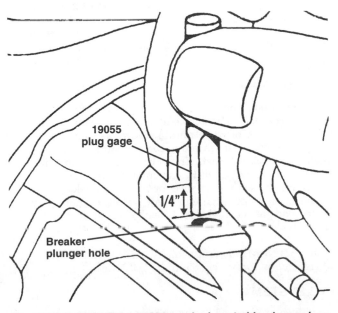

Fig. B529–If B&S gauge 19055 can be inserted in plunger bore 1/4 inch (6.4 mm) or more, bore is worn and must be rebushed.

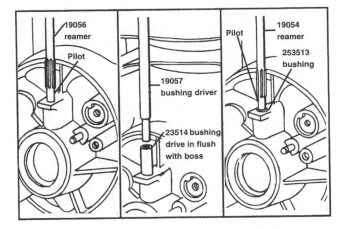

Fig. B530–Views showing reaming plunger bore to accept bushing (left view), installing busing (center) and finish reaming bore of bushing (right).

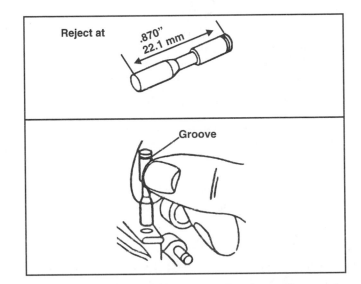

Fig. B531–Insert breaker point plunger into bore with grove toward top.

Armature and module have been manufactured as either one-piece units or as a separable two-piece assembly. The presence of large rivet heads on one side of the armature laminations identifies the two-piece unit. To remove armature and Magnetron module, remove flywheel shroud and armature retaining screws. On one-piece units, disconnect stop switch wire at spade connector. On two-piece units, use a $\frac{3}{16}$-inch (4.8 mm) diameter pin punch to release stop switch wire from module. To remove module on two-piece units, unsolder wires, push module retainer away from laminations and remove module. See Fig. B532.

Solder wires for installation and use RTV sealant to hold ground wires in position.

Armature to flywheel air gap should be 0.010-0.014 inch (0.25-0.36 mm) for two-leg armature or 0.012-0.016 inch (0.30-0.41 mm) for three-leg armature. Ignition timing is not adjustable on these models.

VALVE ADJUSTMENT

To correctly set valve tappet clearance, remove spark plug and, using a suitable measuring tool, rotate crankshaft in normal direction (clockwise at flywheel) so piston is at top dead center on compression stroke. Continue to rotate crankshaft so piston is 1/4-inch (6.4 mm) down from top dead center. This position places the tappets away from the compression release device, if used, on the cam lobe.

Exhaust valve tappet clearance (engine cold) for all models is 0.009-0.011 inch (0.23-0.28 mm). Intake valve tappet clearance (engine cold) for all models except Series 253400 and 255400 engines with electric start is 0.005-0.007 inch (0.13-0.18 mm). On Series 253400 and 255400 engines with electric start, intake valve tappet clearance is 0.009-0.011 inch (0.23-0.28 mm). If a Series 253400 or 255400 engine is equipped with a manual starter and an electric starter, intake valve tappet clearance is 0.005-0.007 inch (0.13-0.18 mm).

Valve tappet clearance is adjusted on all models by carefully grinding end of valve stem to increase clearance or by grinding valve seats deeper and/or replacing the valve or lifter to decrease clearance.

CRANKCASE BREATHER

A crankcase breather is built into the engine tappet chamber cover. A partial vacuum must exist in crankcase to prevent oil seepage past oil seals, gaskets, breaker point plunger or piston rings. Air can flow out of crankcase through breather, but a one-way valve blocks return flow, maintaining necessary vacuum. Breather mounting holes are offset one way. A vent tube connects breather to carburetor air horn for extra protection against dusty conditions.

CYLINDER HEAD

After 100 to 300 hours of engine operation, the cylinder head should be removed and any carbon or deposits should be removed.

COMPRESSION PRESSURE

Briggs & Stratton does not publish compression pressure specifications.

An alternate method of determining internal engine condition and wear is by using a cylinder leak-down tester. The tester is available commercially or through Briggs & Stratton (part No. 19413). The tester uses compressed air to pressurize the combustion chamber, then gauges the amount of leakage past the piston rings and valves. Instructions are included with the tester.

REPAIRS

TIGHTENING TORQUE

Recommended tightening torque specifications are as follows:

Alternator stator	18-24 in.-lb.
	(2.0-2.7 N•m)
Blower housing	75-95 in.-lb.
	(8.5-10.7 N•m)
Breather screws	20-30 in.-lb.
	(2.3-3.4 N•m)
Carburetor mounting screws	65-75 in.-lb.
	(7.3-8.5 N•m)
Connecting rod	See Text
Crankcase cover	See Text
Electric starter	130-150 in.-lb.
	(14.7-17.0 N•m)

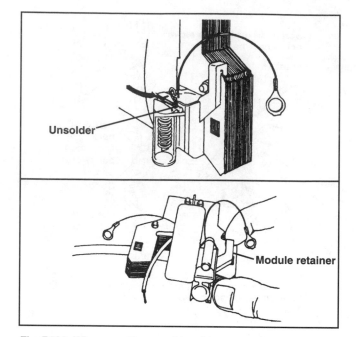

Fig. B532–Wires must be unsoldered to remove Magnetron ignition module.

Fan retainer	130-150 in.-lb.
	(14.7-17.0 N•m)
Flywheel nut:	
170000-250000	65 ft.-lb.
	(88 N•m)
280000	95-105 ft.-lb.
	(129-142 N•m)
Fuel pump	40-50 in.-lb.
	(4.5-5.7 N•m)
Governor lever bolt	35-45 in.-lb.
	(3.9-5.1 N•m)
Ignition module	20-28 in.-lb.
	(2.3-3.2 N•m)
Intake manifold	65-75 in.-lb.
	(7.3-8.5 N•m)
Spark plug	140-200 in.-lb.
	(15.8-22.6 N•m)
Starter gear cover	20-24 in.-lb.
	(2.3-2.7 N•m)
Solenoid ground wire	40-50 in.-lb.
	(4.5-5.7 N•m)

CYLINDER HEAD

Remove fan housing and/or cylinder head cover as required to access the cylinder head. Note the location and lengths of cylinder head retaining screws as they are removed so they can be installed in their original positions.

Clean combustion deposits from the cylinder head using a wooden or plastic scraper. Be careful not to nick or otherwise damage the sealing surface for the head gasket.

Always install a new cylinder head gasket. Do not apply sealer to head gasket. Lightly lubricate threads of cylinder head screws with Led-Plate part No. 93963 or graphite grease. Install screws and tighten in steps or increments of 55 in.-lb. (6.2 N•m) following sequence shown in Fig. B533. Final tightening torque is 165 in.-lb. (19 N•m).

VALVE SYSTEM

The valves are located in the cylinder block. To remove the valves, remove cylinder head. Remove components as

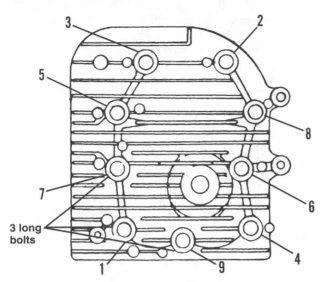

Fig. B333–Tighten cylinder head screws in sequence shown. Note location of three long screws.

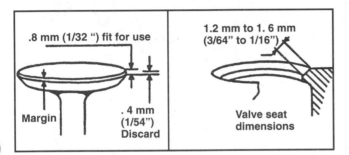

Fig. B534–Valve and seat dimensions.

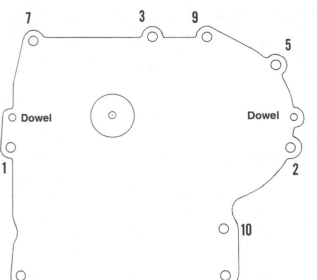

Fig. B535–On 10-bolt crankcase cover/oil pan used on 280000 series engines, it is important to tighten the fasteners in proper sequence to avoid distorting the cover.

required to access the crankcase breather. Remove breather/tappet chamber cover. Rotate the flywheel so piston is at top of the cylinder and both valves are closed or seated. Three methods are used to retain the valve spring on the valve stem. Most engines are equipped with a slotted spring retainer that fits in a groove on the valve stem. The valve end will pass through the large end of the slot. Some engines are equipped with a retaining pin that fits in a hole in the end of the valve stem. The third method uses a split key, automotive-type retainer to retain the valve spring. Compress the valve spring using a suitable valve spring compressor tool. Remove the spring retainer, slide the valve out of the block and remove valve spring.

Some intake valves and all exhaust valves have a face angle of 45°. Seats for these valves should be cut at 46°. Some engine models have intake valves with a 30° face angle. Seats for these valves should be cut at 31°.

Replace valve if margin is 1/64 inch (0.4 mm) or less (Fig. B534). Seat width should be 3/64 to 1/16 inch (1.2-1.6 mm).

All models are equipped with replaceable valve seat inserts. Use a suitable puller to remove damaged or worn inserts. Chill the new insert in a freezer prior to installation. Use the old seat insert as a spacer between the driver and new insert. Be sure the new insert is bottomed in the cylinder block counterbore. Peen around the new insert to prevent it from loosening.

Valve guides are replaceable. Using tool 19204, press in new guide bushing so it is flush with top of guide bore. Valve guide 230655 does not require reaming; however,

other valve guides must be finish reamed using B&S reamer 19233 and reamer guide 19234.

Some engines may be equipped with a Cobalite exhaust valve and exhaust seat insert as well as a rotocoil on the exhaust valve stem. These components are offered as replacement parts for engines used in severe engine service.

CRANKCASE COVER/OIL PAN

On 170000-250000 series engines, tighten crankcase cover or oil pan fasteners in increments of 70 in.-lb. (7.9 N•m) to final torque of 140 in.-lb. (15.8 N•m). Tighten the fasteners in a criss-cross pattern to avoid distorting the cover. On 10-bolt crankcase cover/oil pan used on 280000 series engines, incrementally tighten the fasteners to 200 in.-lb. (22.6 N•m) using the tightening sequence shown in Fig. B535).

NOTE: On 280000 series engines with Code Number of 971120xx or lower, replace cover/pan bolts with current-style part No. 94624 bolts.

CAMSHAFT

The camshaft is supported at both ends in bearing bores machined in crankcase and crankcase cover or oil pan. The camshaft gear is an integral part of camshaft.

Camshaft should be replaced if either journal is worn to a diameter of 0.498 inch (12.66 mm) or less, or if cam lobes are worn or damaged. Cam lobe wear limit is 0.977 inch (24.82 mm) for 170000 and 190000 series engines and 1.184 inch (30.07 mm) for all other engines.

Crankcase, crankcase cover or oil pan must be replaced if bearing bores are 0.506 inch (12.85 mm) or larger, or if tool 19164 enters bearing bore inch (6.4 mm) or more.

The compression release mechanism on camshaft gear holds exhaust valve slightly open at very low engine rpm as a starting aid. Mechanism should work freely and spring should hold actuator cam against pin.

When installing the camshaft in engines with ball bearing main bearings, align timing marks on the camshaft gear and crankshaft counterweight as shown in Fig. B536.

When installing camshaft in engines with integral-type main bearings, align timing marks on camshaft and crankshaft gears as shown in Fig. B537.

If the timing mark is not visible on crankshaft gear, align camshaft gear timing mark with second tooth to the left of crankshaft counterweight parting line as shown in Fig. B538.

PISTON, PIN AND RINGS

Connecting rod and piston are removed from cylinder head end of block as an assembly. To remove, first remove cylinder head as previously outlined. Remove crankcase cover/oil sump and connecting rod cap. Remove any carbon or wear ridge at top of the cylinder to prevent damage to rings or piston during removal. Push the connecting rod and piston out through top of cylinder.

Cylinder bore may be aluminum or a cast iron sleeve. Pistons are designed to run in only one type of bore. Pistons designed for use in a cast iron bore have a dull finish and are stamped with an L on the piston's crown. Some pistons designed for use in an aluminum cylinder bore are chrome plated (shiny finish). Some later-style aluminum-bore pistons are iron-plated and can be identified by their gun metal-blue color. These pistons were first used after Date Code 990101xx. Pistons cannot be interchanged.

Reject piston showing visible signs of wear, scoring and scuffing. After cleaning carbon from top ring groove, insert a new top ring into the groove and measure the side clearance between the ring and ring land with a feeler gauge. Reject the piston if ring side clearance exceeds 0.009 inch (0.23 mm). Reject piston and pin or hone piston pin bore to fit a 0.005 inch (0.13 mm) oversize pin if pin or pin bore exceeds the following service limits. Maximum allowable pin bore out-of-round is 0.0005 inch (0.013 mm). Wear limit for pin bore ID is 0.673 inch (17.09 mm) for 170000 and 190000 series engines, or 0.801 inch (20.34 mm) for all other engines. Wear limit for piston pin diameter is 0.671 inch (17.04 mm) for 170000 and 190000 series engines, or 0.799 inch (20.30 mm) for all other models.

On aluminum bore engines, reject compression rings having an end gap of 0.035 inch (0.90 mm) or more and reject oil rings having an end gap of 0.045 inch (1.14 mm) or more. On cast iron bore engines, reject compression rings having an end gap of 0.030 inch (0.75 mm) or more and reject oil rings having an end gap of 0.035 inch (0.90 mm) or more.

Pistons and rings are available in several oversizes as well as standard. Installation instructions are provided with the ring set. Refer to Figs. B539 and B540 for correct installation of piston rings.

A chrome piston ring set is available for slightly worn standard bore cylinders. No honing or cylinder deglazing is required for these rings. The cylinder bore can be a maximum of 0.005 inch (0.13 mm) oversize when using chrome rings.

If piston has a notch (N–Fig. B541) in piston crown, assemble connecting rod and piston as shown in Fig. B541. Install piston and rod in engine so notch (N) is toward flywheel.

CONNECTING ROD

Connecting rod and piston are removed from cylinder head end of block as an assembly. The aluminum alloy con-

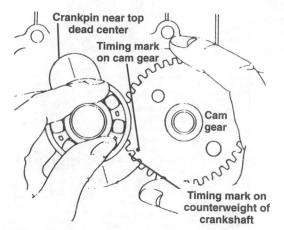

Fig. B536–Align timing mark on cam gear with mark on crankshaft counterweight on ball bearing equipped models.

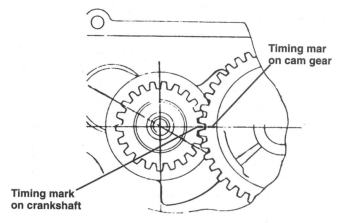

Fig. B537–Align timing marks on cam gear and crankshaft gear on plain bearing models.

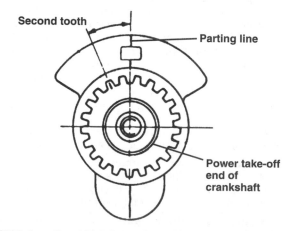

Fig. B538–Location of tooth to align with timing mark on cam gear if mark is not visible on crankshaft gear.

necting rod rides directly on an induction hardened crankshaft crankpin journal. Rod should be rejected if big end of rod is scored or out-of-round more than 0.0007 inch (0.018 mm) or if piston pin bore is scored or out-of-round more than 0.0005 inch (0.013 mm). Replace the connecting rod if either crankpin bore or piston pin bore is worn to, or larger than, sizes given in table.

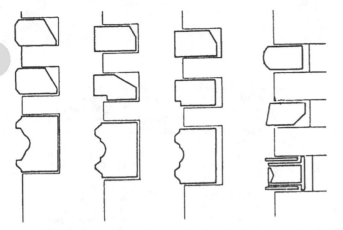

Fig. B539–Refer to above illustration for proper arrangement of piston rings used in engines with aluminum bore.

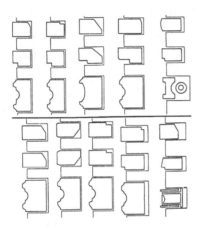

Fig. B540–Refer to above illustration for proper arrangement of piston rings used in engines with cast iron sleeve.

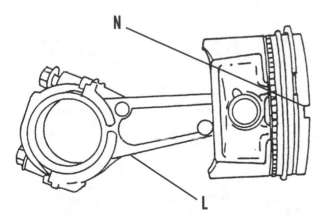

Fig. B541–If piston crown is notched (N), assemble connecting rod and piston as shown while noting relation of long side of rod (L) and notch (N) in piston crown.

Model Series	Crankpin Bore	Pin Bore*
170000	1.095 in. (27.81 mm)	0.674 in. (17.12 mm)
190000	1.127 in. (28.61 mm)	0.674 in. (17.12 mm)
220000, 250000, 280000	1.252 in. (31.8 mm)	0.802 in. (20.37 mm)

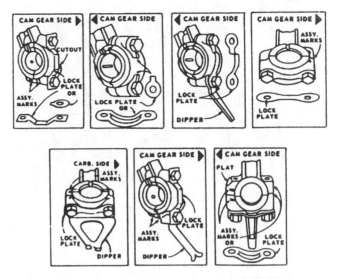

Fig. B542–Install connecting rod in engine as indicated according to type used. Note dipper installation on connecting rod for horizontal crankshaft engine.

*Piston pins that are 0.005 inch (0.13 mm) oversize are available for service. Piston pin bore in rod can be reamed to this size if crankpin bore is within specifications.

Refer to Fig. B542, locate-type of rod being serviced and note installation instructions. If piston has a notch (N—Fig. B541) in piston crown, install connecting rod in piston as shown in Fig. B541. Install piston and rod in engine so notch (N) is toward flywheel.

Refer to the following table for connecting rod screw tightening torque specifications.

Series	Torque
170000	165 in.-lbs. (18.6 N•m)
190000, 220000, 250000	185 in.-lb. (20.9 N•m)
280000 w/equal size rod bolts	185 in.-lb. (20.9 N•m)
280000 w/two sizes of rod bolts	
Small bolt	130 in.-lb. (14.7 N•m)
Large bolt	260 in.-lb. (29.4 N•m)

GOVERNOR

Governor gear and weight unit can be removed after crankcase cover or oil pan is removed. Refer to exploded views of engines in Figs. B543, B544, B545 and B546. Governor weight unit on horizontal crankshaft models rides on a shaft in the crankcase cover. The governor weight unit along with the oil slinger on vertical crankshaft models rides on the end of the camshaft as shown in Fig. B547.

Remove governor lever, cotter pin and washer from outer end of governor lever shaft. Slide governor lever out of bushing toward inside of engine. Governor gear and weight unit can now be removed. Replace the governor lever shaft bushing in crankcase, if necessary, and ream new bushing after installation to 0.2385-0.2390 inch (6.058-6.071 mm). Briggs & Stratton tool 19333 can be used to ream bushing.

Replace the governor lever seal if oil leakage past the seal is evident. Use care not to damage the seal lip when installing the new seal. Wrap thin plastic or cellophane tape over the end of the lever shaft to serve as a seal protector.

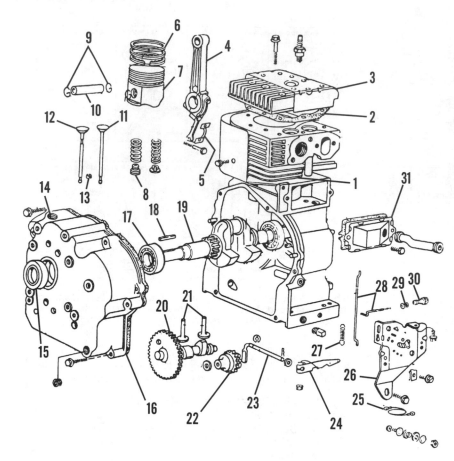

Fig. B543–Exploded view of Series 220000 or 221000 horizontal crankshaft engine assembly. Series 170000, 171000, 176000 and 190000 are similar. Series 222000 is similar, but ball bearings (17) are not used.

1. Cylinder block/crankcase
2. Head gasket
3. Cylinder head
4. Connecting rod
5. Lock plate
6. Piston rings
7. Pisont
8. Rotocoil (exhaust valve)
9. Retainer clips
10. Piston pin
11. Intake valve
12. Exhaust valve
13. Retainers
14. Crankcase cover
15. Oil seal
16. Crankcase gasket
17. Main bearing
18. Key
19. Crankshaft
20. Camshaft
21. Tappet
22. Governor gear
23. Governor crank
24. Governor lever
25. Ground wire
26. Governor control plate
27. Spring
28. Governor rod
29. Spring
30. Nut
31. Breather assy.

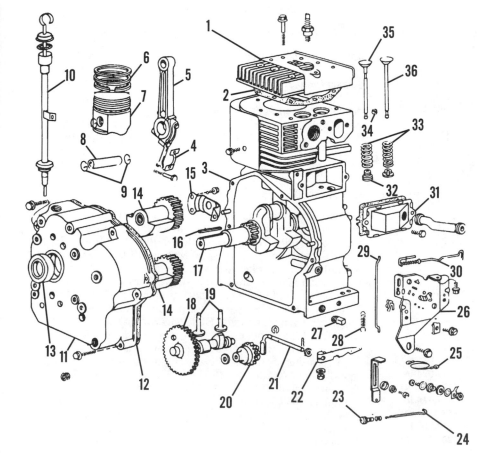

Fig. B544–Exploded view of Series 251000, 252000 or 254000 engine assembly. Series 253000 and 255000 are similar.

1. Cylinder head
2. Head gakset
3. Cylinder block/crankcase
4. Lock plate
5. Connecting rod
6. Piston ring
7. Piston
8. Piston ring
9. Retainer clips
10. Dipstick
11. Crankcase cover
12. Crankcase gasket
13. Oil seal
14. Counterweight & bearing assy.
15. Retainer
16. Key
17. Crankshaft
18. Camshaft
19. Tapper
20. Governor gear
21. Governor crank
22. Governor lever
23. Governor nut & spring
24. Governor control rod
25. Ground wire
26. Governor control pin
27. Drain plug
28. Spring
29. Governor link
30. Choke link
31 Breather assy,
32. Rotocoil (exhaust valve)
33. Valve spring
34. Retainer
35. Exhaust valve
36. Intake valve

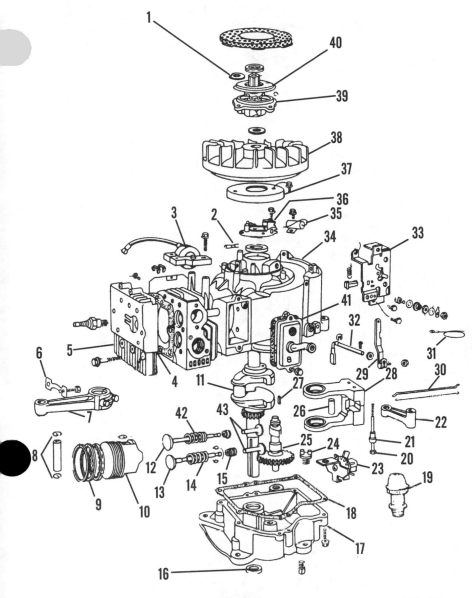

Fig. B545–Exploded view of typical vertical crankshaft engine equipped with Synchro-Balancer. Later models use a solid-state ignition module in place of breaker points and coil assembly.

1. Thrust washer
2. Breaker point plunger
3. Armature assy.
4. Head gasket
5. Cylinder head
6. Lock plate
7. Connecting rod
8. Piston pin & retaining clips
9. Piston rings
10. Piston
11. Crankshaft
12. Intake valve
13. Exhaust valve
14. Retainer
15. Rotocoil (Exhaust valve)
16. Oil sea
17. Oil pan
18. Crankcase gasket
19. Oil minder
20. Cap screw (2)
21. Spacer (2)
22. Link
23. Gorvernor & oil slinger
24. Plug
25. Camshaft
26. Dowel pin (2)
27. Key
28. Counterweight assy.
29. Governor lever
30. Governor link
31. Ground wire
32. Governor crank
33. Choke-A-Matic control
34. Cylinder block/crankcase
35. Condenser
36. Breaker points
37. Cover
38. Flywheel assy.
39. Clutch housing
40. Rewind starter Clutch
41. Breather assy.
42. Valve springs
43. Tappet

CRANKSHAFT AND MAIN BEARINGS

The crankshaft may be supported by bearing surfaces that are an integral part of crankcase, crankcase cover or oil pan, or by ball bearings at each end of crankshaft. The ball bearings are a press fit on the crankshaft and fit into machined bores in the crankcase, crankcase cover or oil pan.

The crankshaft used in models with integral bearings should be replaced or reground if main bearing journals exceed service limits specified in following table.

Crankshaft Reject Sizes

Model	Magneto End Journal	PTO End Journal
170000 and 190000 series	0.997 in.* (25.32 mm)	1.179 in. (29.95 mm)
220000, 250000 and 280000 series	1.376 in. (34.95 mm)	1.376 in. (34.95 mm)

*Models equipped with Synchro-Balancer have a main bearing rejection size for main bearing at magneto side of 1.179 inch (29.95 mm).

Crankshaft for models with ball bearing main bearings should be replaced if new bearings are loose on journals. Bearings should be a press fit.

Crankshaft for all models should be replaced or reground if connecting rod crankpin journal diameter exceeds service limit listed in following table.

Crankshaft Reject Sizes

Model	Crankpin Journal
170000 series	1.090 in. (27.69 mm)
190000 series	1.122 in. (28.50 mm)
220000, 250000, and 280000 series	1.247 in. (31.67 mm)

A connecting rod with undersize big end diameter is available to fit crankshaft that has had crankpin journal reground to 0.020 inch (0.51 mm) undersize.

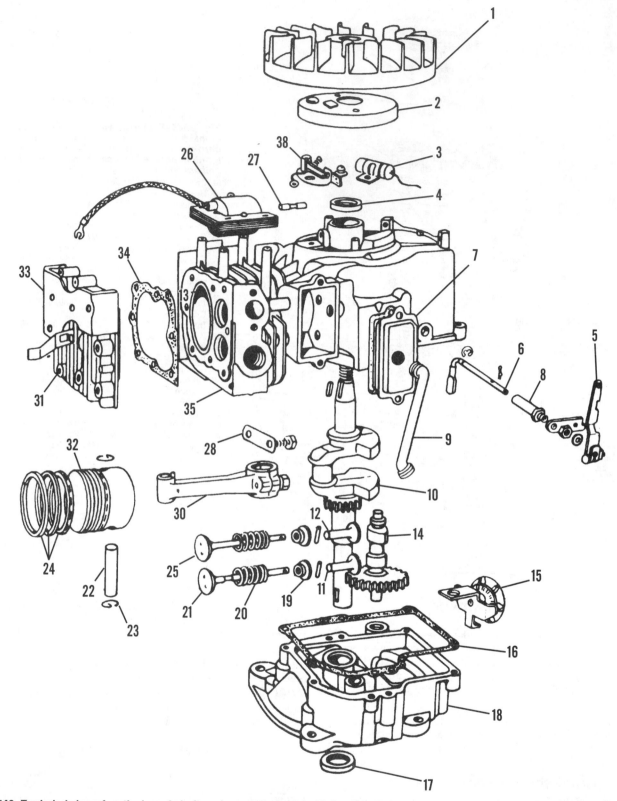

Fig. B546–Exploded view of vertical crankshaft engine not equipped with Synchro-Balancer. Later models are equipped with a solid-state ignition module in place of breaker points and coil assembly.

1. Flywheel	10. Crankshaft	19. Valve spring retainer	28. Rod bolt lock
2. Cover	11. Tappet	20. Valve springs	30. Connecting rod
3. Condenser	12. Valve retaining pins	21. Exhaust valve	31. Cylinder head
4. Oil seal	13. Key	22. Piston pin	32. Piston
5. Governor lever	14. Camshaft	23. Retainer clip	33. Air baffle
6. Governor crank	15. Governor & oil slinger	24. Piston rings	34. Head gasket
7. Breather assy.	16. Crankcase gasket	25. Intake valve	35. Cylinder block/
8. Bushing	17. Oil seal	26. Armature & coil assy.	crankcase
9. Breather vent tube	18. Oil pan	27. Breaker point plunger	38. Breaker points

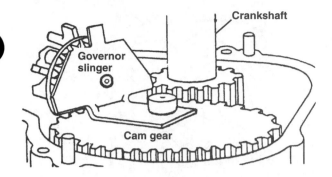

Fig. B547–View of governor weight assembly and oil slinger used on vertical crankshaft models.

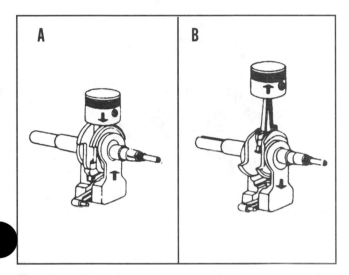

Fig. B548–Drawing showing operating principle of Synchro-Balancer used on some engines. Counterweight oscillates in opposite direction of piston.

On models equipped with integral main bearings, crankcase, crankcase cover or oil pan must be replaced or reamed to accept service bushings if service limits in following table are exceeded.

Main Bearing Reject Sizes

Model	Magneto End Bearing	PTO End Bearing
170000 and 190000 series	1.004 in.* (25.50 mm)	1.185 in. (30.10 mm)
220000, 250000 and 280000 series	1.383 in. (35.13 mm)	1.383 in. (35.13 mm)

*Models equipped with Synchro-Balancer have a main bearing rejection size for main bearing at magneto side of 1.185 inch (30.10 mm).

Install steel-backed aluminum service bushing as follows. Use a suitable tool and, prior to bushing installation, make an indentation in bore of crankcase. Install bushing so oil notches are properly aligned and bushing is flush with bore. Oil hole must be clear after installation. Stake bushing into previously made indentation and finish ream bushing. Do not stake where bushing is split.

When installing DU-type bushing, stake bushing at oil notches in crankcase, but locate bushing so bushing split is

not aligned with an oil notch. On Series 170000 and 190000 models, bushing should be $\frac{3}{32}$ inch (2.4 mm) below face of crankcase bore and $\frac{1}{32}$ inch (0.8 mm) below face of crankcase cover or oil pan. On Series 171700, 191700, 192700, 193700, 194700, 195700 and 196700 models, bushing should be $\frac{1}{64}$ inch (0.4 mm) below face of crankcase bore. On Series 220000, 250000 and 280000 engines, bushing should be $\frac{7}{64}$ inch (2.8 mm) below face of crankcase bore and $\frac{1}{8}$ inch (3.2 mm) below face of crankcase cover or oil pan.

Ball bearing mains are a press fit on the crankshaft and must be removed by pressing the crankshaft out of the bearing. Reject ball bearing if worn or rough. Expand new bearing by heating it in oil and install it on crankshaft with seal side toward crankpin journal.

Crankshaft end play is 0.002-0.008 inch (0.05-0.20 mm). At least one 0.015-inch crankcase gasket must be in place when measuring end play. Additional gaskets in several sizes are available to aid in end play adjustment. If end play is excessive, place shims between crankshaft gear and crankcase on plain bearing models, or on flywheel side of crankshaft if equipped with a ball bearing.

When reinstalling crankshaft, make certain timing marks are aligned (Figs. B536 or B537) and, if equipped with counterbalance weights, refer to ROTATING COUNTERBALANCE SYSTEM paragraphs for counterweight alignment procedure.

CYLINDER

If cylinder bore wear is 0.003 inch (0.08 mm) or more or is 0.0025 inch (0.06 mm) or more out-of-round, cylinder must be replaced or bored to next larger oversize.

Standard cylinder bore diameter is 2.9990-3.0000 inches (76.175-76.230 mm) for Series 170000 and 190000 models. Standard cylinder bore diameter is 3.4365-3.4375 inches (87.287-87.313 mm) for all other models.

Special stones are required to hone aluminum cylinder bore on models so equipped. Follow recommendations and procedures specified by hone manufacturer.

A chrome piston ring set is available for slightly worn standard bore cylinders. No honing or cylinder deglazing is required for these rings. The cylinder bore can be a maximum of 0.005 inch (0.13 mm) oversize when using chrome rings.

SYNCHRO-BALANCER

All vertical crankshaft engines, except Series 220000, 221000 and 222000 models, may be equipped with an oscillating Synchro-Balancer. Balance weight assembly rides on eccentric journals on the crankshaft and move in opposite direction of piston (Fig. B548).

To disassemble balancer unit, first remove flywheel, oil pan, cam gear, cylinder head, and connecting rod and piston assembly. Carefully pry off crankshaft gear and key. Remove the two cap screws holding halves of counterweight together. Separate weights and remove link, dowel pins and spacers. Slide weights from crankshaft (Fig. B549).

To reassemble, install magneto side weight on magneto end of crankshaft. Place crankshaft (PTO end up) in a vise (Fig. B550). Install both dowel pins and place link on pin as shown. Note rounded edge on free end of link must be up. Install PTO side weight, spacers, lock and cap screws. Tighten cap screws to 80 in.-lbs. (9 N•m) and secure with lock tabs. Install key and crankshaft gear with chamfer on inside of gear facing shoulder on crankshaft.

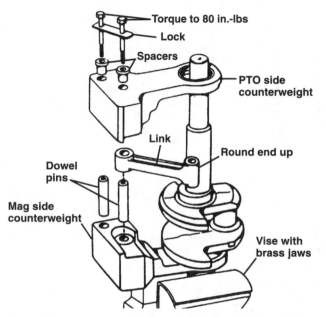

Fig. B549—Exploded view of Synchro-Balancer assembly. Counterweights ride on eccentric journals on crankshaft.

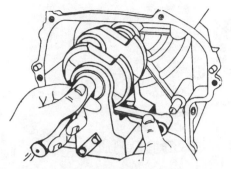

Fig. B551—When installing crankshaft and balancer assembly, place free end of link on anchor pin in crankcase.

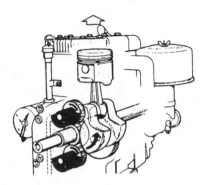

Fig. B552—View rotating counterbalance system used on some models. A gear on the crankshaft drives the counterweight gears.

Fig. B550—Assemble balance units on crankshaft as shown. Install link with rounded edge on free end toward PTO end of crankshaft.

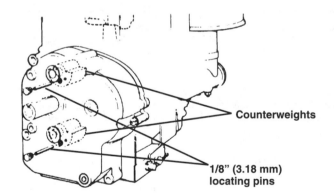

Fig. B553—To properly align coutnerweights, remove two small screws from crankcase cover and insert 1/8-inch (3.2 mm) diameter locating pins.

Install crankshaft and balancer assembly in crankcase, sliding free end of link on anchor pin as shown in Fig. B551. Reassemble engine.

ROTATING COUNTERBALANCE SYSTEM

All horizontal crankshaft engines, except Series 220000, 221000 and 222000 models, may be equipped with two gear-driven counterweights in constant mesh with crankshaft gear. Gears, mounted in crankcase cover, rotate in opposite direction of crankshaft (Fig. B552).

To properly align counterweights when installing cover, remove two small screws from cover and insert ⅛-inch (3.2 mm) diameter locating pins through holes in cover and into timing holes in counterweights as shown in Fig. B553.

With piston at TDC, install cover assembly. Remove locating pins, coat threads of timing hole screws with sealant and install screws with fiber sealing washers.

NOTE: If counterweights are removed from crankcase cover, exercise care in handling or cleaning to prevent loss of needle bearings.

BRIGGS & STRATTON

BRIGGS & STRATTON CORPORATION
Milwaukee, Wisconsin 53201

VANGUARD TWIN-CYLINDER ENGINES

Model Series	No. Cyls.	Bore	Stroke	Displacement	Power Rating
290400, 290700	2	68 mm (2.68 in.)	66 mm (2.60 in.)	480 cc (29.3 cu.in.)	9.4 kW (12.5 hp)
294400, 294700	2	68 mm (2.68 in.)	66 mm (2.60 in.)	480 cc (29.3 cu.in.)	9.4 kW (12.5 hp)
303400, 303700	2	68 mm (2.68 in.)	66 mm (2.60 in.)	480 cc (29.3 cu.in.)	11.9 kW (16 hp)
350400, 350700	2	72 mm (2.83 in.)	70 mm (2.75 in.)	570 cc (34.75 cu.in.)	13.5 kW (18 hp)
351400, 351700	2	72 mm (2.83 in.)	70 mm (2.75 in.)	570 cc (34.75 cu.in.)	14.8 kW (20 hp)
380400, 380700	2	75 mm (2.83 in.)	70 mm (2.97 in.)	627 cc (38.26 cu.in.)	15.6 kW (21 hp)
381400, 381700	2	75 mm (2.97 in.)	70 mm (2.75 in.)	627 cc (38.26 cu.in.)	17.1 kW (23 hp)

NOTE: Metric fasteners are used throughout engine except threaded hole in PTO end of crankshaft, flange mounting holes and flywheel puller holes, which are US threads.

The Vanguard models included in this section are air-cooled, four-stroke, twin-cylinder engines. Series 290400, 294400, 303400, 350400, 351400, 380400 and 381400 have a horizontal crankshaft. Series 290700, 294700, 303700, 350700, 351700, 380700 and 381700 have a vertical crankshaft. All models are equipped with an overhead valve system. Number 1 cylinder is nearer flywheel. Cylinder number is marked on cylinder side nearest flywheel.

Refer to BRIGGS & STRATTON ENGINE IDENTIFICATION INFORMATION section for engine identification. Engine model number as well as the type and code numbers are necessary when ordering parts.

MAINTENANCE

LUBRICATION

The engine is lubricated with oil supplied by a rotor-type oil pump attached to the crankcase cover or oil pan.

Periodically check oil level; do not overfill. Oil dipstick should be screwed in until bottomed for correct oil level reading. Change oil after first eight hours of operation and every 50 hours thereafter under normal operating conditions. Recommended oil change interval is 25 hours if severe service is encountered.

The engine may be equipped with a spin-on oil filter. If so equipped, manufacturer recommends changing oil filter after every 100 hours of operation. Filter should be changed more frequently if engine is operated in a severe environment.

Manufacturer recommends using oil with an API service classification of SH or SJ or any classification formulated to supercede SH or SJ. Use SAE 30 oil for temperatures above 40° F (4° C), SAE 10W-30 oil for temperatures between 0° F (–18° C) and 40° F (4° C), and below 0° F (–18° C), use petroleum based SAE 5W-20 or a suitable synthetic oil. Do not use 10W-40 oil.

Crankcase capacity is 1.65 liters (3.5 pints) if equipped with an oil filter, 1.42 liters (3 pints) if not equipped with a filter.

A low oil pressure switch may be located on the oil filter housing, if so equipped. Switch should be closed at zero pressure and open at 31 kPa (4.5 psi).

FUEL FILTER

The fuel tank is equipped with a filter at the outlet and an inline filter may be installed. Check filters annually and periodically during operating season.

CRANKCASE BREATHER

The engine is equipped with a crankcase breather that provides a vacuum for the crankcase. Vapor from the crankcase is evacuated to the air cleaner. A fiber disk on early models or a reed valve on later models (Fig. B801) acts as a one-way valve to maintain crankcase vacuum. The breather system must operate properly or excessive oil consumption can result. The breather assembly is located in the valley between the cylinders.

On early models with a fiber disc, it should be possible to insert a 1.0 mm (0.045 in.) wire between the disc and breather body; do not use excessive force when measuring

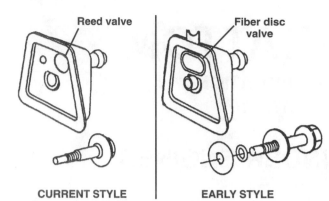

Fig. B801–Later models are equipped with a reed valve in the breather housing while early models are equipped with a fiber disc.

CURRENT STYLE   **EARLY STYLE**

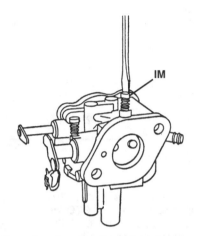

Fig. B802–View showing location of carburetor idle mixture screw on one-barrel carburetor for horizontal crankshaft models.

gap. Disc should not stick or bind during operation. Replace if distorted or damaged.

On later models with a reed valve, check that the valve seats properly. Do not press against reed valve. Replace if distorted or damaged.

Inspect breather tube for leakage.

SPARK PLUG

Recommended spark plug is either an Autolite 3924 or Champion RC12YC. Specified spark plug electrode gap is 0.76 mm (0.030 in.). Tighten spark plug to 20 N•m (180 in.-lb.).

> CAUTION: Briggs & Stratton does not recommend using abrasive blasting to clean spark plugs as this may introduce some abrasive material into the engine that could cause extensive damage.

CARBURETOR

Adjustment

Turn idle mixture screw (IM–Figs. B802 or B803) 1¼ turns out from seated position. Remove air cleaner, carburetor cover and valley cover, if so equipped, for access to governor linkage. Place remote speed control in idle position. Bend throttle restrictor tang shown in Fig. B804 so throttle cannot open greater than open. Run engine until operating temperature is reached. Place remote speed control in idle position. Hold carburetor throttle lever against idle speed adjusting screw and adjust idle speed to 1400 rpm if governed idle spring (S–Fig. B805) is red, or to 1100 rpm if governed idle spring is white. With throttle lever against idle speed adjusting screw, turn idle mixture screw clockwise until a reduction in engine speed is noted and mark screw position. Back out idle mixture screw until engine speed lessens again and mark screw position. Rotate screw so it is halfway between the two marked positions. With throttle lever against idle speed screw, readjust idle speed to 1200 rpm if governed idle spring is red, or to 900 rpm if governed idle spring is white. Release throttle lever. With remote control in governed idle position, bend tab (T–Fig. B805), to obtain 1400 rpm if governed idle spring is red, or to 1100 rpm if governed idle spring is white.

All models are equipped with a fixed high-speed jet. An optional jet for high altitude operation is offered on vertical crankshaft models.

Fig. B803–View showing location of carburetor idle mixture screw on one-barrel carburetor for vertical crankshaft models.

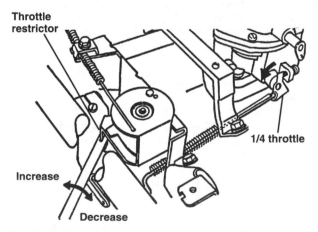

Throttle restrictor

1/4 throttle

Increase

Decrease

Fig. B804–Bend throttle restrictor tang as outlined in text.

Overhaul

One-Barrel Horizontal Crankshaft Models

Refer to Fig. B806 or Fig. B807 for an exploded view of carburetor. On Series 350400 engines, mark choke plate so it can be installed in original position and do not lose detent ball when withdrawing choke shaft. Note the following when assembling carburetor: On all engines except

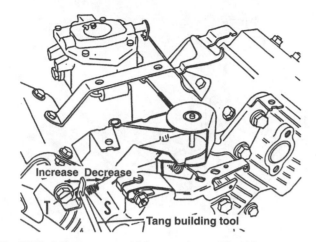

Fig. B805–Adjust governed idle speed as outlined in text.

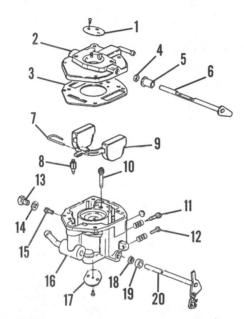

Fig, B806–Exploded view of one-barrel carburetor used on horizontal crankshaft models expect Series 350400.

1. Choke plate	11. Idle mixture screw
2. Cover	12. Idle speed screw
3. Gasket	13. Plug
4. Seal	14. Gasket
5. Spacer	15. Main jet
6. Choke shaft	16. Body
7. Float pin	17. Throttle plate
8. Fuel inlet valve	18. Seal
9. Float	19. Spacer
10. Nozzle	20. Throttle shaft

Series 350400, apply sealant to Welch plug and install choke plate so hole in plate is toward vent tube (Fig. B808). On all models, install throttle shaft seals with lip facing out. Install throttle plate so flat portion (not sharp edge) of chamfers on plate fit against carburetor bore when plate and shaft are installed in carburetor.

On Series 350400 engine, float should be parallel with top cover as shown in Fig. B809. Bend tang on float arm to adjust float level. To adjust float level on all other horizontal crankshaft engines, note if a fuel pump is used because float level is different for gravity-feed or pressure-feed carburetors. Position carburetor a little past vertical as shown in Fig. B810 and press lightly against float pin so fuel valve

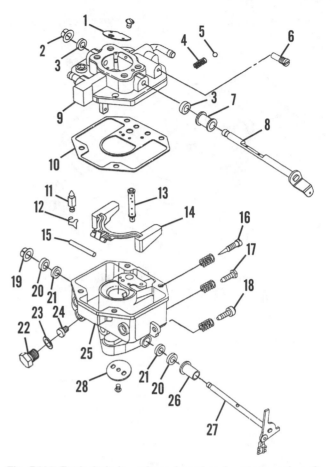

Fig. B807–Exploded view of one-barrel carburetor used on Series 350400 engines.

1. Choke plate	15. Float pin
2. Retiner	16. Idle mixture screw
3. Felt seal	17. Drain screw
4. Spring	18. Idle speed screw
5. Choke shaft detent ball	19. Retainer
6. Idle jet	20. Foam seal
7. Spacer	21. Seal
8. Choke shaft	22. Plug
9. Cover	23. Gasket
10. Gasket	24. Main jet
11. Fuel inlet valve	25. Body
12. Clip	26. Spacer
13. Nozzle	27. Throttle shaft
14. Float	28. Throttle plate

just bottoms against seat. On fuel pump equipped engines, float height (H) should be 1.6 mm ($\frac{1}{16}$ in.). On gravity-feed carburetors, float height (H) should be 2.4 mm ($\frac{3}{32}$ in.). Measure float height at a point on float just before end radius. Adjust float level by bending float tang. Note that spacer between carburetor and intake manifold has an indexing pin that must fit into intake manifold. Tighten carburetor mounting screws to 7 N•m (62 in.-lb.).

One-Barrel Vertical Crankshaft Models

Refer to Fig. B811 for an exploded view of carburetor. On Series 350700, the idle jet is located in side of carburetor as shown in Fig. B812 and the main jet is located in the side of the nozzle stanchion as shown in Fig. B813.

When removing or installing nozzle (Fig. B813) on Series 350700, main jet must be removed. Apply sealant to Welch plug on top of carburetor. Install throttle plate so numbers on plate are down as shown in Fig. B814. Install

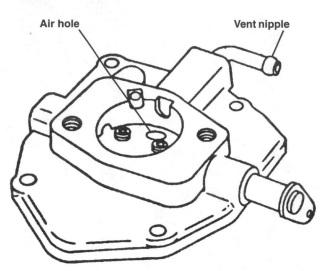

Fig. B808–Install choke plate so hole in plate is toward vent on one-barrel carburetor used on horizontal crankshaft models except Series 350400.

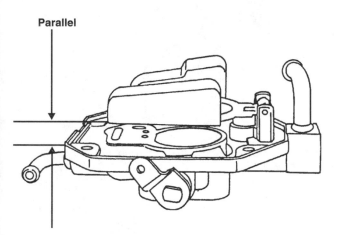

Fig. B809–Float level should be parallel with top cover on carburetor used on Series 350400 engines.

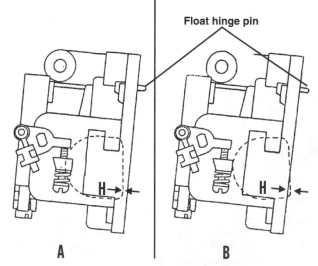

Fig. B810–The one-barrel carburetor used on horizontal crankshaft models except Series 350400, must be held in a near-vertical position as shown when checking float height (H). Fuel pump carburetor is shown in left drawing "A" and gravity feed carburetor is shown in right drawing "B". See text.

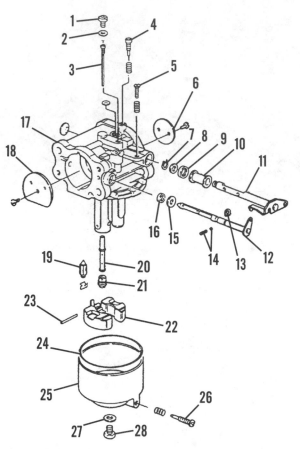

Fig. B811–Exploded view of one-barrel carburetor used on vertical crankshaft models. The idle jet and main jet on Series 350700 engines are located as shown in Figs. B812 and B813.

1. Plug	16. Felt seal
2. Washer	17. Body
3. Idle jet	18. Choke plate
4. Idle mixture screw	19. Fuel inlet
5. Idle speed screw	valve
6. Throttle plate	20. Nozzle
7. Clip	21. Main jet
8. Seal	22. Float
9. Foam seal	23. Pin
10. Spacer	24. Gasket
11. Throttle shaft	25. Fuel bowl
12. Choke shaft	26. Drain screw
13. Clip	27. Gasket
14. Choke detent ball	28. Bowl retainer
15. Washer	

Fig. B812–Idle jet is located on side of carburetor on Series 350700 engines.

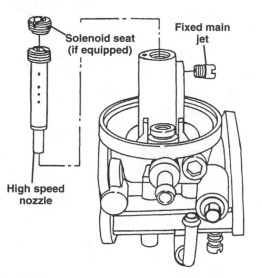

Fig. B813–Main jet is located in side of carburetor nozzle stanchion on Series 350700 engines.

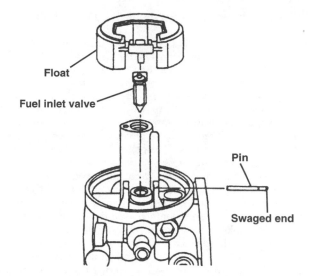

Fig. B816–On Series 350700 engines, install float pin so swaged end is out.

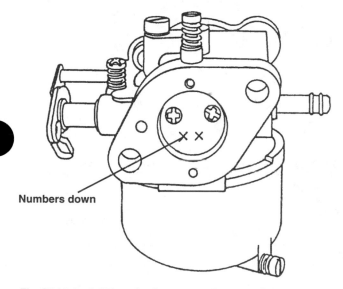

Fig. B814–Install throttle plate so numbers on plate are down.

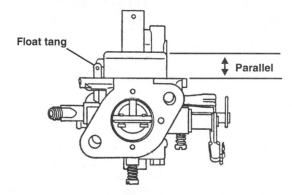

Fig. B817–Float must be level with body surface. Bend float tang to adjust.

be parallel with bowl mating surface. Bend float tang to adjust float level. Note the spacer between carburetor and intake manifold has an indexing pin that must fit into intake manifold. Tighten carburetor mounting screws to 7 N•m (62 in.-lb.).

Two-Barrel Carburetor

Series 351000 and 380000 engines use a two-venturi (two-barrel) side-draft carburetor (Fig. B818). Service procedures are nearly identical for all carburetors in these two series except for idle mixture screw location and main jet sizes. The L and R markings (Fig. B819) on the carburetor float bowl identify the cylinders: L is No. 1 cylinder and R is No. 2 cylinder. Note that the fixed main jets (17–Fig. B818) are not identical. Jet sizes are as follows:

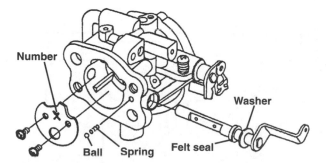

Fig. B815–Install choke plate so number is out and hole is down.

SERIES	MAIN JET
351400	#94 (L) #98 (R)
351700	#98 (L) #100 (R)
380400	#110 (L) #114 (R)
380700	#118 (L) #116 (R)

throttle shaft seals with lip facing out. Install the choke plate so the number is out and the hole is down as shown in Fig. B815. On Series 350700, install float pin so swaged end is out as shown in Fig. B816. To check float level, invert carburetor body as shown in Fig. B817. Float should

When servicing the carburetor, note routing of anit-afterfire solenoid wire when removing the solenoid. Remove idle mixture screw limiter caps (4–Fig. B818) by pulling with pliers; discard if damaged. Discard all used gaskets.

Separate the float bowl (13) from the upper body (6) for access to internal components. The float hinge pin (9) must be removed and installed from the throttle lever side of the carburetor body. Outer end of pin must be installed flush with support post to prevent interference with the float bowl. Remove the float (10), fuel inlet valve (8), idle jets (16), main jets (17) and idle mixture screws (5). Throttle and choke plates (2 and 7) have beveled edges and do not have identifying markings. Mark the plates before removing, and reinstall in the same locations and positions.

Clean dirt and gum deposits from the carburetor with a suitable commercial carburetor cleaner. DO NOT soak plastic, neoprene or rubber parts in solvent. Inspect the carburetor carefully and replace damaged components. Throttle and choke shafts ride directly in carburetor body bores without bushings. Shaft-to-bore wear should not exceed 0.25 mm (0.010 in.). Throttle and choke shafts are replaceable. Carburetor must be replaced if the shaft bores are excessively worn.

Install new throttle and choke shaft seals (19 and 21) with sealing lip facing outward. Lightly coat the threads of throttle and choke plate screws with Loctite 222 or equivalent. Fuel inlet valve (8) is replaceable, but the seat is not. Carburetor must be replaced if the valve seat is damaged. Float level is not adjustable.

If equipped with anti-afterfire solenoid (14), tighten solenoid to 10 N•m (90 in.-lb.). Route the solenoid wire through the hole in No. 1 cylinder shroud. Carburetor-to-engine and air filter-to-carburetor fasteners should be tightened to 7 N•m (65 in.-lb.).

Adjust carburetor as follows: Initial adjustment for idle mixture screws is ¾ turn out from lightly seated position. DO NOT force screws when seating. Start the engine and run until operating temperature is reached (about five minutes). Connect an accurate tachometer to the engine. Set throttle control in the SLOW position. Hold the throttle lever against idle speed stop screw and adjust idle speed to 1200 rpm. While still holding throttle lever against idle speed screw, slowly close (turn clockwise) No. 1 cylinder idle mixture screw until engine speed begins to decrease from lean mixture, then open the mixture screw exactly turn. Check idle speed and readjust to 1200 rpm if necessary. Repeat the mixture screw adjustment for No. 2 cylinder.

Adjust idle speed as follows: If engine has RED governed idle spring, adjust idle speed to 1200 rpm. If engine has WHITE governed idle spring, adjust idle speed to 900 rpm. Release the throttle lever and note idle rpm. If engine has RED governed idle spring, idle speed should be 1750 rpm. If engine has WHITE governed idle spring, idle speed should be 1100 rpm. If necessary, bend governed idle spring tang on throttle control bracket to bring idle speed to correct rpm. With throttle control still in SLOW position and engine rpm at governed idle speed, bend throttle restrictor tang to just contact governor lever (Fig. B820).

Move throttle control to the FAST position; engine should accelerate smoothly. If the engine stumbles, turn the idle mixture screws out (counterclockwise) up to turn to enrich the mixture for smooth acceleration. Install limiter caps on idle mixture screws so that cap stop is midway between stops on carburetor body.

ANTI-AFTERFIRE SYSTEM

Some models are equipped with an anti-afterfire system that stops fuel flow through the carburetor when the ignition switch is in the OFF position. A solenoid inserts a

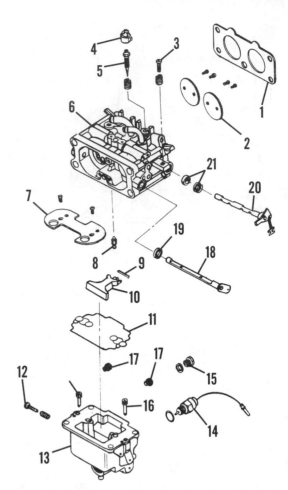

Fig. B818—Exploded view of two-barrel carburetor used on Series 351000 and 380000 engines. Plug (15) is used when not equipped with anti-afterfire solenoid (14).

1. Gasket	12. Fuel drain screw
2. Throttle plates	13. Fuel bowl
3. Idle speed screw	14. Anti-afterfire solenoid
4. Limiter cap	15. Plug
5. Idle mixture screw	16. Idle jets
6. Body	17. Main jets
7. Choke plate	18. Choke shaft
8. Fuel inlet valve	19. Seal
9. Pin	20. Throttle shaft
10. Float	21. Seal assy.
11. Gasket	

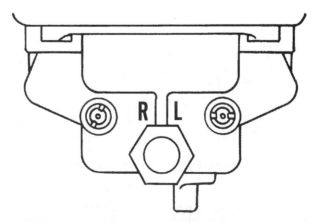

Fig. B819—Fixed main jet location and identification on float bowl of two-barrel carburetor. "R" indicates jet is for No. 2 (right) cylinder and "L" indicates that jet is for No. 1 (left) cylinder. Refer to text.

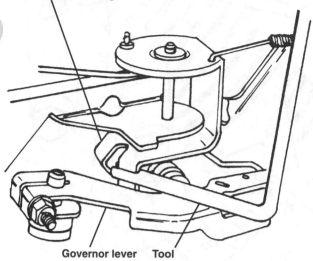

Fig. B820–Adjusting throttle restrictor tang. Refer to text.

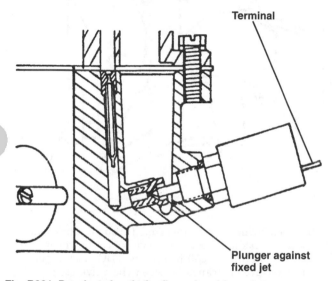

Fig. B821–Drawing of anti-afterfire solenoid used on some carburetors.

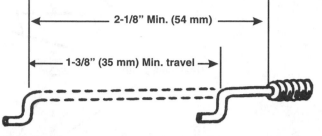

Fig. B822–Remote control wire must extend and travel to dimensions shown above.

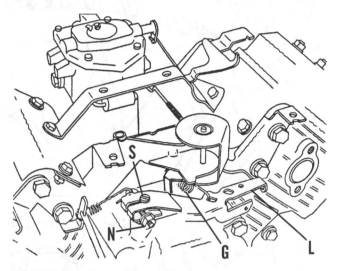

Fig. B823–To adjust governor, loosen governor lever clamp nut (N), rotate governor lever (L) so throttle plate is fully open and hold lever in place. Turn governor shaft (S) counterclockwise and retighten nut.

plunger into the jet to stop fuel flow. The solenoid is attached to the side of the carburetor on horizontal crankshaft engines or to the bottom of the fuel bowl on vertical crankshaft engines. Refer to Fig. B821 for drawing of anti-afterfire system. Solenoid can be removed and tested by connecting a 9-volt battery to solenoid. A faulty solenoid will affect engine performance.

CARBURETOR CONTROL MECHANISM

To ensure proper speed control, measure travel of remote control wire with remote control unit installed. Minimum wire travel is 1⅜ inches as shown in Fig. B822.

To adjust speed control cable, move remote control lever to idle position. Carburetor throttle lever should contact idle speed screw. If not, loosen cable housing clamp and reposition cable housing.

Remote choke control should completely close carburetor choke plate when remote control is in CHOKE position. If necessary, loosen cable clamp and reposition cable to synchronize carburetor choke and remote control.

MECHANICAL GOVERNOR

Most engines are equipped with a mechanical, fly-weight-type governor. To adjust governor linkage, proceed as follows: Remove air cleaner for access to governor linkage. Loosen governor lever clamp nut (N–Fig. B823), rotate governor lever (L) so throttle plate is fully open and hold lever in place. Turn governor shaft (S) counterclockwise as far as possible, then tighten nut (N) to 8 N•m (71 in.-lbs.).

No-load governed top speed is adjusted by bending tang at end of governor spring (G). Normal governed speed is 3600 rpm unless specified otherwise by equipment manufacturer. On remote control engines, governor spring (G) should be attached to oblong hole nearer governor shaft, while governor spring on fixed speed engines should be attached to outer oblong hole on lever.

The governor flyweight assembly is mounted on the end of the camshaft. Refer to CAMSHAFT and GOVERNOR SHAFT sections if internal service is required.

IGNITION SYSTEM

All models are equipped with a Magnetron ignition system.

To check spark, remove spark plug and connect spark plug cable to B&S tester 19051, then ground remaining tester lead to engine. Spin engine at 350 rpm or more. If spark jumps the 4.2 mm (0.166 in.) tester gap, system is functioning properly.

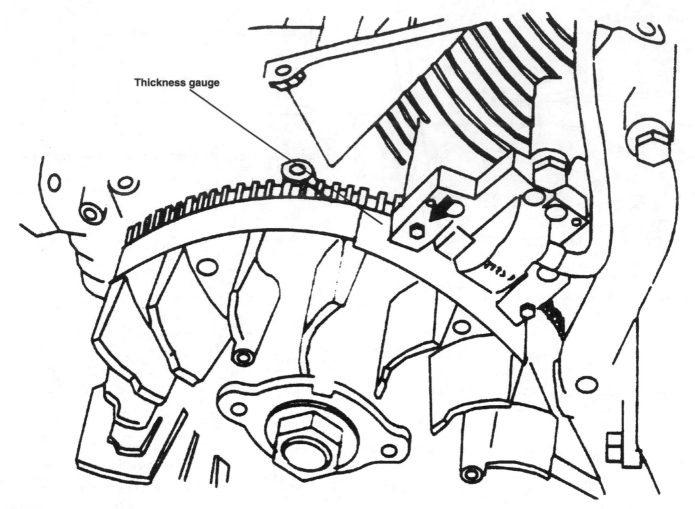

Fig. B824–Adjust armature-to-flywheel air gap.

To remove armature and Magnetron module, remove flywheel shroud and armature retaining screws. Disconnect stop switch wire from module.

When installing armature and module, position armature so air gap between armature legs and flywheel surface is 0.20-0.30 mm (0.008-0.012 in.).

Note that rewind starter cup on Series 350400 and 350700 so equipped, is secured by a screw that must be tightened to 48 N•m (35 ft.-lb.) if removed for access to flywheel.

To prevent cross-fire between the ignition modules (Fig. B824), both stop switch wires running from the modules to the common kill terminal each contain a diode. If any of the following conditions occur when attempting to start or stop the engine, the diode in one or both kill wires is likely faulty:

    a. Will not start due to no spark from either module.

    b. Only runs on one cylinder.

    c. Only shuts off one cylinder.

    d. Continues to run with ignition turned off.

Individual diodes are not replaceable; replace the kill wire if diode is faulty.

VALVE ADJUSTMENT

Adjust valve clearance with engine cold. Remove rocker arm cover. Remove spark plug. Rotate crankshaft so the piston is at top dead center on compression stroke. Using a suitable measuring device inserted through spark plug hole, rotate crankshaft clockwise as viewed at flywheel end so piston is 6.35 mm (0.250 in.) below TDC. Use a feeler gauge to measure clearance between the valve stem and rocker arm. Valve clearance should be 0.10-0.16 mm (0.004-0.006 in.). Loosen locknut (Fig. B825) and turn adjusting screw to obtain desired clearance. Tighten lock screw to 7 N•m (60 in.-lb.). Tighten valve cover screws to 3 N•m (25 in.-lb.).

COMPRESSION PRESSURE

Briggs & Stratton does not publish compression pressure specifications. Compression pressure measured at cranking speed should not vary more than 25 percent between cylinders.

An alternate method of determining internal engine condition is by using a cylinder leak-down tester. The tester is available commercially or from Briggs & Stratton (part No. 19413). Tester uses compressed air to pressurize the combustion chamber, then gauges the amount of leakage past cylinder, piston, rings and valves. Instructions are included with tester.

CYLINDER HEAD

Manufacturer recommends that the cylinder heads be removed and cleaned of deposits after every 500 hours of operation.

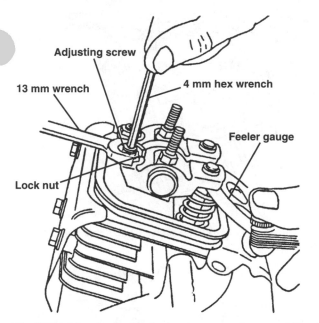

Fig. B825–After loosening locknut, turn rocker arm adjusting screw so valve clearance is 0.10-0.16 mm (0.004-0.006 in,).

REPAIRS

TIGHTENING TORQUE

Recommended tightening torque specifications are as follows:

Alternator stator	2.0 N•m
	(20 in.-lb.)
Carburetor mounting screws	7 N•m
	(60 in.-lb.)
Connecting rod	13 N•m
	(115 in.-lb.)
Crankcase cover/oil pan	17 N•m
	(150 in.-lb.)
Cylinder head	19 N•m
	(165 in.-lb.)
Exhaust flange	17.0 N•m
	(150 in.-lb.)
Flywheel nut	175 N•m
	(130 ft.-lb.)
Governor lever nut	8.0 N•m
	(70 in.-lb.)
Ignition module	3.0 N•m
	(25 in.-lb.)
Intake manifold	16 N•m
	(140 in.-lb.)
Oil pump	7 N•m
	(60 in.-lb.)
Rewind starter	7 N•m
	(60 in.-lb.)
Rocker arm cover	3 N•m
	(25 in.-lb.)
Rocker arm lock screw	7 N•m
	(60 in.-lb.)
Rocker shaft stud	16 N•m
	(140 in.-lb.)
Rocker stud (after Code 96040100)	11.0 N•m
	(100 in.-lb.)
Spark plug	22.5 N•m
	(200 in.-lb.)

CYLINDER HEAD

Cylinder heads are not interchangeable. Cylinder number is cast in area adjacent to the valve springs. To remove the cylinder head, first remove carburetor, intake manifold, muffler, exhaust manifold, air baffles and shields. Remove rocker arm cover, rocker arms and push rods.

NOTE: Do not interchange push rods. Push rods for intake valves are aluminum. Identify position and location of push rods when removing; return the push rods to same locations and positions when reinstalling.

Unscrew cylinder head bolts and remove cylinder head and gasket.

Valve face and seat angles are 45°. Specified seat width is 1.2-1.6 mm (0.047-0.063 in.). Minimum allowable valve margin is 0.4 mm (0.016 in.). See Fig. B826.

The cylinder head is equipped with replaceable valve guides for both valves. Reject the guide if the inside diameter is 6.057 mm (0.2385 in.) or more. Use B&S tool 19274 to remove and install guides. Guides can be installed either way. Top of guide should protrude 7 mm (0.275 in.) as shown in Fig. B827. Use B&S tools 19345 and 19346 to ream valve guide to correct size.

Note the following when reinstalling cylinder head: Do not apply sealer to cylinder head gasket. Sealing washers are used under the heads of the two cylinder head bolts adjacent to the rocker shaft on engines before Code 94050100. Tighten cylinder head bolts using sequence shown in Fig. B828 until final torque reading of 19 N•m (165 in.-lb.) is obtained.

Three styles of rocker arms are used on these engines (Fig. B829). Style 1 rocker arm, used prior to Code 93110100, is stamped steel. Style 2, used between Codes 93110100 and 96040100, is cast aluminum. Style 3, used from Code 96040100, is stamped steel and has its own individual 'saddle' support. Style 3 rocker arm cannot be used on heads designed for Styles 1 or 2. However, Style 3 heads can be installed on earlier engines.

On heads with rocker shaft, the rocker shaft studs are threaded into the cylinder head. Note that rocker shaft stands have offset holes. Hole must be nearer end of shaft as shown in Fig. B830. Tighten studs to 16 N•m (140 in.-lb.) on Style 1 and 2 rocker arm, 11 N•m (100 in.-lb.) on Style 3 arm.

CAMSHAFT

Camshaft and camshaft gear are an integral casting. The governor weight assembly and compression release mechanism are attached to the camshaft. Camshaft, governor and compression release are available only as a unit assembly.

To remove camshaft proceed as follows: Remove engine from equipment and drain crankcase oil. Clean PTO end of crankshaft and remove any burrs or rust. Remove rocker arm push rods and mark them so they can be returned to original position. Unscrew fasteners and remove crankcase cover or oil pan. Rotate crankshaft so timing marks on crankshaft and camshaft gears are aligned (this will position valve tappets out of the way). Remove camshaft and tappets.

Reject size for camshaft bearing journal at flywheel end is 15.933 mm (0.6273 in.); reject size for bearing journal at PTO end is 19.926 mm (0.7845 in.). Reject size for camshaft lobes is 30.25 mm (1.191 in.), except the intake lobe on Series 380000 has a reject size of 31.06 mm (1.223 in.).

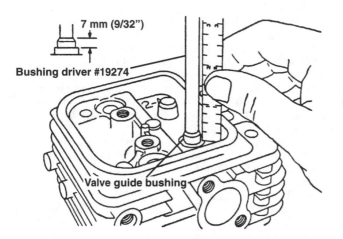

Fig. B826–Valve and valve seat dimension.

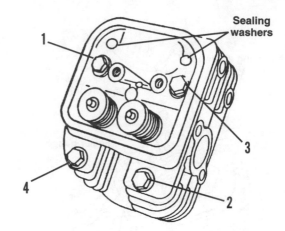

Fig. B828–Follow sequence shown above when tightening cylinder head screws.

Fig. B829–Three different styles of rocker arms used on V-twin engines. Refer to text for correct application.

Fig. B827–Install valve guide so standout is 7.0 mm (0.275) as shown above.

Replace the crankcase if the camshaft bearing bore is 16.08 mm (0.633 in.) or more. Replace crankcase cover or oil pan if camshaft bearing bore is 20.04 mm (0.789 in.) or more.

Be sure compression release and governor components operate freely without binding. Check for loose and excessively worn parts.

Reverse removal procedure to reassemble components. Install camshaft while aligning timing marks (Fig. B831) on crankshaft and camshaft gears. Be sure governor arm is in proper position to contact governor slider on camshaft. Be sure the O-ring (Fig. B832) is in place. Install crankcase cover or oil pan and tighten cover screws to 17 N•m (150 in.-lb.) in sequence shown in Fig. B833. Do not force the mating of the cover with the crankcase. Reassemble remainder of components.

GOVERNOR SHAFT

The governor shaft located in the crankcase cover or oil pan transmits motion from the governor assembly on the camshaft to the governor linkage. The shaft rides in two bushings in the cover. Remove the crankcase cover or oil pan for access to shaft and bushings. Upper bushing is replaceable, but lower bushing is not. If the lower bushing is damaged or excessively worn, replace the crankcase cover or oil pan.

When reinstalling crankcase cover or oil pan, be sure governor arm is in proper position to contact governor slider on camshaft. Complete installation as outlined in CAMSHAFT section.

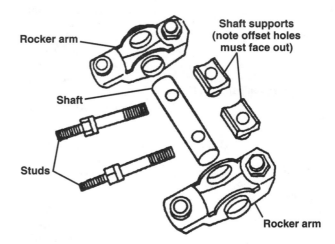

Fig. B830–On heads with rocker shaft, offset hold in shaft supports must be nearer end of rocker shaft.

PISTON, PIN, RINGS AND CONNECTING ROD

To remove piston and rod assembly, drain engine oil and remove engine from equipment. Remove cylinder head as previously outlined. Clean PTO end of crankshaft and remove any burrs or rust. Unscrew fasteners and remove crankcase cover or oil pan. Rotate crankshaft so timing marks on crankshaft and camshaft gears are aligned (this will position valve tappets out of the way). Remove camshaft. Mark rods and caps so they can be installed in original positions. Unscrew connecting rod screws and remove piston and rod.

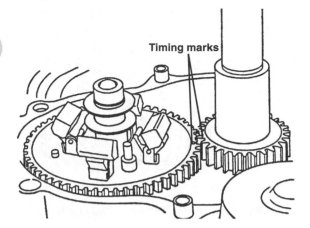

Fig. B831–Timing marks must align after installation of cam-shaft and crankshaft.

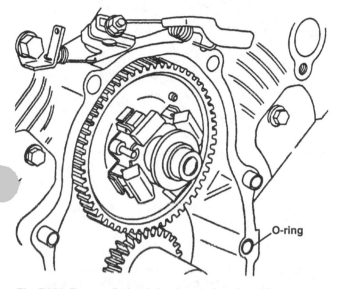

Fig. B832–Be sure O-ring is in place before installing cover.

Reject size for piston ring end gap is 0.76 mm (0.030 in.) for compression and oil rings. The reject size for piston ring side clearance is 0.10 mm (0.004 in.) for compression rings and 0.20 mm (0.008 in.) for oil ring.

Piston pin is a slip fit in piston and rod. Refer to the following table for piston pin and pin bore reject sizes.

Model Series	Piston Pin	Pin Bore
290000-350000	17.06 mm (0.6718 in.)	17.12 mm (0.674 in.)
380000	17.98 mm (0.7078 in.)	18.06 mm (0.711 in.)

The connecting rod rides directly on crankpin. Reject size for rod big end diameter is 37.122 mm (1.4615 in.) and reject size for small end diameter is 17.107 mm (0.6735 in.). A connecting rod with 0.51 mm (0.020 in.) undersize big end diameter is available to accommodate a worn crankpin (machining instructions are included with new rod).

When assembling piston and rod be sure notch or casting mark on piston crown is toward flywheel and OUT side of rod is toward PTO end of engine. Install compression rings

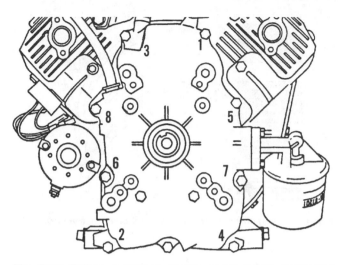

Fig. B833–Follow sequence shown above when tightening crankcase cover or oil pan screws.

with "T" side toward piston crown (Fig. B834). Install piston and rod assembly in engine with notch or casting mark on piston crown toward flywheel (Fig. B835). Install rod cap so marks on rod and cap align and tighten rod screws to 13 N•m (115 in.-lb.).

Install camshaft while aligning timing marks (Fig. B831) on crankshaft and camshaft gears. Be sure governor arm is in proper position to contact governor slider on camshaft. Be sure the O-ring (Fig. B832) is in place. Install crankcase cover or oil pan and tighten screws to 17 N•m (150 in.-lb.) in sequence shown in Fig. B833. Do not force mating of cover with crankcase. Reassemble remainder of components.

CYLINDER BLOCK

If cylinder bore wear exceeds 0.076 mm (0.003 in.) or if out-of-round of bore exceeds 0.038 mm (0.0015 in.), then cylinder should be bored to the next oversize.

Refer to the following table for standard cylinder bore dimensions.

Model Series	Cylinder Bore
290000, 303000	68.00-68.03 mm (2.677-2.678 in.)
350000	72.00-72.03 mm (2.835-2.836 in.)
380000	75.50-75.52 mm (2.9724-2.973 in.)

The crankshaft is supported at the flywheel end by a replaceable bushing in the crankcase. Replace the bushing if bore is 30.086 mm (1.1845 in.) or more on engines before Code 97050100, 35.12 mm (1.383 in.) on engines after Code 97043000. A locating pin secures the bushing in the block. The pin must be driven out before pressing out bushing. Install new bushing so oil holes are aligned. The new locating pin is tapered at both ends; grind off one tapered end. Install pin, tapered end first, using B&S tool 19344 as shown in Fig. B836 until tool bottoms.

Replace the ball bearing in crankcase cover or oil pan if bearing is worn, pitted or turns roughly.

Install oil seal in crankcase so it is flush with outside surface. Install oil seal in crankcase cover or oil pan so seal is 1.6 mm (1/16 in.) below outside surface.

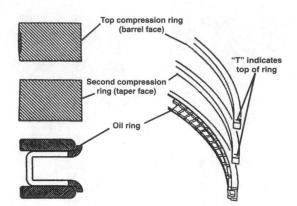

Fig. B834–Drawing showing correct installation of piston rings.

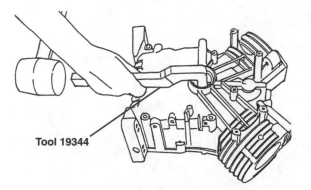

Fig. B836–Install bushing locating pin using B&S tool 19344.

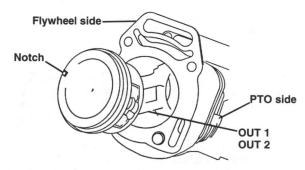

Fig. B835–Install piston and rod so notch or casting mark on piston crown is toward flywheel and "OUT" on rod is toward PTO end of crankshaft.

Fig. B837–Install oil pump rotors so dimples (D) are on the same side.

OIL PUMP

The rotor-type oil pump is located in the crankcase cover or oil pan and driven by the camshaft. Remove crankcase cover or oil pan for access to pump. Note that rotors are installed so dimples (D–Fig. B837) are on same side. Replace any components that are damaged or excessively worn. Tighten oil pump mounting screws to 7 N•m (60 in.-lb.).

When installing crankcase cover or oil pan, be sure governor arm is in proper position to contact governor slider on camshaft. Be sure O-ring (Fig. B832) is in place. Install crankcase cover or oil pan and tighten screws to 17 N•m

(150 in.-lb.) in sequence shown in Fig. B833. Do not force mating of cover with crankcase.

CRANKSHAFT

The crankshaft (39–Fig. B838 or Fig. B839) is supported at the flywheel end by a bushing in the cylinder block and by a ball bearing at the PTO end. Reject crankshaft if worn to 34.92 mm (1.375 in.) or less at PTO bearing journal or if worn to 29.95 mm (1.179 in.) or less at flywheel bearing end. Reject crankshaft if crankpin diameter is worn to 36.96 mm (1.455 in.) or less.

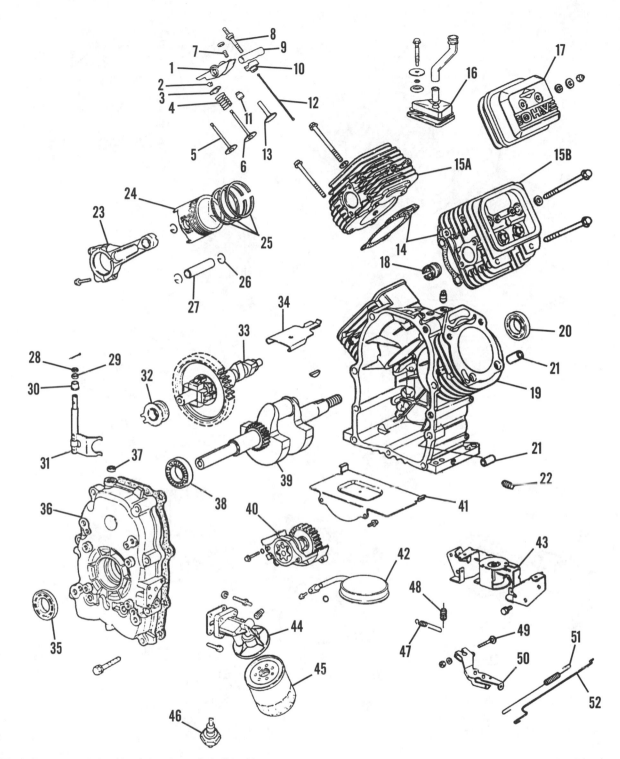

Fig. B838–Exploded view of horizontal crankshaft engine.

1. Rocker arm	15A. Cylinder head (No. 1)	27. Piston ring
2. Retainer	15B. Cylinder head (No. 2)	28. Seal
3. Spring retainer	16. Breather assy.	29. Bushing
4. Valve spring	17. Rocker arm cover	30. Bushing
5. Intake valve	18. Exhaust port liner	31. Governor shaft
6. Exhaust valve	19. Cylinder block	32. Slider
7. Adjusting screw	20. Seal	33. Camshaft
8. Rocker stud	21. Dowel	34. Breather baffle
9. Rocker shaft	22. Oil drain plug	35. Seal
10. Rocker support	23. Connecting rod	36. Crankshaft cover
11. Valve seal	24. Piston	37. Washer
12. Push rod	25. Piston rings	38. Bearing
13. Tappet	26. Retaining rings	39. Crankshaft
14. Head gasket		

40. Oil pump assy.
41. Windage plate
42. Oil pickup
43. Governor bracket
44. Oil filter adapter
45. Oil filter
46. Oil pressure switch
47. Governed idle spring
48. Governor spring
49. Clamp bolt
50. Governor lever
51. Governor link spring
52. Governor link

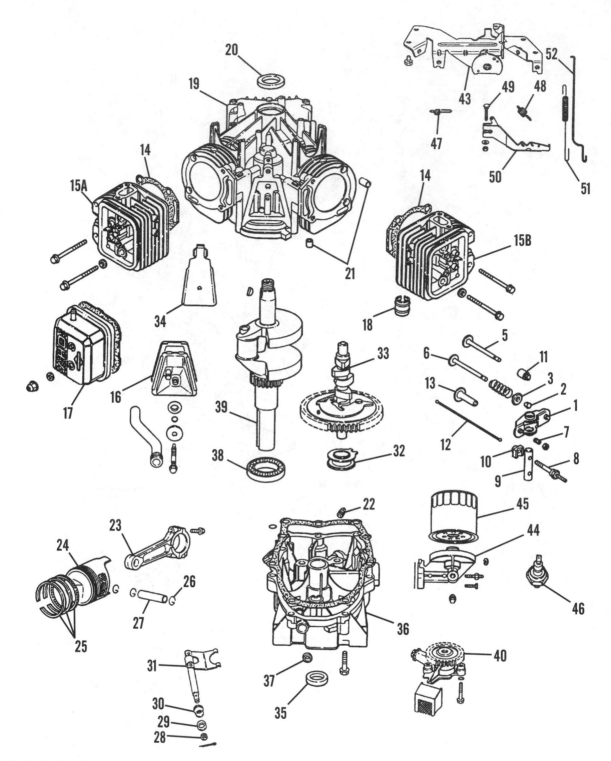

Fig. B839—Exploded view of vertical crankshaft engine. Refer to Fig. B838 for parts identification except: 36. Oil pan.

BRIGGS & STRATTON

SERVICING BRIGGS & STRATTON ACCESSORIES

REWIND STARTER

SINGLE-CYLINDER MODELS
EXCEPT VANGUARD

To replace a broken rewind spring, proceed as follows: Grasp free outer end of spring (S–Fig. BS101) and pull broken end from starter housing. With blower housing removed, bend tangs (T) up and remove starter pulley from housing. Untie knot in rope (R) and remove rope and inner end of broken spring from pulley. Apply a small amount of grease on inner face of pulley. Thread inner end of spring through the notch in the starter housing, and engage the inner end of spring in pulley hub. Place bar in pulley hub,

and turn pulley approximately 13 turns counterclockwise as shown in Fig. BS102. Tie the wrench to the blower housing with wire to hold pulley so hole (H–BS103) in pulley is aligned with rope guide (G) in housing as shown in Fig. BS103. Hook a wire in inner end of rope and thread rope through guide and hole in pulley; then, tie a knot in rope and release the pulley allowing spring to wind rope into pulley groove.

To replace the starter rope only, it is not generally necessary to remove starter pulley and spring. Wind up the spring and install the new rope as outlined in preceding paragraph.

Two different types of starter clutches have been used; refer to exploded view of an early production unit in Fig. BS104 and exploded view of a late production unit in Fig. BS105. The outer end of the late production ratchet (refer

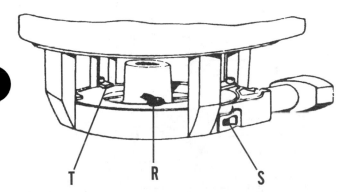

Fig. BS101–View of rewind starter used on single-cylinder engines, except Vanguard models, showing rope (R), spring end (S) and retaining tangs (T).

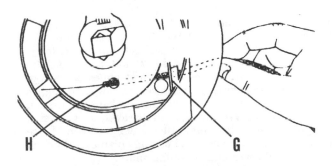

Fig. BS103–Thread rope through (G) in housing and hole (H) in starter pulley with wire hooked in end of rope.

Fig. BS102–Use a square shaft and wrench to wind the rewind starter spring. Refer to text.

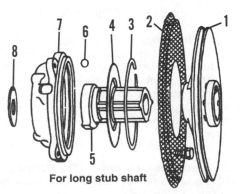

For long stub shaft

Fig. BS104–Exploded view of early production starter clutch unit; refer to Fig. BS107 for "long stub shaft." A late-style unit (Fig. BS105) should be installed when replacing "long" crankshaft with "short" (late production) shaft.

1. Starter rope pulley
2. Roating screen
3. Snap ring
4. Ratchet cover
5. Starter ratchet
6. Steel balls
7. Clutch housing (flywheel nut)
8. Sping washer

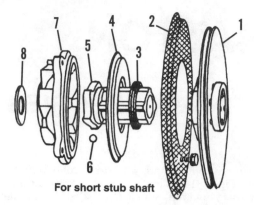

For short stub shaft

Fig. BS105–Exploded view of late production sealed starter clutch unit. Some late-style clutches have a polymer thrust washer between ratchet (5) and housing (7). Some factory-installed clutches have non-metallic composite housing (7) except for threaded nut. All service procedures remain the same.

1. Starter rope pulley	6. Steel balls
2. Rotating screen	7. Clutch housing
3. Snap ring	(flywheel nut)
4. Ratchet cover	8. Spring water
5. Starter ratchet	

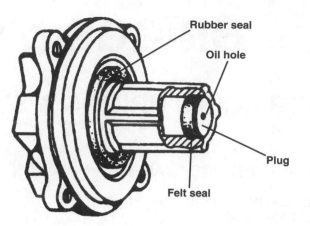

Fig. B106–Cutaway showing felt seal and plug in end of late production starter ratchet (5–Fig. BS105).

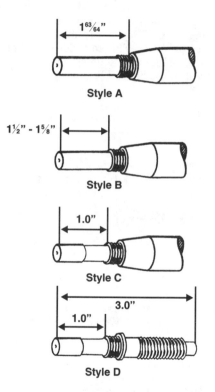

Fig. BS107–Four different styles of crankshaft starter-clutch stub ends used with B&S-design rewind starter. Clutch stub dimensions are measured from end of crankshaft/stub shaft to machined radius at end of stub shank. Refer to text for proper application.

to cut away view in Fig. BS106) is sealed with a felt seal and a retaining plug and a rubber ring is used to seal ratchet to ratchet cover.

To disassemble early type starter clutch unit, refer to Fig. BS104 and proceed as follows: Remove snap ring (3) and lift ratchet (5) and cover (4) from starter housing (7) and crankshaft. Be careful not to lose steel balls (6). Starter housing (7) is also flywheel retaining nut; to remove housing, first remove screen (2) and using B&S flywheel wrench 19114, unscrew housing from crankshaft in counterclockwise direction. When reinstalling housing, be sure spring washer (8) is placed on crankshaft with cup (hollow) side toward flywheel, then install starter housing and tighten securely. Reinstall rotating screen. Place ratchet on crankshaft and into housing and insert the steel balls. Reinstall cover and retaining snap ring.

To disassemble late starter clutch unit, refer to Fig. BS105 and proceed as follows: Remove rotating screen (2) and starter ratchet cover (4). Lift the ratchet (5) from housing and crankshaft and extract the steel balls (6). If necessary to remove housing (7), hold flywheel and unscrew housing in counterclockwise direction using B&S tool 19114. When installing housing, be sure spring washer (8) is in place on crankshaft with cup (hollow) side toward flywheel. Tighten housing securely. Inspect felt seal and plug in outer end of ratchet. Replace the ratchet if seal or plug is damaged, as these parts are not serviced separately. Lubricate the felt with oil and place ratchet on the crankshaft. Insert the steel balls and install ratchet cover, rubber seal and rotating screen.

NOTE: Flyball-type starter clutches (Fig. BS104 and Fig. BS105) are used on four styles of crankshaft stub ends. Refer to Fig. BS107.

If replacing an early-style crankshaft with long stub end (A–Fig. BS107) with a later-style crankshaft (B, C or D), install the late-style (Fig. BS105) starter clutch.

If replacing an early starter clutch (Fig. BS104) with a late-style unit (Fig. BS105), the crankshaft stub end must be shortened to dimension shown for short shaft (Style

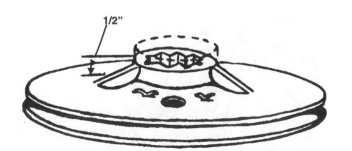

Fig. B108–When installing late-type starter clutch unit as a replacement for early-type, either install new starter rope pulley or cut hub of old pulley to 1/2 inch (12.7 mm) as shown.

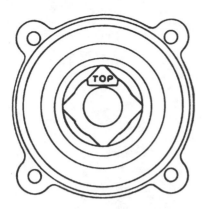

Fig. BS109–When installing blower housing and starter assembly, turn stater ratchet so word "TOP" stamped on outer end of ratchet is toward engine cylinder head.

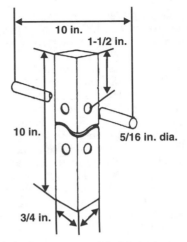

Fig. B112–Use 3/4-inch square stock to fabricate a spring rewind tool to the dimensions shown.

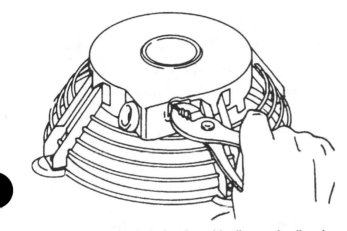

Fig. BS110–Grip outer end of spring with pliers and pull spring out of housing as far as possible. Refer to text.

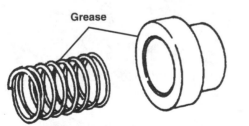

Fig. BS111–Lubricate pulley, spring and adapter with multipurpose grease. Refer to text.

B—Fig. BS107). Bevel the end of the crankshaft approximately $\frac{1}{16}$-inch (1.6 mm) after it is shortened. If starter rope pulley is not being replaced with new style pulley, the old pulley hub must also be shortened to the ½ inch (12.7-mm) dimension shown in Fig. BS108.

Latest Style C and Style D clutch stub shanks are 1.0 inch (25.4 mm) long and are only to be used with late-style clutch (Fig. BS105). Style C is an integral part of the crankshaft, but has the lower inner half of the shank undercut to help prevent debris buildup and subsequent clutch grabbing and starter damage. Style D pilot shaft has a clutch stub identical to Style C, but is a separate shaft that threads into the latest-design crankshafts. Overall length of Style D pilot shaft is 3.0 inch (76 mm).

Replace the clutch-to-flywheel washer if it is cracked or worn. If washer is Belleville design, be sure that high-center inside diameter is toward the clutch.

Prior to inserting clutch over crankshaft stub, thoroughly clean and polish stub shaft and clutch bore. Lightly coat the contact surface of the stub shaft with one to two drops of 10W-30 synthetic engine oil. Insert clutch onto stub shaft with a spinning motion to lubricate the clutch bore. Torque the clutch assembly to the crankshaft. Refer to table below for starter clutch-to-crankshaft tightening torque values.

Series	Torque
170000-250000	65 ft.-lb.
	(88 N•m)
280000	90-100 ft.-lb.
	(122-135 N•m)
400000-420000	150 ft.-lb.
	(203 N•m)

When installing blower housing and starter assembly on horizontal-shaft engines with early-style starter clutch, turn starter ratchet so the word TOP on the ratchet is toward the engine cylinder head (Fig. BS109).

TWIN-CYLINDER MODELS EXCEPT VANGUARD

To remove the rewind starter, remove the four nuts and washers from studs in the blower housing. Separate the starter assembly from blower housing, then separate assembly from blower housing and starter clutch assembly.

To disassemble, remove handle and pin, and allow rope to rewind into housing. Grip end of rope in knot cavity and remove rope. Grip the outer end of the spring with pliers (Fig. BS110) and pull spring out of housing as far as possible. Turn the spring turn and remove from the pulley or bend one of the tangs with B&S tool 19229. Remove starter pulley and detach spring.

Clean spring and housing and oil spring sparingly before reinstallation. If pulley was removed, place a small amount of multipurpose grease on pulley, ratchet spring and ratchet spring adapter (Fig. BS111). Place the ratchet spring, spring adapter and pulley into rewind housing and bend tang using B&S tool 19229 to bend and adjust tang gap to $\frac{1}{16}$ inch (1.6 mm) minimum.

Fabricate a rewind tool (Fig. BS112) and wind pulley counterclockwise until spring is wound tight. Unwind one turn or until hole in pulley for rope knot and eyelet in blower housing are aligned. Lock spring securely in smaller portion of tapered hole. Reinstall rope.

To disassemble starter clutch unit, refer to Fig. BS105 and proceed as follows: Remove rotating screen (2) and starter ratchet cover (4). Lift the ratchet (5) from housing and crankshaft and extract the steel balls (6). If necessary to remove housing (7), hold flywheel and unscrew housing in counterclockwise direction. When installing housing, be sure spring washer (8) is in place on crankshaft with cup (hollow) side toward flywheel; then, tighten housing securely. Inspect felt seal and plug in outer end of ratchet. Replace the ratchet if the seal or plug is damaged, as these parts are not serviced separately. Lubricate the felt with oil and place ratchet on crankshaft. Insert the steel balls and install ratchet cover, rubber seal and rotating screen.

VANGUARD MODELS

Refer to Fig. BS113 for exploded view of the rewind starter. When installing the starter, position starter on the blower housing, then pull out starter rope until dogs engage starter cup. Continue to place tension on rope and tighten starter-mounting screws to 60 in.-lb. (7 N•m).

To install a new rope, proceed as follows. Rope length should be 70 inches (178 cm). Remove starter and extract old rope from the pulley. Allow pulley to unwind then turn pulley counterclockwise until the spring is tightly wound. Rotate pulley clockwise until the rope hole in the pulley is aligned with the rope outlet in the housing. Pass the rope through pulley hole and housing outlet and tie a temporary knot near handle end of rope. Release pulley and allow rope to wind onto pulley. Install rope handle, release temporary knot and allow rope to enter starter.

To disassemble starter, remove rope handle and allow pulley to totally unwind. Remove screw (14–Fig. BS113) and separate retainer (12), dogs (11), springs (10) and brake spring (9) from the pulley. Wear appropriate safety eyewear and gloves before disengaging pulley (7) from starter as spring (6) may uncoil uncontrolled. Place shop towel around pulley and lift pulley out of housing; spring should remain with pulley. Do not attempt to separate spring (6) from cup (5), as they are a unit assembly.

Inspect components for damage and excessive wear. Reverse disassembly procedure to install components. Be sure inner end of rewind spring engages spring retainer adjacent to housing center post. Tighten screw (14) to 70 in.-lb. (8 N•m). Install rope as previously outlined.

NOTE: Repeat failure of starter pulley (7—Fig. BS113) could be the result of excess engine compression caused by incorrect valve tappet clearance or a faulty compression-release mechanism.

12-VOLT STARTER-GENERATOR UNITS

The combination starter-generator functions as a cranking motor when the starting switch is closed. When engine is operating and with the starting switch open, unit operates as a generator. A current-voltage regulator controls generator output and circuit voltage for the battery and various operating requirements. On units where voltage regulator is mounted separately from generator unit, do not mount regulator with cover down, as regulator will not function in this position.

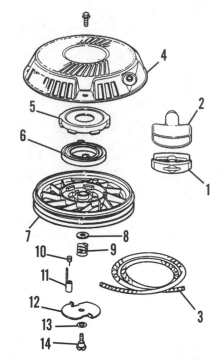

Fig. BS113–Exploded view of rewind starter used on Vanguard models.

1. Insert	8. Washer
2. Rope handle	9. Brake spring
3. Rope	10. Spring
4. Housing	11. Dog
5. Spring cup	12. Retainer
6. Rewind spring	13. Washer
7. Pulley	14. Screw

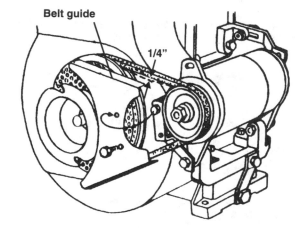

Fig. BS114–View showing starter-generator belt adjustment on models so equipped. Refer to text.

To adjust belt tension, apply approximately 30 pounds (13.6 kg) pull on generator adjusting flange and tighten mounting bolts. Belt tension is correct when a pressure of 10 pounds (44.5 N) applied midway between pulleys will deflect belt inch (6.4 mm). See Fig. BS114. On units equipped with two drive belts, always replace the belts in pairs. A 50-ampere capacity battery is recommended. Starter-generator units are intended for use in temperatures above 0° F (−18° C). Refer to Fig. BS115 for exploded view of starter-generator. Parts and service on starter-generator are available at authorized Delco-Remy service stations.

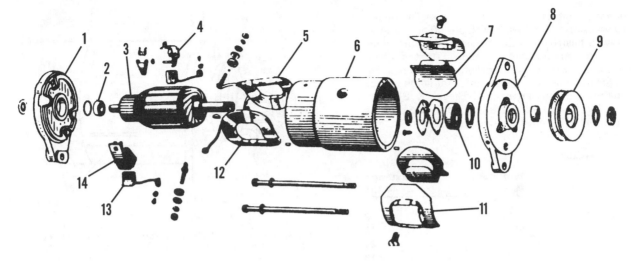

Fig. BS115–Exploded view of Delco-Remy starter generator used on some models.

1. Commutator end frame
2. Bearing
3. Armature
4. Ground brush holder
5. Field coil (left)
6. Frame
7. Pole shoe
8. Drive end frame
9. Pulley
10. Bearing
11. Field coil insulator
12. Field coil (right)
13. Bursh
14. Insulated brush holder

Fig. BS116–Exploded view of 110-volt AC starter motor. A 12-volt DC versionis similar. Rectifier and switch unit (8) is used on 110-volt starter motor only.

1. Pinion gear
2. Helix
3. Armature shaft
4. Drive cup
5. Thrust washer
6. Housing
7. End cap
8. Rectifier & switch unit
9. Bolt
10. Nut

Fig. BS117–Exploded view of 12-volt DC starter motor used on some models.

1. Cap
2. Roll pin
3. Retainer
4. Pinion spring
5. Spring cup
6. Starter gear
7. Clutch assy.
8. Drive end cap assy.
9. Armature
10. Housing
11. Spring
12. Brush assy.
13. Battery wire terminal
14. Commutator end cap assy.

GEAR DRIVE STARTERS

Gear drive starters manufactured by Briggs & Stratton, American Bosch or Mitsubishi may be used, either as a 110-volt AC starter or a 12-volt DC starter. Refer to Figs. BS116 and BS117 for exploded views of starter motors. A properly grounded receptacle should be used with power cord connected to 110-volt AC starter motor. A 32-ampere hour capacity battery is recommended for use with 12-volt starter motor.

CAUTION: Do not clamp starter motor housing in a vise or strike housing as some motors have ceramic field magnets that may be damaged.

To replace a worn or damaged flywheel ring gear, drill out the retaining rivet. Attach the new ring gear using screws provided with new ring gear.

To check for correct operation of starter motor, remove starter motor from engine and place motor in a vise or other holding fixture. Install a 0-5-amp ammeter in power cord to 110-volt AC starter motor. On 12-volt DC motor, connect a 12-volt battery to motor with a 0-50 amp ammeter in series with positive line from battery to starter motor. Connect a tachometer to drive end of starter motor. Determine manufacturer of starter motor and refer to following table for test specifications (note that some motors are tested using a 6-volt battery). If Briggs & Stratton manufactured the 12-volt starter motor, measure housing length (except on Vanguard models) as shown in Fig. BS118.

12-Volt Starter Motor

Starter Motor	Minimum Rpm	Maximum Amps
B&S		
3 in.	6500	18
3 $\frac{1}{16}$ in.	6500	18
3 $\frac{3}{8}$ in.	7000	24
3 $\frac{5}{8}$ in.	6500	18
3 $\frac{13}{16}$ in.	6900	19
3 $\frac{21}{32}$ in.	5000	20
3 $\frac{3}{4}$ in.	6900	19
4 $\frac{3}{8}$ in.	6500	20
4 $\frac{1}{2}$ in.	6500	35
4 $\frac{9}{16}$ in.	6500	35
Vanguard	6500	35
Bosch		
SME-12A-8*	5000	25
SMH-12A-11	4800	16
1965-23-MO- 30-SM	5500	16
Mitsubishi		
MOO1TO2271*, MMO-4FL*,		
MMO-5ML*	6700	16

*Use 6-volt battery for tests.

On OHV engines with solenoid-style starters, remove heavy-gauge solenoid-to-starter cable prior to testing starter motor as outlined in previous paragraph. If tests indicate starter is good, check for faulty solenoid, ignition switch and related starter circuit wiring.

To test solenoid, connect jumper wires from a separate 12-volt power source to the two small terminals on the solenoid. An audible 'click' should be produced indicating solenoid is functioning. As a further test, connect ohmmeter leads to large terminals on solenoid. When solenoid is activated and a 'click' is heard, the ohmmeter should indicate continuity. A meter reading of high resistance or infinity indicates faulty solenoid contacts, and solenoid should be replaced.

To test ignition switch, use an ohmmeter to check for continuity at the switch terminals. Terminal positions for Briggs & Stratton 5-terminal and 6-terminal switches are shown in Fig. BS119. Terminal 1 is internally grounded. Note that terminal positions may be different for switches supplied by manufacturers other than Briggs & Stratton. Refer to the Terminals With Continuity table for switch position and terminal continuity. Replace the switch if test readings indicate a faulty switch.

Terminals With Continuity

Key Position	5-Terminal Switch	6-Terminal Switch
OFF	1-3	1-3-6
RUN	2-5	2-5-6
START	2-4-5	2-4-5

Replace the switch if test readings indicate a faulty switch.

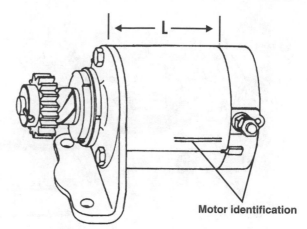

Fig. BS118–On B&S starters, measure length (L) of stater housing to determine correct test specifications. Refer to text.

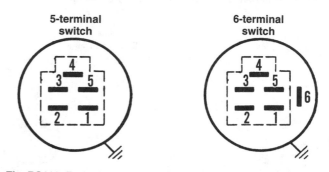

Fig. BS119–Rear view of both the 5-position and 6-position B&S ignition switches.

110-Volt Starter Motor

Starter Motor	Minimum Rpm	Maximum Amps
B&S	6500	2.7
Bosch		
SME-110-C3,		
SME-110-C6		
SME-110-C8	7400	3.5
06026-28-		
M030SM	7400	3
Mitsubishi		
J282188	7800	3.5

If starter motor does not operate satisfactorily, check operation of rectifier in starter control box. If the rectifier and the starter switch are good, disassemble and inspect starter motor.

Two types of rectifiers have been used with 110-volt AC starter motors. The early type is contained in the control box (8–Fig. BS116) mounted on the motor. The later type has four prongs and can be removed from the remote control box. To check rectifier in the control box (8–Fig. BS116), remove the control box from starter motor. Solder a 10,000-ohm, 1-watt resistor to DC internal terminals of rectifier as shown in Fig. BS120. Connect a 0-100 range DC voltmeter to resistor leads. Measure voltage of AC outlet to be used. With starter switch in the "OFF position, a zero reading should be shown on DC voltmeter. With starter switch in the ON position, the DC voltmeter should show a reading that is 0-14 volts lower than AC line voltage measured previously. If voltage drop exceeds 14 volts, replace the rectifier unit.

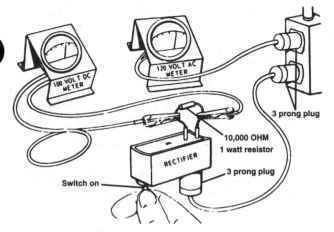

Fig. BS120–View of test connections for 110-volt rectifier. Refer to text for test procedures.

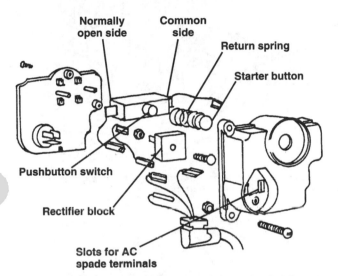

Fig. B121–Exploded view of control unit for 110-volt AC starter motor used on some engines.

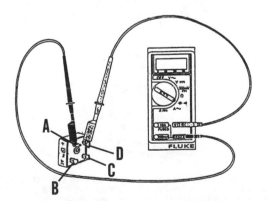

Fig. B122–Identify terminals on rectifier as shown and refer to text for test procedure. Note that "A" is adjacent to "+" on rectifier case.

To check rectifier in remote control box (Fig. BS121), remove back plate on box and remove rectifier. Use a suitable ohmmeter and check continuity between terminals identified in Fig. BS122. If tests are not as indicated in following table, replace the rectifier.

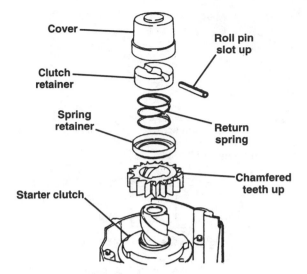

Fig. BS123–Exploded view of starter drive used on some early production starters.

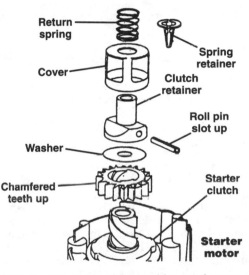

Fig. BS124–Exploded view of starter drive used on some current production starters.

(+) Tester Lead	(–) Tester Lead	Tester Reading
A	B	Infinity
B	A	Continuity
B	C	Infinity
C	B	Continuity
C	D	Continuity
D	C	Infinity
D	A	Continuity
A	D	Infinity

There should be no continuity between any terminal and the rectifier case, otherwise, replace the rectifier.

Disassembly of starter motor is self-evident after inspection of unit and referral to Figs. BS116, BS117, BS123 and BS124. Mark housing and end caps before disassembly and note position of bolts during disassembly so they can be installed in their original positions during assembly.

On Briggs & Stratton motors, minimum brush length is inch (3.2 mm) and minimum commutator diameter is 1.23 inches (31.24 mm) for 12-volt starter and 1.32 inches

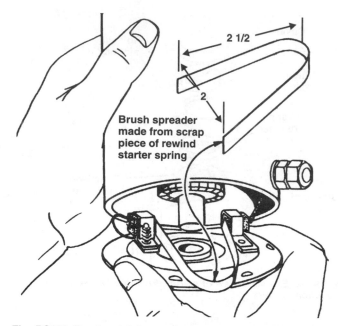

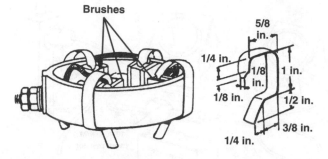

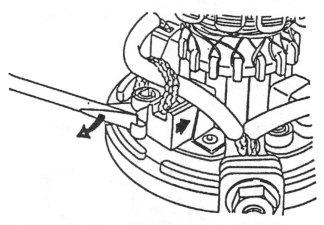

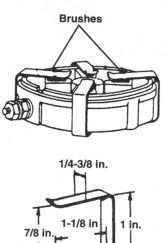

Fig. BS125–Brush retaining tool shown can be fabricated to hold the type of brushes shown when installing motor end cap.

Fig. BS126–To hold brushes shown while assembling starter motor, a brush retainer tool can be fabricated from a piece of rewind starter spring using the dimensions shown.

Fig. BS127–Position end of retaining spring against rear of brush as shown to hold brush in guide.

Fig. BS128–To hold brushes shown while assembling starter motor, a brush retainer tool can be fabricated from a piece of rewind starter spring using the dimensions shown.

(33.53 mm) for 120-volt starter. Lubricate bearings with SAE 20 oil.

If so equipped, be sure to match drive cap keyway to stamped key in housing when sliding armature into motor housing.

Note installation of brushes in Figs. BS125, BS126, BS127 and BS128. If the helix (2–Fig. BS116) is separate, splined end must be toward end of armature shaft as shown in Fig. BS129. Some early starters are equipped with shim washers to limit armature shaft end play to 0.006-0.038 inch (0.15-0.96 mm). Tighten armature shaft nut on models so equipped to 170 in.-lb. (19 N•m). Tighten through-bolts if 10-24 to 40-45 in.-lb. (4.5-5.1 N•m), or if ¼-20 to 45-55 in.-lb. (5.1-6.2 N•m). On models equipped with a retaining pin (Figs. BS123 or BS124), install pin so split is toward end of armature shaft. Note the position of drive components in Figs. BS123 and BS124.

Some electric-start engines have a factory-installed plastic composite flywheel ring gear. This gear requires a different-design starter bendix gear. The compatibility of the ring gear and bendix gear must be maintained to prevent damage. Replacement ring gears are aluminum alloy.

Aluminum ring gears MUST USE Style A bendix gear shown in Fig.BS130.

Style A bendix gear has beveled-edge teeth on one side of the gear. It must be installed with beveled teeth edges toward the ring gear.

Plastic ring gears MUST USE Style B bendix gear. Style B bendix gear has straight-cut teeth with rounded edges on the gaps between the teeth. It must be installed with round-edge gaps toward the ring gear.

Some single-cylinder Series 28xxxx and 31xxxx engines and some Vanguard V-twin engines are equipped with a heavy-duty starter and a steel flywheel ring gear. Refer to Fig. BS131 for exploded view of starter. DO NOT use this starter on engines with aluminum or plastic ring gear, and DO NOT use starter for plastic ring gear engines on engines with steel ring gear.

On engines equipped with a wire ring used as a retainer for the bendix drive (Fig. BS130), ring removal is made easier by using B&S tool 19436. Tool 19435 is used to install the ring.

ALTERNATOR

Note the configuration, color of stator leads and wire connector to identify the alternator type. Refer to Figs. BS132, BS133, BS138, BS139, BS140, BS144, BS148, BS149, BS150, BS151, BS152, BS161, BS162 and BS163.

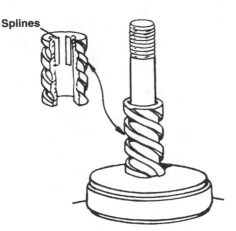

Fig. BS129–Install helix on armature so splines of helix are toward outer end of shaft as shown.

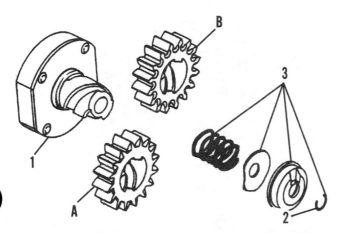

Fig. BS130–Exploded view of starter drive and two different types of drive gears used on later-style starters except those with steel ring gears (see Fig. BS131). Refer to text for starter gear-to-ring gear compatibility.

A. Gear for aluminum
   ring gear
B. Gear for plastic
   ring gear

1. Bendix clutch
2. C-ring retainer
3. Return spring,
   wave washer & cap

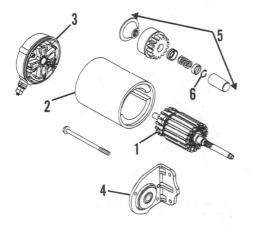

Fig. BS131–Exploded view of 12-volt inertia-drive starter motor and bendix used on single-cylinder Series 28xxx and 31xxx engines and two-cylinder Vanguard engines with steel ring gear. Do not use this starter on engines with plastic or aluminum ring gear.

1. Armature
2. Housing
3. End cap & brushes

4. Drive end
5. Bendix assy.
6. C-ring retainer

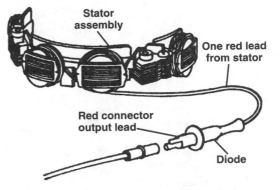

Fig. BS132–Drawing of 3-amp DC alternator used on some models.

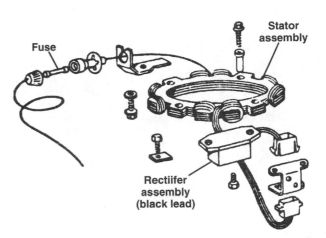

Fig. BS133–Stator and rectifier assemblies used on the 4-amp alternator.

Identify type to be serviced and refer to appropriate following section.

3-AMP DC ALTERNATOR

The 3-amp DC alternator (Fig. BS132) is regulated only by engine speed and provides 2- to 3-amp charging current to maintain battery state of charge.

To check output, connect an ammeter in series with red lead, start engine and run at 2400 rpm. Ammeter should show 2-amp charging current. Increase engine speed to 3600 rpm. Ammeter should show 3-amp charging current. If charging current is not as specified, stop engine and connect an ohmmeter lead to laminations of stator and connect remaining ohmmeter lead to red stator lead. Ohmmeter should indicate continuity. If not, replace the stator. If continuity is indicated, but the system fails to produce charging current, inspect magnets in flywheel.

4-AMP ALTERNATOR

Some engines are equipped with the 4-amp alternator shown in Fig. BS133 that is regulated only by engine speed. A solid-state rectifier and 7-amp fuse are used with this alternator.

If the battery is run down and no output from the alternator is suspected, first check the 7-amp fuse. If the fuse is good, clean and tighten all connections. Disconnect charging lead and connect an ammeter as shown in Fig. BS134. Start the engine and check for alternator output. If ammeter shows no charge, stop engine, remove ammeter and install a test lamp as shown in Fig. BS135. Test lamp should

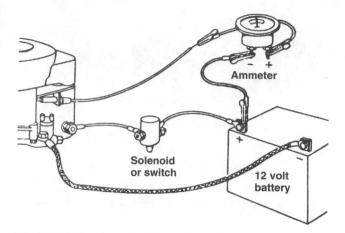

Fig. BS134—Connect ammeter as shown for output test.

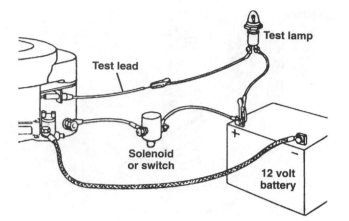

Fig. BS135—Connect a test lamp as shown to test for shorted stator or defective rectifier. Refer to text.

not light. If it does light, the stator or rectifier is defective. Unplug rectifier plug under blower housing. If test lamp does not go out, stator is shorted.

If shorted stator is indicated, use an ohmmeter and check continuity as follows: Touch one test lead to lead inside of fuse holder as shown in Fig. BS136. Touch remaining test lead to each of the four pins in rectifier connector. Unless ohmmeter shows continuity at each of the four pins, stator winding is open and stator must be replaced.

If defective rectifier is indicated, unbolt and remove flywheel blower housing with rectifier. Connect one ohmmeter test lead to blower housing and remaining test lead to the single pin connector in rectifier connector. See Fig. BS137. Check for continuity, then reverse leads and again test for continuity. If tests show no continuity in either direction or continuity in both directions, rectifier is faulty and must be replaced.

5-AMP AC ALTERNATOR

The 5-amp alternator shown in Fig. BS138 provides alternating current that is regulated only by engine speed.

To check alternator, connect a voltmeter to black stator lead and check voltage reading with engine running at 3600 rpm. Voltage reading should be at least 14 volts. If not, replace the stator.

5-AMP AND 9-AMP REGULATED ALTERNATOR

The 5-amp and 9-amp alternators (Fig. BS139) provide regulated charging current. Charging rate is determined by the state of the charge in the battery. Stator is located under the flywheel and output capacity is determined by the size of magnets cast into the flywheel.

Alternator output is determined by the size of the flywheel magnets. Magnets are $\frac{1}{16}$ inch $\times$ $\frac{7}{8}$ inch (18 mm $\times$ 22 mm) on 5-amp flywheels and $\frac{15}{16}$ inch $\times$ $1\frac{1}{16}$ inch (24 mm $\times$ 27 mm) on 16-amp flywheels.

To check stator output, disconnect green connector and connect voltmeter leads to stator lead. With engine running at 3600 rpm, voltmeter should indicate at least 28 VAC for 5-amp systems and 40 VAC for 9-amp systems. If not, replace the stator.

To test regulator, the 12-volt battery must have a minimum charge of 5 volts. Connect an ammeter in series with charging circuit positive (red) lead and run engine at normal operating rpm. Test leads must be connected before starting engine and must not be disconnected while engine

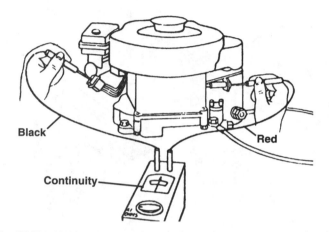

Fig. BS136—Use an ohmmeter to check condition of stator. Refer to text.

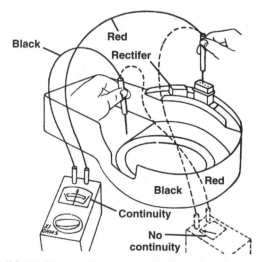

Fig. BS137—If ohmmeter shows continuity in both directions or in neither direction, rectifier is defective.

is running as regulator may be damaged. Ammeter should indicate a charge that will vary according to battery state of charge and capacity of alternator. If no charging current is indicated, check that wires are connected properly and regulator is grounded. Retest and replace the regulator if charge current remains unsatisfactory.

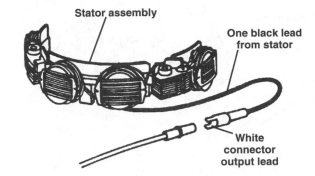

Fig. BS138–Drawing of 5-amp AC alternator used on some models.

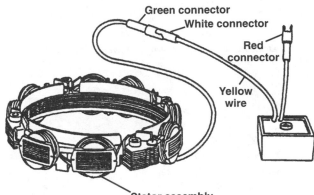

Fig. BS139–Drawing of 5-amp and 9-amp alternator and regulator used on some models.

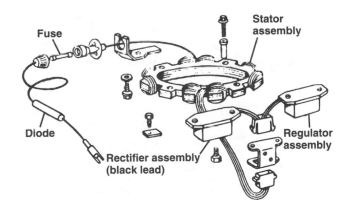

Fig. BS140–Stator, rectifier and regulator assemblies used on 7-amp alternator.

7-AMP ALTERNATOR

The 7-amp regulated alternator (Fig. BS140) is equipped with a solid state rectifier and regulator. An isolation diode is also used on most models.

If engine will not start using the electric starter motor and starter motor is good, install an ammeter in circuit as shown in Fig. BS141. Start engine manually. Ammeter should indicate charge. If the ammeter does not show battery charging taking place, check for defective wiring and, if necessary, proceed with troubleshooting.

If battery charging occurs with the engine running, but the battery does not retain charge, then isolation diode may be defective. The isolation diode is used to prevent battery

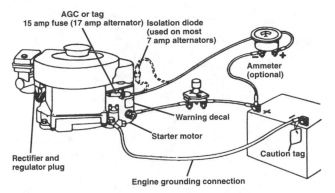

Fig. BS141–Typical wiring diagram for engines equipped with 7-amp alternator system.

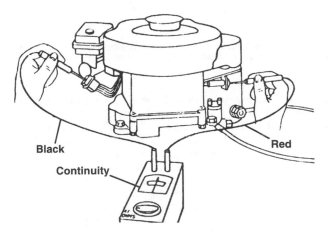

Fig. BS142–Use an ohmmeter to check condition of stator. Refer to text.

drain if alternator circuit malfunctions. After troubleshooting diode, the remainder of the circuit should be inspected to find the reason for excessive battery drain. To check operation of diode, disconnect white lead of diode from fuse holder and connect a test lamp from the diode white lead to negative terminal of battery. The test lamp should not light. If test lamp lights, diode is defective. Disconnect test lamp and disconnect red lead of diode. Test the continuity of the diode with the ohmmeter by connecting the leads of the ohmmeter to the leads of the diode then reverse lead connection. Ohmmeter should show continuity in one direction and an open circuit in the other direction. If readings are incorrect, then diode is defective and must be replaced.

To troubleshoot alternator assembly, proceed as follows: Disconnect white lead of isolation diode from fuse holder and connect a test lamp between positive terminal of battery and fuse holder on engine. Engine must not be started. With connections made, the test lamp should not light. If the test lamp does light, stator, regulator or rectifier is defective. Unplug the rectifier-regulator plug under the blower housing. If the lamp remains lighted, the stator is grounded. If the lamp goes out, the regulator or rectifier is shorted.

If previous test indicated the stator is grounded, check stator leads for defects and repair if necessary. If shorted leads are not found, replace the stator. Check stator for an open circuit as follows: Using an ohmmeter, connect the positive lead to the fuse holder as shown in Fig. BS142 and the negative lead to one of the pins in the rectifier and regulator connector. Check each of the four pins in the connector. The ohmmeter should show continuity at each pin. If

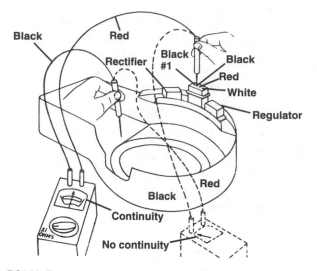

Fig. BS143—Be sure good contact is made between ohmmeter test lead and metal cover when checking rectifier and regulator.

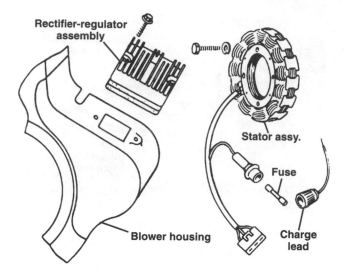

Fig. BS144—Drawing of early 10-amp alternator and rectifier used on some engines.

not, there is an open in the stator and the stator must be replaced.

To test the rectifier, unplug rectifier and regulator connector plug and remove blower housing from engine. Using an ohmmeter, check for continuity between the connector pins connected to black wires and blower housing as shown in Fig. BS143. Be sure good contact is made with the metal of the blower housing. Reverse ohmmeter leads and check continuity again. Ohmmeter should show a continuity reading for only one direction on each plug. If either pin shows a continuity reading for both directions, or if either pin shows no continuity for either direction, then rectifier must be replaced.

To test the regulator unit, repeat procedure used to test rectifier unit except connect ohmmeter lead to pins connected to red wire and white wire. If the ohmmeter shows continuity in either direction for red lead pin, regulator is defective and must be replaced. White lead pin should read as an open on ohmmeter in one direction and a weak reading in the other direction. Otherwise, the regulator is defective and must be replaced.

EARLY 10-AMP ALTERNATOR

Early engines may be equipped with a 10-amp regulated alternator that uses a solid state rectifier-regulator. The early 10-amp system is identified by a fuse in the system (Fig. BS144). To check charging system, disconnect charging lead from battery. Connect a DC voltmeter between the charging lead and ground as shown in Fig. BS145. Start engine and run at 3600 rpm. A voltmeter reading of 14 volts or above indicates alternator is functioning. If the reading is less than 14 volts, stator or rectifier-regulator is defective.

To test stator, disconnect stator plug from rectifier-regulator. Run engine at 3600 rpm and connect AC voltmeter leads to AC terminals in stator plug as shown in Fig. BS146. Voltmeter reading above 20 volts indicates stator is good. A reading less than 20 volts indicates stator is defective.

To test rectifier-regulator, make certain charging lead is connected to battery and stator plug is connected to rectifier-regulator. Check voltage across battery terminals with DC voltmeter (Fig. BS147). If the voltmeter reading is 13.8 volts or higher, reduce battery voltage by connecting a 12-volt load lamp across battery terminals. When

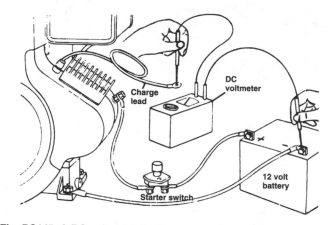
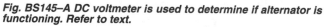

Fig. BS145—A DC voltmeter is used to determine if alternator is functioning. Refer to text.

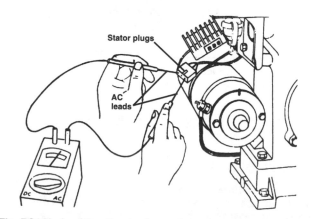

Fig. BS146—An AC voltmeter is used to test stator.

battery voltage is below 13.5 volts, start engine and operate at 3600 rpm. The voltmeter reading should rise. If battery is fully charged, reading should rise above 13.8 volts. If voltage does not increase or if voltage reading rises above 14.7 volts, rectifier-regulator is defective and must be replaced.

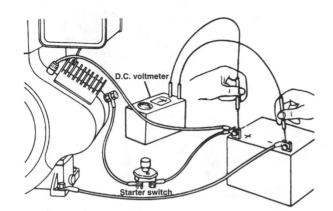

Fig. BS147–A DC voltmeter is used to check battery voltage. Refer to text for rectifier-regulator test.

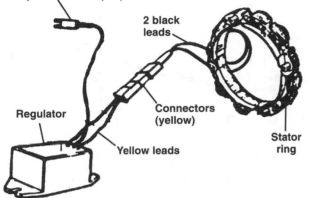

Fig. BS148–Drawing of 10, 13 and 16-amp alternator used on some later models.

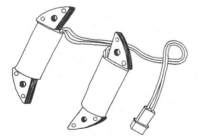

Fig. BS149–Drawing of new-style 10-amp stator used on Series 184500 Vanguard engines. This stator uses the same rectifier-regulator as the system shown in Fig. BS148.

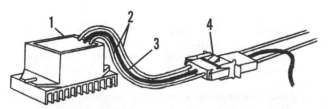

Fig. BS150–Drawing of new-style 20-amp charging system rectifier-regulator and connector used on some Vanguard V-twin engines. Stator is similar to stator shown in Fig. BS148.

1. Rectifier-regulator
2. AC input-yellow
3. DC output-red
4. Connector

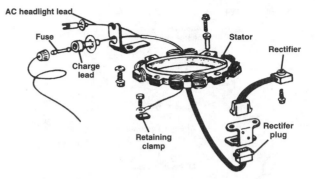

Fig. BS151–Drawing of stator and recifier assemblies used on early dual-circuit alternator system.

LATER 10, 13, 16 AND 20-AMP ALTERNATOR

The 10, 13, 16, and 20-amp alternators (Fig. BS148) provide regulated charging current. Charging rate is determined by state of charge in battery. Stator is located under the flywheel. The size of the magnets cast into the flywheel determines the output capacity of the system.

Magnets are $\frac{11}{16}$ inch $\times$ $\frac{7}{8}$ inch (18 mm $\times$ 22 mm) on 10-amp flywheels, $\frac{11}{16}$ inch $\times$ $1\frac{1}{16}$ inch (18 mm $\times$ 27 mm) on 13-amp flywheels, $\frac{15}{16}$ inch $\times$ $1\frac{1}{16}$ inch (24 mm $\times$ 27 mm) on 16-amp flywheels and $\frac{29}{32}$ inch $\times$ $1\frac{3}{32}$ inch (23 mm $\times$ 27.5 mm) on 20 amp flywheels.

To check stator output, disconnect yellow wire connector and connect voltmeter leads to pins for stator leads. With engine running at 3600 rpm, voltmeter should indicate at least 20 VAC for 10-amp and 13-amp systems, 30 VAC for 16-amp systems and 26 VAC for 20-amp systems. If not, replace the stator.

To test regulator, the 12-volt battery must have a minimum of 5-volt charge. Connect an ammeter in series with charging circuit positive (red) lead and run engine at normal operating rpm. Test leads must be connected before starting the engine and must not be disconnected while the engine is running as the regulator may be damaged. Ammeter should indicate a charge that will vary according to battery state of charge and capacity of alternator. If no charging current is indicated, check that wires are connected properly and regulator is grounded. Retest and replace regulator if charge current remains unsatisfactory.

Some Series 185400 engines have a 10-amp regulated charging system that uses the stator pictured in Fig. BS149. Service procedures are the same as for other 10-amp systems described previously except for the following caution.

CAUTION: When removing the flywheel, DO NOT install flywheel-puller bolts deeper than thickness of the flywheel, or stator damage may result.

Some Vanguard V-twin engines use a 20-amp regulated charging system (Fig. BS150). The heat-sink fins on the rectifier-regulator base must receive unrestricted flow of cooling air for the system to provide proper output. Test procedures are the same as for the B&S 16-amp regulated system described previously.

EARLY DUAL CIRCUIT ALTERNATOR

A dual circuit alternator may be used on some early engines. The early dual circuit system is identified by a fuse in the system (Figs. BS151 or BS152). The dual circuit alternator has one circuit to provide charging current to

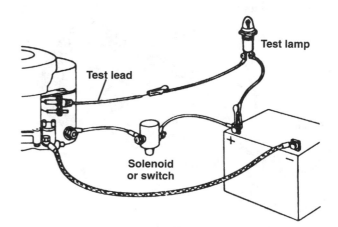

Fig. BS152–Typical wiring diagram for engines equipped with a dual-circuit alternator system.

Fig. BS153–Connect ammeter as shown for output test.

Fig. BS154–Connect a test lamp as shown to test for short in stator or rectifier. Refer to text.

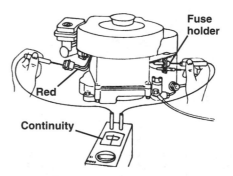

Fig. BS155–Use an ohmmeter to check charging lead for continuity. Refer to text.

maintain battery state of charge and a separate circuit to provide alternating current for lights. The amount of current produced is regulated only by engine speed.

The charging circuit supplies alternating current through a solid state rectifier that converts the alternating current to direct current to maintain battery state of charge.

The lighting circuit provides alternating current to the lights.

The stator is located under the flywheel. A single ring of magnets cast into the flywheel creates the magnetic field for both circuits.

Current for lights is available only when engine is operating. Twelve-volt lights with a total rating of 60 to 100 watts may be used. With a rating of 70 watts, voltage rises from 8 volts at 2400 rpm to 12 volts at 3600 rpm.

Battery charging current connection is made through a 7-amp fuse mounted in a fuse holder. Current for lights is available at plastic connector below fuse holder. The 7-amp fuse protects the 3-amp charging alternator and rectifier from burnout due to reverse polarity battery connections. The 5-amp lighting alternator does not require a fuse.

To check charging alternator output, install an ammeter in circuit as shown in Fig. BS153. Start engine and operate it at 3000 rpm. Ammeter should indicate charging. If not, and the fuse is known to be good, test for short in stator or rectifier as follows: Disconnect charging lead from battery and connect a small test lamp between battery positive terminal and fuse cap as shown in Fig. BS154. DO NOT start engine. Test lamp should not light. If it does light, stator's charging lead is grounded or rectifier is defective. Unplug rectifier plug under blower housing. If test lamp goes out, rectifier is defective. If test lamp does not go out, stator charging lead is grounded.

If the test indicates the stator charging lead is grounded, remove the blower housing, flywheel, starter motor and retaining clamp, then examine length of red lead for damaged insulation or obvious shorts in lead. If bare spots are found, repair with electrical tape and shellac. If the short cannot be repaired, replace the stator. Charging lead should also be checked for continuity as follows: Touch one lead of ohmmeter to lead at fuse holder and other ohmmeter lead to red lead pin in connector as shown in Fig. BS155. If the ohmmeter does not show continuity, charging lead is open and the stator must be replaced. Charging coils should be checked for continuity as follows: Touch ohmmeter test leads to the two black lead pins as shown in Fig. BS156. If the ohmmeter does not show continuity, the

charging coils are defective and the stator must be replaced. Test for grounded charging coils by touching one test lead of ohmmeter to a clean ground surface on the engine and the other test lead to each of the black lead pins as shown in Fig. BS157. If ohmmeter shows continuity, charging coils are grounded and stator must be replaced.

To test the rectifier, use an ohmmeter and check for continuity between each of the three lead pin sockets and blower housing. See Fig. BS158. Reverse ohmmeter leads and check continuity again. Ohmmeter should show a continuity reading for one direction only on each lead socket.

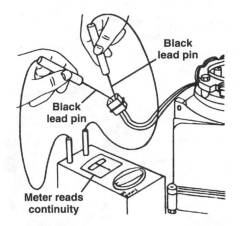

Fig. BS156–Connect an ohmmeter as shown to check charging coils for an open circuit. Meter should show continuity.

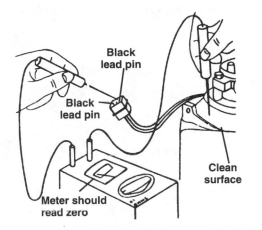

Fig. BS157–Connect an ohmmeter as shown to check charging coils for a grounded circuit. Refer to text.

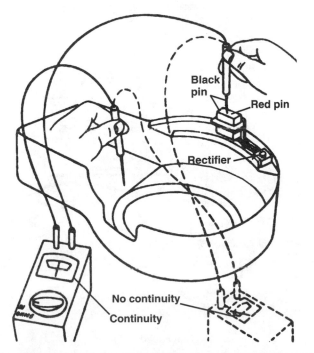

Fig. BS158–If ohmmeter shows continuity in both directions or neither direction, rectifier is defective.

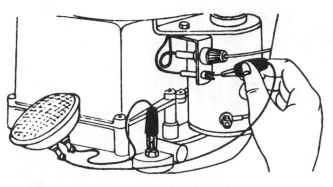

Fig. BS159–A load lamp is used to test AC lighting circuit output.

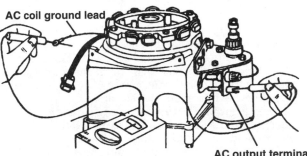

Fig. BS160–Connect an ohmmeter as shown to check AC lighting circuit for continuity. Refer to text.

If any pin socket shows continuity reading in both directions or neither direction, the rectifier is defective and must be replaced.

To test the AC lighting circuit, connect a load lamp to the AC output plug and ground as shown in Fig. BS159. Load lamp should light at full brilliance at medium engine speed. If the lamp does not light or is very dim at medium speeds, remove the blower housing and flywheel. Disconnect ground end of AC coil from retaining clamp screw (Fig. BS160). Connect ohmmeter between ground lead of AC coil and AC output terminal as shown in Fig. BS160. Ohmmeter should show continuity. If not, the stator must be replaced. Be sure the AC ground lead is not touching a grounded surface, then check continuity from AC output terminal to engine ground. If the ohmmeter indicates continuity, the lighting coils are grounded and the stator must be replaced.

LATER DUAL CIRCUIT ALTERNATOR

Dual circuit alternator (Fig. BS161) has one circuit to provide charging current to maintain battery state of charge and a separate circuit to provide alternating current for lights. The amount of current produced is regulated only by engine speed.

The charging circuit supplies alternating current through a solid-state rectifier that converts the alternating current to direct current to maintain battery state of charge.

The lighting circuit provides alternating current to the lights.

The stator is located under the flywheel. A single ring of magnets cast into the flywheel creates the magnetic field for both circuits.

To test charging circuit output, connect an ammeter in series with the charging circuit lead (red wire). Start and

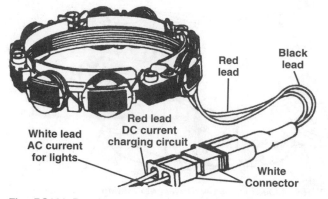

Fig. BS161–Drawing of later dual-circuit alternator used on some models with lights.

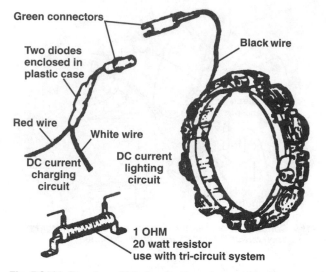

Fig. BS162–Drawing of tri-circuit alternator used on some models with lights and electric PTO clutch.

run engine at 2400 rpm. Ammeter should indicate 2-amp charging current. Increase engine speed to 3600 rpm. Ammeter should indicate 3-amp charging current. If no charging current is indicated, check the diode in the connector. Attach ohmmeter lead to charging circuit connector pin in plug (a bump on the plug identifies the diode). Stick a pin through the red charging circuit wire just behind the plug and connect remaining ohmmeter lead to pin. Note reading then reverse leads. Ohmmeter should indicate continuity in only one position. If not, replace the plug assembly. If diode is good, but system still does not show a charge, replace stator.

To test lighting circuit, connect an AC voltmeter in series with stator lighting circuit lead (black wire) and ground. Run engine at 3600 rpm. Voltmeter reading should be at least 14 volts. Replace the stator if there is insufficient voltage.

TRI-CIRCUIT ALTERNATOR

The tri-circuit alternator (Fig. BS162) consists of a single ring of magnets cast into the flywheel that provides a magnetic field for the stator located under the flywheel. The stator produces alternating current and has a single output lead. Circuit separation is achieved by the use of a positive (+) diode and a negative (–) diode. The charging lead diode rectifies negative (-) 12 VDC (5 amps at 3600 rpm) for lighting. This same charge lead contains a second diode that rectifies positive (+) 12 VDC (5 amps at 3600 rpm) for battery charging and external loads. Some equipment manufacturers incorporate one or both diodes in wiring harness. Check wiring diagram for models being serviced for diode location.

To test alternator output, connect an AC voltmeter in series between stator output lead and ground. Start and run engine at 3600 rpm. Voltmeter should register 28 volts AC or more. Voltage will vary with engine rpm. If charge current is not indicated, replace the stator.

To check diodes, disconnect charge lead from stator output lead. Connect ohmmeter lead to connector pin and connect remaining lead to the white (lighting circuit) wire. Reverse connections. Ohmmeter should indicate continuity in one position only. If not, replace the diode. Repeat the procedure on red wire (charging circuit).

QUAD CIRCUIT ALTERNATOR

The quad circuit alternator (Fig. BS163) provides 8-amp positive (+) DC from the red regulator lead and 8-amp negative (–) DC from the black regulator lead. Note that the black regulator wire changes to a white wire at white connector. Charging rate is determined by the state of the charge in battery. Stator is located under the flywheel and

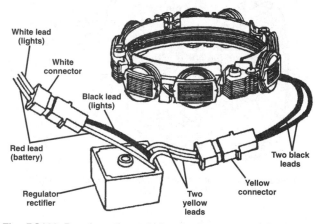

Fig. BS163–Drawing of quad-circuit alternator used on some models.

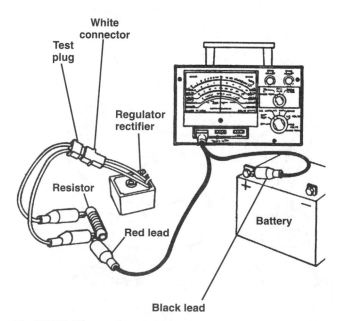

Fig. BS164–The regulator lighting circuit can be checked using a 1-ohm, 20-watt resistor connected as shown. Refer to text.

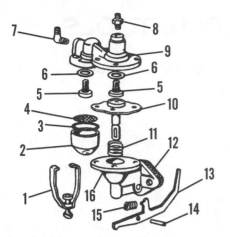

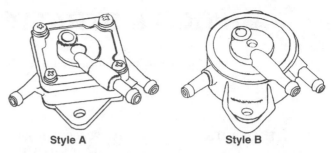

Style A   **Style B**

Fig. BS167—Drawing showing vacuum-operated fuel pumps used on some models. Early models appear as Style A, with aluminum square-shaped housing. Later models, Style B, have circular-shaped housings and are made out of plastic.

Fig. BS165—Exploded view of diaphragm-type fuel pump used on some engines.

1. Yoke assy.
2. Filter bowl
3. Gasket
4. Filter screen
5. Pump valves
6. Gaskets
7. Elbow fitting
8. Connector
9. Fuel pump head
10. Pump diaphragm
11. Diaphragm spring
12. Gasket
13. Pump lever
14. Lever pin
15. Spring
16. Fuel pump body

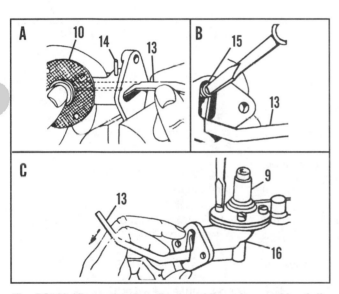

Fig. BS166—Views showing disassembly and assembly of diaphragm-type fuel pump. Refer to text for procedure and to Fig. BS165 for exploded view of pump and parts identification.

output capacity is determined by the size of magnets cast into the flywheel.

To check stator output, disconnect yellow connector and connect voltmeter leads to pins for stator leads. With engine running at 3600 rpm, voltmeter should indicate at least 30 VAC. If not, replace the stator.

To test regulator output, the 12-volt battery must have a minimum of 5-volt charge. Connect an ammeter in series with charging circuit positive (red) lead and start and run engine at normal operating rpm. Test leads must be connected before starting the engine and must not be dis-

connected while the engine is running as the regulator may be damaged. Ammeter should indicate a charge that will vary according to battery state of charge and capacity of alternator. If no charging current is indicated, check that wires are connected properly and regulator is grounded. Retest and replace the regulator if charge current remains unsatisfactory.

To check lighting circuit of regulator, obtain a 1-ohm, 20-watt resistor. Use a suitable jumper wire and connect to white connector of regulator as shown in Fig. BS164. Connect an ammeter between resistor and battery as shown. Run engine at 3600 rpm just long enough to produce test reading. Ammeter should indicate approximately 8 amp, if not replace regulator.

FUEL PUMP

A diaphragm-type mechanical fuel pump is available on many models as optional equipment. Refer to Fig. BS165 for an exploded view of the pump.

To disassemble pump, refer to Figs. BS165 and BS166; then, proceed as follows: Remove clamp (1), fuel bowl (2) and screen (4). Remove screws retaining upper body (9) to lower body (16). Pump valves (5) and gaskets (6) can now be removed. Drive pin (14) out to either side of body (16), then press diaphragm (10) against spring (11) as shown in view A, Fig. BS166, and remove lever (13). Diaphragm and spring (11–Fig. BS165) can now be removed.

To reassemble, place diaphragm spring in the lower body and place the diaphragm on the spring, being sure spring enters cup on bottom side of diaphragm and slot in shaft is at right angle to pump lever. Then, compress the diaphragm against the spring as shown in view A, Fig. BS166, and insert hooked end of lever with hole in lower body and drive pin into place. Then, insert lever spring (15) into body and push outer end of spring into place over hook on arm of lever as shown in view B. Hold lever downward as shown in view C while tightening screws holding upper body to lower body. When installing pump on engine, apply a liberal amount of grease on lever (13) at point where it contacts lobe on crankshaft.

Some models use a vacuum-operated fuel pump (Fig. BS167). The pump has a maximum lift of 12 inches (30.5 cm). Vacuum pulses from the engine's crankcase actuate the pump diaphragm.

Pump can be disassembled and cleaned, but no service parts are available. Replace the pump if it is faulty.

BRIGGS & STRATTON SPECIAL TOOLS

The following special tools are available from Briggs & Stratton Central
Parts Distributors.

TOOL KITS

19138—Valve seat insert puller for all models and series so equipped.

19184—Main bearing service kit for Series 170000 and 190000.

19205—Cylinder hone kit for all aluminum bore (Kool-Bore) engines.

19211—Cylinder hone kit for all cast iron cylinder engines.

19228—Main bearing tool kit for all twin-cylinder engines with integral and DU-type main bearings, except Vanguard.

19232—Valve guide puller/reamer kit for Series 170000, 190000, 220000, 250000, 280000, 300000, 320000 and twin-cylinder engines, except Vanguard.

19237—Valve seat cutter kit for most models and series.

19245—Special tap set for cleaning threads in 2-piece Flo-jet carburetors.

19343—Valve seat cutter kit for Vanguard OHV engines.

19407—Ball main bearing service kit for Series 185400-245400 Vanguard single-cylinder engines.

19460—Carburetor socket set for main jet housing on Intek V-twin engines.

PLUG GAUGES

19055—Check breaker plunger bore on Model 23C and Series 170000, 190000 and 220000.

19117—Check main bearing bore on Models 19, 19D, 23, 23A, 23C, 23D and Series 190000, 200000 and 230000.

19151—Check valve guide bores on Models 19, 19D, 23, 23A, 23C, 23D and Series 170000, 190000, 200000,

230000, 240000, 250000, 300000, 320000 and twin-cylinder engines, except Vanguard.

19164—Check camshaft bearings on Series 170000, 190000, 220000 and 250000.

19219—Check integral or DU-type main bearing bore on twin-cylinder engines.

19377—Check magneto-side main bearing bore on Series 161400 Vanguard single-cylinder engine.

19378—Check main bearing bores on Series 26x700 Vanguard single-cylinder engines.

19380—Check main bearing bores on Vanguard.

19381—Check valve guide bores on Vanguard.

19382—Check valve guides on Vanguard V-twins and single-cylinder Series 185400-245400 engines.

19383—Check camshaft bearings on Vanguard single-cylinder Series 161400 and 26x700 engines.

19384—Check camshaft bearings on Vanguard.

19386—Check PTO-side main bearing bore on Vanguard V-twins.

REAMERS

19056—Breaker plunger bushing reamer for 170000, 190000, 220000 and 250000.

19058—Finish reamer for breaker plunger bushing for Series 170000, 190000, 220000 and 250000.

19173—Finish reamer for main bearings for Series 170000 and 190000.

19174—Counterbore reamer for main bearings for Series 170000, 171000, 190000 and 191000.

19175—Finish reamer for main bearings for Series 170000, 171000, 190000 and 191000.

19183—Valve guide reamer for bushing installation for Models 19, 19D, 23, 23A, 23C, 23D and Series 170000, 190000, 200000, 220000, 230000, 240000, 251000, 300000 and 320000.

19231—Valve guide bushing reamer for Models 19 and 23 and Series 170000, 190000, 200000, 220000, 230000, 240000, 250000, 300000, 320000 and twin-cylinder engines.

19281—Counterbore reamer for main bearings for Series 170000 and 190000.

19333—Valve guide bushing finish reamer for Series 170000, 190000, 200000, 230000, 240000, 250000, 280000, 300000, 320000 and twin-cylinder engines, except Vanguard.

19346—Valve guide bushing reamer for Vanguard.

19444—Finish reamer for Vanguard V-twin valve guides.

PILOTS

19096—Pilot for main bearing reamer for Series 170000, 171000, 190000 and 191000.

19127—Expansion pilot for valve seat counterbore cutter for Models 19 and 23 and Series 170000, 190000, 200000, 220000, 230000, 240000, 300000, 320000 and twin-cylinder engines.

19130—"T" handle for 19127 pilot.

REAMER GUIDE BUSHING

19192—Guide bushing for valve guide reaming for Models 19 and 23 and Series 170000, 190000, 200000, 220000, 230000, 240000, 251000, 300000 and 320000.

19201—Guide bushing for main bearing reaming for Series 171000 and 191000.

19222—Guide bushing for main bearing reaming for tool kit 19228 for twin-cylinder engines.

19234—Guide bushing for main bearing reaming for tool kit 19232 for twin-cylinder engines.

19282—Guide bushing for main bearing reaming for Series 170000 and 190000.

19301—Guide bushing for main bearing reaming for Series 170000 and 190000.

19345—Guide bushing for valve guide reaming for Vanguard.

PILOT GUIDE BUSHINGS

19168—Pilot guide bushing for main bearing reaming for Series 170000 and 190000.

19169—Pilot guide bushing for main bearing reaming for Series 170000 and 190000.

19220—Pilot guide bushing for main bearing reaming for tool lit 19228 for twin-cylinder engines.

COUNTERBORE CUTTERS

19131—Counterbore valve seat cutter for Models 19, 19D, 23, 23A, 23D and Series 190000, 200000, 230000 and 240000.

CRANKCASE SUPPORT JACK

19123—To support crankcase when removing or installing main bearings on Series 170000 and 190000.

19227—To support crankcase when removing or installing DU-type main bearings on twin-cylinder engines.

CYLINDER BORE GAUGE

19404—Stabilized telescoping gauge measures bores to 3.5 inches (90 mm).

DRIVERS

19057—To install breaker plunger bushing on Series 170000, 190000, 220000 and 250000.

19136—To install valve seat inserts on all engines.

19179—To install main bearing on Series 170000 and 190000.

19344—To install main bearing retaining pin on Vanguard.

19349—To install main bearing on Vanguard.

19367—To install valve guides on Vanguard.

19450—To main bearing on magneto side in Vanguard V-twin after Code 970430xxx.

ELECTRICAL

19359—Shunt used in troubleshooting alternator charging systems.

19464—Digital multimeter recommended for testing.

FLYWHEEL PULLERS

19068—Flywheel removal on Models 19, 19D, 23, 23A, 23C, 23D and Series 190000, 200000, 230000, 240000 300000 and 320000.

19165—Flywheel removal on Series 170000, 190000 and 250000.

19203—Flywheel removal on Models 19 and 23 and Series 190000, 200000, 220000, 230000, 240000, 250000, 280000, 300000, 320000 and twin-cylinder engines.

VALVE SPRING COMPRESSOR

19063—Valve spring compressor for all models and series, except Vanguard.

19347—Valve spring compressor for Vanguard.

PISTON RING COMPRESSOR

19070—Piston ring compressor for Vanguard.

19230—Piston ring compressor for all models and series, except Vanguard.

STARTER MOTOR

19435—C-ring installation tool for late-style bendix drives.

19436—C-ring removal tool for late-style bendix drives.

STARTER WRENCH

19114—All models and series with rewind starter.

19161—All models and series with rewind starter (to be used with -inch torque wrench).

19244—To remove, install and torque rewind starter clutches.

BENDING TOOL

19229—Governor tang bending tool, except Vanguard.

19352—Governor tang bending tool for Vanguard.

IGNITION SPARK TESTER

19368—Test ignition spark for all models.

BRIGGS & STRATTON CENTRAL
PARTS DISTRIBUTORS

(Arranged Alphabetically by States)
These franchised firms carry extensive stocks of repair parts. Contact them
for name of the nearest service distributor.

Power Equipment Company
Phone (602) 272-3936
#7 North 43rd Avenue
Phoenix, Arizona 85107

Pacific Western Power
Phone (415) 692-3254
1565 Adrain Road
Burlingame, California 94010

Power Equipment Company
Phone (805) 684-6637
1045 Cindy Lane
Carpinteria, California 93013

Pacific Power Equipment Company
Phone (303) 744-7891
1441 W. Bayaud Avenue #4
Denver, Colorado 80223

Central Power Systems of Florida
Phone (813) 253-6035
1114 W. Cass St.
Tampa, Florida 33606

Sedco, Inc.
Phone (770) 925-4706
4305 Steve Reynolds Blvd.
Norcross, Georgia 30093

Small Engine Clinic, Inc.
Phone (808)488-0711
98019 Kam Highway
Aiea, Hawaii 96701

Midwest Engine Warehouse
Phone (630) 833-1200
515 Romans Road
Elmhurst, Illinois 60126

Diamond Engine Sales
Phone (913) 888-8828
11421 Electron Drive
Lenexa, Kansas 66219

Commonwealth Engine, Inc.
Phone (502) 263-7026
11421 Electron Drive
Louisville, Kentucky 40229

Delta Power Equipment Co.
Phone (504) 465-9222
755 E. Airline Highway
Kenner, Louisiana 70062

Atlantic Power
Phone (508) 543-6911
77 Green Street
Foxboro, Massachusetts 02035

Wisconsin Magneto, Inc.
Phone (612) 323-7477
800 McKinley Street
Anoka, Minnesota 55303

Original Equipment, Inc.
Phone (406) 245-3081
905 Second Avenue North
Billings, Montana 59101

Midwest Engine Warehouse of Omaha
Phone (402) 891-1700
10606 S. 144th Street
Omaha, Nebraska 68138

Atlantic Power
Phone (732) 356-8400
650 Howard Avenue
Somerset, New Jersey 08873

Preferred Power, Inc.
Phone (704) 598-1010
6509-A Northpark Blvd.
Charlotte, North Carolina 28216

Central Power Systems
Phone (614) 876-3533
2555 International Street
Columbus, Ohio 43228

Engine Warehouse, Inc.
Phone (405) 364-6868
2701 Venture Drive
Norman, Oklahoma 73069

Brown & Wiser, Inc.
Phone (503) 692-0330
9991 S. W. Avery Street
Tualatin, Oregon 97062

Three Rivers Engine Distributors
Phone (412) 321-4111
1411 Beaver Avenue
Pittsburgh, Pennsylvania 15233

Engine Power Distributors
Phone (901) 345-0300
3250 Millbranch Road
Memphis, Tennessee 38116

Grayson Company, Inc.
Phone (214) 630-3272
1234 Motor Street
Dallas, Texas 75207

Engine Warehouse, Inc.
Phone (713) 937-4000
7415 Empire Central Drive
Houston, Texas 77040

Frank Edwards Company
Phone (801) 281-4660
3653 South 500 West
Salt Lake City, Utah 84115

RBI Corporation
Phone (888) 724-0101
10201 Cedar Ridge Drive
Ashland, Virginia 23005

Wisconsin Magneto, Inc.
Phone (414) 445-2800
4727 N. Teutonia Avenue
Milwaukee, Wisconsin 53209

CANADIAN DISTRIBUTORS

Briggs & Stratton Canada, Inc.
Phone (604) 520-1294
1360 Cliveden Avenue
Delta, British Columbia V3M 6K2

Briggs & Stratton Canada, Inc.
Phone (905) 795-2632
301 Ambassador Drive
Mississauga, Ontario L5T 2J3

KAWASAKI

Model	No. Cyls.	Bore	Stroke	Displacement	Power Rating
FB460V	1	89 mm (3.5 in.)	74 mm (2.9 in.)	460 cc (28.1 cu. in.)	9.3 kW (12.5 hp)

ENGINE LUBRICATION

Model FB460V is a four-stroke, single-cylinder, air-cooled engine with a vertical crankshaft. The engine is equipped with a pressurized lubrication system and a reciprocating balancer.

MAINTENANCE

Lubrication

Check the engine oil level prior to operation. Maintain the oil level between the reference marks on the dipstick with the dipstick just touching the first threads. Do not screw the dipstick in to check oil level (Fig. KW101).

Engine oil should meet or exceed latest API service classification. Use oil of suitable viscosity for the expected air temperature range during the period between oil changes.

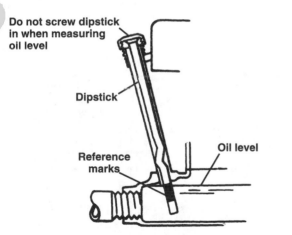

Fig. KW101–View showing procedure to check crankcase oil level. Refer to text.

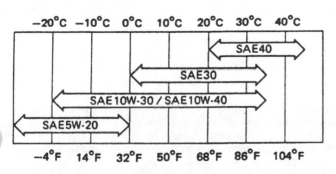

Fig. KW102–Engine oil viscosity should be based on expected air temperature as indicated in chart above.

Refer to the temperature/viscosity chart shown in Fig. KW102.

If the engine is not equipped with an oil filter, change the engine oil after every 25 hours of operation or yearly, whichever comes first. On models equipped with an oil filter, change the oil and filter after every 50 hours of operation or yearly, whichever comes first.

Drain the oil while the engine is warm. Crankcase oil capacity is approximately 1.4 L (3 pt.). Check the oil level using the dipstick after running the engine momentarily.

Oil pressure is regulated by an oil pressure relief valve located inside the crankcase beside the oil pump. Oil pressure should be 29.4 kPa (4.3 psi) at 3000 rpm.

Air Filter

Remove and clean the air filter element after every 25 hours of operation, or more often when operating in extremely dusty conditions. Replace the paper element (5–Fig. KW103) after every 300 hours of operation. Replace either filter element if damaged.

To remove the filter elements (4 and 5), remove the wing bolts (1) and washers (2). Remove the cover (3), foam precleaner element and paper element.

Clean the foam element in a solution of warm water and liquid detergent. Squeeze out excess water and allow to air dry. DO NOT wash the paper element. Apply a light coat of engine oil to the foam element and squeeze out excess oil.

Clean the paper element by tapping gently to remove dust. DO NOT use compressed air to clean the element. Inspect the paper element for damage. Reinstall by reversing the removal procedure.

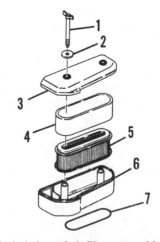

Fig. KW103–Exploded view of air filter assembly.

1. Wing bolt
2. Washer
3. Cover
4. Foam element
5. Paper element
6. Housing
7. O-ring

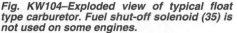

Fig. KW104–Exploded view of typical float type carburetor. Fuel shut-off solenoid (35) is not used on some engines.

1. Choke shaft	22. Main air jet
2. Spring	23. Screw
3. Ring	24. Choke plate
4. Seal	25. Fuel inlet needle
5. Ring	26. Clip
6. Idle speed screw	27. Main nozzle
7. Spring	28. Bleed pipe
8. Throttle shaft	29. Main jet
9. Throttle plate	30. Float
10. Screw	31. Pin
11. Spring	32. Gasket
12. Ring	33. Float bowl
13. Seal	34. Washer
14. Screw	35. Fuel shut-off
15. Retainer plate	solenoid
16. Pilot jet	36. Drain screw
17. O-ring	37. Spring
18. Spring	38. O-ring
19. Pilot screw	39. Washer
20. Cap	40. Special bolt
21. Pilot air jet	

Crankcase Breather

Crankcase pressure is vented through the crankcase breather on the top side of the crankcase. A reed valve is located in the breather assembly. Replace the reed valve if the reed is damaged. Be sure the drain hole in the crankcase is open.

Spark Plug

Recommended spark plug is NGK BPR5ES or Champion RN11YC.

Remove, clean and set the spark plug after every 100 hours of operation. Specified spark plug gap is 0.6-0.7 mm (0.024-0.028 in.).

Carburetor

All models are equipped with a side draft carburetor. Check the carburetor whenever poor or erratic performance is noted.

Recommended engine idle speed is 1325-1475 rpm. Adjust the idle speed by turning the idle speed screw (6–Fig. KW104) clockwise to increase the idle speed or counterclockwise to decrease the idle speed.

Adjust the throttle control as follows: Place the engine throttle lever in the fast position. Insert a 6 mm ($^{15}/_{64}$-inch) drill bit through the hole (H–Fig. KW105) in the speed control lever (7) and bracket (8). Loosen the throttle cable housing clamp screw (10), pull the cable housing tight and retighten the cable clamp screw.

Rotate the choke lever screw (9) on the back side of the bracket so there is a gap between the screw and choke control lever, then turn it back in until the screw just touches

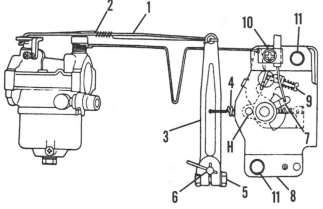

Fig. KW105–View of external governor linkage.

1. Governor-to-carburetor rod	7. Speed control lever
2. Spring	8. Control plate
3. Governor lever	9. Choke setting screw
4. Tension spring	10. Clamp bolt
5. Clamp bolt	11. Screws
6. Governor shaft	

the lever. Remove the drill bit. With the throttle control lever in the choke position, the carburetor choke plate should be closed, if not, repeat the adjustment procedure.

Initial adjustment of the pilot air screw (19–Fig. KW104) is 1⅛ turns open from a lightly seated position. Make final adjustment with engine at operating temperature and running.

Adjust the pilot screw to obtain maximum engine idle speed, then turn the pilot screw out counterclockwise an

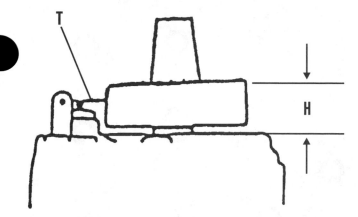

Fig. KW106–Float height (H) should be parallel with fuel bowl mounting surface of carburetor body. If float height is adjustable, bend float tab (T) to adjust float height.

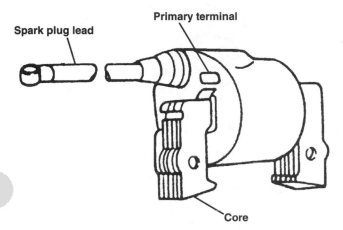

Fig. KW107–View of ignition coil showing location of primary terminal, spark plug lead and iron core.

additional ¼ turn. Adjust the idle speed screw (6) so the engine idles at 1325-1475 rpm.

Main fuel mixture is controlled by a fixed jet (29). Different size main jets are available for high altitude operation.

Disassembly of the carburetor is self-evident upon examination of the unit and reference to Fig. KW104.

Clean carburetor parts except the plastic components using carburetor cleaner. Do not clean the jets or passages with drill bits or wire as enlargement of the passages could affect calibration of the carburetor. Rinse the parts in warm water to neutralize the carburetor cleaner's corrosive action and dry with compressed air.

When assembling the carburetor, note the following. Place a small drop of nonhardening sealant such as Permatex #2 on the throttle and choke plate retaining screws. The float should be parallel with the body when the carburetor is inverted as shown in Fig. KW106. If equipped with a white plastic float, float height is not adjustable. Replace any components that are damaged and adversely affect the float position. On models with an adjustable float, bend the float tab to adjust the float height.

Governor

A gear-driven flyweight governor is located inside the engine crankcase. Before adjusting the governor linkage,

make certain all linkage is in good condition and the tension spring (4–Fig. KW105) is not stretched.

To adjust the external linkage, place the engine throttle control in FAST position. The spring (2) around the governor-to-carburetor rod must pull the governor lever (3) and throttle lever toward each other. Loosen the governor lever clamp bolt (5) and turn the governor shaft (6) clockwise as far as possible. Tighten the clamp bolt nut.

Maximum no-load engine speed should be 3275-3425 rpm unless specified otherwise by the equipment manufacturer. Adjust the maximum no-load engine speed as follows: Run the engine until normal operating temperature is reached. Align the holes in the speed control lever (7) and bracket (8) and insert a 6mm ($^{15}/_{64}$ inch) drill bit. Run the engine under no load and determine the engine speed using an accurate tachometer. If engine speed is not 3275-3425 rpm, loosen the bracket retaining screws (11) and reposition the bracket to obtain the desired engine speed. Retighten screws and recheck engine speed. Check choke operation as outlined in the CARBURETOR section.

Ignition System

The engine is equipped with a transistor ignition system. Regular maintenance is not required. Ignition timing is not adjustable. The ignition coil is located outside the flywheel. The air gap between the ignition coil and flywheel should be 0.30 mm (0.012 in.).

To test the ignition coil, remove the cooling shrouds and disconnect the spark plug cable and primary lead wire (Fig. KW107). Connect ohmmeter test leads between the coil core (ground) and high tension (spark plug) terminal. Secondary coil resistance should be 10,000-18,000 ohms. Remove the test lead connected to the high tension terminal and connect the lead to the coil primary terminal. Primary coil resistance should be 0.4-0.8 ohms. If readings vary significantly from specifications, replace the ignition coil.

To test the control unit, install a new or good control unit and check engine operation. An accurate test procedure is not available due to the wide range of tester results that can result when testing the unit.

Valve Adjustment

Valves and seats should be refaced and stem clearance adjusted after every 300 hours of operation. Refer to VALVE SYSTEM in the REPAIRS section for service procedure and specifications.

CYLINDER HEAD AND COMBUSTION CHAMBER

Minimum compression reading is 296 kPa (43 psi).

NOTE: When checking compression pressure, the spark plug high tension lead must be grounded or the electronic ignition could be damaged.

A leaking cylinder head gasket, worn piston rings and cylinder bore or poorly seated valves are indicated by lower than standard compression reading. Excessive carbon build-up on the piston and cylinder head are indicated by a high compression reading.

REPAIRS

TIGHTENING TORQUES

Recommended tightening torques are as follows:

Connecting rod . . . . 20 N•m
(177 in.-lb.)
Cylinder head . . . . 37 N•m
(27 ft.-lb.)
Flywheel. . . . . 88 N•m
(65 ft.-lb.)
Oil pan. . . . . 20 N•m
(177 in.-lb.)
Oil pump cover . . . . 20 N•m
(177 in.-lb.)

CYLINDER HEAD

To remove the cylinder head, remove the cylinder head shroud. Clean the engine to prevent entrance of foreign material. Loosen the six cylinder head bolts and the three cylinder head stud nuts in ¼-turn increments following the sequence shown in Fig. KW108 until all bolts are loose enough to remove by hand.

Remove the spark plug and clean carbon and other deposits from the cylinder head. Place the cylinder head on a flat surface and check the entire sealing surface for warpage. If warpage exceeds 0.4 mm (0.015 in.), replace the cylinder head. Slight warpage may be repaired by lapping the cylinder head. In a figure eight pattern, lap the head on a flat surface against 200 grit and then 400 grit emery paper.

Reinstall the cylinder head and tighten the bolts and nuts evenly to the specified torque following the sequence in Fig. KW108.

VALVE SYSTEM

Clearance between the valve stem and valve tappet (cold) should be 0.10-0.16 mm (0.0039-0.0063 in.) for intake and exhaust valves. If clearance is not as specified, remove the valve and grind the end of the valve stem to increase clearance. To reduce the clearance, machine the valve seat so the valve sits lower.

Valve face and seat angles are 45° for intake and exhaust. Valve seating surface should be 1.0-1.6 mm (0.039-0.063 in.). Minimum valve margin is 0.6 mm (0.02 in.).

Minimum valve stem diameter is 7.912 mm (0.3115 in.) for intake valve and 7.919 mm (0.3118 in.) for exhaust valve. Maximum valve stem bend is 0.03 mm (0.0012 in.). If the valve stem bend exceeds the specification, replace the valve.

Valve spring free length should be 43.3 mm (1.705 in.) for intake valve spring and 39.0 mm (1.535 in.) for exhaust valve spring.

Maximum valve guide inside diameter for the replaceable valve guides is 8.062 mm (0.3174 in.). If the guide inside diameter is greater than specified, use a valve guide puller to remove the guide. Press new guides into the guide bore until the top surface of the guide is 30 mm (1.18 mm) from the cylinder head mating surface on cylinder.

CONNECTING ROD

Connecting rod and piston are removed as an assembly after removing the cylinder head and oil pan. Remove carbon and ring ridge if present from the top of the cylinder before removing the piston. Remove the connecting rod bolts and connecting rod cap (7–Fig. KW109), then push the connecting rod and piston out through the top of the cylinder. Remove the retaining rings (4) and push the piston pin (5) out of the piston to separate the piston from the connecting rod.

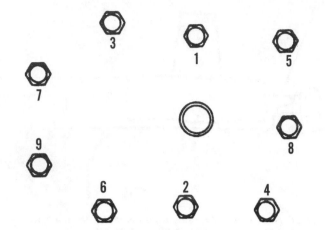

Fig. KW108–Tighten cylinder head bolts in sequence shown.

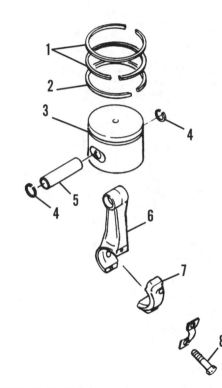

Fig. KW109–Exploded view of piston and connecting rod assembly.

1. Compression rings
2. Oil control ring
3. Piston
4. Retaining rings
5. Piston ring
6. Connecting rod
7. Connecting rod cap
8. Connecting rod bolts

Connecting rod rides directly on the crankshaft journal. Maximum allowable inside diameter for connecting rod big end bearing surface is 37.02 mm (1.4575 in.). Maximum connecting rod-to-crankpin clearance is 0.09 mm (0.0035 in.). A connecting rod is available with 0.50 mm (0.020 in.) undersize big end for use with undersize crankshaft crankpin. Refer to the CRANKSHAFT AND BALANCER section.

Maximum inside diameter of connecting rod small end is 21.01 mm (0.827 in.). Maximum allowable connecting rod-to-piston pin clearance is 0.03 mm (0.0012 in.).

When reassembling, install the piston on the connecting rod so the arrow on top of the piston is toward the MADE

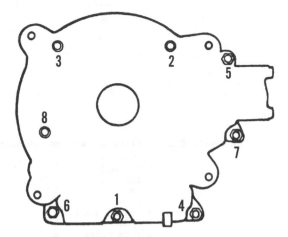

Fig. KW110–Tighten the oil pan bolts in the sequence shown.

IN JAPAN side of the connecting rod. Install the piston and connecting rod in the cylinder so the arrow on top of the piston is toward the flywheel side of the engine. Tighten the connecting rod cap bolts to 20 N•m (177 in.-lb.).

PISTON, PIN AND RINGS

Piston and connecting rod are removed as an assembly after removing cylinder head and oil pan. Refer to CONNECTING ROD section for removal and installation procedure.

After separating the piston and connecting rod, carefully remove the piston rings and clean the carbon and other deposits from the piston surface and piston ring lands.

> CAUTION: Exercise extreme care when cleaning the piston rings lands. Do not damage the squared edges or widen the piston ring grooves. If piston ring lands are damaged, replace the piston.

Maximum inside diameter of pin bore in piston is 21.03 mm (0.828 in.). Minimum piston pin outside diameter is 20.98 mm (0.826 in.). Maximum piston-to-pin clearance is 0.05 mm (0.0020 in.).

To check piston ring grooves for wear, insert a new ring in the ring groove and use a feeler gauge to measure ring side clearance in groove. Replace the piston if the side clearance exceeds 0.16 mm (0.006 in.) for the top ring, 0.14 mm (0.005 in.) for the second ring or 0.19 mm (0.007 in.) for the oil ring.

Insert each ring squarely in the cylinder bore about 25 mm (1 in.) below the cylinder top and measure the ring end gap. The maximum allowable end gap is 0.70 mm (0.028 in.) for compression rings and 1.20 mm (0.047 in.) for the oil control ring. If the piston ring gap is greater than specified, check the cylinder bore for wear.

During reassembly, install the piston on the connecting rod so the arrow on top of the piston is toward the MADE IN JAPAN side of the connecting rod. Use new snap rings to retain piston pin in the piston.

When installing piston rings install the oil ring spacer first, then install the side rails. Position the side rail end gaps 180° apart. Install the second compression ring and top compression ring on the piston with R, N or NPR mark on the ring toward the piston crown. Stagger the piston ring end gaps 180° apart, but do not align with the side rail end gaps. Lubricate the piston and cylinder with engine

oil. Use a ring compressor to compress the rings when installing the piston in the cylinder. Be sure the arrow on the top of the piston points toward the flywheel side of the engine.

CYLINDER, CRANKCASE, MAIN BEARINGS AND SEALS

The cylinder and crankcase are an integral casting. Standard cylinder bore diameter is 88.90-89.00 mm (3.500-3.504 in.). The cylinder bore wear limit is 89.06 mm (3.506 in.). The cylinder can be bored or honed to fit an oversize piston. Oversize pistons are available.

The main bearing on the PTO side is an integral bushing in the oil pan. Main bearing on the flywheel side is a ball bearing.

Maximum inside diameter for integral bearing bore in the oil pan is 35.069 mm (1.3807 in.). Bearing on the flywheel side should be a press fit on the crankshaft and in the bearing bore of the crankcase.

Replace the crankshaft seals when damaged. Install the seals with the open side facing the inside of the engine and press in until flush with the crankcase or oil pan. Pack the seals with lithium-base grease prior to crankshaft installation.

When installing the oil pan, tighten the retaining screws to 20 N•m (177 in.-lb.). Tighten the mounting screws in the sequence shown in Fig. KW110.

CRANKSHAFT AND BALANCER

The crankshaft is supported on the flywheel side by a ball main bearing and on the PTO side by a plain bearing in the oil pan. A reciprocating balancer is used on all models.

To remove the crankshaft, remove the shrouds, fan housing, flywheel, cylinder head and oil pan. Remove the piston and connecting rod assembly. Remove the governor shaft retaining pin and remove the governor shaft. Rotate the crankshaft until the timing marks on the camshaft gear and crankshaft gear are aligned, then remove the camshaft. Remove the valve tappets. Identify the tappets so they can be reinstalled in the original position. Rotate the crankshaft carefully until the crankpin is down toward the balancer weight. Unbolt and remove the balancer support shaft (16–Fig. KW111). Remove the crankshaft and balancer assembly from the crankcase.

To disassemble the balancer, remove the spacer (1–Fig. KW112), gear (7), spacer (6) and link rods (2) from the crankshaft (4) and balancer (9) wrist pins.

Clean and inspect all parts for damage. Refer to the following table for crankshaft main journal minimum diameter:

PTO end . . . . **34.919 mm**
                                                                            (1.3747 in.)
Flywheel end . . . . **34.945 mm**
                                                                            (1.3758 in.)

Main journals cannot be resized. Refer to the CYLINDER, CRANKCASE, MAIN BEARINGS AND SEALS section for main bearing dimensions. Measure crankshaft runout at the main journals. Replace the crankshaft if runout exceeds 0.05 mm (0.002 in.). The crankshaft cannot be straightened.

Crankpin journal minimum diameter is 36.95 mm (1.455 in.). Crankpin can be reground to accept an undersize connecting rod. Refer to the CONNECTING ROD section.

Measure outside diameter of the crankshaft balancer link rod journals (A–Fig. KW113), inside diameter of the

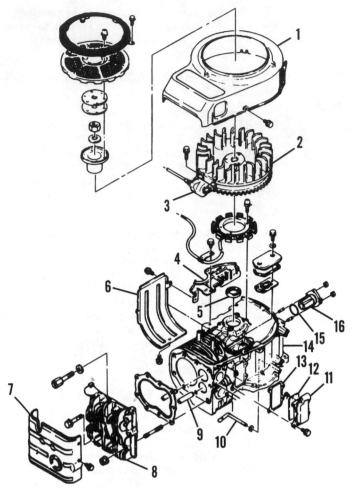

Fig. KW111–Exploded view of crankcase assembly.
1. Blower housing
2. Flywheel
3. Ignition coil
4. Shroud
5. Oil seal
6. Cooling shroud
7. Cooling shroud
8. Cylinder head
9. Valve guide
10. Governor shaft
11. Valve chamber cover
12. Cover
13. Gasket
14. Cylinder block & crankcase
15. O-ring
16. Balancer gear

big end and small end of the balancer link rods (B), inside diameter of the support shaft bushing (D) and the outside diameter of support shaft (E). Refer to the following table for wear limit specifications and replace parts when necessary.

Link rod journal OD	53.950 mm (2.1240 in.)
Link rod big end ID	54.121 mm (2.1307 in.)
Link rod small end ID	12.06 mm (0.475 in.)
Support shaft bushing ID	26.097 mm (1.0274 in.)
Support shaft OD	25.927 mm (1.0208 in.)

The balancer link rod bushing (3–Fig. KW112) is replaceable. When installing a new link rod bushing, press the bushing into the link rod from the side opposite the oil grooves (G–Fig. KW114). Position the seam (S) of the bushing 90° from the centerline (C) of the link rod. Install the bushing so the depth (D) below the machined surface of rod is 0.5 mm (0.020 in.).

Support shaft bushing (10–Fig. 112) is replaceable. When installing a new support shaft bushing, make sure the oil hole in the bushing is aligned with the oil passage in the balancer.

To assemble the crankshaft and balancer, install the balance weight (W–Fig. KW113) with the oil hole (O) toward the flywheel side of the crankshaft. Install the link

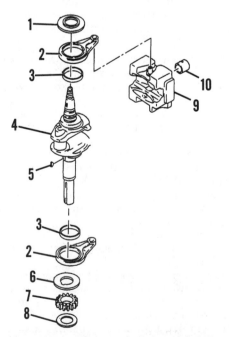

Fig. KW112–Exploded view of the crankshaft and balancer assembly.

1. Spacer	6. Spacer
2. Link rod	7. Gear
3. Bushing	8. Shim
4. Crankshaft	9. Balancer counterweight
5. Key	10. Bushing

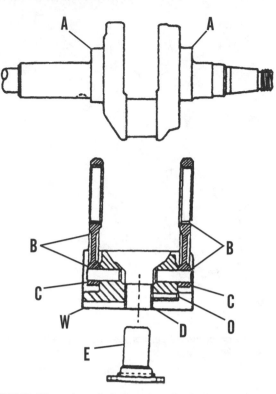

Fig. KW113–View of crankshaft and engine balancer wear check points. Refer to text.

A. Crankshaft journals
B. Link rod bearings
C. Wrist pins
D. Support shaft bushing
E. Support shaft

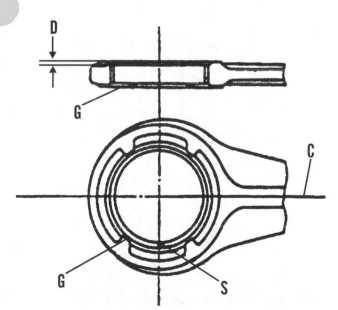

Fig. KW114–Bushing in big end of balancer link rod is replaceable. Refer to text for special installation instructions.

C. Link rod centerline
D. Bushing depth
G. Oil grooves
S. Bushing seam

rods (B) with the oil grooves facing away from the crankwebs. Install the spacer (6–Fig. KW112) with the chamfered face toward the link rod. Install the spacer (1–Fig. KW112) so the conical face is out. Install the balancer assembly with the crankshaft in the crankcase being careful not to damage the crankshaft oil seal. Align

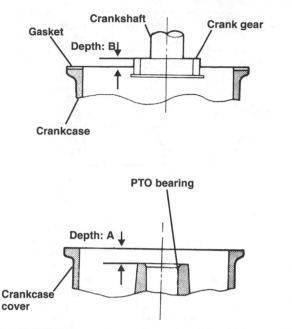

Fig. KW115–Refer to text to determine shim thickness for correct crankshaft end play.

the balancer weight with the hole in the crankcase and insert the support shaft (16–Fig. KW111). Install the connecting rod and piston. Rotate the crankshaft until the piston is at top dead center.

Install the valve tappets in their original bores. Align the timing marks on the crankshaft gear and camshaft gear and install the camshaft. Measure the distance from the oil pan mounting surface to the PTO shaft bearing edge as shown at (A–Fig. KW115) and note dimension. Measure the distance from the crank gear end of the crankshaft to the crankcase gasket surface with gasket installed as shown (B) and note the dimension. Subtract dimension B from dimension A and refer to the chart shown in Fig. KW116 to determine correct thickness of shim (8–Fig. KW112) needed to provide 0.09-0.22 mm (0.004-0.008 in.) crankshaft end play after assembly.

Make sure the governor weights are closed. Align the oil pump shaft convex with the camshaft end groove, align the governor gear teeth with the cam gear teeth and install the oil pan. Tighten the oil pan screws to the specified torque following the sequence shown in Fig. KW110.

CAMSHAFT AND BEARINGS

Camshaft is supported at each end in bearings that are an integral part of the crankcase or oil pump cover. Refer to the CRANKSHAFT AND BALANCER section for camshaft and valve tappet removal. Mark the tappets so they can be installed in their original positions if reused.

Camshaft minimum lobe height for intake and exhaust lobes is 35.40 mm (1.3937 in.).

Bearing journal minimum diameter is 19.907 mm (0.7837 in.) for PTO end of camshaft and 15.907 mm (0.6263 in.) for flywheel end.

Camshaft bearing bore maximum inside diameter is 20.071 mm (0.7902 in.) for oil pump cover bearing and 16.068 mm (0.6326 in.) for crankcase bearing.

When installing the camshaft and tappets, be sure the tappets are installed in their original position. If the camshaft is replaced, the tappets should also be replaced.

317

Difference in depth: A–B	Part Number of Shim	Thickness of Shim
1.92 to 1.99 mm (0.0755 to 0.0748 in.)	92025-2153	1.74 mm (0.0685 in.)
1.85 to 1.92 mm (0.0728 to 0.0755 in.)	92025-2152	1.67 mm (0.0629 in.)
1.78 to 1.85 mm (0.0700 to 0.0728 in.)	92025-2151	1.60 mm (0.0629 in.)
1.71 to 1.78 mm (0.0673-0.0700 in.)	92025-2150	1.53 mm (0.0602 in.)
1.64 to 1.71 mm (0.0645 to 0.0673 in.)	92025-2149	1.46 mm (0.0574 in.)
1.57 to 1.64 mm (0.0618 to 0.0645 in.)	92025-2148	1.39 mm (0.0547 in.)
1.50 to 1.57 mm (0.0590 to 0.0618 in.)	92025-2147	1.32 mm (0.0519 in.)
1.43 to 1.50 mm (0.0562 to 0.0590 in.)	92025-2146	1.25 mm (0.0492 in.)
1.36 to 1.43 mm (0.0535 to 0.0562 in.)	92025-2145	1.18 mm (0.0464 in.)

Fig. KW116–Chart showing recommended shim for correct crankshaft end play.

Make sure the timing marks on the camshaft gear and crankshaft gear are aligned.

GOVERNOR

The internal centrifugal flyweight governor is mounted in the oil pan and driven by the camshaft gear.

To remove the governor assembly, remove the oil pan from the crankcase. Use two screwdrivers to snap the governor gear and flyweight assembly off the governor stub shaft. The governor unit will be damaged when removed and must be replaced if removed. Be sure to install the thrust washer between the gear and oil pan. Install the governor by pushing down until it snaps onto the locating groove.

If removed, install the governor shaft and arm in the side of the crankcase and attach the cotter pin.

Refer to MAINTENANCE section for external governor linkage adjustment.

LOW OIL SENSOR

Some engines are equipped with a low oil sensor that may be located as shown in Fig. KW117. The oil sensor activates a low oil pressure warning light if oil pressure falls below 29.4 kPa (4.3 psi).

OIL PUMP AND RELIEF VALVE

The engine is equipped with an oil pump (4–Fig. KW118) attached to the oil pan. The trochoid oil pump draws oil through a filtering screen and inlet into the pump chamber. Pressurized oil is pumped to the PTO main journal, into and through the crankshaft to lubricate the connecting rod bearing, lower balancer link rods

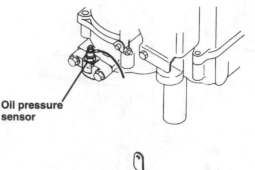

Fig. KW117–An oil pressure sender may be installed in one of the locations shown.

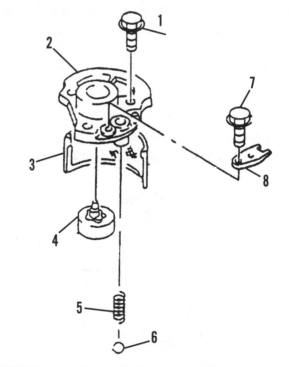

Fig. KW118–Exploded view of oil pump assembly.

1. Bolt
2. Oil pump cover
3. Filter screen
4. Oil pump rotors
5. Spring
6. Pressure relief ball
7. Bolt
8. Cover

and crankpin. Oil at the crankpin is passed through a metered orifice in the connecting rod and is sprayed onto the piston to cool the piston. Return oil lubricates the flywheel end bearing.

To remove the oil pump, remove the oil pan. Refer to the CAMSHAFT AND BEARINGS section and check the camshaft bearing diameter in the oil pump cover. Remove the

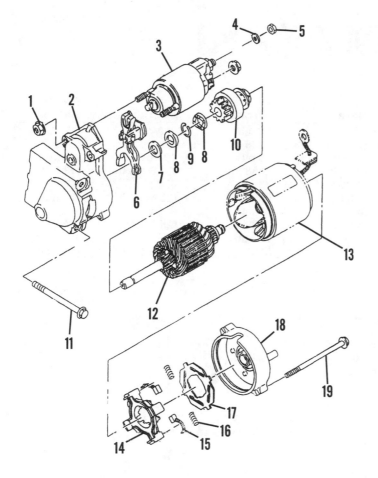

Fig. KW119–Exploded view of electric starter motor used on some models.

1. Nut
2. Drive housing
3. Solenoid
4. Washer
5. Nut
6. Yoke
7. Washer
8. Stop
9. Circlip
10. Starter drive
11. Bolt
12. Armature
13. Frame
14. Brush holder
15. Brush
16. Spring
17. Insulator plate
18. End cap
19. Bolt

oil pump cover and inspect the oil screen. Capscrews retaining the oil pressure relief valve cover are treated with locking compound. Remove only if required. Inspect seating of the ball in the relief valve.

Inspect oil pump components and refer to the following specifications:

Outer rotor diameter (min.)	28.9 mm (1.149 in.)
Outer rotor shaft (min.)	12.63 mm (0.497 in.)
Outer rotor thickness (min.)	11.92 mm (0.470 in.)
Pump cover bore (max.)	29.15 mm (1.148 in.)
Pump cover bore depth (max.)	12.14 mm (0.478 in.)

Pump shaft bore (max.)	12.76 mm (0.502 in.)
Pump shaft diameter (min.)	12.63 mm (0.497 in.)
Relief valve spring free length	19.0 mm (0.750 in.)

Reinstall by reversing the removal procedure. Tighten oil pump cover screws to 20 N•m (177 in.-lb.).

ELECTRIC STARTER

Refer to Fig. KW119 for an exploded view of the electric starter motor used on some models. Maximum no-load current draw at 6000 rpm is 50 amps.

KAWASAKI

Model	No. Cyls.	Bore	Stroke	Displacement	Power Rating
FC290V	1	78 mm (3.07 in.)	60 mm (2.36 in.)	286 cc (17.4 cu. in.)	6.7 kW (9 hp)
FC400V	1	87 mm (3.43 in.)	68 mm (2.68 in.)	404 cc (24.6 cu. in.)	9.7 kW (13 hp)
FC401V	1	89 mm (3.50 in.)	68 mm (2.68 in.)	423 cc (25.8 cu. in.)	9.7 kW (13 hp)
FC420V	1	89 mm (3.50 in.)	68 mm (2.68 in.)	423 cc (25.8 cu. in.)	10.5 kW (14 hp)
FC540V	1	89 mm (3.50 in.)	86 mm (3.38 in.)	535 cc (32.6 cu. in.)	12.8 kW (17 hp)

All models are four-stroke, overhead-valve, single-cylinder, air-cooled engines with a vertical crankshaft. Splash lubrication is used on Model FC290V, while an oil pump provides pressure lubrication on Models FC400V, FC401V, FC420V and FC540V. Engine serial number plate is located on the flywheel blower housing.

MAINTENANCE

LUBRICATION

Check engine oil level prior to operation. Maintain oil level between reference marks on dipstick with dipstick just touching first threads. Do not screw dipstick in to check oil level (Fig. KW201).

Engine oil should meet or exceed latest API service classification. Use oil of suitable viscosity for the expected air temperature range during the period between oil changes. Refer to temperature/viscosity chart shown in Fig. KW202.

On models without an oil filter, change engine oil after every 50 hours of operation or yearly, whichever comes first. On models equipped with an oil filter, change oil and filter after every 100 hours of operation or yearly, whichever comes first. Drain oil while engine is warm. Crankcase oil capacity for FC290V is approximately 1.1 L (2.3 pt.). Crankcase oil capacity for FC400V, FC401V and FC420V is approximately 1.3 L (2.75 pt.) with filter. Crankcase oil capacity for FC540V is approximately 1.6 L (3.4 pt.) with filter. Check oil level using dipstick after running engine momentarily.

Models FC400V, FC401V, FC420V and FC540V may be equipped with an oil pressure sensor located on the oil filter adapter, if equipped with an oil filter, or on the oil passage cover if not equipped with an oil filter. Switch should be closed at zero pressure and open at 29.4 kpa (4.3 psi). Switch is connected to a warning device.

AIR FILTER

Remove and clean the air filter element after every 25 hours of operation, or more often if operating in extremely dusty conditions. Replace the paper element (5—Figs. KW203 and KW204) after every 300 hours of operation. Replace either filter element anytime it is damaged.

To remove filter elements (4 and 5), remove the retaining knob or wing bolts (1) and washers (2). Remove the filter cover (3), foam precleaner element and paper element. Clean

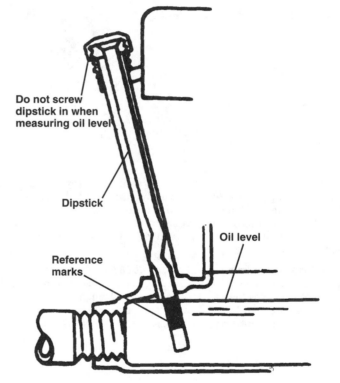

Fig. KW201–View showing procedure to check crankcase oil level. Refer to text.

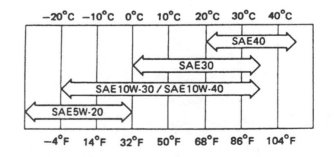

Fig. KW202–Engine oil viscosity should be based on expected air temperature as indicated in chart above.

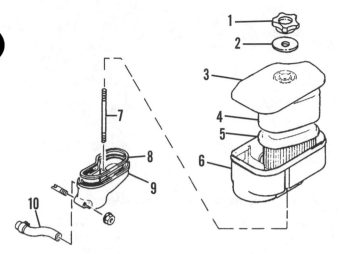

Fig. KW203–Exploded view of air filter assembly used on Model FC290V.

1. Knob
2. Washer
3. Cover
4. Foam element
5. Paper element
6. Housing
7. Stud
8. Gasket
9. Base
10. Breather hose

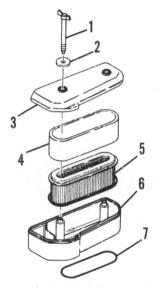

Fig. KW204–Exploded view of air filter assembly used on Models FC400V, FC401V, FC420V and FC540V.

1. Wing bolt
2. Washer
3. Cover
4. Foam element
5. Paper element
6. Housing
7. O-ring

foam element in a solution of warm water and liquid detergent, then squeeze out excess water and allow to air dry. DO NOT wash paper element. Apply light coat of engine oil to foam element and squeeze out excess oil. Clean paper element by tapping gently to remove dust. DO NOT use compressed air to clean the element. Inspect paper element for damage. Reinstall by reversing the removal procedure.

CRANKCASE BREATHER

Crankcase pressure is vented to the cylinder head. A reed valve is located on the top of the cylinder on Model FC290V or in the rocker arm chamber on all other models. Replace the reed valve if tip of reed stands up more than 0.2 mm

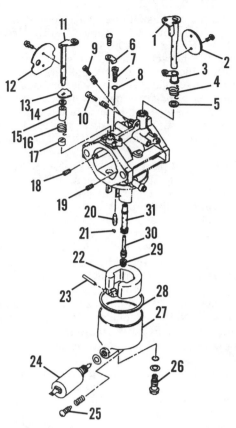

Fig. KW205–Exploded view of typical float-type carburetor used on all models. Fuel shut-off solenoid (24) is not used on some engines.

1. Throttle shaft
2. Throttle plate
3. Ring
4. Spring
5. Seal
6. Retainer plate
7. Pilot jet
8. O-ring
9. Pilot screw
10. Idle speed screw
11. Choke shaft
12. Choke plate
13. Plate
14. Seal
15. Ring
16. Spring
17. Ring
18. Pilot air jet
19. Main air jet
20. Fuel inlet needle
21. Clip
22. Plate
23. Pin
24. Fuel shut-off solenoid
25. Drain screw
26. Special bolt
27. Float bowl
28. Gasket
29. Main jet
30. Bleed pipe
31. Main nozzle

(0.008 in.) on Model FC290V or 2.0 mm (0.080 in.) on all other models, or if reed is damaged or worn excessively.

SPARK PLUG

Recommended spark plug is NGK BPR5ES or Champion RN11YC.

Remove, clean and set the spark plug after every 100 hours of operation. Specified spark plug gap is 0.7-0.8 mm (0.028-0.031 in.).

CARBURETOR

All models are equipped with a float side draft carburetor. Check carburetor whenever poor or erratic performance is noted.

Recommended engine idle speed is 1450-1650 rpm. Adjust the idle speed by turning the idle speed screw (10–Fig. KW205) clockwise to increase the idle speed or counterclockwise to decrease the idle speed.

Adjust throttle control as follows: Place engine throttle lever in fast position. Insert a 6 mm ($^{15}\!/_{64}$-inch) drill bit through the hole (H–Fig. KW206) in speed control lever (7) and bracket (8). Loosen throttle cable housing clamp screw (10), pull cable housing tight and retighten cable clamp screw. Rotate choke lever screw (9) on back side of bracket so there is a gap between screw and choke control lever, then turn the screw back in until it just touches the lever. Remove drill bit. With throttle control lever in choke position, carburetor choke plate should be closed, if not, repeat procedure.

Initial adjustment of pilot air screw (7–Fig. KW205) is 1½ turns open from a lightly seated position. Make the final adjustment with the engine at operating temperature and running. Adjust pilot screw to obtain the maximum engine idle speed, then turn pilot screw out counterclockwise an additional ¼ turn. Adjust the idle speed screw (10) so the engine idles at 1450-1650 rpm.

Main fuel mixture is controlled by a fixed main jet (29). Different size main jets are available for high altitude operation.

Remove the float bowl (27–Fig. KW205) for access to internal components. Note that pilot jet (7) is pressed into carburetor body on some FC540V engines.

Clean carburetor parts except plastic components using carburetor cleaner. Do not clean jets or passages with drill bits or wire as enlargement of the passages could affect carburetor calibration. Rinse the parts in warm water to neutralize the corrosive action of the carburetor cleaner and dry with compressed air.

When assembling the carburetor, note the following. Place a small drop of nonhardening sealant such as Permatex #2 or equivalent on throttle and choke plate retaining screws. Float should be parallel with body when carburetor is inverted as shown in Fig. KW207. If equipped with white plastic float, float height is not adjustable; replace any components that are damaged or excessively worn and adversely affect the float position. On models with an adjustable float, bend the float tab to adjust the float height. On Models FC290V and FC540V, measure float drop (D–Fig. KW208). Float drop should be 10.5-12.5 mm (0.413-0.492 in.). Bend tab on back of float arm to adjust float drop.

GOVERNOR

A gear-driven, flyweight governor is located inside the engine crankcase. Before adjusting governor linkage, make certain all linkage is in good condition and that tension spring (4–Fig. KW206) is not stretched.

To adjust external linkage, place engine throttle control in the FAST position. Spring (2) around governor-to-carburetor rod must pull governor lever (3) and throttle lever toward each other. Loosen governor lever clamp bolt (5) and turn governor shaft (6) clockwise as far as possible. Tighten clamp bolt nut.

Maximum no-load engine speed should be 3275-3425 rpm unless specified otherwise by equipment manufacturer. Adjust maximum no-load engine speed as follows: Run engine until normal operating temperature is reached. Align holes in speed control lever (7) and bracket (8) and insert a inch drill bit through hole (H). Run engine under no load and determine engine speed using an accurate tachometer. If engine speed is not 3275-3425 rpm, loosen bracket retaining screws (11) and reposition bracket to obtain desired engine speed. Retighten screws and recheck engine speed. Check choke operation as outlined in the CARBURETOR section.

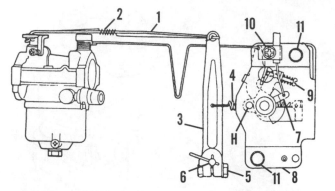

Fig. KW206–View of the external governor linkage used on all models.

1. Governor-to-carburetor rod
2. Spring
3. Governor lever
4. Tension spring
5. Clamp bolt
6. Governor shaft
7. Speed control lever
8. Control plate
9. Choke setting screw
10. Clamp bolt
11. Screws

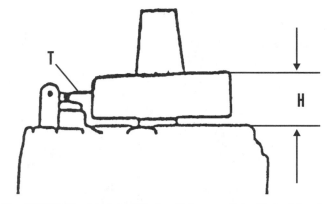

Fig. KW207–Float height (H) should be parallel with fuel bowl mounting surface of carburetor body. If float height is adjustable, bend float tab (T) to adjust float height.

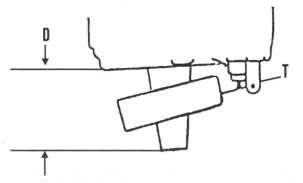

Fig. KW208–On models FC290V and FC540V, flat drop (D) should be 10.5 mm (0.4313-0.492 in.). Bend tab on back of float arm to adjust float drop.

IGNITION SYSTEM

All models are equipped with an electronic ignition system and regular maintenance is not required. Ignition timing is not adjustable. Ignition coil is located outside flywheel. Air gap between ignition coil and flywheel should be 0.30 mm (0.012 in.).

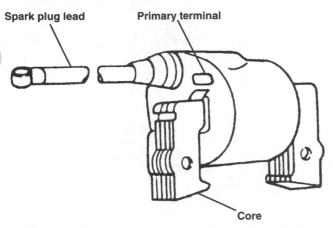

Fig. KW209—View of ignition coil showing location of primary terminal, spark plug lead and iron core.

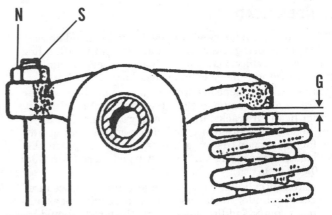

Fig. KW211—Valve clearance gap (G) is adjusted by loosening nut (N) and rotating adjusting screw (S). Valve clearance should be 0.15 mm (0.006 in.).

compression stroke. Remove rocker arm cover. Valve clearance gap (G–Fig. KW211) for both valves should be 0.15 mm (0.006 in.). Loosen nut (N) and turn adjusting screw (S) to obtain desired clearance. Tighten nut to 20 N•m (177 in.-lb.) and recheck adjustment.

CYLINDER HEAD AND COMBUSTION CHAMBER

Standard compression reading should be 483 kPa (71 psi).

NOTE: When checking compression pressure, spark plug high tension lead must be grounded or electronic ignition could be damaged.

Excessive carbon build-up on piston and cylinder head are indicated by higher than standard compression reading. A leaking cylinder head gasket, worn piston rings and cylinder bore, or poorly seated valves are indicated by lower than standard compression reading.

REPAIRS

TIGHTENING TORQUE

Recommended tightening torque specifications are as follows:

Connecting rod	20 N•m
	(177 in.-lb.)
Crankshaft (PTO end)	38 N•m
	(28 ft.-lb.)
Cylinder head:	
FC290V	24 N•m
	(212 in.-lb.)
All other models..	52 N•m
	(38 ft.-lb.)
Flywheel:	
FC290V	86 N•m
	(63 ft.-lb.)
FC540V	172 N•m
	(126 ft.-lb.)
All other models	137 N•m
	(101 ft.-lb.)
Oil drain plug	23 N•m
	(204 in.-lb.)
Oil pan	26 N•m
	(19 ft.-lb.)

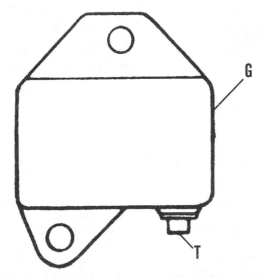

Fig. KW210—All models are equipped with the ignition control unit shown. Refer to text for test procedure.

To test ignition coil, remove cooling shrouds and disconnect spark plug cable and primary lead wire (Fig. KW209). Connect ohmmeter test leads between coil core (ground) and high tension (spark plug) terminal. Secondary coil resistance should be 10.9k-16.3k ohms. Remove the test lead connected to high tension terminal and connect lead to coil primary terminal. Primary coil resistance should be 0.48-0.72 ohms. If readings vary significantly from specifications, replace the ignition coil.

To test control unit, refer to Fig. KW210 and disconnect all electrical leads. Connect positive ohmmeter lead to terminal (T) and negative ohmmeter lead to the ground lead or control unit case (G) according to model being serviced. Ohmmeter reading should be 400-600 ohms. Reverse leads. Ohmmeter reading should be 60-100 ohms. If ohmmeter readings are not as specified, replace the control unit.

VALVE ADJUSTMENT

Clearance between the valve stem ends and rocker arms should be checked and adjusted after every 300 hours of operation. Engine must be cold for valve adjustment. Rotate crankshaft so the piston is at top dead center on the

CYLINDER HEAD

To remove cylinder head, remove cylinder head shroud and blower housing. Remove carburetor and muffler. Remove rocker arm cover, loosen cylinder head mounting bolts evenly and remove cylinder head and gasket.

Remove carbon deposits from combustion chamber being careful not to damage gasket sealing surface. Inspect cylinder head for cracks, nicks or other damage. Place cylinder head on a flat surface and check entire sealing surface for distortion using a feeler gauge. Replace the cylinder head if sealing surface is warped more than 0.05 mm (0.002 in.).

To reinstall cylinder head, reverse removal procedure. Surfaces of cylinder head gasket are coated with a sealant and do not require additional sealant. Push rods should be installed in their original positions. Tighten cylinder head screws in sequence shown in Fig. KW212 to initial torque of 18 N•m (159 in.-lb.) on Model FC290V and 32 N•m (24 ft.-lb.) on all other models. On Model FC290V, tighten screws 3 N.m (27 in.-lb.) at a time following sequence in Fig. KW212. On all other models, tighten screws 7 N•m (5 ft.-lb.) at a time following sequence in Fig. KW212. Final torque is 24 N•m (18 ft.-lb.) on Model FC290V and 52 N•m (38 ft.-lb.) on all other models. Adjust valve clearance as outlined in MAINTENANCE section.

VALVE SYSTEM

Remove cylinder head as outlined above. Remove rocker arm shaft (21–Fig. KW213) and rocker arms (6 and 7). Compress valve springs using a suitable valve spring compressor, and remove collet halves (8). Remove the retainers (9), springs (10) and valves (19 and 20). Remove the valve stem seals (11) from top of valve guides.

NOTE: Removal of valve stem seal will damage the seal. Replace the seals whenever they are removed.

Check all parts for damage. Refer to the following specifications:

Rocker arm shaft OD—
  Wear limit . . . . 12.94 mm
  (0.509 in.)

Rocker arm ID—
  Wear limit . . . . 13.07 mm
  (0.515 in.)

Valve spring free length—
  Minimum allowable:
  FC290V . . . . 31.00 mm
  (1.220 in.)
  All other models . . . . 37.50 mm
  (1.476 in.)

Valve guide ID—
  Wear limit . . . . 7.07 mm
  (0.278 in.)

Replace the valves if the stem is warped more than 0.03 mm (0.001 in.) or if valve margin is less than 0.60 mm (0.020 in.). Valve stem ends should be ground square. Valve face and seat angles are 45° for intake and exhaust. Valve seating surface should be 0.80 mm (0.031 in.) for Model FC290V, 1.10-1.46 mm (0.039-0.057 in.) for all other models. Seats can be narrowed using a 30° stone or cutter. Lap valves into the seats to ensure proper contact. Seats should contact center of valve face.

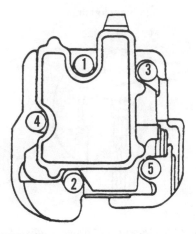

Fig. KW212–Tighten cylinder head bolts in sequence shown.

Valve guides (14) can be replaced using suitable valve guide driver. Press guides into cylinder head until snap ring (13) just contacts cylinder head. Ream new guides with a 7 mm valve guide reamer. Valve guide finished inside diameter should be 7.000-7.015 mm (0.2756-0.2762 in.).

CONNECTING ROD

The connecting rod (16–Fig. KW214 or Fig. KW215) and piston are removed as an assembly after removing the cylinder head and oil pan. Remove carbon and ring ridge if present from the top of the cylinder before removing piston. Remove connecting rod bolts and connecting rod cap, then push connecting rod and piston out through top of cylinder. Remove retaining rings (18) and push piston pin (17) out of the piston to separate piston from the connecting rod.

Connecting rod rides directly on the crankshaft journal. Maximum allowable inside diameter for connecting rod big end bearing surface is 35.567 mm (1.4003 in.) for Model FC290V and 41.068 mm (1.6169 in.) for all other models. Maximum connecting rod-to-crankpin clearance is 0.14 mm (0.006 in.). A connecting rod is available with 0.50 mm (0.020 in.) undersize big end for use with undersize crankshaft crankpin. Refer to CRANKSHAFT AND BALANCER section.

Maximum inside diameter of connecting rod small end is 19.059 mm (0.7540 in.) for Model FC290V, and 22.059 mm (0.8685 in.) for all other models. Maximum allowable connecting rod-to-piston pin clearance is 0.08 mm (0.003 in.).

When reassembling, install piston on connecting rod so arrow on top of piston is toward the "MADE IN JAPAN" side of connecting rod. Install piston and connecting rod in cylinder so arrow on top of piston is toward flywheel side of engine. Tighten connecting rod cap bolts to 20 N•m (180 in.-lb.).

PISTON, PIN AND RINGS

Piston and connecting rod are removed as an assembly after removing cylinder head and oil pan. Refer to CONNECTING ROD section for removal and installation procedure.

After separating piston and connecting rod, carefully remove piston rings and clean carbon and other deposits from piston surface and piston ring lands.

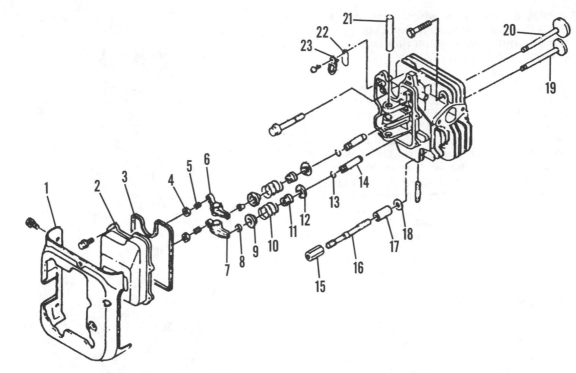

Fig. KW213–Exploded view of cylinder head assembly.

1. Shroud
2. Rocker arm cover
3. Gasket
4. Locknut
5. Adjusting screw
6. Rocker arm, intake

7. Rocker arm, exhaust
8. Retainer
9. Retainer
10. Valve spring
11. Seal
12. Plate

13. Snap ring
14. Valve guide
15. Nut
16. Stud
17. Bushing
18. Washer

19. Exhaust valve
20. Intake valve
21. Rocker arm shaft
22. Breather valve
23. Retainer plate

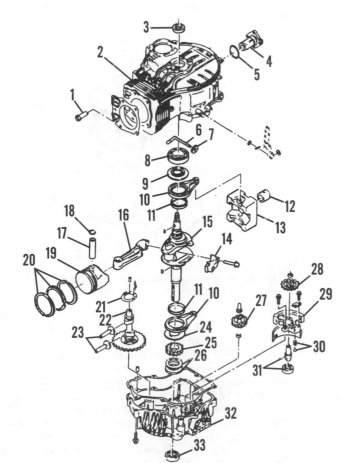

Fig. KW214–Exploded view of FC400V, FC401V, FC420V and FC540V engines. Model FC290V is similar, but bushing (12) is not replaceable. Refer to Fig. KW215 for Model FC290V.

1. Check valve
2. Cylinder block & crankcase
3. Oil seal
4. Counterweight support shaft
5. O-ring
6. Governor shaft
7. Washer
8. Main bearing
9. Spacer
10. Link rod
11. Bushing
12. Bushing
13. Balancer counterweight
14. Rod cap
15. Crankshaft
16. Connecting rod
17. Piston pin

18. Snap ring
19. Piston
20. Piston rings
21. Compression release mechanism
22. Camshaft assy.
23. Valve tappets
24. Spacer
25. Gear
26. Shims
27. Governor flyweight assy.
28. Gear
29. Oil pump housing
30. Oil pressure relief valve
31. Oil pump rotors
32. Oil pan
33. Oil seal

CAUTION: Exercise extreme care when cleaning piston rings lands. Do not damage squared edges or widen piston ring grooves. If piston ring lands are damaged, replace the piston.

Maximum inside diameter of pin bore in piston is 19.031 mm (0.7493 in.) for Model FC290V and 22.037 mm (0.8676 in.) for all other models. Piston pin outside diameter wear limit is 18.981 mm (0.7473 in.) for Model FC290V, and 21.977 mm (0.8652 in.) for all other models. Maximum piston-to-pin clearance is 0.05 mm (0.0020 in.) for Model FC290V, and 0.06 mm (0.0024 in.) for all other models.

To check piston ring grooves for wear, insert a new ring in the ring groove and use a feeler gauge to measure ring side clearance in the groove. On Model FC290V, replace the piston if side clearance exceeds 0.16 mm (0.006 in.) for top ring, 0.14 mm (0.005 in.) for second ring or 0.19 mm (0.007 in.) for oil ring. On all other models, replace the piston if side clearance exceeds 0.17 mm (0.007 in.) for top ring, 0.15 mm (0.006 in.) for second ring or 0.20 mm (0.008 in.) for oil ring.

Insert each ring squarely in cylinder bore about 25 mm (1 in.) below top of cylinder and measure ring end gap. On Model FC290V, maximum allowable end gap is 0.70 mm (0.028 in.) for compression rings and 1.20 mm (0.047 in.) for oil control ring. On Models FC420V and FC540V, the maximum allowable end gap is 0.90 mm (0.035 in.) for compression rings and 1.30 mm (0.051 in.) for the oil control ring. If the piston ring gap is greater than specified, check cylinder bore for wear.

During assembly, install piston on connecting rod so the arrow on top of the piston is toward the MADE IN JAPAN side of connecting rod. Use NEW snap rings (18—Fig. KW214 or Fig. KW215) to retain piston pin in piston. Install oil ring spacer (3—Fig. KW216) first, then install side rails (4). Position side rail end gaps 180° apart. Install the second ring (2) and first ring (1) on piston with R, N or NPR mark on ring facing up. Stagger piston ring end gaps 180° apart, but do not align with side rail end gaps. Lubricate piston and cylinder with engine oil. Use a suitable ring compressor to compress rings when installing piston in cylinder. Be sure that arrow on top of piston faces flywheel side of engine.

CYLINDER, CRANKCASE, MAIN BEARINGS AND SEALS

Cylinder and crankcase are an integral casting. Standard cylinder bore diameter is 77.98-78.00 mm (3.070-3.071 in.) for Model FC290V, and 88.90-89.00 mm (3.500-3.504 in.) for all other models. Cylinder bore wear limit is 78.067 mm (3.0735 in.) for Model FC290V, and 89.076 mm (3.5069 in.) for all other models. Cylinder can be bored or honed to fit an oversize piston. Oversize pistons are available.

The main bearing on PTO side is a replaceable bushing in the oil pan on Model FC290V, while an integral bushing is a part of the oil pan on all other models. Main bearing on the flywheel side of all models is a ball bearing.

On Model FC290V, maximum outside diameter of bushing in oil pan is 30.125 mm (1.1860 in.). If bushing replacement is required, press out the old bushing. Install new bushing so grooves (G—Fig. KW217) point toward inside of oil pan and split (T) in bushing is located as shown in Fig. KW217. The bearing on the flywheel side should be a press fit on crankshaft and in bearing bore of crankcase.

On Models FC400V, FC401V, FC420V and FC540V, maximum inside diameter for integral bearing bore in oil

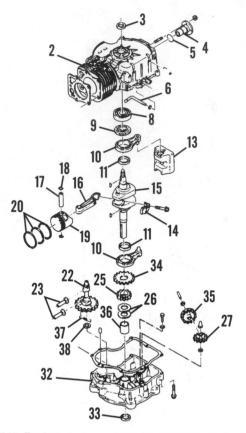

Fig. KW215—Exploded view of Model FC290V. Refer to Fig. KW214 for parts identification except for the following:

34. Governor drive gear
35. Oil slinger
36. Bushing
37. Compression release spring
38. Shim

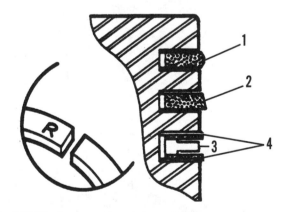

Fig. KW216—Cross-sectional view of piston showing correct installation of piston rings. Refer to text.

1. Top ring
2. Second ring
3. Spacer
4. Side rails

pan is 35.069 mm (1.3807 in.) for FC400V, FC401V and FC420V, and 38.056 mm (1.4983 in.) for FC540V. Bearing on flywheel side should be a press fit on crankshaft and in bearing bore of crankcase.

Replace the crankshaft seals (3 and 33—Fig. KW214 or Fig. KW215) if worn or damaged. Install seals with open side facing inside of engine and press in until flush with crankcase or oil pan. Pack seals with lithium-base grease prior to crankshaft installation.

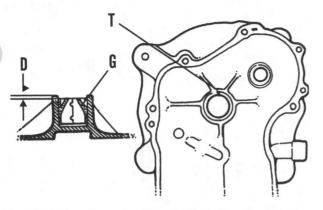

Fig. KW217–Install new bushing on FC290V engine so grooves (G) point toward inside of oil pan and split (T) in bushing is located as shown. Bushing depth (D) must be 1 mm (0.030 in.) below surface.

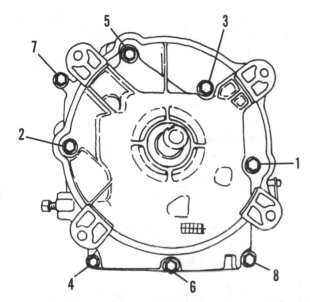

Fig. KW218–Oil pan screws on FC290V engines must be tightened evenly to specified torque following the sequence shown.

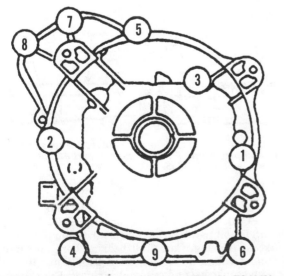

Fig. KW219–Oil pan screws on FC400V, FC401V, FC420V and FC540V engines must be tightened evenly to specified torque following the sequence shown.

When installing oil pan, tighten retaining screws to 26 N•m (19 ft.-lb.). On all models, tighten mounting screws in the sequence shown in Fig. KW218 or KW219.

CRANKSHAFT AND BALANCER

The crankshaft is supported on flywheel side by a ball main bearing, and on the PTO side by a plain bearing in the oil pan. A reciprocating balancer is used on all models.

To remove crankshaft, remove shrouds, fan housing, flywheel, cylinder head and oil pan. Rotate crankshaft until timing marks on camshaft gear and crankshaft gear are aligned, then remove camshaft and gear. Remove valve tappets (23–Fig. KW214); identify tappets so they can be reinstalled in original position. Remove connecting rod and piston. Unbolt and remove counterweight support shaft (4). Remove crankshaft and balancer assembly from crankcase.

To disassemble balancer, remove collar (9), gear (25), spacer (24) and link rods (10) from crankshaft (15) and balancer (13) wrist pins.

Clean and inspect all parts for damage. Refer to the following table for crankshaft main journal minimum diameter:

FC290V

PTO end	29.922 mm
	(1.1780 in.)
Flywheel end.	29.940 mm
	(1.1787 in.)

FC540V

PTO end	37.904 mm
	(1.4923 in.)
Flywheel end	34.945 mm
	(1.3758 in.)

All other models

PTO end	34.919 mm
	(1.3747 in.)
Flywheel end	34.945 mm
	(1.3758 in.)

Main journals cannot be resized. Refer to CYLINDER, CRANKCASE, MAIN BEARINGS AND SEALS section for main bearing dimensions. Measure crankshaft runout at the main journals. Replace the crankshaft if runout exceeds 0.05 mm (0.002 in.). Crankshaft cannot be straightened.

Crankpin journal minimum diameter is 35.428 mm (1.3948 in.) for Model FC290V and 40.928 mm (1.6113 in.) for all other models. Crankpin can be reground to accept undersize connecting rod. Refer to the CONNECTING ROD section.

Measure outside diameter of the crankshaft balancer link rod journals (A–Fig. KW220), inside diameter of big end and small end of balancer link rods (B), inside diameter of the support shaft bushing (D) and outside diameter of support shaft (E). Refer to the following table for wear limit specifications and replace the parts when necessary.

Link rod journal OD—

FC290V	46.953 mm
	(1.8485 in.)
FC540V	57.941 mm
	(2.2811 in.)
All other models	53.950 mm
	(2.1240 in.)

Link rod big end ID—

FC290V	7.121 mm
	(1.8552 in.)

FC540V . . . . 58.153 mm
(2.2895 in.)

All other models . . . . 54.121 mm
(2.1307 in.)

Link rod small end ID—
All models . . . . 12.06 mm
(0.475 in.)

Support shaft bushing ID—
All models . . . . 26.097 mm
(1.0274 in.)

Support shaft OD—
All models . . . . 25.927 mm
(1.0208 in.)

Balancer link rod (10—Fig. KW214 and KW215) may be equipped with a replaceable bushing. When installing a new link rod bushing, press bushing into link rod from side opposite oil grooves (G—Fig. KW221). Position seam (S) of bushing 90° from centerline (C) of link rod. Install bushing so the depth (D) below the machined surface of the rod is 0.5 mm (0.020 in.).

The support shaft bushing (D) is replaceable on all models except Model FC290V. When installing new support shaft bushing, make sure that oil hole in bushing is aligned with oil passage in balancer.

To assemble crankshaft and balancer, install balance weight (W–Fig. KW220) with oil hole (O) toward flywheel side of crankshaft. Install link rods (B) with oil grooves facing away from crank webs. Install the spacer (24–Fig. KW214) on Models FC400V, FC401V, FC420V and FC540V with the chamfered face toward link rod. On Model FC290V, install the governor gear (34–Fig. KW215) with the chamfered face toward link rod. On all models, install spacer (9–Fig. KW214 or KW215) so conical face is out. On all models, install balancer assembly with the crankshaft into the crankcase, being careful not to damage crankshaft oil seal. Align balancer weight with hole in crankcase and insert support shaft (4). Install connecting rod and piston. Rotate crankshaft until piston is at top dead center.

Install valve tappets in their original bores. Align timing marks on crankshaft gear and camshaft gear and install camshaft. Install oil pan with original shims (26), then use a dial indicator to measure crankshaft end play. Add or remove shims when necessary to obtain the specified end play of 0.09-0.22 mm (0.004-0.009 in.).

CAMSHAFT AND BEARINGS

Camshaft is supported at each end in bearings that are integral part of crankcase or oil pan. Refer to CRANKSHAFT AND BALANCER section for camshaft and valve tappet removal. Mark tappets so they can be installed in their original positions if reused.

Camshaft minimum lobe height for intake and exhaust lobes is 27.08 mm (1.066 in.) for FC290V engine, 37.10 mm (1.461 in.) for FC540V engine or 36.75 mm (1.446 in.) for all other model engines.

Bearing journal minimum diameter for FC290V engine is 13.922 mm (0.5481 in.) for PTO end of camshaft and 15.921 mm (0.6268 in.) for flywheel end. Bearing journal minimum diameter for FC400V, FC401V and FC420V engines is 20.912 mm (0.8233 in.) for PTO end of camshaft and 19.912 mm (0.7839 in.) for flywheel end. Bearing journal minimum diameter for FC540V engine is 20.91 mm (0.823 in.) for both ends of camshaft.

Camshaft bearing bore maximum inside diameter for FC290V engine is 14.054 mm (0.5533 in.) for oil pan bearing and 16.055 mm (0.6321 in.) for crankcase bearing.

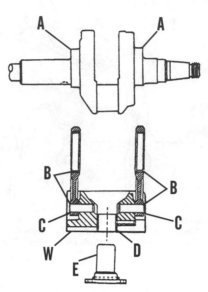

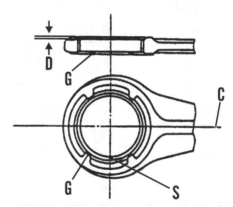

Fig. KW220–View of crankshaft and engine balancer wear check points. Refer to text.

A. Crankshaft journals
B. Link rod bearings
C. Wrist pins
D. Support shaft bushing
E. Support shaft

Fig. KW221–Bushing in big end of balancer link rod is replaceable. Refer to text for special installation instruction.

C. Link rod centerline
D. Bushing depth
G. Oil grooves
S. Bushing seam

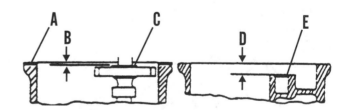

Fig. KW222–Refer to text to determine shim thickness to adjust camshaft end play on all FC290V engines and FC540 engines prior to serial number 014455.

Camshaft bearing bore maximum inside diameter for FC400V, FC401V and FC420V engine is 21.076 mm (0.8298 in.) for oil pan bearing and 20.076 mm (0.790 in.) for crankcase bearing. Camshaft bearing bore maximum inside diameter for FC540V engine is 21.076 mm (0.8298 in.) for both crankcase and oil pan bearings.

Camshaft end play must be adjusted on all FC290V engines and FC540V engines prior to serial number 014455

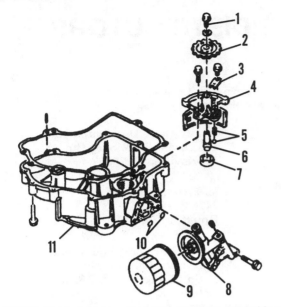

Fig. KW223—Exploded view of engine oil pump assembly used on all models except FC290V.

1. Cap screw	6. Pump inner rotor
2. Drive gear	7. Pump outer rotor
3. Retainer plate	8. Filter base
4. Pump housing	9. Oil filter
5. Pressure relief	10. O-rings
valve assy.	11. Oil pan

whenever camshaft, oil pan or crankcase is replaced. Correct end play is 0.20 mm (0.008 in.). Adjust end play by changing the thickness of shim located between oil pan and camshaft. To calculate correct shim thickness, position camshaft and oil pan gasket on crankcase as shown in Fig. KW222. Measure distance (B) from gasket (A) to thrust face (C) on camshaft. Measure distance (D) from oil pan face to top of camshaft bearing boss (E). For FC290V engine, subtract measurement (B) from measurement (D). For FC540V engine, add measurement (B) to measurement (D). For either engine, subtract 0.20 mm (0.008 in.) from the result of the above calculation to determine required shim thickness. Install shim (38—Fig. KW215) on camshaft thrust face (C—Fig. KW222).

When installing camshaft and tappets, be sure that tappets are installed in their original position. If the camshaft is replaced, the tappets should also be replaced. Make sure that timing marks on the camshaft gear and crankshaft gear are aligned.

GOVERNOR

The internal centrifugal flyweight governor (27—Figs. KW214 and KW215) is mounted in the oil pan. On Model FC290V, the governor is gear driven by gear (34—Fig. KW215) on the crankshaft, while the governor on all other models is driven by the camshaft gear. The governor gear on Model FC290V also drives the oil slinger gear (25—Fig. KW215).

To remove governor assembly, remove oil pan from crankcase. Use two screwdrivers to snap governor gear and flyweight assembly off governor stub shaft. Governor unit will be damaged when removed and must be replaced if removed. Be sure to install thrust washer between gear and oil pan. Install governor by pushing down until it snaps onto the locating groove.

If removed, install governor shaft and arm in the side of the crankcase and attach the cotter pin.

Refer to the MAINTENANCE section for external governor linkage adjustment.

OIL PUMP AND RELIEF VALVE

All models except FC290V are equipped with an oil pump. Model FC290V is equipped with an oil slinger gear.

The trochoid oil pump (Fig. KW223) used on Models FC400V, FC401V, FC420V and FC540V is mounted in the oil pan (11).

To remove oil pump, first separate oil pan from the cylinder block. Remove pump drive gear (2). Remove pump housing mounting cap screws and withdraw pump housing (4) and inner rotor shaft (6) together from oil pan. Remove retainer plate (3) and relief valve ball and spring (5).

Inspect seating of relief valve ball. Measure relief valve spring free length. Replace the spring if free length is less than 19.00 mm (0.748 in.).

Measure diameter of outer rotor shaft (6); wear limit is 12.63 mm (0.497 in.). Measure inside diameter of rotor shaft bearing surface in pump housing; wear limit is 12.76 mm (0.502 in.).

To reinstall pump, reverse removal procedure. Lubricate parts with engine oil.

ELECTRIC STARTER

Place alignment marks on pinion housing, frame and end cover before disassembly so they can be reinstalled in original position. Replace the brushes if the length is less than 8.5 mm (0.33 in.) on Model FC290V, 6 mm (0.24 in.) on Models FC400V, FC401V and FC420V, or 10.5 mm (0.41 in.) on Model FC540V.

KAWASAKI CENTRAL PARTS DISTRIBUTORS

(Arranged Alphabetically by States)

These franchised firms carry extensive stocks of repair parts. Contact them
for name of dealer in their area who will have replacement parts.

Artesco, Inc.
2949 E. Washington Street
Phoenix, AZ 85034

Bee Tee Equipment Sales
21075 Alexander Crt., Unit H
Hayward, CA 91754

T M C Power Equipment, Inc.
2051 Saturn Street
Monterey Park, CA 91754

Colorado Outdoor Power Equip.
1441 W. Bayaud, Suite 1 A
Denver, CO 80223

Engine Power Supply
3685 Old Winter Garden Road
Orlando, FL 32805

Power Systems Div. E. C Dist.
4499 Market Street
Boise, ID 83705

Remco Power Equipment Company
2100 West 16th Street
Broadview, IL 60135

Strietters II Distributors
1333 Street Road #2 West
La Porte, IN 46350

A-1 Distributors Ltd.
2600 Hwy. 75 North
Sioux City, IA 51102

Parrish Implement Co., Inc.
913 E. Liberty
Louisville, KY 40204

Gulf Engine & Equipment
2306 Engineers Road
Belle Chasse, LA 70037

C V Foster Equipment Co.
2502 Hartford Road
Baltimore, MD 21218

D & S Sales
197 Main Street
Agawan, MA 01001

Plymouth Air Cooled Equip, Inc.
587 W. Ann Arbor Trail
Plymouth, MI 48170

Fowler Electric Co.
2208 W 94 Street
Bloomington, MN 55431

Pro Engine Sales
Route 206 S of Ross Corner
Augusta, NJ 07822

Arbordale Power Products
480 Dodge Road
Getzville, NY 14068

Dixie Sales Co. Inc.
335 North Greene
Greensboro, NC 27402

Power Equipment Company
4050 W. Main Avenue
Fargo, ND 58103

Hayward Distributing Co.
460 Neilston Street
Columbus, OH 43215

Brown Engine & Equipment
4315 S. Robinson
Oklahoma City, OK 73109

E C Distributing Company
2122 Northwest Upshur
Portland, OR 97210

Stull Company
701 4th Avenue
Corapolis, PA 15108

Sullivan Brothers Inc.
Creek Road & Langoma Ave.
Elverson, PA 19520

Trinity Metro Distributors Inc.
100 Lewisville W. Shop Ctr.
Lewisville, TX 75067

M & M Distributing
7476 Harwin
Houston, TX 77036

Industrial Energy Equipment
145 North Highway 89
N. Salt Lake City, UT 84054

Northwest Motor Parts
2930 6th Avenue
Seattle, WA 98124

Morley Murphy
700 Morley Road
Green Bay, WI 54303

Morley-Murphy
8500 W. Bradley Road
Milwaukee, WI 53224

CANADA

Oliver Industrial Supply Ltd.
236 36th Street
Lethbridge, ALB T1J 4B2

Coast Dieselec Ltd.
101 11471 Blacksmith Place
Richmond, BC V7A 4T7

Coast Dieselec Ltd.
10 1235 Shawson Drive
Mississauga, ONT L4W 1C4

Oliver Agricultural Supply
140 East 4th Avenue
Regina, SASK S4P 3B2

KOHLER

Model	No. Cyls.	Bore	Stroke	Displacement	Power Rating
CH11, CV11	1	87 mm (3.43 in.)	67 mm (2.64 in.)	398 cc (24.3 cu. in.)	8.2 kW (11 hp)
CH12.5, CV12.5	1	87 mm (3.43 in.)	67 mm (2.64 in.)	398 cc (24.3 cu. in.)	9.33 kW (12.5 hp)
CH14, CV14	1	87 mm (3.43 in.)	67 mm (2.64 in.)	398 cc (24.3 cu. in.)	10.5 kW (14 hp)
CH15, CV15	1	90 mm (3.55 in.)	67 mm (2.64 in.)	426 cc (26.0 cu. in.)	11.2 kW (15 hp)
CV16	1	90 mm (3.55 in.)	67 mm (2.64 in.)	398 cc (26.0 cu. in.)	11.9 kW (16 hp)

NOTE: Metric fasteners are used throughout engine.

The Kohler engines covered in this section are four-stroke, air-cooled, single-cylinder engines using an overhead valve system. Engine identification numbers are located on a decal affixed to flywheel fan shroud.

MAINTENANCE

LUBRICATION

Periodically check oil level; do not overfill. To check oil level, seat the dipstick cap on the oil fill tube. Remove the dipstick and check oil level on dipstick. Oil level should be up to, but not over, the "F" mark on the dipstick.

Manufacturer recommends using oil with an API service rating of SG or SH, or any rating formulated to supercede SG or SH. Use SAE 10W-30 oil for temperatures above 0° F (−18° C). When operating in temperatures below 32° F (0° C), SAE 5W-20, 5W-30 or 10W-30 oil may be used, except 10W-30 oil should not be used below 0° F (−18° C). Do not use SAE 10W-40 oil in any temperature.

In overhauled or new engines or short blocks, use SAE 10W-30 oil for the first 5 hours of operation, then change oil according to ambient temperature requirements. Recommended oil change interval after 5-hour break-in is every 100 hours of operation. Oil should be drained while engine is warm.

It is recommended that a new oil filter be installed at each oil change. Apply a light coating of clean engine oil to filter gasket. Install oil filter until the rubber gasket contacts the filter adapter plate, then tighten an additional turn.

Crankcase oil capacity is approximately 2.1 quarts (2.0 L) with the oil filter.

The engine may be equipped with a low-oil sensor. The sensor circuit may be designed to stop engine or trigger a warning device if oil level is low.

AIR FILTER

The engine is equipped with a foam precleaner element and paper air filter. Service the precleaner after every 25 hours of operation and the air filter after every 100 hours of operation. Service more frequently when the engine is operated in severe conditions.

Clean precleaner element by washing in soapy water. Allow to dry then apply clean engine oil. Squeeze out excess oil.

The air filter should be replaced rather than cleaned. Do not wash or direct pressurized air at the filter.

After performing air cleaner maintenance on horizontal-shaft engines, insure the inner air cleaner cover (Fig. KO200A) is properly installed so that the baffle on the back of the inner air filter cover does not interfere with the spit-back tray on the air cleaner base. Interference at this point can prevent the air filter cover from sealing properly. Note the spit-back tray is standard equipment on horizontal-shaft engines beginning with serial No. 2512100014; earlier horizontal-shaft engines will benefit by being upgraded with this spit-back control tray.

NOTE: Vertical-shaft engines prior to serial No. 2813402183: It is recommended that a short stud seat, part No. 230046, be installed over the air filter stud above the air filter element wing nut (Fig. KO200B) to prevent the wing nut from loosening during engine operation. Engines after this serial number are equipped with this seal from the factory. Insure that the seal is in place prior to installing air cleaner cover.

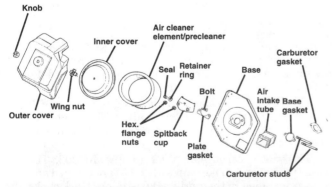

Fig. KO200A–Exploded view of air filter components on CH engines with spitback tray on air filter base. Inner cover must not interfere with spitback tray, or cover will not seal.

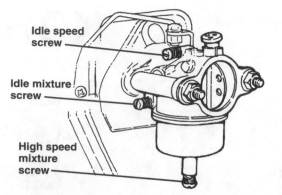

Fig. KO200B–Exploded view of air filter components on CV engines showing position of short seal over inner wing nut. Seal prevents wing nut from loosening.

FUEL FILTER

If so equipped, periodically inspect fuel filter. If dirty or damaged, replace the filter.

CRANKCASE BREATHER

A breather valve is attached to the top of the cylinder head under the rocker cover. A tube connects valve cover to the air cleaner base to allow crankcase vapors to be burned by the engine. Inspect and clean breather valve as needed to prevent or remove restrictions.

SPARK PLUG

The recommended spark plug is Champion RC12YC or equivalent. The specified electrode gap is 1.0 mm (0.040 in.). Tighten spark plug to 38-43 N•m (28-32 ft.-lbs.).

NOTE: Manufacturer does not recommend spark plug cleaning using abrasive grit as grit may enter engine.

CARBURETOR

Initial setting of idle mixture screw (Fig. KO201) is 1¼ turns out on Models CH11 and CH12.5, 1¾ turns out on Model CH14, and one turn out on all CV models. Initial setting of high-speed mixture screw is 1½ turns out on Models CH11 and CH12.5, and 1¼ turns out on Model CH14 (there is no high-speed mixture screw on CV models). Final adjustment of mixture screws should be made with engine at normal operating temperature. Adjust idle speed screw so engine idles at 1500 rpm on CH models and at 1200 rpm on CV models, or at speed specified by equipment manufacturer. Turn the idle mixture screw counterclockwise until engine rpm decreases and note screw position. Turn screw clockwise until engine rpm decreases again and note screw position. Turn screw to midpoint between the two noted positions. Reset idle speed screw if necessary to obtain desired idle speed.

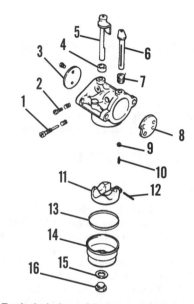

Fig. KO201–View of carburetor showing adjustment points. High-speed mixture screw is not used on CV models. Some models may be equipped with a fuel shutoff solenoid valve on bottom of fuel bowl.

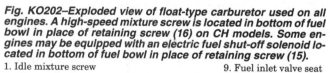

Fig. KO202–Exploded view of float-type carburetor used on all engines. A high-speed mixture screw is located in bottom of fuel bowl in place of retaining screw (16) on CH models. Some engines may be equipped with an electric fuel shut-off solenoid located in bottom of fuel bowl in place of retaining screw (15).

1. Idle mixture screw
2. Idle speed screw
3. Throttle plate
4. Throttle shaft dust seal
5. Throttle shaft
6. Choke shaft
7. Return spring
8. Choke plate
9. Fuel inlet valve seat
10. Fuel inlet valve
11. Float
12. Float shaft
13. Gasket
14. Fuel bowl
15. Gasket
16. Retaining screw

To adjust high-speed mixture screw (Fig. KO201) on CH models, run engine at maximum speed under load. Slowly rotate high-speed mixture screw in until engine speed decreases, then turn screw out turn.

A fixed main jet controls the high-speed mixture on CV models. No optional jets are offered, although a high altitude kit may be available for non-EPA/CARB compliant engines.

To disassemble carburetor, refer to Fig. KO202. The edges of throttle and choke plates (3 and 8) are beveled and must be reinstalled in their original positions. Mark choke and throttle plates before removal to ensure correct assembly. Use a suitably sized screw to pull out the fuel inlet seat

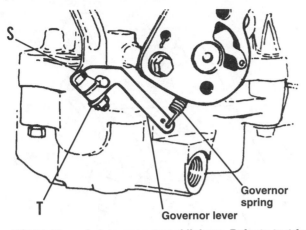

Fig. KO203–View of governor external linkage. Refer to text for adjustment procedure.

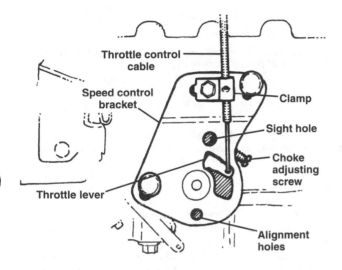

Fig. KO204A–View of typical speed control linkage on CV models. Refer to text for adjustment procedure.

if seat is to be replaced. Do not reinstall a seat that has been removed. Use a sharp punch to pierce the Welch plug and pry plug from carburetor body. Be careful to prevent the punch from contacting and damaging the carburetor body.

Clean all parts in carburetor cleaner and blow out all passages with compressed air. Be careful not to enlarge any fuel passages or jets as the calibration of the carburetor may be altered.

Press new fuel inlet seat into carburetor body so seat is bottomed. Apply Loctite 609 to throttle plate retaining screw. Be sure throttle plate is properly seated against carburetor bore before tightening screw. Be sure choke shaft properly engages detent spring on carburetor. Locking tabs on choke plate must straddle choke shaft. Use a sealant on the Welch plug.

On CV-16 engines with a self-relieving choke, the original design choke lever housing has a cavity on the underside allowing the lever to pivot around the stop pin. In dirty or dusty operation, the cavity can accumulate dirt, hindering both movement and travel of the choke lever. Periodically remove the choke housing and clean the cavity, or replace housing with the manufacturer's upgraded choke repair kit (part No. 12 757 32) which has an exposed cavity, preventing dirt buildup.

IGNITION

The engine is equipped with a breakerless, electronic magneto ignition system. The electronic ignition module is mounted outside the flywheel. The ignition switch grounds the module to stop the engine. There is no periodic maintenance or adjustment required with this ignition system.

Air gap between module and flywheel should be 0.20-0.30 mm (0.008-0.012 in.). Loosen module retaining screws and position module to obtain desired gap. Tighten screws to 4 N•m (35 in.-lbs.) for used engines or to 6.2 N•m (55 in.-lbs.) on a new engine cylinder block.

If ignition module fails to produce a spark, check for faulty kill switch or grounded wires. Measure resistance of ignition module secondary using an ohmmeter. Connect one test lead to the spark plug terminal of a high-tension wire and other the test lead to the module core laminations. Resistance should be 7900-10,850 ohms. If resistance is low or infinite, replace the module.

GOVERNOR

A flyweight governor is located in the crankcase. The governor gear is driven by the camshaft gear. Refer to the REPAIRS section for overhaul information.

To adjust governor linkage, proceed as follows: Loosen the governor lever clamp nut (T–Fig. KO203) and push the governor lever so throttle is wide open. Turn the governor shaft (S) counterclockwise as far as possible and tighten the clamp nut.

The engine should never run at speeds exceeding 3750 rpm. Maximum high-speed setting depends on engine application. Use a tachometer to check engine speed.

To adjust high idle speed setting on CV models, first loosen throttle control cable clamp (Fig. KO204A). Move the equipment speed control lever to the FAST position. Align the hole in throttle lever with hole in speed control bracket by inserting a pencil or drill bit through the holes. Pull up on throttle control cable shield to remove slack and tighten cable clamp.

Start the engine and allow it to reach operating temperature. Align hole in throttle lever with hole in speed control bracket as previously outlined. Loosen speed control bracket mounting screws and move bracket up (toward flywheel) to decrease high idle speed or down (toward PTO) to increase high idle speed. When desired speed is obtained, tighten control bracket screws to 10.7 N•m (95 in.-lbs.) on a new short block or to 7.3 N•m (65 in.-lbs.) on all other engines.

On CH models, the governor spring end should be located in following specified hole from end of governor lever for specified high idle speed: outer hole for 3800 rpm, second hole for 3600 rpm, third hole for 3400 rpm, fifth hole for 3200, sixth hole for 3000 rpm. Note that throttle end of governor spring is attached to third hole from top of throttle lever for 3800 rpm and first hole for all other speeds.

Governor sensitivity is adjusted by positioning governor spring in different holes in governor lever arm. On CV models, it is recommended that spring be installed in the hole closest to governor shaft if high idle speed is 3600 rpm or less. If high idle speed is greater than 3600 rpm, use the second hole that is farthest from governor cross shaft. On CH models, governor sensitivity is adjusted by reattaching governor spring to another hole in governor arm. Move spring to an outer hole on arm to decrease governor sensitivity.

On vertical-shaft engines with governed idle control (Fig. KO204B), if idle speed adjustment is necessary, manually move the governor lever so the throttle shaft (5—Fig. KO202) is tight against idle speed stop screw (2). Check idle speed with a tachometer and adjust idle speed stop screw to obtain 900-1000 rpm. Release the governor lever and allow engine to return to governed idle speed. If idle speed is not within equipment manufacturer's specification, turn governed idle speed adjusting screw (Fig. KO204B) clockwise to increase idle speed or counterclockwise to decrease speed.

VALVE CLEARANCE

All models are equipped with hydraulic valve lifters that automatically maintain proper valve clearance. No periodic adjustment is required.

REPAIRS

TIGHTENING TORQUE

Recommended tightening torque values are as follows:

Air cleaner base	9.9 N•m
	(88 in.-lb.)
Charging stator	4.0 N•m
	(35 in.-lb.)
Connecting rod	See Text
Crankcase cover/oil pan	24.4 N•m
	(216 in.-lb.)
Cylinder head	40.7 N•m
	(30 ft.-lb.)
Rocker arm pedestal	9.9 N•m
	(88 in.-lb.)
Flywheel	66 N•m
	(49 ft.-lb.)
Fuel pump*	7.3/9.0 N•m
	(65/80 in.-lb.)
Governor lever	9.9 N•m
	(88 in.-lb.)
Ignition module*	4.0/6.2 N•m
	(35/55 in.-lb.)
Muffler	24.4 N•m
	(216 in.-lb.)
Oil drain plug	8.0 N•m
	(70 in.-lb.)
Oil sentry switch	8.0 N•m
	(70 in.-lb.)
Oil pump cover*	4.0/6.2 N•m
	(35/55 in.-lb.)
Spark plug	38.0-43.4 N•m
	(28-32 ft. in.-lb.)
Speed control bracket*	7.3/10.7 N•m
	(65/95 in.-lb.)
Starter drive pinion	15.3 N•m
	(135 in.-lb.)
Valve cover*	7.3/10.7 N•m
	(65/95 in.-lb.)

*When installing self-tapping fasteners into new unthreaded holes, use higher torque value; use lower torque value for installation into previously tapped holes and weld nuts.

FUEL PUMP

Some engines may be equipped with a mechanically operated diaphragm fuel pump. An eccentric on the engine camshaft actuates the fuel pump. Individual components

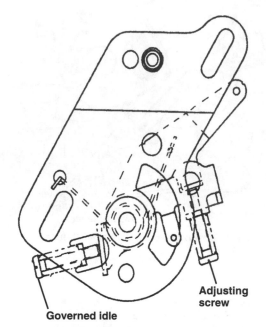

Fig. KO204B–View of throttle control on engines with governed idle. Refer to text for adjustment procedure.

are not available; pump must be replaced as a unit assembly.

When installing fuel pump assembly, make certain that fuel pump lever is positioned to the right side of camshaft. Damage to fuel pump and engine may result if the lever is positioned on left side of camshaft. Tighten fuel pump mounting screws to 9.0 N•m (80 in.-lbs.) for first-time installation on new short block. On all other engines, tighten mounting screws to 7.3 N•m (65 in.-lbs.).

When repairing an engine with oil leaking around fuel pump mounting pad, or if fuel pump body is cracked, visually inspect mounting pad face. If mounting face has machined surface, a spacer must be installed between fuel pump gasket and mounting pad face to prevent recurring damage. The spacer is furnished in the manufacturer's replacement fuel pump kit.

CYLINDER HEAD

To remove cylinder head, remove air cleaner assembly and base. Detach speed control linkage and fuel line. Unbolt and remove carburetor and muffler. Remove recoil starter, blower housing and cylinder head air baffles and shields. Remove rocker arm cover. Rotate crankshaft so the piston is at top dead center on the compression stroke. Push rods and rocker arms should be marked so they can be reinstalled in their original position. Unscrew cylinder head bolts and remove cylinder head and gasket.

To disassemble, remove spark plug. Remove breather retainer (14—Fig. KO205) and reed (15). Push the rocker shaft (13) out the breather side of rocker arm bridge (12) and remove the rocker arms (11). Use a valve spring compressor tool to compress the valve springs. Remove the split retainers (2), release the spring tension and remove valves from cylinder head.

Clean combustion deposits from cylinder head and inspect for cracks or other damage. Check cylinder head surface for flatness; replace the head if warped more than 0.076 mm (0.003 in.).

To assemble cylinder head components, reverse disassembly procedure. Be sure rocker pedestal (12) is installed

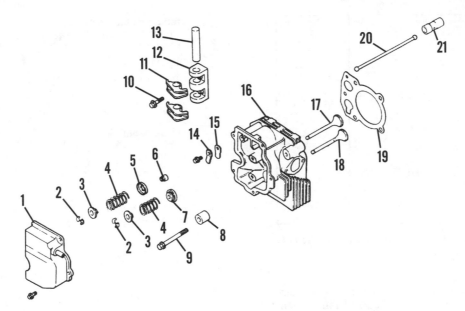

Fig. KO205—Exploded view of cylinder head and valve components. Exhaust valve rotator (7) is used on early production CV model engines before S.N. 1933593554.

1. Valve cover
2. Split retainer
3. Spring retainer
4. Valve spring
5. Spring seat
6. Valve seal (intake)
7. Valve rotator (exhaust)
8. Spacer
9. Head bolt
10. Screw
11. Rocker arm
12. Rocker bridge
13. Rocker shaft
14. Retainer plate
15. Breather reed
16. Cylinder head
17. Intake valve
18. Exhaust valve
19. Head gasket
20. Push rod
21. Valve lifter

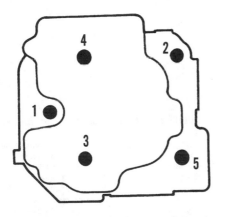

Fig. KO206—Follow sequence shown when tightening cylinder head bolts. Refer to text.

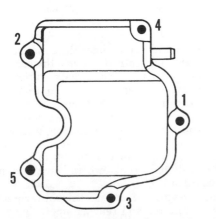

Fig. KO207—Follow sequence shown when tightening valve cover mounting screws. Refer to text.

with small counterbored hole toward exhaust port side of cylinder head. Tighten rocker pedestal mounting screws to 9.9 N•m (88 in.-lbs.). Install a new stem seal (6) on the intake valve; do not reuse the old seal.

NOTE: New cylinder head bolts should always be installed. The rust-preventative coating on the bolts affects torque retention, and most of the coating wears off the threads once bolts are installed and tightened. Attempting to reuse bolts results in loss of torque retention, and will likely cause short term head gasket failure.

Reverse removal procedure to reinstall head. Tighten cylinder head screws in increments of 14 N•m (10 ft.-lbs.) following sequence shown in Fig. KO206 until final torque of 41 N•m (30 ft.-lbs.) is reached. Install push rods in their original position, compress valve springs and snap push rods underneath rocker arms.

Silicone sealant is used as a gasket between valve cover and cylinder head. GE Silmate-type RTV-1473 or RTV-108 sealant is recommended. The use of a silicone removing solvent is recommended to remove old silicone gasket, as scraping the mating surfaces may damage them and could cause leaks. Apply a 1.6 mm (in.) bead of sealant to gasket surface of the cylinder head. Follow tightening sequence shown in Fig. KO207 and tighten the valve cover screws to 10.7 N•m (95 in.-lbs.) if a new cylinder head is installed, or to 7.3 N•m (65 in.-lbs.) if the original head is installed.

VALVE SYSTEM

Clean valve heads and stems with a wire brush. Inspect each valve for warped or burned head, pitting or worn stem and replace when required.

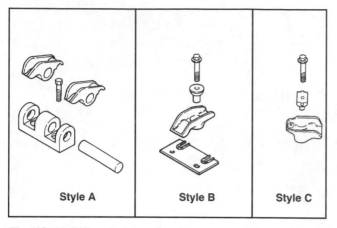

Fig. KO208–Different styles of rocker arms and pivots. Refer to text.

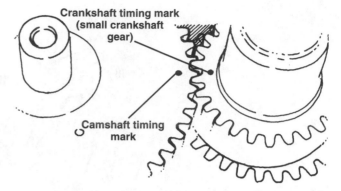

Fig. KO209–Align timing mark on small crankshaft gear with timing mark on camshaft gear.

Valve face and seat angles are 45° for intake and exhaust. Replace valve if valve margin is less than 1.5 mm (0.060 in.) after grinding valve face.

Specified valve stem-to-guide clearance is 0.038-0.076 mm (0.0015-0.0030 in.) for intake valve and 0.050-0.088 mm (0.0020-0.0035 in.) for exhaust valve. Specified new valve stem diameter is 6.982-7.000 mm (0.2749-0.2756 in.) for intake and 6.970-6.988 mm (0.2744-0.2751 in.) for exhaust. Specified new valve guide inside diameter for either valve is 7.033-7.058 mm (0.2769-0.2779 in.). Maximum allowable valve guide inside diameter is 7.134 mm (0.2809 in.) for intake guide and 7.159 mm (0.2819 in.) for exhaust guide. Valve guides are not replaceable; however, the guides can be reamed to accept valves with 0.25 mm oversize stem.

On late production CV engines, starting with serial number 1933503554, the exhaust valve rotator (7–Fig. KO205) has been eliminated and a new spring seat with different length valve spring is used in its place. Free length of the new valve spring is 55.8 mm (2.197 in.), and spring is color coded green for identification. Free length of the early production exhaust valve spring is 48.69 mm (1.917 in.).

Note that three different styles of rocker arms and pivots (Fig. KO208) are used. Engines with serial No. 2617200734 and higher use the latest Style "C." If rocker arm replacement is required due to valve train wear, Style "B" can be upgraded to Style "C" with engine manufacturer's retrofit kit. Engines with Style "A" components can only be upgraded to Style "C" by installing a complete new cylinder head.

CAMSHAFT AND HYDRAULIC LIFTERS

To remove camshaft, first rotate crankshaft so the piston is at top dead center on the compression stroke. Remove the rocker cover, compress the valve springs and disengage the push rods from rocker arms. Remove push rods while marking them so they can be returned to their original positions. Remove crankcase cover or oil pan mounting screws, then pry cover or oil pan from crankcase at prying lugs located on cover or oil pan. Rotate crankshaft so timing marks on crankshaft and camshaft gears are aligned. Remove camshaft from the crankcase. Identify the valve lifters as either intake or exhaust so they can be returned to original position, then remove lifters from crankcase.

The camshaft is equipped with a compression reduction device to aid starting. The lever and weight mechanism on

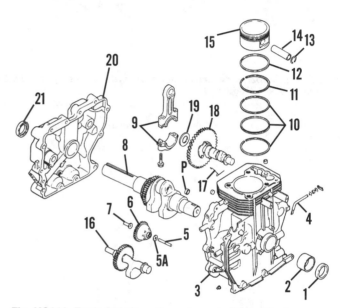

Fig. KO210–Exploded view of crankcase/cylinder block assembly of CH models.

1. Oil seal	12. Top compression ring
2. Main bearing	13. Snap ring
3. Crankcase/cylinder block	14. Piston ring
4. Governor cross shaft	15. Piston
5. Governor gear shaft	16. Balance shaft &
5A. Thrust washer	gear assy.
6. Governor gear assy.	17. Compression release
7. Governor pin	spring
8. Crankshaft	18. Camshaft & gear assy.
9. Connecting rod	19. Shim
10. Oil control ring	20. Crankshaft cover
11. Second compression ring	21. Cover

the camshaft gear moves a pin inside the exhaust cam lobe. During starting the pin protrudes above the cam lobe and forces the exhaust valve to stay open longer thereby reducing compression. At running speeds the pin remains below the surface of the cam lobe. Inspect mechanism for proper operation.

Inspect camshaft and lifters for scoring, pitting and excessive wear. Minimum cam lobe height is 8.96 mm (0.353 in.) for intake lobe and 9.14 mm (0.360 in.) for exhaust lobe. If the camshaft is replaced, the new valve lifters should also be installed.

If the hydraulic valve lifters are noisy after engine has run for several minutes and reached operating temperature, it is probably an indication that contamination is preventing the lifter check ball from seating or there is

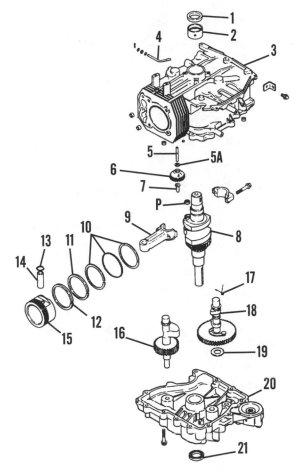

Fig. KO211–Exploded view of crankcase/cylinder block assembly of CV models.

1. Oil seal	12. Top compression ring
2. Main bearing	13. Snap ring
3. Crankcase/cylinder block	14. Piston ring
4. Governor cross shaft	15. Piston
5. Governor gear shaft	16. Balance shaft &
5A. Thrust washer	gear assy.
6. Governor gear assy.	17. Compression release
7. Governor pin	spring
8. Crankshaft	18. Camshaft & gear assy.
9. Connecting rod	19. Shim
10. Oil control ring	20. Oil pan
11. Second compression ring	21. Oil seal

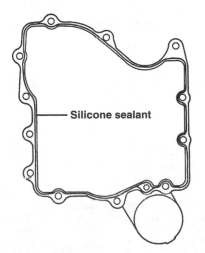

Fig. KO212–Apply silicone sealant in a 1.6 mm (1/16 in.) bead around crankcase cover mating surface as shown.

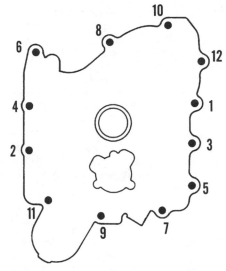

Fig. KO213–Follow sequence shown when tightening crankcase cover or oil pan mounting screws.

internal wear in the lifter. Individual parts are not available for the hydraulic lifters. Lifters should be replaced when faulty.

Current production engines are equipped with new style "quick-purge" lifters that reduce the lifter pump-up time and resultant noisy operation during engine start-up. The new style lifters, part No. 25 351 01, are available for service replacement on all engines.

Lubricate lifter bores with oil and install hydraulic lifters in their original position. The exhaust lifter bore is closest to crankcase gasket surface.

Install camshaft, aligning timing marks (Fig. KO209) on crankshaft and camshaft gears as shown. Camshaft end play is adjusted with shims (19–Fig. KO210 or KO211), which are installed between the camshaft and crankcase cover or oil pan. To determine camshaft end play, install camshaft with an original thickness shim in the crankcase. Attach end play checking tool KO-1031 to crankcase and use a feeler gauge to measure clearance between the shim and checking tool. Camshaft end play should be 0.076-0.127 mm (0.003-0.005 in.). Install different thickness shim as necessary to obtain desired end play.

No gasket is used with crankcase cover or oil pan. Apply a 1.6 mm (1/16 in.) bead of silicone gasket sealant (GE Silmate RTV-108, RTV-1473 or equivalent) around crankcase cover or oil pan mating surface as shown in Fig. KO212. Tighten crankcase cover or oil pan screws to 24.4 N•m (216 in.-lbs.) using sequence shown in Fig. KO213.

After completing assembly of engine, rotate crankshaft slowly and check for compression. If there is compression, valves are seating and the engine may be started.

PISTON, PIN AND RINGS

The piston and connecting rod are removed as an assembly. Remove cylinder head and camshaft as previously outlined. Remove balance shaft from crankcase. Remove carbon deposits and ring ridge (if present) from top of cylinder before removing piston and rod assembly. Remove connecting rod cap and push connecting rod and piston out of cylinder. Remove piston pin retaining rings and separate piston and rod.

To determine piston clearance in cylinder, measure piston skirt diameter at a point 6 mm (0.24 in.) from bottom of skirt and perpendicular to piston pin bore. Measure cylinder bore inside diameter at point of greatest wear, approximately 63 mm (2.5 in.) below top of cylinder and perpendicular to piston pin. The difference between the two measurements is piston clearance in bore, which should be 0.041-0.044 mm (0.0016-0.0017 in.).

Piston and rings are available in standard size and oversizes of 0.25 and 0.50 mm (0.010 and 0.020 in.). Standard piston skirt diameter is 86.941-86.959 mm (3.4229-3.4236 in.), and wear limit is 86.814 mm (3.418 in.).

Specified piston pin bore is 19.006-19.012 mm (0.7483-0.7485 in.), and wear limit is 19.025 mm (0.749 in.). Specified piston pin diameter 18.995-19.000 mm (0.7478-0.7480 in.), and wear limit is 18.994 mm (0.7478 in.). Piston-to-piston pin clearance should be 0.006-0.017 mm (0.0002-0.0007 in.).

Insert new rings in piston ring grooves and measure ring side clearance using a feeler gauge. Piston ring side clearance should be 0.040-0.105 mm (0.0016-0.0041 in.) for the top compression ring; 0.040-0.072 mm (0.0016-0.0028 in.) for the second compression ring; 0.551-0.675 mm (0.0217-0.0266 in.) for oil control ring. Replace the piston if side clearance is excessive.

The specified piston ring end gap for compression rings is 0.30-0.50 mm (0.012-0.020 in.). Maximum allowable ring end gap in a used cylinder is 0.77 mm (0.030 in.).

When assembling piston rings on piston, install oil control ring expander (Fig. KO214) first and then the side rails. Install compression rings so side marked with the pip mark is toward the piston crown and stripe on face of ring is to the left of end gap. The second compression ring has a bevel on inside of ring and has a pink stripe on face of ring. The top compression ring has a barrel face and has a blue stripe on face of ring. Stagger ring end gaps evenly around the piston.

Lubricate piston and cylinder with oil, then use a ring compressor tool to install the piston and rod. Be sure the arrow on the piston crown is toward the flywheel side of the crankcase as shown in Fig. KO215. Refer to CONNECTING ROD section for connecting rod tightening torque. Install balance shaft, camshaft and cylinder head as outlined in the appropriate sections.

CONNECTING ROD

Piston and connecting rod are removed as an assembly as outlined in PISTON, PIN AND RINGS section. Remove piston pin retaining rings and separate piston and rod.

Replace the connecting rod if bearing surfaces are scored or excessively worn. Specified connecting rod small end diameter is 19.015-19.023 mm (0.7486-0.7489 in.), and wear limit is 19.036 mm (0.7495 in.). Specified connecting rod-to-piston pin running clearance is 0.015-0.028 mm (0.0006-0.0011 in.).

Specified connecting rod-to-crankpin bearing clearance is 0.030-0.055 mm (0.0011-0.0022 in.), and maximum allowable clearance is 0.07 mm (0.0025 in.). A connecting rod with 0.25 mm (0.010 in.) undersize big end is available. The undersized rod can be identified by the drilled hole located in lower end of the rod.

Specified rod side clearance on crankpin is 0.18-0.41 mm (0.007-0.016 in.).

To reinstall connecting rod and piston assembly, reverse the removal procedure. Be sure that arrow mark on top of piston is toward flywheel side of crankcase (Fig. KO215).

NOTE: Three different style connecting rod bolts are used (Fig. KO216). Each style bolt has a differ-

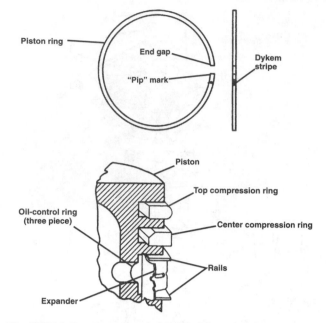

Fig. KO214—Cross-sectional view of piston showing correct installation of piston rings. Refer to text for details.

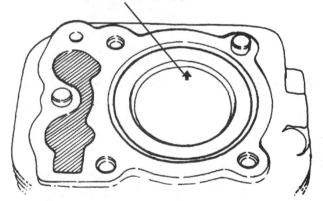

Fig. KO215—Piston must be installed with arrow pointing toward flywheel side of engine.

ent tightening torque. Refer to Fig. KO216 to identify rod bolts and their respective torque values.**

Refer to the PISTON, PIN AND RINGS section and reverse removal procedure to install remainder of components.

GOVERNOR

The engine is equipped with a flyweight mechanism mounted on governor gear (6–Figs. KO210 or KO211). Remove crankcase cover or oil pan (20) for access to governor gear. Inspect gear assembly for excess wear and damage. The governor gear is held onto governor shaft (5) by molded tabs on the gear. When gear is removed, the tabs are damaged and replacement of governor gear will be required. Gear and flyweight are available only as a unit assembly. If governor gear shaft (5) requires replacement, tap new shaft into crankcase so it protrudes 32.64-32.84

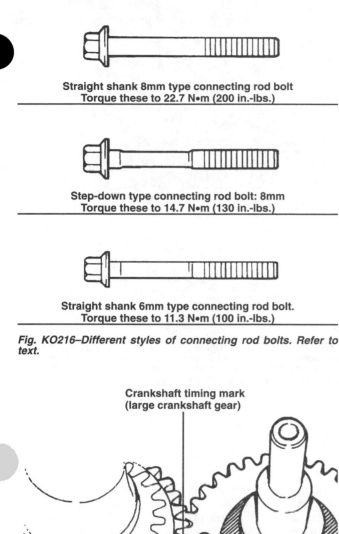

Straight shank 8mm type connecting rod bolt
Torque these to 22.7 N•m (200 in.-lbs.)

Step-down type connecting rod bolt: 8mm
Torque these to 14.7 N•m (130 in.-lbs.)

Straight shank 6mm type connecting rod bolt.
Torque these to 11.3 N•m (100 in.-lbs.)

Fig. KO216–Different styles of connecting rod bolts. Refer to text.

Crankshaft timing mark
(large crankshaft gear)

Balance shaft timing mark

Fig. KO217–When assembling engine, align timing mark on large crankshaft gear with timing mark on balance shaft gear.

mm (1.285-1.293 in.) above crankcase boss. Remove the cotter pin to remove governor lever shaft (4). Inspect the shaft oil seal in crankcase bore and replace when necessary.

No gasket is used with crankcase cover or oil pan. Apply a 1.6 mm (¹⁄₁₆ in.) bead of silicone gasket sealant (GE Silmate RTV-108, RTV-1473 or equivalent) around crankcase cover or oil pan mating surface as shown in Fig. KO212. Tighten crankcase cover or oil pan screws to 24.4 N•m (216 in.-lbs.) using sequence shown in Fig. KO213. Adjust governor as previously outlined in MAINTENANCE section.

CRANKSHAFT

To remove crankshaft, remove starter and flywheel. Remove crankcase cover or oil pan, piston, connecting rod and camshaft as previously outlined. Remove balance shaft.

Remove crankshaft from crankcase. The crankshaft rides in a replaceable bushing (2–Fig. KO210 or KO211) in the crankcase and in an integral bearing in the crankcase cover or oil pan.

NOTE: When replacing a vertical-shaft crankshaft, short block, or engine, insure that the threads on PTO bolt removed from old crankshaft are compatible with threads in new crankshaft. Some equipment manufacturers have requested "inch" threads instead of metric. Some engine Spec Numbers could have either thread.

Specified main journal diameter at flywheel end is 44.913-44.935 mm (1.7682-1.7691 in.), and wear limit is 44.84 mm (1.765 in.). Bearing inside diameter at flywheel end is 44.965-45.003 mm (1.7703-1.7718 in.), and wear limit is 45.016 mm (1.7723 in.). Crankshaft-to-bearing running clearance should be 0.03-0.09 mm (0.0012-0.0035 in.). When replacing the main bearing, make certain that oil hole in bearing aligns with oil passage in crankcase.

Specified main journal diameter at PTO end is 41.915-41.935 mm (1.6502-1.6510 in.), and wear limit is 41.86 mm (1.648 in.). Crankshaft-to-oil pan bore running clearance should be 0.03-0.09 mm (0.0012-0.0035 in.).

Maximum allowable main journal taper is 0.020 mm (0.0008 in.) and maximum allowable out-of-round is 0.025 mm (0.0010 in.). Main journals cannot be machined undersize.

Specified standard crankpin diameter is 38.958-38.970 mm (1.5338-1.5343 in.). Minimum allowable crankpin diameter is 38.94 mm (1.533 in.). Maximum allowable crankpin taper is 0.012 mm (0.0005 in.) and maximum allowable out-of-round is 0.025 mm (0.0010 in.). Crankpin can be ground to accept a connecting rod that is 0.25 mm (0.010 in.) undersize. Plug (P–Fig. KO210 or KO211) should be removed after machining operation so oil passages can be cleaned thoroughly. Use a suitable screw puller to extract the plug. Be sure the new plug does not leak.

Maximum allowable crankshaft runout is 0.15 mm (0.006 in.) measured at PTO end of crankshaft with crankshaft supported in engine. Maximum allowable crankshaft runout is 0.10 mm (0.004 in.) measured at any point on the crankshaft with the crankshaft supported in V-blocks.

To install crankshaft, reverse the removal procedure. Install balance shaft, aligning timing marks on large crankshaft gear and balance shaft gear as shown in Fig. KO217. Install camshaft, aligning timing marks on small crankshaft gear and camshaft gear as shown in Fig. KO209. No gasket is used with crankcase cover or oil pan. Apply a 1.6 mm (¹⁄₁₆ in.) bead of silicone gasket sealant (GE Silmate RTV-108, RTV-1473 or equivalent) around crankcase cover or oil pan mating surface as shown in Fig. KO212. Tighten crankcase cover or oil pan screws to 24.4 N•m (216 in.-lbs.) using sequence shown in Fig. KO213. Tighten flywheel retaining nut to 66 N•m (49 ft.-lbs.).

CYLINDER/CRANKCASE

Cylinder bore standard diameter is 87.000-87.025 (3.4252-3.4262 in.), and wear limit is 87.063 mm (3.4277 in.). Maximum bore out-of-round is 0.12 mm (0.005 in.). Maximum bore taper is 0.05 mm (0.002 in.). Cylinder can be bored to accept an oversize piston.

Install crankshaft oil seals in crankcase and oil pan using seal driver KO-1036. Force seal into crankcase or oil pan until tool bottoms.

OIL PUMP

A gerotor oil pump is located in the crankcase cover of CH models or oil pan of CV models. The oil pump is driven by the engine balance shaft. Oil pump rotors (9–Fig. KO218) can be removed for inspection after removing pump cover (11) from bottom of crankcase cover or oil pan. The crankcase cover or oil pan must be removed for access to oil pick-up or oil pressure regulator valve (5 through 7).

Check oil pump rotors and oil pan cavity for scoring or excessive wear. Pressure relief valve body (7) and piston (6) must be free of scratches or burrs. Relief valve spring (5) free length should be approximately 25.20 mm (0.992 in.).

Lubricate the oil pump cavity and pump rotors with engine oil during assembly. Install new O-ring (10) in groove in crankcase cover or oil pan. Install pump cover (11) and tighten mounting screws to 6.2 N•m (55 in.-lbs.) on a new crankcase cover or oil pan or 4.0 N•m (35 in.-lbs.) on a used crankcase cover or oil pan.

No gasket is used with crankcase cover or oil pan. Apply a 1.6 mm ($\frac{1}{16}$ in.) bead of silicone gasket sealant (GE Silmate RTV-108, RTV-1473 or equivalent) around crankcase cover or oil pan mating surface as shown in Fig. KO212. Tighten crankcase cover or oil pan screws to 24.4 N•m (216 in.-lbs.) using the sequence shown in Fig. KO213.

OIL SENSOR

Some engines are equipped with an Oil Sentry oil pressure monitor. The system uses a pressure switch installed in one of the main oil galleries of the crankcase cover or oil pan, or on the oil filter adapter. The pressure switch is designed to break contact as oil pressure increases to normal pressure, and to make contact when oil pressure decreases within the range of 20-35 kPa (3-5 psi). When switch contacts close, either the engine will stop or a low oil warning light will be activated, depending on engine application.

To check sensor pressure switch, a regulated supply of compressed air and a continuity tester are required. With

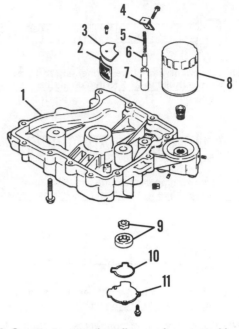

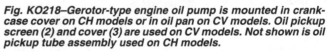

Fig. KO218–Gerotor-type engine oil pump is mounted in crankcase cover on CH models or in oil pan on CV models. Oil pickup screen (2) and cover (3) are used on CV models. Not shown is oil pickup tube assembly used on CH models.

1. Crankcase cover/oil pan	7. Relief valve body
2. Oil pick-up screen	8. Oil filter
3. Cover	9. Inner & outer rotors
4. Relief valve bracket	10. O-ring
5. Relief valve spring	11. Pump cover
6. Relief valve piston	

zero pressure applied to switch, tester should indicate continuity across switch terminal and ground. When pressure is increased through range of 20-35 kPa (3-5 psi), switch should open and tester should indicate no continuity. If switch fails test, install new switch.

KOHLER

SERVICING KOHLER ACCESSORIES

REWIND STARTERS

When servicing rewind starter, refer to the Fig. KA100 and Fig. KO102 to identify the starter used on the engine, then refer to the appropriate paragraph for service procedure.

EATON OVERHAUL

Exploded view of clockwise starter is shown in Fig. KA100. To disassemble starter, first release tension of rewind spring as follows: Hold starter assembly with pulley facing up. Pull starter rope until notch in pulley is aligned with rope hole in cover. Use thumb pressure to prevent pulley from rotating. Engage rope in notch of pulley and slowly release thumb pressure to allow spring to unwind until all tension is released.

When removing rope pulley, use extreme care to keep starter spring confined in housing. Replace starter spring if it is cracked, distorted or broken. If starter spring is to be replaced, carefully remove it from housing, noting direction of rotation of spring before removing. Check pawl, brake, spring, retainer and hub for wear and replace when necessary. If the starter rope is worn or frayed, remove from the pulley, noting the direction it is wrapped on the pulley. Replace the rope and install pulley in the housing, aligning notch in pulley assembly with rope outlet in housing. Align notch in pulley hub with hook in end of spring. Use a wire bent to form a hook to aid in positioning the spring in the hub.

After securing pulley assembly in housing, engage rope in notch and rotate pulley at least two full turns in the same direction it is pulled to properly preload the starter spring. Pull rope to fully extended position. Rope will fully

rewind when the handle is released if spring is properly preloaded.

Before installing starter on engine, check the teeth in the starter driven hub (165–Fig. KA101) for wear and replace the hub if necessary.

COMMAND AND LATER MAGNUM MODELS OVERHAUL

Command models may be equipped with the rewind starter shown in Fig. KA102. To disassemble starter, remove the rope handle and allow the rope to wind into the starter. Remove retaining screw from center of starter, and separate starter components. To disengage rewind spring from the starter housing, rotate pulley two turns clockwise. Wear appropriate safety eyewear and gloves to prevent injury should rewind spring uncoil uncontrolled. The rewind spring is contained in cup (9) and manufacturer recommends installation of a new spring and cup if spring uncoils from cup.

Assemble starter before installing rope. Lubricate rewind spring before installation. Apply a small amount of grease on brake spring (4) ends. Apply Loctite 271 to threads of center screw (1) and tighten to 7.4-8.5 N•m (65-75 in.-lbs.). Use the following procedure to install rope. With the starter assembled except for the rope, rotate the pulley six turns counterclockwise and stop when the rope hole on pulley is aligned with rope outlet on the starter housing. Hold pulley so it cannot rotate and insert the rope through rope outlet and attach rope end to pulley. Attach rope handle and release pulley. Check starter operation.

12-VOLT GEAR DRIVE STARTERS

Four types of gear drive starters are used on Kohler engines. Refer to Figs. KA103, KA104, KA106, KA107, KA108, KA109 and KA110 for exploded views of the starter motors and drives.

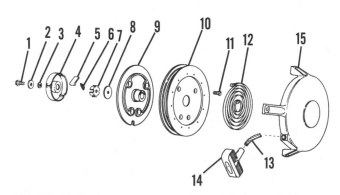

Fig. KA100–Exploded view of Eaton rewind starter used on some models.

1. Retainer screw	9. Pulley hub
2. Brake washer	10. Pulley
3. Spacer	11. Screw
4. Retainer	12. Recoil spring
5. Pawl	13. Rope
6. Spring	14. Handle
7. Brake	15. Starter housing
8. Thrust washer	

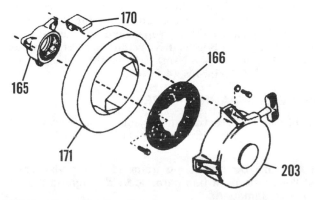

Fig. KA101–View showing rewind starter and starter hub.

165. Starter hub	171. Air director
166. Screen	203. Rewind starter
167. Bracket	

Fig. KA102–Exploded view of rewind starter used on Command and later Magnum models.

1. Screw	7. Pawl springs
2. Washer	8. Pulley
3. Pawl retainer	9. Rewind spring & cup
4. Brake spring	10. Rope
5. Washer	11. Starter housing
6. Pawls	

TWO-BRUSH COMPACT-TYPE

To disassemble the starting motor, clamp mounting bracket in a vise. Remove the through-bolts (H–Fig. KA103) and slide commutator end plate (J) and frame assembly (A) off the armature. Clamp the steel armature core in a vise and remove the Bendix drive (E), drive end plate (F), thrust washer (D) and spacer (C) from the armature (B).

Replace the brushes if unevenly worn or worn to a length of inch (7.9 mm) or less. To replace the ground brush (K), drill out rivet, then rivet new brush lead to end plate. Field brush (P) is soldered to the field coil lead.

Reassemble by reversing disassembly procedure. Lubricate bushings with a light coat of SAE 10 oil. Inspect Bendix drive pinion and splined sleeve for damage. If Bendix is in good condition, wipe clean and install completely dry. Tighten Bendix drive retaining nut to a torque of 130-150 in.-lbs. (15-18 N•m). Tighten through-bolts (H) to a torque of 40-55 in.-lbs. (4-7 N•m).

PERMANENT MAGNET-TYPE

To disassemble starting motor, clamp mounting bracket in a vise and remove through-bolts (19–Fig. KA104).

CAUTION: Do not clamp frame (11) in a vise or strike frame as it has ceramic field magnets that may be damaged.

Carefully slide the end cap (10) and frame (11) off armature. Clamp steel armature core in a vise and remove nut

Fig. KA103–Exploded view of two-brush compact gear drive starting motor.

A. Frame & field coil assy.	J. Commutator end plate
B. Armature	K. Ground brush
C. Spacer	L. Terminal nuts
D. Thrust washer	M. Lockwashers
E. Bendix drive assy.	N. Flat washer
F. Drive end plate	O. Insulating washer
G. Lockwasher	P. Field brush
H. Through-bolt	

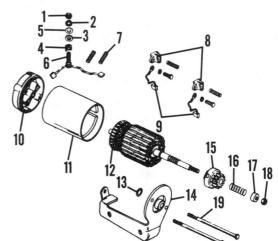

Fig. KA104–Exploded view of permanent magnet-type starting motor.

1. Terminal nut	10. Commutator end cap
2. Lockwasher	11. Frame & magnets
3. Insulation washer	12. Armature
4. Terminal insulator	13. Thrust washer
5. Flat washer	14. Drive end plate
6. Terminal stud &	15. Drive assy.
input brushes	16. Anti-drift spring
7. Brush springs (4)	17. Spacer
8. Brush holders	18. Nut
9. Brushes	19. Through-bolt

(18), spacer (17), anti-drift spring (16), drive assembly (15), end plate (14) and thrust washer (13) from armature (12).

The two input brushes are part of terminal stud (6). Remaining two brushes (9) are secured with cap screws. When reassembling, lubricate bushings with American Bosch lubricant LU3001 or equivalent. Do not lubricate starter drive. Use rubber band or clip shown in Fig. KA105

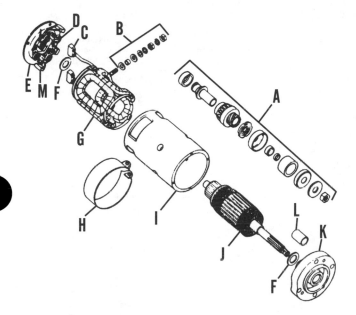

Fig. KA105–A brush retaining clip can be fabricated as shown to hold brushes in end cap during starter assembly.

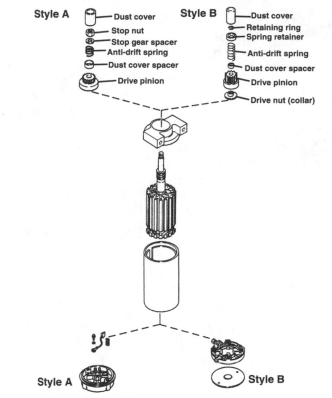

Fig. KA107–Exploded view of late-style inertia drive permanent magnet of four-brush starter motor showing both styles of brush end plates and Bendix drives.

Fig. KA106–Exploded view of four-brush starting motor with Bendix drive.

A. Bendix drive assy.	H. Cover
B. Terminal stud	I. Frame
C. Field brushes	J. Armature
D. Brush springs	K. Drive end plate
E. Commutator end plate	L. Bushing
F. Thrust washer	M. Ground brushes
G. Field coil	

to hold brushes in position until started in the commutator. Cut and remove rubber band after assembly. Tighten through-bolts to 80-95 in.-lbs. (8-10 N•m). Apply Loctite to threads of nut (18) and tighten to 135 in.-lbs. (15.2 N•m).

FOUR-BRUSH BENDIX DRIVE

To disassemble starter motor, remove screws securing drive end plate (K–Fig. KA106) to frame (I). Carefully withdraw armature and drive assembly from frame assembly. Clamp the steel armature core in a vise and remove Bendix drive retaining nut. Remove drive assembly (A), end plate (K) and thrust washer from armature (J). Remove the cover (H). Remove screws securing end plate (E) to frame. Pull the field brushes (C) from brush holders, then remove the end plate assembly.

The two ground brush leads are secured to the end plate (E), and the two field brush leads are soldered to field coils. Replace the brush set when worn.

Inspect bushing (L) in end plate (K), and replace the bushing if necessary. When assembling, lubricate bushings with light coat of SAE 10 oil. Lightly lubricate Bendix drive splines with Kohler Drive Lube part No. 52 357 01 or equivalent.

Note the starter can be installed with the Bendix in engaged or disengaged position. Do not attempt to disengage Bendix if it is in the engaged position.

Fig. KA107 shows the late-style inertia-drive (Bendix) permanent magnet four-brush starter motor. This motor comes in two styles as identified in Fig. KA107. Repair procedures are similar to those for early-style motor shown in Fig. KA106. To access retaining ring on the style "B" Bendix, extend drive pinion fully. Grasp the dust cover tip with pliers, then pull dust cover free. The retaining ring and Bendix assembly can now be removed. A stop nut retains the style "A" Bendix.

SOLENOID-SHIFT STARTERS

Manufacturer recommends a minimum 500-hour or annual, whichever occurs first, maintenance schedule for solenoid-shift starters. The starter should be disassembled, cleaned, inspected and lubricated as necessary. Drive splines should be lightly lubricated with Kohler Bendix Drive Lubricant part No. 52 357 01 or equivalent. Solenoid shift lever and shaft should be lubricated with Shifter Shaft Lubricant part No. 52 357 02 or equivalent.

If starter will not engage the flywheel and crank the engine, the problem could be caused by an accumulation of

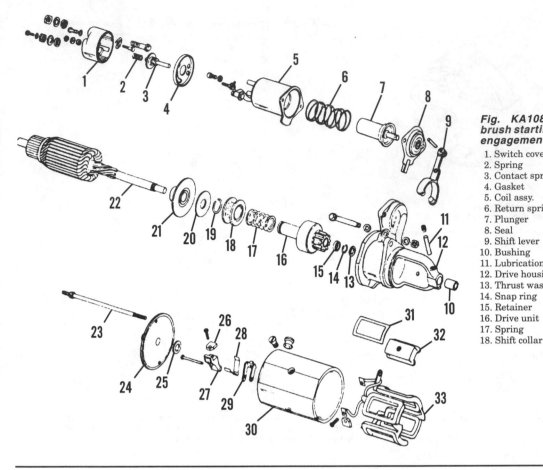

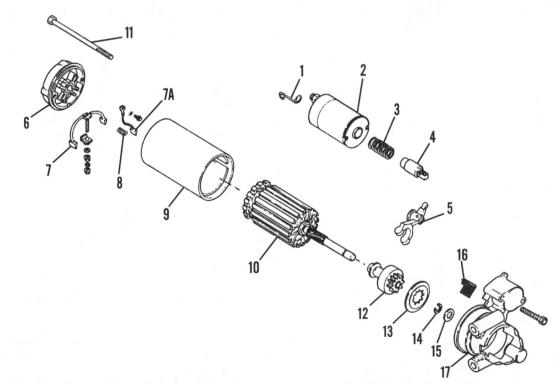

Fig. KA108—Exploded view of four brush starting motor with solenoid shift engagement.

1. Switch cover
2. Spring
3. Contact spring
4. Gasket
5. Coil assy.
6. Return spring
7. Plunger
8. Seal
9. Shift lever
10. Bushing
11. Lubrication wick
12. Drive housing
13. Thrust washer
14. Snap ring
15. Retainer
16. Drive unit
17. Spring
18. Shift collar
19. Snap ring
20. Brake washer
21. Center bearing
22. Armature
23. Through-bolt
24. End plate
25. Thrust washer
26. Brushes (4)
27. Insulated brush holder
28. Brush spring
29. Ground brush
30. Frame
31. Field coil insulator
32. Pole shoe
33. Field coil assy.

Fig. KA109—Exploded view of permanent magnet-type starter with solenoid shift engagement.

1. Clip
2. Solenoid
3. Spring
4. Plunger
5. Shift lever
6. Commutator end cap
7. Terminal stud & input brushes
7A. Brush
8. Brush springs (4)
9. Frame & magnets
10. Armature
11. Through-bolts
12. Drive assy.
13. Seal
14. Retainer
15. Thrust washer
16. Dust cover
17. Drive housing

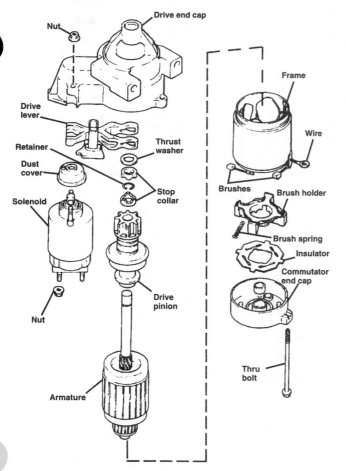

Fig. KA110—Exploded view of late-style Nippon Denso solenoid shift-type starter motor.

dirt or debris in the solenoid and/or starter. This is especially true for vertical-shaft and/or high-hour usage engines.

NOTE: Engine cranking speed must be 200 rpm minimum for proper starting.

SOLENOID SHIFT-TYPE

K-Series

Refer to Fig. KA108 for exploded view of starting motor. To disassemble, unbolt and remove solenoid switch assembly (items 1 through 6). Remove through-bolts (23), end plate (24) and frame (30) with brushes (26), brush holders (27 and 29) and field coil assembly (33). Remove screws retaining center bearing (21) to drive housing (12), remove shift lever pivot bolt, raise shift lever (9) and carefully withdraw armature and drive assembly. Drive unit (16) and center bearing (21) can be removed from armature (22) after snap ring (14) and retainer (15) are removed. Drive out shift lever pin and separate plunger (7), seal (8) and shift lever (9) from drive housing. Any further disassembly is obvious after examination of unit. Refer to Fig. KA108. Replace the brushes (26), center bearing (21) and bushings in end plate (24) and drive housing (12) as needed.

Magnum And Command Series

Refer to Fig. KA109 for an exploded view of the starter.

CAUTION: Do not clamp frame (9) in a vise or strike frame as it has ceramic field magnets that may be damaged.

To disassemble starter, detach clip (1) then unscrew and remove solenoid. Mark frame (9), end cap (6) and drive housing (17) so they can be assembled in the original position. Unscrew through-bolts and separate starter components. Detach retainer (14) from armature to remove drive unit (12) from shaft.

The two input brushes are part of terminal stud (7). Remaining two brushes (7A) are secured with cap screws. Replace the brushes as needed. The clip shown in Fig. KA105 can be fabricated to hold brushes in end cap during assembly.

Nippon Denso

An exploded view of starter is shown in Fig. KA110. To disassemble, remove the solenoid nuts and solenoid. Remove two through-bolts and commutator end cap. Remove insulator and brush springs from the brush holder, then slide brushes from holder and remove holder. Slide the farm off armature. Remove armature and drive lever assembly from drive end cap, then separate drive lever from armature. Be careful not to lose the drive end cap thrust washer when removing the lever and armature. Pry the two-piece stop collar off the armature shaft retainer. Remove the retainer and discard it.

Clean, inspect and replace the starter components as necessary. If brushes require replacement, Brush Kit part No. 52 221 01 contains the needed brushes, springs, and instructions to replace the frame-fastened brushes. Solenoid is not serviceable and must be replaced if faulty.

To assemble starter, slide the drive pinion onto the armature shaft. Insert the rear stop collar on the armature shaft. Place a NEW retaining ring into armature shaft groove. Insert the front stop collar on the armature shaft, and using two pair of pliers, mash the two collars together by applying an even force over the retainer. Make sure the drive end cap thrust washer is installed between the stop collar and end cap. Complete assembly in reverse order of disassembly.

FLYWHEEL ALTERNATORS

3-AMP ALTERNATOR

The 3-amp alternator consists of a permanent magnet ring with five or six magnets on flywheel rim and a stator assembly attached to crankcase. A diode is located in the charging output lead. See Fig. KA111.

To avoid damage to the charging system, the following precautions must be observed:
1. Negative post of battery must be connected to engine ground and correct battery polarity must be observed at all times.
2. Prevent alternator leads (AC) from touching or shorting.
3. Remove battery or disconnect battery cables when recharging battery with battery charger.
4. Do not operate engine for any length of time without a battery in system.
5. Disconnect plug before electric welding is done on equipment powered by, and in common ground with, the engine.

Troubleshooting

Defective conditions and possible causes are as follows:
1. No output. Could be caused by:

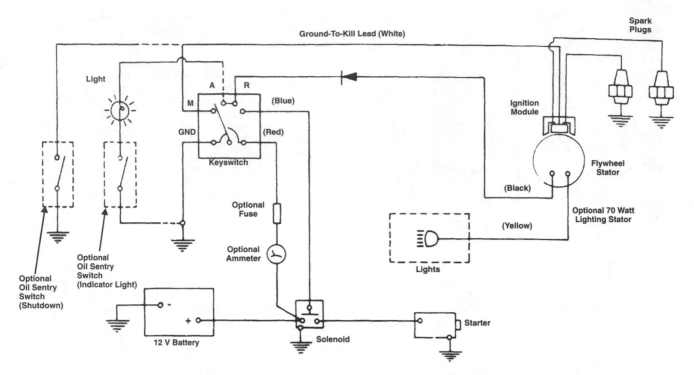

Fig. KA111—Typical electrical wiring diagram for engines equipped with 3-amp unregulated charging system.

a. Faulty windings in stator.
b. Defective diode.
c. Broken lead wire.
2. No lighting. Could be caused by:
a. Shorted stator wiring.
b. Broken lead.

If "no output" condition is the trouble, run following tests:

1. Connect ammeter in series with charging lead. Start engine and run at 2400 rpm. Ammeter should register 2-amp charge. Run engine at 3600 rpm. Ammeter should register 3-amp charge.

2. Disconnect battery charge lead from battery, measure resistance of lead to ground with an ohmmeter. Reverse ohmmeter leads and take another reading. One reading should be about mid-scale with meter set at R × 1. If both readings are high, the diode or stator is open.

3. Expose diode connections on the battery charge lead. Check resistance on stator side to ground. Reading should be 1 ohm. If zero ohms, the winding is shorted. If infinity ohms, the stator winding is open or lead wire is broken.

If "no lighting" condition is the trouble, use an AC voltmeter and measure the open circuit voltage from the lighting lead to ground with engine running at 3000 rpm. If 15 volts, wiring may be shorted.

Check resistance of lighting lead to ground. If 0.5 ohms, stator is good, zero ohms indicates shorted stator and a reading of infinity indicates stator is open or lead is broken.

3/6 AMP ALTERNATOR

The 3/6-amp alternator consists of a permanent magnet ring with six magnets on flywheel rim and a stator assembly attached to crankcase. Two diodes are located in battery charging lead and auxiliary load lead. See Fig. KA112.

To avoid damage to the charging system, the following precautions must be observed:

1. Negative post of battery must be connected to engine ground and correct battery polarity must be observed at all times.
2. Prevent alternator leads (AC) from touching or shorting.
3. Remove battery or disconnect battery cables when recharging battery with battery charger.
4. Do not operate engine for any length of time without a battery in system.
5. Disconnect plug before electric welding is done on equipment powered by, and in common ground with, the engine.

Troubleshooting

Defective conditions and possible causes are as follows:
1. No output. Could be caused by:
a. Faulty windings in stator.
b. Defective diode.
c. Broken lead wire.
2. No lighting. Could be caused by:
a. Shorted stator wiring.
b. Broken lead.

If "no output" condition is the trouble, run following tests:

1. Disconnect auxiliary load lead and measure voltage from lead to ground with engine running at 3000 rpm. If 17 volts or more, stator is good.

2. Disconnect battery-charging lead from battery. Measure voltage from charging lead to ground with engine running at 3000 rpm. If 17 volts or more, stator is good.

3. Disconnect battery charge lead from battery and auxiliary load lead from switch. Measure resistance of both leads to ground and take another reading. One reading should be about mid-scale with meter set at R × 1. If both readings are low, diode is shorted. If both readings are high, diode or stator is open.

4. Expose diode connections on battery charge lead and auxiliary load lead. Check resistance on stator side of diodes to ground. Reading should be 0.5 ohm. If zero ohms,

APPLICATION DIAGRAM

ENGINE DIAGRAM

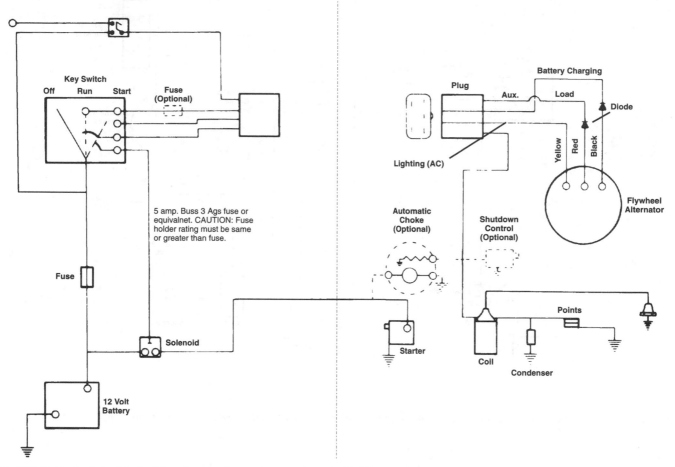

Fig. KA112–Typical electrical wiring diagram for engines equipped with 3/6-amp alternator.

winding is shorted. If infinity ohms, stator winding is open or lead wire is broken.

If "no lighting" condition is the trouble, disconnect lighting lead and measure open circuit voltage with an AC voltmeter from lighting lead to ground with engine running at 3000 rpm. If 22 volts or more, stator is good. If less than 22 volts, wiring may be shorted.

Check resistance of lighting lead to ground. If 0.5 ohms, stator is good, zero ohms indicates shorted stator and a reading of infinity indicates stator is open or lead is broken.

10-, 15-, 20-, 25-AMP ALTERNATOR

Some engines may be equipped with a 10-, 15-, 20- or 25-amp alternator. Alternator output is controlled by a solid state rectifier-regulator. See Figs. KA113, KA114, KA115, KA116 and KA117 for wiring diagrams typical of most models.

Rectifier-regulator for 15-, 20- and 25-amp charging systems can be tested with Tester part No. 25 761 20. Instructions are included with the tester. If tester is not available, or if servicing a 10-amp system, use the test procedure that follows:

To avoid damage to charging system, the following precautions must be observed:

1. Negative post of battery must be connected to engine ground and correct battery polarity must be observed at all times.

2. Rectifier-regulator must be connected in common ground with engine and battery.
3. Disconnect leads at rectifier-regulator if electric welding is to be done on equipment in common ground with engine.
4. Remove battery or disconnect battery cables when recharging battery with battery charger.
5. Do not operate engine with battery disconnected.
6. Prevent possible grounding of AC leads.

Operation

Alternating current (AC) produced by the alternator is changed to direct current (DC) in the rectifier-regulator. The rectifier-regulator electronically "senses" the counter-voltage created by the battery, and controls or limits the charging rate accordingly. No adjustments are possible on alternator charging system. Faulty components must be replaced. Note the rectifier-regulators used on 10-amp and early 15-amp systems are similar in appearance (Fig. KA118), but units are not interchangeable.

Refer to the following troubleshooting paragraph to help locate possible defective parts.

Troubleshooting

Defective conditions and possible causes are as follows:
1. No output. Could be caused by:
   a. Faulty windings in stator.
   b. Defective diode(s) in the rectifier.
   c. Rectifier-regulator not properly grounded.

APPLICATION DIAGRAM

ENGINE DIAGRAM

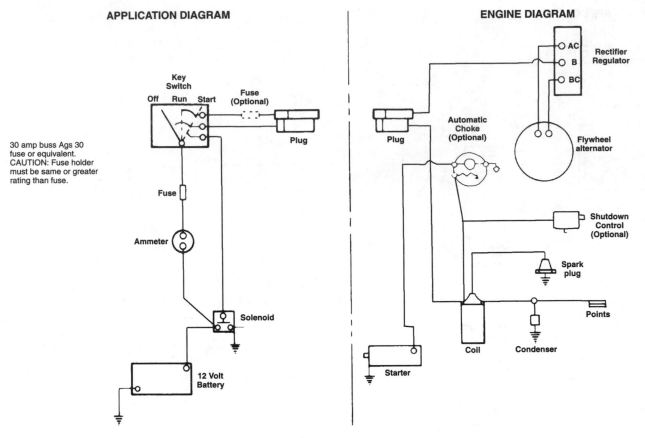

Fig. KA113–Typical electrical wiring diagram for engines equipped with 15-amp alternator and breaker point ignition.

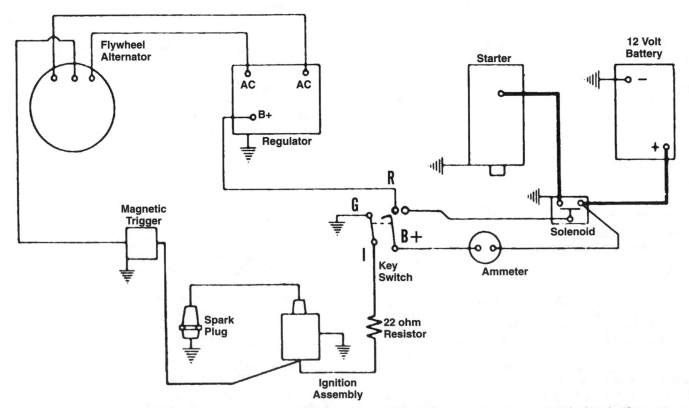

Fig. KA114–Typical electrical wiring diagram for engines equipped with early 15-amp flywheel alternator and breakerless ignition system. The 10-amp alternator is similar.

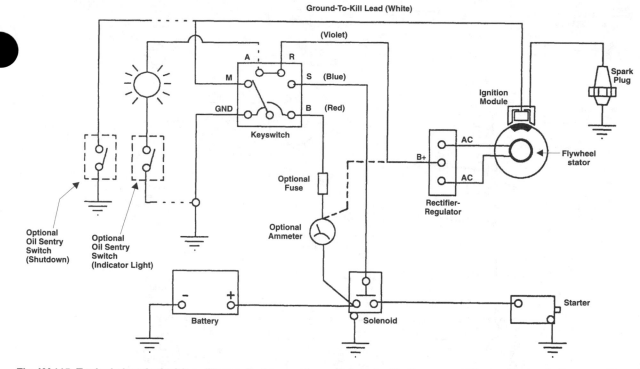

Fig. KA115–Typical electrical wiring diagram for later engines equipped with 15-amp and 25 amp flywheel alternator. Note that B+ wire (dashed line) from rectifier-regulator on 25-amp system is routed to ammeter rather than key switch.

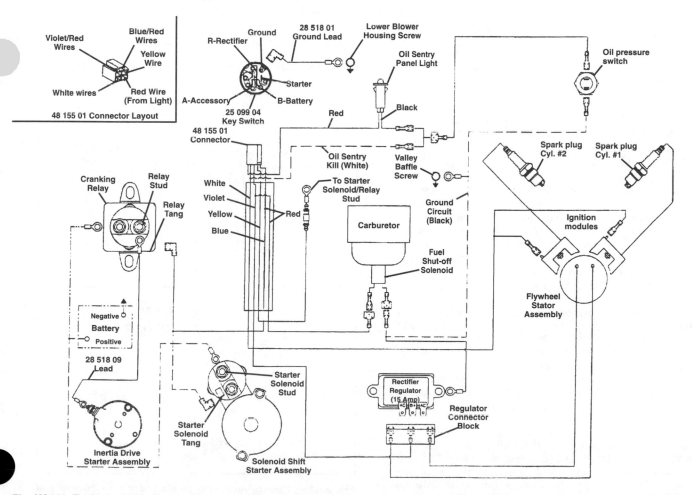

Fig. KA116–Typical wiring diagram for overhead cam engines equipped with 15-amp regulated charging system and engine-mounted control panel.

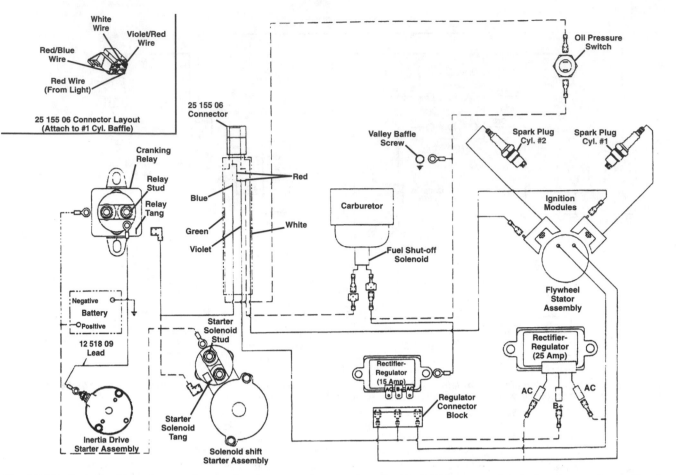

Fig. KA117—Typical wiring diagram for overhead cam engines equipped with 15/25-amp regulated charging system without engine-mounted control panel.

  d. Battery fully discharged or less than 4 volts.
2. Full charge-no regulation. Could be caused by:
  a. Defective rectifier-regulator.
  b. Defective battery.

If "no output" condition is the trouble, disconnect B+ cable from rectifier-regulator. Connect a DC voltmeter between B+ terminal on rectifier-regulator and engine ground. Start engine and operate at 3600 rpm. Voltage should be above 13.8 volts. If reading is above zero volts but less than 13.8 volts, check for defective rectifier-regulator. If reading is zero volts, check for defective rectifier-regulator or defective stator by disconnecting AC leads from rectifier-regulator and connecting an AC voltmeter to the two AC leads.

Check AC voltage with engine running at 3600 rpm. If reading is less than 20 volts (10-amp alternator) or 28 volts (15-amp alternator), stator is defective. If reading is more than 20 volts (10-amp alternator) or 28 volts (15-amp alternator), rectifier-regulator is defective.

If "full charge-no regulation" is the condition, use a DC voltmeter and check B+ to ground with engine operating at 3600 rpm. If reading is over 14.7 volts, rectifier-regulator is defective. If reading is under 14.7 volts but over 14.0 volts, alternator and rectifier-regulator are satisfactory and battery is probably defective (unable to hold a charge).

If a 25-amp regulator failure is encountered on a Command twin-cylinder engine with a serial number beginning with '25' or lower, the engine might need to be upgraded to allow more cooling air over the regulator fins. Regulator kits available for service include all necessary

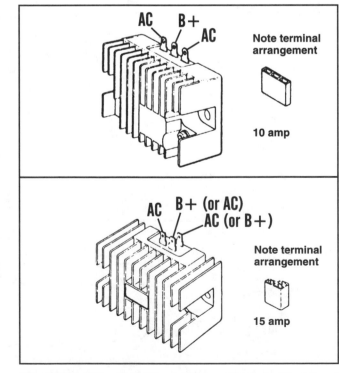

Fig. KA118—View of rectifier-regulators used on 10-amp and early 15-amp alternators. Although similar in appearance, units must not be interchanged.

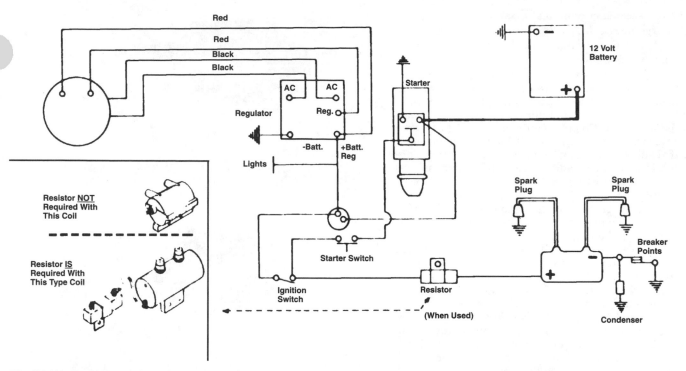

Fig. KA119–Typical electrical wiring diagram for two-cylinder engines equipped with 30-amp alternator charging systems. The 30-amp alternator on single-cylinder engines is similar.

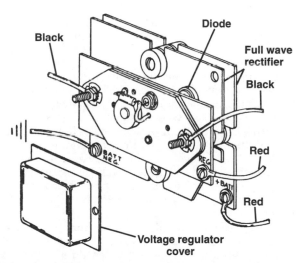

Fig. KA120–Rectifier-regulator used with 30-amp flywheel alternator, showing wire connections. Refer also to Fig. KA119.

components and instructions to properly complete this upgrade.

30-AMP ALTERNATOR

A 30-amp flywheel alternator, consisting of a permanent field magnet ring (on flywheel) and an alternator stator (on bearing plate on single-cylinder engines or gear cover on two-cylinder engines), is used on some models. Alternator output is controlled by a solid-state rectifier-regulator.

To avoid damage to charging system, the following precautions must be observed:

1. Negative post of battery must be connected to engine ground and correct battery polarity must be observed at all times.

2. Rectifier-regulator must be connected in common ground with engine and battery.

3. Disconnect wire from rectifier-regulator terminal marked "BATT. NEG" if electric welding is to be done on equipment in common ground with engine.

4. Remove battery or disconnect battery cables when recharging battery with battery charger.

5. Do not operate engine with battery disconnected.

6. Prevent possible grounding of AC leads.

Operation

Two black wires carry alternating current (AC) produced by alternator to a full wave bridge rectifier where it is changed to direct current (DC). Two red stator wires serve to complete a circuit from regulator to secondary winding in the stator. A zener diode is used to sense battery voltage and control a silicone controller rectifier (SCR). The SCR functions as a switch to allow current to flow in the secondary winding in stator when battery voltage exceeds a specific level.

An increase in battery voltage increases the current flow in secondary winding in stator. This increased current flow in secondary winding brings about a corresponding decrease in AC current in primary winding, thus controlling output.

When battery voltage decreases, zener diode shuts off the SCR and no current flows to secondary winding. Maximum AC current is produced in primary winding at this time.

Troubleshooting

Refer to Figs. KA119 or KA120 for wiring diagram. Defective conditions and possible causes are as follows:

1. No output.
   a. Faulty windings in stator.
   b. Defective diode(s) in rectifier.
2. No charge (when normal load is applied to battery).

a. Faulty secondary winding in stator.

3. Full charge-no regulation.

a. Faulty secondary winding in stator.

b. Defective regulator.

If "no output" is the trouble, check stator windings by disconnecting all four stator wires from rectifier-regulator. Check resistance on R × 1 scale of ohmmeter. Connect ohmmeter leads to the two red stator wires. About 2.0 ohms should be indicated. Connect ohmmeter leads to the two black stator wires. Approximately 0.1 ohm should be indicated. If readings are not within specified values, replace the stator. If ohmmeter readings are correct, stator is good and trouble is in rectifier-regulator. Replace the rectifier-regulator.

If "no charge when normal load is applied to battery" is the trouble, check stator secondary winding by disconnecting red wire from the REG terminal on rectifier-regulator. Operate engine at 3600 rpm. Alternator should now charge at full output. If full output of at least 30 amps is not attained, replace the stator.

If "full charge-no regulation" is the trouble, check stator secondary winding by removing both red wires from rectifier-regulator and connecting ends of these two wires together. Operate engine at 3600 rpm. A maximum 4-amp charge should be noted. If not, stator secondary winding is faulty. Replace the stator. If maximum 4-amp charge is indicated, stator is good and trouble is in rectifier-regulator. Replace the rectifier-regulator.

BRAKING STATOR

Some CV11-16 engines are equipped with a braking stator for safety purposes. The stator rapidly stops the engine when the seat safety switch is activated. The stator is designed to 'short-circuit' upon activation, creating an increased magnetic drag on the flywheel.

The 15-amp stator shown in Fig. KA121 has a short pigtail lead attached to each of the AC-lead terminals. When the seat safety switch is activated, it completes a circuit through these pigtail leads, shorting the AC windings. Refer to the equipment manufacturer's instructions to test the seat switch circuit.

The 3-amp/70 watt stator (Fig. KA122) has a third wire that connects to the seat safety switch circuit.

Troubleshooting

Faulty conditions and possible causes are as follows:

1. No charge to battery.

a. Faulty windings in stator.

b. Faulty diode in stator.

2. No lights.

a. Faulty lights.

b. Loose connections or shorts in wiring.

c. Stator winding shorted.

3. No lights or battery charging.

a. Braking lead is shorted.

b. Stator is shorted.

c. Stator or lighting lead is open.

If no charge to battery is the trouble, run the engine at 3400 rpm and measure voltage across battery terminals with a DC voltmeter. If voltage is 12.5 volts or higher, the charging system is satisfactory. If voltage is less than 12.5 volts, stator or diode is probably defective.

Disconnect charging lead (black) from wiring harness. Run engine at 3400 rpm and measure voltage from charging lead to ground with a DC voltmeter. If voltage is 5 volts or

Fig. KA121–Typical 15-amp braking stator for single-cylinder Command vertical-shaft engines.

Fig. KA122–Typical 3-amp/70-watt braking stator for single-cylinder Command vertical-shaft engines.

more, stator winding is satisfactory. If voltage is less than 5 volts, test stator for open or shorted circuit as follows:

With charging lead disconnected from wiring harness and engine stopped, measure resistance from charging lead to ground with an ohmmeter. Reverse the meter test lead connections and measure resistance again. In one test, the resistance should be infinity (open circuit). In the other test, very low resistance should be measured. If resistance is low in both directions, the diode is shorted. If resistance is infinity in both directions, the diode or stator winding is open.

If no lighting is the problem, disconnect the lighting lead (yellow) from the wiring harness. Run the engine at 3400 rpm and measure voltage from lighting lead to ground with an AC voltmeter. If voltage is 13 volts or more, stator is satisfactory. Check for loose connections or shorts in wiring harness. If voltage is less than 13 volts, test stator with an ohmmeter as follows:

With lighting lead (yellow) disconnected from the wiring harness and engine stopped, measure resistance from the lighting lead to ground with an ohmmeter. If resistance is approximately 0.15 ohms, stator winding is satisfactory. If resistance is 0 ohms, stator winding is shorted. Replace the stator. If resistance is infinity, stator or lighting lead is open. Replace the stator.

If no lights and no charge to battery are the problem, perform braking system test as follows: Disconnect braking lead (green) from the wiring harness. Run engine at 3400 rpm and measure voltage from braking lead to ground with an AC voltmeter. If voltage is 35 volts or more, stator is satisfactory. Check the unit that grounds the braking lead for short circuit. If voltage is less than 35 volts, test stator as follows:

With braking lead disconnected and engine stopped, measure resistance from braking lead to ground using an ohmmeter. If resistance is approximately 0.2-0.4 ohms, stator is satisfactory. If resistance is 0 ohms, stator is shorted. If resistance is infinity, stator or lighting lead is open. Replace stator.

KOHLER CENTRAL PARTS DISTRIBUTORS

(Arranged Alphabetically by States)
These franchised firms carry extensive stocks of repair parts. Contact them
for name of dealer in their area who will have replacement parts.

Auto Electric & Carburetor Company
Phone: (205) 323-7155
2625 4th Avenue South
Birmingham, Alabama 35233

Loftin Equipment Company
Phone: (602) 272-9466
12 N. 45th Avenue
Phoenix, Arizona 85043

H.G. Makelim Company
Phone: (714) 978-0071
1520 South Harris Ct.
Anaheim, California 92806

H.G. Makelim Company
Phone: (650) 873-4757
219 Shaw Road
S. San Francisco, California 94080

Spitzer Industrial Products Company
Phone: (303) 287-3414
6601 N. Washington Street
Thornton, Colorado 80229

Gardner, Inc.
Phone: (904) 262-1661
5200 Sunbeam Road
Jacksonville, Florida 32257

Small Engine Clinic
Phone: (808) 488-0711
98019 Kam Hwy.
Aiea, Hawaii 96701

E.C. Power Systems
Phone: (208) 342-6541
4499 Market Street
Boise, Idaho 83705

Medart, Inc.
Phone: (314) 422-3100
2644 S. 96th Street
Edwardsville, Kansas 66111

Engines Southwest
Phone: (318) 222-3871
1255 N Hearne Street
Shreveport, Louisiana 71162

W.J. Connell Company
Phone: (508) 543-3600
65 Green Street
Foxboro, Massachusetts 02035

Central Power Distributors, Inc.
Phone: (612) 576-0901
1101 McKinley Street
Anoka, Minnesota 55303

Medart, Inc. - St. Louis
Phone: (314) 343-0505
100 Larkin Williams Ct.
Fenton, Missouri 63026

Original Equipment, Inc.
Phone: (406) 245-3081
905 Second Avenue, North
Billings, Montana 59103

Gardner, Inc. - New Jersey
Phone: (609) 860-8060
106 Melrich Road
Cranbury, New Jersey 08512

Gardner, Inc. - Ohio
Phone: (614) 488-7951
1150 Chesapeake Avenue
Columbus, Ohio 43212

E.C. Power Systems
Phone: (503) 224-3623
1835 NW 21st Avenue
Portland, Oregon 97296

Pitt Auto Electric Company
Phone: (412) 766-9112
2900 Stayton Street
Pittsburgh, Pennsylvania 15212

Medart, Inc. -Memphis
Phone: (314) 343-0505
4365 Old Lamar
Memphis, Tennessee 38118

Waukesha-Pearce Industries, Inc.
Phone: (713) 551-0463
12320 South Main Street
Houston, Texas 77235

E.C. Power Systems
Phone: (801) 886-1424
Unit A, 3683 W 2270 South
Salt Lake City, Utah 84120

Chesapeake Engine Distributors
Phone: (804) 550-2231
10241 Sycamore Drive
Ashland, Virginia 23005

E.C. Power Systems
Phone: (253) 872-7011
6414 S. 196th Street
Kent, Washington 98032

Central Power Distributors, Inc.
Phone: (414) 250-1977
N90 W14635 Commerce Dr.
Mcnomoncc Falls, Wisconsin 53051

Kohler Company
Engine Division
Phone: (414) 457-4441
Kohler, Wisconsin 53044

CANADIAN DISTRIBUTORS

Lotus Equipment Sales, Ltd.
Phone: (403) 253-0822
Bay 120, 5726 Burleigh Cres. SE
Calgary, Alberta T2H 1Z8

Yetman's Ltd.
Phone: (204) 586-8046
949 Jarvis Avenue
Winnipeg, Manitoba R2X 0A1

CPT Canada Power Technologies, Ltd.
Phone: (905) 890-6900
161 Watline Avenue
Mississauga, Ontario L4Z 1P2

TECUMSEH
4-STROKE ENGINES
(Except Vector & Overhead Valve Engines)

Model	Bore	Stroke	Displacement	Power Rating
ECV100	2.625 in. (66.68 mm)	1.844 in. (46.84 mm)	9.98 cu. in. (164 cc)	
H30	2.500 in. (63.50 mm)	1.844 in. (46.84 mm)	9.05 cu. in. (148 cc)	3.0 hp (2.2 kW)
H35	2.500 in. (63.50 mm)	1.938 in. (49.23 mm)	9.51 cu. in. (156 cc)	3.5 hp (2.6 Kw)
H50, HH50	2.625 in. (66.68 mm)	2.250 in. (57.15 mm)	12.18 cu. in. (229 cc)	5.0 hp (93.7 Kw)
H60, HH60, HSK60	2.625 in. (66.68 mm)	2.500 in. (63.50 mm)	13.53 cu. in. (222 cc)	6.0 hp (4.5 kW)
HS40	2.625 in. (66.68 mm)	1.938 in. (49.23 mm)	10.49 cu. in. (172 cc)	4.0 hp (3.0 kW)
HS50 (early)	2.812 in. (71.43 mm)	1.938 in. (49.23 mm)	12.04 cu. in. (197 cc)	5.0 hp (3.7 kW)
HS50 (later)	2.795 in. (71 mm)	1.938 in. (49.23 mm)	11.90 cu. in. (195 cc)	5.0 hp (3.0 kW)
HSSK50 (early)	2.812 in. (71.43 mm)	1.938 in. (49.23 mm)	12.04 cu. in. (197 cc)	5.0 hp (3.7 kW)
HSSK50 (later)	2.795 in. (71 mm)	1.938 in. (49.23 mm)	11.90 cu. in. (195 cc)	5.0 hp (3.0 kW)
LEV80	2.313 in. (58.75 mm)	1.844 in. (46.84 mm)	7.75 cu. in. (127 cc)	3 hp (2.2 kW)
LEV100	2.625 in. (66.68 mm)	1.844 in. (46.84 mm)	9.98 cu. in. (164 cc)	4.0 hp (3.0 kW)
LEV115	2.795 in. (71 mm)	1.844 in. (46.84 mm)	11.32 cu. in. (185 cc)	5.0 hp (3.73 kW)
LEV120	2.795 in. (71 mm)	1.938 in. (49.23 mm)	11.90 cu. in. (195 cc)	5.0 hp (3.73 kW)
TNT100	2.625 in. (66.68 mm)	1.844 in. (46.84 mm)	9.98 cu. in. (164 cc)	4.0 hp (3 kW)
TNT120	2.812 in. (71.43 mm)	1.938 in. (49.23 mm)	12.04 cu. in. (197 cc)	5.0 hp (3.7 kW)
TVM125	2.625 in. (66.68 mm)	2.250 in. (57.15 mm)	12.18 cu. in. (229 cc)	5.0 hp (3.7 kW)
TVM140	2.625 in. (66.68 mm)	2.500 in. (63.50 mm)	13.53 cu. in. (222 cc)	6.0 hp (4.5 kW)
TVS75	2.313 in. (58.74 mm)	1.844 in. (46.84 mm)	7.75 cu. in. (127 cc)	3.0 hp (2.2 kW)
TVS90	2.500 in. (63.50 mm)	1.844 in. (46.84 mm)	9.05 cu. in. (148 cc)	3.5 hp (2.6 kW)
TVS100	2.625 in. (66.68 mm)	1.844 in. (46.84 mm)	9.98 cu. in. (164 cc)	4.0 hp (3.0 kW)
TVS105 (early)	2.625 in. (66.68 mm)	1.938 in. (49.23 mm)	10.49 cu. in. (172 cc)	4.0 hp (3.0 kW)
TVS105 (later)	2.795 in. (71 mm)	1.844 in. (46.84 mm)	11.32 cu. in. (185 cc)	5.0 hp (3.73 kW)

(continued)

Model	Bore	Stroke	Displacement	Power Rating
TVS115 (early)	2.812 in. (71.44 mm)	1.844 in. (46.84 mm)	11.45 cu. in. (188 cc)	4.5 hp (3.3 kW)
TVS115 (later)	2.795 in. (71 mm)	1.844 in. (46.84 mm)	11.32 cu. in. (185 cc)	5.0 hp (3.73 kW)
TVS120 (early)	2.812 in. (71.43 mm)	1.938 in. (49.23 mm)	12.04 cu. in. (197 cc)	5.0 hp (3.8 kW)
TVS120 (later)	2.795 in. (71 mm)	1.938 in. (49.23 mm)	11.90 cu. in. (195 cc)	5.0 hp (3.8 kW)
TVXL115 (early)	2.812 in. (71.44 mm)	1.844 in. (46.84 mm)	11.45 cu. in. (188 cc)	4.5 hp (3.3 kW)
TVXL115 (later)	2.795 in. (71 mm)	1.844 in. (46.84 mm)	11.32 cu. in. (185 cc)	5.0 hp (3.73 kW)

Fig. T1–View of a typical Tecumseh engine identification number.

ECH	Exclusive Craftsman Horisontal Crankshaft
ECV	Exclusive Craftsman Vertical Crankshaft
H	Horizontal Crankshaft
HH	Horizontal Crankshaft Heavy Duty (Cast Iron)
HHM	Horizontal Crankshaft Heavy Duty (Cast Iron) Medium Frame
HM	Horzontal Crankshaft Medium Frame
HS	Horizontal Crankshaft Small Frame
HSK	Horizontal Crankshaft Snow King
HSSK	Horizontal Crankshat Snow King Small Frame
LAV	Lightweight Aluminum Vertical Crankshaft
LEW	Low Emissions Vertical Crankshaft
OHM	Overhead Valve Horizontal Crankshaft Medium Frame
OVH	Overhead Valve Vertical Crankshaft Medium Frame
OVRM	Overhead Valve Vertical Crankshaft Rotary Mower
TNT	Toro N'Tecumseh
TVM	Tecumseh Vertical Crankshaft (Medium Frame)
TVS	Tecumseh Styled Vertical Crankshaft
TVXL	Tecumseh Vertical Crankshaft Extra Life
V	Vertical Crankshaft
VH	Vertical CrankshaftHeavy Duty (Cast Iron)
VLV	Vector Lightweight Vertical Crankshaft
VN	Vertical Crankshaft Medium Frame

EXAMPLE

Engine model and specification numbers TVS90-4356A

TVS	Techumseh Styled Vertical Crankshaft
90	Indicates 9 cubic inch displacement
43056A	Is the specification number uses to identify engine parts

Engine serial number 8310C

8	First digit is the year of manufacture (1978)
310	Indicates calendar day of that year (310th day or November 6, 1978)
C	Represents the line and shift on which the engine was built at the factory

Fig. T2–Table showing Tecumseh engine model number and se-rial number interpretation.

ENGINE IDENTIFICATION

Engines must be identified by the complete model number, including the specification number in order to obtain correct repair parts. Engine identification numbers, including the model number, specification number and serial number, are located on the blower housing or on a tag attached to the engine. The numbers are stamped in an identification plate or directly in the metal as shown in Fig. T1. On some later models, engine identification information is provided on a decal. Remove top cover bezel on LEV series engines for access to the decal on the blower housing.

The engine model number identifies the basic engine family. Refer to Fig. T2 for a breakdown and example of a typical Tecumseh engine model number.

The specification number specifies the parts configuration of the engine, as well as cosmetic details such as paint color and decals. The specification number also determines governor speed settings depending on the engine's application, i.e., lawnmower, tractor, pump, etc.

The serial number provides information concerning the manufacturing of the engine. Refer to Fig. T2 for a breakdown of a typical serial number.

Note that some engines are classified using the term "frame." Tecumseh classifies the basic engine structure according to the type of metal, either aluminum or cast iron, used to manufacture the engine crankcase and the metal in the cylinder bore. A small frame engine is made of aluminum with an aluminum cylinder bore. A medium frame engine is made of aluminum and has a cast iron liner in the cylinder bore. A heavy frame engine is made of cast iron with a cast iron cylinder bore.

It is important to transfer the blower housing or identification tag from the original engine to a replacement short block assembly so unit can be identified when servicing.

If selecting a replacement engine and model or type number of the old engine is not known, refer to chart in Fig. T3 and proceed as follows:
1. List the corresponding number that indicates the crankshaft position.
2. Determine the horsepower needed.
3. Determine the primary features needed. (Refer to the Tecumseh Engines Specification Book No. 692531 for specific engine variations.)
4. Refer to Fig. T2 for Tecumseh engine model number and serial number interpretation.

Note that new short blocks are identified by a tag marked SBH (Short Block Horizontal) or SBV (Short Block Vertical).

1st DIGIT	2nd & 3rd DIGIT	4th DIGIT	5th & 6th DIGIT	7th DIGIT
CRANKSHAFT POSITION	HORSEPOWER OR 2 CYCLE	PRIMARY FEATURES	ENGINE VARIATION NUMBER	REVISION LETTER
8 - Vertical 9 - Horizontal	00 = 2 Cycle 02 = 3 H.P. 03 = 3.5 H.P. 04 = 4 H.P. 05 = 5 H.P. 06 = 6 H.P. 07 = 7 H.P. 08 = 8 H.P. 10 = 10 H.P. 12 = 12 H.P. 14 = 14 H.P. 16 = 16 H.P. 18 = 18 H.P.	1 = Rotary Mower 2 = Industrial 3 = Snow King 4 = Mini Bike 5 = Tractor 6 = Tiller 7 = Rider 8 = Rotary Mower	00 thru 99 00 thru 99 00 thru 99 00 thru 99 00 thru 99 00 thru 99 00 thru 99 00 thru 99	

(EXAMPLE) 8 0 4 1 0 1 A

Fig. T3–Reference chart used to select or identify Tecumseh replacement engines.

MAINTENANCE

LUBRICATION

Vertical crankshaft engines are equipped with a barrel and plunger type oil pump. Horizontal crankshaft engines are equipped with a dipper type oil slinger attached to the connecting rod.

Oil level should be checked after every five hours of operation. Maintain oil level at lower edge of filler plug or at "FULL" mark on dipstick.

Engine oil should meet or exceed latest API service classification. Use SAE 30 or SAE 10W-30 motor oil for temperatures above 32° F (0° C). Use SAE 5W-30 or SAE 10W for temperatures below 32° F (0° C). Manufacturer explicitly states: DO NOT USE SAE 10W-40 motor oil.

Oil should be changed after the first two hours of engine operation (new or rebuilt engine) and after every 25 hours of operation thereafter.

AIR FILTER

The filter element may be made of foam or paper, or a combination of both foam and paper. The recommended maintenance interval depends on the type of filter element.

Foam type filter elements should be cleaned, inspected and re-oiled after every 25 hours of engine operation, or after three months, whichever occurs first. Clean the filter in soapy water then squeeze the filter until dry (don't twist the filter). Inspect the filter for tears and holes or any other opening. Discard the filter if it cannot be cleaned satisfactorily or if the filter is torn or otherwise damaged. Pour clean engine oil into the filter, then squeeze the filter to remove the excess oil and distribute oil throughout the filter.

Paper type filter elements should be replaced annually or more frequently if the engine operates in a severe environment, such as extremely dusty conditions. A dirty filter element cannot be cleaned and must be discarded.

CRANKCASE BREATHER

Three types of crankcase breather have been used: an integral breather, a top-mounted breather and a side-mounted breather.

Side-Mounted Crankcase Breather

This type of breather is located in the valve tappet cover (C–Fig. T4). A disc valve regulates pressure in the crankcase. Unscrew retaining screws to remove breather.

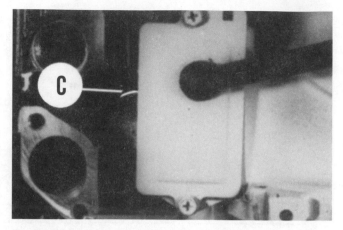

Fig. T4–On some engines, crankcase breather is located in valve tappet cover (C).

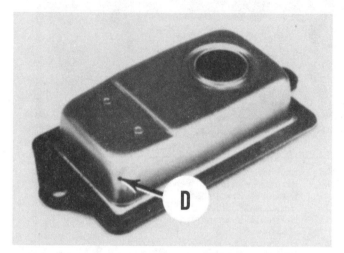

Fig. T5–Drain hole (D) must be down when installing valve tappet cover.

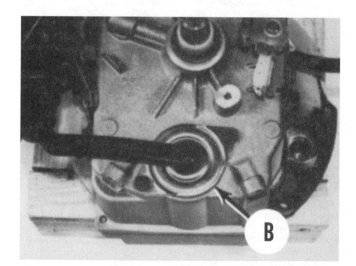

Fig. T6–View of top-mounted crankcase breather used on some engines with a vertical crankshaft.

On some engines breather can be separated for access to internal filter element, while on other engines, breather is a unit assembly. On unit type breather, a removable filter element resides inside breather. A barb inside the housing

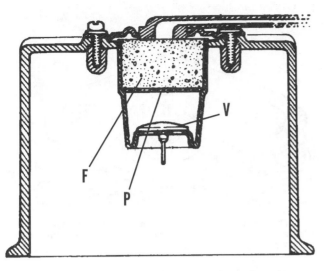

Fig. T7–Cross-section of top-mounted crankcase breather.

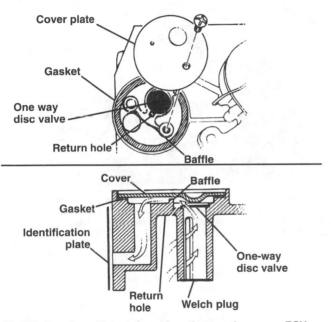

Fig. T8–Drawing of integral type breather used on some ECV series engines.

holds element in place. Insert a smooth blade between the barb and filter element to remove element. Clean filter element in a suitable solvent.

Install either type breather so the drain hole (D–Fig. T5) is down. Some units have two gaskets located between the breather and engine. Install both gaskets if so equipped.

Top-Mounted Crankcase Breather

Some vertical crankshaft engines are equipped with a crankcase breather (B–Fig. T6) mounted on top of the crankcase. Remove flywheel for access to the crankcase breather. Unscrew the breather cover and lift out the breather assembly. Remove and clean filter element (F–Fig. T7) in a solvent. Inspect check valve (V) for damage. Removal may damage the valve. Lubricate stem of new check valve to ease installation. Install baffle plate (P) above check valve.

Integral Crankcase Breather

An integral breather is found on some ECV series engines. This type of breather is mounted on top of the crankcase and functions using passages in the crankcase (Fig. T8). Gases are vented out the back of the crankcase, sometimes behind the identification plate.

Remove flywheel for access to crankcase breather. Check for blocked passages and a damaged valve. A replacement parts set is available.

SPARK PLUG

Refer to owner's manual or spark plug manufacturer's recommendations for recommended spark plug. Note that engine application may affect recommended spark plug.

A resistor type plug may be required in some localities. Specified spark plug electrode gap for all models is 0.030 inch (0.76 mm). Tighten spark plug to 18-20 ft.-lb. (24.5-27 N•m) torque.

CARBURETOR

Several different carburetors are used on these engines. Refer to the appropriate paragraph for model being serviced.

Tecumseh Diaphragm Carburetor

Refer to model number stamped on the carburetor mounting flange and to Fig. T9 for an exploded view of the Tecumseh diaphragm carburetor.

Initial adjustment of idle mixture and main fuel mixture screws from a lightly seated position is one turn open. Clockwise rotation leans the mixture and counterclockwise rotation richens the mixture.

Final adjustment is made with the engine at operating temperature and running. Operate engine at rated speed and adjust main fuel mixture screw (20–Fig. T9) for smoothest engine operation. Operate engine at idle speed and adjust idle mixture screw (16) for smoothest engine idle. If engine does not accelerate smoothly, slight adjustment of the main fuel mixture screw may be required. Engine idle speed should be approximately 1800 rpm.

To clean the fuel strainer in the fuel inlet fitting, remove the inlet needle and seat (31–Fig. T9) and reverse flush with compressed air and solvent. The inlet needle seat fitting is metal with a neoprene seat, so the fitting (and enclosed seat) should be removed before carburetor is cleaned with a commercial solvent. Welch plug (24) should be removed to expose drilled passage for cleaning. A small chisel or scratch awl should be used to remove Welch plugs. Do not use wire or drill bit to clean orifices or passages.

Inspect the inlet lever spring (27) and replace if damaged. Inspect diaphragm (32) for damage.

When reassembling the carburetor, note the following: The stamped line on the carburetor throttle plate should be toward top of carburetor, parallel with throttle shaft and facing outward as shown in Fig. T10. Flat side of choke plate should be toward the fuel inlet fitting side of carburetor. Mark on choke plate should be parallel to shaft and should face inward when choke is closed.

Install a new Welch plug by tapping the crown of the plug with a hammer and punch that is slightly larger in diameter than the Welch plug. A correctly installed Welch plug is flat; a concave plug may leak. Apply a light coat of sealant such as fingernail polish to outer edge of Welch plug after installation.

Diaphragm (32–Fig. T9) should be installed with rounded head of center rivet up toward the inlet needle

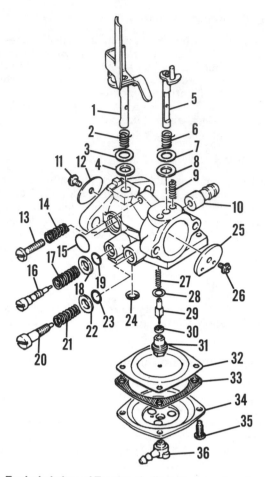

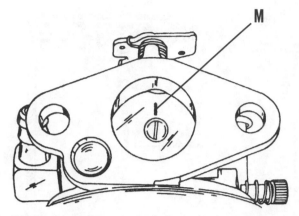

Fig. T10–The mark (M) on throttle plate should be parallel to the throttle shaft and outward as shown. Some models may also have mark at 3 o'clock position.

Fig. T11–If carburetor flange is marked with an "F", diaphragm (32–Fig. T9) and gasket (33) should be installed in order shown in Fig. T9. If carburetor is not marked with an "F", diaphragm and gasket must be installed in order shown in Fig T12.

Fig. T9–Exploded view of Tecumseh diaphragm carburetor. Refer also to Figs. T11 and T12.

1. Throttle shaft	19. O-ring
2. Spring	20. High-speed mixture screw
3. Washer	21. Spring
4. Felt washer	22. Washer
5. Choke shaft	23. O-ring
6. Spring	24. Welch plug
7. Washer	25. Choke plate
8. Felt washer	26. Screw
9. Spring	27. Spring
10. Fuel inlet fitting	28. Washer
11. Screw	29. Fuel inlet valve
12. Throttle plate	30. Fuel inlet valve seat
13. Idle speed screw	31. Fuel inlet nut
14. Spring	32. Diaphragm
15. Welch plug	33. Gasket
16. Idle mixture screw	34. Cover
17. Spring	35. Screw
18. Washer	36. Fitting

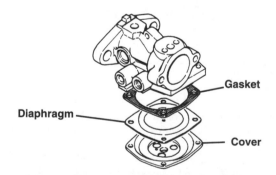

Fig. T12–If carburetor flange is not marked with an "F" (see Fig. T11), diaphragm and gasket should be installed in order shown.

(29) regardless of size or placement of washers around the rivet.

On carburetors marked with a "F" as shown in Fig. T11, gasket (33–Fig. T9) must be installed between diaphragm (32) and cover (34). All other models are assembled as shown in Fig. T12, with gasket between diaphragm and carburetor body.

Tecumseh Standard Float Carburetor

Refer to Fig. T13 for an exploded view of the Tecumseh standard float carburetor.

Initial adjustment of idle mixture screw (16–Fig. T13) and main fuel mixture screw (35) from a lightly seated po-

sition is one turn open. Clockwise rotation leans mixture and counterclockwise rotation richens mixture.

Final adjustment is made with the engine at operating temperature and running. Operate engine at rated speed and adjust main fuel mixture screw (35) for smoothest engine operation. Operate engine at idle speed and adjust idle mixture screw (16) for smoothest engine idle. If the engine does not accelerate smoothly, slight adjustment of main fuel mixture screw may be required.

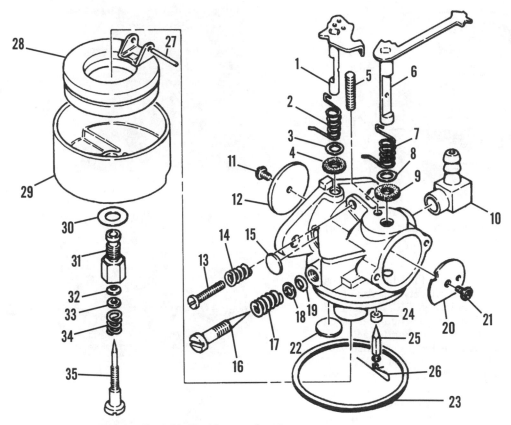

Fig. T13–Exploded view of Tecumseh adjustable float type carburetor.

1. Throttle shaft
2. Spring
3. Washer
4. Felt washer
5. Spring
6. Choke shaft
7. Spring
8. Washer
9. Felt washer
10. Fuel inlet fitting
11. Screw
12. Throttle plate
13. Idle speed screw
14. Spring
15. Welch plug
16. Idle mixture screw
17. Spring
18. Washer
19. O-ring
20. Choke plate
21. Screw
22. Welch plug
23. Gasket
24. Fuel inlet valve seat
25. Fuel inlet valve
26. Clip
27. Float pin
28. Float
29. Fuel bowl
30. Washer
31. Fuel bowl nut
32. O-ring
33. Washer
34. Spring
35. High speed mixture screw

Fig. T14–Do not attempt removal of main nozzle (N).

Fig. T15–Fuel inlet seat (T) must be installed so grooved side is toward body and flat side is out as shown.

The carburetor must be disassembled and all neoprene or Viton rubber parts removed before the carburetor is immersed in cleaning solvent. Do not attempt to reuse any expansion plugs (15 and 20). Install new plugs if any are removed for cleaning. Do not attempt to remove nozzle (N—Fig. T14) as it is pressed into position and movement will affect carburetor operation.

The fuel inlet valve needle (25—Fig. T13) seats against a Viton seat that must be removed before cleaning. The seat can

be removed by blowing compressed air in from the fuel inlet fitting or by using a hooked wire. The grooved face of valve seat should be in toward bottom of bore and the valve needle should seat on smooth side of the Viton seat (Fig. T15).

Install the throttle plate (12–Fig. T13) with the two stamped marks out and at 12 and 3 o'clock positions. The 12 o'clock line should be parallel with the throttle shaft and toward top of carburetor. Install choke plate (20) with flat side down toward bottom of carburetor.

Fuel inlet fitting (10) is pressed into the body on some models. Start fitting into body, then apply a light coat of Loctite sealant to shank and press fitting into position. Install the fuel valve retaining clip (26) on the float tab so the long end is toward the choke end of the carburetor.

11/64 in. drill bit

Rim

Fig. T16–Measure float level by positioning an 11/64-inch drill bit between rim on carburetor body and float.

Fig. T17–Float height can be set using Tecumseh float tool 670253A as shown.

With carburetor inverted, measure float height by positioning an $\frac{11}{64}$-inch diameter drill bit between rim on carburetor body and float as shown in Fig. T16. Position drill bit so it is opposite the fuel inlet valve. The outer edge of the float should just contact the drill bit. Bend the float tab to adjust the float height. The float height can also be set using Tecumseh float tool 670253A as shown in Fig. T17.

Install fuel bowl so indented part of bowl (N–Fig. T18) is located under the fuel inlet fitting.

Be sure to use correct parts when servicing the carburetor. Some fuel bowl gaskets are square section, while others are round. The bowl retainer nut (Fig. T19) contains a drilled passage for fuel to the high speed metering needle. The fuel bowl retaining nut may have one or two holes adjacent to the hex. If a replacement nut is required, the new nut must have the same number of holes as the original nut.

Tecumseh Automagic and Dual System Float Carburetors

Refer to Fig. T20 or Fig. T21 for an exploded view of Automagic or Dual System carburetor. Neither type carburetor is equipped with a choke plate. Dual System carburetors are equipped with a primer bulb (10–Fig. T21) on the side, while some Automagic carburetors are equipped with a primer bulb (26–Fig. T20) on the fuel bowl retaining nut. Automagic carburetors are not equipped with mixture screws. Some Dual System carburetors are equipped with a high-speed mixture screw (27–Fig. T21) in the fuel bowl retaining nut.

NOTE: Some carburetors on low-emission engines are equipped with caps to prevent adjustment of mixture screws. Mixture adjustment should be performed only if approved by Tecumseh.

Refer to Fig. T22 for operating principles of Automagic carburetor. Dual System carburetor operation is similar. On carburetors equipped with a primer bulb, air pressure from the primer bulb forces fuel through the main jet and up the nozzle, thereby enriching the air:fuel mixture for starting.

Follow service procedures outlined in previous section on Tecumseh float carburetors when servicing Automagic or Dual System carburetor. On Dual System carburetors, install the primer bulb and retainer by pushing the bulb

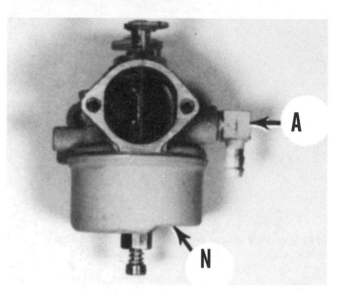

A

N

Fig T18–Indented part of float bowl (N) should be located under the fuel inlet fitting.

Fig. T16–Fuel bowl retaining nut has drilled passages. Be sure replacement nut is same as defective nut.

and retainer into the carburetor using a ¾ inch deep well socket.

Tecumseh Low-Emission Carburetor

Some engines are equipped with a low-emission carburetor that enables the engine to comply with CARB (California Air Resources Board) and EPA emission requirements. The carburetor is equipped with a fixed main jet (26–Fig. T23) and a fixed idle jet (13) that is covered by a cap (12).

When servicing carburetor, refer to service procedures for Tecumseh float carburetors while also noting the following: Upper O-ring (22) may remain in carburetor body. Remove O-ring from body. Before installing nozzle (23), place both O-rings on nozzle before inserting nozzle in carburetor body. Install the primer bulb (10) and retainer (11)

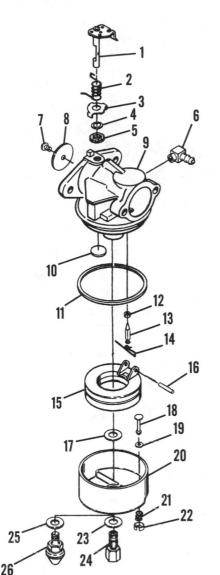

Fig. T20–Exploded view of Automagic carburetor.

1. Throttle shaft	14. Clip
2. Spring	15. Float
3. Plate	16. Pin
4. Washer	17. Washer
5. Felt washer	18. Drain valve
6. Fuel inlet fitting	19. Washer
7. Screw	20. Fuel bowl
8. Throttle plate	21. Spring
9. Body	22. Clip
10. Welch plug	23. Washer
11. Gasket	24. Fuel bowl nut
12. Fuel inlet seat	25. Washer
13. Fuel inlet valve	26. Primer

by pushing the bulb and retainer into the carburetor using a inch deep well socket.

SPEED CONTROL PANEL

Engines with a vertical crankshaft may be equipped with a speed control panel that is a separate component adjacent to the carburetor (Fig. T24 or T25). Two styles of speed control panels are used. Depending on the speed control style, engine speed may be adjusted either by bending tabs as shown in Fig. T24 or by rotating adjusting screws shown in Fig. T26.

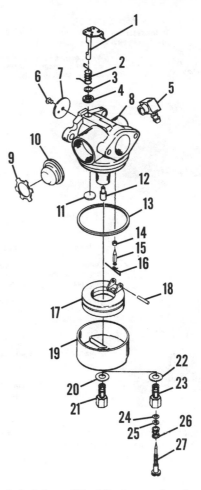

Fig. T21–Exploded view of Dual System carburetor.

1. Throttle shaft	15. Fuel inlet valve
2. Spring	16. Clip
3. Washer	17. Float
4. Felt washer	18. Pin
5. Fuel inlet fitting	19. Fuel bowl
6. Screw	20. Washer
7. Throttle plate	21. Fuel bowl nut
8. Body	22. Washer
9. Retainer	23. Fuel bowl nut
10. Primer bulb	24. O-ring
11. Welch plug	25. Washer
12. Spacer	26. Spring
13. Gasket	27. High-speed
14. Fuel inlet seat	mixture screw

If the panel is equipped with slots for the panel mounting screws (S–Fig. T25), the position of the panel must be adjusted so the linkage is synchronized. To adjust panel position, loosen mounting screws (S). Insert rod (R) through holes in panel, choke actuating lever and choke as shown, then retighten mounting screws. Check operation. Adjust idle speed screw (16–Fig. T26) and high speed stop screw (18) according to equipment manufacturer specifications.

To adjust speed adjustment tabs on panels so equipped, move speed control lever to high speed position. Insert a rod through the pin holes (Fig. T24) in panel and speed control lever. Bend high-speed tab using Tecumseh tool 670326 or equivalent so engine runs at speed specified by equipment manufacturer. Remove rod from holes and move speed control lever to low speed position. Bend low speed tab so engine idles at speed specified by equipment manufacturer.

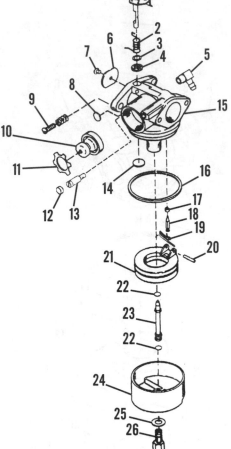

Before Start

Throttle butterfly

Before starting fuel fills well to level maintained in float bowl.

When engine is stopped prime well refills instantly to prepare for next starting cycle.

Air bleed

Main jet

Run

With throttle open, starter rotates engine creating low pressure in venturi causing fuel to rise empty-ing rich starting mixture during first starting revolutions.

Higher pressure air through bleed vent facilitates rapid movement of prime charge.

When engine is running, air from bleed vent and fuel from main jet are pulled directly up nozzle tube.

Prime charge cannot form in well while engine is running.

Fig. T22—The "Automagic" carburetor provides a rich starting mixture without using a choke plate. Mixture will be changed by operating with a dirty air filter or by incorrect float setting.

GOVERNOR

All engines are equipped with a mechanical (flyweight) type governor. To adjust the governor linkage, refer to Figs. T27 through T41 and loosen governor lever screw (S). Rotate governor shaft clamp counterclockwise as far as possible on vertical crankshaft engines; clockwise on horizontal crankshaft engines. On all models, move the governor lever (L) until carburetor throttle shaft is in wide open position, then tighten governor lever clamp screw.

Binding or worn governor linkage will result in hunting or unsteady engine operation. An improperly adjusted carburetor will also cause a surging or hunting condition.

Refer to Figs. T27 through T41 for views of typical mechanical governor speed control linkage installations.

IGNITION SYSTEM

A magneto ignition system with breaker points or a capacitor-discharge ignition (CDI) may be used according to model and application. Refer to appropriate paragraph for model being serviced.

Breaker-Point Ignition System

Breaker-point gap at maximum opening should be 0.020 inch (0.51 mm) for all models. Marks are usually located on stator and mounting post to facilitate timing (Fig. T42).

Ignition timing can be checked and adjusted to occur when piston is at specific location (BTDC) if marks are missing. Refer to the following specifications for recommended timing.

Fig. T23—Exploded view of low emission type carburetor.

1. Throttle shaft	15. Carburetor body
2. Spring	16. Gasket
3. Washer	17. Fuel inlet seat
4. Felt washer	18. Fuel inlet valve
5. Fuel inlet fitting	19. Clip
6. Throttle plate	20. Hinge pin
7. Screw	21. Float
8. Welch plug	22. O-ring
9. Idle speed screw	23. Nozzle
10. Primer bulb	24. Fuel bowl
11. Retainer	25. Washer
12. Plug	26. Fuel bowl nut &
13. Idle mixture screw	main jet
14. Welch plug	

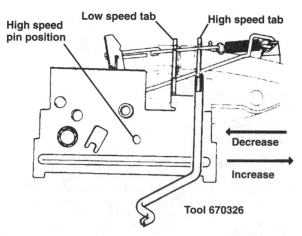

Fig. T24—Refer to text for adjustment of speed control tabs.

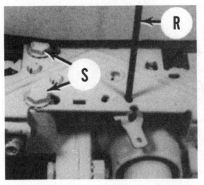

Fig. T25–View of speed control panel. Refer to text for adjustment.

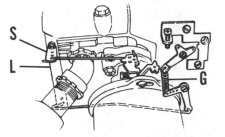

Fig. T29–View of governor mechanism on medium frame, horizontal crankshaft engines showing location of governor spring (G), governor lever (L) and adjusting screw (S).

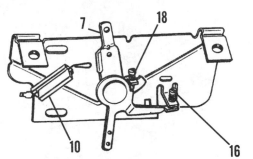

Fig. T26–Drawing of underside of speed control panel.

7. Control panel
10. Ignition stop switch

16. Idle speed stop
18. High-speed stop

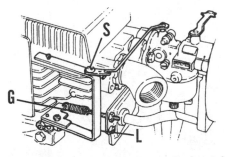

Fig. T30–View of governor mechanism on horizontal crankshaft engines for constant speed application showing location of governor spring (G), governor lever (L) and adjusting screw (S).

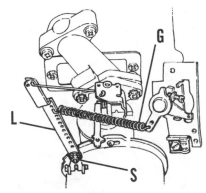

Fig. T27–View of governor mechanism on light frame, horizontal crankshaft engines showing location of governor spring (G), governor lever (L) and adjusting screw (S).

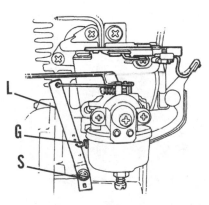

Fig. T31–View of governor mechanism on horizontal crankshaft engines on Snow King engines showing location of governor spring (G), governor lever (L) and adjusting screw (S).

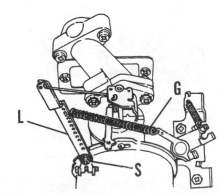

Fig. T28–View of governor mechanism on light frame, horizontal crankshaft engines for recreational vehicle application showing location of governor spring (G), governor lever (L) and adjusting screw (S).

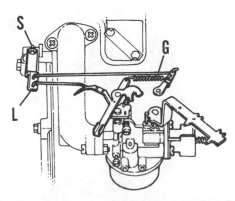

Fig, T32–View of governor mechanism on medium frame, horizontal crankshaft engines on Snow King engines showing location of governor spring (G), governor level (L) and adjusting screw (S).

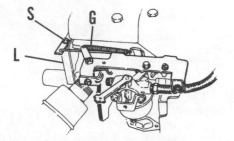

Fig. T33–View of governor mechanism on horizontal crankshaft engines on Snow King engines showing location of governor spring (G), governor lever (L) and adjusting screw (S).

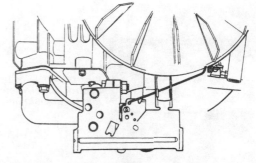

Fig. T37–View of governor mechanism on Model TVS115 engine with "snap in" speed control.

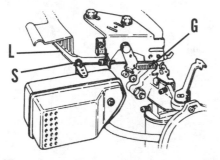

Fig. T34–View of governor mechanism on medium frame, horizontal crankshaft engines showing location of governor spring (G), governor lever (L) and adjusting screw (S).

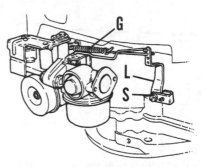

Fig. T38–View of governor mechanism on Model TNT100 engine showing location of governor spring (G), governor lever (L) and adjusting screw (S).

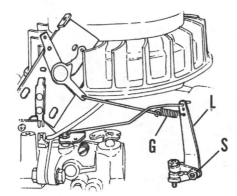

Fig. T35–View of governor mechanism on vertical crankshaft engines showing location of governor spring (G), governor lever (L) and adjusting screw (S).

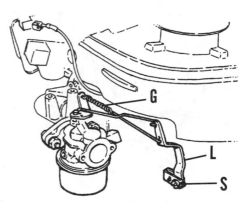

Fig. T39–View of governor mechanism of Model TNT120 engine showing location of governor spring (G), governor lever (L) and adjusting screw (S).

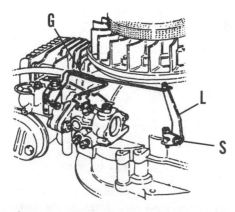

Fig. T36–View of governor mechanism on vertical crankshaft engines showing location of governor spring (G), governor lever (L) and adjusting screw (S).

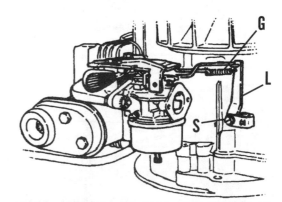

Fig. T40–View of governor mechanism on Model TVS engines with a fully adjustable carburetor showing location of governor spring (G), governor lever (L) and adjusting screw (S).

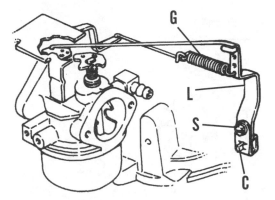

Fig. T41–View of governor mechanism on Model TVM engines showing location of governor spring (G, governor lever (L) and adjusting screw (S).

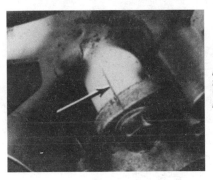

Fig. T42–View of ignition marks on engines with a breaker-point ignition system.

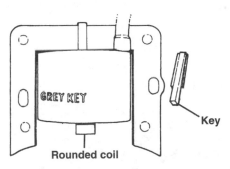

Fig. T43–Drawing of ignition coil and flywheel key used on engines equipped with a breaker-point ignition system and an external ignition coil. Coil is marked "GREY KEY" and key is colored grey.

GREY KEY
Rounded coil
Key

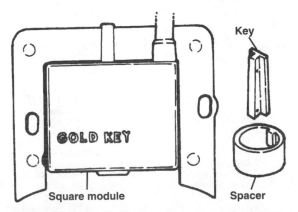

Fig. T44–Drawing of ignition coil, flywheel key and spacer used on some engines with a solid-state ignition system. Coil is marked "GOLD KEY" and key is colored gold.

GOLD KEY
Square module
Key
Spacer

Model	Piston Position BTDC
ECV100, HS40, TNT100, TNT120, TVS105	0.035 in. (0.89 mm)
HS50, TVS120	0.050 in. (1.27 mm)
H30, H35, TVS75, TVS90	0.065 in. (1.65 mm)
H50, HH50, H60, HH60, TVM125, TVM140	0.080 in. (2.03 mm)

Engines equipped with breaker-point ignition have the ignition points and condenser mounted under the flywheel, and the coil and laminations mounted outside the flywheel. This system is identified by the round shape of the coil (Fig. T43) and a stamping "Grey Key" in the coil to identify the correct flywheel key.

The correct air gap setting between the flywheel magnets and the coil laminations is 0.0125 inch (0.32 mm). Use Tecumseh gauge 670297 or equivalent thickness plastic strip to set gap.

Solid-State Ignition System

The Tecumseh solid-state ignition system does not use ignition breaker points. The only moving part of the system is the rotating flywheel with the charging magnets. Engines with solid-state (CDI) ignition have all the ignition components sealed in a module and located outside the flywheel. There are no components under the flywheel except a spring clip to hold the flywheel key in position. This system is identified by the square shape module and a stamping "Gold Key" to identify the correct flywheel key. See Fig. T44.

The correct air gap setting between the flywheel magnets and the laminations on ignition module is 0.0125 inch (0.32 mm). Insert 0.0125 inch (0.32 mm) feeler gauge (such as Tecumseh gauge 670297) between the flywheel magnet and ignition module armature legs. Loosen armature retaining screws and push armature legs against feeler gauge, then tighten armature retaining screws.

FLYWHEEL BRAKE

A flywheel brake is used on some engines that will stop the engine within three seconds when the mower safety handle is released. The ignition circuit is grounded also when the brake is actuated. On electric start models, an interlock switch prevents energizing the starter motor if the brake is engaged.

Refer to FLYWHEEL BRAKE in REPAIRS section for adjustment and service.

VALVE ADJUSTMENT

Clearance between valve tappet and valve stem (engine cold) is 0.008-0.012 inch (0.20-0.30 mm) for intake and exhaust valves for Models H50, HH50, H60, HH60, TVM125 and TVM140. Valve tappet clearance for all other models is 0.004-0.008 inch (0.10-0.20 mm) for intake and exhaust valves.

To check and adjust clearance, remove the valve tappet chamber cover (37–Fig. T45 or 30–Fig. T46). It may be necessary to remove the carburetor and muffler for access to the tappet chamber. Rotate crankshaft so piston is at top dead center on compression stroke. Measure clearance between valve stem and tappet with a feeler gauge. If clearance is less than specified, remove valve and carefully grind valve stem end as necessary to obtain specified clearance. To reduce the clearance, reface the valve and valve seat or replace the valve.

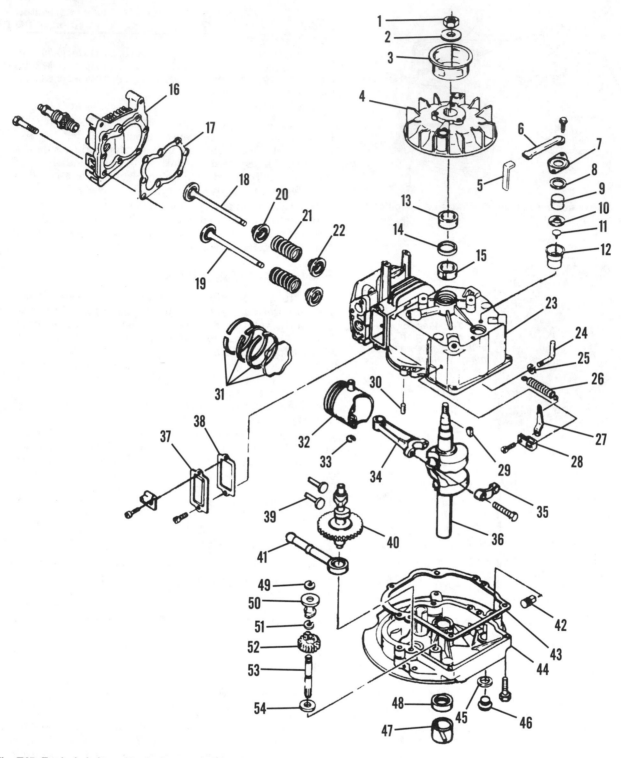

Fig. T45–Exploded view of typical engine with a vertical crankshaft.

1. Nut
2. Belleville washer
3. Starter cup
4. Flywheel
5. Elbow
6. Breather tube
7. Cover
8. Gasket
9. Filter
10. Baffle
11. Valve
12. Housing
13. Spacer
14. Oil seal

15. Bushing
16. Cylinder head
17. Gasket
18. Intake valve
19. Exhaust valve
20. Valve seal
21. Spring
22. Retainer
23. Crankcase
24. Governor shaft
25. Washer
26. Governor spring
27. Governor lever
28. Clamp

29. Key
30. Dowel pin
31. Piston rings
32. Pistons
33. Retaining ring
34. Connecting rod
35. Rod cap
36. Crankshaft
37. Tappet cover
38. Gasket
39. Tappets
40. Camshaft
41. Oil pump

42. Drain plug
43. Gasket
44. Oil pan
45. Gasket
46. Drain plug
47. Bushing
48. Oil seal
49. Snap ring
50. Governor spool
51. Snap ring
52. Flyweight assy.
53. Governor shaft
54. Washer

Fig. T46–Exploded view of typical engine with a horizontal crankshaft.

1. Oil seal (camshaft)
2. Oil seal
3. Governor shaft
4. Washer
5. Flyweight assy.
6. Snap ring
7. Governor spool
8. Snap ring
9. Crankcase cover
10. Gasket
11. Piston rings
12. Retaining ring
13. Piston
14. Connecting rod
15. Thrust washer
16. Tappets
17. Camshaft
18. Crankshaft
19. Rod cap
20. Oil dipper
21. Key
22. Cylinder head
23. Gasket
24. Intake valve
25. Exhaust valve
26. Spring
27. Retainer
28. Dowel pin
29. Breather tube
30. Tappet cover
31. Gasket
32. Filter
33. Breather
34. Gasket
35. Clamp
36. Governor lever
37. Drain plug
38. Crankcase
39. Washer
40. Governor shaft
41. Shroud
42. Oil seal
43. Spacer
44. Flywheel
45. Starter cup
46. Belleville washer
47. Nut

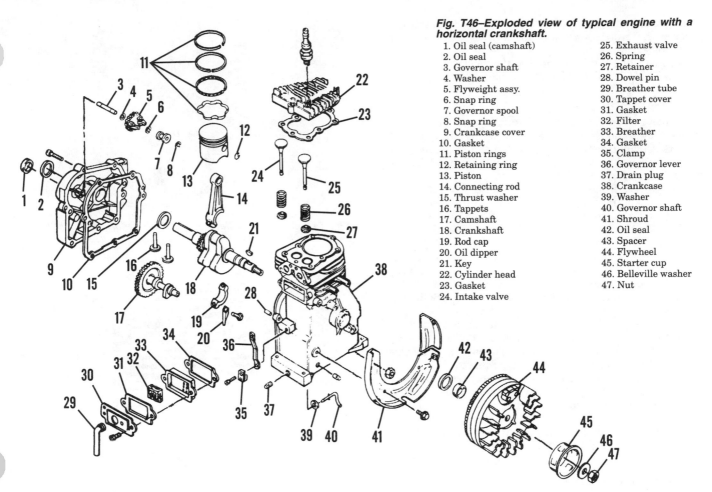

REPAIRS

TIGHTENING TORQUE

Recommended tightening torque specifications are as follows:

Carburetor to
intake pipe. . . . . 70 in.-lb.
(8 N•m)

Connecting rod:
H50, H60, HSK60,
TVM125, TVM140. . . . . 170 in.-lb.
(19.2 N•m)

All other models. . . . . 105 in.-lb.
(11.5 N•m)

Cylinder head . . . . 200 in.-lb.
(23 N•m)

Flywheel:
ECV, H30, H35, HS40,
LAV, TNT, TVS, TVXL. . . . . 37.5 ft.-lb.
(51 N•m)

H50, H60, LEV, TVM . . . . 40 ft.-lb.
(54 N•m)

HH50, HH60. . . . . 52.5 ft.-lb.
(71 N•m)

External ignition . . . . 58 ft.-lb.
(79 N•m)

Gear reduction cover. . . . . 75-110 in.-lb.
(9-12 N•m)

Gear reduction housing . . . . 100-144 in.-lb.
(11-16 N•m)

Intake pipe to cylinder. . . . . 72-96 in.-lb.
(8-11 N•m)

Crankcase cover/oil pan . . . . 125 in.-lb.
(14 N•m)

Spark plug. . . . . 18-20 ft.-lb.
(24.5-27 N•m)

FLYWHEEL

On models so equipped, disengage flywheel brake as outlined in FLYWHEEL BRAKE section. If flywheel has tapped holes, use a suitable puller to remove flywheel. If no holes are present, screw a knock-off nut onto crankshaft so there is a small gap between nut and flywheel. Gently pry against bottom of flywheel while tapping sharply on nut.

On engines originally equipped with a breaker-point ignition system and an external ignition coil, the ignition coil is round and stamped "GREY KEY" as shown in Fig. T43. The flywheel key is colored grey.

The ignition coil on some engines equipped with an electronic ignition (often used as a replacement for the external coil on the breaker-point ignition system) has a square shape and is stamped "GOLD KEY" as shown in Fig. T44. A gold colored flywheel key must be used with this ignition coil for proper ignition timing. A spacer must also be installed on the crankshaft.

Install a stepped flywheel key so the stepped end is toward the engine. Install a tapered flywheel key so the big end is toward the engine. If a spacer is used, install the spacer so the protrusion fits in the keyway and is toward the end of the crankshaft.

After installing flywheel, tighten flywheel nut to torque listed in TIGHTENING TORQUE table.

CYLINDER HEAD

To remove cylinder head (16–Fig. T45 or 22–Fig. T46), remove blower housing and all interfering shrouds and brackets. Clean area around cylinder head to prevent entrance of foreign material. Unscrew cylinder head screws and remove cylinder head and gasket.

Clean carbon from cylinder head being careful not to damage gasket mating surface. Use a straightedge to check cylinder head for distortion. If cylinder head is warped more than 0.005 inch (0.13 mm), replace the cylinder head.

A new head gasket should be installed when installing cylinder head. Do not apply any type of sealant to the head gasket. Some cylinder head screws are equipped with flat washers, while some screws are equipped with a Belleville washer (B—Fig. T47) as well as a flat washer (W). The Belleville washer must be installed so the concave side is toward the screw threads. On H50 and H60 series engines, install cylinder head screws equipped with a Belleville washer in the locations shown in Fig. T48.

Tighten the cylinder head screws on engines with eight cylinder head screws in the sequence shown in Fig. T49. Tighten the cylinder head screws on engines with nine cylinder head screws in the sequence shown in Fig. T50. Tighten cylinder head retaining screws evenly in 50 in.-lb. (5.6 N•m) increments to a final torque of 200 in.-lb. (23 N•m).

CRANKCASE COVER

Some horizontal crankshaft models are equipped with a ball bearing at the PTO end of the crankshaft. On Models H30 through HS50 the ball bearing is retained in the crankshaft cover, while on Models H50, H60, HH50 and HH60, the bearing is pressed on the crankshaft.

Before removing the crankcase cover on Models H30 through HS50, measure oil seal depth then remove the oil seal. Detach snap ring (Fig. T51) from the crankshaft and remove crankcase cover. A screw on the inside of the cover secures the main bearing. When installing cover, press new seal in to same depth as old seal before removal.

To remove the crankcase cover on Models H50, H60, HH50 and HH60, refer to Fig. T52 and note location of bearing lock screws. Loosen locknuts and rotate protruding ends of lock screws counterclockwise. The inner ends of the lock screws will move away from the bearing (Fig. T53) thereby allowing withdrawal of the cover from the crankshaft and bearing.

Install crankcase cover with a new gasket. Tighten crankcase cover screws evenly to 125 in.-lb. (14 N•m).

VALVE SYSTEM

To remove valves, first remove the cylinder head as previously outlined. Remove the valve tappet chamber cover. Rotate crankshaft so piston is at top dead center on compression stroke. Compress the valve spring and remove the spring retainer. Remove spring and valve from cylinder block.

Remove carbon from valve head and stem. Inspect valve and valve seat for evidence of pitting, overheating, distortion or other damage. If valve is in useable condition, valve face should be reground. Valve face angle is 45° and valve

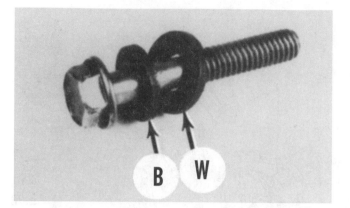

Fig. T47–Install Belleville washer (B) and flat washer (W) on cylinder head screw as shown.

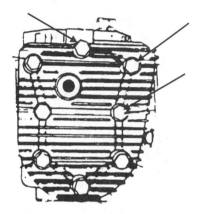

Fig. T48–On H50 and H60 series engines, install cylinder head screws and equipped with a Belleville washer in the locations shown.

Fig. T49–Tighten cylinder head screws in sequence shown on engines equipped with eight cylinder head screws.

seat angle is 46° for intake and exhaust. Replace valve if valve head margin is less than inch (0.79 mm) after grinding. Valve seats are not replaceable.

Refer to following table for specified valve seat width:

Fig. T50–Tighten cylinder head screws in sequence shown on engines equipped with nine cylinder head screws.

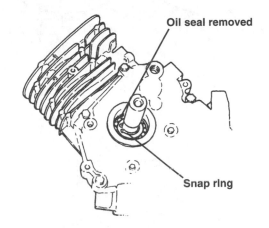

Fig. T51–On Models H30 through HS50 equipped with a ball bearing at PTO end, a snap ring retains bearing on crankshaft.

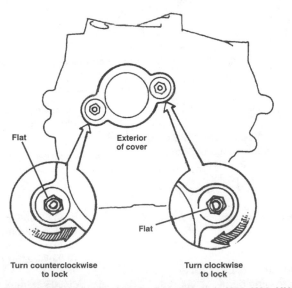

Fig. T52–View showing bearing locks on Models H50, H60, HH50 and HH60 equipped with ball bearing main bearings. Locks must be released before removing crankcase cover. Refer to Fig. T53 for interior view of cover and locks.

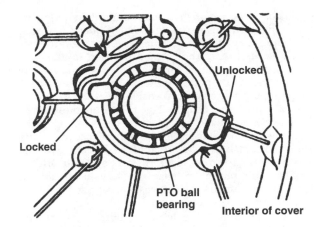

Fig. T53–Interior view of crankcase cover and ball bearing locks used on Models H50, H60, HH50 and HH60.

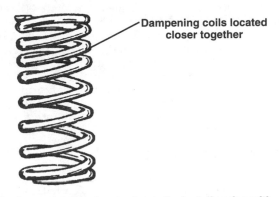

Fig. T54–If valve spring has dampening coils, install spring with dampening coils against the cylinder block (away from valve spring retainer).

Model	Valve Seat Width
H50, HH50, H60, HH60, TVM125, TVM140	0.042-0.052 in. (1.07-1.32 mm)
LEV100, LEV115 LEV120	0.066-0.086 in. (1.68-2.18 mm)
All other models	0.035-0.045 in. (0.89-1.14 mm)

Valve stem guides are cast into cylinder block and are not replaceable. If excessive clearance exists between valve stem and guide, guide should be reamed and a new valve with an oversize stem installed. The valve seats must be refaced after reaming valve guides to align the seat to the guide.

When installing the valves, make certain the valves are installed in the correct location. Valves marked "EX" are exhaust and valves marked "I" are intake. If valve spring has dampening coils (Fig. T54), the spring must be installed with the dampening coils against the cylinder block (away from the valve cap and retainer).

CAMSHAFT

Remove the crankcase cover/oil pan for access to the camshaft. When removing camshaft, align timing marks

(Fig. T55 or T56) on camshaft gear and crankshaft gear to relieve valve spring pressure on camshaft lobes. On models with compression release, it is necessary to rotate crankshaft three teeth past the aligned position to allow compression release mechanism to clear the exhaust valve tappet. Mark the tappets if they are removed so they can be installed in their original location.

The camshaft and camshaft gear are an integral part which rides on journals at each end of camshaft. Camshaft on some models also has a compression release mechanism mounted on camshaft gear which lifts exhaust valve at low cranking rpm to reduce compression and aid starting. Spring on compression release mechanism should snap weight against camshaft. Compression release mechanism and camshaft are serviced as an assembly only.

Replace the camshaft if lobes or journals are worn or scored. Always replace the tappets when installing a new camshaft. Standard camshaft journal diameter is 0.6230-0.6235 inch (15.824-15.837 mm) for Models H50, HH50, H60, HH60, TVM125 and TVM140, and 0.4975-0.4980 inch (12.637-12.649 mm) for all other models.

On models equipped with the barrel and plunger type oil pump, an eccentric on the camshaft actuates the pump. Refer to the OIL PUMP paragraph.

When installing camshaft, align crankshaft and camshaft timing marks as shown in Fig. T55. If there is no timing mark on the crankshaft gear, align the keyway in the crankshaft with the timing mark on the camshaft gear. If the crankshaft is equipped with a ball bearing or the crankshaft gear is pressed on (no keyway), align the crankshaft gear tooth that is beveled or has a punch mark (Fig. T56) with the mark on the camshaft.

PISTON, PIN AND RINGS

Piston and connecting rod assembly is removed from cylinder head end of engine. Remove cylinder head and crankcase cover/oil pan. Before removing piston, remove any carbon or ring ridge from top of cylinder to prevent ring breakage. Remove connecting rod cap screws, and push piston and rod out of the cylinder.

Aluminum alloy pistons are equipped with two compression rings and one oil control ring. Insert each piston ring squarely into the cylinder and measure ring end gap with a feeler gauge. If ring end gap exceeds specification, check the cylinder bore for excessive wear. Refer to following table for specified piston ring end gap:

Model	Piston Ring End Gap
LEV80	0.005-0.013 in.
	(0.13-0.33 mm)
LEV100, LEV115, LEV120	0.005-0.024 in.
	(0.13-0.61 mm)
TNT120	0.007-0.017 in.
	(0.18-0.43 mm)
All Other Models	0.010-0.020 in.
	(0.25-0.50 mm)

After cleaning the piston ring grooves, install a new ring in the groove and measure side clearance between the ring and ring land with a feeler gauge. Replace the piston if ring side clearance is excessive. Standard ring side clearance in ring grooves is listed in the following table:

Model	Ring Side Clearance
H30, H35, TVS75, TVS90:	
Compression rings	0.002-0.005 in.
	(0.05-0.13 mm)

Fig. T55—View of timing marks (M) on crankshafts and camshaft gears.

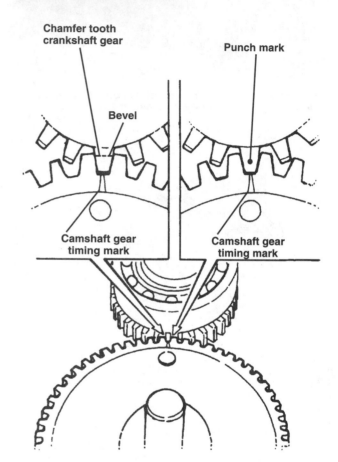

Fig. T56—Drawing of timing marks used on crankshaft equipped with a ball bearing.

Oil control ring	0.0005-0.0035 in.
	(0.013-0.089 mm)
ECV100, H50, H60, HH50, HH60, HS40, HS50, HSK60, HSSK50, LEV115, TNT100, TNT120, TVM125, TVM140, TVS100, TVS105, TVS115, TVS120, TVXL115:	
Compression rings	0.002-0.005 in.
	(0.05-0.13 mm)
Oil control ring	0.001-0.004 in.
	(0.03-0.10 mm)
LEV100, LEV115, LEV120:	
Compression rings	0.005 in. max.
	(0.13 mm)
Oil control ring	0.0035 in. max.
	(0.09 mm)

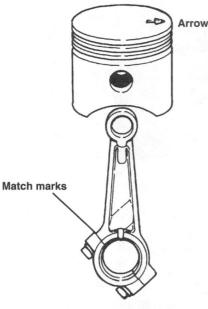

Fig. T57–If piston crown is marked with an arrow, assemble piston and rod as shown.

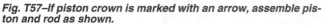

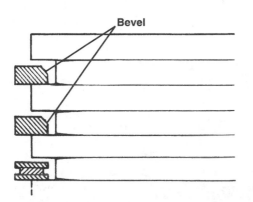

Fig. T58–Top ring and some second compression rings have an inside bevel that must face up toward piston crown. If second ring has a notch on outer diameter, it should face down toward piston skirt.

Piston skirt-to-cylinder clearances are listed in the following table:

Model	Piston Clearance
ECV100, H30, H35, HS40, HS50, HSSK50	0.0040-0.0058 in. (0.102-0.147 mm)
LEV115, TNT100, TNT120, TVS90, TVS100, TVS105, TVS115, TVS120, TVXL115	0.0040-0.0058 in. (0.102-0.147 mm)
H50, H60, HSK60, TVM125, TVM140	0.0030-0.0048 in. (0.076-0.123 mm)
HH50, HH60	0.0015-0.0055 in. (0.038-0.140 mm)
LEV80	0.0025-0.0045 in. (0.064-0.114 mm)
LEV100, LEV115, LEV120	0.003-0.006 in. (0.076-0.152 mm)
TVS75	0.0025-0.0043 in. (0.064-0.110 mm)

Standard piston diameters measured at piston skirt 90° from piston pin bore are listed in the following table:

Model	Piston Diameter
ECV100, HS40, TNT100, TVS100, TVS105 (early)	2.6202-2.6210 in. (66.553-66.573 mm)
H30, H35, TVS90	2.4952-2.4960 in. (63.378-63.398 mm)
H50, H60, HSK60, TVM125, TVM140	2.6212-2.6220 in. (66.578-66.599 mm)
HH50, HH60	2.6205-2.6235 in. (66.561-66.637 mm)
HS50 (early), HSSK50 (early), TNT120, TVS115, TVS120 (early), TVXL115	2.8072-2.8080 in. (71.303-71.323 mm)
HS50 (later), HSSK50 (later), LEV115, TVS105 (later), TVS115, TVS120, (later), TVXL115	2.790-2.791 in. (70.866-70.891 mm)
LEV80, TVS75	2.3092-2.3100 in. (58.654-58.674 mm)
LEV100	2.620-2.622 in. (66.548-66.599 mm)
LEV115, LEV120	2.790-2.791 in. (70.866-70.891 mm)

Piston pin should be a tight push fit in piston pin bore and connecting rod pin bore. Pin is retained by retainer clips at each end of piston pin bore. If piston crown is marked with an arrow, note correct assembly of rod and piston in Fig. T57.

If the top compression ring has an inside bevel, install the ring with the bevel facing up toward piston crown (Fig. T58). The second compression ring may have either an inside bevel or an outside notch. If the second ring has an inside bevel, install it with bevel facing up (Fig. T58). If ring is notched on the outer diameter, install ring so notch is down toward piston skirt. The oil control ring can be installed with either side up.

NOTE: Piston rings used on emission compliant engines have a narrower width than the rings used on standard non-compliant engines. Be sure piston rings are designed for use on engine being overhauled. Using rings designed for an emission compliant engine in a standard engine will result in ring breakage due to the wider ring grooves.

Stagger ring end gaps equally around circumference of piston before installation. If the area adjacent to the valves has been machined (trenched) as shown in Fig. T59, position the piston rings on the piston so the end gaps are staggered and none of the end gaps will coincide with the machined area. This will prevent a piston ring end from catching the machined surface during installation.

When installing connecting rod and piston assembly, align the match marks (casting projections) on connecting rod and cap as shown in Fig. T60. Install piston and connecting rod so match marks on rod face out toward the power take-off (PTO) end of crankshaft.

CONNECTING ROD

The aluminum alloy connecting rod rides directly on crankshaft crankpin.

371

Fig. T59–If engine has a machined (trenched) area adjacent to the valves, stagger piston ring end gaps so they are not aligned with trenched area.

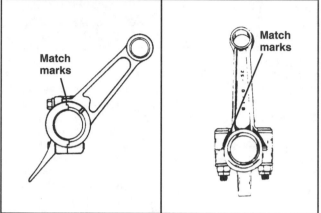

Fig. T60–View of rod match marks used on engines.

Refer to the following table for standard crankpin journal diameter:

Model	Crankpin Diameter
ECV100, H30, LEV80, LEV115, TNT100, TVS75, TVS90, TVS100, TVS105, TVS115, TVXL115	0.8610-0.8615 in. (21.869-21.882 mm)
H35, HS40, HS50, HSSK50	0.9995-1.0000 in. (25.390-25.400 mm)
LEV100, LEV115, LEV120, TNT120, TVS105, TVS120	0.9995-1.0000 in. (25.390-25.400 mm)
H50, HH50, H60, HH60, HSK60, TVM125, TVM140	1.0615-1.0620 in. (26.962-26.975 mm)

Standard inside diameter for connecting rod big end is listed in the following table (if engine has external ignition, check list for a different specification than engines not so equipped):

Model	Rod Big End Diameter
ECV100, H30, LEV80, LEV115, TNT100, TVS75, TVS90, TVS100, TVS105, TVS115, TVXL115	0.8620-0.8625 in. (21.895-21.908 mm)
H35, HS40, HS50, HSSK50	1.0005-1.0010 in. (25.423-25.425 mm)
LEV100, LEV115, LEV120, TNT120, TVS105, TVS120	1.0005-1.0010 in. (25.413-25.425 mm)
H50, HH50, H60, HH60, HSK60, TVM125, TVM140	1.0630-1.0636 in. (27.000-27.013 mm)

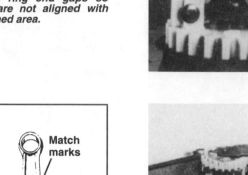

Fig. T61–View of governor used on engines with vertical crankshaft.

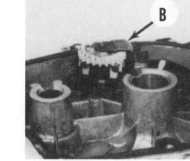

Fig T62–View of governor used on engines with horizontal crankshaft.

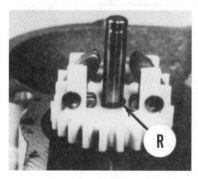

Fig. T63–Detach snap ring (R) to remove flyweight assembly.

Connecting rod bearing-to-crankpin journal clearance should be 0.0005-0.0015 inch (0.013-0.038 mm) for all models.

Assemble connecting rod and piston as outlined in previous section. Tighten connecting rod screws to 170 in.-lb. (19.2 N•m) torque on H50, H60, HSK60, TVM125 and TVM140 engines or to 105 in.-lb. (11.5 N•m) torque on all other models.

GOVERNOR

On most engines with a vertical crankshaft and low horsepower horizontal crankshaft engines, the governor is retained on the shaft by snap ring (R–Fig. T61). On larger horizontal crankshaft engines, the governor is retained by bracket (B–Fig. T62).

To remove spool, detach either upper snap ring or bracket. Detach lower snap ring (R–Fig. T63) to remove flyweight assembly. A washer (W–Fig. T64) is located under the flyweight assembly. On some engines, a spacer (S–Fig. T65) is located under washer (W).

On later small frame engines and replacement shafts, no snap rings are used on the governor shaft. The governor is held in place by a boss on the governor shaft. The flyweights and gear are available only as a unit assembly.

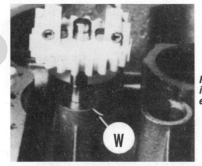

Fig. T64–A thrust washer is located under the governor gear.

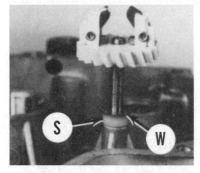

Fig. T65–Some engines are equipped with a spacer (S) under thrust washer (W).

Fig. T66–Install governor shaft so height is as specified in text.

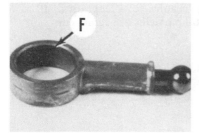

Fig. T67–Install oil pump so chamfer (F) is toward camshaft.

The governor shaft is pressed into the crankcase cover or oil pan and may be replaced if the mounting boss is not damaged or the hole is not enlarged. To remove the governor shaft, clamp the shaft in a vise and using a soft mallet, drive the crankcase cover or oil pan off the shaft. Do not attempt to twist governor shaft out of boss. Twisting will enlarge the hole.

Apply Loctite 271 (red) to end of new shaft. If shaft is retainerless design, position washer and governor gear assembly on shaft before installing shaft, then press in shaft until the governor gear has 0.010-0.020 inch (0.25-0.50 mm) axial play. If snap rings are used on the governor shaft, press shaft into crankcase cover or oil pan until the

height above boss (Fig. T66) is as specified in the following table:

Model	Governor Shaft Height
H50, HH50, H60, HH60	1⁷⁄₁₆ in. (36.51 mm)
TVM125, TVM140	1¹⁹⁄₃₂ in. (40.48 mm)
All other models	1²¹⁄₆₄ in. (33.73 mm)

OIL PUMP

Vertical crankshaft engines are equipped with a barrel and plunger type oil pump located in the oil pan. An eccentric on the camshaft drives the oil pump.

Chamfered side of drive collar (Fig. T67) should be toward camshaft gear. Oil pumps may be equipped with two chamfered sides, one chamfered side or with flat boss as shown. Be sure installation is correct.

CRANKSHAFT, MAIN BEARINGS AND SEALS

Always note oil seal depth and seal lip direction before removing oil seal from crankcase or cover. New seal must be pressed into seal bore to the same depth as old seal before removal on all models.

Refer to CONNECTING ROD section for specified crankshaft crankpin journal diameters.

Crankshaft main bearing journals on some models ride directly in the aluminum alloy bores in the cylinder block and crankcase cover or oil pan. Other engines are originally equipped with replaceable steel backed bronze bushings, and some are originally equipped with a ball type main bearing at the PTO end of crankshaft. On Models H50, H60, HH50 and HH60, the bearing is pressed on the crankshaft.

Standard diameters for main bearing bores are listed in the following table (if engine has external ignition, check the list for a different specification than engines not so equipped):

Model	Main Bearing Inside Diameter
ECV100, TVS75, TVS90	0.8755-0.8760 in. (22.238-22.250 mm)
ECV100 (external ignition), H30, LEV80, TVS75 (external ignition), TVS90 (external ignition),TNT100, TVS100:	
Crankcase side	1.0005-1.0010 in. (25.413-25.425 mm)
Cover (flange) side	0.8755-0.8760 in. (22.238-22.250 mm)
H35, H50, H60, HH50, HH60, HS40, HS50, HSK60, HSSK50	1.0005-1.0010 in. (25.413-25.425 mm)
LEV100, LEV115, LEV120, TNT120,TVM125, TVM140, TVS105, TVS115, TVS120, TVXL115	1.0005-1.0010 in. (25.413-25.425 mm)

Standard diameters for crankshaft main bearing journals are shown in the following table (if engine has external ignition, check the list for a different specification than engines not so equipped):

Model	Main Bearing Journal Diameter
ECV100, TVS75, TVS90	0.8735-0.8740 in. (22.187-22.200 mm)

ECV100 (external ignition), H30,
  LEV80, TVS75 (external ignition),
  TVS90 (external ignition), TNT100,
  TVS100:	

Crankcase side	0.9985-0.9990 in. (25.362-25.375 mm)
Cover (flange) side	0.8735-0.8740 in. (22.187-22.200 mm)
H35, H50, H60, HH50, HH60, HS40, HS50, HSK60, HSSK50	0.9985-0.9990 in. (25.362-25.375 mm)

LEV100, LEV115, LEV120,
  TNT120, TVM125, TVM140,
  TVS105, TVS115, TVS120 . . . .
	0.9985-0.9990 in.
	(25.362-25.375 mm)

Main bearing clearance should be 0.0015-0.0025 inch (0.038-0.064 mm). Crankshaft end play should be 0.005-0.027 inch (0.13-0.069 mm) for all models.

On models equipped with a ball bearing, inspect the bearing and replace when damaged. On Models H50, H60, HH50 and HH60, the bearing must be pressed on or off crankshaft journal using a suitable press or puller.

When installing crankshaft, align crankshaft and camshaft gear timing marks as shown in Fig. T55. If there is no timing mark on the crankshaft gear, align the keyway in the crankshaft with the timing mark on the camshaft gear. If the crankshaft is equipped with a ball bearing or the crankshaft gear is pressed on (no keyway), align the crankshaft gear tooth that is beveled or has a punch mark (Fig. T56) with the mark on the camshaft.

CYLINDER AND CRANKCASE

Cylinder and crankcase are an integral casting on all models. Cylinder should be honed and fitted to nearest oversize piston and ring set that is available if cylinder is scored, tapered or out-of-round more than 0.005 inch (0.13 mm).

Standard cylinder bore diameters are listed in the following table (if engine has external ignition, check the list for a different specification than engines not so equipped):

Model	Cylinder Bore Diameter
H30, LEV80, TVS75	2.3125-2.3135 in. (58.738-58.763 mm)
H30, H35, TVS90	2.5000-2.5010 in. (63.500-63.525 mm)
ECV100, H50, H60, HH50, HH60, HS40, HSK60	2.6250-2.6260 in. (66.675-66.700 mm)
LEV100, TNT100, TVM125, TVM140, TVS100, TVS105	2.6250-2.6260 in. (66.675-66.700 mm)

HS50 (later), HSSK50 (later),
  LEV115, LEV120, TVS115 (later),
  TVS120 (later), TVXL115 (early) . . . .
	2.795-2.796 in.
	(70.993-71.018 mm)

HS50 (early), HSSK50 (early),
  TNT120, TVS115 (early),
  TVS120 (early), TVXL115 (early) . . . .
	2.8120-2.8130 in.
	(71.425-71.450 mm)

Refer to PISTON, PIN AND RINGS section for correct piston-to-cylinder block clearance. Note also that cylinder block used on Models H50, HH50, TVM125 and TVM140 has been "trenched" to improve fuel flow and power (Fig. T59).

The proper crosshatch pattern must be restored in the cylinder bore when installing new piston rings. A rigid hone is recommended for reconditioning or resizing the cylinder. Use honing stones and lubrication recommended by the hone manufacturer to produce the correct cylinder wall finish. Operate hone at 300-700 rpm and with an up and down movement that will produce the desired crosshatch pattern. Always check availability of oversize piston and ring sets before honing cylinder.

After honing, the cylinder and crankcase must be thoroughly cleaned to remove all abrasive particles. Honing grit is extremely abrasive and will result in rapid wear to all internal components if not completely removed. Use a stiff brush with a solution of detergent and hot water to clean the cylinder wall and crankcase. Clean until all traces of honing grit and metal particles are removed.

TECUMSEH

Model	No. Cyls.	Bore	Stroke	Displacement	Power Rating
OHV14	1	3.56 in. (90.4 mm)	3.00 in. (76.2 mm)	29.9 cu. in. (490 cc)	14 hp (10.4 kW)
OHV145	1	3.56 in. (90.4 mm)	3.00 in. (76.2 mm)	29.9 cu. in. (490 cc)	14.5 hp (10.8 kW)
OHV15	1	3.56 in. (90.4 mm)	3.00 in. (76.2 mm)	29.9 cu. in. (490 cc)	15 hp (11.2 kW)
OHV155	1	3.56 in. (90.4 mm)	3.00 in. (76.2 mm)	29.9 cu. in. (490 cc)	15.5 hp (11.6 kW)
OHV16	1	3.56 in. (90.4 mm)	3.00 in. (76.2 mm)	29.9 cu. in. (490 cc)	16 hp (11.9 kW)
OHV165	1	3.56 in. (90.4 mm)	3.00 in. (76.2 mm)	29.9 cu. in. (490 cc)	16.5 hp (12.3 kW)
OHV17	1	3.56 in. (90.4 mm)	3.00 in. (76.2 mm)	29.9 cu. in. (490 cc)	17 hp (12.7 kW)

All models are four-stroke, overhead valve, single-cylinder gasoline engines equipped with a vertical crankshaft. The aluminum alloy cylinder and crankcase assembly is equipped with a cast iron cylinder sleeve that is an integral part of the cylinder. Lubrication is provided by a rotor-type oil pump that is operated by a camshaft-driven shaft.

Engine model number, serial number and specification number are stamped into the cooling shroud or on a decal. Always furnish the correct engine model, serial and specification numbers when ordering parts.

MAINTENANCE

LUBRICATION

The engine is equipped with a rotor-type oil pump that is located in the bottom of the oil pan. A driveshaft driven by the camshaft turns the rotor in the oil pump to force oil up the center of the camshaft. The pressurized oil lubricates

the top main bearing and top camshaft bearing. Oil is sprayed out of a hole between the camshaft and main bearings to lubricate the connecting rod and other internal parts.

Oil level should be checked before initial start-up and at five-hour intervals. Maintain oil level at "FULL" mark on dipstick.

Recommended oil change interval is every 50 hours of normal operation. Oil should be drained when engine is warm. Manufacturer recommends using oil with API service classification SJ. Use SAE 30 oil for temperatures above 32° F (0° C) and SAE 5W-20 or 10W-30 for temperatures below 32° F (0° C).

Replace the oil filter after every 100 hours of operation or more frequently if engine is operated in adverse conditions.

CRANKCASE BREATHER

The engine is equipped with a reed-valve crankcase breather located in the side of the crankcase. Unscrew retaining screws to remove breather.

When assembling the breather, position reed valve (1–Fig. T901) against the crankcase. Place the stop plate (2) over the reed valve with notch, if so equipped, toward PTO. If the stop plate has a mark on one side, position the stop plate so mark is out. Secure reed valve and stop plate with a screw, then install the breather baffle and cover.

SPARK PLUG

The recommended spark plug is a Champion RN4C. Recommended electrode gap is 0.030 in. (0.76 mm). Tighten spark plug to 21 ft.-lb. (28 N•m).

CARBURETOR

The engine is equipped with a Walbro LMK float carburetor. The carburetor has a fixed main jet. Carburetors on early engines may be equipped with an adjustable idle mixture screw, while later engines have a fixed idle mixture jet.

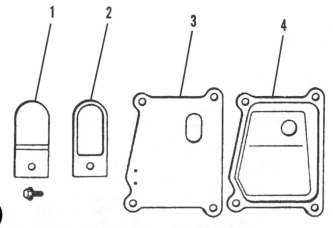

Fig. T901—Exploded view of crankcase breather.
1. Reed plate
2. Stop plate
3. Baffle
4. Cover

Initial setting of idle mixture screw (12–Fig. T902), on carburetors so equipped, is one turn out. With engine at normal operating temperature and equipment control lever in "SLOW" position, adjust idle speed screw (9) to desired engine idle speed. With engine running at idle speed, turn the idle mixture screw clockwise until engine speed just starts to drop. Note screw position. Turn the idle mixture screw counterclockwise until engine speed just starts to drop again. Note the screw position, then turn screw to midpoint between the noted screw positions. If engine will not accelerate cleanly, slightly enrich the mixture by turning the idle mixture screw counterclockwise. If necessary, readjust the idle speed screw.

To disassemble the carburetor, remove the fuel bowl (18–Fig. T902), pivot pin (14) and float (16), fuel inlet valve (15) and idle mixture screw (12). Choke shaft (1) and throttle shaft (5) can be removed after removing screws from choke plate (4) and throttle plate (13).

Clean the carburetor using a commercial carburetor cleaning solvent and compressed air. Inspect components and discard any parts that are damaged or excessively worn. The fuel inlet valve (15) is available for service, but the carburetor body must be replaced if the valve seat is damaged.

The main jet is located in the side of the center fuel leg. Do not remove the main jet unless it is damaged or installation of a high altitude jet is required. To remove main jet, carefully drive jet into fuel leg; do not damage surrounding metal. Using a punch slightly larger than new jet, force jet into hole in leg so it is flush with leg surface.

When assembling carburetor, note the following: Do not deform the Welch plug (10) during installation; it should be flat. Seal outer edges of plug with nonhardening sealer. Install throttle return spring (7) so square end is up. With throttle shaft installed, both ends of spring should be to the left of center boss as viewed from throttle end of carburetor. Install choke and throttle plates so numbers are on outer face when choke or throttle plate is in closed position. Float height is not adjustable. Refer to SPEED CONTROL section to synchronize speed control mechanism and adjust governed engine speeds.

SPEED CONTROL

Use the following procedure to synchronize remote speed control and engine speed control assembly, and also adjust high and low idle speeds. Before starting procedure, be sure linkage is in good condition, including bushings in levers.

Loosen throttle control cable clamp screw (Fig. T903). Move the equipment speed control lever to the FAST position. Align the hole in throttle lever with hole in speed control bracket by inserting a drill bit or rod through the holes. Remove the slack in the control cable and tighten cable clamp. Be sure speed control will operate through full travel from full choke to wide-open throttle. At full throttle there should be a gap of 0.040-0.070 inch (1.02-1.78 mm) as shown in Fig. T903. Bend tab to adjust gap. Start the engine and allow to reach operating temperature. Adjust governed idle speed by turning idle speed screw shown in Fig. T903. Bend high-speed adjustment tab using Tecumseh tool 670326 to adjust high speed governed no-load speed.

GOVERNOR

All models are equipped with a mechanical flyweight type governor located inside the oil pan.

To adjust external governor linkage (Fig. T904), stop engine and loosen the screw (S) securing governor lever and

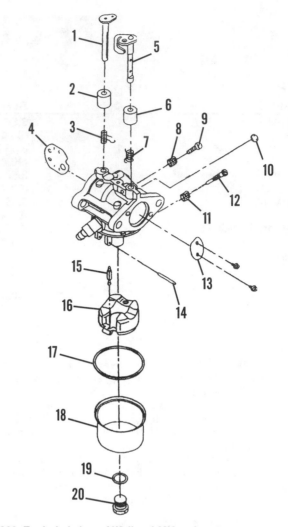

Fig. T902–Exploded view of Walbro LMK carburetor.

1. Choke shaft
2. Dust seal
3. Spring
4. Choke plate
5. Throttle shaft
6. Dust seal
7. Spring
8. Spring
9. Idle speed screw
10. Welch plug
11. Spring
12. Idle mixture screw
13. Throttle plate
14. Float pin
15. Fuel inlet valve
16. Float
17. Gasket
18. Fuel bowl
19. Washer
20. Washer

High speed adjustment tab

Idle speed screw

Alignment hole

Choke lever air gap (.40-.70") (1.02-1.778 mm) bend tab to adjust

Tool #670326

Fig. T903–Refer to text for speed control adjustment procedure.

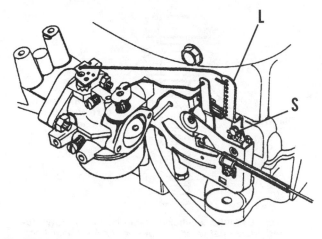

Fig. T904–Refer to text for adjustment of governor linkage.

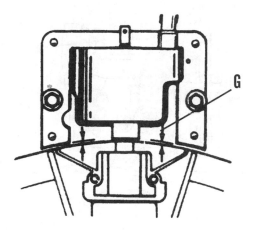

Fig. T905–Air gap (G) between coil legs and flywheel should be 0.0125 inch (0.32 mm).

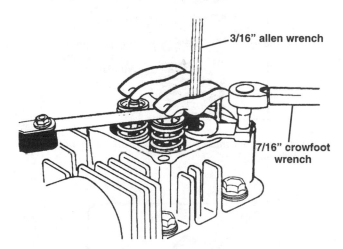

Fig. T906–Use a feeler gauge to correctly set valve clearance. Refer to text.

governor clamp. Push governor lever (L) to fully open carburetor throttle. Turn governor clamp counterclockwise as far as it will go. While holding clamp and lever in this position, tighten screw.

Refer to SPEED CONTROL section to adjust governed engine speeds.

IGNITION SYSTEM

A solid-state ignition system is used on all models. Ignition system has no moving parts and is considered satisfactory if a spark will jump a $\frac{1}{8}$ inch (3.2 mm) air gap when engine is cranked at 125 rpm.

Ignition module is mounted outside of the flywheel. Air gap setting (G–Fig. T905) between ignition module and flywheel magnets is 0.0125 inch (0.32 mm). To set air gap, loosen module mounting screws, move module as necessary and retighten screws.

VALVE ADJUSTMENT

Engine must be cold for valve adjustment. Remove rocker arm cover. Position crankshaft at TDC on compression stroke. Be sure both valves are closed. If not, rotate flywheel one revolution clockwise.

Valve clearance for both valves should be 0.004 inch (0.10 mm). Loosen setscrew at center of pivot nut and turn pivot nut to obtain desired clearance (Fig. T906). Tighten setscrew to 110 in.-lb. (12.4 N•m). Rotate crankshaft two turns so it is at TDC on compression stroke and recheck adjustment.

REPAIRS

TIGHTENING TORQUE

Recommended tightening torque values are as follows:

Connecting rod bolts	210 in.-lb.
	(24 N•m)
Oil pan	125 in.-lb.
	(14 N•m)
Cylinder head bolts	230 in.-lb.
	(26 N•m)
Flywheel nut	58 ft.-lb.
	(79 N•m)
Intake pipe	95 in.-lb.
	(10.7 N•m)
Rocker arm studs	190 in.-lb.
	(21.5 N•m)
Rocker cove	55 in.-lb.
	(6.2 N•m)
Spark plug	21 ft.-lb.
	(28 N•m)

CYLINDER HEAD

Always allow engine to cool completely before removing cylinder or loosening cylinder head bolts. To remove cylinder head, remove blower housing and air baffle, carburetor and intake pipe, and muffler. Turn flywheel to position the piston at top dead center of compression stroke. Remove rocker arm cover (1–Fig. T907). Loosen pivot nut setscrew (7) and unscrew pivot nuts (8). Remove the rocker arms (9). Mark pivot nuts and rocker arms so they can be installed in their original locations. Unscrew rocker arm studs (10) and remove push rod guide plate (11). Remove cylinder head retaining bolts and remove cylinder head.

Thoroughly clean cylinder head and inspect for cracks or other damage. Position cylinder head on a flat plate and use a feeler gauge to check flatness of head gasket sealing surface. Replace the cylinder head if warpage exceeds 0.005 inch (0.13 mm).

Use a new head gasket when installing cylinder head. Install Belleville washer on cylinder head bolt with crown up toward bolt head, then install flat washer (Fig. T908). Tighten the head bolts following the sequence shown in

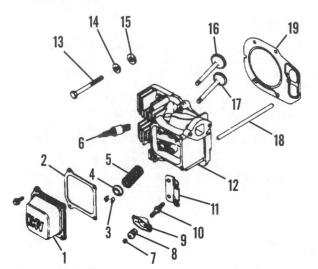

Fig. T907–Exploded view of cylinder head assembly.

1. Rocker arm cover
2. Gasket
3. Valve keeper
4. Valve spring retainer
5. Valve spring
6. Spark plug
7. Setscrew
8. Pivot nut
9. Rocker arm
10. Rocker arm stud
11. Push rod guide plate
12. Cylinder head
13. Head bolt
14. Belleville washer
15. Washer
16. Intake valve
17. Exhaust valve
18. Push rod

Fig. T909. Tighten the bolts in 60 in.-lb. (6.7 N•m) increments to a final torque of 230 in.-lb. (26 N•m).

VALVE SYSTEM

Valve seats are machined directly in the cylinder head. Seats should be cut at a 46° angle and valve faces cut or ground at a 45° angle. Valve seat width should be $\frac{3}{64}$-inch (1.2 mm).

Clean all combustion deposits from valves. Replace valves that are burned, excessively pitted, warped or if valve head margin after grinding is less than $\frac{1}{32}$-inch (0.8 mm). Valves should be lapped to their seats using fine lapping compound.

Valve spring free length should be 1.980 inches (50.29 mm). It is recommended that valve springs be replaced when the engine is overhauled. The valve spring dampening coils are coils wound closer together at one end than the other (Fig. T910). Install spring so end with closer coils is against the cylinder head.

Valve guides can be reamed to 0.3432-0.3442 inch (8.717-8.743 mm) for use with oversize valve stems.

OIL PUMP

All engines are equipped with a rotor-type oil pump located in the oil pan (Fig. T911) and driven by the camshaft via a driveshaft. A relief valve is located in the side of the oil pan.

Remove engine from the equipment for access to oil pump cover. Remove cover and extract pump rotors. Mark rotors so they can be reinstalled in their original position. Replace any components that are damaged or excessively worn. Be sure the O-ring is installed before installing cover. Tighten oil pump cover screws to 55 in-lb. (6.2 N•m).

BALANCER SHAFTS

The engine is equipped with two balancer shafts (15 and 16–Fig. T912) that ride directly in the crankcase and oil

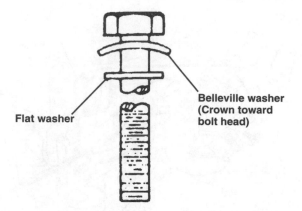

Fig. T908–Install Belleville washer on head bolt with crown toward bolt head. Install flat washer with sharp edge toward bolt head.

Flat washer

Belleville washer (Crown toward bolt head)

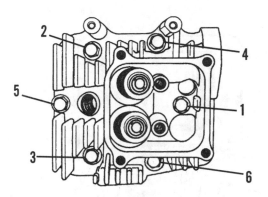

Fig. T909–Tighten cylinder head bolts in sequence shown.

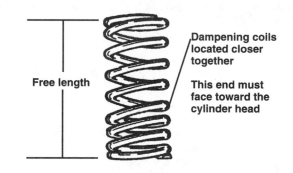

Dampening coils located closer together

This end must face toward the cylinder head

Free length

Fig. T910–Valve spring must be installed with dampening coil end positioned against the cylinder head.

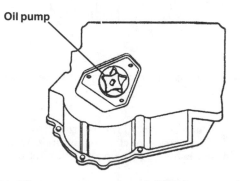

Oil pump

Fig. T911–Oil pump rotors are accessible after removing cover on bottom of oil pan.

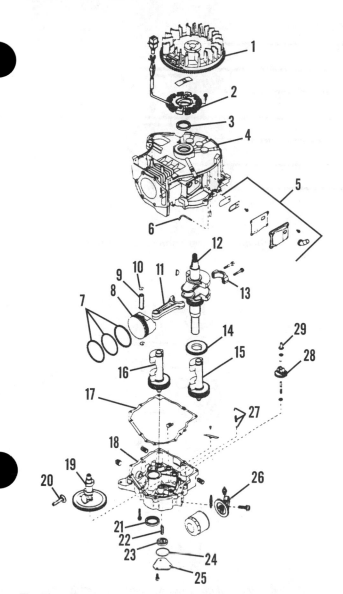

Fig. T912–Exploded view of engine internal components.

1. Flywheel
2. Alternator coil
3. Oil seal
4. Crankcase
5. Breather assy.
6. Governor lever
7. Piston rings
8. Piston
9. Piston pin
10. Retaining rings
11. Connecting rod
12. Crankshaft
13. Rod cap
14. Balancer drive gear
15. Balancer gear (wide gear)
16. Balancer gear (thin gear)
17. Gasket
18. Oil pan
19. Camshaft
20. Tappet
21. Oil seal
22. Pump shaft
23. Oil pump rotor
24. O-ring
25. Cover
26. Oil filter adapter
27. Oil pressure relief valve
28. Governor
29. Spool

pan bores. Drain oil and remove oil pan for access to the balancer shafts.

A gear (14–Fig. T912) on the crankshaft drives the balancer shaft with the thicker gear, which in turn drives the balancer shaft with the thinner gear. Note the position and configuration of the gears in Fig. T913. Thin balancer gear has one timing mark and wide balancer gear has two timing marks. Install the balancer gears so timing marks are aligned as shown in Fig. T913.

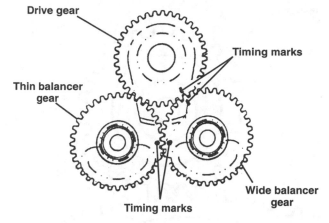

Fig. T913–Install balancer gears so timing marks are aligned as shown.

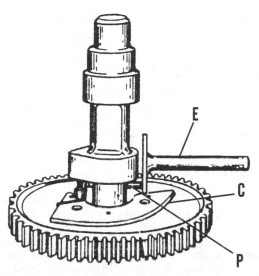

Fig. T914–Compression release pin (P) extends during starting to hold exhaust valve (E) off its seat.

CAMSHAFT

Camshaft and camshaft gear are an integral part which can be removed from the engine after removing the cylinder head, push rods, oil pan and balancer shafts. Identify the position of the tappets as they are removed so they can be reinstalled in original position if reused.

Camshaft bearings are an integral part of crankcase and oil pan or crankcase cover. Camshaft journal diameter should be 0.6235-0.6240 inch (15.84-15.85 mm). Camshaft bearing inside diameter should be 0.6245-0.6255 inch (15.86-15.89 mm). Clearance between camshaft journal and camshaft bearing should not exceed 0.003 inch (0.08 mm). Inspect camshaft lobes for pitting, scratches or excessive wear and replace when necessary. Tappets should be replaced whenever a new camshaft is installed.

Camshaft is equipped with a compression release mechanism (Fig. T914) to aid starting. Compression release mechanism parts should work freely with no binding or sticking. Parts are not serviced separately from camshaft.

When installing camshaft, be sure that timing marks on camshaft gear and crankshaft gear are aligned as shown in Fig. T915.

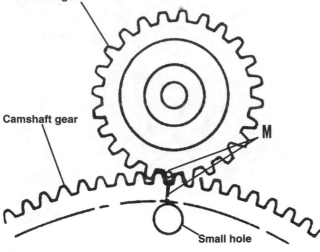

Fig. T915–View of crankshaft and camshaft timing marks (M).

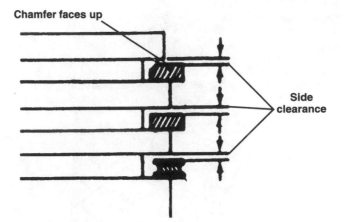

Fig. T916–Inside chamfer on top compression ring must face piston crown.

PISTON, PIN AND RINGS

Piston and connecting rod are removed as an assembly. Remove cylinder head and camshaft as previously outlined. Remove connecting rod cap. Remove carbon or ring ridge (if present) from top of cylinder before removing piston. Push the connecting rod and piston out top of cylinder.

Standard piston skirt diameter, measured at bottom of skirt 90° from piston pin bore, is 3.562-3.563 inches (90.47-90.50 mm) for all models. Specified clearance between piston skirt and cylinder wall is 0.0015-0.0030 inch (0.038-0.076 mm). Oversize pistons are available. Oversize piston size should be stamped on top of piston.

To check piston ring grooves for wear, clean carbon from ring grooves and install new rings in grooves. Use a feeler gauge to measure side clearance between ring land and ring. Specified side clearance is 0.0020-0.0040 inch (0.051-0.102 mm) for compression rings and 0.0009-0.0029 inch (0.023-0.074 mm) for oil control ring. Replace the piston if ring side clearance is excessive.

Ring end gap should be 0.012-0.022 inch (0.30-0.56 mm) for all rings.

Rings must be installed on piston as shown in Fig. T916. Stagger ring end gaps around piston. Lubricate piston and cylinder with engine oil prior to installing piston. Be sure that arrow on top of piston points toward push rod side of engine. Match marks on connecting rod and cap must be toward open side of crankcase after installation and must align when installing cap on rod.

CONNECTING ROD

Piston and connecting rod are removed as an assembly. Refer to previous section to remove piston and connecting rod.

Connecting rod rides directly on crankshaft crankpin. Inside diameter of connecting rod bearing bore at crankshaft end should be 1.6234-1.6240 inches (41.234-41.250 mm).

GOVERNOR

Governor weight and gear assembly is driven by camshaft gear and rides on a replaceable shaft that is pressed into engine crankcase or crankcase cover.

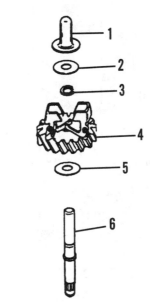

Fig. T917–Exploded view of governor flyweight assembly.

1. Thrust spool
2. Washer
3. Snap ring
4. Governor gear & weight assy.
5. Washer
6. Stud

Governor gear, flyweights and shaft (Fig. T917) are serviced only as an assembly. If governor gear shaft is replaced, press new shaft into oil pan boss so exposed shaft length is 1.350-1.365 inches (34.29-34.67 mm).

Adjust external linkage as outlined in MAINTENANCE section.

CRANKSHAFT, MAIN BEARINGS AND SEALS

To remove crankshaft, first remove all shrouds. Remove the flywheel. Remove connecting rod and piston as previously outlined, then remove crankshaft.

Main bearings are integral part of crankcase and oil pan or crankcase cover. Main bearing inside diameter should be 1.6265-1.6270 inches (41.313-41.326 mm).

Standard crankshaft main journal diameter is 1.6245-1.6250 inches (41.262-41.275 mm) for each end. Standard crankpin journal diameter is 1.3740-1.3745 inches (34.900-34.912 mm).

Crankshaft end play should be 0.0025-0.0335 inch (0.064-0.851 mm).

CYLINDER AND CRANKCASE

A cast iron liner is permanently cast into the aluminum alloy cylinder and crankcase assembly. Standard piston bore inside diameter is 3.562-3.563 inches (90.47-90.50 mm). If cylinder taper or out-of-round exceeds 0.004 inch (0.10 mm), cylinder should be bored to nearest oversize for which piston and rings are available.

Cylinder may be manufactured oversize at the factory. A cylinder bored oversize at the factory may be identified by oversize number stamped on cylinder head mating surface of cylinder. For instance, a cylinder manufactured 0.010-inch oversize is stamped ".010".

FUEL PUMP

The engine may be equipped with a diaphragm fuel pump to transfer fuel from the fuel tank to the carburetor. A pulse line connected to the crankcase provides pressure pulses to operate the pump. A repair kit is available to rebuild the pump.

TECUMSEH
SERVICING TECUMSEH ACCESSORIES

12 VOLT STARTING AND CHARGING SYSTEMS

Some Tecumseh engines may be equipped with 12 volt electrical systems. Refer to the following paragraphs for servicing of Tecumseh electrical units and 12 volt Delco-Remy starter-generator used on some models.

12 VOLT STARTER MOTOR (BENDIX DRIVE)

Refer to Fig. TE101, TE102, TE103 or TE104 for an exploded view of 12-volt starter motor and Bendix drive unit used on some engines. To identify starter, refer to service number stamped on end cap.

To disassemble starter shown in Fig. TE101, remove nut (1) and separate drive assembly from armature shaft. Remove through-bolts (22) and separate end plates (14 and 20) and armature (16) from the frame (17).

When assembling starter motor shown in Fig. TE101, use spacers (15) of varying thickness to obtain an arma-

ture end play of 0.005-0.015 inch (0.13-0.38 mm). Note the following tightening torque specifications:

Armature nut (1):	
Starters 29965, 32468,	
32468A, 32468B, 33202	100 in.-lbs.
	(11.3 N•m)
Starter 32510	130-150 in.-lbs.
	(14.7-16.9 N•m)
Starter 32817	170-220 in.-lbs.
	(19.2-24.8 N•m)
Through-bolts (22):	
Starters 29965, 32468,	
32468A, 32468B, 33202	30-35 in.-lbs.
	(3.4-3.9 N•m)
Starter 32510	45-50 in.-lbs.
	(5.0-5.6 N•m)
Starter 32817	35-44 in.-lbs.
	(3.9-5.0 N•m)

To perform no-load test for starter motors 29965, 32468 and 32468A, use a fully charged 6-volt battery. Maximum current draw should not exceed 25 amps at 6 volts. Minimum rpm is 6500.

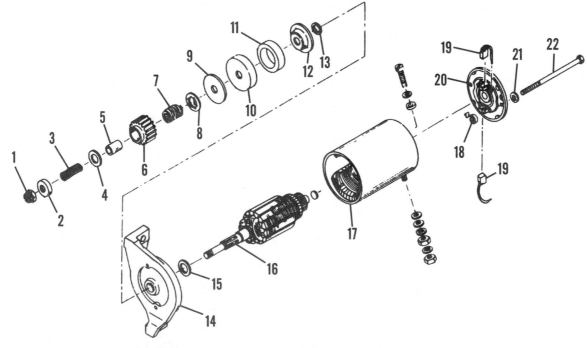

Fig. TE101—Exploded view of 12-Volt electric starter used on early model engines.

1. Nut	7. Screw shaft	13. Thrust bushing	18. Brush spring
2. Pinion stop	8. Stop washer	14. Drive end cap	19. Brush
3. Spring	9. Thrust washer	15. Spacer washer	20. End cap
4. Washer	10. Cushion	16. Armature	21. Washer
5. Anti-drift sleeve	11. Rubber cushion	17. Frame & field	22. Bolt
6. Pinion gear	12. Thrust washer	coil assy.	

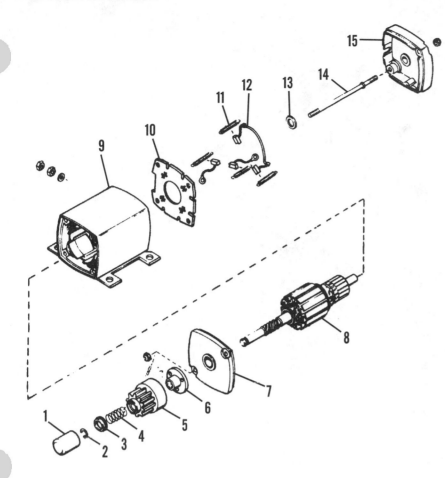

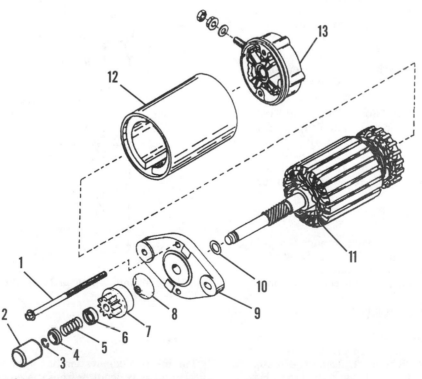

Fig. TE102—Exploded view of 12-volt starter motor used on some later models. Components on 110-volts starter are similar.

1. Dust cover
2. Clip
3. Spring retainer
4. Spring
5. Pinion
6. Retainer
7. Drive end cap
8. Armature
9. Housing
10. Brush card
11. Brush spring
12. Brush
13. Thrust washer
14. Through-bolt
15. End cap

Fig. TE103—Exploded view of 12-volt starter motor used on some later models.

1. Through bolt
2. Dust cover
3. Clip
4. Spring retainer
5. Spring
6. Spring seat
7. Pinion
8. Retainer
9. Drive end cap
10. Washer
11. Armature
12. Housing
13. End cap

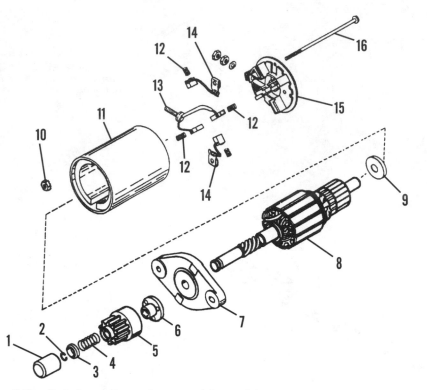

Fig. TE104–Exploded view of 12-volt starter motor used on some later models.

1. Dust cover	5. Pinion	9. Washer	13. Brush
2. Clip	6. Retainer	10. Nut	14. Brush
3. Spring retainer	7. Drive end cap	11. Housing	15. End cap
4. Spring	8. Armature	12. Brush spring	16. Through bolt

No-load test for Models 32468B and 33202 requires a fully charged 12-volt battery. Maximum current draw should not exceed 25 amps at 11.8 volts. Minimum rpm is 8000.

No-load test for starter motors 32510 and 32817 must be performed with a 12-volt battery. Maximum current draw should not exceed 25 amps at 11.5 volts. Minimum rpm is 8000.

To disassemble starter motors 33605, 33606 and 33835 shown in Fig. TE102. Remove end cap (1) and clip (2). Separate the drive components from the armature shaft. Remove nuts from through-bolts (14) and separate end plates (7 and 15) and armature (8) from the housing (9). Note that stops on through-bolts (14) are used to secure brush card (10) in housing (9).

Through-bolts must be installed with stops toward end cover (15).

Maximum current draw with starter on engine should not exceed 55 amps at a minimum of 850 rpm for starters 33605 and 33606 or 70 amps at a minimum of 600 rpm for starter 33835. Cranking test should not exceed 10 seconds.

ALTERNATOR CHARGING SYSTEMS

The engine may be equipped with an alternator to provide battery charging direct current, or provide electricity for accessories, or both. The alternator coils may be located under the flywheel, or on some models with an external ignition module, the alternator coils are attached to the legs of the ignition coil. Rectification is accomplished either with a rectifier panel, regulator-rectifier unit, external or internal, or by an inline diode contained in the harness.

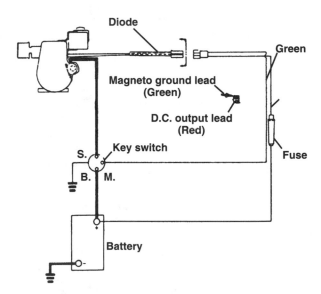

Fig. TE105–Wiring diagram of 3 amp direct current system with inline diode.

Inline Diode System

The inline diode system has a diode connected into the alternator wire leading from the engine. See Fig. TE105. The system produces approximately 3 amps direct current. The diode rectifies the alternating current produced by the alternator into direct current. A 6 amp fuse provides overload protection.

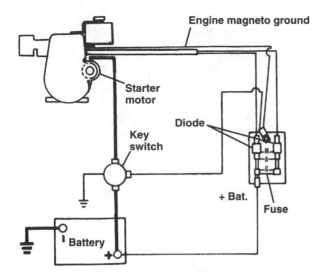

Fig. TE106–Wiring diagram of typical 3 amp alternator and rectifier pan charging system.

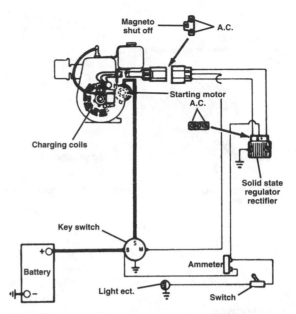

Fig. TE108–Wiring diagram of typical 7, 10 or 20 amp alternator and regulator-rectifier charging system.

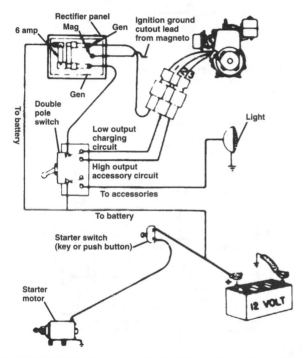

Fig. TE107–Wiring diagram of typical 7 amp alternator and rectifier panel charging system. The double pole switch in one position reduces output to 3 amps for charging or increasing output to 7 amps in other position to operate accessories.

To check the system, disconnect the harness connector. Connect positive lead of a DC voltmeter to the red wire connector terminal, and ground the negative tester lead to engine. At 3600 rpm engine speed, voltmeter reading should be at least 11.5 volts. If engine speed is less, the voltmeter reading will be less.

If voltage reading is unsatisfactory, check the alternator coils by taking an AC voltage reading. Connect one tester lead between the diode and engine, and ground the other tester lead to the engine. At engine speed of 3600 rpm, voltage reading should be 26 volts, otherwise the alternator is defective. If the engine cannot attain 3600 rpm, voltage reading will be less.

Another type of inline diode system provides 3 amps direct current and 5 amps alternating current. This system has a two-wire pigtail consisting of a red wire and a black or yellow wire; the diode is inline with the red wire. To test system, check voltage at pigtail connector. At engine speed of 3600 rpm (less engine speed will produce less voltage), voltage at the red wire terminal should be 11 volts DC on OHV models or 13 volts DC on all other models. Voltage at the black or yellow wire terminal should be 22 volts AC on OHV models or 13 volts AC on all other models.

If voltage reading is unsatisfactory, check alternator coils by taking an AC voltage reading. Connect one tester lead to the red wire between the diode and engine, and ground the other tester lead to the engine. At engine speed of 3600 rpm, voltage reading should be 24.5 volts on OHV models or 29 volts on all other models, otherwise alternator is defective. If the engine cannot attain 3600 rpm, voltage reading will be less.

Rectifier Panel Systems

The charging system shown in Fig. TE106 has a maximum charging output of about 3 amperes at 3600 rpm. No current regulator is used on this low output system. The rectifier panel includes two diodes (rectifiers) and a 6 ampere fuse for overload protection.

The system shown in Fig. TE107 has a maximum output of 7 amperes. To prevent overcharging the battery, a double pole switch is used in low output position to reduce the output to 3 amperes for charging the battery. Move the switch to high output position (7 amperes) when using accessories.

To test systems, remove rectifiers and test them with either a continuity light or an ohmmeter. Rectifiers should show current flow in one direction only. Alternator output can be checked using an induction ammeter over the positive lead wire to battery.

7, 10 and 20 Amp External Regulator-Rectifier System

The system shown in (Fig. TE108) may produce 7, 10 or 20 amperes and uses a solid state regulator-rectifier out-

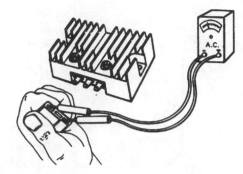

Fig. TE109–Connect DC voltmeter as shown when checking the regulator-rectifier.

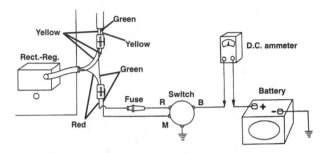

Fig. TE110–Connect AC voltmeter to AC leads as shown when checking alternator coils.

side the flywheel that converts the generated alternating current to direct current for charging the battery. The regulator-rectifier also allows only the required amount of current flow for existing battery conditions. When the battery is fully charged, current output is decreased to prevent overcharging the battery.

To test 7 or 10 amp system, disconnect B+ lead and connect a DC voltmeter as shown in Fig. TE109. With engine running at 3000 rpm, voltage should be at least 14 volts on 7 amp system and 16 volts on 10 amp system. If reading is excessively high or low, regulator-rectifier unit may be defective. To check alternator coils, connect an AC voltmeter to the AC leads as shown in Fig. TE110. With engine running at 3000 rpm check AC voltage. Alternator is defective if voltage is less than 18 volts on 7 amp system or 19 volts on 10 amp system.

To test 20 amp system, disconnect B+ lead and connect a DC voltmeter as shown in Fig. TE109. With headlights on or another load on system so battery voltage is less than 12.5 volts, run engine from 2500 rpm to full throttle. If voltmeter indicates a voltage rise, system is good.

To check alternator coils, connect an AC voltmeter to the AC leads as shown in Fig. TE110. With engine running at 3000 rpm check AC voltage. Alternator is defective if voltage is less than 38 volts. With B+ wire connected in series with a DC ammeter as shown in Fig. TE111, alternator is defective if meter indicates less than 13 amps at 2500 rpm, 15 amps at 3000 rpm and 17 amps at 3600 rpm. The regulator-rectifier is defective if battery voltage exceeds 14.8 volts with the battery fully charged.

16 Amp External Regulator System

It is not possible to perform an open-circuit DC test. To check alternator, disconnect red DC wire from regulator. See Fig. TE112. Connect AC voltmeter leads to terminals of regulator as shown in Fig. TE112. At engine speed of 3600 rpm (less engine speed will produce less voltage), voltage should be at least 31.5 volts AC. If voltage reading is less, the alternator is defective. If voltage reading is satisfactory and a known to be good battery is not charged by the system, then the regulator-rectifier unit is defective. Regulator is defective if battery voltage exceeds 15 volts with battery fully charged.

Internal Regulator-Rectifier System

The regulator-rectifier unit is epoxy covered or epoxied in an aluminum box and mounted under the blower housing. Units are not interchangeable. Three systems may be used that produce 5, 7 or 20 amps at full throttle.

Fig. TE111–On 20 amp system, connect a DC ammeter as shown when checking regulator-rectifier as outlined in text.

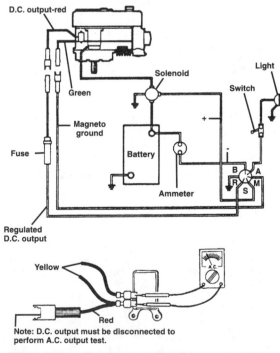

Note: D.C. output must be disconnected to perform A.C. output test.

Fig. TE112–Wiring diagram of 16 amp alternator with external regulator.

It is not possible to perform an open-circuit DC test. To check the alternator, remove regulator-rectifier unit from blower housing, then reinstall the blower housing. Do not run engine without the blower housing installed. Connect AC voltmeter leads to AC terminals of regulator-rectifier unit as shown in Fig. TE113. At engine speed of 3600 rpm (less engine speed will produce less voltage), voltage

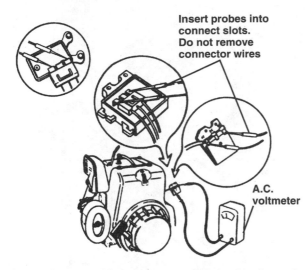

Fig. TE113–Connect AC voltmeter to AC leads of regulator-rectifier to check alternator output. Note that three types of internal regulator-rectifier units have been used.

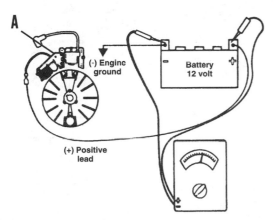

Fig. TE114–Connect a DC voltmeter to battery as shown to test output of alternator (A) on engines equipped with an external ignition system.

should be at least 28 volts AC for 5 amp system, 23 volts AC for 7 amp system and at least 45 volts for 20 amp system. If voltage reading is less, the alternator is defective. If voltage reading is satisfactory and a known to be good battery is not charged by the system, then the regulator-rectifier unit is defective. On 20 amp systems, regulator-rectifier is defective if battery voltage exceeds 14.8 volts with battery fully charged.

External Ignition Module Alternator

Engines with an external ignition may have an alternator coil attached to the ignition module. The alternator produces approximately 350 milliamperes for battery charging. To check alternator output, connect a DC voltmeter to battery (battery must be in normal circuit) as shown in Fig. TE114. Run engine. Voltage should be higher when engine is running, or alternator is defective.

MOTOR-GENERATOR

The combination motor-generator (Fig. TE115) functions as a cranking motor when the starting switch is closed. When the engine is operating and starting switch is open, the unit operates as a generator. Generator output

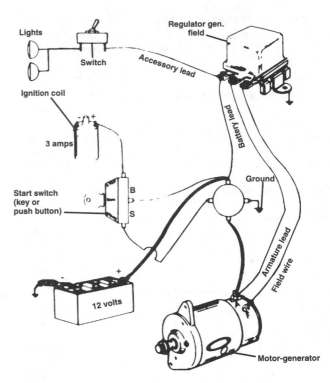

Fig. TE115–Wiring diagram of typical 14 amp output current-regulator and motor-generator system. The 7 amp output system is similar.

and circuit voltage for battery and various accessories are controlled by the current-voltage regulator.

To determine cause of abnormal operation, motor-generator should be given a no-load test or a generator output test. The generator output test can be performed with the motor-generator on or off the engine. The no-load test must be performed with the motor-generator off the engine.

Motor-generator test specifications are as follows:

Delco-Remy Motor-Generator 1101980

Brush spring tension	24-32 oz.
	(680-900 g)
Field draw:	
Amperes	1.52-1.62
Volts	12
Cold output:	
Amperes	12
Volts	14
Rpm	4950
No-load test:	
Amperes (max)	18
Volts	11
Rpm (min)	2500
Rpm (max)	2900

CURRENT-VOLTAGE REGULATORS

Two types of current-voltage regulators are used with the motor-generator system. One is a low output unit that delivers a maximum of 7 amps. The high output unit delivers a maximum of 14 amps.

The low output (7 amp) unit is identified by its four connecting terminals (three on one side of unit and one on underside of regulator). The battery ignition coil has a 3 amp draw. This leaves a maximum load of 4 amps that may be used on accessory lead.

The high output (14 amp) unit has only three connecting terminals (all on side of unit). So with a 3 amp draw for battery ignition coil, a maximum of 11 amps can be used for accessories.

Regulator service test specifications are as follows:

Delco-Remy Regulator 1118988 (7 amp)

Ground polarity	Negative
Cut-out relay:	
Air gap	0.020 in. (0.5 mm)
Point gap	0.020 in. (0.5 mm)
Closing voltage, range	11.8-14.0
Adjust to	12.8
Voltage regulator:	
Air gap	0.075 in. (1.9 mm)
Setting volts, range	13.6-14.5
Adjust to	14.0

Delco-Remy Regulator 1119207 (14 amp)

Ground polarity	Negative
Cut-out relay:	
Air gap	0.020 in. (0.5 mm)
Point gap	0.020 in. (0.5 mm)
Closing voltage, range	11.8-13.5
Adjust to	12.8
Voltage regulator:	
Air gap	0.075 in. (1.9 mm)
Voltage setting @ °F.	
	14.4-15.4 @ 65°
	14.2-15.2 @ 85°
	14.0-14.9 @ 105°
	13.8-14.7 @ 125°
	13.5-14.3 @ 145°
	13.1-13.9 @ 165°
Current regulator:	
Air gap	0.075 in. (1.9 mm)
Current setting	13-15

RATCHET STARTER

On models equipped with the ratchet starter, refer to Fig. TE116 and move release lever to the RELEASE position to remove tension from the main spring. Remove starter assembly from the engine. Remove left-hand thread screw (26), retainer hub (25), brake (24), washer (23) and six starter dogs (22). Note position of starter dogs in hub (21). Remove the hub (21), washer (20), spring and housing (12), spring cover (18), release gear (17) and retaining ring (19) as an assembly. Remove retaining ring, then carefully separate these parts.

CAUTION: Do not remove main spring from housing (12). The spring and housing are serviced only as an assembly.

Remove snap rings (16), spacer washers (29), release dog (14), lock dog (15) and spring (13). Winding gear (8), clutch (4), clutch spring (5), bearing (6) and crank handle (2) can be removed after first removing the retaining screw and washers (10, 30 and 9).

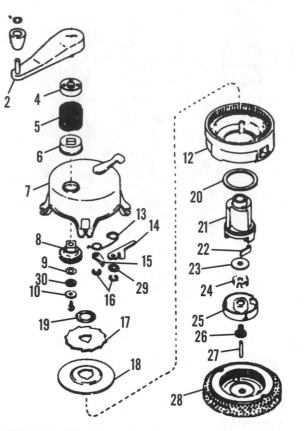

Fig. TE116—Exploded view of a ratchet starter assembly used on some engines.

2. Handle	18. Spring cover
4. Clutch	19. Retaining ring
5. Clutch spring	20. Hub washer
6. Bearing	21. Starter hub
7. Housing	22. Starter dog
8. Wind gear	23. Brake washer
9. Wave washer	24. Brake
10. Clutch washer	25. Retainer
12. Spring & housing	26. Screw (L.H.)
13. Release dog spring	27. Centering ring
14. Release dog	28. Hub & screen
15. Lock dog	29. Spacer washers
16. Dog pivot retainers	30. Lockwasher
17. Release gear	

Reassembly procedure is the reverse of disassembly. Centering pin (27) must align screw (26) with crankshaft center hole.

REWIND STARTERS

FRICTION SHOE TYPE

To disassemble the starter, hold starter rotor (12–Fig. TE117) securely with thumb pressure and remove the four screws securing flanges (1 and 2) to cover (15). Remove the flanges and release thumb pressure enough to allow the spring to rotate the pulley until the spring (13) is unwound. Remove retaining ring (3), washer (4), spring (5), slotted washer (6) and fiber washer (7). Lift out the friction shoe assembly (8, 9, 10 and 11), then remove second fiber washer and slotted washer. Withdraw the rotor (12) with rope from the cover and spring. Remove the rewind spring from cover and unwind the rope from rotor.

Inspect all parts for wear or damage and replace when necessary. To function properly, the ends of the friction

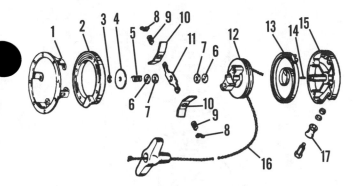

Fig. TE117–Exploded view of typical friction shoe rewind starter.

1. Mounting flange
2. Flange
3. Retaining ring
4. Washer
5. Spring
6. Slotted washer
7. Fiber washer
8. Spring retainer
9. Spring
10. Friction shoe
11. Actuating lever
12. Rotor
13. Rewind spring
14. Centering spring
15. Cover
16. Rope
17. Roller

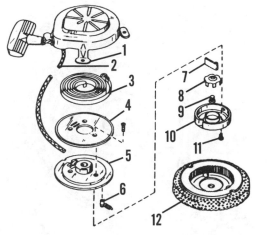

Fig. TE119–Exploded view of dog type rewind starter assembly used on some models. Some units are equipped with three starter dogs (7).

1. Housing
2. Rope
3. Rewind spring
4. Pulley half
5. Pulley half & hub
6. Retainer spring
7. Starter dog
8. Brake
9. Brake screw
10. Retainer
11. Retainer screw
12. Hub & screen assy.

is installed properly for correct starter rotation. If properly installed, sharp ends of friction shoes will extend when rope is pulled.

Remove brass centering pin (14) from cover shaft, straighten pin if necessary, then reinsert pin of its length into cover shaft. When installing starter on engine, centering pin will align starter with center hole in end of crankshaft.

DOG TYPE

Teardrop Housing

Note shape of starter housing in Fig. TE118, TE119 or TE121. The pulley may be secured with either a retainer screw (9–Fig. TE118 or 11–Fig. TE119) or retainer pin (11–Fig. TE121). Refer to following paragraphs for service. To disassemble the starter shown in Fig. TE118 and equipped with retainer screw (9), release preload tension of rewind spring by removing rope handle and allowing rope to wind into starter. Remove retainer screw (9), retainer (8) and spring (7). Remove dog (6) and spring (5). Remove pulley with spring. Wear appropriate safety eyewear and gloves before disengaging keeper (2) and rewind spring (3) from pulley as spring may uncoil uncontrolled.

To reassemble, reverse the disassembly procedure. Spring (3) should be lightly greased. Assemble starter but install rope last as follows: Turn pulley counterclockwise until tight, then allow to unwind so hole in pulley aligns with rope outlet as shown in Fig. TE120. Insert rope through starter housing and pulley hole, and tie a knot in rope end. Install the rope handle and allow the rope to wind onto pulley.

Some models use centering pin (10) to align starter with starter cup. Place nylon bushing (11) on pin (10), then bottom the pin in the hole in retainer screw (9). Pin and bushing should index in end of crankshaft when installing starter on engine.

To disassemble starter shown in Fig. TE119 and equipped with retainer screw (11), pull starter rope until notch in pulley half (5) is aligned with rope hole in housing (1). Hold pulley and prevent from rotating. Engage rope in

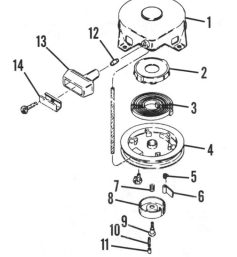

Fig. TE118–Exploded view of typical dog type rewind starter with teardrop shaped housing (1) using retainer screw (9). Some starters may have three starter dogs (6).

1. Housing
2. Spring keeper
3. Rewind spring
4. Pulley
5. Spring
6. Dog
7. Brake spring
8. Retainer
9. Screw
10. Centering pin
11. Nylon bushing
12. Rope coupler
13. Handle
14. Insert

shoes (10) must have a sharp edge. Sharpen or replace the shoes as necessary.

When reassembling, lubricate the rewind spring, cover shaft and center bore in rotor with a light coat of Lubriplate or equivalent. Install the rewind spring so windings are in same direction as removed spring. Install the rope on the rotor, then place rotor on the cover shaft. Make certain the inner and outer ends of the spring are correctly hooked on the cover and rotor. Preload the rewind spring by rotating the rotor two full turns. Hold rotor in preload position and install flanges (1 and 2). Install washers (6 and 7), friction shoe assembly, spring (5), washer (4) and retaining ring (3). Make certain friction shoe assembly

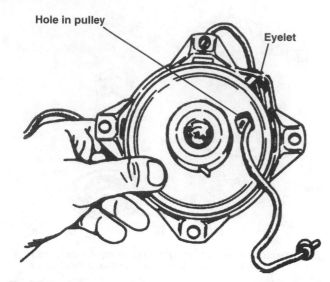

Fig. TE120–Insert rope through starter housing eyelet and hole in pulley then tie knot in rope end.

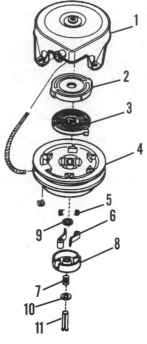

Fig. TE121–Exploded view of typical dog type rewind starter with teardrop shaped housing (1) using retainer pin (11).

1. Housing
2. Spring keeper
3. Rewind spring
4. Pulley
5. Spring
6. Dog
7. Brake spring
8. Retainer
9. Washer
10. Washer
11. Pin

notch and allow pulley to slowly rotate so rewind spring will unwind. Remove components as shown in Fig. TE119. Note direction rewind spring is wound. Wear appropriate safety eyewear and gloves when working with rewind spring as spring may uncoil uncontrolled.

Reassemble by reversing the disassembly procedure. Preload rewind spring by turning pulley two turns with rope.

To disassemble starter equipped with retainer pin (Fig. TE121), release preload tension of rewind spring by removing rope handle and allowing rope to wind into starter. Remove the retainer pin (11) by supporting pulley on a one-inch deep well socket then driving out pin using a inch punch. Remove spring (7) and retainer (8). Remove dog (6) and spring (5). Remove the pulley (4) with spring. Wear appropriate safety eyewear and gloves before disengaging keeper (2) and rewind spring (3) from pulley as spring may uncoil uncontrolled.

To reassemble, reverse the disassembly procedure. Spring (3) should be lightly greased. Assemble the starter but install rope last. Drive in retainer pin (11) until seated against shoulder of housing.

To install rope, rotate pulley counterclockwise until tight, then allow to unwind so hole in pulley aligns with rope outlet as shown in Fig. TE120. Insert rope through starter housing and pulley hole, and tie a knot in rope end. Install the rope handle and allow the rope to wind onto the pulley.

Medium Frame Engines

These engines may be equipped with the starter shown in Fig. TE122. To disassemble starter, release preload tension of rewind spring by removing rope handle and allowing rope to wind into starter. Remove retainer screw (11), dog cam (10), spring (9), and washer (8). Detach E-rings (7) and remove the dogs (6) and springs (5). Remove pulley with spring. Wear appropriate safety eyewear and gloves before disengaging keeper (2) and rewind spring (3) from pulley as spring may uncoil uncontrolled.

To reassemble, reverse the disassembly procedure. Spring (3) should be lightly greased. Install springs (5) so dogs (6) are held in against pulley. Assemble the starter but install rope last as follows: Turn pulley counterclockwise until tight, then allow to unwind so hole in pulley

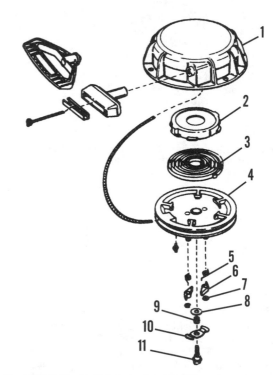

Fig. TE122–Exploded view of rewind starter used on VM and HM engines.

1. Housing
2. Spring keeper
3. Rewind spring
4. Pulley
5. Spring
6. Dog
7. E-ring
8. Washer
9. Spring
10. Dog cam
11. Screw

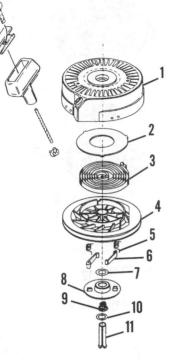

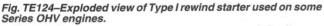

Fig. TE123–Exploded view of "stylized" rewind starter.

1. Starter housing
2. Cover
3. Rewind spring
4. Pulley
5. Springs (2)
6. Dogs (2)
7. Plastic washers (2)
8. Retainer pawl
9. Brake spring
10. Metal washer
11. Pin

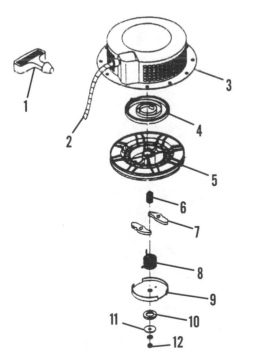

Fig. TE124–Exploded view of Type I rewind starter used on some Series OHV engines.

1. Rope handle
2. Rope
3. Starter housing
4. Rewind spring
5. Rope pulley
6. Spring
7. Pawl
8. Spring
9. Retainer
10. Washer
11. Washer
12. Nut (metric)

aligns with rope outlet as shown in Fig. TE120. Insert rope through starter housing and pulley hole, and tie a knot in the rope end. Install the rope handle and allow the rope to wind onto pulley.

Stylized Starter

The stylized starter is shown in Fig. TE123. To disassemble starter, remove rope handle and allow rope to wind into starter. Position a suitable sleeve support (a ¾ inch deep socket) under retainer pawl (8). Using a ⁵⁄₁₆ or ¼-inch punch, drive the pin (11) free of starter. Remove brake spring (9), retainer (8), dogs (6) and springs (5). Wear appropriate safety eyewear and gloves before disengaging pulley from starter as spring may uncoil uncontrolled. Place shop cloth around pulley and lift pulley out of housing; spring should remain with pulley.

Inspect components for damage and excessive wear. Reverse disassembly procedure to install components. Rewind spring coils wind in clockwise direction from outer end. Wind the rope around the pulley in counterclockwise direction as viewed from retainer side of pulley. Be sure inner end of rewind spring engages spring retainer adjacent to the housing center post. Use two plastic washers (7). Install a new pin (11) so top of pin is ⅛ inch (3.2 mm) below top of starter. Driving pin in too far may damage retainer pawl.

Series OHV Engines

Two designs have been used on Series OHV engines. The Type I rewind starter is shown in Fig. TE124 and Type II rewind starter is shown in Fig. TE125. Refer to appropriate following section.

Type I

To disassemble the rewind starter, pull out the rope handle and tie a temporary knot in the rope so it cannot rewind. Remove the rope handle, untie temporary knot and allow the rope to wind into the housing. Unscrew metric nut (12 Fig. TE124) and remove components (6 through 11). Place shop cloth around the pulley (5) and lift the pulley out of the housing; spring (4) should remain with the pulley. If the spring must be removed from the pulley, position the pulley so the spring side is down and against floor, and tap the pulley to dislodge spring.

Reassemble starter by reversing the disassembly procedure while noting the following: Apply light coating of grease to the sides of the rewind spring and pulley. Install the spring in the pulley so coil direction is counterclockwise from outer spring end.

Using a new rope of same length and diameter as the original, attach the rope handle on the rope. Install other end of rope through the guide bushing of the housing and through the hole in pulley groove (pulley is separate from housing). Pull the rope through the pulley hole and tie a knot in the end. Pull the knot into the pulley hole. Wind the rope clockwise on pulley as viewed from pawl side.

Install the pulley in starter housing. While holding the pulley in the housing, rotate pulley counterclockwise until the tang on pulley engages the hook on inner end of rewind spring. Hook a loop of rope into pulley notch and preload the rewind spring by turning the pulley four full turns counterclockwise. Remove the rope from notch and allow the pulley to slowly turn clockwise as the rope winds on the pulley and the handle returns to the guide bushing on the housing.

Refer to Fig. TE124 and install components (6 through 12). Install the return spring (8) with bent end hooked into hole of pulley hub and looped end toward outside. Then, mount the ratchet retainer so loop end of return spring extends through slot. Rotate the retainer slightly clockwise until ends of slots just begin to engage the ratchets. Press down on the retainer, install the washer and nut.

Type II

To disassemble starter, remove the rope handle and allow the rope to wind into the starter. Unscrew the center retaining screw (12–Fig. TE125) and separate starter components. To disengage the rewind spring (4) from the starter housing, rotate the pulley two turns clockwise. Wear appropriate safety eyewear and gloves to prevent injury should the rewind spring uncoil uncontrolled. The rewind spring is contained in cup (3).

Assemble starter before installing the rope. Lubricate the rewind spring before installation. Apply a small amount of grease on the brake spring (9) ends. Assemble each pawl (7) and spring (6) so spring end pushes the pawl toward the center. Apply Loctite 242 (blue) to threads of center screw (12) and tighten to 70 in.-lb. (8 N•m).

Use the following procedure to install the rope. With the starter assembled except for the rope, rotate the pulley four to five turns counterclockwise and stop when rope hole on pulley is aligned with rope outlet on starter housing. Hold the pulley so it cannot rotate and insert the rope through rope outlet in housing and hole in pulley. Tie a knot at inner end of rope, then pull rope knot against pulley. Attach rope handle and slowly release the pulley. Check starter operation.

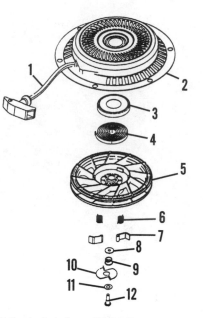

Fig. TE125–Exploded view of Type II rewind starter used on Series OHV engines.

1. Rope	7. Pawl
2. Starter housing	8. Washer
3. Spring cup	9. Brake spring
4. Rewind spring	10. Retainer
5. Rope pulley	11. Washer
6. Spring	12. Screw

TECUMSEH CENTRAL PARTS DISTRIBUTORS

(Arranged Alphabetically by States)
These franchised firms carry extensive stocks of repair parts. Contact them
for name of the nearest service distributor.

Billou's, Inc.
Phone (209) 784-4102
1343 S. Main
Porterville, California 93257

Pacific Power Equipment Company
Phone (303) 744-7891
1441 W. Bayaud Ave., Unit 4
Denver, Colorado 80223

Smith Engines Inc.
Phone (407) 855-5764
2303 Premier Row
Orlando, Florida 32807

Small Engine Clinic, Inc.
Phone (808) 841-3800
1728 Homerule Street
Honolulu, Hawaii 96819

Industrial Engine & Parts
Phone (847) 263-0500
50 Noll Street
Waukegan, Illinois 60085

Medart Engines of Kansas
Phone: (913) 422-3100
2644 S. 96th Street
Edwardsville, Kansas 66111

Engines Southwest
Phone (318) 222-3871
1255 N. Hearne, P.O. Box 67
Shreveport, Louisiana 71161

W.J. Connell Company
Phone (508) 543-3600
65 Green St., Rt. 106
Foxboro, Massachusetts 02035

Central Power Distributors, Inc.
Phone (612) 576-0901
1101 McKinley St.
Anoka, Minnesota 55303

Medart Engines of St. Louis
Phone: (314) 343-0505
100 Larkin Williams Industrial Ct.
Fenton, Missouri 63026

Gardner, Inc.
Phone: (609) 860-8060
106 Melrich Rd.
Cranbury, New Jersey 08512

Smith Engines Inc.
Phone (704) 392-3100
4250 Golf Acres Dr., P.O. Box 668985
Charlotte, North Carolina 28266

Gardner, Inc.
Phone (614) 488-7951
1150 Chesapeake Ave.
Columbus, Ohio 43212

Power Equipment Systems
Phone (503) 585-6120
1645 Salem Industrial Drive N.E., P.O.
Box 669
Salem, Oregon 97308

Pitt Auto Electric Company
Phone: (412) 766-9112
2900 Stayton Street
Pittsburgh, Pennsylvania 15212

Frank Edwards Company
Phone (801) 281-4660
3653 S. 500 West
Salt Lake City, Utah 84115

Power Equipment Systems
Phone (206) 763-8902
88 South Hudson, P.O. Box 3901
Seattle, Washington 98124

CANADIAN DISTRIBUTORS

CPT Canada Power Technology, Ltd.
Phone (403) 453-5791
13315 146th Street
Edmonton, Alberta T5L 4S8

CPT Canada Power Technology, Ltd.
Phone (416) 890-6900
161 Watline Ave.
Mississauga, Ontario L4W 2T7

TRANSMISSION REPAIR

PEERLESS
SERIES 700 TRANSMISSION
OVERHAUL

The Series 700 transmission may be equipped with four or five speeds forward and one reverse. The transmissions are very similar except that on 4-speed units, gears (11 and 32-Fig. PT1-1) are not used. The output sprockets (19) and brake assembly may be located on either side of the transmission. Service procedures are similar for all models. The following procedure is for the 5-speed unit.

To disassemble the transmission, place the shift lever in NEUTRAL then remove the shift lever and safety starting switch, if so equipped. Refer to Fig. PT1-1 and remove the setscrew (5), spring (4) and detent ball (3). Remove the six capscrews (1) and lift off the cover (2). Pull the shifter assembly (27) upward and remove it from the case. See Fig. PT1-2.

Lift both gear and shaft assemblies straight upward out of the case (23–Fig. PT1-1). Move the reverse sprockets (18 and 22) together until the bushing (7), thrust washer (8) and reverse drive sprocket (22) can be removed from the countershaft (28) and chain (21). Remove the chain and

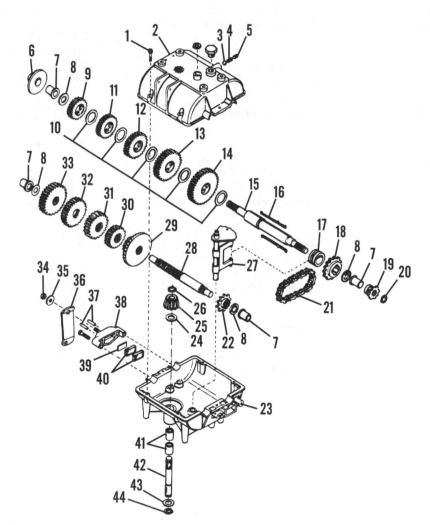

Fig. PT1-1–Exploded view of typical 5-speed Series 700 Peerless transmission. Series 700 4-speed is similar. Refer to text.

1. Capscrew (6)	12. Third speed gear	23. Transmission case	34. Adjusting nut
2. Cover	13. Second speed gear	24. Thrust washer	35. Washer
3. Detent ball	14. First speed gear	25. Input bevel gear	36. Brake lever
4. Spring	15. Output & brake shaft	26. Snap ring	37. Actuating pins
5. Setscrew	16. Shifter (drive) keys	27. Shifter assy.	38. Brake holder
6. Brake disc	17. Shifter collar	28. Countershaft	39. Backup plate
7. Flange bushing	18. Reverse driven sprocket	29. Bevel spur (first drive) gear	40. Brake pads
8. Thrust washer	19. Output sprocket	30. Second drive gear	41. Needle bearings
9. Fifth speed gear	20. Snap rin	31. Third drive gear	42. Input shaft
10. Thrust washer	21. Chain	32. Fourth drive gear	43. Thrust washer
11. Fourth speed gear	22. Reverse drive sprocket	33. Fifth drive gear	44. Snap ring

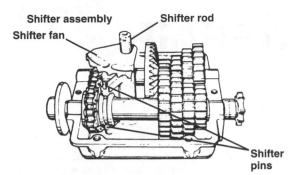

Fig. PT1-2–Series 700 transmission with cover removed. Shift rod, fan fork and pins are removed as an assembly.

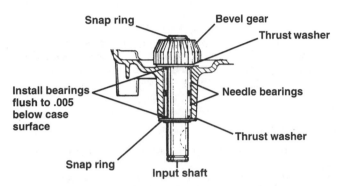

Fig. PT1-3–Input shaft needle bearings must be installed flush to 0.005 inch (0.13 mm) below case surface.

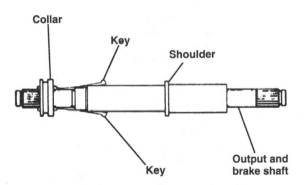

Fig. PT1-4–Install shift collar and shifter (drive) keys on output shaft as shown. Thick side of collar must face shoulder on shaft.

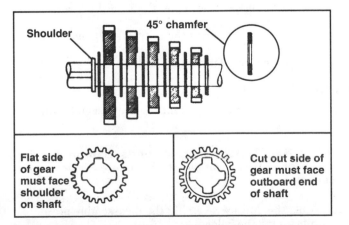

Fig. PT1-5–View showing correct installation of thrust washers and gears on output shaft. The 45° inside chamfer on thrust washers must face the shoulder on the shaft.

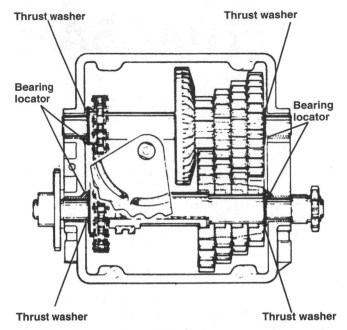

Fig. PT1-6–Make certain that thrust washers are in position shown and that bearing locator tangs are seated in notches in case.

separate the shaft assemblies. Remove the bushing, thrust washer, spur gears (33, 32, 31 and 30) and bevel spur gear (29) from the countershaft (28).

Remove the brake disc (6), bushing (7), thrust washer (8), spur gears (9, 11, 12, 13 and 14) and thrust washers (10) from the output and brake shaft (15). Remove the snap ring (20), output sprocket (19), bushing (7), thrust washer (8) and reverse driven sprocket (18) from the opposite end of the shaft. Slide the shifter collar (17) and shifter drive keys (16) from the shaft. Remove the snap ring (26), input bevel gear (25) and thrust washer (24), then withdraw the input shaft (42) from the bottom of the case. Unbolt and remove the brake assembly (34-40).

Clean and inspect all parts and replace any showing damage. If needle bearings (41) are being replaced, press the bearings in until they are flush to 0.005 inch (0.13 mm) below the case surfaces. See Fig. PT1-3.

Apply a light coat of EP lithium grease to the bearings, shafts and gears, then reassemble by reversing the disassembly procedure. Refer to Fig. PT1-4 and install the shifter collar and shifter key on the output and brake shaft. The thick side of the collar must face the shoulder on the shaft. When installing the gears and thrust washers (9-14–Fig. PT1-1), the flat side of gears and the 45° inside chamfer on the thrust washers must face the shoulder on the shaft. See Fig. PT1-5. The reverse drive sprocket (22–Fig. PT1-1) must be installed with the large hub side of the sprocket facing toward the bevel spur gear (29).

Make certain that thrust washers are installed in the positions shown in Fig. PT1-6 and the bearing locator tangs are seated in notches in the case. Install the shifter assembly, then cover the gears, shaft, reverse sprocket and chain with 12 oz. (0.34 kg) of EP lithium grease. Install the cover (2–Fig. PT1-1) and tighten the capscrews (1) to a torque of 90-100 in.-lb. (10-11 N•m). Install the detent ball (3), spring (4) and setscrew (5) and tighten the setscrew two full turns below flush. Replace brake pads (40) when necessary and install brake assembly.

TRANSAXLE REPAIR

MTD
(SERIES 618)

The Series 618 MTD transaxle provides forward and reverse motion. A belt drive couples the transaxle to the variable speed pulley.

OVERHAUL

Disassembly

1. Thoroughly clean the exterior of the transaxle case.
2. Remove the input pulley from the input shaft (6–Fig. TR1-1).
3. Remove the brake caliper assembly, brake disc (10) and key.
4. Remove all the capscrews retaining the upper case half (4) to the lower case half (48).
5. Separate the upper case half from the lower case half.

NOTE: Note the position of the shim washers so the proper gear backlash can be maintained.

6. Remove the wire ring (1), if so equipped.
7. Remove the snap ring (2), washer (3), gear (8) and thrust washer (7).
8. Remove the input shaft (6) and bearings (5) as needed.
9. Remove the shifter assembly (16).
10. Lift the drive /brake shaft (14) and gear assembly out as an assembly and disassemble if needed.
11. Lift the axle shafts and differential assembly out as an assembly.

NOTE: On later models, the differential assembly, differential gear and axles must be serviced as a unit assembly. Individual components are not available. These units are identified by nonreplaceable screws securing the differential housing to the gear.

12. On early models, remove the screws (Fig. TR1-2) retaining the differential housing to the differential gear.
13. Remove the snap rings (33–Fig. TR1-1), cross shaft (39) and spider gears (31).
14. Remove the nuts (32).
15. Remove the side gears (30).
16. Pull the axles out of the housing and gear assembly.

Reassembly

1. Reassemble by reversing the disassembly procedure while noting the following:
   a. Apply grease to the gears and shafts during assembly to prevent galling.
   b. Backlash between the input gear (8) and the bevel gears (19 and 21) should be 0.006-0.015 inch (0.15-0.38 mm). Adjust the shim washer thickness to obtain desired backlash.

   c. Before installing the upper case half, pack the transaxle housing with 10 ounces (296 mL) of lithium-based grease.

PEERLESS

SERIES 910

The 910 series transaxle provides one forward speed and one reverse speed. The transaxle model number is located on a tag (I–Fig. TR1-3) attached to the right side of the transaxle housing just below the brake assembly.

Overhaul

Disassembly

Refer to Fig. TR1-4 when performing the following procedure.

1. Thoroughly clean the exterior of the transaxle case.
2. Remove the wheel assemblies and brake components as outlined in the equipment section.
3. Drain the lubricant.
4. Remove the pulley from the input shaft.
5. Move the shift lever to the NEUTRAL position.
6. Remove the shift lever from the shift shaft.
7. Remove the neutral switch, if so equipped.
8. Remove any brackets attached to the cases.
9. Unscrew and remove the upper case (6–Fig. TR1-4).
10. Disassembly of the transaxle is evident after inspection and referral to Fig. TR1-4. Note the following:
   a. Do not lose the detent ball (5) and spring (4) when removing the shift arm (17).
   b. Note that two snap rings (34) are used to secure the side gears (33) on the axles.
11. Detach the snap ring (1) to remove the input shaft (8) assembly.
12. Detach the snap ring (12) and separate the pinion gear (11) from the shaft.
13. If necessary, remove the input shaft needle bearings (7).
14. Use a suitable tool to drive the bearings (30) out of the bearing sleeves (29).
15. Inspect components for damage.

Assembly

1. Lubricate all internal components before assembly with Bentonite grease.

NOTE: Manufacturer recommends Bentonite grease for transaxle lubrication. Do not use EP Lithium grease.

2. Assemble the unit by reversing the disassembly procedure while noting the following:
   a. Be sure the bushings and quad rings fit in the case properly.

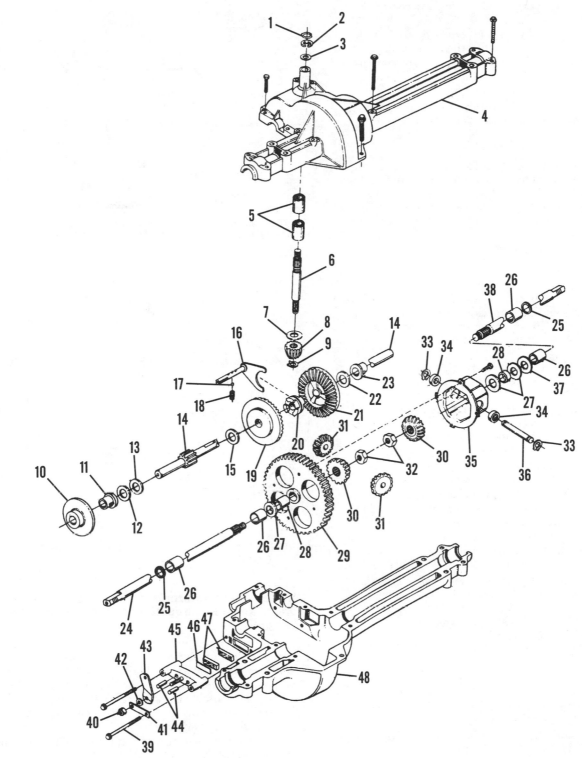

Fig. TR1-1–Exploded view of MTD Series 618 transaxle. The differential asssembly, gear and axles are available only as a unit assembly on later models.

1. Circlip	13. Washer	25. Seal	37. Shim washer
2. E-ring	14. Drive shaft	26. Sleeve bearing	38. Axle (right)
3. Shim washer	15. Thrust bearing	27. Washer	39. Bolt
4. Upper housing	16. Shift fork	28. Spacer	40. Nut
5. Needle bearing	17. Detent ball	29. Differential gear	41. Bracket
6. Input shaft	18. Detent spring	30. Gear	42. Washer
7. Thrust washer	19. Gear (small ID)	31. Axle gear	43. Brake lever
8. Gear	20. Clutch collar	32. Nut	44. Actuating pins
9. Snap ring	21. Gear (large ID)	33. Snap ring	45. Caliper
10. Brake disc	22. Washer	34. Thrust bearing	46. Plate
11. Flange bearing	23. Flange bearing	35. Differential housing	47. Pads
12. Shim washer	24. Axle (left)	36. Cross shaft	48. Lower housing

b. Install the new bearings (30) so they are centered in the sleeves.

c. Install the upper bearing (7) so it is flush with the outer case surface and install the lower bearing so it is 0.150 inch (3.81 mm) from the inside case surface.

NOTE: Manufacturer recommends Bentonite grease for transaxle lubrication. Do not use EP Lithium grease.

d. With gear assemblies installed in lower case half, pack the lower case half around the gears and shafts with 18 ounces (533 mL) of Bentonite grease. Grease should be present in the recesses (R) of the case, but there should not be grease between bearing blocks (36) and case.

e. Tighten the case screws to 100 in.-lb. (11.3 N•m).

SERIES 915

The 915 series transaxle provides five forward speeds and one reverse speed. The transaxle model number is located on a tag (I–Fig. TR1-3) attached to the right side of the transaxle housing just below the brake assembly.

Overhaul

Disassembly

Refer to Fig. TR1-5 when performing the following procedure.

1. Thoroughly clean the exterior of the transaxle case.
2. Remove the wheel assemblies and brake components as outlined in the equipment section.
3. Drain the lubricant from the transaxle.
4. Remove the pulley from the input shaft.
5. Move the shift lever to the NEUTRAL position and remove the shift lever from the shift shaft.
6. Remove the neutral switch, if so equipped.
7. Remove any brackets attached to the cases.
8. Unscrew and remove the upper case (4–Fig. TR1-5).
9. Remove the differential and axle assembly from the case and disassemble as needed. Note that two snap rings (51) are used to secure the side gears (50) on the axles.
10. Remove the shift/brake shaft (27) assembly.
11. Remove the brake disc (59).
12. Refer to Fig. TR1-5 and separate the remainder of the components.
13. If necessary, remove the needle bearing (41) in the bevel gear (40).
14. Remove the countershaft (13) assembly. Refer to Fig. TR1-5 and disassemble the components.
15. Withdraw the shift fork (21) while being careful not to lose the detent ball (23) and spring (22).
16. Detach the snap ring (2) and remove the input shaft (6) assembly.
17. Detach the snap ring (10) and separate the pinion gear (9) from the shaft.
18. If necessary, remove the input shaft needle bearings (5).
19. Inspect the components for damage.

Assembly

1. Lubricate all internal components before assembly with Bentonite grease.

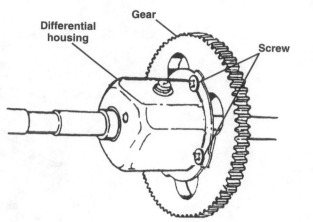

Fig. TR1-2–Early models are identified by the removable screws securing the differential housing ot the differential gear.

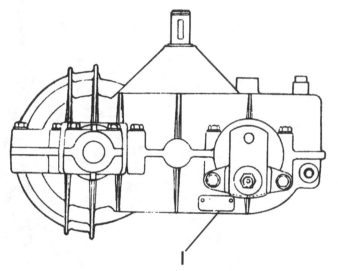

Fig. TR1-3–The transaxle identification tag (I) is located on the side of the case.

NOTE: Manufacturer recommends Bentonite grease for transaxle lubrication. Do not use EP Lithium grease.

2. Assemble the unit by reversing the disassembly procedure while noting the following:

a Install the upper bearing (5–Fig. TR1-5) so it is flush with the outer case surface and install the lower bearing so it is 0.135-0.150 inch (3.43-3.81 mm) from the inside case surface.

b. Install a new bearing (41) so it is flush with the small gear side of the bevel gear (40).

c. Washer (11) is thicker than washer (19).

d. When assembling the gears (33, 35, 36 and 38) on the shift/brake shaft (27), place the rounded side of the thrust washers next to the cutout side of the gears as shown in Fig. TR1-6.

e. Coat the brake disc splines on the shift/brake shaft (27–Fig. TR1-5) with Lubriplate before installing the brake disc (59) on the shaft.

f. Install the brake pads (58) and the backup plate (60) in the case before installing the shift/brake shaft assembly.

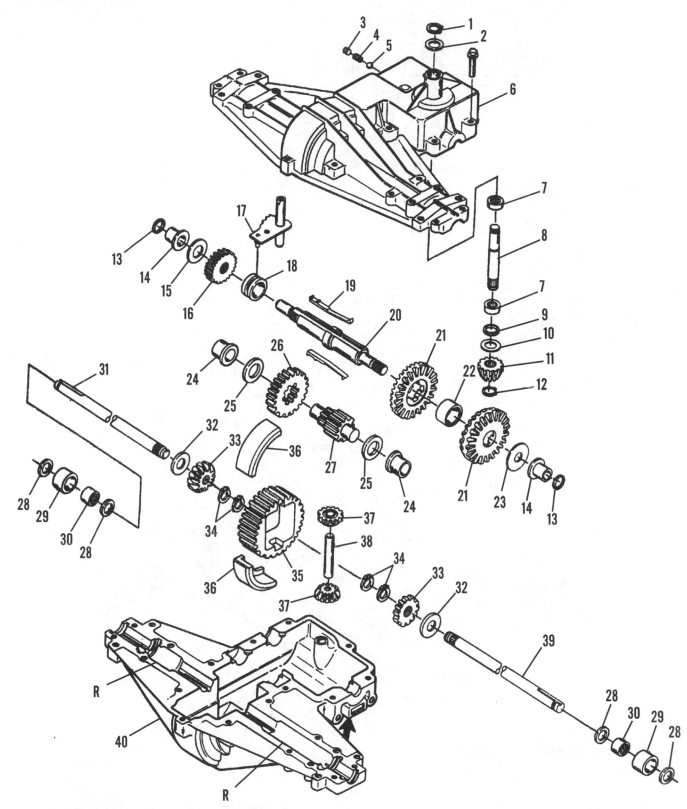

Fig. TR1-4–Exploded view of Peerless Model 910 transaxle. Note that brake assembly may be located on either side of transaxle.

1. Snap ring	11. Pinion gear	21. Bevel gear	31. Axle
2. Washer	12. Snap ring	22. Spacer	32. Thrust washer
3. Plug	13. Quad ring	23. Thrust washer	33. Side gear
4. Detent spring	14. Bushing	24. Bushing	34. Snap rings
5. Detent ball	15. Thrust washer	25. Thrust washer	35. Ring gear
6. Upper case half	16. Gear	26. Gear	36. Bearing block
7. Needle bearing	17. Shift arm	27. Pinion shaft	37. Pinion gear
8. Input shaft	18. Shift collar	28. Quad ring	38. Pinion shaft
9. Quad ring	19. Shift key	29. Sleeve	39. Axle
10. Thrust washer	20. Shift/brake shaft	30. Bearing	40. Lower case half

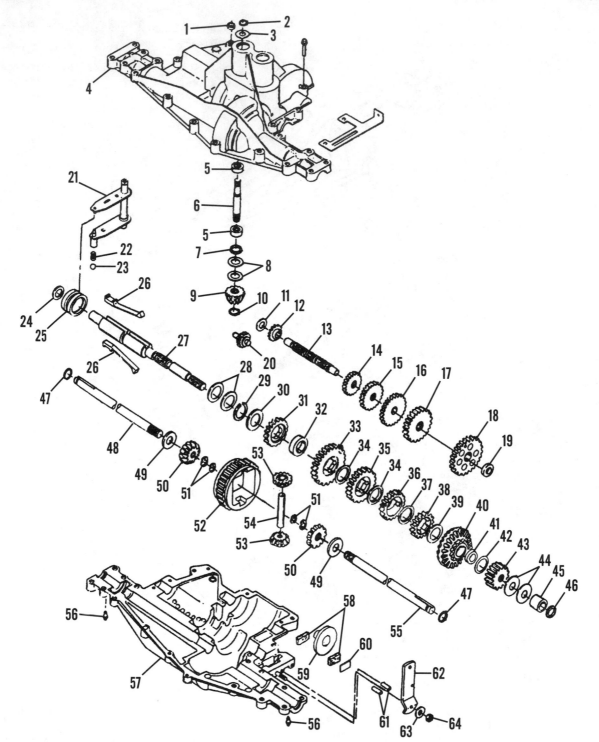

Fig. TR1-5—Exploded view of Peerless Model 915 transaxle.

1. Quad ring
2. Snap ring
3. Washer
4. Upper case half
5. Needle bearing
6. Input shaft
7. O-ring
8. Thrust washer
9. Pinion gear
10. Snap ring
11. Thrust washer
12. Gear
13. Countershaft
14. Gear
15. Gear
16. Gear

17. Gear
18. Bevel gear
19. Thrust washer
20. Reverse idler
21. Shift fork
22. Detent spring
23. Detent ball
24. Thrust washer
25. Shift collar
26. Shift key
27. Shift brake shaft
28. Thrust washer
29. Snap ring
30. Washer
31. Gear
32. Spacer

33. Gear
34. Thrust washer
35. Gear
36. Gear
37. Thrust washer
38. Gear
39. Thrust washer
40. Bevel gear
41. Needle bearing
42. Thrust washer
43. Gear
44. Thrust washer
45. Bushing
46. Quad ring
47. Quad ring
48. Axle

49. Thrust washer
50. Side gear
51. Snap rings
52. Ring gear
53. Pinion gear
54. Pinion shaft
55. Axle
56. Grease fitting
57. Lower case half
58. Brake pads
59. Brake disc
60. Backup plates
61. Pins
62. Brake lever
63. Washer
64. Nut

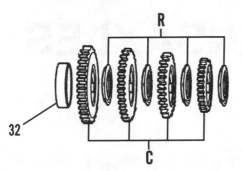

Fig. TR1-6–When assembling gears and thrust washers on shift/brake shaft, note location of spacer (32), cutout (C) of gears and rounded side (R) of thrust washers.

g. Be sure the bushing (45) and the quad ring (46) fit in the case properly.

NOTE: Manufacturer recommends Bentonite grease for transaxle lubrication. Do not use EP Lithium grease.

h. With the gear assemblies installed in the lower case half, pack the lower case half around the gears and shafts with 18 ounces (533 mL) of Bentonite grease.
i. Tighten the case screws to 100 in.-lb. (11.3 N•m).
j. Using a hand-held grease gun, inject one or two shots of grease into the grease fittings (56) at the outer axle ends.

HYDROSTATIC TRANSAXLES

EATON
(MODEL 778)

OPERATION

Eaton Model 778 hydrostatic transaxle uses a variable displacement, reversible flow, ball piston pump and one fixed displacement, ball piston motor to provide infinite speed and torque output. Two units, one each per rear axle, are used to provide steering on a riding mower. The transaxle is equipped with an internal, disc brake.

Riding mower ground speed is regulated by changing the oil delivery of the variable displacement pump. This is accomplished by changing the position of the cam ring in which the pump ball pistons operate. The system operates as a closed loop. Any oil lost from the closed loop is replaced by oil from the reservoir.

TROUBLESHOOTING

The following problems and possible causes may be used as an aid in locating and correcting transmission problems.
1. Loss of power or transmission will not operate in either direction.
    a. Slipping or broken drive belt.
    b. Broken speed control linkage.
    c. Low transmission oil level.
    d. Wrong transmission oil or water contaminated oil.
    e. Transmission oil temperature too hot.
    f. Transmission roll release valve in the wrong position.
    g. Plugged oil filter.
    h. Faulty pressure relief valve.
    i. Damaged transmission pump and/or motor.
    j. Drive pulley slipping on the transmission input shaft.
    k. Internal damage to the reduction gear assembly.
2. Transmission operating too hot.
    a. Low transmission oil level.
    b. Wrong transmission oil.
    c. Defective cooling fan.
    d. Blocked transmission cooling fins.
    e. Faulty roll release valve.
    f. Overloaded tractor.
    g. Worn transmission pump and/or motor.
3. Transmission jerks when starting.
    a. Faulty control linkage.
    b. Incorrect oil.
    c. Faulty belt.
    d. Air in the hydraulic circuit.
    e. Faulty bypass valve.
    f. Faulty transaxle motor.
4. Transmission operates in one direction only.
    a. Faulty control linkage.
    b. Air in the hydraulic circuit.
5. Tractor creeps when in NEUTRAL.
    a. Worn or misadjusted control linkage.

OVERHAUL

Disassembly

1. Remove the fan, pulley, and all external brackets, levers and fittings.
2. Thoroughly clean the outside of the unit.
3. Drain the oil from the unit.

> **NOTE: During disassembly, mark components so they may be returned to their original position.**

> **NOTE: The axle housing assembly must be removed to gain access to the hydrostatic motor (29–Fig. HX1-1).**

4. Remove the capscrews securing the axle housing (7) and withdraw the axle housing and planetary assembly (1-16) from the hydrostatic housing (31).

> **CAUTION: Be very careful not to dislodge the hydrostatic motor assembly. The spring-loaded balls (27) are a selective fit in the motor rotor (29) and must be installed in a matching bore in the rotor if removed.**

5. Remove the planetary assemblies from the axle housing (Fig. HX1-2).

> **NOTE: The primary sun gear (17–Fig. HX1-1) may remain in the motor bore.**

6. Use the following procedure to remove the axle from the housing:
    a. Remove the outer snap ring (1–Fig. HX1-1).
    b. Remove the inner snap ring (9) and thrust washer (8).

> **CAUTION: Do not damage the splines on the axle when performing the following step.**

    c. Press or drive the axle toward the outer end of the axle housing and remove the axle, bearing (2) and oil seal (3).
    d. Separate the bearing and seal from the axle. Removal of the snap ring on the middle of the axle is not necessary.
7. Disassemble the planetary assemblies (Fig. HX1-2).
8. Remove the brake disc (19–Fig. HX1-1) and brake backup plate (18).
9. Remove the primary sun gear (17) from the motor (29) bore.
10. Remove the brake pad (21).
11. Unscrew the adapter ring retaining screws and remove the adapter ring (24). To remove the brake shaft and seal, proceed as follows:
    a. Drive out the retaining pin (23).
    b. Remove the brake shaft (25).
    c. Remove the seal (26).

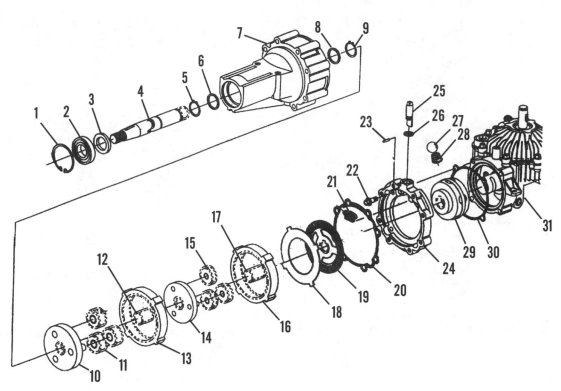

Fig. HX1-1–Exploded view of axle housing, planetary gear and motor assemblies.

1. Snap ring
2. Bearing
3. Oil seal
4. Axle
5. Snap ring
6. Thrust washer
7. Axle housing
8. Thrust washer
9. Snap ring
10. Secondary carrier
11. Planetary gears
12. Secondary sun gears
13. Secondary ring gear
14. Primary carrier
15. Planetary gears
16. Primary ring gear
17. Primary sun gear
18. Backup plate
19. Brake disc
20. Gasket
21. Brake pad
22. Screw
23. Pin
24. Adapter
25. Brake shaft
26. Seal
27. Ball
28. Spring
29. Motor rotor
30. Gasket
31. Transaxle housing

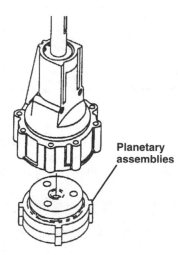

Fig. HX1-2–Remove the planetary assemblies as a unit.

12. Place a large rubber band or similar device around the motor rotor (29) to hold the spring-loaded ball pistons (27) in their bores. Carefully withdraw the motor assembly. Due to a selective fit, if the balls are removed they must be returned to their original rotor bores.

NOTE: The buttons (11–Fig. HX1-3) may fall out during cover removal.

13. Unscrew the pump cover (9) retaining screws and remove the pump cover.

14. Remove the buttons (11) from the cover.

15. Remove the snap ring (1).

16. Tap or press the input shaft (2) and bearing (4) out of the cover by forcing the shaft toward the outside of the cover. Shaft and bearing assembly is available only as a unit assembly.

17. Drive the input shaft seal (8) out of the cover bore.

18. Remove the control shaft (15) and the cam ring insert (14) from the cam ring (16).

19. Place a wide rubber band or similar device around the pump rotor (12) to hold the ball pistons (13) in their bores. The balls are a selective fit in the rotor and must be installed in their matching bore if removed from the rotor.

20. Carefully lift the pump rotor from the housing.

21. Remove the charge pressure relief valve spring (18) and ball (17).

22. Do not remove the dampening pistons (1–Fig. HX1-4).

23. Push the pins on the dump valve actuator (3) together, then remove the actuator and spring (4).

24. Remove the snap ring (6) and remove the actuator pin (5).

25. Remove the filter (2).

Inspection

Clean all components in clean solvent. Inspect components for damage.

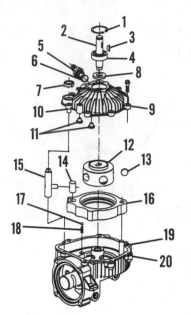

Fig. HX1-3–Exploded view of cover and pump assemblies. The input shaft and bearing are available only as a unit assembly.

1. Snap ring
2. Input shaft
3. Key
4. Bearing
5. Fitting
6. Gasket
7. Seal
8. Seal
9. Cover
10. Dowel
11. Buttons
12. Pump rotor
13. Ball
14. Pin
15. Control shaft
16. Cam ring
17. Pressure relief ball
18. Spring
19. Dowel
20. Transaxle housing

When removing the ball pistons from the pump and motor rotors, number the rotor bores and place the balls in a plastic ice cube tray or egg carton with cavities numbered to correspond to rotor bores. Piston balls and rotor bores must be smooth and free of any irregularities. Pump and motor rotors and balls are unit assemblies as the balls are selectively fitted to the rotor bores.

Assembly

NOTE: Lubricate all components with clean transaxle oil prior to assembly.

1. Apply molybdenum grease to the seal (7–Fig. HX1-4) and install it onto the actuator pin (5).
2. Install the actuator pin into the bore in the housing.
3. Install the snap ring (6) onto the actuator pin.
4. Install the dump valve actuator (3) and spring (4) into the housing. Check for proper operation.
5. Trim the lip off a new filter as shown in Fig. HX1-5 so the filter abuts with the motor race in the housing.
6. Carefully install the filter so the tabs on the ends fit into grooves in the housing. Push on the metal frame, not the filter element.
7. Install the charge pressure relief valve (17–Fig. HX1-3) and spring.
8. Install the pump rotor, balls, dowel (19) and cam ring (16).
9. Remove the rubber band holding the balls in the pump rotor.
10. Install the pivot pin (14) on the control shaft (15) stub shaft.

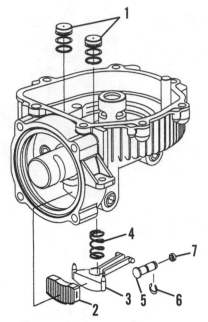

Fig. HX1-4–Exploded view showing dump valve actuator and dampening valve assemblies.

1. Dampening valves
2. Filter
3. Dump valve actuator
4. Spring
5. Pin
6. Snap ring
7. Seal

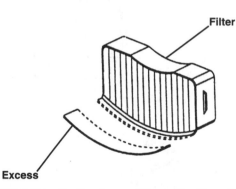

Fig. HX1-5–Trim the lip of a new filter so the filter will fit properly in the transaxle housing.

11. Install the control shaft assembly into the notch on the cam ring (16) and into the housing (20).
12. Install the cover seal (8) so the lip is to the inside of the cover.
13. Install the control shaft seal (7) so the lip is to the inside of the cover.
14. Press or drive the input shaft and bearing into the cover so the bearing is bottomed in the bore.
15. Be sure the snap ring (1) is firmly seated in the cover after installing the input shaft assembly. Be sure the shaft turns without binding.
16. Hold the buttons (11) in place with petroleum jelly.
17. Clean the mating surfaces of the cover and housing using alcohol. Be sure the surfaces are free of all oil residue.
18. Apply a $\frac{1}{16}$-$\frac{1}{8}$ inch bead of liquid gasket, such as Loctite 518 Master Gasket, on the housing mating surface. Allow the liquid gasket to cure as specified by the manufacturer.
19. Install the cover while aligning the shafts. Carefully rotate the input shaft so it engages the pump rotor.

Fig. HX1-6–Tighten the cover retaining screws in the sequence shown.

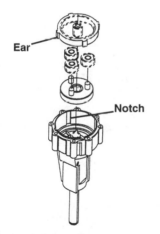

Bevel

Fig. HX1-7–Install the ring gears so the beveled edge is toward the threaded end of the axle.

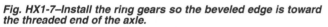

Ear

Notch

Fig. HX1-8–Install the ring gears so the ears on the ring gears fit into the notches in the axle housing.

20. With all components engaged in the cover and housing, mate the cover and housing so the index dowel (10) in the cover fits in the hole in the housing.

21. Tighten the cover screws to 125 in.-lb. (14 N•m) using the sequence shown in Fig. HX1-6. Tighten the screws again to the specified torque.

22. Carefully install the motor rotor (29–Fig. HX1-1) in the housing and remove the rubber band used to retain the ball pistons in the rotor.

23. Install a new seal (26) in the adapter ring (24), then install the brake shaft (25) and retaining pin (23).

24. Install the gasket (30) and adapter ring (24) onto the housing. Tighten the adapter ring retaining screws to 124 in.-lb. (14 N•m).

Inner axle end

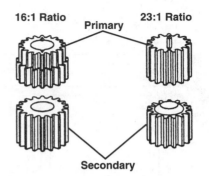

Primary

16:1 Ratio

23:1 Ratio

Secondary

Fig. HX1-9–Planetary gearsets have been produced with 16:1 or 23:1 ratios. Identify and install the sun gears as shown.

25. Install the thrust washer (6) into the axle housing.

26. If removed, install the snap ring (5) in the center groove on the axle.

27. Install the axle into the axle housing.

28. Install the thrust washer (8) and snap ring (9). The flat side of the snap ring must be toward the splined end of the axle.

NOTE: Be sure to protect the lips of the seal when performing the following step.

29. Install the oil seal (3) with the open side toward the inside of the axle housing.

30. Install the bearing (2) and snap ring (1).

31. Install the planetary gears onto the secondary gear carrier (10).

32. Install the secondary gear carrier and planetary gears onto the splined end of the axle.

33. Install the secondary ring gear (13) into the axle housing with the beveled edge (Fig. HX1-7) toward the outer end of the axle. The ears on the ring gear must fit into the axle housing notches (Fig. HX1-8).

34. Identify the primary and secondary sun gears by referring to Fig. HX1-9. Note the relationship of the gears with respect to the inner and outer axle ends.

35. Install the secondary sun gear (12–Fig. HX1-1) into the secondary planetary gears.

36. Install the primary planetary gears (15) onto the primary gear carrier (14).

37. Install the primary gear carrier and planetary gears onto the secondary sun gear.

38. Install the primary ring gear (16) into the axle housing with the beveled edge (Fig. HX1-7) toward the outer threaded axle end.

39. Install the primary sun gear (17–Fig. HX1-1) into the primary planetary gears.

40. Install the backup plate (18) into the axle housing.

41. Install the brake disc (19) onto the primary sun gear (17). The side coated with friction material must be next to the backup plate.

42. Install the brake pad (21) into the recess in the adapter ring. The pad must fit in the notch on the brake shaft (25).

43. Remove the rubber band holding the balls in the motor rotor.

44. Position the gasket (20) on the axle housing and install the axle housing onto the transaxle housing. First insert

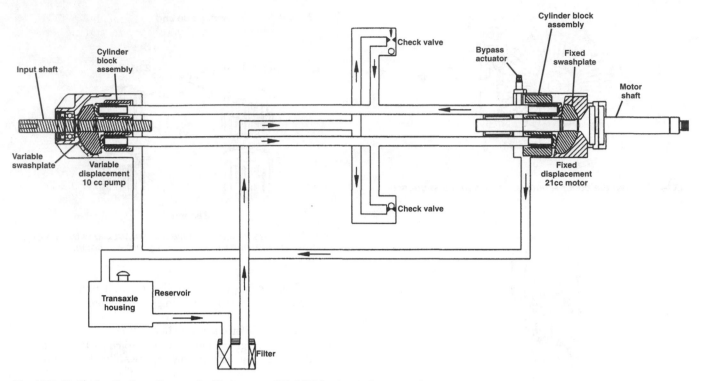

Fig. HX1-10–Hydraulic flow diagram for Hydro-gear 310-2400 hydrostatic transaxle.

the primary sun gear into the motor rotor bore, then rotate the axle housing so the screw holes align.

45. Tighten the axle housing capscrews to 125 in.-lb. (14 N•m).

46. Fill the transaxle with SAE 20W-50 engine oil.

HYDRO-GEAR
(MODEL 310-2400)

OPERATION

Two Hydro-gear 310-2400 units are used on a riding lawn mower with each unit driving a rear wheel. Because each transaxle is operated independently, the machine may be turned within a "zero radius".

The hydrostatic transaxle consists of a variable volume, reversible swashplate, axial piston pump connected in a closed loop to a fixed displacement, axial piston motor. The hydrostatic pump is driven by the engine, and the motor is connected to the motor shaft. The motor shaft transfers power to the brake shaft through a set of bevel gears. A gear on the brake shaft drives the final drive gear mounted on the axle. A multi-disc brake is mounted on the brake shaft. The axle drives one of the tractor wheels.

The hydrostatic pump inlet is connected to the transaxle housing internal reservoir, allowing the pump to make up any oil that is lost from the closed loop system during operation. Refer to Fig. HX1-10 for a circuit diagram. Make-up oil is drawn from the reservoir through an oil filter screen that is mounted in the transaxle housing.

Hydrostatic motor speed is controlled by hydrostatic pump rpm and the angle of the pump swashplate. As the angle of the pump swashplate is increased from the neutral zero degree position, the length of each pump piston stroke increases and more oil is pumped to the motor. Because the motor is a fixed displacement unit, it must turn faster in order to accept the increased flow from the pump.

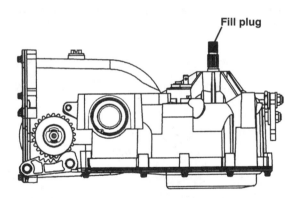

Fig. HX1-11–Drawing showing location of the fill plug.

When the pump swashplate angle decreases, the opposite effect takes place and motor speed decreases.

The hydrostatic pump turns in the same direction all the time. The hydrostatic motor is capable of turning in both directions. Motor direction of rotation is reversed by reversing the pump swashplate angle which reverses the flow of oil being pumped to the motor. When the control lever is in NEUTRAL, there is no pump swashplate tilt and no pump piston stroke.

Any oil lost internally from the closed loop system is replaced by oil from the internal oil reservoir. Reservoir oil will pass through the check valve when the transmission oil pressure is not sufficient to keep the check valve closed.

LUBRICATION

The hydraulic fluid is contained in the transaxle. Recommended fluid is SAE 20W-50 engine oil. The transaxle capacity is 79 fl. oz. (2336 mL). To check or fill the transaxle, clean the area around the fill plug (Fig. HX1-11), then unscrew the fill plug. To check the oil level, measure from the

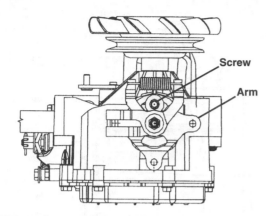

Fig. HX1-12–On models so equipped, loosen the screw and rotate the control arm to perform the neutral adjustment procedure.

boss surface to the oil. The oil level should be 1⅞ inches (78 mm). Run the unit for approximately one minute, then re-check the oil lever.

PURGE AIR IN TRANSAXLE

Air trapped inside the transaxle during overhaul or service must be purged for proper operation and to prevent internal damage.

1. Position the machine on a level surface.
2. Move the bypass or pressure release lever to the disengaged position.
3. Run the engine at slow idle speed.
4. Move the speed control lever alternately to the full forward and full reverse positions three times. Keep the lever in the forward or reverse position for five seconds each time.
5. Move the speed control lever to NEUTRAL.
6. Move the bypass or pressure release lever to the engaged position.
7. Move the throttle control to full throttle, then operate the speed control lever so the machine moves forward and reverse alternately at least five feet in each direction. The speed control lever must be at the maximum speed position. Operate the machine three times in each direction.
8. Repeat the purging procedure as needed until the machine operates smoothly.

NEUTRAL ADJUSTMENT

NOTE: Two types of transaxle control levers are used. On some units, the neutral adjustment is performed using the control linkage on the machine. Refer to the manufacturer's section in this manual.

Perform the following procedure if it is necessary to perform the neutral adjustment using the transaxle operating lever.

1. Be sure all machine control linkage is disconnected from the transaxle operating lever.
2. Run the engine and note if the rear wheel rotates. The wheel should not rotate, indicating the transaxle is in NEUTRAL. If the wheel rotates, perform the following steps.
3. Stop the engine.
4. Loosen the control arm holding screw (Fig. HX1-12).

5. Move the control arm, restart the engine and note the change in wheel movement. Stop the engine and move the control arm as needed.
6. After achieving no wheel movement, tighten the holding screw to 18-22 ft.-lb. (25-30 N•m).

BRAKE ADJUSTMENT

The hydrostatic transaxle is equipped with brake discs inside a housing on the side of the transaxle housing. Check for correct brake adjustment using the following procedure.

1. Insert a feeler gauge between two brake discs through the opening on the underside of the housing (Fig. HX1-13).
2. Measure the gap between the brake discs. The gap should be 0.025-0.030 inch (0.64-0.76 mm), or as specified by the manufacturer of the machine.
3. Rotate the brake lever retaining nut to obtain the specified gap.

TROUBLESHOOTING

When troubleshooting the hydrostatic drive system, always check the easiest and most obvious items first. Some problems which may occur during operation of hydrostatic transmission and their possible causes are as follows:

1. Lack of drive or limited speed in both directions.
   a. Broken or misadjusted control linkage.
   b. Slipping or broken transmission drive belt.
   c. Leaking or stuck open bypass valve.
   d. Low oil level.
   e. Plugged oil filter.
   f. Internal leakage of high pressure fluid due to wear of pump or motor.
   g. Final drive failure.
2. Lack of drive or limited speed in one direction.
   a. Damaged or binding control linkage.
   b. Movement of pump swashplate being restricted in one direction.
   c. Charge check valve not seating.
3. Noisy operation.
   a. Low oil level.
   b. Excessive loading.
   c. Misadjusted brake.
   d. Loose parts.
   e. Damage bypass valve linkage.
4. Hot operation.
   a. Debris buildup.
   b. Low oil level.
   c. Excessive loading.
   d. Misadjusted brake.

OVERHAUL

1. Before disassembling the transmission, thoroughly clean the exterior of the unit.
2. Remove the fill plug and drain oil from the transaxle.
3. Remove the input pulley and fan.
4. Remove the control arm assembly (79 or 87–Fig. HX1-13).
5. Remove the brake housing (29) and brake disc assembly.
6. On models so equipped, remove the parking brake components (23-26).
7. Remove the back cover (5).
8. Remove the retaining ring (1) and oil seal (2).
9. Remove the retaining ring (22) and oil seal (21).
10. Remove the snap ring (20).

11. Remove the brake shaft (4), bearing (19) and bevel gear (3).

12. Remove the wheel hub (53).

13. Remove the snap ring (52) and seal (51).

14. Remove the snap ring (42) and seal plug (43). Tap on the end of the axle to dislodge the plug.

15. Remove the snap ring (44) from the axle.

16. Remove the axle and bearings (45 and 50).

17. Note the location of the bushings (46 and 48). Remove the bushings and ring gear (47).

18. Remove the lower cover (76).

19. Remove and discard the oil filter (75).

20. Remove the bevel gear (64).

21. Remove the motor shaft (68) and bearing (66).

22. Remove the three screws attaching the center section (73) to the housing.

NOTE: Pump cylinder may stick to the center section during removal. Separate the pump cylinder from the center section while removing the center section.

23. Remove the center section (73) with the motor cylinder (69).

NOTE: Springs will force the center section out of position. Do not allow the pistons to fall out of the motor cylinder.

24. Separate the thrust block bearing (67) and the motor cylinder (69) from the center section.

25. Remove the pump cylinder (62), spring (61), washer (60) and thrust bearing (58).

26. Remove the swashplate (55), control lever (57) and guide (56).

27. Remove the snap ring (14) and seal (15).

28. Push out the input shaft (59) with bearing (18) toward the outside of the housing.

29. Do not remove the check valve plug on the center section (5). Check the torque of the check valve plug. Recommended tightening torque is 200-360 in.-lb. (23-41N•m).

INSPECTION

Thoroughly clean all parts before inspection. Be sure to clean all sealant from the back cover, lower cover and housing.

Inspect the pistons and cylinder bores for damage. The pump and motor cylinder blocks are serviced as complete assemblies. Check the polished surfaces of the center section (73) and cylinder blocks for wear, scoring or scratches.

Inspect the bearings, bushings and contact surfaces on the shaft for damage. Inspect the gears for damage. Inspect the cradle bearings (Fig. HX1-14) in the center section for damage. The cradle bearings are not removable.

ASSEMBLY

NOTE: Be sure to lubricate all components with oil before assembly.

1. Install a new control arm seal (41–Fig. HX1-15).

2. Install the control arm (57).

3. Install the bearing (18) and retaining ring (17) onto the input shaft (59).

4. Install the input shaft into the housing. Install the spacer (16), seal (15) and snap ring (14).

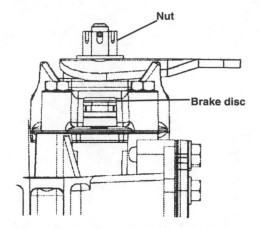

Fig. HX1-13–Refer to text for brake adjustment procedure on models equipped with a disc type brake.

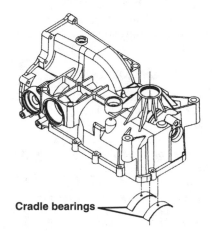

Fig. HX1-14–The cradle bearings in the housing are not removeable.

5. Install a new bypass acutator seal (8), then install the actuator (63), arm (6) and retaining ring (7).

6. Install the slot guide (56) onto the control arm (57).

7. Install the swashplate assembly (55) and thrust bearing (58). Be sure the thin race contacts the swashplate and the thick race will contact the pistons. Operate the control arm to be sure the swashplate moves freely.

8. Install the washer (60) and spring (61).

9. Install the pump piston and cylinder assembly (62).

10. Position the bypass actuator (63) so it is centered in the housing.

11. Install the dowel pins (70).

12. Install the bypass plate (71) into the center section (73).

13. Install the center section (73) and motor piston and cylinder assembly (69) into the housing. Install the three center section retaining screws and tighten to 44-58 ft.-lb. (60-79 N•m).

14. Install the thrust bearing (67). Be sure the thick race contacts the pistons.

NOTE: Be sure the splines on the motor shaft and in the motor cylinder are properly aligned when installing the motor shaft.

15. Install the motor shaft (68), bearing (66) and retaining ring (65).

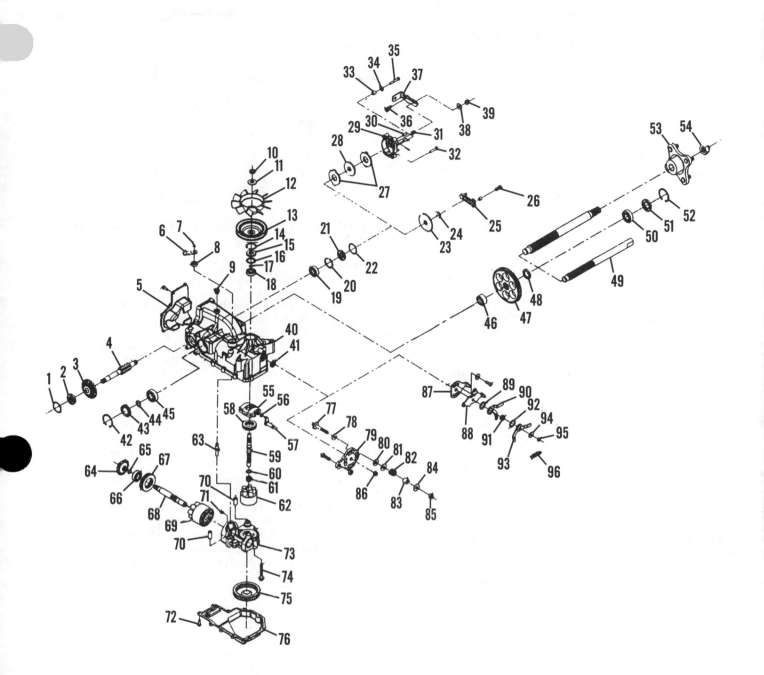

Fig. HX1-15—Exploded view of Hydro-gear 310-2400 hydrostatic transaxle. A left side (L) unit is shown.

1. Retaining ring
2. Seal
3. Bevel gear (19T)
4. Brake shaft
5. Back cover
6. Bypass control arm
7. Retaining ring
8. Seal
9. Oil fill plug
10. Locknut
11. Washer
12. Fan
13. Input pulley
14. Snap ring
15. Seal
16. Spacer

17. Retaining ring
18. Ball bearing
19. Ball bearing
20. Snap ring
21. Seal
22. Retaining ring
23. Brake rotor
24. Retaining ring
25. Brake arm
26. Screw
27. Brake disc
28. Brake rotor
29. Brake housing
30. Brake actuating pins
31. Compression spring
32. Screw

33. Spacer
34. Washer
35. Screw
36. Spring
37. Bracket
38. Washer
00. Castellated nut
40. Housing
41. Seal
42. Snap ring
43. Seal
44. Retaining ring
45. Ball bearing
46. Bushing
47. Ring gear
48. Bushing
49. Axle

50. Ball bearing
51. Seal
52. Snap ring
53. Wheel hub
54. Nut
55. Swashplate
56. Slot guide
57. Control arm
58. Thrust bearing
59. Input shaft
60. Washer
61. Spring
62. Pump piston & cylinder assy.
63. Bypass actuator
64. Bevel gear (14T)
65. Retaining ring

66. Ball bearing
67. Thrust bearing
68. Motor shaft
69. Motor piston & cylinder assy.
70. Dowel pins
71. Bypass plate
72. Screw
73. Center section
74. Screw
75. Oil filter
76. Lower cover
77. Stud
78. Friction disc
79. Control arm
80. Friction disc
81. Washer

82. Spring
83. Spacer
84. Washer
85. Locknut
86. Locknut
87. Control arm
88. Return arm
89. Nylon washer
90. Inner arm
91. Spacer
92. Nylon washer
93. Outer arm
94. Washer
95. Locknut
96. Spring

Fig. HX1-16–Apply a bead of RTV sealant to the lower cover as shown.

RTV sealant

Fig. HX1-17–Apply a bead of RTV sealant to the back cover as shown.

16. Install the 14-tooth bevel gear (64) onto the motor shaft.

17. Install a new filter (75).

18. Apply a bead of automotive-type RTV sealant to the lower cover as shown in Fig. HX1-16. Install the lower cover. Tighten the retaining screws to 110-150 in.-lb. (12.4-17 N•m).

19. Install the ring gear (47–Fig. HX1-15) and bushings (46 and 48). Use a screwdriver to hold the gear and bushings in position until the insertion of the axle.

20. Install the bearing (45) and axle (49).

21. Install the retaining ring (44) onto the axle.

22. Install the seal (43) and snap ring (42).

NOTE: Protect the seal (51) by installing a seal protector sleeve or tape on the sharp edges on the axle.

23. Install the bearing (50), seal (51) and snap ring (52).

24. Position the 19-tooth bevel gear (3) in the housing, then install the brake shaft (4) and bearing (19) into the housing.

25. Install the snap ring (20), seal (21) and retaining ring (22).

26. Install the brake assembly. On units equipped with a disc type brake, tighten the brake housing (29) retaining screws to 80-120 in.-lb. (9-13.6 N•m).

27. Apply a bead of automotive-type RTV sealant to the back cover as shown in Fig. HX1-17. Install the back cover. Tighten the retaining screws to 110-150 in.-lb. (12.4-17 N•m).

28. Install the control arm assembly (79 or 87–Fig. HX1-15).

29. Install the input pulley and fan. Tighten the pulley retaining nut to 30-43 ft.-lb. (41-58 N•m).

30. Fill the transaxle with oil as described in the Lubrication section.

31. After installation of the unit in the machine, perform the following:

    a. Tighten the wheel hub retaining nut, if so equipped, to 200-295 ft.-lb. (271-400 N•m).

    b. Perform the brake adjustment procedure.

    c. Purge air from the transaxle.

    d. Perform the neutral adjustment procedure.

Genuine John Deere Service Literature

For ordering information, call John Deere at 1-800-522-7448.
All major credit cards accepted.

PARTS CATALOG

The parts catalog lists service parts available for your machine with exploded view illustrations to help you identify the correct parts. It is also useful in assembling and disassembling.

OPERATOR'S MANUAL

The operator's manual provides safety, operating, maintenance, and service information about John Deere machines.

The operator's manual and safety signs on your machine may also be available in other languages.

TECHNICAL AND SERVICE MANUALS

Technical and service manuals are service guides for your machine. Included in the manual are specifications, diagnosis, and adjustments. Also illustrations of assembly and disassembly procedures, hydraulic oil flows, and wiring diagrams.

Component technical manuals are required for some products. These supplemental manuals cover specific components.

FUNDAMENTALS OF SERVICE MANUALS

These basic manuals cover most makes and types of machines. FOS manuals tell you how to SERVICE machine systems. Each manual starts with basic theory and is fully illustrated with colorful diagrams and photographs. Both the "whys" and "hows" of adjustments and repairs are covered in this reference library.